D1413405

the bureaucratic state

public affairs and administration
(editor: James S. Bowman)
vol. 6

Garland reference library
of social science
vol. 166

the public affairs and administration
series: James S. Bowman, editor

the bureaucratic state
an annotated bibliography

Robert D. Miewald

foreword by Christian Soe

Garland Publishing, Inc. • New York & London
1984

Library of Congress Cataloging in Publication Data

Miewald, Robert D.
  The bureaucratic state.

  (Public affairs and administration series ; 6)
(Garland reference library of social science ; v. 166)
  Includes index.
    1. Bureaucracy—Bibliography.   2. Public administration—
Bibliography.   3. Comparative government—
Bibliography.   I. Title.   II. Series.   III. Series: Garland
reference library of social science ; v. 166.
  Z7164.A2M53   1984   016.351′001   82–49154
  [JF1351]
  ISBN 0–8240–9155–8

Cover design by Laurence Walczak

Printed on acid-free, 250-year-life paper.
Manufactured in the United States of America

Jmb
5-24-89

contents

series foreword

The twentieth century has seen public administration come of age as a field and practice. This decade, in fact, marks the one hundredth anniversary of the profession. As a result of the dramatic growth in government, and the accompanying information explosion, many individuals—managers, academicians and their students, researchers—in organizations feel that they do not have ready access to important information. In an increasingly complex world, more and more people need published material to help solve problems.

The scope of the field and the lack of a comprehensive information system has frustrated users, disseminators, and generators of knowledge in public administration. While there have been some initiatives in recent years, the documentation and control of the literature have been generally neglected. Indeed, major gaps in the development of the literature, the bibliographic structure of the discipline, have evolved.

Garland Publishing, Inc., has inaugurated the present series as an authoritative guide to information sources in public administration. It seeks to consolidate the gains made in the growth and maturation of the profession.

The Series consists of three tiers:
1. core volumes keyed to the major subfields in public administration such as personnel management, public budgeting, and intergovernmental relations;
2. bibliographies focusing on substantive areas of administration such as community health; and
3. titles on topical issues in the profession.

Each book will be compiled by one or more specialists in the area. The authors—practitioners and scholars—are selected in open competition from across the country. They design their work to include an introductory essay, a wide variety of bibliographic materials, and, where appropriate, an information re-

source section. Thus each contribution in the collection provides a systematic basis for managers and researchers to
make informed judgments in the course of their work.

Since no single volume can adequately encompass such a
broad, interdisciplinary subject, the Series is intended as a
continuous project that will incorporate new bodies of literature as needed. The titles in preparation represent the initial
building blocks in an operating information system for public
affairs and administration. As an open-ended endeavor, it is
hoped that not only will the Series serve to summarize knowledge in the field but also will contribute to its advancement.

This collection of book-length bibliographies is the product
of considerable collaboration on the part of many people. Special appreciation is extended to the editors and staff of Garland Publishing, Inc., to the individual contributors in the Public
Affairs and Administration Series, and to the anonymous re-
viewers of each of the volumes. Inquiries should be made to
the Series Editor:

James S. Bowman
Tallahassee

foreword

The purists looking for the ultimate definition of bureaucracy are likely to be discouraged by this compilation. There are 2,700 items listed and, from a cursory examination, there may be about as many meanings attached to the word. For better or worse, it is clear that one does not have to be a certified expert in order to expound upon the nature of bureaucracy. Should we then be appalled by this chaos in the academic marketplace? Of course not, since as Miewald points out in the introduction, our fascination with government really means that there is still something that is not bureaucratic. The time to worry is when bureaucracy is not a major topic of everyday discussion or when it is of special concern only to the scholarly.

As for the scholars, a bibliography as vast as this project will mean different things to different groups. However, it would appear to be a special boon for students of comparative government. It has become a commonplace among observers of modern politics, in whatever part of the globe, that the bureaucracy is the heart of government. But just what does that mean? If bureaucrats are political actors, as everyone agrees, how do they acquire their power? After all, there are few societies which, on the surface, openly condone the rule by clerks.

Finding the answer to such a question would seem to be at the top of the agenda for comparative government. To be sure, the "comparative administration" movement did produce a large number of works on various countries and, for a while, system building was all the rage. But that movement, if not obsessed with the exotic or overexcited by theoretical pretensions, at least did not produce a completely clear picture of the "bureaucratic state." Perhaps then it is appropriate that we begin over again. This bibliography indicates that the resources for a number of fresh approaches are readily available.

Most of all, this work should protect us from parochialism. Bureaucracy is all around us, regardless of time or clime. The arrangement of the material supports the editor's contention that bureaucracy is more a frame of mind, a way of thinking, than it is anything more tangible. Finding out why we behave as we do in systems of authority will help to unlock a number of doors in the comparative study of government.

Christian Soe
California State University
Long Beach

introduction

The term "bureaucratic state" seems straightforward enough. Everybody knows about bureaucracy and, as the heft of this volume shows, many are eager to share that knowledge. However, problems emerge once we try to set the metes and bounds of the modern bureaucratic state. Surely one ought to begin with the literature of public administration, the discipline whose concern is the care and feeding of the bureaucrat. But an understanding of bureaucracy cannot be confined to a governmental organization chart. Bureaucracy as a "cracy," as a form of government, is fairly insubstantial. It is, literally, government by desks, or by the pieces of paper on the desk. But we cannot learn enough by looking at the objective paraphernalia of bureaucracy—the routines, the regulations, the red tape—or even at the clerks behind the desk.

Bureaucracy is the way people relate to one another and to nature. As Max Weber informed us, the power of bureaucracy is based primarily on the willingness of society to accept it. A bureaucratic state, that is, requires a bureaucratic society. Therefore, to comprehend bureaucracy, one must move out of the government office into the larger world in order to examine the lives of ordinary people. The private firm, the educational system, the patterns of interpersonal relationships, the church, and even the family, are part of the bureaucratic state. Or perhaps the bureaucratic state is only a more visible part of the bureaucratic society.

In either case, for citizens and scholars alike, the major concern is the active nature of bureaucracy. It is never at rest; it is always in flux. In the nineteenth century, it was quite common for writers to express dismay over the "encroachments" of bureaucracy. Today, we have summed up this movement in more scholarly language as the process of "bureaucratization." Bureaucracy never "is"; it is always "becoming." The threat which has stimulated two centuries of literature is that it will not remain in its place but instead will spill over into all areas of life, with awful consequences for the individual.

Some writers are inclined to argue that we are doomed, that bureaucracy has become an autonomous force that can never stop until it encompasses every social action. In Ralph Hummel's view, the "bureaucratic culture" cannot co-exist peaceably with the larger society.[1] Since few people have openly advocated more bureaucracy—politicians do not campaign for it, revolutionaries do not present it as their utopia, and managers do not vow to "turn this company into a real bureaucracy"—there may be some validity to the gloomiest predictions.

Most people, however, are not ready to concede that the course of history leads inexorably to one big bureau. Bureaucracy is expansive, but it can be managed. In this sense, the identification of bureaucracy is made at the margins, at the interface of bureaucracy and something that is not bureaucracy. The true definition of bureaucracy, then, is not so much in the hard, tangible "thing," but rather in the pressure it exerts on other values. In algebraic terms, bureaucracy plus or minus x equals a desirable state of human affairs, be it greater efficiency in the organization, more political democracy, heightened human dignity, a healthier personality, or the broadest form of rationality.

All this means that the boundaries of bureaucracy cannot be found within the literature of a single discipline. Moreover, at no single point in time can one determine a reliable standard for bureaucracy. Bureaucracy is dynamic, never static, and the exact quality of the x in the equation—that which is not bureaucracy—is always under review. The aim of this bibliography, therefore, is not so much the exploration of the bureaucratic state itself, but rather the identification of those areas in modern society where the tension between bureaucracy and its alternatives are the greatest. In short, where does one begin to look for the active manifestations of the bureaucratic state?

the state of the art

The search is no easier today than it was in 1846 when Robert von Mohl, the German political scientist, wrote what is generally acknowledged as the first scholarly treatment of this new word "bureaucracy":

> For a relatively short time now, the talk in every place and at the most diverse occasions has been about "bureaucracy," and, as a rule, not in a favorable or moderate sense. Indeed, classes and individuals whose views and goals otherwise diverge greatly are united in their complaints about this common enemy. What then is the precise concept behind this word, which has been condemned as barbaric by the linguists? Is its recent usage proof of a new form of state and society? Or is it only a designation making us more conscious of something which has been around for a long time? Is it perhaps only a meaningless figure of speech, now in vogue, but in a short time to be viewed as stale and out-of-date? But if not the latter, how does science and how does life relate to the thing which the word signifies?"[2] (Author's translation)

Now after 137 years, the only part of Mohl's interrogation we can answer with much certainty is that the word was not a passing fad. We all are aware of bureaucracy, even if there is no complete agreement of all of its dimensions or what, if anything, we can do about it.

Even a sampling of the many items written about it, however, has to be based on reasonable premises. A significant bibliography, most of all, must be as inclusive as possible. This assumption immediately brings up the issue of whether there is now a "state of the art" which can be used to exclude the irrelevant. Social scientists have tended to argue that a precise standard must be set. Friedrich and Cole, in their 1932 study of Swiss administration, stated the scientific credo clearly:

> The man in the street is an enemy of the political scientist, but the politician and the political propagandist are far worse. It is an almost hopeless task to cleanse words, which are essential for our work, of the layers of surface associations which deft orators have heaped upon them. Bureaucracy is one of those words.[3]

During the intervening decades, many scholars have tried to sanitize the word and, in the process, probably remove it from the everyday lives of those very "men in the street" and politicians who should be the center of study. Thus, although some sociologists have demonstrated empirically that bureaucrats are really more creative than other people and that citizens are personally pleased with their contacts with bureaucracy, public concern about bureaucracy has not disappeared.

Academics, moreover, may find it difficult to approach the subject of bureaucracy in a completely objective manner. For many years, American writers on public administration simply denied that there was such a thing. At most, it was a figment of the fevered imagination of reactionary robber barons. Such an attitude is not strange since the founders of public administration had as their mission the creation of a bureaucracy in the United States. C. Wright Mills argued persuasively that an affinity between scholarship and bureaucracy still exists.[4]

I deny, in other words, that we are at a point where an orthodox definition of bureaucracy can be defended. Our understanding of the word is still at a rather primitive stage and the major research assignment is the distillation of commonalities from its several usages. For example, when the editor of *Water and Waste Disposal* launches a tirade against the bureaucrats in the Environmental Protection Agency, is he talking about a problem that would make sense to a Polish sociologist? When a physician fumes about the bureaucrats in the Food and Drug Administration, is there something relevant to the study of economic development in Malaysia or can it contribute in any way to an appreciation of the frustration expressed by sculptors working with urban planners?

The time hardly seems ripe for an academy of savants, perhaps composed of contributors to the *Administrative Science Quarterly*, who could impose a standard definition of bureaucracy. It would be rejected by the indignant legislator, the frustrated social worker, the disillusioned foreign service officer and, most of all, "the man in the street." The best we can do at the present is examine the usage of the word from the viewpoint of the users. Bureaucracy is still "the talk in every place and at the most diverse occasions." This bibliography is an attempt to sketch the length and breadth of the concept as a prologue to further work in the field. The authors cited may be predominantly political scientists, public administrators, and sociologists, but educators, business people, chemists, artists, and even mad poets are also represented.

The items contained in this work were selected largely on the basis of their having "bureaucracy" or some cognate in the title. I took this as evidence that the author had named something significant and, in most cases, had related that something to the *x*, to the non-bureaucratic factor. Of course, complete reliance on this simple guide to the literature would be, well, very bureaucratic and would exclude, among other things, the works of Karl Marx and Max Weber. Therefore, other important items, particularly in the period before 1960, have been included. In general, however, I agree with Dwight Waldo who, in a recent review article, said that this "spate" of works with bureaucracy in the title "is not an accident but a phenomenon of some importance, reflecting important developments and concerns."[5]

If the items had been arranged chronologically, the acceleration in the use of the concept of bureaucracy would become evident. It is no "spate" we have here; rather, as part of a long-range trend, bureaucracy has become a unifying concept in a number of areas. The more we study it, the more it spreads. My job here has been to search out and identify the most important of those places and diverse occasions. Some clusters of usage have already become part of the language of social science: representative bureaucracy, street-level bureaucracy, the bureaucratic politics model in foreign affairs, the professional-bureaucracy debate. Other areas have resulted from "the shock of recognition" as teachers, judges, writers, doctors, or other groups which had felt that bureaucracy was someone else's affair sensed that it had become, or is becoming, a major problem for them.

Of course, serious scholars of bureaucracy predominate, especially in comparative government. But I have imposed no rule that would exclude "the man on the street," the demagogue, or indeed, the true crank (and bureaucracy is something cranks can really get their teeth into). The following items cover what I believe is a large percentage of the many books, articles, tracts, screeds, and impolite outbursts, written in English, over the last 150 years. However motley the whole may appear, however different the exact definitions of the term, there is agreement on the essence of bureaucracy. The categories I have used can, I hope, help us in the digestion of all the material that has been produced about this thing called bureaucracy.

a user's guide

The bureaucratic state, it was argued, is more than the government office and its inhabitants. It is part of a larger social phenomenon which sustains and causes the expansion of a particular style of administration. Therefore, the lines between public and private, between state and society are often blurred. The literature on bureaucracy, although drawn from a number of sources tends to coalesce around certain issues. The greatest number of these issues do concern purely political questions, but the larger impact of bureaucratization must also be taken into account. The following categories are intended to show the major areas of tension between bureaucracy and the non-bureaucratized parts of modern society.

I. *General*. This section includes bibliographies and general surveys of the meaning of the concept of bureaucracy.

II. *The Study of Bureaucracy*. As the entries in this section indicate, there is no standard way to approach the study of bureaucracy. The early works in English are generally expressions of discontent with government, although thinkers such as John Stuart Mill (Items 77 and 78) and Walter Bagehot (Item 35) incorporated bureaucracy into larger theories of politics.

The two major schools of thought on bureaucracy are the Marxist and the Weberian. Both claim to present an objective analysis of the subject, yet both have a strong ideological component. The gravest questions are posed by and for the Marxists: did Marx foresee or even understand the significance of bureaucracy; do bureaucrats form a distinct social class; how does one explain or justify the nearly total bureaucratization of those states claiming to be Marxist?

Weber, while striving for great precision in the study of

bureaucracy, has also caused confusion among later students. Much mischief has resulted from ripping the "ideal type" of bureaucracy from the rich and complex context of Weber's views of the progressive rationalization of Western society. Efforts have been made to operationalize the elements of the Weberian model, with varying degrees of success.

The question of bureaucracy has also been examined with intense rigor by modern social scientists. Much discussion has been devoted to finding the best way of measuring, in quantitative terms, the existence of bureaucracy. The latest major development in the study of bureaucracy has been the rapid growth in the number of works produced by the political economists such as Niskanen (Item 259). The image of bureaucrats as rational largely in terms of their own self-interest has opened up a new dimension in the study of large organizations.

III. *The Problem of Bureaucracy.* Bureaucracy is commonly portrayed as a threat to such values as individuality, creativity, or democracy. The items in the first section illuminate what it means to live the bureaucratic life; if Hummel (Item 322) is correct, it is a grim existence. A more specific problem, first addressed by Robert Merton (Item 373) is the "bureaucratic personality." Are bureaucrats born that way or are they produced by the society and the organization?

Bureaucracy as a form of government, so it is argued, endangers all traditional forms of politics. The democratic West is as much a bureaucratic polity as the collectivist East. But even though we are sure that the bureaucrats exercise a great deal of power, there is lack of agreement about the exact sources of that power. In this section are a number of authors who explore the dimensions of the political power of administrators. An excellent place to begin is Eisenstadt's work on bureaucratization and debureaucratization (Item 395).

While much of the politics-of-administration literature deals with major issues in high places, a recent source of concern is the more mundane contacts between citizen and clerk—the "bureaucratic encounter" as some call it. Michael Lipsky's model (Item 484) of the "street-level bureaucrat" has stimulated much interest in how bureaucracy defines our everyday lives.

Finally, there are some who insist that we can change the

negative aspects of bureaucracy. In fact, the more optimistic suggest that we have to do very little since bureaucracy will wither away. Warren Bennis (Item 519) has done much to popularize the coming "death of bureaucracy."

IV. *American Bureaucracy.* As the first part of this section indicates, Americans love to denounce their bureaucracy. Many of these attacks may seem rather insubstantial, but they persist despite the eloquent defenses of administration by such writers as Appleby (Item 567) or Goodsell (Item 607). Americans do not seem to be ready to believe anything but the worst about those "awful bureaucrats."

The federal bureaucracy excites the most concern and few politicians take off for Washington without promising to do something about the "fourth branch of government." The items represent a thorough review of the problems of controlling the national bureaucracy.

Beginning in the 1960s, the notion of "representative bureaucracy" (Item 916) gained great popularity. If the bureaucracy is the heart of political action, then all participants ought to have access to it. Some writers argue that access has always been there and so the bureaucracy has been more democratic than the traditional branches.

When administration is asked to regulate parts of society, the cry of bureaucratic despotism is sure to be heard. The items in this part indicate that no matter what the administrators do, they are often condemned both by the friends and opponents of active government. No one seems pleased with the way bureaucracy handles its regulatory function.

Washington is not the only home for bureaucrats and the sub-national governments have their share of bureaucracy. States and cities provide the opportunity for comparative analyses in terms of several variables of bureaucratization. Of recent interest is the way in which municipal officials, according to bureaucratic rules, determine the distribution of public goods and services. See Items 997, 1028, and 1045 for examples.

V. *Bureaucracy in International Affairs.* Students of international relations have found it useful to look at the participants in world politics as bureaucracies. In particular, a major explanation for the failure of foreign policy efforts, especially by the United States, has become known as the "bureaucratic politics" model. Developed by Graham Allison (Item 1086) and Morton Halperin (Item 1107) the model has been applied to a number of cases in international affairs.

VI. *Historical Bureaucracies.* Bureaucracy existed long before it was named. In fact, in large measure, we have a written history only because of the diligent record keeping of ancient clerks. In this section are items covering various historical administrative systems. Those bureaucracies which flourished before the nineteenth century are featured although, as in the case of the Chinese, such a cutoff date is quite arbitrary. Wittfogel's monumental study of Oriental systems (Item 1205) indicates the sorts of lessons that can be drawn from pre-industrial societies.

VII. *Comparative Study of Bureaucracy.* Students of comparative government probably account for the largest increase in the work on bureaucracy. How comparative much of this material really is can be debated; much of it consists of professorial travelogues about the latest exotic place to be visited by the writer. Comparative administration, in fact, was little more than development administration, with a great deal of attention devoted to problems of administration in the Third World. Perhaps the most interesting question raised by these scholars is whether the bureaucracy, as a political actor, helps or hinders the development of other centers of political power (Item 1274).

VIII. *National Studies.* Comparative administration did precious little comparing. Most of the literature concentrated on a single administrative system. One is struck, however, by the different aspects emphasized by students in various parts of the world. For example, the works on the People's Republic of China tend to stress the ongoing problems of bureaucracy within a revolutionary context (Item 1394). In India, a major question is the "commitment" of administrators to development and democracy (Item 1435). For students of Latin America, the "bureaucratic authoritarianism" model (Item 1851) is important.

IX. *Bureaucratic Management.* The management of large organizations has often been examined through the prism of bureaucratic theory. Leadership style, management philosophy, organization size, environmental factors, and internal power plays are some of the aspects that have been tested in order to emphasize elements of organizational effectiveness in public and private settings. Some of the works here, such as that of Blau (Item 2038) and Gouldner (Item 2062) are among the true classics of administrative science.

X. *Bureaucracy and the Control of Knowledge.* Although no one seems sure of the exact outcome, bureaucracy is seen as playing a major role in the emerging "knowledge society." Authorities from Weber to Simon have viewed bureaucracy as an information-processing and rational decision-making instrument. But if knowledge is power, that power can be used to advance parochial or personal interests. Thus, many of the innovations of the knowledge revolution—zero-base budgeting (Item 2131), social indicators (Item 2134), computers (2138), and evaluation (2144)—have not had the effect that their advocates expected.

XI. *Bureaucracy in Business.* As a matter of course, business leaders are fond of denouncing government bureaucracy. The more thoughtful among them, however, have recognized that their own organizations are susceptible to the process of bureaucratization. Moreover, as Bendix (Item 2173) and Goldman and Van Houton (Item 2183) have shown, business leaders have used bureaucracy as an effective means for the preservation of their power and social status.

XII. *Criminal Justice.* "Bureaucratic justice" strikes many as a contradictory concept. Yet a growing number of jurists, lawyers, and police officers now admit that aspects of the criminal justice system, from arrest to conviction to incarceration, are taking shape as a highly routinized bureaucracy. As Litrell (Item 2230) argues, the system places people caught up in it into a number of categories.

XIII. *Education.* Educators, from the primary grades through the university, face special tensions in doing their jobs. As professionals, they are dedicated to freeing each student from ignorance; as bureaucrats, they are paid to produce a uniform product. As indicated by the large volume of books and articles by teachers, this struggle has assumed a significant role, and there seems to be little doubt about which side is winning. An even harsher argument says that the

teachers, as bureaucrats, are instruments to control a poten-
tially unruly society. The thesis posed by Katz (Item 2287) is
an indictment of American education as a tool for suppressing
the lower class.

XIV. *The Environment.* Raw nature seems to be an area
immune to bureaucratization. The administration of the environment now poses a number of special problems, as indicated by the collection edited by Baden and Stroup (Item
2361). In particular, those stewards of the environment, the
farmers, have found themselves caught up in a complex organizational system which makes a mockery of their self-image as
independent yeomen.

XV. *The Health Care System.* Doctors, nurses, and other
health care personnel feel most acutely the pressures on their
personal autonomy caused by the need for the greater organization of a complex technology. The physician, in particular, is
an example of the once "free professional" who must operate
within a structured context. Heydebrand, in his study of the
modern hospital (Item 2408) suggests, however, that the system may be evolving into a new form of post-bureaucratic
organization.

XVI. *Labor.* The labor movement has always provided a number of examples to support the Iron Law of Oligarchy. Unions,
in the eyes of critics, tend to lose their radical edge and become just another set of self-serving bureaucracies. Van
Tine's work (Item 2443) on the "making of the labor bureaucrat" traces this development in the United States.

XVII. *Military Affairs.* The military is a bureaucracy with
feet of clay. No matter how well organized an army may be the
irrationality of warfare is always lurking in the background and
military leaders know that bureaucratic armies are usually de-
feated by forces that possess the mysterious and not altogether predictable elements of morale and esprit. Addi-
tionally, the exact shape of a nation's military posture is
dictated not so much by the state of the art of war as it is by
the politicking of the bureaucrats in uniform. Beard (Item
2448) and Bergerson (2449) make this case about the American military.

XVIII. *Professionals and Bureaucracy.* The probability of
conflict between professionals and the bureaucracy has often

been discussed by sociologists as well as the members of various professions. A powerful chemistry is at work here, although it is not clear what the exact nature of the reaction will be. For every writer (*e.g.*, Item 2486) who believes that there is an inevitable conflict between professionals and the organization, there is another (*e.g.*, Item 2505) who sees the two factors as quite compatible.

XIX. *Religion and Philanthropy.* Weber's theory of bureaucracy arose out of his investigation of ancient religion. Organized religion, or in a larger sense, organized kindness, still poses many riddles for the pious and for scholars. A recent empirical work is presented in Item 2523.

XX. *Science and Technology.* Scientists and technologists harbor a number of suspicions about organized research. At the same time, their projects are now so complex and so costly that administration has become a necessary step in pushing back the frontiers of human knowledge. As the editor of *Bioscience* (Item 2549) lamented, the age of heroism in science is over. Whether this also means the end of free inquiry is another matter. Salsburg and Heath (Item 2556) suggest that the uncertainty of science and the certitude of bureaucracy may result in bad public policy.

XXI. *Social Services.* Welfare workers and other members of the "helping professions" are particularly conscious of the pressures of bureaucracy. Because they lack the autonomy of doctors and other traditional professionals, they are especially dependent upon the organization, usually a public one, for the conduct of their work. It is that same organization which, in their eyes, often prevents the provision of services to the neediest clients. For an overview, see Item 2589.

XXII. *Arts and Humanities.* The artist is the antithesis of the dull, sober bureaucrat. All the more painful, then, is the recognition that today's artist or writer depends upon an elaborate infrastructure to sustain the creative process. Arian (Item 2610) illustrates this development in the musical field. Another interesting feature is the view of the future utopias (or dystopias) held by writers (Items 2616 and 2617).

XXIII. *Bureaucratic Responsibility.* The traditional conclusion of any work on public administration is the old question:

"How to catch the conscience of the bureaucrat?" As Friedrich (Item 2652) and Finer (Item 2650) showed in their famous exchange, the means may be external, such as the ombudsman, or internal, as in a personal sense of moral responsibility.

XXIV. *A Little Humor.* Bureaucracy is an inviting target for the satirist. Unfortunately, the quality of the humor has not always been overly impressive since the bureaucracy is so good at satirizing itself. Only a comic genius could produce some of the memos and regulations that are cranked out, in all seriousness, by the bureaus. Parkinson's Law (Item 2702) was the most successful example of the tongue-in-cheek approach to bureaucracy and it encouraged a number of imitators.

a final word

If the worst fears of the critics of bureaucracy are realized, all the categories discussed here, based as they are on some tension between bureaucracy and its opposite, will be made obsolete when all of human existence becomes one big predictable routine. Indeed, a bibliography on bureaucracy would be as reasonable as a bibliography on, say, "things in general." We are far from that point, if this work is any measure. If anything, we are more conscious than ever of the pressure of bureaucracy, and with consciousness comes the realization that there are alternatives to further bureaucratization.

notes

1. Ralph Hummel, *The Bureaucratic Experience* (New York: St. Martin's, 1977).

2. Robert von Mohl, "Ueber Bureaukratie," *Zeitschrift für gesamte Staatswissenschaft* 3 (1846), 330.

3. Carl Friedrich and Taylor Cole, *Responsible Bureaucracy: A Study of the Swiss Civil Service* (Cambridge, Mass.: Harvard University Press, 1932), 1.

4. C. Wright Mills, *The Sociological Imagination* (New York: Oxford University Press, 1959).

5. Dwight Waldo, "Organization Theory: Revisiting the Elephant," *Public Administration Review* 38 (1978), 593.

the bibliography

I. GENERAL

A. Bibliographies

1. Coppa and Avery Consultants. BUREAUCRATIC ORGANIZATIONS:
    A GUIDE TO THE LITERATURE. Monticello, Ill.: Vance
    Bibliographies, 1980. 11 pp.

    Contains items on bureaucracy in the United States
    written between 1901 and the mid-1970s.

2. Coppa and Avery Consultants. THE APPLICATION OF SYSTEMIC
    THEORIES TO BUREAUCRATIC ORGANIZATIONS. Monticello,
    Ill.: Vance Bibliographies, 1981. 12 pp.

    Concentrates on the application of systems theory to the
    study of bureaucratic organizations.

3. Eisenstadt, S.N. "Bureaucracy and Bureaucratization: A
    Trend Report." CURRENT SOCIOLOGY, 7 (1958), 99-164.

    Includes a review essay on the literature and a bibli-
    ography of over 600 items. The main trends in current re-
    search are represented. The essay deals with the causes
    of bureaucratization, as expounded by writers since Max
    Weber. A major theme is the dilemma of bureaucracy: mas-
    ter or servant?

4. Library of Congress, Division of Bibliography. LIST OF
    REFERENCES ON BUREAUCRACY, mimeograph. Washington,
    D.C.: 1922. 4 pp.

    Identifies references to bureaucracy in English, Ger-
    man and French sources through 1922.

5. Library of Congress, Division of Bibliography. A LIST OF
    REFERENCES ON BUREAUCRACY, mimeograph. Washington, D.C.:
    1931. 8 pp.

    An update of Item 4.

6. Mohapatra, Manindra, and David R. Hager. STUDIES OF PUB-
    LIC BUREAUCRACY: A SELECTED CROSS-NATIONAL BIBLIOGRAPHY.
    Monticello, Ill.: Council of Planning Librarians, 1977.
    149 pp.

    Covers work since 1960. The emphasis is on comparative
    and developmental administration.

7. Sheriff, Peta. "The Sociology of Public Bureaucracies,
    1965-1975." CURRENT SOCIOLOGY, 24, No. 2 (1976), 1-
    174.

    A bibliography of over 300 items covering the recent
    literature on public administration. A trend report notes
    the uncertain boundaries of the sociology of bureaucracy.
    It is still a new field of specialization without a spec-
    ific focus.

                    B. Bureaucracy: An Overview

8. Albrow, Martin. BUREAUCRACY. New York: Praeger, 1970.
    157 pp.

    Traces the development of bureaucracy, as a word and as
    a concept, from its "invention" in 1764 by de Gournay to
    the present. The use of the term in the popular and the
    scholarly literature of the 19th century is emphasized.
    Marx and Weber are seen as major contributors to current
    discussions of bureaucracy. Today, bureaucracy as a con-
    cept in the social sciences may have been stretched to
    cover too much, but it is still a useful way to identify
    a range of issues concerning the relationships of indiv-
    iduals to abstract organizations. The search for a per-
    fectly pure definition of bureaucracy would be quixotic;
    the word would lose that vitality gained through its use
    in everyday speech.

9. Aylmer, G.E. "Bureaucracy." THE NEW CAMBRIDGE MODERN
    HISTORY: COMPANION VOLUME, Vol. XIII. Edited by Peter
    Burke. Cambridge: Cambridge University Press, 1979.

    Presents a general history of the development of bur-
    eaucracy from the 16th century to the present. An im-
    portant theme is the difficulty of making comparisons
    about administrative systems from different historical
    periods.

10. Bendix, Reinhard. "Bureaucracy." INTERNATIONAL ENCYCLO-
    PEDIA OF THE SOCIAL SCIENCES, Vol. II. Edited by David
    Sills. New York: Macmillan, 1968.

    Treats the historical development of bureaucracy as a
    form of government.

11. Blau, Peter. BUREAUCRACY IN MODERN SOCIETY. New York:
    Random House, 1956. 127 pp.

    Summarizes the major sociological theories about bur-
    eaucracy. Specialization, hierarchy, written rules and
    impersonality are the characteristics of that form of or-
    ganization. The bureaucratic structure in turn induces
    a particular type of behavior among its members. Bureau-
    cracy and democracy, as organizing systems, can be dis-
    tinguished according to either's basic principle: effic-
    iency or freedom of dissent. Too much emphasis on effic-
    iency can be dysfunctional.

12. Blau, Peter, and Marshall W. Meyer. BUREAUCRACY IN MOD-
    ERN SOCIETY, 2nd. ed. New York: Random House, 1971.
    180 pp.

    A revision of Item 11.

13. Carr, Cecil. "Bureaucracy." CHAMBER'S ENCYCLOPEDIA.
    London: George Newnes, 1959.

    Bureaucracy described as a governmental phenomenon,
    with emphasis on the situation in Great Britain.

14. Emmerich, Herbert. "Bureaucracy." ENCYCLOPAEDIA BRITAN-
     NICA. Chicago: Encyclopaedia Britannica, Inc., 1960.

     Bureaucracy is described as an unhealthy condition that
     society must ever guard against.

15. Friedrich, Carl J. "Bureaucracy." ENCYCLOPEDIA AMERICA-
     NA. New York: Americana Corporation, 1980.

     Public bureaucracy can be held responsible only when
     there exists a functioning constitution.

16. Jacoby, Henry. THE BUREAUCRATIZATION OF THE WORLD.
     Berkeley: University of California Press, 1973.   241 pp.

     Attempts to illuminate the forces shaping a central soc-
     ial issue of the 20th century. The roots of bureaucracy
     are found in the absolute monarchy and in the Enlighten-
     ment reaction to feudalism. The growth of rationalism
     has created a social form which pervades both the economy
     and the polity. The durability of bureaucracy is illus-
     trated by the Russian/Soviet example. Antibureaucratic
     thought and other reactions to the "administered world"
     are described. This book is a translation from the orig-
     inal German.

17. Kamenka, Eugene, and Martin Krygier, eds. BUREAUCRACY:
     THE CAREER OF A CONCEPT. London: Edward Arnold, 1979.
     165 pp.

     A collection of original essays concerning the emergence
     of the concept of bureaucracy as an analytical tool in the
     social sciences. The contributions of Saint-Simon, Marx,
     Weber, Lenin, and Trotsky are described. The role of the
     bureaucracy in modern Marxist thought is covered, partic-
     ularly in terms of the "new class" argument. Contains
     Item 529.

18. Kolodziej, E.A. "Bureaucracy." NEW CATHOLIC ENCYCLO-
     PEDIA. New York: McGraw-Hill, 1967.

     On the knowledge and expertise of officials as a chal-
     lenge to democracy.

19. Laski, Harold J. "Bureaucracy." ENCYCLOPEDIA OF THE
    SOCIAL SCIENCES, Vol. III. New York: Macmillan, 1930.

    Defines bureaucracy as a form of government in which the
    experts and other permanent officers have monopolized ex-
    ecutive power, to the detriment of the liberties of citi-
    zens. If left to their own devices, officials will become
    a caste with a narrow point of view. Political control
    of the experts is necessary.

20. Merton, Robert, Alisa P. Gray, Barbara Hockey, and Hanan
    C. Selvin, eds. READER IN BUREAUCRACY. Glencoe, Ill.:
    Free Press, 1952. 464 pp.

    A collection of original essays and previously published
    work on several aspects of bureaucracy. The articles
    concern recent research on American and Western European
    conditions, with emphasis on public organizations. The-
    oretical concepts as well as specific cases are included.
    The personality of the bureaucrat and its pathologicial
    manifestations are also covered. Contains Items 142 and
    148.

21. Morstein Marx, Fritz. "Bureaucracy." INTRODUCTION TO
    POLITICS. Edited by Roy Peel and Joseph Roucek. New
    York: Thomas Y. Crowell, 1941.

    Discusses the political problems associated with modern
    bureaucracy.

22. Mouzelis, Nicos P. ORGANISATION AND BUREAUCRACY: AN AN-
    ALYSIS OF MODERN THEORIES. Chicago: Aldine, 1968.
    230 pp.

    Divides the literature on formal organizations between
    the theorists of bureaucracy--Marx, Weber, Michels--and
    the management scientists--Taylor, the "human relations"
    school, and decision-making theorists. Recent trends in-
    dicate a convergence of these two lines of thought. The
    concern for organizational effectiveness must be broad-
    ened to take into account the impact of bureaucracy on
    the entire society.

23.   Mouzelis, Nicos P.   "Bureaucracy."   ENCYCLOPAEDIA BRITAN-
      NICA. Chicago: Encyclopaedia Britannica, Inc., 1974.

      Sees purposive design and goal specification as crucial
      criteria of bureaucracy. Classical and managerial the-
      orists are described. The two research traditions are
      now converging.

24.   Mouzelis, Nicos P.   ORGANISATION AND BUREAUCRACY: AN AN-
      ALYSIS OF MODERN THEORIES, rev. ed. London: Routledge
      and Kegan Paul, 1976. 234 pp.

      A revision of Item 22.

25.   Newland, Chester A.   "Bureaucracy: Characteristics and
      Problems." PUBLIC PERSONNEL REVIEW, 21 (Jan., 1963).
      24-29.

      Examines the popular and analytical meanings attached
      to the concept of bureaucracy. A common theme in the
      literature is the tendency of organizations to replace
      ends with means.

26.   Peabody, Robert L., and Francis E. Rourke.   "Public Bur-
      eaucracies." HANDBOOK OF ORGANIZATIONS. Edited by
      James March. Chicago: Rand McNally, 1965.

      Review "research which has focused upon public bureau-
      cracies and present a summary of the state of existing
      knowledge about such organizations." The emphasis is on
      the unique features of public agencies. The place of
      bureaucratic power in democratic theory is summarized.

27.   Riggs, Fred.   "Introduction: Shifting Meanings of the
      Term 'Bureaucracy.'" INTERNATIONAL SOCIAL SCIENCE
      JOURNAL, 31 (1979), 563-84.

      Relying on Albrow (Item 8), identifies eleven major
      meanings of the word "bureaucracy." The definitions are
      compared with those found in major dictionaries and in
      the article by Stone (Item 29). Scholars must adopt more
      precise terms when trying to describe the things now
      covered by that overworked word.

28. Stewart, Phyllis L., and Nancy Wityak. "Bureaucracy."
     ACADEMIC AMERICAN ENCYCLOPEDIA. Princeton, N.J.: Arete
     Publishing, 1981.

     On bureaucracy in government and industry.

29. Stone, Robert C. "Bureaucracy." A DICTIONARY OF THE
     SOCIAL SCIENCES. Edited by Julius Gould and William
     L. Kolb. New York: Free Press, 1964.

     Social science tends to follow variations of the Web-
     erian definition of bureaucracy.

30. Walcott, Charles. "Bureaucracy." DICTIONARY OF AMERI-
     CAN HISTORY, rev. ed. New York: Charles Scribner's,
     1976.

     Discusses problems associated with the growth of the
     American civil service.

31. Waldo, Dwight. "Bureaucracy." COLLIER'S ENCYCLOPEDIA.
     New York: Crowell-Collier Publishers, 1962.

     Says that bureaucracy has both a neutral and an emo-
     tional meaning. A historical sketch of bureaucracy is
     given. The work of Weber and later social scientists
     is emphasized.

32. Yeager, Mary A. "Bureaucracy." ENCYCLOPEDIA OF AMERICAN
     ECONOMIC HISTORY: STUDIES OF THE PRINCIPAL MOVEMENTS
     AND IDEAS, Vol. III. Edited by Glenn Porter. New York:
     Charles Scribner's, 1980.

     Traces the history of the concept of bureaucracy, with
     emphasis on the management of public and private organ-
     izations in the United States.

II. THE STUDY OF BUREAUCRACY

A. Early Discussions of Bureaucracy (Pre-1930)

33. Allen, Carleton. "Bureaucracy Triumphant." QUARTERLY
    REVIEW, 240 (1923), 246-61.

    Deplores the undermining of the traditional English
    constitution through the unrestrained use of authority
    by appointed officials.

34. Allen, Carleton. "Bureaucracy Again." QUARTERLY REVIEW,
    244 (1925), 38-52.

    A review of Marriott's *The English Constitution in
    Transition*.

35. Bagehot, Walter. THE ENGLISH CONSTITUTION. London: Chap-
    man and Hall, 1867. 348 pp.

    Cautions the British against too much admiration for the
    continental model of administration. Bureaucracy may be
    efficient, but it has unavoidable defects, tending to a
    sort of "under-government in point of quality" and "over-
    government in point of quantity." In contrast to the
    specialist, the generalist will be better able to grasp
    the "floating vapours of knowledge" that shapes the char-
    acter of a nation.

36. Baker, Benjamin. "An 'American Federation of Business'
    Could Check Growth of Bureaucracy." ANNALIST, 30 (1926),
    619.

    A businessman urges greater unity in the fight against
    the proliferation of bureaucratic regulations.

11

37. "Benevolent Bureaucracy: Is It Managing Our Forests?"
     OUTLOOK, 139 (1925), 565-66.

     A critical look at the U.S. Forest Service.

38. Bent, Silas. "Bureaucracy Triumphant: Government by Com-
     mission at Washington." CENTURY, 112 (1926), 180-89.

     Is alarmed by the delegation of authority to federal
     commissions for the regulation of the economy.

39. Bent, Silas. "Bureaucracy Triumphant." STRANGE BEDFEL-
     LOWS: A REVIEW OF POLITICS, PERSONALITIES, AND THE
     PRESS. New York: Horace Liveright, 1928.

     An elaboration of the theme in Item 38.

40. Beveridge, Albert. "Republic or Bureaucracy?" SATURDAY
     EVENING POST, 196 (March 15, 1924), 33, 189-90. 193-94,
     197.

     A U.S. senator denounces the increased governmental in-
     terference with the prerogatives of business.

41. Blackie, J.S. "Prussia and the Prussian System." WEST-
     MINSTER REVIEW, 37 (1842), 134-71.

     In one of the first uses of the concept of bureaucracy
     in English, the administrative style is seen as one of the
     most illiberal features of Prussian government, turning
     the citizens into "mere clods, political nullities."

42. Bourne, Jonathan. "The Growing American Bureaucracy."
     REVIEW OF REVIEWS, 46 (1912), 201-06.

     A U.S. senator claims that the executive branch has
     grown in power at the expense of Congress.

43. Bourne, Jonathan. "The Menace of Bureaucracy." COLLIER'S,
     54 (December 26, 1914), 30.

     Appointed officials have too much discretion.

44. Bourne, Jonathan. "Freedom Menaced by Bureaucracy."
    PUBLIC, 18 (1915), 174.

    An appointed officialdom is a threat to the political
    liberties of Americans.

45. Brater, Karl. "Bureaucracy." CYCLOPAEDIA OF POLITICAL
    SCIENCE, POLITICAL ECONOMY, AND THE POLITICAL HISTORY
    OF THE UNITED STATES. Edited by John J. Lalor. Chi-
    cago: M.B. Cary, 1883.

    A translation of a German political scientist's defin-
    ition of bureaucracy. Essentially, it is a "system of
    over-government." This tendency to meddle leads to a
    number of other bureaucratic evils.

46. "Bureaucracy." DICTIONARY OF POLITICAL ECONOMY. Edited
    by R.H.I. Palgrave. London: Macmillan, 1894.

    Contrasts bureaucracy with the laissez-faire economic
    system.

47. "Bureaucracy." JOURNAL OF COMPARATIVE LEGISLATION AND
    INTERNATIONAL LAW, 11 (1929), 152-54.

    Compares administrative law in the U.S. and Great
    Britain.

48. "Bureaucracy and Salaries." SPECTATOR, 125 (1920), 458-
    59.

    The size of the payroll for the British civil service
    has risen alarmingly since WWI.

49. "Bureaucracy in the Making." NEW REPUBLIC, 16 (1918),
    94-96.

    Events during WWI have led to the decay of the legis-
    lature and the increase in executive power.

50. "Bureaucratic Authority." SOLICITOR'S JOURNAL, 72 (1928), 492-93.

     Appointed officials in Britain have assumed ever greater degrees of judicial authority.

51. Cecil, Robert. "The Growth of Bureaucracy." SATURDAY RE-VIEW, 111 (1911), 449-50.

     Defines bureaucracy as "the uncontrolled power of ministers and officials."

52. Couzens, James. "How to Kill Bureaucracy." COLLIER'S, 75 (March 28, 1925), 27.

     A U.S. Senator warns against federal centralizations.

53. Curtin, Thomas. "Military Bureaucracy and Revolution." NATIONAL REVIEW, 70 (1917), 304-13.

     Imperial Germany is described as a military bureaucracy.

54. Dickinson, John. "Administrative Law and the Fear of Bureaucracy." AMERICAN BAR ASSOCIATION JOURNAL, 14 (1928), 513-16, 597-602.

     Explains to lawyers this new term "administrative law." Despite the necessity of expert administration, Americans fear bureaucracy

55. Eaton, Dorman. CIVIL SERVICE IN GREAT BRITAIN. New York: Harper and Brothers, 1881. 82 pp.

     Defends the civil service movement against the charge that the reform would lead to a bureaucratic system like those in Europe. A proper civil service system would actually limit bureaucracy by opening public offices to every eligible person.

56. "The Encroaching Bureaucracy." QUARTERLY REVIEW, 221 (1914), 51-75.

     On centralization in British government.

57.   "Encroachments of Bureaucracy." SPECTATOR, 117 (1916).
        650-51.

        Suggests that the British government is on a dangerous
        course with the plans for reorganization of labor ex-
        changes.

58.   "The Encroachments of Bureaucracy." LAW JOURNAL, 68
        (1929), 309.

        On Hewart's *The New Despotism* (Item 70).

59.   "The Failure of Bureaucracy." NEW REPUBLIC, 15 (1918),
        305-06.

        Discusses the many deficiencies of wartime administra-
        tion in Washington.

60.   Fergusson, Harvey. "Out Where Bureaucracy Begins."
        NATION, 121 (1925), 112-14.

        Reports that those hearty folks in the Western states
        live under a modified form of socialism because of the
        heavy involvement of the federal government in their ac-
        tivities.

61.   Finer, Herman. THE BRITISH CIVIL SERVICE: AN INTRODUC-
        TORY ESSAY. London: The Fabian Society, 1927. 96 pp.

        Claims that, "in the continental sense, England has
        no bureaucracy." The word, as a reproach, is used rare-
        ly in Great Britain.

62.   Freeman, W. Marshall. "Our Bureaucratic Autocrats."
        ENGLISH REVIEW, 48 (1929), 387-93.

        British cabinet ministers have surrendered their auth-
        ority to appointed civil servants.

63.   Hale, Charles W. BUREAUCRACY AND PATERNALISM THREATEN-
        ING THE UNITED STATES: THEIR SURE AND DANGEROUS

ACCOMPLISHMENT SHOWN IN PENDING AND THREATENED LEGISLA-
TION. Indianapolis: n.p., 1921. 16 pp.

A tract against the regulation of the practice of medicine.

64. Garner, James W. INTRODUCTION TO POLITICAL SCIENCE. New
     York: American Book, 1910. 616 pp.

     Classifies administration as bureaucratic or popular.
     The bureaucratic version is dominated by an elite of pro-
     fessionally trained officials.

65. Garner, James W. "Bureaucracy." CYCLOPEDIA OF AMERICAN
     GOVERNMENT. Edited by A. McLaughlin and A.B. Hart.
     New York: P. Smith, 1914.

     Outlines strengths and weaknesses of bureaucracy as a
     form of public administration.

66. Ghose, Nagendra. COMPARATIVE ADMINISTRATIVE LAW, WITH
     SPECIAL REFERENCE TO THE ORGANIZATION AND LEGAL POSI-
     TION OF THE ADMINISTRATIVE AUTHORITIES IN BRITISH IN-
     DIA. Calcutta: Butterworth, 1919. 704 pp.

     Includes a historical sketch of bureaucracy in India.

67. Goodnow, Frank. COMPARATIVE ADMINISTRATIVE LAW. New
     York: G.P. Putnam's, 1903. 327 pp.

     Defines bureaucracy as a system of administration that
     "relies entirely or mainly upon professional officers."
     Such a system is incompatible with civil liberty.

68. Green, Alice Stopford. "Growing Bureaucracy and Parlia-
     mentary Decline." NINETEENTH CENTURY, 47 (1900),
     839-46.

     Argues that the vote for women is an irrelevant issue
     since parliamentary power has been usurped by the bur-
     eaucracy; women would be "flocking in when the fair is
     over." Instead, women should develop the ability to
     keep watch on the bureaus.

69. Griffith, Sanford. "Germany's Bureaucratic Blight."
    OUTLOOK, 60 (1927), 696.

    A report on governmental problems in Weimar Germany.

70. Hewart, Gordon. THE NEW DESPOTISM. New York: Cosmopol-
    itan Books, 1929. 311 pp.

    The Lord Chief Justice of England describes the pern-
    icious effects of "administrative law." Bureaucrats have
    encroached upon the prerogatives of the courts, thus un-
    dermining the whole notion of the rule of law. Several
    recent statutes delegating excessive power to the bureau-
    cracy are discussed.

71. Houghton, Bernard. BUREAUCRATIC GOVERNMENT: A STUDY IN
    INDIAN POLITY. London: P.S. King and Son, 1913. 200
    pp.

    Criticizes the British system of administration in In-
    dia. It is an efficient machine which destroys the spir-
    it of those whom it administers. Bureaucratic formalism
    undermines any feeling of devotion to government. Lord
    Curzon was largely responsible for this unhappy develop-
    ment.

72. Long, Robert. "Democracy, Bureaucracy and Doles: A Let-
    ter from Berlin." FORTNIGHTLY REVIEW, 115 (1921), 1-16.

    Observations on conditions in Weimar Germany.

73. Lowell, Abbott L. PUBLIC OPINION AND POPULAR GOVERNMENT.
    New York: Longmans, Green and Co., 1913. 415 pp.

    Contains several references to the popular animosity
    toward bureaucracy in the United States. In general,
    there is little danger of such an institution gaining
    power in this country.

74. McSwain, John J. "Bureaucratic Government versus Repre-
    sentative Government." CONGRESSIONAL RECORD, 67 (1926),
    4889-92.

On the inflexibility of the military in the development
of air power. According to Billy Mitchell, military education is the root cause of bureaucracy.

75. Mencken, H.L. "Life under Bureaucracy." PREJUDICES.
     London: Jonathan Cape, 1927.

     Says that "it is the invariable habit of bureaucracies,
     at all times and everywhere, to assume ... that every
     citizen is a criminal." The only way to protect oneself
     is to acquire "pull."

76. Michels, Robert. POLITICAL PARTIES: A SOCIOLOGICAL STUDY
     OF THE OLIGARCHICAL TENDENCIES OF MODERN DEMOCRACY.
     London: Eden and Cedar Paul, 1915. 416 pp.

     Because of the "Iron Law of Oligarchy," even the most
     democratically based organization will eventually be con-
     trolled by a leadership elite. The organization becomes
     more bureaucratic as the unit is seen as an end in itself.
     The resulting "bureaucratic spirit" will corrupt the char-
     acter and engender moral poverty. Attempts at decentral-
     ization only lead to the creation of a multitude of small
     oligarchies.

77. Mill, John Stuart. ON LIBERTY. London: J.W. Parker,
     1859. 207 pp.

     Among the reasons for limiting government is the dis-
     couragement of bureaucratic power. The more activities
     the officials control, the less initiative the citizens
     will show. The vitality of the people is too often sac-
     rificed to the needs of the state machinery.

78. Mill, John Stuart. CONSIDERATIONS ON REPRESENTATIVE
     GOVERNMENT. London: Parker, Son and Bourn, 1861.
     365 pp.

     Defines bureaucracy as a system in which "the work of
     government has been in the hands of governors by profes-
     sion." While such a system has many advantages, it be-
     comes a victim of its own routines. The control of the
     professional staff is a problem for democracy.

79. "The Monotony of Bureaucracy." SATURDAY REVIEW, 125
       (1918), 337-38.

       Associates socialism with the deadening effects of bur-
       eaucracy.

80. Mosca, Gaetano. THE RULING CLASS. New York: McGraw-Hill,
       1939. 514 pp.

       Defines bureaucracy as a political system in which a
       larger portion of the total wealth supports the military
       and the public services. The bureaucracy is seen as the
       tool of the dominant class in society. Individual lead-
       ership is minimized. The other type of state is the
       "feudal," with power less centralized and specialized.

81. Muir, Ramsey. PEERS AND BUREAUCRATS: TWO PROBLEMS OF
       ENGLISH GOVERNMENT. London: Constable, 1910. 243 pp.

       Disabuses the English of the notion that they do not
       have a bureaucracy. The English bureaucrats are a highly
       qualified group, but they are "liable to certain defects,
       inherent in all bureaucracies." In any case, the further
       expansion of bureaucracy is inevitable.

82. Palmerston, Viscount. "Letter to Queen Victoria, Febru-
       ary 25, 1838." THE LETTERS OF QUEEN VICTORIA, Vol. I,
       1837-1843. Edited by Arthur Benson and Viscount Esher.
       London: John Murray, 1907.

       Lectures the Queen about the meaning of the new word,
       "bureaucracy."

83. "Peers and Bureaucrats." SPECTATOR, 105 (1910), 652-53.

       Review of Muir, Item 81.

84. Pettingill, Samuel B. "Government by Bureaucrats."
       NOTRE DAME LAWYER, 1 (1925-26), 24-29.

       Deplores the granting of judicial and legislative pow-
       er to administrators.

85. Pound, Ezra. "Bureaucracy, the Flail of Jehovah."
     IMPACT: ESSAYS ON IGNORANCE AND THE DECLINE OF AMER-
     ICAN CIVILIZATION. Chicago: H. Regnery, 1960.

     An article written in 1928. Officials and their offic-
     iousness make life miserable for citizens.

86. Saxon, John. "Autocratic Bureaucracy." OUTLOOK, 55
     (1925), 126-37.

     On the British civil service.

87. von Schulte, Friedrich. "Bureaucracy and Its Operation
     in Germany and Austria-Hungary." CONTEMPORARY REVIEW,
     37 (1880), 432-58.

     Describes the administrative structure and personnel
     of the major German states.

88. Sharp, Walter. "The Political Bureaucracy of France
     since the War." AMERICAN POLITICAL SCIENCE REVIEW,
     22 (1928), 301-23.

     Finds that French administration is undergoing rapid
     change. The two major reform efforts emphasize decen-
     tralization and the improvement in the morale of the
     civil service. Whether these movements will bear fruit
     remains to be seen.

89. "The Spread of Bureaucracy." CONGRESSIONAL RECORD, 62
     (1922), 10798-99.

     Reprint of an editorial from the Chicago *Tribune* de-
     nouncing the growth in government expenditures.

90. Watson, W.F. "The Rise of the Official Class: An An-
     alysis of the Growth of Bureaucratic Officialism in
     the Trade Unions and the Labour Party." FORTNIGHTLY
     REVIEW, 124 (1925), 363-73.

     Says that socialism will lead to a large bureaucratic
     establishment, as events within the Labour Party show.

91. Webb, Sidney, and Beatrice Webb. STATUTORY AUTHORITIES
     FOR SPECIAL PURPOSES: WITH A SUMMARY OF THE DEVELOP-
     MENT OF LOCAL GOVERNMENT STRUCTURES. London: Longmans,
     Green, 1922. 521 pp.

     Include a discussion of the impact of a centralized ad-
     ministration on British local government.

92. Wedd, H.G. "The Rise of Bureaucracy, or the Growing In-
     terference of the Government Officials with the Liberty
     of the Subject." LAW JOURNAL, 68 (1929), 220-21.

     On conditions in Great Britain.

93. Willoughby, W.F. PRINCIPLES OF PUBLIC ADMINISTRATION.
     Washington, D.C.: Brookings Institution, 1927. 720 pp.

     In this early public administration textbook, bureau-
     cracy is defined as a personnel system. As such, "there
     can be nothing to justify the prejudices which exist in
     the United States against what is known as bureaucracy."

          B. Marxist Perspectives on Bureaucracy

94. Andreski, Stanislav. "Society, Bureaucrats and Business-
     men." SURVEY, 25 (Autumn, 1980), 112-26.

     Sees bureaucracy as a form of white-collar "parasitism."
     The phenomenon occurs in all large organizations, but it
     is stimulated by Marxist doctrine, with its emphasis on
     collective action. Marxism also denies that those who
     are supported by public resources in a socialist state
     can be exploiters.

95. Arato, Andrew. "Understanding Bureaucratic Centralism."
     TELOS, 35 (1978), 73-87.

     Discusses the inadequacy of classical Marxist doctrine
     in explaining the centralizing tendencies of the social-
     ist state. In a reformulation of Marxist concepts, it
     is argued that Stalinism was both the formative process
     and the first stage of bureaucratic centralism.

96. Bendix, Reinhard. "Socialism and the Theory of Bureau-
     cracy." CANADIAN JOURNAL OF ECONOMICS AND POLITICAL
     SCIENCE, 16 (1950), 501-14.

     Shows how classical revolutionary socialists attempted
     to deal with the problem of bureaucracy. Marx's ideas
     on freedom and the organization are examined.

97. Bookchin, Murray. "On Neo-Marxism, Bureaucracy and the
     Body Politic." TOWARD AN ECOLOGICAL SOCIETY. Mont-
     real: Black Rose Books, 1980.

     Criticizes Herbert Marcuse and other 20th-century
     Marxists for their failure to deal with the illiberal
     implications of Marxist ideas about authority and the
     social structure.

98. Draper, Hal. KARL MARX'S THEORY OF REVOLUTION. Vol. I:
     STATE AND BUREAUCRACY (in two volumes). New York:
     Monthly Review Press, 1977. 728 pp.

     The first part of a multi-volume treatment of the pol-
     itical theory of Karl Marx. In this part, the argument
     is made that Marx saw the state as indistinguishable from
     its bureaucratic organs. In analyzing the early writings
     and later works on political questions, however, one can
     make a distinction between "bureaucratism" or the attitude
     of public officials and "bureaucracy" as an active polit-
     ical force. The implications of Marx's ideas for later
     socialist thought is considered.

99. Eisenstadt, S.N., and Klaus von Beyme. "Bureaucracy."
     MARXISM, COMMUNISM, AND WESTERN SOCIETY: A COMPARATIVE
     ENCYCLOPEDIA, Vol. I. New York: Herder and Herder,
     1972.

     Include a brief survey of the contributions of major
     thinkers to a Marxist study of bureaucracy. Current
     Soviet approaches to the question of bureaucracy are em-
     phasized. Bureaucracy is perceived by the Soviets as a
     problem peculiar to capitalism.

100. Fainstein, Susan S., and Norman I. Fainstein. "The Pol-
      itical Economy of American Bureaucracy." MAKING BUR-
      EAUCRACIES WORK. Edited by Carol Weiss and Allen H.
      Barton. Beverly Hills, Cal.: Sage, 1980.

      Using a Marxist structuralist approach, argue that the
      deficiencies of bureaucracy are rooted in the capitalist
      economy. Attacks on bureaucracy are to the advantage of
      business because they weaken government's ability to im-
      prove the status of the deprived classes. Powerful pri-
      vate interests will continue to escape democratic con-
      trol because of the weakness of government. The most
      non-controversial agencies are those which serve capital-
      ism and the dominant class in America.

101. Glaberman, Martin. "Structuralism as Defense of the Bur-
      eaucratic Status Quo: A Dialectical Critique of Althus-
      serian Theory." REVIEW OF SOCIAL THEORY, 3 (1975),
      3-12.

      Critiques the thought of the French neo-Marxist,
      Louis Althusser.

102. Goldman, Paul, and Donald R. Van Houten. "Managerial
      Strategies and the Worker: A Marxist Analysis of Bur-
      cracy." SOCIOLOGICAL QUARTERLY, 18 (1977), 108-25.

      Note the absence of a sociology of organizations in
      classical and modern Marxist theory. There is, however,
      the potential for a Marxist model of bureaucracy which
      might challenge the Weberian perspective. In such a new
      model, capitalist strategies of good management can be
      viewed as mechanisms for controlling the work force and,
      consequently, the working class.

103. Goldman, Paul. "Sociologists and the Study of Bureau-
      cracy." INSURGENT SOCIOLOGIST, 8 (1978), 21-30.

      Calls the traditional sociology of organizations a con-
      servative body of thought. A Marxist approach offers a
      better way of dealing with the dynamics of change, as
      well as serving the needs of the members.

104. Hearn, Francis. "Rationality and Bureaucracy: Maoist
      Contributions to a Marxist Theory of Bureaucracy."
      SOCIOLOGICAL QUARTERLY, 19 (1978), 37-54.

      Contends that the ideal of bureaucracy found in Maoist
      thought provides the basis for a Marxist alternative to
      the Weberian model. This model challenges the notion
      that bureaucracy and revolution are contradictory.

105. Hegedus, Andras. SOCIALISM AND BUREAUCRACY. New York:
      St. Martin's, 1976. 193 pp.

      A collection of previously published articles which ex-
      amine the question of bureaucracy in socialist states.
      Centralization has led to the degradation of socialist
      ideals. The works of Marx and Lenin are reviewed and
      alternatives to bureaucratism are considered.

106. Heydebrand, Wolf. "Organizational Contradictions in Pub-
      lic Bureaucracies: Toward a Marxian Theory of Organiza-
      tions." SOCIOLOGICAL QUARTERLY, 18 (1977), 83-107.

      Uses Marxist categories and propositions to outline an
      alternative theory of organizations. Organization con-
      trol structures and newer forms of organizing work ac-
      tivity such as professional status groups represent di-
      alectical tension. The organizational contradictions pre-
      dicted by Marx are discussed in terms of the American
      judiciary.

107. Hodges, Donald C. THE BUREAUCRATIZATION OF SOCIALISM.
      Amherst: University of Massachusetts Press, 1981.
      210 pp.

      Argues that the bureaucratization of the socialist
      state can be explained in Marxist terms. In socialist
      systems, science becomes a major factor of production.
      The emphasis on scientific control leads to the rise of
      a new ruling elite.

108. Horowitz, Irving Louis. "Slouching toward the Brave
      New World: Bureaucracy, Administration, and State
      Power." MARXIST PERSPECTIVES, 3 (Spring, 1980), 142-
      157.

Claims that the doctrines of public administration are meant to rationalize society for domination by the managers.

109. Kaminski, Antoni. "State Bureaucracy and Parliamentary Democracy in the Development of a Liberal-Democratic State." POLISH SOCIOLOGICAL BULLETIN, 38 (1977), 37-48.

Examines the role of bureaucracy in the creation of the modern capitalist economy and society.

110. Krygier, Martin. "'Bureaucracy' in Trotsky's Analysis of Stalinism." SOCIALISM AND THE NEW CLASS: TOWARDS THE ANALYSIS OF STRUCTURAL INEQUALITY WITHIN SOCIAL-IST SOCIETIES. Edited by Marian Sawer. Bedford Park: Australasian Political Studies Association, 1978.

On Trotsky's attack on the Stalinist bureaucracy.

111. Lazreg, Mariha. "Bureaucracy and Class: The Algerian Dialectic." DIALECTICAL ANTHROPOLOGY, 1 (1975-76), 295-305.

Argues that a social category such as bureaucracy does not constitute a social class. Algeria is used to prove that bureaucracy is not a class in the Marxist sense.

112. Lefort, Claude. "What Is Bureaucracy?" TELOS, 22 (1974-75), 31-65.

Analyzes current theoretical approaches to the study of bureaucracy, with emphasis on the thought of Marx and Weber.

113. Lenin, V.I. STATE AND REVOLUTION. New York: International Publishers, 1932. 103 pp.

Originally published in 1917. The nature of the post-revolutionary state is explored. The old bureaucratic machinery must be broken up and replaced by an administrative system based on the participation of the masses.

114. Lenin, V.I. "Better Fewer, But Better." COLLECTED WORKS
      OF LENIN, Vol. XXXIII. Moscow: Progress Publishers,
      1966.

      An article of 1923, suggesting how growing bureaucrat-
      ism can be combated in the Soviet Union. The basic prob-
      lem is that Russians, although capable of great revolu-
      tionary acts, have not shown the same creativity in ad-
      ministration.

115. Liebich, André. "On the Origins of a Marxist Theory of
      Bureaucracy in the *Critique of Hegel's 'Philosophy of
      Right'*" POLITICAL THEORY, 10 (1982), 77-93.

      Argues that Marx's critique of Hegel (Item 120) is of
      limited value as a general abstract commentary on the
      role of modern bureaucracy. It is better understood
      as a reflection of conditions in Germany in the 1840s.

116. Lukács, Georg. "Tribune or Bureaucrat?" ESSAYS ON RE-
      ALISM. Cambridge, Mass.: MIT Press, 1980.

      A translation of the 1940 article on capitalist lit-
      erature, using Lenin's two types of ideologues--revolu-
      tionary tribune or bureaucrat. Come the revolution, the
      writers will be able to free themselves from their bur-
      eaucratic roles and become true artists for the masses.

117. Mandel, Ernest. ON BUREAUCRACY: A MARXIST ANALYSIS.
      London: IMG Publications, 1973. 40 pp.

118. Mandel, Ernest. "Why the Soviet Bureaucracy Is Not a
      New Ruling Class." MONTHLY REVIEW, 31 (July-August,
      1979), 63-79.

      Argues that Trotsky was correct in rejecting the idea
      of a bureaucratic class in the Soviet Union.

119. Marx, Karl. "Comments on the Latest Prussian Censor-
      ship Instruction." COLLECTED WORKS OF KARL MARX AND
      FREDERICK ENGELS, Vol. I. New York: International
      Publishers, 1975.

      Marx's first comments on bureaucracy, from 1842.

120. Marx, Karl. "Contributions to the Critique of Hegel's Philosophy of Law." COLLECTED WORKS OF KARL MARX AND FREDERICK ENGELS, Vol. III. New York: International Publishers, 1975.

An attack on the political philosophy of Hegel and particularly his positive view of state administration. Hegel idealized the Prussian bureaucracy and made it the "universal class" in his political system. Marx rejected the inherent superiority of public officials. Bureaucracy tends to become a state within the state. For individual bureaucrats, the pursuit of career goals is more important than public objectives.

121. Mićunović, Dragoljub. "Bureaucracy and Public Communication." PRAXIS: YUGOSLAV ESSAYS IN THE PHILOSOPHY AND METHODOLOGY OF THE SOCIAL SCIENCES. Edited by Mihailo Markovic and Gajo Petrovic. Dordrecht: D. Reidel, 1979.

Understands Marx as asserting that the source of bureaucratic power is official secrecy. An effective form of public communication is then the enemy of bureaucracy. True socialism demands an honest and independent media so that the public can understand what officials are doing. The comments of Marx on the evils of censorship substantiate this need.

122. Mollenkopf, John. "Untangling the Logics of Urban Service Bureaucracies: The Strange Case of the San Francisco Municipal Railway." INTERNATIONAL JOURNAL OF HEALTH SERVICES, 9 (1979), 255-68.

Combines Marxist and public choice theory to assess the reasons for a bureaucratic failure.

123. Osterfeld, D. "The Bureaucracy Problem." FREEMAN, 29 (1979), 178-89.

Insists that bureaucracy is inevitable in socialist society because of the absence of market information. The work of Hegedus (Item 105) is discussed.

124. Papaioannou, Kostas. "Marx and the Bureaucratic State."
      DISSENT, 16 (1969), 252-62.

      Says that Marx did not understand bureaucracy, and so
      Marxism is incapable of explaining the rise of the tot-
      alitarian state.

125. Perez-Diaz, Victor M. STATE, BUREAUCRACY AND CIVIL
      SOCIETY: A CRITICAL DISCUSSION OF THE POLITICAL THE-
      ORY OF KARL MARX. London: Macmillan, 1978. 117 pp.

      Contends that the state bureaucracy and the polity
      were never treated by Marx in any systematic way. The
      concept of bureaucracy in Marx's early and mature writ-
      ings is explored. Integrating the work on Hegel and the
      regime of Louis Napoleon, it is possible to construct a
      Marxist view of bureaucracy as an ideological defense
      of the bourgeois class. The bureaucracy remains an area
      of conflict for social interests.

126. Renault, Gregory. "From Bureaucracy to *L'Imaginaire*:
      Cornelius Castoriadis' Immanent Critique of Marxism."
      CATALYST, 13 (1979), 72-90.

      Examines the Greek writer's critique of Marx and the
      question of bureaucracy. The criticism emerges from
      Marxist premises and thus does not overcome the intrin-
      sic weaknesses of the Marxist worldview.

127. Sewart, John J. "Alvin Gouldner's Challenge for Socio-
      logy and Marxism: The Problem of Bureaucracy." PAC-
      IFIC SOCIOLOGICAL REVIEW, 24 (1981), 441-60.

      Describes Gouldner's contributions to a critical soc-
      iology within the context of Western Marxism.

128. Singer, Brian. "The Early Castoriadis: Socialism, Bar-
      barism and the Bureaucratic Thread." CANADIAN JOUR-
      NAL OF POLITICAL AND SOCIAL THEORY, 3 (1979), 35-56.

      Reviews the early work of a Greek critic of the Marx-
      ist position on bureaucracy.

129. Tadić, Ljubomir. "Bureaucracy--Reified Organization."
      PRAXIS: YUGOSLAV ESSAYS IN THE PHILOSOPHY AND METHOD-
      OLOGY OF THE SOCIAL SCIENCES. Edited by Mihailo Mar-
      kovic and Gajo Petrovic. Dordrecht: D. Reidel, 1979.

      Accepts the Weberian definition of bureaucracy as lead-
      ing to alienation and the degradation of knowledge into
      that which is practical. Most Western writers go on to
      conclude that there is no way to escape this sort of
      lifeless fate. However, the Yugoslav version of Marx-
      ism does offer hope. A democratic, socialist self-gov-
      ernment can provide for a fluid, creative social process
      which rejects the supremacy of rigid institutions and
      hierarchy.

130. Trotsky, Leon. "The Terror of Bureaucratic Self-Preser-
      vation." WRITINGS OF LEON TROTSKY, Vol. VII. Edited
      by George Breitman and Bev Scott. New York: Pathfind-
      er Press, 1970.

      Only worldwide revolution can pressure the proletar-
      iat of the Soviet Union to rise up against their bureau-
      cratic masters.

131. Trotsky, Leon. "Against Bureaucracy, Progressive and
      Unprogressive." PROBLEMS OF EVERYDAY LIFE: AND OTHER
      WRITINGS ON SCIENCE AND CULTURE. New York: Monad
      Press, 1973.

      A 1923 article on conditions in the Soviet Union.

132. Trotsky, Leon. "Bureaucratic Tendencies." WRITINGS OF
      LEON TROTSKY, Vol. XIII. Edited by George Breitman.
      New York: Pathfinder Press, 1979

      Even the Trotskyites are guilty of creating bureau-
      cracy within their own organization.

133. Trotsky, Leon. "The Stalinist Bureaucracy in Straits."
      WRITINGS OF LEON TROTSKY, Vol. V. Edited by George
      Breitman and Sarah Lovell. New York: Pathfinder
      Books, 1973.

      Soviet bureaucracy has become even more repressive.

134.   Trotsky, Leon.   "On the Foreign Policy of the Stalinist
       Bureaucracy." WRITINGS OF LEON TROTSKY, Vol. V.   Ed-
       ited by George Breitman and Sarah Lovell. New York:
       Pathfinder Books, 1973.

       Stalin stirs up foreign intrigue in order to justify
       a repressive state machine.

135.   Trotsky, Leon.   "The Stalinist Bureaucracy and the Kirov
       Assassination: A Reply to Friends in America." WRIT-
       INGS OF LEON TROTSKY, Vol. VII.   Edited by George
       Breitman and Bev Scott. New York: Pathfinder Books,
       1971.

       An article of 1934 describing the bureaucratic dictat-
       orship not as a new class but as "a distorted expression
       of the dictatorship of the proletariat," which needs a
       permanent political crisis in order to survive.

136.   Trotsky, Leon.   "Where Is the Stalinist Bureaucracy Lead-
       ing the USSR?" WRITINGS OF LEON TROTSKY, Vol. VII.
       Edited by George Breitman and Bev Scott. New York:
       Pathfinder Books, 1971.

       An article of 1935 arguing that the workers must force
       the bureaucracy to reform itself before foreign enemies
       attack the Soviet Union.

137.   Trotsky, Leon.   "The Soviet Bureaucracy and the Spanish
       Revolution." WRITINGS OF LEON TROTSKY, Vol. VIII.
       Edited by George Breitman and Naomi Allen. New York:
       Pathfinder Press, 1970.

       An article of 1937 claiming the Soviets are sabotag-
       ing the Spanish revolution.

138.   Wittfogel, Karl.   "The Ruling Bureaucracy of Oriental
       Despotism: A Phenomenon That Paralyzed Marx." REVIEW
       OF POLITICS, 15 (1953), 350-59.

       Argues that Marx misunderstood the significance of
       the "Asiatic Society" as a social system.

139. Zamoshkin, I.A. "Ideological and Theoretical Discus-
     sions Surrounding the Problems of Bureaucracy." SOV-
     IET LAW AND GOVERNMENT, 10 (1971), 99-123.

     Explores the ideological elements of the "systems-
     functionalist" approach to organization theory in the
     capitalist societies.

140. Zamoshkin, I.A. "Bureaucracy and the Individual." SOV-
     IET REVIEW, 2 (August, 1961), 20-38.

     Presents the Soviet view of the impact of bureaucratic
     organizations on American life. The individual is de-
     tached from work and suffers from a sense of alienation.
     Capitalist social science has no answers to this prob-
     lem.

C. The Weberian Model

141. Arora, Ramesh. "Bureaucracy and the Political System:
     The Weberian Persepctive." CHINESE JOURNAL OF ADMIN-
     ISTRATION, 21 (1973), 1-7.

     A general discussion of Weber's political theory.

142. Burin, Frederic S. "Bureaucracy and National Socialism:
     A Reconsideration of Weberian Theory." READER IN BUR-
     EAUCRACY. Edited by Robert Merton, Ailsa Gray, Bar-
     bara Hockey, and Hanan Selvin. Glencoe, Ill.: Free
     Press, 1952.

     Describes how the Nazis were able to dominate the Ger-
     man bureaucracy, despite Weber's predictions about the
     resistance of administration to political control. Sev-
     eral techniques of "nazification" are listed. Through
     these means the civil service was converted into an arm
     of the party.

143. Churchward, L.G. "Bureaucracy--USA:USSR." COEXISTENCE,
     5 (1968), 201-10.

     Compares the two countries through a Weberian perspec-
     tive.

144. Constas, Helen. "Max Weber's Two Conceptions of Bur-
      eaucracy." AMERICAN JOURNAL OF SOCIOLOGY, 63 (1958),
      400-09.

      Notes ambiguities in Weber's ideas about the charis-
      matic model of bureaucracy. In particular, he failed
      to see that the charismatic system does not necessarily
      evolve into a legal-rational bureaucracy. It may re-
      main as the basis of a totalitarian structure.

145. Corpuz, Onofre D. "Theoretical Limitations of Max Web-
      er's Systematic Analysis of Bureaucracy." PHILIPPINE
      JOURNAL OF PUBLIC ADMINISTRATION, 1 (1957), 342-49.

      Finds several weaknesses in the Weberian analysis of
      the relationship between democracy and bureaucracy. A
      review of the model indicates no logical reason why a
      democratic society could not develop a responsible ad-
      ministrative structure.

146. Delany, William. "The Development and Decline of Patri-
      monial and Bureaucratic Administrations." ADMINISTRA-
      TIVE SCIENCE QUARTERLY, 7 (1963), 458-501.

      Evaluates the usefulness of Weber's theory for the
      study of modern organizations. Although the theory
      failed to predict the decline of bureaucracy in the U.S.
      and elsewhere, it is still a valid research tool.

147. Diamant, Alfred. "The Bureaucratic Model: Max Weber
      Rejected, Rediscovered, Reformed." PAPERS IN COMPAR-
      ATIVE PUBLIC ADMINISTRATION. Edited by Ferrel Heady
      and Sybil Stokes. Ann Arbor: University of Michigan,
      Institute of Public Administration, 1962.

      Concedes that Weber may have had something useful to
      say after all. The ideal type of bureaucracy might be
      applied in the comparative administration field.

148. Friedrich, Carl J. "Some Observations on Weber's Analy-
      sis of Bureaucracy." READER IN BUREAUCRACY. Edited
      by Robert Merton, Ailsa Gray, Barbara Hockey, and Han-
      an Selvin. Glencoe, Ill.: Free Press, 1952.

Expresses a number of reservations about Weber's ideal type. The notion of progressive rationalization is just one more version of the movement of society toward some unsubstantiated goal. The ideal type is a tool of dubious value in social research.

149. Gerth, H.H., and C. Wright Mills, eds. FROM MAX WEBER: ESSAYS IN SOCIOLOGY. New York: Oxford University Press, 1946. 490 pp.

Still the main source of Weber's ideal type of bureaucracy for most American writers. An introductory essay places Weber's work in perspective. The article, "Politics as Vocation," gives some indication of Weber's view of the political process.

150. Kaplan, Berton H. "Notes on a Non-Weberian Model of Bureaucracy: The Case of Development Bureaucracy." ADMINISTRATIVE SCIENCE QUARTERLY, 13 (1968), 471-83.

Suggests that the Weberian model, with its emphasis on organizational efficiency and effectiveness, must be refined and expanded for use in studying organizations designed for social development. Community disintegration and ego impairment are special constraints in development. Major structural patterns of a development bureaucracy are proposed.

151. Katz, Fred E., James Britton, Hsi Chih Chang, Virginia L. Fisher, Graeme Fraser, Helga Shen, Merced Ramos, and James E. Watson. "Do Administrative Officials Believe in Bureaucracy? A Pilot Study." SOCIOLOGICAL INQUIRY, 37 (1967), 205-09.

Operationalize elements of Weber's ideal type and apply a test to public officials. There was little association between rank and bureaucratic orientation. There was a tendency for longer service to decrease the official's belief in the value of strictly bureaucratic procedures.

152. Khan, Mohammed. "Bureaucracy: Theoretical Background and Developments." INDIAN JOURNAL OF PUBLIC

ADMINISTRATION, 23 (1977) 218-41.

Traces developments in sociological theory from Weber
to the present. The major criticisms of Weber are described. Also analyzed is the utility of Weberian concepts in developing countries.

153. Maneker, Jerry S. "An Extension of Max Weber's Theory
       of Bureaucracy." REVISTA INTERNACIONAL DE SOCIOLOGIA,
       30 (1973), 55-61.

       Argues that, in charitable organizations, the elements
       of charismatic authority may coexist with more formal
       bureaucratic features.

154. Mansfield, Roger. "Bureaucracy and Centralization: An
       Examination of Organizational Structure." ADMINISTRA-
       TIVE SCIENCE QUARTERLY, 18 (1973), 477-88.

       Considers the contention that the Weberian model is no
       longer useful in the study of organizations. The method-
       ology of the critics is evaluated and other empirical
       studies are examined. The data reinforce the utility of
       Weber's concepts.

155. Miller, Jon. "Social-Psychological Implications of Web-
       er's Model of Bureaucracy: Relations Among Expertise,
       Control, Authority, and Legitimacy." SOCIAL FORCES,
       49 (1970), 91-101.

       Tests Weber's propositions among public school person-
       nel. The model is useful in explaining the relation-
       ships among several variables in organization life.

156. Mommsen, Wolfgang J. THE AGE OF BUREAUCRACY: PERSPEC-
       TIVES ON THE POLITICAL SOCIOLOGY OF MAX WEBER. Lon-
       don: Basil Blackwell and Mott, 1974. 125 pp.

       Describes the central role of bureaucratization in Max
       Weber's concept of modern politics. The ideal type of
       bureaucracy was "deliberately designed by Weber in such
       a way as to underline those elements which he considered
       particularly relevant in regard to the future destinies

of individualistic, liberal societies of the West." In
his personal orientation, Weber is described a "a liberal in despair" who was passionately dedicated to preserv-
ing humane values against social forces opposed to autonomous individuality. Weber's concept of plebiscitarian
democracy is examined.

157. Mommsen, Wolfgang J. "Toward the Iron Cage of Future
     Serfdom? On the Methodological State of Max Weber's
     Ideal-Typical Concept of Bureaucratization." TRANS-
     ACTIONS OF THE ROYAL HISTORICAL SOCIETY, 30 (1980),
     157-81.

     Discusses Weber's ideal type as a tool for historical
     analysis. The ideal type was not a presentation of re-
     ality nor did it have a full equivalent in empirical re-
     ality. The ideal type of bureaucracy was designed to
     1) assess the properties of the pure model of bureau-
     cratic institutions, 2) identify those factors causing
     the inherent dynamism of bureaucracy, or, bureaucrat-
     ization and, 3) the contrast of bureaucracy with alter-
     native forms of social organization. The notion of pro-
     gressive bureaucratization is as useful to history as it
     is to sociology.

158. North, Gary. "Statist Bureaucracy in the Modern Econ-
     omy." FREEMAN, 20 (1970), 16-28.

     Uses Weber's theory of bureaucracy as a basis for
     speculation about the fate of Western civilization.

159. Presthus, Robert V. "Weberian vs. Welfare Bureaucracy
     in Traditional Society." ADMINISTRATIVE SCIENCE QUART-
     ERLY, 6 (1961), 1-24.

     Points out the problems in applying the Weberian model
     to developing countries, in this case, the Turkish state
     coal monopoly. The welfare bureaucracy, in which formal
     objectives are secondary, may be common in non-Western
     society.

160. Rieger, Hans G. "The Mechanics of Bureaucracy: An Essay
     in Social Cybernetics." INDIAN JOURNAL OF PUBLIC

ADMINISTRATION, 12 (1966), 175-94.

Discusses bureaucracy as an information-processing system. The rational or Weberian model is useful in such an
approach.

161. Rudolph, L.I., and S.H. Rudolph. "Authority and Power
      in Bureaucratic and Patrimonial Administration: A Re-
      visionist Interpretation of Weber on Bureaucracy."
      WORLD POLITICS, 31 (1979), 195-227.

      Argue that the Weberian model needs revision to take
      into account the positive effects of fairly stable ele-
      ments of patrimonialism in administration.

162. Toren, Nina. "Bureaucracy and Professionalism: A Recon-
      sideration of Weber's Thesis." ACADEMY OF MANAGEMENT
      REVIEW, 1 (July, 1976), 36-46.

      Reviews recent research on professionals within bur-
      eaucracy. The evidence indicates that Weber has been
      vindicated since professionalism and bureaucracy may be
      positively related in organization structure and in the
      personal orientation of members.

163. Udy, Stanley H. "'Bureaucracy' and 'Rationality' in
      Weber's Organization Theory." AMERICAN SOCIOLOGICAL
      REVIEW, 24 (1959), 791-95.

      Separates the bureaucratic and the rational variables
      in Weber's model. The two sets are not positively re-
      lated, based on data from non-industrial societies. A
      way of including informal elements within the model is
      described.

164. Verma, S.L. "The Role of Bureaucracy in a Socialist Soc-
      iety." CHINESE JOURNAL OF ADMINISTRATION, 22 (1974),
      1-8.

      Argues that the Weberian model fails to provide a sat-
      isfactory explanation for the expanding role of bureau-
      cracy in socialist countries.

165. "Max Weber on Bureaucratization in 1909." Appendix to
J.P. Mayer. MAX WEBER AND GERMAN POLITICS: A STUDY
IN POLITICAL SOCIOLOGY. London: Faber and Faber, 1944.

A translation of Weber's remarks to a group of German
scholars. He expressed dismay at the lack of a way to
resist bureaucratization, to "keep a portion of mankind
free from this parcelling-out of the soul."

166. Weber, Max. THE THEORY OF SOCIAL AND ECONOMIC ORGANIZA-
TIONS. Edited by Talcott Parsons. New York: Oxford
University Press, 1947. 436 pp.

A translation of Part I of *Wirtschaft und Gesellschaft*. It contains a discussion of bureaucracy in the
section entitled "Legal Authority with a Bureaucratic
Administrative Staff."

167. Weber, Max. ECONOMY AND SOCIETY. Edited by Guenther
Roth and Claus Wittich. New York: Bedminster Press,
1968. 3 vols., 1,462 pp.

A translation of *Wirtschaft und Gesellschaft*, Weber's
most elaborate treatment of the role of bureaucracy in
modern society. This edition contains as an appendix
the article, "Parliament and Government in a Reconstruc-
ted Germany," which is a proposal for a democratic politics in post-WWI Germany. The article expresses Weber's thoughts on the possibility of the political control of bureaucracy.

168. "The Sociology of Organization: Bureaucracy and Ration-
ality in Organizations." MAX WEBER AND SOCIOLOGY TO-
DAY. Edited by Otto Stammer and Kathleen Morris.
Oxford: Basil Blackwood, 1971.

A summary of papers presented about Weber's contributions to organization theory.

169. Wright, Erik. "To Control or to Smash Bureaucracy:
Weber and Lenin on Politics, the State, and Bureaucracy." BERKELEY JOURNAL OF SOCIOLOGY, 19 (1974-75),
69-108.

Compares Weber's "Parliament and Government in a Re-
constructed Germany" (Item 167) with Lenin's *State and
Revolution* (Item 113). For both writers, a central issue was the control of the state apparatus. A theory
is needed to integrate the perspectives and contributions
of both men since the analysis of public bureaucracy has
advanced very little since they wrote in 1917.

D. Current Approaches

170. Arora, Ramesh, and Augusto Ferreros. "A Dimensional Ap-
     proach to the Ecology of Public Bureaucracy--An Adden-
     dum to John Forward." INDIAN JOURNAL OF PUBLIC ADMIN-
     ISTRATION, 18 (1972), 200-15.

     Propose an empirical framework for the ecological in-
     vestigation of bureaucracy. A factor analysis of 25
     ecological variables revealed six distinct dimensions
     to the character of public bureaucracies. The public
     organization does not operate in a vacuum but is in con-
     stant interaction with its environment.

171. Becker, Theodore M., and Peter R. Meyers. "Empathy and
     Bravado: Interviewing Reluctant Bureaucrats." PUBLIC
     OPINION QUARTERLY, 38 (1974-75), 605-13.

     Based on their experience in doing research in Chicago,
     offer advice on how researchers can obtain information
     held by bureaucrats. Both supportive and assertive tac-
     tics may have to be used in order to influence public em-
     ployees to cooperate in interviews.

172. Blau, Peter. "The Research Process in the Study of *The
     Dynamics of Bureaucracy*." SOCIOLOGISTS AT WORK. Ed-
     ited by Phillip E. Hammond. New York: Basic Books,
     1964.

     Discusses the problems of doing field work in a public
     organization. See Item 2038.

173. Bohlke, Robert, and Kenneth Winetrout. BUREAUCRATS AND
     INTELLECTUALS: A CRITIQUE OF C. WRIGHT MILLS.

Springfield, Mass.: American International College, 1963. 25 pp.

A critique of the organization theory of C. Wright Mills (Item 194).

174. Britan, Gerald M. "Some Problems of Field Work in the Federal Bureaucracy." ANTHROPOLOGICAL QUARTERLY, 52 (1979), 211-20.

Discusses the difficulties of carrying out anthropological research within large, formal organizations.

175. Britan, Gerald M., and Ronald Cohen, eds. HIERARCHY AND SOCIETY: ANTHROPOLOGICAL PERSPECTIVES ON BUREAU-CRACY. Philadelphia: Institute for the Study of Human Issues, 1980. 186 pp.

Original essays apply anthropological techniques to the study of complex organizations. Includes Items 180, 551, 872 and 1422.

176. Brown, Richard H. "Bureaucracy as Praxis: Toward a Political Phenomenonology of Formal Organizations." ADMINISTRATIVE SCIENCE QUARTERLY, 23 (1978), 365-82.

Presents an ethnomethodological approach to an understanding of concepts such as "rationality," "legitimacy," and "authority" within formal organizations. Rational actions are created by participants through actions that in themselves are non-rational. A reinterpretation of Marx's category of labor helps to explain this aspect of organizational behavior, and points the way to a theoretical convergence with "sociologies of consciousness."

177. Caldwell, Lynton K. "Biology and Bureaucracy: The Coming Confrontation." PUBLIC ADMINISTRATION REVIEW, 40 (1980), 1-12.

Attempts to apply the findings of sociobiology to the study of administration. Modern government and its bureaucracy are being threatened by our growing knowledge about the biology of human behavior.

178.   Chapman, Richard A. "The Real Cause of Bureaucracy."
        ADMINISTRATION, 12 (1964), 55-60.

        Finds that there are two broad categories of theories
        of bureaucracy: the technical ones which see it as a
        matter of size, and functional ones which see bureaucracy
        as a social or political phenomenon. Properly consid-
        ered, the values and attitudes of a society will be the
        major determinant of the level of bureaucracy.

179.   Denich, Bette. "On the Bureaucratization of Scholar-
        ship in American Anthropology." DIALECTICAL ANTHRO-
        POLOGY, 2 (1977), 153-57.

        Criticizes the perversion of anthropology because of
        its close association with large organizations, partic-
        ularly the modern university.

180.   Denich, Bette. "Bureaucratic Scholarship: The New An-
        thropology." HIERARCHY AND SOCIETY: ANTHROPOLOGICAL
        PERSPECTIVES ON BUREAUCRACY. Philadelphia: Institute
        for the Study of Human Issues, 1980.

        Discusses the implications of the bureaucratization
        of anthropological research.

181.   Gold, David. "A Criticism of an Empirical Assessment of
        the Concept of Bureaucracy on Conceptual Independence
        and Empirical Evidence." AMERICAN JOURNAL OF SOCIO-
        LOGY, 70 (1964), 223-25.

        Finds fault with Richard Hall's operationalization of
        the concept of bureaucracy (Item 184).

182.   Gouldner, Alvin W. "Metaphysical Pathos and the Theory
        of Bureaucracy." AMERICAN POLITICAL SCIENCE REVIEW,
        49 (1955), 496-507.

        Takes to task the critics of the large organization.
        Much modern theory about bureaucracy is pessimistic and
        fatalistic. The study of bureaucracy is shaped by a
        "pathos of pessimism," causing it to become a modern
        version of the "dismal science."

183. Hajjar, Sami. "Towards Understanding the Concept of Bureaucratic Rationality." INDIAN JOURNAL OF PUBLIC ADMINISTRATION. 19 (1973), 148-62.

Criticizes traditional views of rationality and puts forth the concept of "projective rationality" in describing bureaucratic behavior.

184. Hall, Richard H. "The Concept of Bureaucracy: An Empirical Assessment." AMERICAN JOURNAL OF SOCIOLOGY, 69 (1963), 32-40.

Views bureaucracy as consisting of several dimensions which exist along a continuum from more to less bureaucratic.

185. Hall, Richard H., and Charles R. Tittle. "A Note on Bureaucracy and Its 'Correlates.'" AMERICAN JOURNAL OF SOCIOLOGY, 72 (1966), 267-72.

Attempt to relate the degree of bureaucratization in an organization to a number of dimensions. The degree of bureaucratization seems to be associated with the relation of the organization to objects, as opposed to ideas.

186. Hall, Richard H. "Bureaucratic Functioning." HANDBOOK OF APPLIED SOCIOLOGY: FRONTIERS OF CONTEMPORARY RESEARCH. Edited by Marvin Olsen and Michael Micklin. New York: Praeger, 1981.

Reviews the latest research on the improvement of the performance of bureaucracy. Problems of effectiveness, change, and responsiveness are explored.

187. Hinings, C.R., D.S. Pugh, D.J. Hickson, and C. Turner. "An Approach to the Study of Bureaucracy." SOCIOLOGY, 1 (1967), 61-72.

Describe an operational definition of the dimensions of bureaucracy. An "overall specialization scale" was derived from the study of 52 work organizations.

188. Hood, Christopher, and Eileen Sutcliffe. "The Faces of
      Bureaucracy." NEW SOCIETY, 50 (1979), 186-87.

      Describe the system called "bureaumetrics" which can
      be used to distinguish among types of government agen-
      cies (see Item 189).

189. Hood, Christopher, and Andrew Dunsire, with the assis-
      tance of K. Suky Thompson. BUREAUMETRICS: THE QUAL-
      ITATIVE COMPARISON OF BRITISH CENTRAL GOVERNMENT
      AGENCIES. University: University of Alabama Press,
      1981. 312 pp.

      Develop a method for the quantification of differences
      among government departments. Bureaumetrics involves
      the determination of appropriate indices to be used in
      interorganizational comparisons. The method is applied
      to the agencies of the British government. It promises
      to provide government reformers with useful information.
      In an appendix, a computer program for drawing the
      "faces" of various bureaucracies is described.

190. Inbar, Michael. "Toward Valid Computer Simulations of
      Bureaucratized Decisions." SIMULATION AND GAMES, 7
      (1976), 243-60.

      Conceives of the bureaucracy as a computer program.
      Simulation of an organization's decision-making system
      can be adapted to provide information about social con-
      trol or improved efficiency.

191. Inbar, Michael. ROUTINE DECISION-MAKING: THE FUTURE OF
      BUREAUCRACY. Beverly Hills, Cal.: Sage, 1979. 239
      pp.

      Sees bureaucracy as a decision-making system; under
      normal conditions it functions much like a "social com-
      puter." The improvement of bureaucracy requires the re-
      cognition of this feature. A central matter is the prob-
      lem of maintaining organizational routines.   In the or-
      ganization of the future, many more decisions will be
      made by the computers, with little loss in consumer sat-
      isfaction.

192. Krohn, Roger. "Conflict and Function: Some Basic Issues in Bureaucratic Theory." BRITISH JOURNAL OF SOCIOLOGY, 22 (1971) 115-32.

     Argues that questions of conflict and function are basic sociological issues often reflected in studies of bureaucracy. The works of Melville Dalton and Michel Crozier are examined as examples. Both authors wind up using the "informal organization" as a major explanation of formal operations. Why then does the formal organization endure as a theoretical attraction?

193. Miller, Michael, and Charles Thomas. "The Bureaucratization Process and Its Effects: A Simulation." TEACHING SOCIOLOGY, 2 (1974), 43-56.

     Bureaucracy as a simulation exercise.

194. Mills, C. Wright. THE SOCIOLOGICAL IMAGINATION. New York: Oxford University Press, 1959. 234 pp.

     Sees social science methods as a subset of bureaucratic techniques. In particular, the "bureaucratic ethos" encourages researchers to increase the reputation and the efficiency of bureaucratic forms of domination. In this manner, social science provides an ideological justification for authority. This trend violates the real essence of sociological scholarship.

195. Mohan, Raj P. "Some Theoretical Implications of Status in Bureaucracy." INTERNATIONAL REVIEW OF HISTORY AND POLITICAL SCIENCE, 8 (November, 1971), 99-110.

     Contends that formal and informal statuses are both important in the study of organizations.

196. Parker, R.S. "Public Administration as the Study of Bureaucracy." PUBLIC ADMINISTRATION(SYDNEY), 15 (1956), 25-37.

     Suggests the greater application of sociological theory to the study of public administration.

197. Pundir, Jagdish. "Understanding Bureaucracy." EMERGING SOCIOLOGY, 1 (1979), 56-78.

     Examines the work of Weber, Mertin, Blau, and Bendix.

198. Ray, Joseph. "Reflections of a Professor Turned Bureaucrat." PUBLIC ADMINISTRATION REVIEW, 19 (1959), 238-42.

     Points out some of the differences between the theory and practice of public administration.

199. Rowney, Don. "Bureaucratic Development and Social Science History." SOCIAL SCIENCE HISTORY, 2 (1978), 379-84.

     Reviews some of the disciplinary paradigms used in the study of bureaucracy and suggests further collaboration among the social sciences.

200. Samuel, Yitzhak, and Bilha F. Mannheim. "A Multidimensional Approach toward a Typology of Bureaucracy." ADMINISTRATIVE SCIENCE QUARTERLY, 15 (1970), 216-28

     Present a method for describing, classifying, and comparing the bureaucratization of formal organizations. The four universal characteristics of bureaucracy are intensity of structural control, functionalization, normativity, and interlevel impersonality. Objective indices for these and other variables were analyzed with data from 30 industrial plants. Six types of bureaucracy were identified: rudimentary, interpersonal, balanced, emergent, technical, and managerial.

201. Santos, Conrado R. "A Theory of Bureaucratic Authority." CANADIAN PUBLIC ADMINISTRATION, 21 (1978), 243-67.

     Sees two bodies of thought on the question of bureaucratic authority: the structuralist Weberian perspective and the behavioralist Barnard-Simon view. Another definition of bureaucratic authority is presented. Such authority is ultimately dependent upon the sovereign political authority of the jurisdiction.

202.   Selznick, Philip. "An Approach to a Theory of Bureau-
          cracy." AMERICAN SOCIOLOGICAL REVIEW, 8 (1943), 47-
          54.

       Considers bureaucracy as a potential problem in any
       large organization. There is a need to find ways for
       "blocking the bureaucratic drift."

203.   Siffin, William J. "'Bureaucracy:' The Problem of Meth-
          odology and the 'Structural' Approach." JOURNAL OF
          COMPARATIVE ADMINISTRATION, 2 (1971), 471-503

       Discusses the use of structural-functional approaches
       in the study of comparative administration.

204.   Sjoberg, Gideon, and Paula Miller. "Social Research on
          Bureaucracy: Limitations and Opportunities." SOCIAL
          PROBLEMS, 21 (1973), 129-43.

       Inquire into the difficulties of studying inherently
       secretive organizations. Much sociological research
       takes for granted the rational nature of the organiza-
       tion, thus attributing too much meaning to the formal
       statements of members.

205.   Somit, Albert. "Bureaucratic Realpolitik and the Teach-
          ing of Administration." PUBLIC ADMINISTRATION REVIEW,
          16 (1956), 292-95.

       Argues that the organization is "the scene of an un-
       ending and sometimes desperate battle for personal sur-
       vival, power and prestige." Potential bureaucrats should
       be instructed in the art of administrative survival, al-
       though we now lack a systematic theory about this aspect
       of administration.

206.   Spencer, Gary. "Methodological Issues in the Study of
          Bureaucratic Elites: A Case Study of West Point."
          SOCIAL PROBLEMS, 21 (1973), 90-103.

       Presents a model to explain why bureaucratic elites
       shun outside researchers. Social scientists must assert
       their right to investigate such groups.

207. Ugalde, Antonio. "A Decision Model for the Study of
      Public Bureaucracies." POLICY SCIENCES, 4 (1973), 75-
      84.

      Derives a model of bureaucracy, or implementation,
      from a concept called "series of decisions." Any de-
      cision in a series can be either programming or imple-
      mentation. A hypothesis based on the time between pro-
      gramming and implementation is put forward. A case of
      health administration in Colombia is used to indicate
      the utility of the model.

208. Warwick, Dennis. BUREAUCRACY. London: Longman, 1974.
      158 pp.

      Contends that the images of bureaucracy will always
      be very emotive since they touch on basic questions of
      power and domination. In the study of bureaucracy, soc-
      iologists tend to stress matters of less importance to
      the administrators. Special reference is made to the
      bureaucratization of British education.

            E. The Political Economy of Bureaucracy

209. Arnold, R. Douglas. "Legislators, Bureaucrats, and Lo-
      cational Decisions." PUBLIC CHOICE, 37 (1981), 107-
      32.

      Examines the forces which determine the geographical
      distribution of federal funds to the states. See Items
      262 and 777.

210. Alexander, Tom. "Why Bureaucracy Keeps Growing." FOR-
      TUNE, 99 (May 7, 1979), 164-66.

      Summarizes the theory of "political economy."

211. Beck, J.H. "Budget-Maximizing Bureaucracy and the Ef-
      fects of State Aid on School Expenditures." PUBLIC
      FINANCE QUARTERLY, 9 (1981), 159-82.

      Argues that, because of the role of the bureaucracy in
      making the budget, state aid is not passed on to voters
      as local tax relief.

212.   Bennett, James T., and Manuel Johnson. "Bureaucratic
       Imperialism: Some Sobering Statistics." INTERCOLLE-
       GIATE REVIEW, 13 (Winter-Spring, 1978), 101-03.

       On the growth of the federal civil service.

213.   Benson, Bruce L. "Why Are Congressional Committees Dom-
       inated by 'High-Demand' Legislators--A Comment on Nis-
       kanen's View of Bureaucrats and Politicians." SOUTH-
       ERN ECONOMIC REVIEW, 48 (1981), 68-77

       Attempts to reconcile some differences in Niskanen's
       view (Item 259) of high-demand and vote-maximizing leg-
       islators in the budgetary process.

214.   Borcherding, Thomas E., ed. BUDGETS AND BUREAUCRATS:
       THE SOURCES OF GOVERNMENT GROWTH. Durham, N.C.: Duke
       University Press, 1977. 291 pp.

       A collection of original essays by economists. The
       question under consideration is the role of bureaucrats
       in the expansion of the public sector. To what extent
       is the size of government a reflection of public demands
       or of the self-interest of public employees? Contains
       Items 215, 222, 263.

215.   Borcherding, Thomas E., Winston Bush, and Robert Spann.
       "The Effects of Public Spending on the Divisibility
       of Public Outputs in Consumption, Bureaucratic Power,
       and the Size of the Tax-Sharing Group." BUDGETS AND
       BUREAUCRATS. Edited by Thomas E. Borcherding. Dur-
       ham, N.C.: Duke University Press, 1977.

       Consider several sources of bureaucratic power in the
       determination of levels of public spending. Public ser-
       vice activism, either as voters, members of cartel-like
       civil service systems, or participants in the budgetary
       process are discussed.

216.   Borjas, George J. "Wage Determinants in the Federal Gov-
       ernment: The Role of Constituents and Bureaucrats."
       JOURNAL OF POLITICAL ECONOMY, 88 (1980), 1110-47.

       Studies wage differentials among U.S. government

employees. The salaries appear to be better in those agencies with small, well-organized constituencies.

217. Breton, Albert, and Ronald Wintrobe. "The Equilibrium Size of a Budget-Maximizing Bureau: A Note On Niskanen's Theory of Bureaucracy." JOURNAL OF POLITICAL ECONOMY. 83 (1975), 195-207.

Argue that Niskanen's model (Item 259) is appropriate to only a small number of bureaus. The real power of bureaucracy is in the control of information. The political subordination of administration depends upon the ability of outsiders to manipulate information.

218. Breton, Albert, and Ronald Wintrobe. "Bureaucracy and State Intervention: Parkinson's Law?" CANADIAN PUBLIC ADMINISTRATION, 22 (1979), 208-26.

Consider explanations for the growth of government. Bureaucrats maximize power, but not by increasing the size of the budget. Instead, they strive to acquire the loyalty of their subordinates, interest groups and the media.

219. Breton, Albert, and Ronald Wintrobe. THE LOGIC OF BUR-EAUCRATIC CONDUCT: A ECONOMIC ANALYSIS OF COMPETITION, EXCHANGE, AND EFFICIENCY IN PRIVATE AND PUBLIC ORGAN-IZATIONS. Cambridge: Cambridge University Press, 1982. 195 pp.

Develop a theory of bureaucratic supply based on the relationships between superiors and subordinates. This relationship is not a matter of formal authority, rules, control, or commands; rather, it is a question of exchange as subordinates decide whether their compliance is worth their while. The elements of the model are trust, selective behavior, and bureaucratic competition. The model is tested in the explanation of production differentials among firms.

220. Brownfeld, Allan. "The Inherent Inefficiency of Government Bureaucracy." FREEMAN, 27 (1977), 361-67.

On why government cannot produce efficiently.

221. Buchanan, James, and Gordon Tullock. "The Politics and
      Bureaucracy of Planning." THE POLITICS OF PLANNING:
      A REVIEW AND CRITIQUE OF CENTRALIZED ECONOMIC PLAN-
      NING. Edited by A.L. Chickering. San Francisco: In-
      stitute of Contemporary Issues, 1976.

      Look at the motivation of those involved in the making
      and implementation of plans. The chances for success of
      the planning process are rather slim.

222. Bush, Winston, and Arthur T. Denzau. "The Voting Behav-
      ior of Bureaucrats and Public Sector Growth." BUDGETS
      AND BUREAUCRATS: THE SOURCES OF GOVERNMENT GROWTH. Dur-
      ham, N.C.: Duke University Press, 1977.

      Explore the question whether public employees vote in
      large numbers for candidates favoring greater government
      expenditure. Such a factor would be in keeping with the
      theory that minorities with intense preferences have a
      disproportionate influence in elections. The small num-
      ber of empirical studies on the topic are reviewed.

223. Chamberlain, John. "The Compleat Bureaucrat." NATIONAL
      REVIEW, 18 (1966), 75-76.

      Review of Tullock, *The Politics of Bureaucracy* (Item
      279.

224. Chan, Kenneth S. "A Behavioral Model of Bureaucracy."
      SOUTHERN ECONOMIC JOURNAL, 45 (1979), 1188-94.

      Shows that voter participation is a critical factor in
      the theory of bureaucratic monopoly. In particular,
      when voter participation is considered, the lack of com-
      petition in government is "neither necessary nor suffic-
      ient for the growth of bureaucracy."

225. Chant, John F., and Keith Acheson. "The Choice of Mon-
      etary Instruments and the Theory of Bureaucracy."
      PUBLIC CHOICE, 12 (1972), 13-33.

      Investigate how the Bank of Canada makes monetary pol-
      icy. Many of the bank's actions seem to have a stronger
      rationale in bureaucratic behavior than in principles

of monetary policy. The possibilities for the enhance-
ment of the prestige and autonomy of officials are strong
motivators.

226. Cremer, J. "A Partial Theory of the Optimal Organization
       of a Bureaucracy." BELL JOURNAL OF ECONOMICS, 11
       (1980), 683-93.

      Develops an economic model to describe the relation-
ship of public organizations with their environments.

227. Dahl, Robert, and Charles Lindblom. POLITICS, ECONOMICS,
       AND WELFARE: PLANNING AND POLITICO-ECONOMIC SYSTEMS RE-
       SOLVED INTO BASIC SOCIAL PROCESSES. New York: Harper
       and Row, 1953. 557 pp.

      Discuss bureaucracy, or hierarchy, as one of the four
central sociopolitical processes at work in the modern
economy. As distinct from other processes, bureaucracy
is based on leaders having a great deal of unilateral
power over non-leaders. Bureaucratic organizations are
highly rational and efficient means for the solution of
a certain class of problems. There are a variety of
costs, however, associated with bureaucracy and it would
be unwise for a society to rely entirely on that form
in the direction of social planning.

228. Davis, David Howard. "Consensus or Conflict: Alterna-
       tive Strategies for the Bureaucratic Bargainer." PUB-
       LIC CHOICE, 13 (1972), 21-29.

      Explores the making of foreign policy as a series of
bargains struck among participants from different departments. Actors can attempt to build coalitions (the
rule of consensus) or to defeat the "enemy" (the rule
of conflict). Economic theory is applied to the bar-
gaining process.

229. Downs, Anthony. INSIDE BUREAUCRACY. Santa Monica:
       Rand, 1964. 29 pp.

      See Item 233.

230. Downs, Anthony. A THEORY OF BUREAUCRACY. Santa Monica: Rand, 1964. 13 pp.

See Item 233.

231. Downs, Anthony. "A Theory of Bureaucracy." AMERICAN ECONOMIC REVIEW, 55 (1965), 439-46.

Presents a theory of bureaucracy based on the idea that officials are motivated, in part, by their own self-interest.

232. Downs, Anthony. BUREAUCRATIC STRUCTURE AND DECISION MAKING. Santa Monica: Rand, 1966. 171 pp

See Item 233.

233. Downs, Anthony. INSIDE BUREAUCRACY. Boston: Little, Brown, 1967. 292 pp.

Sets forth a number of hypotheses about decision-making within large organizations. A basic premise of the study is that bureaucrats (members of large organizations who are employed full-time and whose output cannot be measured in any market) attempt to maximize a number of personal and social goals. The emphasis on a particular type of goal distinguishes different types of officials. Bureaucrats may be classified as climbers, conservers, advocates, zealots, and statesmen. The actual performance of any bureau, and particularly its growth or decline, is a function of the combination of personality types within it. The public interest may not be served by the bureaucracy unless it is in the interest of the officials that it be served.

234. Faith, Roger L. "Rent-Seeking Aspects of Bureaucratic Competition." TOWARD A THEORY OF THE RENT-SEEKING SOCIETY. Edited by James Buchanan and Robert Tollison. College Station: Texas A&M Press, 1980.

Rent seeking is defined as using the power of the state for the redistribution of wealth. In this sense, competition among bureaucracies can be viewed as the interaction of rational, rent-seeking individuals.

235.   Fiorina, Morris P., and Roger G. Noll. "Voters, Bureau-
       crats, and Legislators: A Rational Choice Perspective
       on the Growth of Bureaucracy." JOURNAL OF PUBLIC ECON-
       OMICS, 9 (1978), 239-54.

       Develop a model for explaining bureaucratic expansion
       as a result of the rational decisions by voters, members
       of Congress, and administrators. The chances of stopping
       the growth of government through formal reform techniques
       are not good.

236.   Fiorina, Morris P., and Roger G. Noll. "Voters, Legis-
       lators, and Bureaucracy." AMERICAN ECONOMIC REVIEW,
       68 (1978), 256-63.

       Outlines a model for explaining why rational actors
       will contribute to the growth of an excessively bureau-
       cratic government. The model is based on the idea of an
       alliance between legislators and bureaucrats.

237.   Flowers, Marilyn, and Richard Stroup. "Coupon Rationing
       and Rent-Seeking Bureaucrats." PUBLIC CHOICE, 34
       (1979), 473-79.

       Inquire into the conditions under which bureaucrats
       would be induced to support commodity rationing.

238.   Fort, Rodney, and John Baden. "The Federal Treasury as
       a Common Pool and the Development of a Predatory Bur-
       eaucracy." BUREAUCRACY VS. ENVIRONMENT. Edited by
       John Baden and Richard Stroup. Ann Arbor: University
       of Michigan Press, 1981.

       Argue that there are no mechanisms which can restrain
       the rational bureaucrat from expanding the budget. An
       economizing official is in fact penalized. A predatory
       bureaucracy is proposed. This budgetary instrument would
       be funded from money it saved by decreasing the program
       costs of other agencies. Its survival would depend upon
       its effective attack on other bureaus.

239.   Forte, Francesco, and Alberto Di Pierro. "A Pure Model
       of Public Bureaucracy." PUBLIC FINANCE, 35 (1980).
       91-100.

Modify the Weberian model to show that bureaucrats, contrary to Niskanen (Item 259), prefer excess input to excess output.

240. Friedman, Milton. "The Market Versus the Bureaucrats." INDIVIDUALITY AND THE NEW SOCIETY. Edited by Abraham Kaplan. Seattle: University of Washington Press, 1970.

Urges greater reliance on the market as a solution to social problems. The failure of government programs in education and welfare indicate that bureaucracy is no panacea.

241. Goodin, Robert E. "The Logic of Bureaucratic Back Scratching." PUBLIC CHOICE, 21 (1975), 53-67.

Suggests that inter-bureaucracy cooperation is more common than conflict as officials attempt to maximize their personal values.

242. Goodin, Robert E. "Rational Politicians and Rational Bureaucrats in Washington and Whitehall." PUBLIC AD-MINISTRATION, 60 (1982), 23-41.

Finds weaknesses in the Niskanen model (Item 259) of bureaucratic behavior, especially in terms of supply and demand of services and the motivation of the partici-pants. A revised model is presented and tested with British and American cases.

243. Hettich, Walter. "Bureaucrats and Public Goods." PUB-LIC CHOICE, 21 (1975), 15-25.

Contends that there are limitations to the implication of the Niskanen model (Item 259) about the overproduc-tion of public goods. Insufficient attention is given to the motivation of the bureau's sponsor.

244. Holcombe, Randall, and Edward Price. "Price Optimality and the Institutional Structure of Bureaucracy." PUB-LIC CHOICE, 33 (1978), 55-59.

Devise a bureaucratic supply curve.

245. Hutcheson, John, and James E. Prather. "Economy of
       Scale or Bureaucratic Entropy? Implications for Met-
       ropolitan Governmental Reorganization." URBAN AFFAIRS
       QUARTERLY, 15 (1979), 164-82.

       Examines the relationship between the number of city
       employees and city population. The size of the bureau-
       cracy seems to increase faster than population, suggest-
       ing diseconomies of scale. There is little support for
       the idea that the consolidation of government units would
       lead to economies of scale in the provision of public
       services. A mix of centralized and decentralized func-
       tions in the metropolitan area may be more economical.

246. Judge, Ken. "Resource Allocation in the Welfare State:
       Bureaucrats or Process?" JOURNAL OF SOCIAL POLICY,
       8 (1979), 371-82.

       Reviews the reports of the Institute of Economic Af-
       fairs, a British advocate of the market instrument.

247. Kristensen, Ole P. "The Logic of Political Bureaucrat-
       ic Decision-Making as a Cause of Governmental Growth:
       Or Why Expansion of Public Programs is a 'Private
       Good' and Their Restriction Is a 'Public Good.'"
       EUROPEAN JOURNAL OF POLITICAL RESEARCH, 8 (1980), 249-
       64.

       Claims that the logic of government decision-making
       implies that "spenders" will always be in a stronger
       position than "cutters."

248. McCaleb, Thomas S. "Bureaucratic Performance and Bud-
       getary Reward: A Test of the Hypothesis with an Alt-
       ernative Specification." PUBLIC CHOICE, 31 (1977),
       143-45.

       A test of Warren's "Bureaucratic Performance and Bud-
       getary Reward," Item 282.

249. McFadden, Daniel. "The Revealed Preferences of a Public
       Bureaucracy: Theory." BELL JOURNAL OF ECONOMICS, 6
       (1975), 401-16.

Inquires to what extent decisions affecting utilities
are controlled by simple investment criteria.

250. McFadden, Daniel. "The Revealed Preferences of a Gov-
     ernment Bureaucracy: Empirical Evidence." BELL JOUR-
     NAL OF ECONOMICS, 7 (1976), 55-72.

     Looks at the California Division of Highways to test
     the proposition established in Item 249. The routing
     decisions of the bureau were largely determined by cost-
     benefit considerations.

251. McKenzie, Richard, and Hugh Macaulay. "A Bureaucratic
     Theory of Regulation." PUBLIC CHOICE, 35 (1980), 297-
     313.

     Contend that "much regulation is purposively designed
     by public bureaucracies to make the public sector in-
     efficient, increasing the relative attractiveness of the
     public sector."

252. Magaddino, Joseph, and Roger Meiners. "Bureaucracy and
     Grants-in-Aid." PUBLIC CHOICE, 34 (1979), 467-71.

     Apply public choice theory to explain the growth of
     intergovernmental transfers of money.

253. Martin, Dolores, and Richard B. McKenzie. "Bureaucrat-
     ic Profits, Migration Costs, and the Consolidation of
     Local Government." PUBLIC CHOICE, 23 (1975), 95-100.

     Apply an economic model of bureaucratic behavior to
     the question of local government consolidation. Bureau-
     crats will absorb whatever financial benefits derive from
     consolidation.

254. Messerlin, Patrick A., "The Political Economy of Pro-
     tectionism: The Bureaucratic Case." WELTWIRTSCHAFT-
     LICHES ARCHIV, 117 (1981), 469-96.

     Elaborates a theory which predicts the role of bureau-
     cracy in the policy decisions regarding free trade or
     protectionism.

255. Miller, Gary J. "Bureaucratic Compliance as a Game on
      the Unit Square." PUBLIC CHOICE, 29 (1977), 37-51.

      Sees that the traditional concept of formal hierarchy
      is obsolete since subordinates tend to act as decision-
      makers in their own right. The game on the unit square
      may be one way of integrating the idea of authority with
      the reality of employee autonomy. The members are play-
      ers in a game manipulated by superiors within the hier-
      archy.

256. Milward, H. Brinton. "Policy Entrepreneurship and Bur-
      eaucratic Demand Creation." WHY POLICIES SUCCEED OR
      FAIL. Edited by Helen Ingram and Dean Mann. Beverly
      Hills, Cal.: Sage, 1980.

      Looks at the factors encouraging bureaus, as producers,
      to create a demand for their services. The creation of
      a state housing finance agency is used to support a mod-
      el of government growth.

257. von Mises, Ludwig. BUREAUCRACY. New Haven, Conn.: Yale
      University Press, 1944. 125 pp.

      Distinguishes between the "market principle" and the
      "budget principle" as mechanisms for the determination
      of the social value of organizations. Since bureaucracy
      is free of market discipline, it receives little reli-
      able information from the outside world. Bureaucratic
      management, therefore, is a style which cannot be val-
      idated by economic calculations. The hallmark of bur-
      eaucracy is the subservience to internal rules rather
      than concern about actual productivity. Free enterprise
      is the answer for bureaucratic mismanagement and for the
      proper evaluation of the worth of organizations.

258. Niskanen, William. "The Peculiar Economics of Bureau-
      cracy." AMERICAN ECONOMIC REVIEW, 58 (1968), 293-
      305.

      Posits a model to explain the behavior of "maximizing
      bureaucrats."

259. Niskanen, William. BUREAUCRACY AND REPRESENTATIVE GOV-
     ERNMENT. Chicago: Aldine, 1971. 241 pp.

     Seeks to explain how the supply of public goods and
     services is the result of personal preferences and in-
     dividual calculations by bureaucrats. Bureaucrats are
     motivated by self-interest, and the structure of govern-
     ment tends to encourage the expansion of the public sec-
     tor as a means for individual advancement. The legisla-
     ture, as the sponsor for the bureaucrats, bears a spec-
     ial responsibility for the excessive production of pub-
     lic goods. Alternative ways of structuring government
     in order to provide better incentives to the participants
     are discussed.

260. Niskanen, William. BUREAUCRACY: SERVANT OR MASTER? Lon-
     don: Institute of Economic Affairs, 1973. 103 pp.

     Contains a summary of the author's arguments made in
     Item 259. Commentaries by British scholars and polit-
     icians are appended.

261. Niskanen, William. "Bureaucrats and Politicians." JOUR-
     NAL OF LAW AND ECONOMICS, 18 (1975), 617-43.

     Reviews a number of suggested modifications and empir-
     ical tests of the theory of bureaucracy described in
     Item 259.

262. Oppenheimer, Joe A. "Legislators, Bureaucrats, and Loc-
     ational Decisions and Beyond: Some Comments." PUBLIC
     CHOICE, 37 (1981), 133-40.

     Comment on Item 209.

263. Orzechowski, William. "Economic Models of Bureaucracy:
     Survey, Extensions, and Evidence." BUDGETS AND BUR-
     EAUCRATS: THE SOURCES OF GOVERNMENT GROWTH. Durham,
     N.C.: Duke University Press, 1977.

     Reviews a number of models of the economic behavior of
     members of bureaus. The three models under considera-
     tion suggest that bureaucrats benefit from their mono-
     poly position in supplying goods and services.

264. Ott, Mack. "Bureaucracy, Monopoly, and the Demand for
      Municipal Services." JOURNAL OF URBAN ECONOMICS, 8
      (1980), 362-82.

      Constructs a model of municipal budgeting. Using Nis-
      kanen's model (Item 259), it is argued that bureaucrats
      apply pressure on politicians in order to maximize their
      salaries.

265. Pasour, E.C., and Marc A. Johnson. "Bureaucratic Pro-
      ductivity: The Case of Agricultural Research Revisit-
      ed." PUBLIC CHOICE, 39 (1982) 301-17.

      Discounts the conclusions of Ruttan (Item 273) and
      others about the value of agricultural research. That
      product is largely a private good and thus is unlike
      most public services.

266. Pierce, Lawrence. "Organizational Constraints and Pub-
      lic Bureaucracy." POLITICAL SCIENCE ANNUAL, Vol. V.
      Edited by Cornelius Cotter. Indianapolis: Bobbs-
      Merrill, 1974.

      Discusses the public choice approach to bureaucratic
      behavior. Organizations are viewed as collections of
      self-interested individuals who join together to accomp-
      lish a variety of objectives.

267. Pierce, William S. "Bureaucratic Politics and the Labor
      Market." PUBLIC CHOICE, 37 (1981), 307-20.

      Argues that the external labor market may mean that
      governments are staffed by incompetent drones or un-
      scrupulous careerists.

268. Pierce, William S. BUREAUCRATIC FAILURE AND PUBLIC EX-
      PENDITURE. New York: Academic Press, 1981. 318 pp.

      Searches for reasons for the failure of the public
      sector to reflect the best interests of the citizens.
      Several hypotheses are presented to explain the weak-
      nesses of non-market organizations, and examples of bur-
      eaucratic failures are examined. The private sector is
      more effective in disciplining organization behavior.

269. Pomerehne, Werner, and Bruno Frey. "Bureaucratic Behavior in Democracy: A Case Study." PUBLIC FINANCE, 33 (1978), 98-112.

Examine the role of bureaucrats as voters. Data are from Swiss elections.

270. Roberts, Paul C. "The Political Economy of Bureaucratic Imperialism." INTERCOLLEGIATE REVIEW, 12 (Fall, 1976), 3-11.

Speculates why bureaucracy is opposed to the notion of "private individuals." Sweden and West Africa are examples of the failure to eliminate the market system.

271. Romer, Thomas, and Howard Rosenthal. "The N-Prisoners' Dilemma: A Bureaucratic-Setter Solution." AMERICAN POLITICAL SCIENCE REVIEW, 72 (1978), 1364-65.

Propose an institutional solution to the N-prisoners' dilemma.

272. Romer, Thomas, and Howard Rosenthal. "Bureaucrats versus Voters: On the Political Economy of Resource Allocation by Direct Democracy." QUARTERLY JOURNAL OF ECONOMICS, 93 (1979), 563-87.

Describe a model for allowing participation by voters in making allocative decisions. The model is tested by data from elections in Oregon school districts.

273. Ruttan, Vernon. "Bureaucratic Productivity: The Case of Agricultural Research." PUBLIC CHOICE, 35 (1980), 529-47.

Finds that public units involved in agricultural research produce a high rate of return on the money invested in them. The reason for this may be the level of decentralization in this area. The conclusions are disputed in Item 265.

274. Ruttan, Vernon. "Bureaucratic Productivity: The Case of
      Agricultural Research Revisited--A Rejoinder." PUBLIC
      CHOICE, 39 (1982), 319-29.

      A reply to Pasour and Johnson, Item 265.

275. Schuettinger, Robert. "Bureaucracy and Representative
      Government: A Review Analysis." MIDWEST REVIEW OF PUB-
      LIC ADMINISTRATION, 7 (1973), 17-22.

      A review essay on Niskanen, Item 259.

276. Stockfisch, Jacob A. THE POLITICAL ECONOMY OF BUREAU-
      CRACY. New York: General Learning Press, 1972. 24 pp.

      Argues that "the bureaucracy problem in its purest form
      is a 'monopoly problem' unique to instrumentalities of
      the state." Bureaucrats have no incentives to economize
      in the use of public resources. In their dual roles as
      bureaucrats and professionals, they are encouraged to
      maximize their share of the budget so they can practice
      their profession better.

277. Stockfisch, Jacob A. ANALYSIS OF BUREAUCRATIC BEHAVIOR:
      THE ILL-DEFINED PRODUCTION PROCESS. Santa Monica:
      Rand, 1976. 16 pp.

      On the peculiar features of bureaucratic production.

278. Toma, Mark, and Eugenia Toma. "Bureaucratic Responses
      to Tax Limitation Amendments." PUBLIC CHOICE, 35
      (1980), 333-48.

      Contend that there will be variations in the actual
      taxpayer benefits derived through the passage of tax
      limitation amendments.

279. Tullock, Gordon. THE POLITICS OF BUREAUCRACY. Washing-
      ton, D.C.: Public Affairs Press, 1965. 228 pp.

      Uses the idea of "politics" to explain why bureaucracy
      is inefficient and constantly expanding. Bureaucratic

politics is a function of superior-subordinate relationships within a hierarchy. The careers of officials depend upon pleasing the bosses, thus leading to timidity
and makework. This situation is in contrast to the "economic" relations among freely contracting individuals.

280. Tullock, Gordon. "Dynamic Hypothesis on Bureaucracy."
    PUBLIC CHOICE, 19 (1974), 127-31.

    Suggests an economic explanation for the growth of gov-
    ernment. Essentially, bureaucracy begets bureaucracy.

281. Tullock, Gordon. "Bureaucracy and the Growth of Govern-
    ment." THE TAMING OF GOVERNMENT: MICRO/MACRO DISCIP-
    LINES ON WHITEHALL AND TOWN HALL. London: Institute
    of Economic Affairs, 1979.

    Argues that bureaucracy is as much a cause as it is a
    product of government growth.

282. Warren, Ronald S. "Bureaucratic Performance and Budget-
    ary Reward: A Reply and Reformulation." PUBLIC CHOICE,
    31 (1977), 139-41.

    See Item 248.

283. Weber, W., and W. Weigel. "Government Bureaucracy: A
    Survey in Positive and Normative Theory." ACTA OEC-
    ONOMIA, 24 (1980), 341-56.

    Survey the economic deficiencies of the monopoly pos-
    ition of bureaucracy. Zero-base budgeting is advanced
    as a way of overcoming many of the defects in government
    production.

284. West, E.G. "Educational Slowdown and Public Investment
    in 19th-Century England: A Study of the Economics of
    Bureaucracy." EXPLORATIONS IN ECONOMIC HISTORY, 12
    (1975), 61-87.

    Applies political economy theory to the early growth
    of public education. Included in the calculations are
    the costs of the negative impact on private schools
    through a "crowding out" process.

III. THE PROBLEM OF BUREAUCRACY

A. Life in the Bureaucracy

285. Anderson, Barry. "Reaction to a Study of Bureaucracy
and Alienation." SOCIAL FORCES, 49 (1971), 614-20.

Critique of Bonjean and Grimes, Item 296.

286. Bendix, Reinhard. "Bureaucracy: The Problem and Its Setting." AMERICAN SOCIOLOGICAL REVIEW, 12 (1947), 493-
507.

Views bureaucracy as a special problem for its members,
in terms of compliance with formal authority versus individual initiatives.

287. Bacharach, Samuel B., and J. Lawrence French. "Role-
Allocation Processes in Public Bureaucracies: External Political Pressures, Internal Differentiation, and
the Perception of Recruitment and Promotion." ADMIN-
ISTRATION AND SOCIETY, 12 (1981), 399-426.

Find that civil service examinations are adopted in
order to enhance bureaucratic autonomy from outside control.

288. Bensman, Joseph, and Bernard Rosenberg. "The Meaning
of Work in Bureaucratic Society." IDENTITY AND ANX-
IETY. Edited by Maurice Stein, Arthur Vidich, and
David White. Glencoe, Ill.: Free Press, 1960.

Argue that bureaucracy forces a change in the personality of its members and, consequently, in "the dominant
character-structure of the society." The personality becomes a commodity to be rationalized.

289. Bensman, Joseph, and Arthur Vidich. "Power Cliques in
      Bureaucratic Society." SOCIAL RESEARCH, 29 (1962),
      467-74.

      Find that much of the coordination within an organ-
      ization comes about through informal cliques. The way
      in which these informal groups operate, as well as their
      implications for the individual, are discussed.

290. Bensman, Joseph, and Bernard Rosenberg. MASS, CLASS,
      AND BUREAUCRACY: THE EVOLUTION OF CONTEMPORARY SOC-
      IETY. Englewood Cliffs, N.J.: Prentice-Hall, 1963.
      548 pp.

      An introductory sociology text, with the bureaucrat-
      ization of society as the focus.

291. Bensman, Joseph, and Bernard Rosenberg, eds. SOCIOLOGY:
      INTRODUCTORY READINGS IN MASS, CLASS, AND BUREAUCRACY.
      New York: Praeger, 1975. 455 pp.

      A collection of previously published work.

292. Benveniste, Guy. BUREAUCRACY. San Francisco: Boyd and
      Fraser, 1977. 247 pp.

      Argues that bureaucratic failures are the responses
      of people within organizations to the uncertainty they
      are expected to overcome. In view of this uncertainty,
      it is better to do nothing, and call it planning or an-
      alysis, than to accept the probability of failure. In
      general, bureaucrats play games to cope with uncertain-
      ty. The solution to bureaucracy would be a method of
      reducing the costs of risk-taking for people within the
      organization, such as increasing job security. An elab-
      orate and novel system for achieving this protection is
      presented.

293. Blalack, Richard. "Dehumanization and Cybernetic Bur-
      eaucracies." BUSINESS AND SOCIETY, 16 (Spring, 1976),
      29-34.

      Suggests the externalization of control systems as an
      antidote to the dehumanization of work.

294. Blau, Peter M. "Co-operation and Competition in a Bur-
     eaucracy." AMERICAN JOURNAL OF SOCIOLOGY, 59 (1954),
     530-35.

     Compares two groups of public employees. Competitive-
     ness and productivity are inversely related for groups,
     but they are directly related for individuals within the
     competitive groups. Anxiety over production inhibits the
     performance of the group, while cooperation increases
     group cohesion.

295. Bonjean, Charles, and Michael D. Grimes. "Bureaucracy
     and Alienation: A Dimensional Approach." PROCEEDINGS
     OF THE SOUTHWESTERN SOCIOLOGICAL ASSOCIATION, 19
     (1968), 127-31.

     Do not find a direct relationship between bureaucracy
     and alienation, after surveying several occupational
     types, from salaried workers to business people.

296. Bonjean, Charles, and Michael D. Grimes. "Bureaucracy
     and Alienation: A Dimensional Approach." SOCIAL FOR-
     CES, 48 (1970), 365-73.

     Do not find support for the thesis that there is a di-
     rect relationship between bureaucracy and alienation.

297. Bonjean, Charles, and Michael D. Grimes. "Some Issues
     in the Study of Bureaucracy and Alienation." SOCIAL
     FORCES, 49 (1971), 622-29.

     Discuss problems in the definition and measurement of
     alienation.

298. Bozeman, Barry, and William E. McAlpine. "Goals and
     Bureaucratic Decision-Making: An Experiment." HUMAN
     RELATIONS, 30 (1977), 417-29.

     Conduct an experiment with undergraduate subjects to
     see how individual goal achievement is integrated with
     group activity.

299. Britan, Gerald M. BUREAUCRACY AND INNOVATION: AN ETH-
      NOGRAPHY OF POLICY CHANGE. Beverly Hills, Cal.: Sage,
      1981. 167 pp.

      Looks at the dynamics of bureaucratic change through
      a field study in the Experimental Technology Incentive
      Program (ETIP), a program set up to promote a better re-
      lationship between innovation and public policy. It was
      concluded that innovation often fails because the main
      goal of the organization is not rational accomplishment
      of goals but instead the survival of the individual and
      the organization. Agencies are not concerned with effic-
      iency or effectiveness, unless those factors are also
      in their political interest.

300. Chackerian, Richard. "Why Human Relations Increases
      Bureaucratization." PUBLIC ADMINISTRATION REVIEW,
      36 (1976), 688-89.

      Reviews a Japanese study which indicates that indus-
      trial relations in that country, while stressing worker
      satisfaction, are more centralized and formalistic.

301. Chapman, Ivan. "The 'War' of Bureaucracy with Society."
      FREE INQUIRY IN CREATIVE SOCIOLOGY, 7 (1979), 73-76.

      Discusses the limitations on creative thought imposed
      by the ideology of bureaucracy.

302. Cleveland, Harlan. "Survival in a Bureaucratic Jungle."
      REPORTER, 14 (April 5, 1956), 29-32.

      A veteran civil servant gives some hints about success.
      Officials must be able to manage while maintaining their
      political support.

303. Cohen, Harry. THE DEMONICS OF BUREAUCRACY: PROBLEMS OF
      CHANGE IN A GOVERNMENT AGENCY. Ames: Iowa State Uni-
      versity Press, 1965. 276 pp.

      Reports a case study of a state employment agency,
      along the lines of the Blau study (Item 2068). The
      purpose is to see how and why bureaucrats deviate from
      prescribed norms and to what effect.

304. Cohen, Harry. "The Tin Soldiers of Bureaucracy." MAN-
AGEMENT REVIEW, 61 (April, 1972), 2-9.

Discusses why bureaucracy prevents people at the low-
est levels from performing more productively.

305. Colley, John W. "Boldness Could Lighten Bureaucratic
Burdens." OFFICE, 81 (January, 1975), 59-60.

Claims that the accountants are not to blame for the
red tape in government.

306. Cooper, John L. THE ANTI-GRAVITY FORCE: A STUDY OF THE
NEGATIVE IMPACT OF PUBLIC BUREAUCRACY ON SOCIETY. Du-
buque, Iowa: Kendall/Hunt, 1981. 141 pp.

Argues that bureaucracy weakens the "social gravity"
or consensus that holds society together. The federal
bureaucracy, in particular, continues to usurp societal
power because of its crucial linkage role between the
state and society. The individual becomes atomized and
dependent upon the formal authority of the state.

307. Crozier, Michel. "Power Relationships in Modern Bureaucracies." INDIAN JOURNAL OF PUBLIC ADMINISTRATION, 7
(1961), 32-38.

See Item 309.

308. Crozier, Michel. "Human Relations at the Management
Level in a Bureaucratic System of Organization."
HUMAN ORGANIZATION, 20 (Summer, 1961), 51-64.

Examines management relations in French industry. See
Item 309.

309. Crozier, Michel. THE BUREAUCRATIC PHENOMENON. Chicago:
University of Chicago Press, 1964. 320 pp.

Describes an in-depth study of the operation of two
French organizations. Bureaucracy is a function of the
larger culture which manifests itself as members of an
organization attempt to preserve a sphere for independent

action. The response of the organization to worker autonomy is often maladaptive or dysfunctional. The attempt
of the organization to impose control systems becomes
self-defeating and the inability for corrective action
generates more bureaucracy. "A bureaucratic organization
is an organization that cannot correct its behavior by
learning from its errors." The more complex the organization, the more likely it is that workers will be able
to maintain their autonomy.

310. DeCotiis, Allen, and Gerald Grysak. "Role Orientation
      and Job Satisfaction in a Public Bureaucracy." SOUTH-
      ERN REVIEW OF PUBLIC ADMINISTRATION, 5 (1981), 22-33.

      Sample attitudes of state government personnel and of-
      fer managerial strategies for improving satisfaction in
      the job.

311. Deutscher, Isaac. "Roots of Bureaucracy." CANADIAN
      SLAVIC STUDIES, 3 (1969) 453-72.

      Argues that modern bureaucracy stems from the division
      between intellectual work and manual labor.

312. Deutscher, Isaac. "Roots of Bureaucracy." THE SOCIAL-
      IST REGISTER, 1969. Edited by Ralph Milibrand and
      John Saville. London: Merlin, 1969.

      Finds the roots of bureaucracy in the basic division
      between the managers and the managed, in the antagonism
      between brainwork and manual labor. Revolution will
      not succeed until managers are forced to concentrate
      on, in Marxist terms, the administration of "things,"
      not people.

313. Didion, Joan. "Bureaucrats." THE WHITE ALBUM. New
      York: Simon and Shuster, 1979.

      Finds very ominous the assurances given that the bur-
      eaucrats really know what they are doing. They seem
      to be so damn cheerful about their ability to control
      the world.

314. Ferkiss, Victor, Murray Bookchin, and Max Lerner. "Symposium on Bureaucracy, Centralization, Decentralization." TECHNOLOGY, POWER, AND SOCIAL CHANGE. Edited by Charles Thrall and Jerold Starr. Lexington, Mass.: Lexington Books, 1972.

     Three scholars assess the impact of bureaucracy and hierarchy on human freedom.

315. Ferrarotti, Franco. "The Struggle of Reason against Total Bureaucratization." TELOS, 27 (1976), 157–69.

     Discusses the view of the sociologist, Max Horkheimer, that modern attitudes toward authority are determined by the middle-class family.

316. Foster, John L., and Judson H. Jones. "Rule Orientation and Bureaucratic Reform." AMERICAN JOURNAL OF POLITICAL SCIENCE, 22 (1978), 348–63.

     Examine the argument that the structure of large, bureaucratic organizations determines the officials' petty allegience to rules. Based on material from the Atlanta Model Cities program, it was found that the structure was not a major determinant of rule orientation. Career orientation was the best explanation of rule orientation.

317. Foster, John L. "Role Orientation in Bureaucracy." SOUTHERN REVIEW OF PUBLIC ADMINISTRATION, 3 (1980), 487–513.

     Develops a typology of bureaucratic orientations.

318. Frisbie, Parker. "Measuring the Degree of Bureaucratization at the Societal Level." SOCIAL FORCES, 53 (1975), 563–73.

     Uses aggregate data to develop an index of the level of bureaucratization for purposes of cross-national comparison.

319. Gibson, R. Oliver. "The Person and the Bureaucracy."
      JOURNAL OF APPLIED BEHAVIORAL RESEARCH, 5 (1969), 104-
      08.

      Inquires how the individual can maintain an identity
      in the university bureaucracy.

320. Harrison, Frank. "Bureaucratization: Perceptions of
      Role Performance and Organizational Effectiveness."
      JOURNAL OF POLICE SCIENCE AND ADMINISTRATION, 3 (1975),
      319-26.

      Surveys 221 supervisors in law enforcement agencies to
      confirm that the more bureaucratic the organization, the
      lower the perception of member role performance.

321. Homans, George. "Bureaucracy as Big Brother." SENTI-
      MENTS AND ACTIVITIES. New York: Free Press, 1962.

      Thoughts on Whyte's *The Organization Man*.

322. Hummel. Ralph P. THE BUREAUCRATIC EXPERIENCE. New York:
      St. Martin's, 1977. 238 pp. Second edition, 1982.
      282 pp.

      Sees bureaucracy as a "new culture" which is in con-
      flict with normal human life in the larger society. Be-
      cause of its pervasiveness, this form of organization is
      eroding the bases of other values. The growth of the
      bureaucratic culture has radically transformed psycho-
      logical, linguistic, and political forces in modern soc-
      iety. Because bureaucracy is ultimately incapable of
      dealing with basic human questions, we face a "terminal
      world." Ways of transcending bureaucracy are discussed.

323. Jackall, Robert. "The Control of Public Faces in a Com-
      mercial Bureaucratic Work Situation." URBAN LIFE, 6
      (1977), 277-302.

      Describes the consequences of creating "public faces"
      by people employed in the banking industry.

324. Jackall, Robert. WORKERS IN A LABYRINTH: JOBS AND SUR-
     VIVAL IN A BANK BUREAUCRACY. Montclair, N.J.: Allan-
     held, Osmun, 1978. 190 pp.

     Interviews clerical workers in a large commercial bank.
     The central theme is the pressure of work on people at
     lower levels and the ways in which they attempt to ad-
     just to the organization.

325. Jansen, Robert B. THE ABC'S OF BUREAUCRACY. Chicago:
     Nelson-Hall, 1978. 228 pp.

     A guide to the mysteries of life within the bureau-
     cracy by a former insider. Although the bureaucracy is
     often sluggish and unresponsive, it is also a source of
     stability in government and in society. The true sur-
     vivor must recognize that not much, good or bad, is like-
     ly to happen. A tour through the maze of bureaucracy is
     conducted.

326. Jaques, Elliot A. A GENERAL THEORY OF BUREAUCRACY.
     New York: Halsted, 1976. 412 pp.

     Attempts to "build a general theoretical construction
     of how social institutions and human nature affect each
     other, with special reference to bureaucracy." Bureau-
     cracy, by itself, is neither centralizing nor dehuman-
     izing. As dependent institutions, they take their char-
     acter from the groups that employ them. Bureaucracy may
     be inevitable in an industrial society, but many of its
     negative features can be mitigated through the "inter-
     active participation" of its members. The theory is
     applied to industry, commerce, public administration,
     education, religious institutions, and the military.

327. Kamenka, Eugene, and Alice Ehr-Soon Tay. "Freedom, Law
     and the Bureaucratic State." BUREAUCRACY: THE CAREER
     OF A CONCEPT. Edited by Eugene Kamenka and Martin
     Krygier. London: Edward Arnold, 1979.

     Discuss the roots of modern disenchantment with tech-
     nically proficient administration, especially in social-
     ist countries. Public law, based on the rights of in-
     dividuals, has been replaced by administrative regula-
     tions.

328.   Kaufman, Harold F. "Community and Bureaucracy in the
       Modern World." JOURNAL OF SOCIAL RESEARCH, 11 (1968),
       49-63.

       Compares bureaucracy to primary groups in terms of pure
       instrumental organizations versus those which are regard-
       ed by their members as intrinsically valuable.

329.   Kaufman, Herbert. RED TAPE: ITS ORIGINS, USES, AND
       ABUSES. Washington, D.C.: Brookings Institution,
       1977. 100 pp.

       Inquires into the durability of this thing often de-
       nounced as "red tape." Red tape derives from our insis-
       tence on equitable government activity in so many areas.
       It is also indicative of our mistrust of government.
       There is no cure for red tape; the best we can do is to
       lessen some of its worst manifestations.

330.   Krasner, William. "How to Live with the Bureaucracy--
       And Win." NEW SOCIETY, 12 (1968), 116-18.

       Helpful hints on how to cope with the big organization.

331.   Krislov, Samuel. "Organizational Theory: Freedom and
       Constraint in a Large-Scale Bureaucracy." EMPATHY
       AND IDEOLOGY: ASPECTS OF ADMINISTRATIVE ORGANIZATION.
       Edited by Charles Press and Alan Arian. Chicago:
       Rand McNally, 1966.

       Absolves modern organization theory of the charge that
       it desires a dehumanized bureaucracy. It is by no means
       clear that the theory despises the individual. It may
       prize conformity, but the objects, the members of the or-
       ganization, will continue to resist too much control of
       their behavior.

332.   Kvale, Steinar. "Examinations: From Ritual through Bur-
       eaucracy to Technology." SOCIAL PRAXIS, 3 (1975),
       187-206.

       Argues that examinations for selection or placement
       have moved through several stages, from ritual, to a
       means of entry, to a form of constant evaluation.

333. Litwak, Eugene. "Reference Group Theory, Bureaucratic Career, and Neighborhood Primary Group Cohesion." SOCIOMETRY, 23 (May, 1960), 27-84.

Examines how the orientation of the subject toward a bureaucratic career influences relationships with other reference groups.

334. Marvick, Dwaine. "Expectations Concerning Power in a Bureaucratic Arena." ADMINISTRATIVE SCIENCE QUARTERLY, 2 (1958), 542-49.

Tests how members of an organization develop an orientation toward power.

335. O'Mahoney, Joseph. "Bureaucracy Trend toward Collectivism." COMMERCIAL AND FINANCIAL CHRONICLE, 165 (1947), 873, 987.

Argues that government, business, and unions are all becoming more centralized, posing a threat to individual freedom.

336. Parker, R.S. "The Bureaucratic Revolution." AUSTRALIAN QUARTERLY, 27 (December, 1955), 9-22.

Urges adjustment to the realities of the modern world, including the big organization.

337. Peterson, William, ed. AMERICAN SOCIAL PATTERNS: STUDIES OF RACE RELATIONS, POPULAR HEROES, UNION DEMOCRACY AND GOVERNMENT BUREAUCRACY. Garden City, N.Y.: Doubleday, 1956. 263 pp.

Contains selections from Blau, Item 2068.

338. Ray, Verne F., ed. SYSTEMS OF POLITICAL CONTROL AND BUREAUCRACY IN HUMAN SOCIETIES: PROCEEDINGS OF THE 1958 ANNUAL SPRING MEETING OF THE AMERICAN ETHNOLOGICAL SOCIETY. Seattle: American Ethnological Society, 1958. 63 pp.

A collection of papers by anthropologists.

339.   Savells, Jerald. "The Americanization of the Bureaucrat-
       ic Ethos." PERSONNEL JOURNAL, 51 (1972), 835-39.

       Argues that increasing bureaucratization leads to ali-
       enation.

340.   Sayre, Wallace. "Unhappy Bureaucrats: Views Ironic,
       Hopeful, Indignant." PUBLIC ADMINISTRATION REVIEW,
       18 (1958), 239-45.

       A review essay on books about life in the modern or-
       ganization by Parkinson, Argyris, and Whyte. The am-
       biguous attitudes of the 1950s are highlighted.

341.   Schuman, David. BUREAUCRACIES, ORGANIZATIONS, AND AD-
       MINISTRATION: A POLITICAL PRIMER. New York: Macmil-
       lan, 1976. 235 pp.

       Takes a critical look at the impact of bureaucracy on
       people and society, and suggests ways of reform.

342.   Smith, Michael P. "Self-Fulfillment in a Bureaucratic
       Society: A Commentary on the Thought of Gabriel Mar-
       cel." PUBLIC ADMINISTRATION REVIEW, 29 (1969), 25-
       32.

       Discusses the writings of the French existentialist,
       Gabriel Marcel. Marcel saw bureaucratic expansion as
       driving out genuine human relationships from society.
       The individual must avoid becoming trapped in the ster-
       ile world of techniques. Those techniques deny the
       "ethic of love" for one's fellow human being.

343.   Smith, Pringle. "Eight Games the System Plays: Or, How
       to Psych Out the Bureaucracy." MS, 4 (February, 1976),
       97-100.

       On how the bureaucracy resists change.

344.   Thompson, Victor. BUREAUCRACY AND THE MODERN WORLD.
       Morristown, N.J.: General Learning Press, 1976. 141
       pp.

Stresses the difference between individual and organizational rationality within bureaucracies. The bureaucratic system is incapable of accomplishing some of its
goals because of the inherent limitations of its mode of
rationality. Bureaucracy creates order at the expense
of innovation. Neither can it afford to be truly com-
passionate.

345. Torrey, E. Fuller. "The Bureaucrat's New Clothes: A
    Cautionary Tale." PSYCHOLOGY TODAY, 11 (July, 1977),
    95.

    On the busy but pointless career of a public servant.

346. Vachell, Horace. "Bureaucrats." LITTLE TYRANNIES.
    London: Cassell, 1940.

    Fumes about some minor bureaucratic idiocies.

347. Waddell, Jack. "Resurgent Patronage and Lagging Bureau-
    cracy in a Papago Off-Reservation Community." HUMAN
    ORGANIZATION, 29 (1970), 37-42.

    Examines the changes in social relationships from a
    patron-client connection to a bureaucratic one among
    American Indians employed in a modern industrial plant.

348. Watson, Gordon. "The Problem of Bureaucracy: A Summary."
    JOURNAL OF SOCIAL ISSUES, 1 (December, 1945), 69-72.

    Enumerates several points about modern bureaucracy.

349. Watson, Gordon. "Bureaucracy as Citizens See it."
    JOURNAL OF SOCIAL ISSUES, 1 (December, 1945), 4-13.

    Based on interviews with 240 citizens. When asked
    their reaction to the word "bureaucracy," most expressed
    a disapproving attitude.

350. White, Orion. "Human Freedom and Bureaucratic Con-
    straint." PUBLIC ADMINISTRATION REVIEW, 26 (1966),
    217-22.

Review essay on Golembiewski's *Men, Management, and Morality*. The book is a refreshing way out of the fog of the "bureaucratic pathos" in scholarship.

351.   Wilson, James Q. "The Bureaucracy Problem." PUBLIC IN-
        TEREST, 6 (1967), 3-9.

        Argues that there are limits to the use of bureaucracy
        as a solution to social problems. Unhappily, most of us
        do not see these limits and thus feel that the bureau-
        cracy is incompetent.

352.   Yessian, Mark H. "Coping within the Bureaucracy: A Way
        to Keep the Juices Flowing." BUREAUCRAT, 7 (Summer,
        1978), 48-49.

        Claims that the dedicated official can avoid frustra-
        tion. Public servants are advised to be aware of their
        options.

B.   The Bureaucratic Personality

353.   Baker, Sally, Amitai Etzioni, Richard Hansen, and Marvin
        Sontag. "Tolerance for Bureaucratic Structure: The-
        ory and Measurement." HUMAN RELATIONS, 26 (1973), 775-
        86.

        Attempt to measure the personality factors influencing
        the worker's tolerance for bureaucratic features of the
        work setting. A Tolerance for Bureaucratic Structure
        (TBS) scale is constructed involving four areas: atti-
        tude toward rules and regulations, attitude toward auth-
        ority, orientation toward task, and orientation toward
        delayed gratification.

354.   Bronzo, Anthony, and Daniel J. Baer. "Leadership and
        Bureaucratic Tendency Measures as Predictors of Fresh-
        man Dropouts from AFROTC." PSYCHOLOGICAL REPORTS,
        22 (1968), 232.

        Develop a test which seems to be successful in predict-
        ing who will leave an ROTC program.

355. Cohen, Louis, and R. Harris. "Personal Correlates of
     Bureaucratic Orientation." BRITISH JOURNAL OF EDUCA-
     TIONAL PSYCHOLOGY. 42 (1972), 300-04.

     Apply Gordon's (Item 361) School Environment Prefer-
     ence Schedule (SEPS) to preteen children. A bureau-
     cratic orientation is correlated with dogmatism, con-
     servatism, neuroticism, and extroversion.

356. Dailey, Charles A. ASSESSMENT OF LIVES: PERSONALITY
     EVALUATION IN A BUREAUCRATIC SOCIETY. San Francisco:
     Jossey-Bass, 1971. 243 pp.

     Criticizes the personality assessment techniques that
     stress standardization and objectivity. These tests
     also do not permit much contact between the assessor
     and the assessee. Such methods are designed to fit in
     with the goals of the bureaucratic organization. A more
     humanistic approach—the "life history" model—is des-
     cribed.

357. Guyot, James F. "Government Bureaucrats are Different."
     PUBLIC ADMINISTRATION REVIEW, 22 (1962), 195-202.

     Describes the administration of personality tests to
     public and private managers. Government officials score
     higher in achievement motivation; they tend to be less
     motivated by the desire of acceptance by colleagues.
     Both groups were about equal in their orientation toward
     power.

358. Gordon, Leonard. "Correlates of Bureaucratic Orienta-
     tion." MANPOWER AND APPLIED PSYCHOLOGY, 2 (Winter,
     1968), 54-59.

     Discusses the validity of a measure for bureaucratic
     orientation.

359. Gordon, Leonard, and Akio Kikuchi. "The Measurement
     of Bureaucratic Orientation in Japan." INTERNATIONAL
     REVIEW OF APPLIED PSYCHOLOGY, 19 (1970), 133-40.

     Apply the WEPS (see Item 360) to a group of Japanese

students. Those with a strong bureaucratic orientation
were inclined to favor conformist behavior.

360.   Gordon, Leonard. "Measurement of Bureaucratic Orienta-
        tion." PERSONNEL PSYCHOLOGY, 23 (1970), 1-11.

        Describes the construction of the Work Environment
        Preference Schedule (WEPS) as a measure of bureaucratic
        orientation. The scales measure attributes associated
        with the characteristics of bureaucracy: self-subord-
        ination, compartmentalization, impersonalization, rule
        conformity, and traditionalism. The "bureaucratic per-
        sonality" seems to be a personality construct in its own
        right.

361.   Gordon, Leonard. "Bureaucratic Values and ROTC Re-En-
        rollment." PSYCHOLOGICAL REPORTS, 26 (1970), 570.

        Administers a test of bureaucratic orientation to stu-
        dents in ROTC. Those who volunteered to re-enroll also
        scored as more bureaucratic.

362.   Grosof, Elliott. "Social Class Background of College
        Seniors and Anticipated Behavior in Bureaucratic
        Structure." AMERICAN CATHOLIC SOCIOLOGICAL REVIEW,
        25 (1962), 224-35.

        Examines the attitudes of college students from var-
        ious social backgrounds toward bureaucracy. Little
        difference was found, indicating the power of college
        in the socialization of future managers.

363.   "Hail to Thee, Blithe Bureaucrat." MANAGEMENT REVIEW,
        68 (January, 1979), 56.

        On the work of Melvin Kohn (Item 367), showing the
        bureaucrat to be flexible and creative.

364.   Kakkar, S.B. "Correlates of Bureaucratic Orientation."
        INDIAN JOURNAL OF PSYCHOLOGY, 47 (1972), 47-54.

        Applies Gordon's (Item 360) Work Environment Prefer-
        ence Schedule (WEPS) and Cattlett's Sixteen Personality

Factor test to Indian teachers.

365. Khalique, Nazre. "Bureaucratic Orientation: A Cross-
      Cultural Study." PSYCHOLOGIA, 17 (1974), 71-74.

      Compares Pakistani with American and Japanese students
      using the WEPS (Item 360). Pakistani females were more
      bureaucratic than their American counterparts.

366. Kiefer, Christie. "The Psychological Interdependence
      of Family, School, and Bureaucracy in Japan." AMER-
      ICAN ANTHROPOLOGIST, 72 (1970), 66-75.

      Looks at the examination system as a rite which intro-
      duces children to the peer-group values of the larger
      society.

367. Kohn, Melvin L. "Bureaucratic Man: A Portrait and an
      Interpretation." AMERICAN SOCIOLOGICAL REVIEW, 36
      (1971), 461-74.

      Reports on interviews with 3,101 employees in civilian
      occupations. There was a tendency for people in bureau-
      cratic organizations "to be more intellectually flexible,
      more open to new experience, and more self-directed in
      their values" than those in non-bureaucratic settings.
      This may be because of the higher educational status of
      bureaucrats. The occupational characteristics of gov-
      ernment work--security, income, and the nature of the
      job--are also important factors.

368. Kohn, Melvin L. "Bureaucratic Man." NEW SOCIETY, 18
      (1971), 820-24.

      More on the survey (Item 367) that found bureaucrats
      to be more flexible and less conforming than people in
      non-bureaucratic occupations.

369. Lane, Robert E. "Businessmen and Bureaucrats." SOCIAL
      FORCES, 32 (1953), 145-52.

      Examines the bases of differences between businessmen
      and government officials.

370. Maas, Henry S., Charles H. Price, and George E. Davis. "Personal-Social Disequilibria in a Bureaucratic System." PSYCHIATRY, 16 (1953), 129-37.

     Theorize that people in the military have a personality structure congruent with a stable organization. When the organization is disrupted, as in a time of rapid expansion during mobilization, the members suffer from mental stress.

371. March, C. Paul, Robert Dolen, and William Riddick. "Anomia and Communication Behavior: The Relationship between Anomia and Utilization of Three Public Bureaucracies." RURAL SOCIOLOGY, 32 (1967), 435-45.

     Suggest that anomic individuals will have fewer contacts with government. The hypothesis was only partially confirmed by the data.

372. Meerlo, Abraham. "Saint Bureaucratius." AFTERMATH OF OF PEACE: PSYCHOLOGICAL ESSAYS. New York: International Universities Press, 1946.

     Speculates on the rise of the bureaucratic personality in the modern world.

373. Merton, Robert. "Bureaucratic Structure and Personality." SOCIAL FORCES, 18 (1940), 560-69.

     Suggests lines of research into the interaction between individual personality and the demands of the formal organization. The need for conformity, while necessary for an efficient operation, may create the sort of person who behaves inefficiently in specific contexts.

374. Miner, John B. "Changes in Student Attitudes toward Bureaucratic Role Expdctations during the 1960s." ADMINISTRATIVE SCIENCE QUARTERLY, 16 (1971), 351-64.

     Compares student attitudes from the late and early 1960s. The later students had more negative attitudes toward a role in the bureaucracy. They were more negative toward authority firgures and toward assuming a

managerial position. "It appears that the Protestant
ethic is declining in influence, but that it is not being replaced by a social ethic."

375. Miner, John B. "Student Attitudes toward Bureaucratic
      Role Prescriptions and Prospects for Managerial Talent
      Shortages." PERSONNEL PSYCHOLOGY, 27 (1974), 605-13.

      Finds that business administration majors are less in-
      clined to choose a managerial career or to perform ef-
      fectively within a bureaucratic setting. This fore-
      shadows a lack of managerial talent for adequate staff-
      ing of the existing organization system.

376. Presthus, Robert. THE ORGANIZATIONAL SOCIETY, rev. ed.
      New York: St. Martin's, 1978. 288 pp.

      Attempts to define the pattern of accommodation made
      by individuals to life in the bureaucracy. The primary
      feature of bureaucracy is the distribution of formal
      authority; the reaction to this authority is the most
      critical variable in organizational accommodation. Based
      on principles of social psychology, three personality
      types within formal organizations are discussed: upward-
      mobiles, indifferents, and ambivalents.

377. Reismann, Leonard. "A Study of Role Conceptions in Bur-
      eaucracy." SOCIAL FORCES, 27 (1949), 305-10.

      Analyzes the interaction of personality types and bur-
      eaucratic structure and roles.

378. Sage, George H. "American Values and Sport: Formation
      of a Bureaucratic Personality." JOURNAL OF PHYSICAL
      EDUCATION AND RECREATION, 49 (October, 1978), 42-44.

      Contends that organized sports are unrelated to the
      factor of playfulness. Instead, they are agents for the
      deliberate socialization of people into accepting bureau-
      cracy as the dominant form of organization. Team sports
      help to internalize the bureaucratic ethic while the
      rationalization of play leads to centralization and elit-
      ism.

379.   Sieber, Timothy. "Schooling, Socialization and Group
       Boundaries: A Study of Informal Social Relations in
       the Public Domain." URBAN ANTHROPOLOGIST, 7 (1978),
       67-98.

       Examines the ways in which different school systems
       introduce children to appropriate patterns of bureau-
       cratic behavior.

380.   Sieber, Timothy. "Schoolrooms, Pupils, and Rules: The
       Role of Informality in Bureaucratic Socialization."
       HUMAN ORGANIZATION, 38 (1979), 273-82.

       Shows how informal modes of teaching serve in the pro-
       cess of cultural transmission. In urban schools, formal
       types of behavior are encouraged through subtle, infor-
       mal clues from teachers. School display non-bureaucrat-
       ic traits in order to move student behavior in the di-
       rection of accepting bureaucratic authority.

381.   Williams, Norma M., Gideon Sjoberg, Andree E. Sjoberg.
       "The Bureaucratic Personality: An Alternative View."
       JOURNAL OF APPLIED BEHAVIORAL SCIENCE, 16 (1980), 389-
       405.

       Explore the function of secrecy, loyalty, and subord-
       ination in the development of the social self of the bur-
       eaucrat.

       C.   Toward a Theory of Bureaucratic Politics

382.   Aberbach, Joel D., Robert D. Putnam, and Bert A. Rock-
       man, with the collaboration of Thomas Anton, Samuel
       Eldersveld, and Ronald Inglehart. BUREAUCRATS AND
       POLITICIANS IN WESTERN DEMOCRACIES. Cambridge, Mass.:
       Harvard University Press, 1981. 308 pp.

       Present the results of of interviews with over 1,400
       civil servants and politicians in the United States,
       Great Britain, France, West Germany, Italy, the Nether-
       lands, and Sweden. In general, these two groups are
       different in their outlook and orientation. Politicians
       are more sensitive to broad social issues, while civil

servants are concerned with interest group relations and
specific problem solving. Politicians are more likely to
endorse partisan causes than are bureaucrats. Among the
countries studied, there was the highest degree of elite
overlap in the U.S., with the lines between the two camps
being somewhat blurred.

383. Argyriades, Demetrios. "Reconsidering Bureaucracy as
      Ideology." STRATEGIES FOR ADMINISTRATIVE REFORM. Ed-
      ited by Gerald E. Caiden and Heinrich Siedentopf. Lex-
      ington, Mass.: Lexington Books, 1982.

      Argues that the centralization of power in the state
      began as a reform effort. Public administration was pro-
      pelled by a belief in the value of state action. The
      allure of the bureaucracy, however, is declining as
      other centers of power deny the total legitimacy of the
      state.

384. Baaklini, Abdo I. "Legislative Reform? Or the Bureau-
      cratisation of the Legislature." ADMINISTRATION, 24
      (1976), 138-58.

      Contends that the imposition of traditional public ad-
      ministration doctrine on the legislature may have a bad
      effect. The logics of the legislature and the bureau-
      cracy are incompatible.

385. Barnard, Chester I. "Bureaucracy in a Democracy." AMER-
      ICAN POLITICAL SCIENCE REVIEW, 44 (1950), 990-1004.

      Review essay on Charles Hyneman's *Bureaucracy in a
      Democracy*, Item 408.

386. Bendix, Reinhard. "Bureaucracy and the Problem of Pow-
      er." PUBLIC ADMINISTRATION REVIEW, 5 (1945), 194-209.

      Inquires whether bureaucracy is an autonomous source
      of power or the tool of other social forces. Paradox-
      ically, bureaucracy is powerful, yet incapable of de-
      termining how that power should be used. The same pro-
      fessionalism that gives it power also makes it a sub-
      servient tool.

387. Birnbaum, Pierre. "State, Centre, and Bureaucracy."
      GOVERNMENT AND OPPOSITION, 16 (1981), 58-77.

      Suggests that the rise of the state is dependent upon
      the nature of the classes and groups in a society which
      do or do not permit a strong central bureaucracy.

388. Brecht, Arnold. "Bureaucratic Sabotage." ANNALS OF THE
      AMERICAN ACADEMY OF POLITICAL AND SOCIAL SCIENCE, 189
      (1937), 48-57.

      Identifies the ways in which officials can defeat the
      directives of political leadership. Intentional acts
      of sabotage by groups may be avoided through the divers-
      ification of the membership of the civil service.

389. Brecht, Arnold. "How Bureaucracies Develop and Func-
      tion." ANNALS OF THE AMERICAN ACADEMY OF POLITICAL
      AND SOCIAL SCIENCE, 292 (1954), 1-10.

      Attempts to clarify the meaning of bureaucracy as "gov-
      ernment by officials." Two types of power are identi-
      fied: first, the constitutional or legal right to make
      or enforce laws and, second, the actual power to achieve
      or prohibit certain actions by government. By further
      indicating whether these sorts of power are used proper-
      ly or improperly, there are eight types of bureaucratic
      polities. The factors which move a bureaucracy from one
      type to another are discussed.

390. Burns, Tom. "Sovereignty, Interests, and Bureaucracy
      in the Modern State." BRITISH JOURNAL OF SOCIOLOGY,
      31 (1980), 491-506.

      Argues that the politicization of the bureaucracy can
      be traced to the decline of the notion of sovereignty.

391. Cousins, Norman. "The Bureaucrats and Mr. 1069." SAT-
      URDAY REVIEW, 5 (January 21, 1978), 4.

      Sees the case of the man who wanted to change his name
      to a number as another sign of the sorry shape of citi-
      zenship in the modern world.

392. Davis, James W. AN INTRODUCTION TO PUBLIC ADMINISTRA-
    TION: POLITICS, POLICY, AND BUREAUCRACY. New York:
    Free Press, 1974. 336 pp.

    An introductory public administration text which em-
    phasizes the role of administration in politics, prim-
    arily at the national level.

393. Divine, D.R. "A Political Theory of Bureaucracy."
    PUBLIC ADMINISTRATION, 57 (1979), 143-58.

    Argues that the structure of public bureaucracies
    is indicative of the value of justice. The bureau
    is an expression of the polity's conception of justice.

394. Dorsey, John T. "Administrators: Bureaucrats and Pol-
    icy-Makers." GOVERNMENT AND POLITICS: AN INTRODUC-
    TION TO POLITICAL SCIENCE. Edited by Alex Dragnich
    and John C. Wahlke. New York: Random House, 1966.

    A general discussion of bureaucracy in modern politi-
    cal systems, including the less developed world. Ef-
    ficiency and responsibility are posited as the two fun-
    damental criteria for evaluating bureaucracy.

395. Eisenstadt, S.N. "Bureaucracy, Bureaucratization, and
    Debureaucratization." ADMINISTRATIVE SCIENCE QUART-
    ERLY, 4 (1959), 302-36.

    Attempts to reconcile the views of bureaucracy as a
    tool and as an expansive social force. Bureaucratiza-
    tion and debureaucratization are described as corruptions
    of the idea of bureaucracy as a neutral social instru-
    ment. Bureaucratization includes the extension of the
    power of the bureaucratic organization over many areas
    beyond its initial purpose, the growing internal regi-
    mentation within the organization, the formalization
    of these areas by the bureaucracy and, in general, a
    strong emphasis by the bureaucracy on the enhancement
    of its power. The proper condition of administrative
    equilibrium depends on the relationship of the bureau-
    cracy with the environment.

396. Eisenstadt, S.N. "Bureaucratization, Markets, and Power
      Structure." TRANSACTIONS OF THE WESTERMARCK SOCIETY,
      10 (1964), 241-55.

      Offers two definitions of bureaucracy and of bureau-
      cratization. The extent of bureaucratization seems to
      be dependent on the structure of markets within a soc-
      iety. In general, the conditions necessary for check-
      ing the growth of bureaucracy exist mostly within the
      democratic societies.

397. Eisenstadt, S.N. "Bureaucracy, Bureaucratization, Mark-
      ets and Power Structure." ESSAYS ON COMPARATIVE IN-
      STITUTIONS. New York: John Wiley, 1965.

      A summary and expansion of the ideas from Item 3 and
      Item 396.

398. Ellis, Ellen. "Man versus Bureaucracy." FORUM, 111
      (1949), 257-60, 321-26.

      Outlines the problem of political control of bureau-
      cracy and suggest solutions.

399. Franklin, Julian H. "Bureaucracy and Freedom." MAN IN
      CONTEMPORARY SOCIETY, Vol. I. Prepared by the Contemp-
      orary Civilization Staff of Columbia College. New
      York: Columbia University Press, 1955.

      Sees bureaucracy as an inevitable part of modern gov-
      ernment. Bureaucratic routine, as a social problem, is
      in contrast to the flexibility of democracy. The offic-
      ial mind is naturally conservative. However, by over-
      coming our anxieties, we can turn bureaucracy into a
      useful tool for humane ends.

400. Friedrich, Carl J. CONSTITUTIONAL GOVERNMENT AND DEMOC-
      RACY: THEORY AND PRACTICE IN EUROPE AND AMERICA. Bos-
      ton: Ginn, 1946. 695 pp.

      Views constitutionalism as the basis of civilized gov-
      ernment. Bureaucracy, in turn, is the basis of true con-
      stitutionalism.

401. Friedrich, Carl J. "Bureaucracy Faces Anarchy" CANAD-
      IAN PUBLIC ADMINISTRATION, 13 (1970), 219-31.

      Argues that the limits of bureaucratization have prob-
      ably been reached. Further extension of the process of
      rationalization will provoke a reaction from the public.

402. Friedrich, Carl J. "Reflections on Democracy and Bureau-
      cracy." FROM POLICY TO ADMINISTRATION. Edited by J.
      A.G. Griffith. London: George Allen and Unwin, 1976.

      Discusses the need for more inspirational political
      leadership to avoid the possibility of a bureaucratic
      breakdown.

403. Goldwin, Robert A., ed. BUREAUCRATS, POLICY ANALYSTS,
      STATESMEN: WHO LEADS? Washington, D.C.: American En-
      terprise Institute for Public Policy Research, 1980.
      133 pp.

      A collection of essays which inquire into the question
      of who is leading whom? At the present, government is
      under attack again from anti-political reformers, this
      time in the guise of policy analysts. An applied social
      science, although unjustified by the knowledge base, is
      a threat to supercede the skills of the politicians.

404. Greenwood, Royston, and C.R. Hinings. "Contingency The-
      ory and Public Bureaucracies." POLICY AND POLITICS,
      5 (1976), 159-80.

      Suggest that contingency theory, so valuable in look-
      ing at the economic survival of the firm, can also be ap-
      plied to the political survival of the bureau. The ex-
      tent to which political pressure affects the organiza-
      tion structure of the bureau is considered.

405. Greenwood, Royston. "Politics and Public Bureaucracies:
      A Reconsideration." POLICY AND POLITICS, 6 (1978),
      403-20.

      Reformulates the thesis of Item 404 and demonstrates
      that parts of public bureaucracies are affected by pol-
      itical pressure.

406.   Holden, Matthew. "'Imperialism' in Bureaucracy." AMER-
        ICAN POLITICAL SCIENCE REVIEW, 60 (1966), 943-51.

        Concludes that administrators are inspired to increase
        the scope of their jurisdictions because of a desire to
        preserve or expand their constituencies. Among the fac-
        tors that will determine their imperialistic attempts
        are the disposition of the agency, the occasions for re-
        allocation, and the modes of resolution of inter-agency
        disputes.

407.   Hyneman, Charles. "Bureaucracy and the Democratic Sys-
        tem." LOUISIANA LAW REVIEW, 6 (1945), 309-49.

        Defines bureaucracy and democracy as well as their in-
        terrelationship, based on a review of the New Deal ex-
        perience and the most recent literature in political
        science.

408.   Hyneman, Charles. BUREAUCRACY IN A DEMOCRACY. New York:
        Harper and Brothers, 1950.   586 pp.

        Examines the problems of bureaucracy in the federal
        government, with the primary concern being the consid-
        eration of "what can be done to make our federal bur-
        eaucracy function as the faithful servant of the Amer-
        ican people?" Structural means of ensuring political
        supremacy over bureaucracy are reviewed. Presidential
        authority, augmented by central staff agencies such as
        the Bureau of the Budget, are emphasized. The creation
        of a "central council" made up of the president and cer-
        tain members of Congress is the final recommendation for
        dealing with the fragmentation of the federal system.

409.   Johnson, A.W. "Public Policy: Creativity and Bureaucra-
        cy." CANADIAN PUBLIC ADMINISTRATION, 21 (1978), 1-15.

        Argues that the real source of creativity in govern-
        ment is the individual bureau or ministry. Cooperative
        agreements with other agencies tend to compromise po-
        tentially novel approaches to a policy area. The ele-
        ments which favor creativity in the individual human
        mind are also at work on a collective basis. The use
        of committees has a negative effect on creativity.

410. Kernaghan, Kenneth. "Responsible Public Bureaucracy:
     A Rationale and a Framework for Analysis." CANADIAN
     PUBLIC ADMINISTRATION, 16 (1973), 572-603.

     Argues that administrative responsibility must be seen
     in conjunction with bureaucratic power. In light of this
     connection, subjective responsibility must be stressed.
     Reforms such as MBO offer ways for improving the level
     of subjective responsibillity.

411. Lane, Edgar. "Interest Groups and Bureaucracy." ANNALS
     OF THE AMERICAN ACADEMY OF POLITICAL AND SOCIAL SCI-
     ENCE. 292 (1954), 104-10.

     Inquires whether bureaucrats, with their ties to pres-
     sure groups, can really be expected to represent the pub-
     lic interest.

412. Lipset, Seymour M. "Bureaucracy and Social Reform."
     RESEARCH STUDIES OF THE STATE COLLEGE OF WASHINGTON,
     17 (1949), 11-17.

     Looks at the question of how reformers and the leaders
     of socialist governments can impose their will on the
     civil service. This study seems to indicate that the
     efforts of establishing popular control can be thwarted
     by a determined bureaucracy.

413. Mayntz, Renate. "Public Bureaucracies and Policy Imple-
     mentation." INTERNATIONAL SOCIAL SCIENCE JOURNAL, 31
     (1979), 633-45.

     Discovers that public agencies are not mere tools in
     the implementation process. On occasion, they must use
     their discretion to adapt to the real world by taking
     account of features overlooked by legislators.

414. Morstein Marx, Fritz. "The Bureaucratic State--Some
     Remarks on Mosca's Ruling Class." REVIEW OF POLITICS,
     11 (1939), 457-72.

     Summarizes the contributions of "Mosca, the diagnos-
     tician of the bureaucratic state." See Item 80.

415. Morstein Marx, Fritz. "Bureaucracy and Consultation."
      REVIEW OF POLITICS, 1 (1939), 84-100.

      Sees as a major problem in policy making the "insul-
      arity of mind" caused by organizational separatism.
      Greater intra- and inter-departmental communication is
      recommended. Organizational self-criticism will stim-
      ulate creative thinking.

416. Morstein Marx, Fritz. "Bureaucracy and Dictatorship."
      REVIEW OF POLITICS, 3 (1941), 100-17.

      Describes bureaucracy as a check on totalitarian ex-
      cesses.

417. Morstein Marx, Frtiz. THE ADMINISTRATIVE STATE: AN IN-
      TRODUCTION TO BUREAUCRACY. Chicago: University of
      Chicago Press, 1957. 202 pp.

      Reviews the problems of bureaucracy in the emerging
      "administrative state" in Western society. Four types
      of bureaucracy are identified: guardian, caste, patron-
      age, and merit bureaucracies. Civil service concepts
      in Europe and the U.S. are examined. The major prob-
      lems of democracy concern the subordination of technic-
      cal competence to popular control.

418. Partridge, P.H. "An Evaluation of Bureaucratic Power."
      PUBLIC ADMINISTRATION (SYDNEY), 33 (1974), 99-116.

      Agrees that bureaucracy is a major wielder of power
      in government, but such power is not a unidimensional
      thing. The evaluation of bureaucratic power must take
      into account a number of variables.

419. Peters, B. Guy. "Insiders and Outsiders: The Politics
      of Pressure Group Influence on Bureaucracy." ADMIN-
      ISTRATION AND SOCIETY, 9 (1977), 191-218.

      Develops a typology for studying the relationships of
      pressure groups and administration. The categories
      range from the formal, legitimate contacts--as in the
      Scandanavian countries--to the sporadic and illegitimate
      ones, as are common in developing countries.

420. Peters, B. Guy. THE POLITICS OF BUREAUCRACY: A COMPAR-
      ATIVE PERSPECTIVE. New York: Longman, 1978. 246 pp.

      Outlines an approach to the comparative study of ad-
      ministration in the Western democracies. Systems the-
      ory is used to identify the relationships between ad-
      ministration and environment and the connection of bur-
      eaucracy with other political institutions. The recruit-
      ment practice of bureaucracy is a major linkage with the
      political culture of a society. The political dimen-
      sions of administrative accountability are stressed.

421. Peters, B. Guy. "Bureaucracy, Politics, and Public Pol-
      icy." COMPARATIVE POLITICS, 11 (1979), 339-58.

      Review essay on books by Dogan, Grindle, Schumaker,
      and Mayntz and Scharpf.

422. Peters, B. Guy. "The Problem of Bureaucratic Govern-
      ment." JOURNAL OF POLITICS, 43 (1981), 56-82.

      Investigates the nature of bureaucratic involvement
      in public policy. Several approaches to the question
      are reviewed. While administration may provide govern-
      ment, it cannot provide the necessary leadership. The
      fragmentation of bureaucracy in industrialized nations
      leads to decreased popular control as well as to inef-
      fective government policies. Neither politics nor ad-
      ministration seems capable of providing direction to
      public policy.

423. Putnam, Robert D. "Bureaucrats and Politics." NEW SOC-
      IETY, 27 (1974), 63-65.

      Describes the differing attitudes about their roles
      in public affairs of British, Italian, and German bur-
      eaucrats. An Index of Tolerance for Politics distin-
      guishes between "classical" and "political" bureaucrats.
      The British and Germans were more inclined to accept
      their role in the political process.

424. Robson, William A. "Bureaucracy and Democracy." THE
      CIVIL SERVICE IN BRITAIN AND FRANCE. London: Hogarth
      Press, 1956.

Indicates some problems in "bringing public administration into organic relations with the aspirations and the needs of democratic government." Integration, communication, and participation are essential in narrowing the gap between governors and the governed.

425. Roche, John P., and Stephen Sachs. "The Bureaucrat and the Enthusiast: An Exploration of the Leadership of Social Movements." WESTERN POLITICAL QUARTERLY, 8 (1955), 248-61.

Identifies two leadership types within social movements. The bureaucrat concentrates on organizational aspects of the movement.

426. Rubenstein, Richard L. "The Bureaucratization of Torture." JOURNAL OF SOCIAL PHILOSOPHY, 13 (September, 1982), 31-51.

Looks at the increased use of torture by government to deal with dissidents. Torture is not new, but there is a threat from its routinization, rationalization, and bureaucratization.

427. Saito, Shoji. "The Structure of Modern Society and Bureaucracy." JAPANESE SOCIOLOGICAL REVIEW, 9 (October, 1958), 2-16.

Sees bureaucracy as a product of capitalism and of a mass society. It leads to the alienation of people and prevents them from standing on their own.

428. Schaffer, Bernard. "Insiders and Outsiders: Insideness, Incorporation, and Bureaucratic Politics." DEVELOPMENT AND CHANGE, 11 (1980), 187-210.

Discusses the bureaucratization of politics. Modern politics cannot be understood apart from its considerable bureaucratic component. Bureaucracy, therefore, is not truly external to the political process, but instead is an active ingredient in its several manifestations. The old myths must be reexamined.

429. Schneck, Rodney, Douglas Russell, and Ken Scott. "The
      Effects of Ruralism, Bureaucratic Structure, and Econ-
      omic Role on Right-Wing Extremism." CANADIAN JOURNAL
      OF POLITICAL SCIENCE, 7 (1974), 155-65.

      Find little difference between the old and new middle
      classes (business versus bureaucracy) in terms of affin-
      ity with extremist political movements.

430. Smith, Gordon. "A Model of the Bureaucratic Culture."
      POLITICAL STUDIES, 22 (1974), 31-43.

      Generates a model for the examination of the bureau-
      cratic component of a nation's political culture. The
      model can be applied to Western Europe.

431. Strouse, James C. "Bureaucracy, Failure, and the Gueril-
      la Bureaucrat." MAKING GOVERNMENT WORK: ESSAYS IN
      HONOR OF CONLEY H. DILLON. Edited by James C. Strouse,
      Richard P. Claude, and John D. Huss. Washington, D.C.:
      University Press of America, 1981.

      Suggests that the success or failure of a government
      policy is often a matter of chance. Bureaucracy is ill
      prepared to adapt to this world of chance and so its
      performance becomes routinized. The innovative worker
      then becomes alienated.

432. Thompson, Victor. "Bureaucracy in a Democratic Society."
      PUBLIC ADMINISTRATION AND DEMOCRACY: ESSAYS IN HONOR
      OF PAUL H. APPLEBY. Edited by Roscoe Martin. Syra-
      cuse, N.Y.: Syracuse University Press, 1965.

      Argues that the logic, or "doctrinal basis," of bur-
      eaucracy poses special problems for a democracy. New
      tension has arisen as we have moved from an agrarian
      to an industrial society. We need an administrative
      doctrine that better fits with an open, pluralistic soc-
      iety.

433. Tripathi, Harihar N. "Democratic Socialism and Bureau-
      cracy." INDIAN JOURNAL OF POLITICAL SCIENCE, 26
      (1965), 32-38.

Maintains that democratic socialism is a feasible alternative to totalitarian domination in an era of advanced technological society.

434. Urwick, Lyndall. "Bureaucracy and Democracy." PUBLIC
     ADMINISTRATION, 14 (1936), 134-42.

     Suggests that many of the problems of bureaucracy can
     be eliminated through improved training of officials in
     the science of administration.

435. Vidich, Arthur. "Political Legitimacy in Bureaucratic
     Society: An Analysis of Watergate." SOCIAL PROBLEMS,
     42 (1975), 778-811.

     Argues that bureaucratic society does not depend upon
     a dominant system of legitimacy. Nixon and Watergate
     provide an example.

436. Waldo, Dwight. DEMOCRACY, BUREAUCRACY AND HYPOCRISY.
     Berkeley: University of California, Institute of Gov-
     ernmental Studies, 1977. 23 pp.

     Sums up a lifetime of wrestling with the central prob-
     lem of public administration: the reconciliation of bur-
     eaucracy with democracy. No answers are given. But
     many political scientists, economists, conservatives,
     and some liberals, are just as confused--and hypocrit-
     ical to boot.

437. Weber, Alfred. "Bureaucracy and Freedom." MODERN RE-
     VIEW, 2 (1948), 176-86.

     Advocates a new form of socialism to deal with the in-
     creasing pressure on individuals from bureaucratic organ-
     izations.

438. Wheare, Kenneth. "Bureaucracy in a Democracy." PUBLIC
     ADMINISTRATION, 29 (1951), 144-50.

     A review essay on Hyneman's *Bureaucracy in a Democ-
     racy*, Item 408.

439. Wiltse, Charles M. "The Representative Function of Bur-
       eaucracy." AMERICAN POLITICAL SCIENCE REVIEW, 35
       (1941), 510-16.

       Sees modern bureaucracy as a unifying force between,
       on the one hand, the executive and the legislature, and
       on the other hand, the citizen, either as a member of a
       group or as an individual. It can serve best of all as
       an arena for the representation of functional interests,
       a feature which should be strengthened.

440. Wurzburg, Frederic. "Bureaucratic Decay." JOURNAL OF
       COMPARATIVE ADMINISTRATION, 1 (1970), 387-97.

       Reviews the evidence pointing to a decline in bureau-
       cratic authority in the modern world.

                      D.   Bureaucracy and the Public

441. Anderson, Jack. "How to Outsmart the Bureaucrats."
       PARADE, (July 27, 1980), 6-8.

       Advises the common citizen how to deal with government
       officials.

442. Boekestijn, C. "Stress in Bureaucratic Encounters."
       STRESS AND ANXIETY, Vol. VII.   Edited by Irwin Sar-
       ason and Charles Spielberger.   Washington, D.C:
       Hampshire Publishing, 1980.

       Describes the tensions resulting from contacts between
       clients and officials in a Dutch public agency.

443. Brintnall, Michael. "Caseloads, Performance, and Street-
       Level Bureaucracy." URBAN AFFAIRS QUARTERLY, 16 (1981),
       281-98.

       Inquires whether administrative discretion at lower
       levels is induced by heavy caseloads. Bureaucrats tend
       to handle a heavy caseload by using informal cues about
       priority work.

444. "Bureaux against Bureaucracy." ECONOMIST, 164 (1952),
      486-87.

      Discusses volunteer "citizen advice bureaus" in Brit-
      ain as a reaction to the challenges of the welfare state
      bureaucracy.

445. Bush, Malcolm, and Andrew Gordon. "Client Choice and
      Bureaucratic Accountability: Possibilities for Re-
      sponsiveness in a Social Welfare Bureaucracy." JOUR-
      NAL OF SOCIAL ISSUES, 34, No. 4 (1978), 22-43.

      Ask whether it is possible for clients to select their
      own providers of welfare services. The level of user
      satisfaction was measured when clients were given or re-
      fused some choice in selecting welfare facilities.

446. Catrice-Lorey, Antoinette. "Social Security and Its Re-
      lations with Beneficiaries: The Problem of Bureaucracy
      in Social Administration." BULLETIN OF THE INTERNA-
      TIONAL SOCIAL SECURITY ASSOCIATION, 19 (1966), 286-
      97.

      Describes the sense of alienation between the recip-
      ients of social security and the administration in
      France.

447. Cloward, Richard, and Frances Fox Piven. "The Profes-
      sional Bureaucracies: Benefit Systems as Influence
      Systems." THE ROLE OF GOVERNMENT IN PROMOTING SOC-
      IAL CHANGE. Edited by Murray Silberman. New York:
      Columbia School of Social Work, 1965.

      Argue that citizen participation is largely a ritual
      which hides the continuous expansion of bureaucratic
      power over the lives of the poor. In general, the
      lower class is being deprived of effective political
      power by its dependency on the welfare system.

448. Cohen, Harry. "Buraucratic Flexibility: Some Comments
      on Robert Merton's 'Bureaucratic Structure and Person-
      ality.'" BRITISH JOURNAL OF SOCIOLOGY, 21 (1970),
      390-99.

Examines the conditions under which bureaucrats will be flexible or rigid in their dealings with clients.

449. Collins, William P. "Public Participation in Bureaucratic Decision Making: A Reappraisal." PUBLIC ADMINISTRATION, 58 (1980), 465-77.

Argues that the idea of citizen participation has been misunderstood as a way of legitimizing the activity of the liberal welfare state. Participation, nonetheless, is very important, especially as an indication of the mobilization of diverse interests in society.

450. Comer, John C. "'Street-Level' Bureaucracy and Political Support: Some Findings on Mexican-Americans." URBAN AFFAIRS QUARTERLY, 14 (1978), 207-28.

Concludes that a sample of Mexican-Americans in Omaha did not show dissatisfaction with public services, although they had fewer contacts with agencies. It is not clear from this study that political support is associated with satisfaction with services.

451. Danet, Brenda. "The Language of Persuasion in Bureaucracy: 'Modern' and 'Traditional' Appeals to the Israeli Customs Authorities." AMERICAN SOCIOLOGICAL REVIEW, 36 (1971), 847-59.

Conducts content-analysis of letters to an Israeli office. Appeals on the basis of impersonal norms and altruism distinguished between modern and traditional approaches to authority. Occupation was a better predictor than ethnicity in the choice of strategies for clients.

452. Danet, Brenda, and Harriet Hartman. "On 'Proteksia:' Orientations toward the Use of Personal Influence in Israeli Bureaucracy." JOURNAL OF COMPARATIVE ADMINISTRATION, 3 (1972), 405-34.

Examine the extent of the institutionalization of non-bureaucratic norms in the Israeli public service.

453. Danet, Brenda, and Michael Gurevitch. "Presentation
      of Self in Appeals to Bureaucracy: An Empirical
      Study of Role Specificity." AMERICAN JOURNAL OF SOC-
      IOLOGY, 77 (1972), 1165-90.

      Explore the bureaucratic socialization of clients of
      formal organizations. The data are from contacts with
      Israeli customs officers.

454. Danet, Brenda, and Harriet Hartman. "Coping with Bureau-
      cracy: The Israeli Case." SOCIAL FORCES, 51 (1972),
      7-22.

      Examine the nature of contacts with bureaucrats in
      terms of the social background of clients.

455. Denhardt, Robert B. "Bureaucratic Socialization and Or-
      ganization Accommodation." ADMINISTRATIVE SCIENCE
      QUARTERLY, 13 (1968), 441-50.

      Reports on a study of clients in an Appalachian anti-
      poverty program. The bureaucratic socialization of the
      clients is essential for organizational maintenance.
      Until that occurs, the organization may have to condone
      non-bureaucratic behavior, leading it to integrate the
      values of the local culture.

456. Denhardt, Robert B. "Learning about Bureaucracy." PER-
      SONNEL ADMINISTRATION, 35 (May-June, 1972), 15-19.

      Studies class differences in the acceptance of key
      norms of bureaucratic behavior. Middle-class high school
      students were found to be more knowledgeable about organ-
      izations, but were more independent in their attitudes.
      Lower-class students knew less, but were more likely to
      defer to bureaucratic authority.

457. Denhardt, Robert B. "Subcultural Differences in Bureau-
      cratic Socialization." JOURNAL OF SOCIOLOGY, 3 (1973),
      61-85.

      Finds differences between middle and lower-class stu-
      dents in terms of knowledge about and deference to bur-
      eaucracy.

458. Denhardt, Robert B. "Developing Attitudes toward Bur-
        eaucracy." STATE AND LOCAL GOVERNMENT REVIEW, 12
        (January, 1980), 24-29.

        On bureaucratic socialization.

459. Dornstein, Miriam. "Compliance with Legal and Bureau-
        cratic Rules: The Case of Self-Employed Taxpayers in
        Israel." HUMAN RELATIONS, 29 (1976), 1019-34.

        Tries to determine the reason taxpayers comply with
        formal rules--personal orientation or regard for the
        control system.

460. Goodsell, Charles T. "Bureaucratic Manipulation of Phys-
        ical Symbols: An Empirical Study." AMERICAN JOURNAL
        OF POLITICAL SCIENCE, 21 (1977), 77-91.

        Identifies the symbols or signals used by bureaucratic
        offices in the presentation of the self to the clients.
        The symbols used by officials are designed to evoke the
        emotions of clients in order to enhance legitimacy or to
        expedite business. Variations in the manipulation of
        symbols were found in different offices.

461. Goodsell, Charles T., Raymond Austin, and Karen Hedblom.
        "Bureaucracy Expresses Itself: How State Documents
        Address the Public." SOCIAL SCIENCE QUARTERLY, 62
        (1981), 576-91.

        Sample documents prepared by several state governments
        and compare them in terms of "effectiveness" and "tone
        of voice." Variations were found among states and types
        of documents. Bureaucratic prose need not be obscure or
        offensive and improvements are possible.

462. Goodsell, Charles T. "The Contented Older Client of
        Bureaucracy." INTERNATIONAL JOURNAL OF AGING AND HU-
        MAN DEVELOPMENT, 14 (1981-82), 1-9.

        Interviewed 240 welfare clients. Older clients tend
        to be more satisfied with services and treatment. Per-
        haps this is because of a "pro-elderly" bias among ad-
        ministrators.

463. Gordon, Laura K. "Bureaucratic Competence and Success
      in Dealing with Public Bureaucracies." SOCIAL PROB-
      LEMS, 23 (1975), 197-208.

      Finds that welfare workers had a great deal of discre-
      tion in the determination of eligibility for benefits.
      There appears to be some connection between the bureau-
      cratic competence of the recipients and the level of
      benefits they received.

464. Handelman, Don. "Bureaucratic Transactions: The Devel-
      opment of Official-Client Relationships in Israel."
      TRANSACTION AND MEANING: DIRECTIONS IN THE ANTHROPOL-
      OGY OF EXCHANGE AND SYMBOLIC BEHAVIOR. Edited by Bruce
      Kapferer. Philadelphia: Institute for the Study of
      Human Issues, 1976.

      Questions the notion that contacts with the bureau-
      cracy are purely impersonal. Clients of welfare agen-
      cies were studied to see the patterns by which personal
      contact is added to bureaucratic business.

465. Handelman, Don, and Elliot Leyton. BUREAUCRACY AND
      WORLD VIEW: STUDIES IN THE LOGIC OF OFFICIAL INTERP-
      RETATION. St. John's: Memorial University of New-
      foundland, 1978. 143 pp.

      Use an anthropological approach to the study of "or-
      ganizational connections" of officials and clients. Two
      in-depth case studies show the working out of the bureau-
      cratic worldview and its effect on the ordinary lives of
      the clients.

466. Hirsch, Phil. "Privacy: The Problem Doesn't Alarm Bur-
      eaucrats." DATAMATION, 19 (August, 1973), 86-89.

      On a House hearing into the information held by fed-
      eral agencies.

467. Hudson, James R. "Creating Accountable Public Bureau-
      cracies." JOURNAL OF SOCIOLOGY AND SOCIAL WELFARE,
      1 (1973), 103-05.

468. Janowitz, Morris, and William Delany. "The Bureaucrat and the Public: A Study of Informational Perspectives." ADMINISTRATIVE SCIENCE QUARTERLY, 2 (1957), 141-62.

Measure the different degrees of functional and substantive knowledge (in Mannheim's terms) of federal, state, and local officials in the Detroit area. The subject of knowledge was the attitudes of clients and other members of the public. There was a relation between rank and substantive knowledge. Functional knowledge was associated with contact with clients.

469. Jones, Bryan D., Saadia Greenberg, Clifford Kaufman, and Joseph Drew. "Bureaucratic Response to Citizen-Initiated Contacts: Environmental Enforcement in Detroit." AMERICAN POLITICAL SCIENCE REVIEW, 71 (1977), 148-65.

Attempt to link the individual citizen's contact with a government agency to the response of the agency to the contact. Citizen contacts are stimulated by a need for a service and an awareness that government provides it. The agency generally responds to contacts, but the quality of the response varied with the social characteristics of the neighborhood.

470. Kahn, Robert L., Barbara Gutek, Eugenia Barton, and Daniel Katz. "Americans Love Their Bureaucrats." PSYCHOLOGY TODAY, 9 (June, 1975), 110-13.

A summary of Katz, *et al.*, Item 472.

471. Kahn, Robert L., Daniel Katz, and Barbara Gutek. "Bureaucratic Encounters--An Evaluation of Government Services." JOURNAL OF APPLIED BEHAVIORAL SCIENCE, 12 (1976), 178-98.

Recommend that client satisfaction with administrative contacts should be included in measurements of the quality of life.

472. Katz, Daniel, Barbara Gutek, Robert L. Kahn, and Eugenia Barton. BUREAUCRATIC ENCOUNTERS: A PILOT STUDY IN THE EVALUATION OF GOVERNMENT SERVICES. Ann Arbor:

University of Michigan, Institute for Social Research,
Survey Research Center,1975. 264 pp.

Report on a 1973 national survey designed to investigate three general areas: 1) differences in the utilization of major government services; 2) public evaluation of their contacts with government offices; and
3) the relation of experiences with general attitudes
toward government. Government services tended to be
underutilized by those most in need. Two-thirds of
the respondents expressed satisfaction with their governmental contacts. People's experiences with government are not always congruent with their ideological
beliefs. In general, Americans seem to be satisfied
in their day-to-day dealings with bureaucracy.

473. Katz, Elihu, and Brenda Danet. "Communication between
      Bureaucracy and the Public: A Review of the Litera-
      ture." HANDBOOK OF COMMUNICATION. Edited by Ithiel
      de Sola Pool and Wilbur Schramm. Chicago: Rand Mc-
      Nally, 1973.

      Examine the literature on organizational communication
      to isolate features of official-client relations on the
      micro level. The reciprocal nature of the bureaucratic
      contact is stressed.

474. Katz, Elihu, and Brenda Danet, eds. BUREAUCRACY AND THE
      PUBLIC: A READER IN OFFICIAL-CLIENT RELATIONS. New
      York: Basic Books, 1973. 534 pp.

      A collection of previously published work on the issue
      of contacts between clients and administrators. The
      authors' introduction, "Bureaucracy as a Problem for Soc-
      iology and Society," urges more attention be paid to the
      relationship between bureaucracy and the rest of society.

475. Katz, Joan. "The Games Bureaucrats Play: Hide and Seek
      under the Freedom of Information Act." TEXAS LAW Re-
      VIEW, 48 (1970), 1261-85.

      Argues that the numerous exemptions have made the fed-
      eral Freedom of Information Act a virtual nullity. The
      judges must enforce the law more zealously.

476. Krause, Elliot A. "Functions of a Bureaucratic Ideology: 'Citizen Participation.'" SOCIAL PROBLEMS, 16 (1968), 129-42.

Discusses the idea of "citizen participation" as an ideology directed at influencing a target group, in this case, the clients of the poverty program. The use of the ideology had both intended and unintended consequences.

477. Kweit, Robert W., and Mary G. Kweit. "Bureaucratic Decision-Making: Impediments to Citizen Participation." POLITY, 12 (1980), 647-66.

Examine the conditions under which citizen participation works. Citizens need the resources to enable them to participate. This means that the affluent and those possessing professional qualifications will be more likely to participate. For most citizens, participation is regarded as too costly.

478. Kweit, Mary G., and Robert W. Kweit. IMPLEMENTING CITIZEN PARTICIPATION IN A BUREAUCRATIC SOCIETY: A CONTINGENCY APPROACH. New York: Prager, 1981. 185 pp.

Describe the development of citizen participation, with the emphasis on problems that have been encountered in implementing participation. Three models of participation are presented. Data indicate that the success of participation is not automatic, but is contingent upon a number of other factors.

479. Levin, Jack, and Gerald Taube. "Bureaucracy and the Socially Handicapped: A Study of Lower-Status Tenents in Public Housing." SOCIOLOGY AND SOCIAL RESEARCH, 54 (1970), 209-19.

Investigate the relationship of 452 female tenents in public housing. The result was a pattern of treatment by bureaucrats of the clients as socially handicapped.

480. Lipsky, Michael. "Street-Level Buraucracy and the Analysis of Urban Reform." URBAN AFFAIRS QUARTERLY, 6 (1971), 391-409.

Argues that the nature of the job of the street-level
bureaucrat, especially when dealing with non-voluntary
clients, may account for much of the criticism of urban
administration, as well as the defensiveness of public
employees about such charges. The bureaucrats have developed mechanisms for coping with job-related stress.
These mechanisms, in turn, lead to a deterioration of
relationships with clients.

481. Lipsky, Michael. "Toward a Theory of Street-Level Bur-
     eaucracy." THE STATE, SCHOOL, AND POLITICS. Edited
     by Michael Kirst. Lexington, Mass.: Lexington Books,
     1972.

     Suggests that research is needed viewing the teacher
     as a street-level bureaucrat.

482. Lipsky, Michael. "Toward a Theory of Street-Level Bur-
     eaucracy." THEORETICAL PERSPECTIVES ON URBAN PROB-
     LEMS. Edited by Willis Hawley and Michael Lipsky.
     Englewood Cliffs, N.J.: Prentice-Hall, 1976.

     Claims that the concept of street-level bureaucracy
     is important for the study of urban government since
     these officials may be a cause of the inability of mun-
     icipalities to respond to the demands for service by the
     citizens.

483. Lipsky, Michael. "The Assault on Human Services:
     Street-Level Bureaucrats, Accountability, and the
     Fiscal Crisis." ACCOUNTABILITY IN URBAN SERVICES:
     PUBLIC AGENCIES UNDER FIRE. Edited by Scott Greer,
     Ronald Hedlund, and James Gibson. Beverly Hills,
     Cal.: Sage, 1978.

     Maintains that demands for accountability have led
     managers to impose greater controls over the inevitable
     discretion of low-level officials. The result has been
     further erosion in the service quality of urban admin-
     istration.

484. Lipsky, Michael. STREET-LEVEL BUREAUCRACY: DILEMMAS OF
     THE INDIVIDUAL IN PUBLIC SERVICE. New York: Russell
     Sage, 1980. 244 pp.

Defines the street-level bureaucrat as a worker who in-
teracts with and has wide discretion over the dispensa-
tion of benefits or the allocation of public sanctions.
Examples include employees who work directly with the
public such as teachers, police, legal aid workers, and
social workers. Because of the ambiguity of the goals
within the agencies, these officials have a wide degree
of discretion. The means they develop to deal with the
uncertainties and pressures of their job become, in effect, the public policies of the government. The street-
level bureaucrats are also important in determining the
public's impression of government.

485. Litwak, Eugene, and Henry Meyer. "A Balance Theory of
         Co-ordination between Bureaucratic Organizations and
         Community Primary Groups." ADMINISTRATIVE SCIENCE
         QUARTERLY, 11 (1966), 33-58.

         Discuss the ways in which bureaucracies and community
      primary groups can interact without negative consequences
      for the essential nature of either.

486. Litwak, Eugene, Henry Meyer, and David C. Hollister.
         "The Role of Linkage Mechanisms between Bureaucracies
         and Families: Education and Health as Empirical Cases
         in Point." POWER, PARADIGMS, AND COMMUNITY RESEARCH.
         Edited by Roland Liebert and Allen W. Imershein. Bev-
         erly Hills, Cal.: Sage, 1977.

         Develop a model of social balance to examine the re-
      lationships between formal organization and the primary
      group. The linkages are described in terms of cases con-
      cerned with education, health care, and political activ-
      ity. The maintenance of social distance by either com-
      ponent is important.

487. Lyden, Fremont. "Middle-Class Bureaucracy?" PUBLIC AD-
         MINISTRATION REVIEW, 26 (1966), 234-35.

         Summarizes the arguments of Sjoberg, *et al.* (Item 505)
      and Litwak and Meyer (Item 485). It may be that the
      bureaucracy is a middle-class institution, but those
      class values are the basic one in society. Perhaps the
      lower class will have to adjust to this fact.

488. Lystad, Mary H., and Robert C. Stone. "Bureaucratic
      Mass Media: A Study in Role Definitions." SOCIAL FOR-
      CES, 34 (1956), 356-61.

      Examine how the formal internal communications within
      a bureau may affect the self-perception of its members.
      Those workers with client contacts seemed to be less
      bureaucratic in orientation.

489. Marshall, Thomas R. "The Benevolent Bureaucrat: Polit-
      ical Authority in Children's Literature and Televis-
      ion." WESTERN POLITICAL QUARTERLY, 34 (1981), 389-98.

      Finds that in media oriented toward children, govern-
      ment officials are presented as competent and benevolent.
      They also tend to be pictured as individuals free from
      constant organizational restraints.

490. Mathiesen, Per. "Bureaucratic Categories and Ethnic As-
      criptions: An Analysis of a Norwegian Housing Program
      in a Sami Region." ETHNOS, 43 (1978), 236-45.

      Describes how bureaucracies go about the business of
      classifying people for eligibility for programs designed
      to help a specific ethnic group. In the process, stereo-
      types were transformed from a cognitive to an existential
      level. This represents one mechanism by which majority
      groups exert control over minorities.

491. Mladenka, Kenneth R. "Citizen Demand and Bureaucratic
      Response: Direct Dialing Democracy in a Major Amer-
      ican City." THE POLITICS AND ECONOMICS OF URBAN
      SERVICES. Edited by Robert L. Lineberry. Beverly
      Hills, Cal.: Sage, 1978.

      Analyzes how city officials responded to citizen tele-
      phone contacts. Few citizens complain to administra-
      tors and few of the complaints that are received have
      much impact on the bureaucracy. In general, citizen-
      initiated contacts play an insignificant role in the
      decision-making and resource allocation process in mun-
      icipal government.

492. Neuse, Steven M. "Citizen Participation: Variation in
      Bureaucratic Attitudes." MIDWEST REVIEW OF PUBLIC
      ADMINISTRATION, 14 (1980), 252-68.

      Finds that the attitudes of bureaucrats toward citizen
      participation are related to a number of individual var-
      iables. Professional, organizational, and personal fac-
      tors will determine the perception of the value of par-
      ticipation.

493. Newton, Virgil. THE PRESS AND BUREAUCRACY. Tucson:
      University of Arizona Press, 1961. 8 pp.

      An address on government-press relations.

494. Prottas, Jeffrey M. "The Power of the Street-Level Bur-
      eaucrats in Public Service Bureaucracies." URBAN AF-
      FAIRS QUARTERLY, 13 (1978), 285-312.

      Examines the critical position of the street-level
      bureaucrat for both the organization and the clients.
      As a "boundary actor," the low-level official mediates
      between the formal bureaucracy and its environment. The
      official can manipulate information in order to limit
      formal control.

495. Prottas, Jeffrey M. PEOPLE-PROCESSING: THE STREET-LEVEL
      BUREAUCRAT IN PUBLIC SERVICE BUREAUCRACIES. Lexington,
      Mass.: Lexington Books, 1979. 179 pp.

      Defines the work of the street-level bureaucrat as a
      matter of transforming citizens into clients. The book
      consists of four case studies of the process of categor-
      ization of people through the exercise of lower level
      discretion. Many of the officials use methods which are
      not sanctioned by the organization as they manufacture
      clients.

496. Rice, Mitchell. "Public Policy, Bureaucracy, and Equal-
      ity in the Urban Service Delivery Process." URBAN AF-
      FAIRS QUARTERLY, 16 (1981), 385-91.

      Review essay on Lipsky, Item 484, and Prottas, Item
      495.

497. Robbins, Jane. "The Reference Librarian: A Street-Level
      Bureaucrat? LIBRARY JOURNAL, 97 (1972), 1389-92.

      Applies Lipsky's model (Item 480) to reference librar-
      ians.

498. Rosener, Judy B. "Making Bureaucracy Responsive: A
      Study of the Impact of Citizen Participation and
      Staff Recommendations on Regulatory Decision Making."
      PUBLIC ADMINISTRATION REVIEW, 42 (1982), 339-45.

      Studies the public hearings of the California Coastal
      Commission. The results bring into question the con-
      tention that citizen participation is ineffective or that
      regulatory bodies always take the suggestions of their
      professional staffs.

499. Rothchild, John. "Finding the Facts Bureaucrats Hide."
      WASHINGTON MONTHLY, 3 (January, 1972), 15-27.

      Describes the ways in which administrators have avoided
      full compliance with the Freedom of Information Act. The
      law may have increased bureaucratic paranoia about public
      scrutiny.

500. Rourke, Francis E. "Secrecy in American Bureaucracy."
      POLITICAL SCIENCE QUARTERLY, 72 (1957), 540-64.

      Argues that American bureaucracy has always been rel-
      atively open to the public. However, there are recent
      indications of greater secrecy in administration.

501. Rourke, Francis E. "Bureaucratic Secrecy and Its Con-
      stituents." BUREAUCRAT, 1 (1972), 116-21.

      Finds that bureaucratic secrecy is invaluable to a
      number of political participants beyond the bureaucrats
      themselves. In recent years, the primary beneficiaries
      have been political leaders and representative of private
      interests. Any move, therefore, to make government more
      open will not necessarily enjoy total support from those
      outside the bureaucracy.

502. Scherer, Ursula, and Klaus R. Scherer. "Psychological
      Factors in Bureaucratic Encounters: Determinants and
      Effects of Interactions between Officials and Clients."
      THE ANALYSIS OF SOCIAL SKILL. Edited by W.T. Singleton
      and R.B. Stammers. New York: Plenum, 1980.

      Analyze the "non-verbal and paralinguistic behavior
      of officials" in interactions with clients. The per-
      sonality traits and attitudes of officials and the soc-
      ial class and behavior of clients exert considerable in-
      fluence on the reactions of officials.

503. Sigal, Leon V. "Bureaucratic Objectives and Tactical
      Uses of the Press." PUBLIC ADMINISTRATION REVIEW,
      33 (1973), 336-45.

      Describes the ways in which administrators manipulate
      the press. Officials must choose among several media
      and channels, including covert ones, to get across the
      information favorable to their agency. News reports
      about government activity should not be taken out of
      their political contexts.

504. Singer, Benjamin D. "The Fight against Hyperbureaucra-
      cy." BUSINESS QUARTERLY, 42 (Winter, 1977), 36-39.

      Defines hyperbureaucracy as the replacement of person-
      al contacts with outsiders with complex communications
      technology. This leads to alienated relationships and
      a loss of learning capacity by the organization.

505. Sjoberg, Gideon, Richard A. Brymer, and Buford Farris.
      "Bureaucracy and the Lower Class." SOCIOLOGY AND
      SOCIAL RESEARCH, 50 (1966), 325-37.

      Argue that bureaucracy is the means by which the middle
      and lower classes encounter one another. The bureau-
      cratic orientation of the middle-class individual will
      structure even informal contacts with the lower class.
      Bureaucracy is a way in which the middle class suppresses
      the lower class. Formal organizations are important in
      the study of social stratification, as well as the un-
      derstanding of the maintenance of social order.

506. Smith, Merriman. "Bureaucrat's Escape Hatch: If Caught,
      Blame the Press." NATION'S BUSINESS, 51 (January,
      1963), 23.

      The press is a scapegoat for bureaucratic failures.

507. Stewart, Donald. "The Place of Volunteer Participation
      in a Bureaucratic Organization." SOCIAL FORCES, 29
      (1952), 311-17.

      Studies the role of local draft boards in the Selective
      Service System. The volunteer members have little im-
      pact on the decisions made by the system.

508. Taebel, Delbert. "Strategies to Make Bureaucracies Re-
      sponsive." SOCIAL WORK, 17 (November, 1972), 38-43.

      Argues that efforts by clients to put pressure on the
      street-level bureaucrats are often counterproductive.
      Other options for stimulating responsiveness are sug-
      gested.

509. Taebel, Delbert. "Bureaucratization and Responsiveness:
      A Research Note." MIDWEST REVIEW OF PUBLIC ADMINISTRA-
      TION, 7 (1973), 199-205.

      Maintains that improvements in administrative respon-
      siveness must take into account the needs of particular
      types of clients. One method will not suit all. In
      particular, White's (Item 562) "dialectical bureaucracy"
      may not be appropriate for middle-class, professional
      clients.

510. Theoharis, Athan. "Bureaucrats above the Law: Double-
      Entry Intelligence Files." NATION, 225 (1977), 393-
      97.

      Worries about public access to government documents,
      especially when two sets of records are kept.

511. Vosburgh, William W., and Drew Hyman. "Advocacy and Bur-
      eaucracy: The Life and Times of a Decentralized

Advocacy Program." ADMINISTRATIVE SCIENCE QUARTERLY, 18 (1973), 433-48.

Study a citizen's advocacy program in the ghetto areas of Pennsylvania. Its failure illustrates the difficulty of organizational innovation within a bureaucratic context. Its decentralized and non-bureaucratic nature isolated it from the rest of state government and prevented the documentation of its activities.

512. Weatherley, Richard, and Michael Lipsky. "Street-Level Bureaucrats and Institutional Innovation: Implementing Special Education Reform." HARVARD EDUCATIONAL REVIEW, 47 (1977), 171-97.

Examine how implementation of new programs is affected by the behavior of the lower level bureaucrats responsible for carrying it out. The employees incorporated into their routines a new piece of legislation while continuing to carry out their other responsibilities.

513. Weatherley, Richard, and Michael Lipsky. STREET-LEVEL BUREAUCRATS AND INSTITUTIONAL INNOVATION: IMPLEMENTING SPECIAL EDUCATION REFORM IN MASSACHUSETTS. Cambridge, Mass.: Joint Center for Urban Studies, 1977. 90 pp.

See Item 512.

514. Wunsch, James, Larry Teply, Joel Zimmerman, and Geoffrey Peters. "Civil Commitment as a 'Street-Level' Bureaucracy: Caseload, Professionalization, and Administration." JOURNAL OF HEALTH POLITICS, POLICY, AND LAW, 6 (1981), 285-302.

Apply the street-level bureaucracy theories to an involuntary commitment system. Boards in urban and rural settings differed in the ways in which they modified the statutory requirements.

515. Yarwood, Dean, and Dan Nimmo. "Bureaucratic Roles in Policy Development." PUBLIC ADMINISTRATION AND PUBLIC POLICY. Edited by George Frederickson and Charles Wise. Lexington, Mass.: Lexington Books, 1977.

Suggest the application of role theory to the problems
of citizen participation in administration. That particular middle range theory has many implications for
expanded participation in administrative and political
structures.

E.   Alternatives to Bureaucracy

516.   Abrahamsson, Bengt. BUREAUCRACY OR PARTICIPATION: THE
          LOGIC OF ORGANIZATION. Beverly Hills, Cal.: Sage,
          1977.   236 pp.

          Criticizes the traditional organization theory as un-
          derstating the instrumental nature of organizations.
          They are set up by a particular individual, group, or
          class to achieve certain goals. The humane side of the
          organization has been stressed at the expense of the need
          to get something done. Discussed here is the development
          of organization theory, from Marx, Michels, and Weber,
          to the modern era. Bureaucracy arises when members re-
          place organization goals with individual motives. In
          terms of a Process Model of organization, the argument
          turns to worker participation, self-management, and in-
          dustrial democracy. These devices can be useful ap-
          proaches in the struggle against bureaucracy.

517.   Baptista, Jose. "Bureaucracy, Political System, and
          Social Dynamic." TELOS, 22 (1974-75), 66-84.

          Considers possible alternatives to the bureaucratized
          political system.

518.   Barton, Allen H. "A Diagnosis of Bureaucratic Maladies."
          AMERICAN BEHAVIORAL SCIENTIST, 22 (1979), 483-92.

          Looks for the causes of bureaucratic malfunctioning in
          the areas of personal traits of officials, structural ar-
          rangements, and political control problems. These areas
          are interrelated. Alternative forms of social organiza-
          tion, such as competitive business firms and professional
          service organization, are considered. "The comparison
          of these types of organization suggest that one remedy
          for bureaucracy problem" is turning over areas to profit-
          making firms and professional service providers.

519.   Bennis, Warren G. "Beyond Bureaucracy." TRANS-ACTION,
          2 (July-August, 1965), 31-35.

          Predicts that, "in the next 25 to 50 years we should
       witness and participate in the end of bureaucracy and
       the rise of new social systems better suited to twent-
       ieth century demands of industrialization." The old
       bureaucracy is out of touch with a changing environment
       and with the values of its members. The replacement will
       be an organic-adaptive structure. These will be composed
       of groups of problem-solving experts who come together
       just long enough to solve a particular problem.

520.   Bennis, Warren G. "The Coming Death of Bureaucracy."
          THINK, 32 (November-December, 1966), 32-35.

          Insists that the rigid, hierarchical nature of bureau-
       cracy will cause it to self-destruct and to be replaced
       by a more open, adaptive form of organization.

521.   Bennis, Warren G. "Organizational Developments and the
          Fate of Bureaucracy." INDUSTRIAL MANAGEMENT REVIEW,
          7 (Spring, 1966), 41-55.

          Claims that bureaucracy will not survive much longer
       as the dominant form of human organization. The organ-
       ization of the future will be organic rather than mech-
       anical.

522.   Bennis, Warren G. "The Coming Death of Bureaucracy."
          MANAGEMENT REVIEW, 56 (March, 1967), 19-24.

          A condensation of Item 520.

523.   Bennis, Warren G. "Beyond Bureaucracy." THE TEMPORARY
          SOCIETY. Warren Bennis and Philip E. Slater. New
          York: Harper and Row, 1968.

          Still another version of the obsolescence of bureau-
       cracy.

524. Bennis, Warren G. "Post-Bureaucratic Leadership."
        TRANS-ACTION, 6 (July-August, 1969), 44-52.

        Sees the successor to bureaucracy as "adaptive, rapid-
        ly changing, temporary systems, organized around prob-
        lems-to-be-solved by groups of relative strangers with
        diverse professional skills." In fact, such organiza-
        tions already exist. The leader of the future must be
        "agricultural," that is, devoted to a climate of growth
        and development for subordinates.

525. Bennis, Warren G., ed. AMERICAN BUREAUCRACY. Chicago:
        Aldine, 1970. 187 pp.

        A collection of articles on trends in management or-
        iginally published in *Trans-Action*.

526. Bennis, Warren G. BEYOND BUREAUCRACY: ESSAYS ON THE
        DEVELOPMENT AND EVOLUTION OF HUMAN ORGANIZATIONS.
        New York: McGraw-Hill, 1973. 223 pp.

        Discusses a number of approaches to making large or-
        ganizations more receptive to inevitable change. Be-
        havioral science techniques can be applied to encourage
        organization growth and development.

527. Bennis, Warren G. "Response to Shariff: Beyond Bureau-
        cracy Baiting." SOCIAL SCIENCE QUARTERLY, 60 (1979)
        20-24.

        Whines that the point made by Shariff in Item 555
        may be true, namely, that not many of the great predic-
        tions made in Items 519, 520, 521, 522, 523, 524, 525,
        and 526 appear to be coming true. However, it was very
        unsportsmanlike for Shariff to reveal this.

528. Bjur, Wesley E., and Gerald E. Caiden. "On Reforming
        Institutional Bureaucracies." INTERNATIONAL REVIEW
        OF ADMINISTRATIVE SCIENCES, 44 (1978), 359-65.

        Distinguish between institutional and instrumental
        bureaucracies. The organizations that have become ends
        in themselves--institutionalized--are harder to change.

529. Brown, Robert. "Bureaucracy: The Utility of a Concept."
      BUREAUCRACY: THE CAREER OF A CONCEPT. Edited by Eugene
      Kamenka and Martin Krygier. London: Edward Arnold,
      1979.

      Speculates on the meaning of "bureaucracy" if predic-
      tions such as those of Bennis (Item 519) come true. With
      the dissolution of the rigid command structure, bureau-
      cracy as we have known it would be an unimportant social
      science concept.

530. "Bureaucracy: There's Hope for Better Management." AD-
      MINISTRATIVE MANAGEMENT, 39 (January, 1978), 34-35.

      On reform efforts in federal and state governments.

531. Carlisle, Howard. "Bureaucracy under Attack." ADVANCED
      MANAGEMENT, 36 (July, 1971), 37-45.

      Argues that bureaucracy is no longer appropriate for
      the management of complex technology.

532. Dodds, Harold W. "Bureaucracy and Representative Govern-
      ment." ANNALS OF THE AMERICAN ACADEMY OF POLITICAL AND
      SOCIAL SCIENCE, 189 (1937), 165-72.

      Asks whether we can enjoy expert administration and
      popular government at the same time. The answer is to
      staff the public service with college educated people
      who have been schooled in a dedication to democratic
      ideals. America's universities will have to become ac-
      quainted with government.

533. Doughton, Morgan J. "People Power: Alternative to Run-
      away Bureaucracy." FUTURIST, 14 (April, 1980), 13-22.

      Maintains that setting up formal agencies to solve a
      variety of social problems has been a failure. The local
      community must be energized to help itself. Examples of
      the failure of social services and the successes of self-
      help are presented.

534. Downes, Peter. "Risk Managers Can Stem the Bureaucrats as Political Scientists." BUSINESS INSURANCE, (September 4, 1978), 44.

On how to cure bureaucracy.

535. Duke, Daniel. "Challenge to Bureaucracy: The Contemporary Alternative School." JOURNAL OF EDUCATION THOUGHT, 10 (April, 1976), 34-38.

Views alternative schools as a rejection of traditional forms of public education and a challenge to the very idea of bureaucratic management.

536. Duncan, W. Jack. "Order and Innovation: A New Look at Bureaucracy." PERSONNEL JOURNAL, 51 (1972), 518-23.

Sketches a "synergistic model" for organizations to combine the strengths of bureaucratic and laissez-faire systems. Formal authority can be retained while personal initiative will be enhanced. The rigidity of the hierarchy can be reduced. Such a system will work best where employees are technically and professionally trained.

537. Dvorin, Eugene P., and Robert H. Simmons. FROM AMORAL TO HUMANE BUREAUCRACY. San Francisco: Canfield, 1972. 88 pp.

Express concern about the emphasis on machine-like efficiency in modern administration. Humane values must take precedence over productivity. Administration, as taught and practiced, is concerned with organizational and not human ends. The bureaucrats must be encouraged to pursue a "radical humanism" that stresses human dignity.

538. Ehrle, Raymond. "Management Decentralization: Antidote to Bureaucratic Ills." PERSONNEL JOURNAL, 49 (1970). 296-97.

Believes that while the efficiency of bureaucracy is valuable, it is still possible to decentralize managerial discretion for a better response to the needs of the workers and clients.

539. Hansell, Norris. "Cracking the Bureaucratic Ice." IN-
      NOVATION, 26 (November, 1971), 2-9.

      Suggests some techniques for stopping the "freeze" on
      creativity in big organizations.

540. Hawley, Willis. "The Possibilities of Nonbureaucratic
      Organizations." IMPROVING URBAN MANAGEMENT. Edited
      by Willis Hawley and David Rogers. Beverly Hills,
      Cal.: Sage, 1974.

      Discusses the theoretical limitations to nonbureaucrat-
      ic forms for the delivery of public services. Despite
      the difficulties, it may be possible to devise such means
      for handling some urban services.

541. Jaques, Elliott. "Essential Developments in Bureaucracy
      in the 1980s." JOURNAL OF APPLIED BEHAVIORAL SCIENCE,
      16 (1980), 439-47.

      Sees the 1980s as "a critical decade in which the dem-
      ocratic industrial world will either learn to come to
      grips with the reality of bureaucracy or sink into a con-
      tinuous state of inordinate suffering."

542. Lyden, Fremont. "Beyond Bureaucracy." PUBLIC ADMINIS-
      TRATION REVIEW, 25 (1965), 251-53.

      Comments on Bennis, Item 519.

543. Lyden, Fremont. "Program Change and Bureaucracy." PUB-
      LIC ADMINISTRATION REVIEW, 28 (1968), 278-79.

      On organization designs that promote flexibility.

544. Lyden, Fremont. "Project Management: Beyond Bureaucra-
      cy?" PUBLIC ADMINISTRATION REVIEW, 30 (1970), 435-36.

      Looks at some of the weaknesses in the team approach
      to management.

545. Markert, J. "Bureaucratization of the Alternative
      Youth Programs of the Sixties: A Decade of Change."
      GROUP AND ORGANIZATION STUDIES, 4 (1979), 485-95.

      Looks at the fate of such counter-culture phenomena as
      free health clinics, runaway houses, and hotlines.
      Many of these organizations had to adapt to a changed
      environment once the youth culture faded away.

546. Martin, Carl. "Beyond Bureaucracy." CHILD WELFARE,
      50 (1971), 384-88.

      Foresees a new form of organization that is temporary
      and project oriented. Application of this form to the
      field of health and social services is discussed.

547. Matejko, Alexander. "From the Crisis of Bureaucracy
      to the Challenge of Participation." MANAGEMENT AND
      COMPLEX ORGANIZATIONS IN COMPARATIVE PERSPECTIVE.
      Edited by Raj Mohan. Westport, Conn.: Greenwood,
      1979.

      Argues that bureaucracy is poorly designed to meet
      modern demands since it encourages the institutional-
      ization of mediocrity. Worker participation is the
      preferred organization style.

548. Matejko, Alexander. "The Obsolescence of Bureaucracy."
      RELATIONS INDUSTRIELLES, 35 (1980), 467-93.

      Claims that the bureaucratic style has become self-
      defeating. Realistic alternatives, such as worker con-
      trol, already exist.

549. Meyer, Marshall W. "Debureaucratization?" SOCIAL SCI-
      ENCE QUARTERLY, 60 (1979), 25-34.

      Agrees with Shariff (Item 555) that the end of bureau-
      cracy is not yet in sight. The process of bureaucrat-
      ization is as strong as ever. Despite the widespread
      discontent with bureaucracy, it appears that it will
      be around for some time.

550. Miewald, Robert D. "The Greatly Exaggerated Death of
      Bureaucracy." CALIFORNIA MANAGEMENT REVIEW, 13 (1970),
      65-69.

      Disputes the thesis of Bennis (Item 519) about the de-
      cline of bureaucracy. Bureaucracy is more than a set of
      structural arrangements. It is a form of discipline
      likely to endure in any "post-bureaucratic" environment.

551. Newman, Katherine. "Incipient Bureaucracy: The Develop-
      ment of Hierarchies in Egalitarian Organizations."
      HIERARCHY AND SOCIETY: ANTHROPOLOGICAL PERSPECTIVES
      ON BUREAUCRACY. Philadelphia: Institute for the Study
      of Human Issues, 1980.

      Explores the counter-cultural experiments in nonbureau-
      cratic organization. The workers' collectives were com-
      mitted to equality, but hierarchy tended to emerge. The
      nature of the work was not as important in this as the
      distribution of resources from outside the organization.
      The distinction between paid and unpaid staff became the
      basis of hierarchy.

552. Pace, David, and John Hunter. DIRECT PARTICIPATION IN
      ACTION: THE NEW BUREAUCRACY. Farnsborough: Saxon
      House, 1978. 119 pp.

      Describes an exercise in participative administration
      within a British public agency. It was found that the
      concept of "New Bureaucracy" is viable and necessary.
      The old way of doing business is out of step with the
      needs of the people who work for modern organizations.

553. Pitt, Douglas. "Mr. Illich's Multiplier: The Strange
      'Death' of the Bureaucratic Organization." BRITISH
      JOURNAL OF SOCIOLOGY. 31 (1980), 277-81.

      Questions whether the writer Ivan Illich has any good
      or novel solutions to the problems of the organization
      of the future. Illich is a superficial theorist with
      little to contribute to organization theory. His work
      offers few realistic alternatives.

554. Rothschild-Whitt, Joyce. "The Collectivist Organization:
      An Alternative to Rational-Bureaucratic Models." AM-
      ERICAN SOCIOLOGICAL REVIEW, 44 (1979), 509-27.

      Defines the ideal type of the collective as an option
      to replace traditional organization forms. Collectives
      are not failures to achieve bureaucratic standards, but
      instead are wholly new efforts.

555. Shariff, Zahid. "The Persistence of Bureaucracy." SOC-
      IAL SCIENCE QUARTERLY, 60 (1979), 3-19.

      Claims that the end-of-bureaucracy arguments, such as
      those of Bennis (Item 519), are not supported by the em-
      pirical evidence. Organizations are not responding to
      a changing environment; rather they are modifying that
      environment to fit the organization. Overall, bureau-
      cracy is alive and well. See Item 527 for the response
      from Bennis.

556. Simpson, Richard L. "Beyond Rational Bureaucracy: Chang-
      ing Values and Social Integration in Post-Industrial
      Society." SOCIAL FORCES, 51 (1972), 1-6.

      Predicts the decline of bureaucratic rationality in the
      United States. The rational productive process has made
      available the resources for new groups to pursue non-
      rational values. The elites of activist groups have
      been incorporated into the system, bringing with them
      more diverse values. The moral direction provided by
      the old value system has decreased.

557. Smith, Michael P. "Alienation and Bureaucracy: The Role
      of Participatory Administration." PUBLIC ADMINISTRA-
      TION REVIEW, 31 (1971), 658-64.

      Argues that workers and unorganized clients of bureau-
      cracy are likely to become alienated as they are over-
      whelmed by the routine. Participatory forms of admin-
      istration may provide relief, if they provide to par-
      ticipants a sense of self-expression, a feeling for the
      community, and a belief in the possibility of control-
      ling the organization.

558. Toffler, Alvin. FUTURE SHOCK. New York: Random House 1970. 491 pp.

Enthuses, in a chapter on "Organizations: The Coming Ad-Hocracy," about the demise of bureaucracy and its replacement by temporary work groups. Predictions of a highly regimented future are invalid. Fluidity, change, and movement are the major factors in the coming era. Lockheed's smashing success with its C-5A air transport is presented as an example of future good times.

559. Weiss, Carol H. "Bureaucratic Maladies and Remedies." AMERICAN BEHAVIORAL SCIENTIST, 22 (1979), 477-82.

Lists some of the major deficiencies of public bureaucracy and considers the possibility of reform.

560. Weiss, Carol H., and Allen H. MAKING BUREAUCRACIES WORK. Beverly Hills, Cal.: Sage, 1980. 309 pp.

A collection of essays on bureaucratic reform in the United States.

561. Wesolowski, Zdzislaw. "The Future of Bureaucracy." PERSONNEL ADMINISTRATION, 34 (January-February, 1971), 32-36.

Predicts that the use of automation will cause a drastic change in the whole concept of organization.

562. White, Orion F. "The Dialectical Organization: An Alternative to Bureaucracy." PUBLIC ADMINISTRATION REVIEW, 29 (1969), 32-42.

Urges a new relationship between bureaucracy and clients in such a way as to increase the organization's capacity to respond to a variety of needs. As it is, the bureaucracy tends to transform client needs into rigid procedures. The experiences of a small church-related social agency indicate that client needs can be made the central feature of the organization, with the structure changing to meet new demands.

563. Winthrop, Henry. "Bureaucratization and the Rebirth
      of Community." AMERICAN JOURNAL OF ECONOMICS AND SOC-
      IOLOGY, 23 (1964), 113-29.

      Describes alternatives to the increasing inefficiencies
      of massive bureaucracies. Already the pressure of bur-
      eaucratization and alienation is causing protests from
      individuals. Forms of withdrawal from the system include
      ideological anarchism, subsistence homesteading, and the
      intentional community. The creation of small-scale com-
      munities seems the best option. Perhaps the United Na-
      tions should subsidize experiments in this form.

564. Zorza, Richard. "Challenging Bureaucracy." NEW SOCIETY,
      27 (1974), 460-61.

      Believes that large American organizations will be at-
      tacked from within by the product of the baby boom. The
      new workers will be less tolerant of bureaucratic repres-
      sion and will demand greater democracy on the job.

IV. AMERICAN BUREAUCRACY

A. Bureaucracy, For and Against

565. Allen, Wycliffe (pseudonym). "I Am a Bureaucrat." PAC-
      IFIC SPECTATOR, 4 (1950), 440-45.

      A public employee comes partially out of the closet to
      confess pride in working for government.

566. Anonymous. "How to Become a Bureaucrat." AMERICAN MER-
      CURY, 30 (October, 1936), 143-48.

      Purports to give some insider's advice on how to wal-
      low in the public trough.

567. Appleby, Paul H. BIG DEMOCRACY. New York: Alfred A.
      Knopf, 1945. 197 pp.

      Dedicates this book to the much misunderstood and ma-
      ligned "Bill Bureaucrat." Government is large and com-
      plex, but that only reflects the conditions of the time.
      For all its problems, public administration works well.
      The bureaucracy is under popular control.

568. Appleby, Paul H. "Bureaucracy and the Future." ANNALS
      OF THE AMERICAN ACADEMY OF POLITICAL AND SOCIAL SCI-
      ENCE, 292 (1954), 136-51.

      Exhorts us to forge ever upward and onward in the im-
      provement of public administration. That course is the
      best one if bureaucracy is to be avoided. Government is
      not going to become any simpler, so we must continue to
      cope with complexity.

569. Aswell, James B. "Bureaucratic Government." CONGRES-
      SIONAL RECORD, 67 (1926), 8015-16.

      The federal government is becoming overcentralized and
      out of touch with the people. Jeffersonian principles
      must be revived.

570. Bane, Frank, Maynard Kreuger, and Charles Merriam. "Is
      It True about the Bureaucrat?" UNIVERSITY OF CHICAGO
      ROUND TABLE, 313 (March 19, 1944), 1-24.

      A debate on the merit of public employees.

571. Beard, Charles, and William Beard. "The Case for Bur-
      eaucracy." SCRIBNER'S MAGAZINE, 93 (1933), 209-14.

      Cast aspersions at the critics of bureaucracy and their
      "delirium." Civil servants are as praiseworthy as bus-
      inessmen. The civil service is the "one great moral
      stabilizer now operating in American society."

572. Beck, James. OUR WONDERLAND OF BUREAUCRACY: A STUDY OF
      THE GROWTH OF BUREAUCRACY IN THE FEDERAL GOVERNMENT,
      AND ITS DESTRUCTIVE EFFECT UPON THE CONSTITUTION. New
      York: Macmillan, 1932. 272 pp.

      Defines bureaucracy as "the irrepressible war between
      the individual and the State." As a lawyer and solic-
      itor general under Herbert Hoover, the author is par-
      ticularly appalled by the lack of legal restraints on
      the power of administration. If not an outright viola-
      tion of the Constitution, bureaucracy is at least a sure
      sign of the "decay of the constitutional morality of the
      American people."

573. Belsely, G. Lyle. "Why Bureaucracy is Belittled." PER-
      SONNEL ADMINISTRATION, 9 (January, 1947), 10-13.

      Discusses a number of public attitude surveys about the
      prestige of public employees in the United States. In
      general, the status is not very high.

574.   Bender, George H.   "Bureaucracy Runs Wild."   CONGRES-
       SIONAL RECORD, 86 (1940), Appendix 2765-67.

       Concedes that administration is necessary and that we
       have already had bureaucracy before 1933. But there
       is still cause for alarm about the various alphabet
       agencies "and the dozens of other fantastic growths
       which have mushroomed since the New Deal took office."

575.   Bennett, Marion T.   "Bureaucracy--Causes and Effects."
       CONGRESSIONAL RECORD, 90 (1944), A634-36.

       Contains the thoughts of Everett Dirksen on bureau-
       cracy.

576.   Boren, Lyle H.   "Freedom from Bureaucrats."   CONGRES-
       SIONAL RECORD, 89 (1943), A3958-60.

       Demands that we fight bureaucracy just as we are fight-
       ing our foreign enemies. Americans must resist bureau-
       cratic regimentation and regulation.

577.   "Built-in Bureaucrats."   FREEMAN, 3 (1953), 584-85.

       Complains about the difficulty of getting rid of pos-
       sibly subversive civil servants.

578.   "Bureaucracy and Taxes."   NATIONAL REPUBLIC, 20 (October,
       1932), 10-11.

       Deplores extravagance in government.

579.   "Bureaucratic Bungling Hits Epidemic Levels."   U.S. NEWS
       AND WORLD REPORT, 88 (March 24, 1980), 68-69.

       A report on tomfoolery at all levels of government.

580.   "Bureaucratic Despotism versus State's Rights."   LAWYER
       AND BANKER, 25 (1932), 195-205.

       Lawyers must resist federal centralization.

581. "Bureaucrats Fighting Back." U.S. NEWS AND WORLD RE-
      PORT, 86 (June 11, 1979), 55-57.

      Federal employees taking the initiative.

582. "Bureaucrats on Notice: Shape Up or Else!" U.S. NEWS
      AND WORLD REPORT, 85 (October 23, 1978), 36-37.

      Carter intends to crack down on bureaucrats.

583. "Bureaucrats under Fire." U.S. NEWS AND WORLD REPORT,
      86 (June 11, 1979), 51-57.

      On weakness of the federal civil service.

584. Burger, Alvin. "Bureaucracy and Inflation: Uncle Sam
      Should Follow His Own Advice." TAX DIGEST, 29 (1951),
      221-23.

      Reckless federal spending is the real cause of high
      rates of inflation.

585. Chamberlain, William H. "Bureaucratic Blight." FREE-
      MAN, 17 (1967), 34-41.

      On the evils of big government.

586. Corson, John J. "The Popular View of Bureaucracy."
      PERSONNEL ADMINISTRATION, 9 (January, 1947), 15-17.

      Notes with sadness the fact that the American public
      does not appreciate the quality of its public service.

587. Crider, John. THE BUREAUCRAT. Philadelphia: J.B. Lip-
      pincott, 1944. 373 pp.

      Expresses the urgency of a post-war reduction in the
      size of the federal government. Further steps must be
      taken to ensure political control of administration.
      The trend of expansion must be curbed.

588. "Curb the Bureaucrats!" U.S. NEWS AND WORLD REPORT, 79
       (November 10, 1975), 39-42.

       There is a general feeling among politicians and cit-
       izens at all levels that something has to be done about
       the size of government.

589. Daniels, Jonathan. "I Am a Bureaucrat." ATLANTIC MONTH-
       LY, 173 (April, 1944), 96-101.

       A New Dealer defends the federal government.

590. "A Defense of Bureaucracy." BUSINESS WEEK, (June 23,
       1945), 119.

       A report on Appleby's *Big Democracy*, Item 567.

591. DeNike, J. Harold. "Notes of a Neophyte Bureaucrat."
       HARVARD BUSINESS REVIEW, 22 (1944), 405-14.

       A businessman is highly unimpressed with the quality
       of government and civil servants after wartime service
       with the Office of Price Administration.

592. Derieux, James C. "How to Be a Bureaucrat." COLLIER'S,
       119 (February 8, 1947), 78.

       A little sarcasm about the fat life in Washington.

593. Dickinson, John. "The Perennial Cry of Bureaucracy."
       YALE REVIEW, 24 (1935), 448-63.

       Questions the real motives and targets of those cit-
       izens so lustily denouncing bureaucracy. They may well
       be upset about the substantive programs of the New Deal.

594. Ditter, J. William. "Bureaucratic Ambitions." CONGRES-
       SIONAL RECORD, 87 (1941), A3813-14.

       Claims that President Roosevelt vetoed a public roads
       project because Washington officials wanted to deny to
       the states any control over the money.

595.   Donnelly, Caroline. "Balancing Ideals and Frustrations
       in the Bureaucracy." MONEY, 6 (August, 1977), 54-58.

       Checks out the pluses and minuses of working for the
       federal government.

596.   Dummont, Matthew. "Down the Bureaucracy." TRANS-ACTION,
       7 (October, 1970), 10-14.

       Describes the growing sense of frustration among Wash-
       ington bureaucrats and sees a role for the guerilla ad-
       ministrator.

597.   Edmunds, Sterling. THE FEDERAL OCTOPUS: A SURVEY OF THE
       DESTRUCTION OF CONSTITUTIONAL GOVERNMENT AND OF CIVIL
       AND ECONOMIC LIBERTY IN THE UNITED STATES AND THE RISE
       OF AN ALL-EMBRACING FEDERAL BUREAUCRATIC DESPOTISM.
       Charlottesville, Va.: Michie, 1932. 130 pp.

       Is not the least bit happy about the way things are
       going.

598.   Edmunds, Sterling. "The Growth of the Federal Bureau-
       cratic Tyranny." LAWYER AND BANKER, 26 (1933), 20-29.

       Says that administrative law cannot be reconciled with
       traditional Anglo-Saxon liberties.

599.   Edmunds, Sterling. THE FEDERAL OCTOPUS IN 1933: A SUR-
       VEY OF THE DESTRUCTION OF CONSTITUTIONAL GOVERNMENT
       AND OF CIVIL AND ECONOMIC LIBERTY IN THE UNITED STATES
       AND THE RISE OF AN ALL-EMBRACING FEDERAL BUREAUCRATIC
       DESPOTISM. Charlottesville, Va.: Michie, 1933.   150
       pp.

       Things have not improved since Item 597.

600.   Fanin, Paul. "The Bureaucratic Revolution." CONGRES-
       SIONAL RECORD, 121 (1975), 27340-42.

       Says that government has slowly and silently taken con-
       trol of American business.

601. Farwell, Byron. "No Tears for Bureaucrats." BUREAU-
      CRAT, 9 (Fall, 1980), 10.

      A refutation of Goldman, Item 605. Bureaucrats are
      just not very nice.

602. Ferguson, Homer, and Jonathan Daniels. "Does Bureau-
      cracy Menace America?" TOWN MEETING, 10 (May 11,
      1944), 3-20.

      Transcript of a radio debate.

603. Finer, Herman. "Critics of 'Bureaucracy.'" POLITICAL
      SCIENCE QUARTERLY, 60 (1945), 100-12.

      Review essay on von Mises (Item 257), Crider (Item
      587), Juran (Item 2075), and Sullivan (Item 660). The
      problems and the answers are not as simple as these ex-
      perts make out. And in any case, the infirmities of the
      private organization are no less severe.

604. Freeman, N.B. "Down among the Bureaucrats." NATIONAL
      REVIEW, 29 (1977), 1229.

      On foolishness in Washington.

605. Goldman, Don. "Need a Fall Guy? Blame a Bureaucrat."
      BUREAUCRAT, 9 (Fall, 1980), 7-9.

      Points out that "the civil service is not some foreign
      power." Bureaucrats are the same as anyone else. See
      Item 601 for a comment.

606. Goldwater, Barry. "Bureaucrats Should Follow Laws, Not
      Make Them." CONGRESSIONAL RECORD, 116 (1970), 41591-
      93.

      Says that bureaucrats act as if Congress does not ex-
      ist. Middle-level managers write their own laws, re-
      gardless of the wishes of politicians. This is espec-
      ially true about the Department of Health, Education
      and Welfare.

607. Goodsell, Charles T. THE CASE FOR BUREAUCRACY: A PUBLIC
      ADMINISTRATION POLEMIC. Chatham, N.J.: Chatham House,
      1983. 179 pp.

      Defends American public administration from a variety
      of criticisms, including those from scholars in the
      field. Empirical data are reviewed to show that citizens
      generally are satisfied with government services and that
      public organizations are at least as worthy as private
      ones. The concept of the "bureaucratic mentality" is not
      supported by the evidence. The political power of the
      bureaucracy is not unlimited. Why then, it has to be
      asked, do so many people persist in condemning the modern
      public organization?

608. Hamill, Katherine. "This Is a Bureaucrat." FORTUNE,
      48 (1953), 156-58.

      A day in the life of a member of the Bureau of the Bud-
      get.

609. Hebron, Lawrence. "Why Bureaucracy Keeps Growing."
      BUSINESS WEEK, (November 15, 1976), 23-24.

      Finds the root of the problem to be "the concept of
      government that knows no bounds."

610. Helms, Jesse. "Bureaucratic Absurdities and Citizen
      Harassment." CONGRESSIONAL RECORD, 122 (1976), 22589-
      91.

      In their attempts to build rational categories, the
      bureaucrats create awful absurdities.

611. Hook, Sidney. "Bureaucrats are Human." SATURDAY REVIEW
      OF LITERATURE, 41 (May 17, 1958), 12-14, 41.

      Bureaucrats are just ordinary folk.

612. Hornaday, Mary. "In Defense of Bureaucrats." CHRISTIAN
      SCIENCE MONITOR MAGAZINE SECTION, (June 9, 1943), 2.

      Civil servants perform heroically.

613. Ickes, Harold. "Bureaucrats vs. Business Men." NEW
      REPUBLIC, 109 (August 2, 1943), 131-33.

      Says that bureaucrats and business leaders are not so
      different. And besides, the war effort might be going
      better if there were more bureaucrats in charge.

614. Ickes, Harold. "Ickes Defines--and Defends--the Bureau-
      crats." NEW YORK TIMES MAGAZINE, (January 16, 1944),
      9, 45-47.

      Claims that the much abused bureaucracy is necessary
      for both government and business.

615. Ickes, Harold, Elbert Thomas, and Christian Herter.
      "Bureaucracy in Review." STATE GOVERNMENT, 17 (1944),
      273-75.

      Three public officials comment on Merriam, Item 634.

616. "An Inside Look at Our Runaway Bureaucracy." U.S. NEWS
      AND WORLD REPORT, 83 (October 3, 1977), 22-28.

      On waste and inefficiency in Washington.

617. "Is Bureaucracy Out of Control?" U.S. NEWS AND WORLD
      REPORT, 70 (May 17, 1971), 61-64.

      The federal government continues to grow.

618. Joyner, Conrad. "Crabgrass and Bureaucrats." MIDWEST
      QUARTERLY, 20 (Autumn, 1978), 18-31.

      Criticizes the self-serving nature of the bureaucracy.
      Civil servants are not responsive to political leader-
      ship. As a cure, the protection of civil service laws
      should be eliminated.

619. Kaiser, A.R. "Whither Our Economy? The Trend toward
      Full Bureaucratic Control Must Be Halted Now!"
      TAX OUTLOOK, 4 (October, 1949), 14-16.

A denunciation of federal involvement in the control of the economy.

620. Kaufman, Herbert. "Fear of Bureaucracy: A Raging Pandemic." PUBLIC ADMINISTRATION REVIEW, 41 (1981), 1-9.

Wonders why so many people are so upset with bureaucracy. The evidence and the arguments thrown against bureaucracy are both confused and inconclusive. Perhaps bureaucracy is a symbol of our frustration because, when things are out of joint, we Americans like to believe it is because human agents in control have failed. Today, the guilty ones must be bureaucrats. Such an idea is less frightening than admitting that no one is in charge.

621. Kearney, B.W. "Bureaucracy, the Overshadowing Menace." CONGRESSIONAL RECORD, 96 (1950), A3104.

Wake up, America, and get rid of all that unnecessary administration.

622. Kilpatrick, James. "Unchained Bureaucracy Gone Berserk." NATION'S BUSINESS, 67 (November, 1979), 21-22.

Denounces the arrogance of bureaucracy and calls for more restraints on the power of administrators.

623. Knebel, Fletcher. "Bureaucrats are People." LOOK, 21 (May 14, 1957), 77-78.

A look at the human side of administrators.

624. Langen, Odin. "Bureaucracy Burden Continues." CONGRESSIONAL RECORD, 116 (1970), 7029.

On the size of the federal budget.

625. Lederer, Victor. "Bureaucracy: The Excesses Set Too High a Price." ADMINISTRATIVE MANAGEMENT, 39 (January, 1978), 28-29.

A criticism of American public administration.

626. "Legal Check-Rein on Bureaucracy." LITERARY DIGEST,
      122 (August 8, 1936), 29-30.

      A report on the American Bar Association's counter-
      attack on the New Deal.

627. Lerner, Max. "Notes on Congress and Bureaucracy." PUB-
      LIC JOURNAL: MARGINAL NOTES ON WARTIME AMERICA. New
      York: Viking, 1945.

      Wonders why members of Congress direct so much hostil-
      ity at this thing they call bureaucracy. After all, it
      can be argued that they have some responsibility for the
      existence of much of the executive branch.

628. Leslie, Grey. "Anatomy of Bureaucracy." AMERICAN MER-
      CURY, 91 (December, 1960), 48-55.

      On the character of the bureaucrat: pompous and arro-
      gant.

629. Lewis, Ben W. "Lambs in Bureaucrat's Clothing." HAR-
      PER'S, 191 (1945), 247-51.

      Downplays the dangers of bureaucratic rule in the U.S.

630. Ludlow, Louis. AMERICA GO BUST! AN EXPOSE OF THE FEDERAL
      BUREAUCRACY AND ITS WASTEFUL AND EVIL TENDENCIES. Bos-
      ton: Stratford, 1933. 144 pp.

      American has lost sight of Jeffersonian ideals. There-
      fore, government has grown, imposing a crushing burden
      of taxes on the common people.

631. Ludlow, Louis. "A Resolution to Curb Bureaucracy and
      Unconstitutional Trends of Government." CONGRESSIONAL
      RECORD, 90 (1944), 4288-89.

      A proposal to limit the growth of government.

632. Markey, Morris. "Bureaucracy." AMERICAN MERCURY, 40
      (1937), 291-97.

      Finds little to recommend after a trip to see Wash-
      ington in action.

633. Mathews, David. "The War on Bureaucracy." SOUTHERN
      REVIEW OF PUBLIC ADMINISTRATION, 1 (1977), 247-53.

      The Secretary of Health, Education and Welfare dis-
      cusses the general public discontent with government.

634. Merriam, Charles. "Bureaucracy: What Does it Mean?"
      STATE GOVERNMENT, 17 (1944), 271-75.

      In defense of administration. See Item 615.

635. Miller, Stephen. "Bureaucracy Baiting." AMERICAN
      SCHOLAR, 47 (1978), 205-222.

      Insists that not much is gained by making bureaucracy
      the cause of all modern evils. Especially dangerous
      are those writers who call all forms of social control
      bureaucracy and fail to distinguish among types. The
      administration of the Western democracies, for all the
      faults, is still connected to a free political system.

636. Moley, Raymond. "A Voice from the Bureaucracy." NEWS-
      WEEK, 22 (July 15, 1943), 88.

      Reports on a bureaucrat's disillusionment with the fed-
      eral government.

637. Morrow, Hugh. "Can We Reform Our Bureaucrats?" SATUR-
      DAY EVENING POST, 219 (May 10, 1947), 20-21, 116-19.

      Catalogues the folly going on in Washington.

638. Murphy, Charles J.V. "What's Wrong with Our Federal Bur-
      eaucracy?" READER'S DIGEST, 100 (April, 1972), 77-82.

      On Nixon's attempts to reshape the federal government.

639. Nelson, Michael. "Bureaucracy: The Biggest Crisis of
         All." WASHINGTON MONTHLY, 9 (January, 1978), 51-59.

      Sees a number of problems caused by a listless, self-
      serving bureaucracy in Washington. Public attitudes
      toward the federal government represent one of the major
      domestic crises of our times. From the viewpoint of the
      citizen, bureaucratic behavior is random and arbitrary.
      Politicians of the left and the right can agree on the
      need to do something about the administration of the
      federal government.

640. Nisbit, Robert. "Bureaucracy." PREJUDICES: A PHILO-
         SOPHICAL DICTIONARY. Cambridge, Mass.: Harvard Uni-
         versity Press, 1982.

      Contends that America is in the grips of an always
      expanding bureaucracy that feeds on the need for more
      rationalization. There is no intellectual means for
      challenging its growth.

641. North, James. "My Brief Career as a Bureaucrat." NEW
         REPUBLIC, 180 (February 3, 1979), 21-23.

      Takes a very dim view of the quality of the people who
      work for the federal government.

642. Outland, George E. "The New Personal Devil: Bureaucracy."
         NEW REPUBLIC, 109 (October 25, 1943), 561-63.

      Examines the reasons for the increasingly harsh rhet-
      oric about bureaucracy.

643. Pharo, Eugene. "America's Wet-Nurse Bureaucracy." AMER-
         ICAN MERCURY, 41 (1937), 283-91.

      The growth of government has sapped our inititive.

644. Potter, Ralph. "Where Are the 'Self-Serving' Bureau-
         crats?" BUREAUCRAT, 9 (Summer, 1980), 3-4.

      Argues that bureaucracy is virtually synonymous with
      democracy. Bureaucrats should be proud of that label.

645. Proxmire, William. "Give Bureaucrats Credit." CONGRES-
         SIONAL RECORD, 119 (1973), 38606.

         Federal employees are dedicated, honest, and "a force
         for stability."

646. "Pulliam's Attack on Bureaucrats Fills Front Page." ED-
         ITOR AND PUBLISHER, 104 (November 6, 1971), 14.

         On an Arizona editor's crusade against the federal bur-
         eaucracy.

647. Quillen, James. "The Federal Bureaucracy: See How It
         Grows." CONGRESSIONAL RECORD, 111 (1965), 5350.

         The federal work force has grown at the expense of the
         liberties of citizens.

648. Reed, Daniel. "Bureaucratic Law and the Census." CON-
         GRESSIONAL RECORD, 86 (1940), 2176-77.

         Denounces the bureaucratic highhandedness involved in
         the preparation of the 1940 census. It is another sign
         of bureaucratic encroachments on individual liberty.

649. Romains, Jules. "Bureaucrats at the Multiplication Ta-
         ble." READER'S DIGEST, 47 (September, 1945), 103-06.

         Sees a distinction between bureaucracy and administra-
         tion. Bureaucracy insists on interfering with all parts
         of social life.

650. Sabath, Adolph J. "Who Are the Bureaucrats?" CONGRES-
         SIONAL RECORD, 90 (1944), 2064.

         Demands that the Republicans identify all those evil
         bureaucrats. Chances are, most of them in higher pos-
         itions are Republicans anyway.

651. Samuelson, Robert. "Good-for-Nothing Government: Should
         We Be Badmouthing the Bureaucracy?" NEW REPUBLIC, 17
         (May 15, 1976), 10-14.

Dispels some myths about the federal civil service.

652. Shouse, Jouett. DEMOCRACY OR BUREAUCRACY. Washington,
      D.C.: American Liberty League, 1935. 22 pp.

      The increase in executive power threatens the tradi-
      tional division of powers. The New Deal continues to
      put power in the hands of unelected officials.

653. Snyder, David P. "The Bureaucrat as Scapegoat, and What
      To Do about It." BUREAUCRAT, 6 (Winter, 1977), 112-16.

      Argues that it is bad policy, not bad officials, that
      cause government failures.

654. Stevens, Neil E. "Bureaucracy as a Way of Life." SCI-
      ENCE, 83 (1936), 497-99.

      A defense of federal employees, by a career officer.

655. Sullivan, Lawrence. "The Great American Bureaucracy."
      ATLANTIC MONTHLY, 147 (1931), 137-44.

      The beginning of a continuing tirade about bureaucracy.

656. Sullivan, Lawrence. "The Dead Hand of Bureaucracy."
      FORUM, 89 (1933), 19-25.

      The situation has gotten worse.

657. Sullivan, Lawrence. "Our New System of Bureaucracy."
      FORUM, 91 (1934), 90-95.

      More bad news about government.

658. Sullivan, Lawrence. THE DEAD HAND OF BUREAUCRACY. In-
      dianapolis: Bobbs-Merrill, 1940. 303 pp.

      All the bad tendencies described in Items, 655, 656,
      and 657 have only gotten worse. This is not surprising
      since bureaucracy is a deadly virus gnawing at our sys-
      tem of free enterprise.

659. Sullivan, Lawrence. "Bureaucracy after the War." NA-
      TION'S BUSINESS, 32 (February, 1944), 79.

      No relief in sight.

660. Sullivan, Lawrence. BUREAUCRACY RUNS AMUCK. Indiana-
      polis: Bobbs-Merrill, 1944. 318 pp.

      Still more on the folly of the New Deal.

661. Sumners, Hatton B. "Our Choice--Decentralization of
      Government or Government by a Centralized Bureaucracy."
      CONGRESSIONAL RECORD, 86 (1940), Appendix 2218-21.

      The role of the states has been destroyed by the fed-
      eral government. The governmental capacity of the people
      must be restored.

662. Sumners, Hatton B. "Don't Blame the Bureaucrats." READ-
      ER'S DIGEST, 43 (September, 1943), 1-4.

      Congress started the mess in Washington, through its
      usurpation of the rights of the states.

663. Sumners, Hatton B. "America's Capacity for Self-Govern-
      ment is Being Destroyed by Bureaucracy." AMERICAN BAR
      ASSOCIATION JOURNAL, 30 (January, 1944), 3-5.

      Inveighs against the dangers of centralized government.

664. Switzer, Mary. "Reveries of an Old Bureaucrat." PER-
      SONNEL ADMINISTRATION, 9 (January, 1947), 24-26, 31.

      Reflects on the good work done by her colleagues in
      the federal government.

665. Sypher, Alden H. "Why Bureaucrats Rate Programs above
      People." NATION'S BUSINESS, 54 (March, 1966), 29-30.

      Interprets a survey of federal grant administrators to
      mean that civil servants resent their clients.

666. "That Dreadful Bureaucracy." NEW REPUBLIC, 111 (1944), 361.

    Wonders why the Republicans have such a negative attitude about bureaucracy.

667. Vieg, John. "Democracy and Bureaucracy." PUBLIC ADMINISTRATION REVIEW, 4 (1944), 247-52.

    Review essay on Juran (Item 2075) and Sullivan (Item 660).

668. Vieg, John. "Bureaucracy--Fact and Fiction." ELEMENTS OF PUBLIC ADMINISTRATION. Edited by Fritz Morstein Marx. Englewood Cliffs, N.J.: Prentice-Hall, 1959.

    Concludes that many of the complaints about bureaucracy are based on myths or are the thoughtless reactions of some people against any sort of authority. Increased understanding will make citizens appreciate the conditions under which administrators must work. The "red tape" of government is the best insurance of equal treatment.

669. Watkins, Edgar. "Dangerous By-Products of Bureaucracy." LAWYER AND BANKER, 26 (1933), 3-8.

    On this abomination known as administrative law.

670. Weiss, Carol H. "Efforts at Bureaucratic Reform: What Have We Learned?" MAKING BUREAUCRACIES WORK. Edited by Carol H. Weiss and Allen H. Barton. Beverly Hills, Cal.: Sage, 1980.

    Reviews the major complaints about bureaucracy.

671. "Who Is a Bureaucrat?" PUBLIC MANAGEMENT, 26 (April, 1944), 97.

    Probably just a normal human being. Bureaucrats are just like anyone else, even in local government.

672. "Withering Blight of Bureaucracy." READER'S DIGEST,
      42 (April, 1943), 43.

      Examples of bureaucratic stupidity.

673. Wooddy, Carroll H. "Bureaucracy, Good or Bad." SCHOOL
      LIFE, 20 (January, 1935), 109.

      Lists the pros and cons of bureaucracy.

674. Wriston, Michael J. "In Defense of Bureaucracy." PUB-
      LIC ADMINISTRATION REVIEW, 40 (1980), 179-83.

      Argues that bureaucracy survives and thrives simply
      because of its strengths; it gets the job done. It
      does have weaknesses in receiving feedback and in set-
      ting goals. These and other problems can be overcome
      by concentrating on the functions of selection, motiva-
      tion, and organization.

675. Young, Andrew. "Growth of Government Bureaucracy."
      CRISIS, 82 (1975), 427-30.

      Defends bureaucratic centralization as a means for pro-
      tecting civil rights.

676. Zola, Joan. "Portrait of a Bureaucrat." NATIONAL RE-
      VIEW, 19 (1967), 410-12.

      A synopsis of the career of a bureaucrat.

                  B. The Federal Bureaucracy

                  1. General Discussions

677. Altshuler, Alan A., ed. THE POLITICS OF THE FEDERAL
      BUREAUCRACY. New York: Dodd, Mead, 1968. 452 pp.

      A collection of previously published articles look-
      ing at the federal bureaucracy as a major sub-system
      of the American political system.

678. Altshuler, Alan A., and Norman C. Thomas. THE POLITICS
     OF THE FEDERAL BUREAUCRACY, 2nd. ed. New York: Harper
     and Row, 1977. 379 pp.

     A revision of Item 677.

679. Bent, Silas. "Tangled Bureaucracies." VIRGINIA QUART-
     ERLY REVIEW, 20 (1944), 33-49.

     Traces the growth of American bureaucracy, especially
     since the New Deal.

680. Boyer, William W. BUREAUCRACY ON TRIAL: POLICY MAKING
     BY GOVERNMENT AGENCIES. Indianapolis: Bobbs-Merrill,
     1964. 184 pp.

     Outlines the steps by which the bureaucracy becomes
     involved in the making of public policy. Administra-
     tors are concerned with all parts of the policy-making
     cycle: initiation, preliminary drafting, public partic-
     ipation, final drafting, and reviewing. The initiation
     and participation stages are most important and involve
     the bureaucracy in its heaviest contact with the envir-
     onment. Problems of democratic control of public admin-
     istration are discussed.

681. Browne, William P. POLITICS, PROGRAMS, AND BUREAUCRATS.
     Port Washington, N.Y.: Kennikat, 1980. 190 pp.

     Argues that the bureaucracy is the silent and unchang-
     ing part of the American political process. Politicians
     depend upon the expertise of administrators in the design
     and implementation of public programs. The routines of
     administration, unnoticed by public officials, are the
     real ingredients of policy. Those routines change more
     than might be expected, but they are still the prerog-
     atives of the bureaucrats. This conditions prevails at
     all levels of government.

682. Cleveland, Harlan. "The Case for Bureaucracy." NEW YORK
     TIMES MAGAZINE, (October 27, 1963), 19, 113-14.

     Explodes some myths about government administration.

683. Corbett, D.C. "The Politics of Bureaucracy in the United
      States of America." PUBLIC ADMINISTRATION (SYDNEY),
      32 (1973), 28-41.

      Contends that the specialization and fragmentation
      within the pluralistic American system provides access
      to the administrators from many groups.

684. Dannhauser, Werner. "Reflections on Statesmanship and
      Bureaucracy." BUREAUCRATS, POLICY ANALYSTS, STATES-
      MEN: WHO LEADS? Edited by Robert A. Goldwin. Wash-
      ington, D.C.: American Enterprise Institute for Public
      Policy Research, 1980.

      Doubts whether bureaucracy is the major reason for the
      lack of statesmanship and political leadership in Amer-
      ican politics.

685. Dietsch, Robert W. "The Invisible Bureaucracy." NEW
      REPUBLIC, 164 (February 20, 1971), 19-21.

      Discusses the role of advisory committees in the fed-
      eral government.

686. Farnum, George. "America Confronts Bureaucracy." LAW
      SOCIETY JOURNAL, 7 (1936), 514-19.

      Examines the growth of government activity since WWI.

687. "Federal Bureaucracy Will Grow until We Decide to Cut It
      Down." SATURDAY EVENING POST, 221 (June 4, 1949), 12.

      Views with alarm the growth of the federal government.

688. Foley, Fred. "Effectiveness of Federal Programs: The
      Politics of Bureaucracy." POLITY, 9 (1976), 220-27.

      Review essay on books about policy implementation.

689. Fried, Robert C. PERFORMANCE IN AMERICAN BUREAUCRACY.
      Boston: Little, Brown, 1976. 470 pp.

A public administration textbook that evaluates the
performance of American administration. Performance
includes responsiveness and regard for due process as
well as effectiveness. External and internal constraints
on administrative performance are described.

690. Omitted.

691. Fritschler, A. Lee. "Bureaucracy and Democracy: The
      Unanswered Question." PUBLIC ADMINISTRATION REVIEW,
      26 (1966), 69-74.

      A review essay on books about the bureaucracy in the
      American political process.

692. Fritschler, A. Lee. SMOKING AND POLITICS: POLICYMAKING
      AND THE FEDERAL BUREAUCRACY. New York: Appleton-
      Century-Crofts, 1969. 165 pp. Second edition, Engle-
      wood Cliffs, N.J.: Prentice-Hall, 1975. 180 pp.

      Uses the controversy over the labeling of cigarette
      packages to illustrate the role of the bureaucracy in
      the policy process. Government agencies such as the
      Federal Trade Commission and the Public Health Service
      confronted the powerful "tobacco subsystem." In this
      instance, the bureaucracy played a positive role since
      it was more representative of the will of society and
      less confined by special interests, as compared to the
      elected politicians.

693. Gant, George. "Bureaucracy in the Field." PUBLIC ADMIN-
      ISTRATION REVIEW, 3 (1943), 264-69.

      Reviews several documents discussing the field oper-
      ations of the federal government.

694. Geekie, William J. WHY GOVERNMENT FAILS OR WHAT'S REALLY
      WRONG WITH THE BUREAUCRACY. Roslyn Heights, N.Y.:
      Libra, 1976. 246 pp.

      Chronicles the sorry record of accomplishment compiled
      by many public agencies. The failed bureaucracies are
      victims of "misdesign." Suggestions for citizen efforts
      at improving things are offered.

695. Grabbe, Paul. "Washington Is What We Make It: An Eye-
      witness Report on Bureaucracy." HARPER'S, 189 (1944),
      64-74.

      A look at wartime Washington.

696. Gryski, Gerald. BUREAUCRATIC POLICY MAKING IN A TECH-
      NOLOGICAL SOCIETY. Cambridge, Mass.: Schenkman, 1981.
      243 pp.

      Argues that bureaucracy permeates all aspects of the
      American political system. The environment and struc-
      ture of the federal bureaucracy are analyzed. Big gov-
      ernment and big bureaucracy are here to stay, and the
      problem is to make them more responsive to citizens and
      politicians.

697. Jacob, Charles E. POLICY AND BUREAUCRACY. Princeton,
      N.J.: D. Van Nostrand, 1966. 217 pp.

      Examines the interrelationship of policy and adminis-
      tration in the federal government. The fragmentation
      of leadership in several policy areas is discussed.
      Bureaucrats are seen as playing a major part in the ac-
      complishment of ends beneficial to the general interest.
      They can claim to be as representative of that interest
      as any other part of the policy process.

698. Jain, R.B. "The Bureaucracy: Towards a Responsive Sys-
      tem." AMERICAN GOVERNMENT AND POLITICS. Edited by
      B.K. Shrivastava and Thomas Casstevens. Atlantic
      Highlands, N.J.: Humanities Press, 1980.

      A general description of the American system.

699. Kramer, Fred A. DYNAMICS OF PUBLIC BUREAUCRACY: AN IN-
      TRODUCTION TO PUBLIC ADMINISTRATION. Cambridge, Mass.:
      Winthrop, 1977. 290 pp.

      A textbook in public administration emphasizing the
      administrative side of policy problems in the American
      political system.

700. Kramer, Fred A. PERSPECTIVES ON PUBLIC BUREAUCRACY: A
     READER ON ORGANIZATION. Cambridge, Mass.: Winthrop,
     1973. 199 pp. Second edition, 1977. 220 pp. Third
     edition, 1981. 240 pp.

     Previously published articles on American bureaucracy.

701. Lewis, Eugene. AMERICAN POLITICS IN A BUREAUCRATIC AGE:
     CITIZENS, CONSTITUENTS, CLIENTS AND VICTIMS. Cam-
     bridge, Mass.: Winthrop, 1977. 182 pp.

     Describes the decline of the status of citizen in a
     bureaucratic polity. Participation in a meaningful way
     has deteriorated into acceptance of the roles of constit-
     uent, client, or victim of an organization. The power of
     the state is so diffused among the entities involved in
     separate policy areas that no one is really in charge.
     Americans are well managed, but not well governed. Ex-
     amples of this situation are drawn from economic, wel-
     fare, and military policy.

702. Mainzer, Lewis C. POLITICAL BUREAUCRACY. Glenview,
     Ill.: Scott, Foresman, 1973. 187 pp.

     Seeks to identify ways of controlling the bureaucracy
     without eliminating its positive features. Bureaucracy
     must be evaluated in terms of its competence, its self-
     hood (or humaneness), and its political responsibility.
     The legal and political means available for checking the
     administration are discussed. The question remains
     whether we can have a system which is, at once, effic-
     ient, aware of the dignity of its members, and political-
     ly responsive.

703. Medeiros, James A., and David E. Schmidt. PUBLIC BUR-
     EAUCRACY: VALUES AND PERSPECTIVES. North Scituate,
     Mass.: Duxbury, 1977. 183 pp.

     Discuss American bureaucracy in terms of three ap-
     proaches: the machine, the humane, and the political.
     Each of these approaches is associated with a distinct
     set of values. The need for a model which incorporates
     all three values is stressed.

704. Meier, Kenneth J. POLITICS AND BUREAUCRACY: POLICYMAK-
      ING IN THE FOURTH BRANCH OF GOVERNMENT. North Scit-
      uate, Mass.: Duxbury, 1979. 219 pp.

      Views the growth of bureaucracy as a response to the
      political demands of the public. With this growth, how-
      ever, the bureaucracy has become a major power center in
      the national government. Bureaucracy can be evaluated
      in terms of its responsiveness and competence. The
      traditional control devices available to the other parts
      of government are discussed. Further ways of ensuring
      a responsive yet competent bureaucracy are outlined, in-
      cluding strengthened political institutions, an improved
      merit system, and a better informed public.

705. Minow, Newton H. "The Bureaucracy." THE MAZES OF MOD-
      ERN GOVERNMENT: THE STATES, THE LEGISLATURES, THE BUR-
      EAUCRACY, THE COURTS. Santa Barbara, Cal.: Center for
      the Study of Democratic Institutions, 1964.

      Claims that bureaucracy has failed to keep pace with
      modern technology.

706. Morrow, William L. "Bureaucracy and Politics: Dimensions
      and Dangers." PUBLIC ADMINISTRATION REVIEW, 30 (1970),
      78-84.

      Review essay on books about American government.

707. Nachmias, David, and David H. Rosenbloom. BUREAUCRATIC
      GOVERNMENT USA. New York: St. Martin's, 1980. 269 pp.

      Describe how the three branches of American government
      have become more bureaucratic in response to the growth
      of administration. The political parties and pressure
      groups show signs of the same bureaucratization. As a
      result, citizens have become socialized to accept their
      roles as objects of administration rather than as active
      participants in an open political process. Americans
      have developed a "bureaucratic self" as an adjustment to
      the current realities. The bureaucracy operates as an
      autonomous "fourth branch" of government; because of
      their own bureaucratic character, the other branches
      cannot adjust to changed conditions.

708. Newell, Charldean. "Bureaucratic Politics: Whither Go-
     est Democracy? POLITICAL SCIENCE REVIEWER, 9 (1979),
     231-56.

     Review essay on recent books about American govern-
     ment.

709. Peters, Charles, and Michael Nelson, eds. THE CULTURE
     OF BUREAUCRACY. New York: Holt, Rinehart, and Win-
     ston, 1979. 278 pp.

     A collection of articles originally published in the
     Washington Monthly.

710. Powell, Norman John. RESPONSIBLE PUBLIC BUREAUCRACY IN
     THE UNITED STATES. Boston: Allyn and Bacon, 1967.
     191 pp.

     Examines the meaning of bureaucratic responsibility
     in the American context. Both intragovernmental and
     extragovernmental means of ensuring responsibility are
     discussed. All these means make up a total system that
     is rooted in American political, social, and psycholog-
     ical realities.

711. Rabin, Jack, Gerald Miller, W. Bartley Hildreth, and
     Thomas D. Lynch. "Public Bureaucracy." CONTEMPORARY
     PUBLIC ADMINISTRATION. Edited by Thomas D. Lynch and
     Jack Rabin. New York: Harcourt Brace Jovanovich,
     1981.

     A general discussion of American bureaucracy.

712. Rickover, Hyman. "The Bureaucracy." THE MAZES OF MOD-
     ERN GOVERNMENT: THE STATE, THE LEGISLATURE, THE BUR-
     EAUCRACY, THE COURTS. Santa Barbara, Cal.: Center
     for the Study of Democratic Institutions, 1964.

     Wonders if bureaucracy is compatible with democracy.

713. Ripley, Randall, and Grace Franklin. BUREAUCRACY AND
     POLICY IMPLEMENTATION. Homewood, Ill.: Dorsey, 1982.
     226 pp.

Provide an overview of the policy implementation process from a bureaucratic perspective, using the categories of distributive, regulatory, and redistributive policies. The material covers federal, state, and local
governments. Each policy area tends to operate as an
autonomous entity.

714. Rosen, Bernard. HOLDING GOVERNMENT BUREAUCRACIES AC-
        COUNTABLE. New York: Praeger, 1982. 180 pp.

Explores the dimensions of bureaucratic accountability
in the federal government. The traditional mechanisms
for ensuring accountability--executive control, legislative oversight, citizen participation, the news media,
and the courts--are analyzed. New instruments such as
sunset laws, whistle blowing, inspectors general and
auditing are also discussed. In general, there exists
"an awesome armada of policies, mechanisms, and processes to oversee bureaucracies and bring them to heel when
necessary." An appendix gives examples of how specific
federal agencies are held accountable.

715. Rosenbloom, David H. "Constitutionalism and Public Bur-
        eaucrats." BUREAUCRAT, 11 (Fall, 1982), 54-56.

Argues that in many cases, "constitutional values simply do not mesh well with the values of professionalized
public administration." The bureaucrat's emphasis on
efficiency and program effectiveness often conflicts with
the constitutional values of liberty and individual freedom.

716. Rourke, Francis E., ed. BUREAUCRATIC POWER IN NATIONAL
        POLITICS. Boston: Little, Brown, 1965. 199 pp. Sec-
        ond edition, 1972. 419 pp.

A reader on bureaucratic politics in the federal government.

717. Rourke, Francis E. BUREAUCRACY, POLITICS, AND PUBLIC
        POLICY. Boston: Little, Brown, 1969. 173 pp. Sec-
        ond Edition, 1976. 208 pp.

Maintains that "bureaucratic politics rather than party
politics has become the dominant theater of decisions in
the modern state." The sources of bureaucratic power in
the U.S. are identified. The major factor has been the
inattention of other political actors. Professionalism
and the relations with interest groups are also important sources of strength for the agencies. The role of
the bureaucracy in recent policy failures is considered.

718. Rourke, Francis E. ed. BUREAUCRACY: SOME CASE STUDIES.
      Washington, D.C.: Government Research Corporation, 1976.
      44 pp.

      A collection of articles from the *National Journal*.

719. Salamon, Lester M., and Gary L. Wamsley. "The Federal
      Bureaucracy: Responsivenes to Whom? PEOPLE VS. GOV-
      ERNMENT: THE RESPONSIVENESS OF AMERICAN INSTITUTIONS.
      Edited by Leroy N. Rieselbach. Bloomington: Indiana
      University Press, 1975.

      Argue that the bureaucracy is responsive, if not to the
      general public, then at least to "relevant others." In
      this sense, bureaucracy is no different from other organs
      of government. Paradoxically, however, the agencies that
      are most likely to seek an alliance with stable special
      interests are also the most vulnerable to outside pres-
      sures.

720. Schott, Richard L. THE BUREAUCRATIC STATE: THE EVOLUTION
      AND SCOPE OF THE AMERICAN FEDERAL BUREAUCRACY. Morris-
      town, N.J.: General Learning Press, 1974. 42 pp.

      A basic overview of the history of the federal estab-
      lishment. The contemporary executive branch organiza-
      tion is outlined.

721. Seitz, Steven T. BUREAUCRACY, POLICY, AND THE PUBLIC.
      St. Louis: C.V. Mosby Company, 1978. 216 pp.

      Presents a general discussion of American bureaucracy
      within a structural-functional framework. Problems of
      power in and out of the complex organization are ana-
      lyzed. If administration can be confined to routine

decisions, no political problems arise. However, if the
political organs cannot handle critical decisions, then
the bureaucracy may assume a totalitarian form.

722. Shaw, Albert. "A Growing Bureaucracy." REVIEW OF RE-
      VIEWS, 90 (September, 1934), 17-20.

      Criticizes the National Recovery Act and other New
      Deal programs.

723. Shaw, Albert. "Will Federal Bureaucracy Last?" REVIEW
      OF REVIEWS, 93 (June, 1936), 17-24.

      More on the excesses of the Roosevelt administration.

724. Shefter, Martin. "Party, Bureaucracy and Political
      Change in the United States. POLITICAL PARTIES: DE-
      VELOPMENT AND DECAY. Edited by Louis Maisel and J.
      Cooper. Beverly Hills, Cal.: Sage, 1978.

      Argues that "changes in the relative power of party
      and bureaucracy in the United States are intimately re-
      lated to the process of critical realignment of American
      parties."

725. Wilson, James Q. "The Rise of the Bureaucratic State."
      PUBLIC INTEREST, 41 (Fall, 1975), 77-103.

      Examines the reasons for the growth of American bur-
      eaucracy during 200 years of independence. The relation-
      ship between agency and clientele group accounts for much
      expansion as well as the durability of the existing bur-
      eaucracy.

726. Woll, Peter. AMERICAN BUREAUCRACY. New York: W.W. Nor-
      ton, 1963. 184 pp. Second edition, 1977. 260 pp.

      Sees no reason for despair in the fact that bureaucra-
      cy has become an independent fourth branch of government.
      There is no reason why administration should be subject
      to complete control by executives or legislators. The
      federal administration serves as a check on the other

branches while remaining representative of a variety of
interests. The bureaucracy occupies a responsible position in a system of constitutional democracy.

727. Yates, Douglas. BUREAUCRATIC DEMOCRACY: THE SEARCH FOR
      DEMOCRACY AND EFFICIENCY IN AMERICAN GOVERNMENT. Cam-
      bridge, Mass.: Harvard University Press, 1982. 224 pp.

      Views the United States as a "bureaucratic democracy."
      In such a system, a disproportionate amount of power has
      shifted to chief executives, staff assistants to exec-
      utives, and professional bureaucrats. The contest be-
      tween democracy and efficiency now takes place within
      the bureaucratic arena. A number of proposals for im-
      proving both the democratic functioning and efficiency
      of bureaucratic policymaking are presented.

            2. The President and the Bureaucracy

728. Aberbach, Joel D., and Bert A. Rockman. "Clashing Be-
      liefs within the Executive Branch: The Nixon Admin-
      istration Bureaucracy." AMERICAN POLITICAL SCIENCE
      REVIEW, 70 (1976), 456-68.

      Report on their interviews with 126 high federal ad-
      ministrators about their political beliefs. The career
      bureaucracy contained few Republicans and was ideolog-
      ically opposed to many of the Nixon social proposals.
      Because of the composition of the civil service, pres-
      idential control of the executive branch remains prob-
      lematic.

729. Arnold, Peri. "The 'Great Engineer' as Administrator:
      Herbert Hoover and Modern Bureaucracy." REVIEW OF
      POLITICS, 42 (1980), 329-48.

      On President Hoover as a modern manager.

730. Berkowitz, E.D., and K. McQuaid. "Bureaucrats as 'Soc-
      ial Engineers:' Federal Welfare Programs in Herbert
      Hoover's America." AMERICAN JOURNAL OF ECONOMICS AND
      SOCIOLOGY, 39 (1980), 321-36.

Compare the welfare policy of Hoover and Roosevelt and
find that there was considerable discontinuity between
the two administrations. Hoover stressed efficiency
values in administration, while Roosevelt emphasized the
public role in welfare services.

731. Bonafede, Dom. "The Federal Bureaucracy: An Inviting
      Target." NATIONAL JOURNAL, 7 (1975), 1308.

      On the delight presidents take in criticizing the bur-
      eaucracy.

732. Brower, Brock. "Bureaucrats Redux." HARPER'S, 254
      (March, 1977), 25-26.

      Finds that the Carter administration is full of famil-
      iar faces.

733. Brown, David S. "Reforming the Bureaucracy: Some Sug-
      gestions for the New President." PUBLIC ADMINISTRA-
      TION REVIEW, 37 (1977), 163-70

      Recommends to President Carter a seven-point program
      for making good on his pledge to renew American admin-
      istration. And reform will be difficult; if it is to
      succeed, the bureaucrats will have to be involved.

734. Brown, Roger G. "Party and Bureaucracy: From Kennedy
      to Reagan." POLITICAL SCIENCE QUARTERLY, 97 (1982),
      279-94.

      Examines the impact of presidential actions on the re-
      lationship of party and bureaucracy. In the most recent
      administrations, presidential appointments have not been
      used to bolster the party organization. The president
      tends to manage the bureaucracy without too much help
      from the party.

735. "The Bureaucracy Explosion: Key Campaign Issue." U.S.
      NEWS AND WORLD REPORT, 81 (August 16, 1976), 22-26.

      Ford and Carter promise to do something about the bur-
      eaucracy.

736. "Bureaucracy: Master or Servant?" TIME, 62 (July 20,
      1953), 14.

      On Eisenhower's struggle to control the civil service.

737. "Bureaucratic Maw." NEWSWEEK, 97 (January 26, 1981),
      41-42.

      The continuing problems of presidential control over
      the bureaucracy.

738. "The Bureaucrats Forbear." NATION, 223 (1976), 547-48.

      A report on the early skirmishing between Carter and
      the civil service.

739. Clark, Timothy. "Putting It to the Bureaucrats." NA-
      TIONAL JOURNAL, 11 (1979), 873.

      Concerning Carter's sometimes strained relations with
      the civil service.

740. Cloherty, Jack, and Bob Owens. "Carter's Having a Rough
      Time with the Bureaucrats." INSIDER'S CHRONICLE, 222
      (November 24, 1977), 13.

      Problems with the Carter reforms of administration.

741. "Dug-In Bureaucrats Await New President." U.S. NEWS
      AND WORLD REPORT, 65 (December 30, 1968), 40-41.

      Nixon faces problems with the civil service.

742. "Dug-In Bureaucrats--A Roadblock to Carter." U.S. NEWS
      AND WORLD REPORT, 82 (January 10, 1977), 21-22.

      Now it is Carter's turn; see Item 741.

743. "The Eisenhower Administration Moves to Cut the Bureau-
      cracy Down to Size." SATURDAY EVENING POST, 227
      (September 4, 1954), 12.

744. Garand, James C., and Donald H. Gross. "Toward a Theory
      of Bureaucratic Compliance with Presidential Direc-
      tives." PRESIDENTIAL STUDIES QUARTERLY, 12 (1982)
      195-207.

      Discuss the variations in the degree to which differ-
      ent bureaus comply with presidential orders. Six sets
      of variables are derived from the literature. From
      this, a theory of compliance is constructed. The goals,
      environment, and contextual system of a bureau will de-
      termine a bureau's decision rules about compliance.

745. Gest, Ted. "Carter's New Tactics to Trim Bureaucracy."
      U.S. NEW AND WORLD REPORT, 86 (May 21, 1979), 82.

746. Gest, Ted. "Why Trimming Bureaucracy is No Easy Task."
      U.S. NEWS AND WORLD REPORT, 89 (December 29, 1980), 62.

      About Carter's difficulties in changing bureaucracy.

747. "Government Bureaucracy: Too Snarled to Untangle?" SEN-
      IOR SCHOLASTIC, 109 (May 19, 1977), 6-8, 34.

      On Carter's reorganization plans.

748. Greenfield, Meg. "Reagan versus the Bureaucracies."
      NEWSWEEK, 96 (December 15, 1980), 112.

      A new president takes on an entrenched and fragmented
      bureaucracy.

749. Halperin, Morton H. "The Presidency and Its Interaction
      with the Culture of Bureaucracy." THE SYSTEM: FIVE
      BRANCHES OF AMERICAN GOVERNMENT. Edited by Charles
      Peters and James Fallows. New York: Praeger, 1976.

      Examines the presidential-bureaucratic conflict "that
      pervades all stages of the policy process from the shap-
      ing of the initial agenda through decision-making and
      legislation to details of implementation." Presidents
      are never assured of having their way in any policy area.
      Part of the conflict arises from the dedication of the

officials to the "essence" of their organization--the
bureaucrat's understanding of what the agency should be
involved in.

750. Heclo, Hugh. "Political Executives and the Washington
      Bureaucracy." POLITICAL SCIENCE QUARTERLY, 92 (1977),
      395-424.

      Describes the relationships between political appoint-
      ees and the permanent civil servants. Both come to a
      potentially tense situation with their own strengths and
      weaknesses. The appointees will have to win the support
      of the bureaucrats, but even with that support it is not
      certain that much can be accomplished.

751. Henry, Laurin. "The Presidency, Executive Staffing, and
      the Federal Bureaucracy." THE PRESIDENCY. Edited by
      Aaron Wildavsky. Boston; Little, Brown, 1969.

      Finds that presidents are exerting more influence in
      the appointment of top federal executives. Active con-
      trol of political appointees by the White House staff
      will become more important in presidential affairs.

752. Jones, Rochelle, and Peter Woll. "Carter vs. the Bureau-
      crats: The Interest Vested in Chaos." NATION, 224
      (1977), 402-04.

      Predict that Carter will not be able to shake up the
      bureaucracy. The congressional-bureaucratic alliance
      is highly resistant to change.

753. Kleinschrod, Walter. "Bureaucracy as an Issue." ADMIN-
      ISTRATIVE MANAGEMENT, 33 (April, 1972), 23.

      On the 1972 presidential campaign.

754. Lacy, Alex B. "The White House Staff Bureaucracy."
      TRANS-ACTION, 6 (January, 1968), 50-56.

      Explores the impact of an extended staff on the pres-
      idency. In general, the staff helps the president to

exert his personality as fully as possible. Each president has had a different White House staff arrangement
and has used the people in a different way.

755. Marshall, Eliot. "Efficiency Expert: Carter's Plan to
      Shake Up the Bureaucracy." NEW REPUBLIC, 175 (August
      21, 1976), 15-17.

      On Carter's promise to use zero-base budgeting.

756. Martin, David L. "Presidential Attitudes toward the
      Bureaucracy: The White House Tapes." BUREAUCRAT, 4
      (1975), 223-24.

      Some of Nixon's candid comments on bureaucrats.

757. Milakovich, Michael E. "Bureaucratic Politics in a Year
      of Transition." MIDWEST REVIEW OF PUBLIC ADMINISTRA-
      TION, 11 (1977), 157-59.

      An early assessment of the Carter administration.

758. Murray, Lawrence L. "Bureaucracy and Bipartisanship in
      Taxation: The Mellon Plan Revisted." BUSINESS HISTORY
      REVIEW, 52 (1978), 220-25.

      Claims that the federal tax policy in the 1920s was
      largely the product of a series of bureaucratic decisions
      and not of conservative Republican politics.

759. Nathan, Richard P. "The President and the Bureaucracy
      in Domestic Affairs." THE FUTURE OF THE AMERICAN PRES-
      IDENCY. Edited by Charles Dunn. Morristown, N.J.:
      General Learning Press, 1975.

      Reviews the experiences of the Nixon administration for
      clues about the ways of controlling bureaucracy. Among
      the strategies employed were the New Federalism, the
      creation of a counterbureaucracy, and the emphasis on
      management. An "administrative presidency" was planned
      for Nixon's second term, until events were overtaken by
      Watergate.

760. Neustadt, Richard E. "Politicians and Bureaucrats."
         THE CONGRESS AND AMERICA'S FUTURE. Edited by David
         Truman. Englewood Cliffs, N.J.: Prentice-Hall, 1965.

         Claims that the president and Congress spend too much
         time fighting each other for the control of the national
         government. They should recognize, as politicians, that
         they have a common cause in attacking the real basis of
         many of their problems--the bureaucracy.

761. "New Move to Tame the Bureaucracy." U.S. NEWS AND WORLD
         REPORT, 80 (May 17, 1976), 39.

         Gerald Ford takes on the bureaucracy.

762. "Nixon vs. the Veteran Bureaucrats." BUSINESS WEEK,
         (August 1, 1970), 31.

         On the tension between the political appointees and
         the career civil servants.

763. Patterson, Bradley H. "The White House Staff: The Bash-
         ful Bureaucracy." BUREAUCRAT, 7 (Spring, 1978), 81-84.

         Discusses the dilemma of the president's staff. The
         members must make their leader look good, but do it anon-
         ymously. The White House staff is made up of a collec-
         tion of minibureaucracies, each of which is resentful
         of any endruns.

764. Pemberton, William E. BUREAUCRATIC POLITICS: EXECUTIVE
         REORGANIZATION DURING THE TRUMAN ADMINISTRATION. Col-
         umbia: University of Missouri Press, 1979. 262 pp.

         Describes the progress of the Truman executive reorgan-
         ization program. That program, which drew many of its
         recommendations from the Hoover Commission, was a suc-
         cessful move in strengthening the executive branch.

765. "Pruning Bureaucracy." ENGINEERING NEWS-RECORD, (July
         7, 1977), 13.

         On Carter's proposed reduction in water projects.

766. Randall, Ronald. "Presidential Power versus Bureaucratic
      Intransigence: The Influence of the Nixon Administra-
      tion on Welfare Policy." AMERICAN POLITICAL SCIENCE
      REVIEW, 73 (1979), 795-810.

      Examines the popular idea that presidents are too weak
      to control the bureaucracy. The Nixon administration
      was able to effect changes in policies concerning Aid
      to Families with Dependent Children, despite the oppo-
      sition of the bureaucracy. Analysis reveals that a pres-
      ident has management tools, like a reorganization, which
      can influence bureaucratic behavior.

767. Rourke, Francis E. "Grappling with the Bureaucracy."
      POLITICS AND THE OVAL OFFICE: TOWARDS PRESIDENTIAL
      GOVERNANCE. Edited by Arnold Meltsner. San Francis-
      co: Institute for Contemporary Studies, 1981.

      Suggests ways for the president to exert control over
      the executive branch. It is far from a hopeless task
      since "controlling the bureaucracy may be less difficult
      than it has been in the recent past."

768. Sidey, Hugh. "Tackling the Bumbling Bureaucracy." TIME,
      105 (June 9, 1975), 14.

      Gerald Ford has widespread public support for an as-
      sault on the federal bureaucracy.

769. Singer, James. "Changing of the Guard: Reagan's Chance
      to Remold the Senior Bureaucracy." NATIONAL JOURNAL,
      12 (1980), 2028-31.

      On the future of the Civil Service Reform Act of 1978
      under the Reagan administration.

770. Somers, Herman M. "The Federal Bureaucracy and the
      Change of Administration." AMERICAN POLITICAL SCIENCE
      REVIEW, 48 (1954), 131-51.

      Examines the impact of the change of party leadership
      in 1953. The results indicate that there is a need for
      a true "career" system to make transitions easier.

771. Stanfield, Rochelle. "Bureaucrat Can't Count on His Old
      Allies." NATIONAL JOURNAL, 13 (1981), 525-27.

      On the new rules of the game brought about by the bud-
      get cuts of the Reagan administration.

772. "What the Candidates Say on Bureaucracy." ADMINISTRA-
      TIVE MANAGEMENT, 33 (October, 1972), 18-20.

      Nixon and McGovern discuss how they would reform the
      federal government.

773. Woll, Peter, and Rochelle Jones. "Against One-Man Rule:
      Bureaucratic Defense in Depth." NATION, 217 (1973),
      229-32.

      Believe that the bureaucracy was valuable check on the
      power plays of President Nixon. It was a "vital although
      little noticed safeguard of the democratic system."

774. Woll, Peter, and Rochelle Jones. "The Bureaucracy as a
      Check upon the President." BUREAUCRAT, 3 (1974), 8-20.

      Argue that the bureaucracy should retain as much inde-
      pendence as Congress and the president so that it can
      act fully in the system of checks and balances. Pres-
      idents are often deluded by the belief that they must
      indeed be the "chief administrator."

                 3. Congress and the Bureaucracy

775. Aberbach, Joel D., and Bert Rockman. "Bureaucrats and
      Clientele Groups: A View from Capitol Hill." AMERICAN
      JOURNAL OF POLITICAL SCIENCE, 22 (1978), 818-32.

      Find that House members think that ties between the
      agencies and interest groups are desirable although
      they could become too close. It is not likely that Con-
      gress will act to insulate the bureaus from the groups
      in any serious way.

776. Arieff, Irwin B. "The New Bureaucracy: Growing Staff
      System on Hill Forcing Changes in Congress." CONGRES-
      SIONAL QUARTERLY WEEKLY REPORTS, 37 (1979), 2631-46.

      On the growth and power of congressional staffs.

777. Arnold, R. Douglas. CONGRESS AND BUREAUCRACY: A THEORY
      OF INFLUENCE. New Haven, Conn.: Yale University Press,
      1979. 235 pp.

      Attempts to identify the extent to which members of
      Congress influence the bureaucracy in the making of al-
      locative decisions on federal expenditures. Do certain
      parts of the country benefit more than others? Bureau-
      crats appear to allocate benefits at their disposal in
      a strategic manner in an effort to maintain or expand
      their supporting coalition. Congress and the bureaus
      have developed a mutually advantageous system. The evi-
      dence is relevant to a larger theory of administrative
      responsiveness to congressional influence.

778. "Bureaucrats for the Last Roundup." SATURDAY EVENING
      POST, 215 (March 13, 1943), 215.

      Congress plans to "ride herd" on the bureaucracy.

779. Calvert, Randall, and Barry R. Weingast. "Runaway Bur-
      eaucracy and Congressional Oversight: Why Reforms
      Fail." POLICY STUDIES REVIEW, 1 (1981), 557-64.

      Look at the Federal Trade Commission during the 1970s
      to illuminate the weaknesses of attempts at legislative
      control. The bureaucracy has plenty of resources and is
      involved in making policy because Congress has neither
      the time nor the desire to impose effective oversight.
      Congress must have the will to act decisively.

780. "Capitol Hill's Growing Army of Bureaucrats." U.S. NEWS
      AND WORLD REPORT, 87 (December 24, 1979), 52-55.

      On congressional staffs.

781. "Congress Frets about Its Own Bureaucracy." U.S. NEWS
      AND WORLD REPORT, 84 (May 15, 1978), 21-22.

      On congressional staffs.

782. Coston, Dean W. "Bureaucratic Reactions to Congression-
      al Pressures." BUREAUCRAT, 2 (1973), 269-77.

      Concludes that "the bureaucratic response to congres-
      sional pressure depends on who is pressuring and for
      what." A matrix identifying the many facets of congres-
      sional pressure on the bureaucracy is presented.

783. Dellums, Ronald. "Bureaucratic Accountability Act."
      CONGRESSIONAL RECORD, 119 (1973), 10044-45.

      Asks Congress to crack down on "government lawless-
      ness.

784. "Easy Chairs for Bureaucrats." U.S. NEWS AND WORLD RE-
      PORT, 30 (May 4, 1951), 26.

      Congress intends to get tough with requests for plush
      offices from civil servants.

785. Fiorina, Morris P. "The Case of the Vanishing Margin-
      als: The Bureaucracy Did It." AMERICAN POLITICAL SCI-
      ENCE REVIEW, 71 (1977), 177-81.

      Explains the decline in competition in congressional
      elections. Incumbent members are able to provide con-
      stituent service by cooperating with the bureaucrats.

786. Fiorina, Morris P. "Congressional Control of the Bur-
      eaucracy: A Mismatch of Incentives and Capabilities."
      CONGRESS RECONSIDERED, 2nd. ed. Edited by Lawrence
      Dodd and Bruce Oppenheimer. Washington, D.C.: Wash-
      ington, D.C.: Congressional Quarterly Press, 1981.

      Argues that Congress has the power but not the incen-
      tive for coordinated control of the federal bureaucracy.
      It is unlikely to embrace any major reforms to assert

such control. If Congress is to achieve more control,
the electoral fate of its members will have to depend
on the performance of government.

787. Freeman, J. Lieper. "The Bureaucracy in Pressure Pol-
      itics." ANNALS OF THE AMERICAN ACADEMY OF POLITICAL
      AND SOCIAL SCIENCE, 319 (1958), 10-19.

      Views agencies as pressure groups which attempt to
      promote or oppose legislative policies. Bureaus can
      mobilize the support of a chief executive, employees,
      clients, and interest groups to lobby for or against
      a legislative proposal. The bureaus are also adept at
      utilizing general publicity activities.

788. Gilbert, Charles E., and Max M. Kampelman. "Legislative
      Control of the Bureaucracy." ANNALS OF THE AMERICAN
      ACADEMY OF POLITICAL AND SOCIAL SCIENCE, 292 (1954),
      76-87.

      Discuss the difficulty of legislative oversight by a
      fragmented Congress.

789. Kaiser, Fred M. "Congress Oversees the Bureaucracy."
      BUREAUCRAT, 5 (1976), 357-66.

      Review essay on Ogul, *Congress Oversees the Bureau-
      cracy*, Item 792.

790. Kampelman, Max M. "The Legislative Bureaucracy: Its Re-
      sponse to Political Change." JOURNAL OF POLITICS, 16
      (1954), 539-50.

      Discusses the growth of staff aid for members of Con-
      gress.

791. Lees, J.D. "Legislative Review and Bureaucratic Respon-
      sibility: The Impact of Fiscal Oversight by Congress
      on the American Federal Administration." PUBLIC ADMIN-
      ISTRATION, 45 (1967), 369-86.

      Studies the behavior of committees involved with bud-
      geting.

792. Ogul, Morris S. CONGRESS OVERSEES THE BUREAUCRACY:
      STUDIES IN LEGISLATIVE SUPERVISION. Pittsburgh: Uni-
      versity of Pittsburgh Press, 1976. 237 pp.

      Uses interview data and case studies to examine the
      ways in which Congress oversees the administration. Over-
      sight includes all behavior of legislators or their staffs
      which have an impact on bureaucratic actions. While some
      specific oversight functions do exist, most of the activ-
      ity occurs in a rather sporadic fashion. In a number of
      ways, administrators are alerted to real or potential
      problems and can make the appropriate adjustments in
      order to meet congressional expectations.

793. O'Mahoney, Joseph. "Congress Will Seek to Put a Curb on
      Growing Federal Bureaucracy." CONGRESSIONAL DIGEST,
      22 (1943), 3-5.

      A senator describes the movement afoot in Congress to
      cut back on the size of government while reducing the
      exercise of executive discretion.

794. Reed, Leonard. "The Bureaucracy: The Cleverest Lobby of
      Them All." WASHINGTON MONTHLY, 10 (April, 1978), 49-
      54.

      Contends that the bureaucrats influence legislation,
      despite the desire of the president. The bureaus have
      built-in access to Congress through their relations with
      the various subcommittees. Alliances with the special
      interests also help.

795. Ripley, Randall, and Grace Franklin. CONGRESS, THE BUR-
      EAUCRACY, AND PUBLIC POLICY. Homewood, Ill.: Dorsey,
      1976. 193. Revised edition, 1980. 250 pp.

      Examine the patterns of interaction between Congress
      and the bureaucracy in policy formulation and legitima-
      tion stages. Especially important are the subgovernments
      which make most of the routine decisions in the particu-
      lar substantive policy field. Differences are found de-
      pending upon whether the policy is distributive, regula-
      tory, redistributive, or related to foreign policy. The
      process is inherently conservative and favorable to es-
      tablished interests.

796. Sigel, Leon V. "Official Secrecy and Informal Commun-
      ication in Congressional-Bureaucratic Relations."
      POLITICAL SCIENCE QUARTERLY, 90 (1975), 71-92.

      Describes how administrators manipulate the information
      given to Congress. Outside of official channels, the
      bureaucrats may use the techniques of "bootlegging,"
      informal disclosures to selected members of Congress,
      or the news "leak." Because of such strategic uses
      of information, congressional oversight is weakened.

797. Tax Foundation, Inc. THE LEGISLATIVE BRANCH: THE NEXT
      BILLION DOLLAR BUREAUCRACY. New York: Tax Foundation,
      1976. 27 pp.

      On congressional staffs.

798. Wyden, Peter. "The Man Who Frightens Bureaucrats."
      SATURDAY EVENING POST, 231 (January 31, 1959), 27,
      87-89.

      On the battles with the bureaucracy by Congressman
      Rooney.

                    4. Law and the Lawyers

799. Abramowitz, Michael E. "Bureaucrats and Lawyers--Legal
      Myths and Realities." BUREAUCRAT, 2 (1973), 256-68.

      Looks at the role of lawyers in the policy process,
      especially those of the "why-you-can't" variety. What-
      ever their nature, however, lawyers should not be per-
      mitted to have the final say in making policy.

800. Baldwin, Raymond, and Livingston Hall. "Using Govern-
      ment Lawyers to Animate Bureaucracy." YALE LAW RE-
      VIEW, 63 (1953), 197-204.

      Believe that lawyers can be the "unspoiled citizens
      in government," thus promoting the public interest
      and reminding officials of their duties.

801. Cortner, Richard C. THE BUREAUCRACY IN COURT: COMMEN-
     TARIES AND CASE STUDIES IN ADMINISTRATIVE LAW. Port
     Washington, N.Y.: Kennikat, 1982. 240 pp.

     Discusses the basic issues of administrative law and
     the relationship of the judiciary to administration.
     Six case studies of federal agencies provide the back-
     ground material for a review of the principles of Amer-
     ican administrative law.

802. Dimock, Marshall E. "Administrative Law and Bureaucracy:
     ANNALS OF THE AMERICAN ACADEMY OF POLITICAL AND SOCIAL
     SCIENCE, 292 (1954), 57-64.

     Describes the effects of administrative law on the ef-
     ficiency of bureaucracy.

803. Farber, Mindy. "Tales from the Public Sector: Diary of
     a Bureaucrat." POLICY REVIEW, 22 (Fall, 1982), 167-
     75.

     A lawyer becomes rapidly disenchanted with the waste
     and game-playing in a federal department.

804. Horowitz, Donald L. "The Courts as Monitors of the Bur-
     eaucracy." MAKING BUREAUCRACIES WORK. Edited by Carol
     H. Weiss and Allen H. Barton. Beverly Hills, Cal.:
     Sage, 1980.

     Considers administrative law as a check on bureaucracy.
     Whatever its strengths, the judicial process is not well
     suited for ensuring positive changes.

805. Katzmann, Robert A. "Judicial Intervention and Organ-
     ization Theory: Changing Bureaucratic Behavior and
     Policy." YALE LAW JOURNAL, 89 (1980), 513-37.

     Argues that if judges are going to get involved in
     the administrative process, as they persist in doing,
     then they should know something about modern administra-
     tive theory.

806. Mashaw, Jerry L. "Reforming the Bureaucracy: The Admin-
         istrative Conference Technique." ADMINISTRATIVE LAW
         REVIEW, 26 (1974), 261-68.

         Describes the Administrative Conference of the United
         States as a "moral tutor to the federal administrative
         process."

807. Plumlee, John P. "Lawyers as Bureaucrats: The Impact
         of Legal Training in the Higher Civil Service." PUB-
         LIC ADMINISTRATION REVIEW, 41 (1981) 220-28.

         Compares higher civil servants in terms of their legal
         training to test whether lawyers are dominating govern-
         ment policy making. Lawyers do not outnumber officials
         with different backgrounds. Nor does legal training
         appear to make much difference in attitudes.

808. Rives, Richard T. "Bureaucracy." ALABAMA LAWYER, 5
         (1944), 420-24.

         Feels that basic constitutional safeguards are still
         effective in controlling bureaucracy.

809. Stillman, Richard H. "The Bureaucracy Problem at DOJ."
         PUBLIC ADMINISTRATION REVIEW, 36 (1976), 429-39.

         Discusses management problems within the Department
         of Justice. DOJ is seen as a "decaying bureaucracy."
         Several areas needing reform are mentioned.

810. Tushnet, Mark. "Should Courts Govern? The Law of Public
         Bureaucracy." GOVERNING THROUGH COURTS. Edited by
         Richard Gambitta, Marilynn May, and James Foster. Bev-
         erly Hills, Cal.: Sage, 1981.

         Examines the policy implications of the political the-
         ory espoused by the judges. The U.S. Supreme Court's
         view of public administration as a neutral tool, staffed
         by thoroughly impartial professionals, is used as an il-
         lustration. The courts may not have a completely real-
         istic picture of the realities of American government.

5. The Federal Civil Service

811. Baum, Bernard H. DECENTRALIZATION OF AUTHORITY IN A
     BUREAUCRACY. Englewood Cliffs, N.J.: Prentice-Hall,
     1961. 172 pp.

     Investigates the differences between formal norms and
     actual bureaucratic behavior in the U.S. Civil Service
     Commission. Analysis is made of position-classification
     actions within a system of decentralized authority. The
     problem of decentralization is emphasized.

812. Bendix, Reinhard. "Who Are the Government Bureaucrats?"
     STUDIES IN LEADERSHIP. Edited by Alvin Gouldner.
     New York: Russell and Russell, 1965.

     Examines the characteristics of American public em-
     ployees.

813. Berkowitz, Edward. "Mary E. Switzer: The Entrepreneur
     within the Federal Bureaucracy." AMERICAN JOURNAL OF
     ECONOMICS AND SOCIOLOGY, 39 (1980), 79-81.

     Sketches the career of a long-time federal official
     in the field of social welfare.

814. Brown, David S. "Survey Finds Federal Bureaucracy Too
     Slow." PUBLIC ADMINISTRATION TIMES, 4 (January 15,
     1981), 12.

     Reports on a poll of popular attitudes about the fed-
     eral government. The problem mentioned by the largest
     number of people was that the bureaucracy was slow, pon-
     derous, and incapable of taking immediate action.

815. "Bureaucrats: The Real Power?" U.S. NEWS AND WORLD RE-
     PORT, 82 (May 9, 1977), 59-60.

     A look at the role of the civil service.

816. "Bureaucrats under Fire." NATIONAL JOURNAL, 10 (1978),
      1540-41.

      It is not an easy time to be a federal employee, what
      with tax revolts, civil service reform, and general pub-
      lic hostility in the air.

817. Burnham, Philip. "Bureaucracy and Patronage." COMMON-
      WEAL, 21 (1933), 532-34.

      Considers the Republican fear that the New Deal bureau-
      cracy is being filled by Democrats

818. "As Business Leaders Join the Bureaucracy." U.S. NEWS
      AND WORLD REPORT, 91 (September 28, 1981), 49-50.

      On business executives in the Reagan administration.

819. Clapper, Raymond. "Banker or Bureaucrat?" REVIEW OF
      REVIEWS, 92 (July, 1935), 20-25.

      On Marriner Eccles, head of the Federal Reserve system.

820. Crenson, Matthew A. THE FEDERAL MACHINE: BEGINNINGS OF
      BUREAUCRACY IN JACKSONIAN AMERICA. Baltimore: Johns
      Hopkins Press, 1975. 186 pp.

      Wants to "determine when, how, and why bureaucratic
      forms of organization were superimposed upon the busi-
      ness of the national government." It is argued that the
      administrative innovations by the officials of the Jack-
      son administration marked the real birth of bureaucracy
      in the federal government. Bureaucratization was a re-
      sponse to the decline in the traditional authority of
      public institutions. The changes in government were in
      keeping with a broader transformation of American social
      institutions.

821. Damon, A.L. "Federal Bureaucracy." AMERICAN HERITAGE,
      25 (August, 1974), 65-68.

      On the growth of federal administration.

822. De Lorme, Ronald. "Westward the Bureaucrat: Government Officials on the Washington and Oregon Frontier." ARIZONA AND THE WEST, 22 (1980), 223-36.

Describes the deficiencies of administration in the territories of the Pacific Northwest. The movement for statehood may have been precipitated by local discontent with the caliber of federal officials.

823. Demkovich, Linda. "The Rewards and Frustrations of the Federal Bureaucracy." NATIONAL JOURNAL, 11 (1979), 998-1000.

An undersecretary of Health, Education and Welfare reflects on two years of service with the federal government.

824. Eccles, J.R. THE HATCH ACT AND THE AMERICAN BUREAUCRACY. New York: Vantage Press, 1981. 318 pp.

Traces the factors leading to the passage of the Hatch Act in 1939. This legislation is designed to limit the political participation of federal employees. Originally a response to the expansion of government during the New Deal, the law is no longer appropriate. Civil servants, as citizens, should have the full right of political particpation.

825. Engh, Keith. "The Bureaucrats Return to Business." BUSINESS MANAGEMENT, 35 (February, 1969), 16-21, 63-65.

President Johnson's appointees return to the private sector.

826. "Fair Deal Bureaucrats Do Meet Some of the Strangest People!" SATURDAY EVENING POST, 224 (November 3, 1951), 12.

State Department employees are probably not communists. But they are easily duped.

827. "For Businessmen in the Bureaucracy, Life Is No Bed of of Roses." U.S NEWS AND WORLD REPORT, 85 (September 25, 1978), 56-58.

828. Gawthorp, Louis C. BUREAUCRATIC BEHAVIOR IN THE EXECU-
      TIVE BRANCH: AN ANALYSIS OF ORGANIZATIONAL CHANGE.
      New York: Free Press, 1969. 276 pp.

      Presents a model of bureaucratic change as a function
      of the external environment and internal strains. The
      ways in which members of the federal administration re-
      solve conflicts, develop a sense of loyalty, and respond
      to the forces of change are discussed. Comparisons in
      each of these areas are made with private organizations.
      Hypotheses about bureaucratic responses to innovation
      are generated from a description of decision making.

829. Gourley, Jay. "Bureaucrat's Country Club." WASHINGTON
      MONTHLY, 8 (May, 1976), 45-47.

      On the Federal Executive Institute.

830. Grandjean, Burke D. "History and Career in a Bureaucrat-
      ic Labor Market." AMERICAN JOURNAL OF SOCIOLOGY, 86
      (1981), 1057-92.

      Determines the factors which account for the career
      development of federal civil servants. After consid-
      ering individual, organizational, and historical ef-
      fects, it is concluded that careers seem to depend upon
      achieved individual attributes.

831. "The Great American Bureaucratic Junketing Machine."
      U.S. NEWS AND WORLD REPORT, 85 (December 18, 1978),
      56-60.

      Military and civilian officials are always on the go.

832. "The Great American Bureaucratic 'Perks' Machine." U.S.
      NEWS AND WORLD REPORT, 87 (December 17, 1979), 34-40.

      On the generous fringe benefits of federal personnel.

833. Gryski, Gerald, and Allen R. DeCotiis. "Length of Ser-
      vice as an Influence on Federal Bureaucratic Attitudes
      and Behavior." JOURNAL OF POLITICAL SCIENCE, 9 (1981),
      17-19.

Find some support for the proposition that length of
service in government affects personal attitudes.

834. Harvey, H. "Our Billion-Dollar Bureaucracy Overseas."
      READER'S DIGEST, 62 (April, 1953), 30-34.

      Deplores the large number of federal employees working
      in foreign countries.

835. Haveman, Joel. "The Ballooning of Bureaucracy." NATION-
      AL JOURNAL, 9 (1977), 95.

      On the size of the federal executive branch.

836. Helden, Karl. MR. BUREAUCRAT. New York: Greenwich
      Book Publishers, 1957. 188 pp.

      Describes one man's experiences as a New Deal official.
      Included are several letters of citizens to federal agen-
      cies during the Great Depression.

837. Kollmorgan, Walter M. "Kollmorgan as a Bureaucrat."
      ANNALS OF THE ASSOCIATION OF AMERICAN GEOGRAPHERS,
      69 (1979), 77-89.

      The reflections of a Department of Agriculture employee
      from 1938 to 1945.

838. Landes, Ruth. "What about This Bureaucracy?" NATION,
      161 (1945), 365-66.

      Contends that federal employees are qualified, but
      they suffer from mismanagement.

839. Lewis, Eugene. PUBLIC ENTREPRENEURSHIP: TOWARD A THEORY
      OF BUREAUCRATIC POLITICAL POWER. Bloomington: Indiana
      University Press, 1980. 274 pp.

      Examines the careers of Hyman Rickover, J. Edgar Hoover
      and Robert Moses to show how bureaucracies are shaped by
      the personalities of their most important members.

840. Lynn, Naomi B., and Richard Vaden. "Bureaucratic Re-
        sponse to Civil Service Reform." PUBLIC ADMINISTRA-
        TION REVIEW, 39 (1979), 333-43.

        Investigate the attitudes of civil servants toward the
        Civil Service Reform Act of 1978. There does not seem
        to have been a great deal of support for the reform among
        senior officials. At the same time, this lack of support
        is not enough to doom the changes.

841. McGregor, Eugene B. "Politics and the Career Mobility
        of Bureaucrats." AMERICAN POLITICAL SCIENCE REVIEW,
        68 (1974), 18-26.

        Measures the career mobility of two groups of federal
        officials. It is suggested that career mobility increas-
        es presidential control over bureaucracy. The career of
        most senior federal officials is limited to a single
        bureau which probably contributes to agency autonomy.

842. McLucas, John L. "Requiem for a Bureaucrat." AVIATION
        WEEK AND SPACE TECHNOLOGY, 106 (April 25, 1977), 23.

        A retiring bureaucrat reflects on life in the civil
        service.

843. Marvick, Dwaine. CAREER PERSPECTIVES IN A BUREAUCRATIC
        SETTING. Ann Arbor: University of Michigan Press,
        1954. 150 pp.

        A study of the career patterns of federal civil ser-
        vants.

844. Methuin, Eugene H. "Why Can't Do-Nothing Bureaucrats
        Be Fired?" READER'S DIGEST, 111 (November, 1977),
        119-22.

        Advocates civil service reform so that federal employ-
        ees can be terminated without so much red tape.

845. Michelson, Stephan. "The Working Bureaucrat and the Non-
        working Bureaucracy." AMERICAN BEHAVIORAL SCIENTIST,
        22 (1979), 585-608.

Argues that public programs can fail, regardless of
the quality and intentions of the employees, because
of a lack of theoretical concepts about what can be
accomplished. Top management may be most responsible
for bureaucratic malfunctioning.

846. Murphy, Thomas P. "Political Executive Roles, Policy-
making and Interface with the Career Bureaucracy."
BUREAUCRAT, 6 (Summer, 1977), 96-127.

Reports on a workshop held at the Federal Executive
Institute with top political appointees in the federal
government. The critical role of the assistant secretary is emphasized.

847. Murphy, Thomas P., Donald E. Neuchterlein, and Ronald
J. Stupak. INSIDE THE BUREAUCRACY: THE VIEW FROM THE
ASSISTANT SECRETARY'S DESK. Boulder, Colo.: Westview,
1978. 218 pp.

Assess the position of the assistant secretary as an
extension of presidential power into the executive agencies. These political appointees are part of the creative interface with the career executives. From the
comments given at a symposium of political and career
officials, a portrait of the assistant secretary is constructed. Changes brought about by the administrative
style of the Carter administration are discussed.

848. "New Princes of Privilege are the Bureaucrats." SATUR-
DAY EVENING POST, 224 (October 6, 1951), 10.

Suggests that bureaucrats, as voters, have become a
crucial factor in presidential elections.

849. Ostrow, Ronald J. "Bell Figuring Out How to Outfox the
Bureaucrats." LOS ANGELES TIMES, (November 7, 1977),
Reprinted in PEOPLE AND PUBLIC ADMINISTRATION: CASE
STUDIES AND PERSPECTIVES. Edited by Phillip Present.
Pacific Palisades, Cal.: Palisades, 1979.

Describes how the relations of Attorney General Bell
with the permanent staff of the Justice Department have
gone.

850. Pyle, John W. "Bureaucracy and Politics." BUSINESS AND
      PUBLIC ADMINISTRATION STUDENT REVIEW, 11 (Fall, 1975),
      51-58.

      Defends the Hatch Act restrictions on the political
      participation of federal employees.

851. Ray, J.K. "The American Bureaucratic Establishment."
      INDIAN JOURNAL OF PUBLIC ADMINISTRATION, 21 (1975),
      231-46.

      Argues that the United States is dominated by an elite
      of high officials in government and business who influ-
      ence public policy directions.

852. Robey, Ralph. "Some Facts on Our Federal Bureaucracy."
      NEWSWEEK, 20 (December 21, 1942), 64.

      Rejects President Roosevelt's defense of the federal
      civil service.

853. Rosenbloom, David. "The Rise of 'Participatory Bureau-
      cracy' and the United States Federal Service." CHIN-
      ESE JOURNAL OF ADMINISTRATION, 24 (1975), 14-23.

      Takes an optimistic view of the chances for further
      democratization in American administration.

854. Sayre, Wallace S. "The Recruitment and Training of Bur-
      eaucrats in the United States." ANNALS OF THE AMERI-
      CAN ACADEMY OF POLITICAL AND SOCIAL SCIENCE, 292
      (1954), 39-44.

      Finds a number of weaknesses in the personnel practices
      of the American civil service.

855. Schmidt, Terry, and Terry Margerum. "Working for the
      Feds: A Primer for Would-Be Bureaucrats." MBA, 6
      (December, 1972), 6-8, 52.

      Discuss how to get a job in Washington, and what to
      do with it once you have it.

856. Sebris, Robert. "Bureaucracy and Labor Relations."
     CIVIL SERVICE JOURNAL, 19 (October-December, 1978),
     28-31.

     On labor-management relations in the federal service.

857. Sherwood, Frank P. "The Federal Executive Institute--
     Academy for the Bureaucracy." GOVERNMENT MANAGEMENT
     INTERNSHIPS AND EXECUTIVE DEVELOPMENT: EDUCATION FOR
     CHANGE. Edited by Thomas P. Murphy. Lexington, Mass.:
     Lexington Books, 1973.

     Describes the function of the Federal Executive In-
     stitute. Its most important goal may be the provision
     of future leadership.

858. Stafford, Samuel. "Federal Job Classification: How Much
     Rigidity Can the Bureaucracy Stand?" GOVERNMENT EXECU-
     TIVE, 4 (October, 1972), 19-23.

     On the controversy about a proposal to move to "factor
     ranking" in job classification.

859. Storing, Herbert. "Political Parties and the Bureaucra-
     cy." POLITICAL PARTIES USA. Edited by Robert Goldwin.
     Chicago: Rand McNally, 1964.

     Discusses the significance of the exclusion of partisan
     influences from the federal civil service.

860. Warner, W. Lloyd, and Paul D. Van Riper. "Image of the
     Bureaucrat." THE AMERICAN FEDERAL EXECUTIVE. By W.
     Lloyd Warner, Paul D. Van Riper, Norman H. Martin, and
     Orvis F. Collins. New Haven, Conn.: Yale University
     Press, 1963.

     Review research on business and government executives.
     America has become less caste-like, with recruitment of
     administrative leaders still taking place at the bottom
     of the ladder. Entry into the higher levels of govern-
     ment is not restricted by ascribed characteristics of the
     applicant.

861. "Washington's Bureaucrats: 'Real Rulers of America.'"
     U.S. NEWS AND WORLD REPORT, 77 (November 4, 1974),
     38-48.

     How administrators run the country.

862. Watson, Goodwin. "Bureaucracy in the Federal Govern-
     ment." JOURNAL OF SOCIAL ISSUES, 1 (December, 1945),
     14-31.

     Summarizes the reactions of social scientists to ser-
     vice in the federal government during WWII.

863. Wynia, Bob L. "Federal Bureaucrats' Attitudes toward
     a Democratic Ideology." PUBLIC ADMINISTRATION REVIEW,
     34 (1974), 156-62.

     Studies the attitudes of federal career bureaucrats
     toward certain democratic principles. Several factors
     explain variations in individual attitudes. Among other
     things, the "anti-democratic" attitude is related to the
     type of agency and to length of service. Defense agency
     personnel tend to be more "anti-democratic" than those
     involved in civilian programs.

864. Yessian, Mark R. "The Generalist Perspective in the HEW
     Bureaucracy: An Account from the Field." PUBLIC ADMIN-
     ISTRATION REVIEW, 40 (1980), 138-49.

     Presents a case study of decentralizing authority to
     generalists in HEW field offices. The strategies used
     by the generalists are described. The experiment was
     not an unqualified success.

                    6. Reforming the Bureaucracy

865. Balzano, Michael P. REORGANIZING THE FEDERAL BUREAUCRA-
     CY: THE RHETORIC AND THE REALITY. Washington, D.C:
     American Enterprise Institute for Public Policy Re-
     search, 1977. 43 pp.

     The former director of ACTION reflects on the diffi-
     cultry of changing the federal establishment.

866. Ban, Carolyn, Edie Goldenberg, and Tony Marzotto. "Con-
         trolling the U.S. Federal Bureaucracy: Will SES Make
         a Difference?" STRATEGIES IN ADMINISTRATIVE REFORM.
         Edited by Gerald E. Caiden and Heinrich Siedentopf.
         Lexington, Mass.: Lexington Books, 1982.

         Focus on the creation of the Senior Executive Service
         in the Civil Service Reform Act of 1978. The SES was
         expected to change the relationship between career ex-
         ecutives and political appointees. The implementation
         of the program has been impeded by several factors, in-
         cluding budgetary restraints and the attitudes of the
         executives themselves.

867. "The Battle over Bureaucracy." TIME, 111 (March 6, 1978),
         13-15.

         On the Carter reform proposals.

868. Bonafede, Dom, and Jonathan Cottin. "Nixon in Reorgan-
         ization Plan Seeks to Tighten Control of the Bureau-
         cracy." NATIONAL JOURNAL, 2 (1970), 62-66.

         On Nixon's restructuring of the federal system.

869. Bonafede, Dom. "Bureaucracy, Congress, and Interests
         See Threat in Nixon's Reorganization Plan." NATIONAL
         JOURNAL, 3 (1971), 977-86.

         On the coalition of groups which tend to oppose change
         in government.

870. Bonafede, Dom. "Winding Down the Bureaucracy." NATIONAL
         JOURNAL, 3 (1971), 977-86.

         Discusses efforts to reduce the size of the federal
         government.

871. Britan, Gerald. "Evaluating a Federal Experiment in
         Bureaucratic Reform." HUMAN ORGANIZATION, 38 (1979),
         319-24.

         See Item 299.

872. Britan, Gerald, and Michael Chibnek. "Bureaucracy and
     Innovation: An American Case." HIERARCHY AND SOCIETY:
     ANTRHOPOLOGICAL PERSPECTIVES ON BUREAUCRACY. Edited
     by Gerald Britan and Ronald Cohen. Philadelphia:
     Institute for the Study of Human Issues, 1980.

     Apply anthropological theory to an examination of the
     dynamics of the federal bureaucracy. The question under
     consideration is the resistance to change by groups with-
     in organizations.

873. "Bureaucracy Never Dies." FREEMAN, 5 (1954), 44-45.

     Is not fooled by the change of the Reconstruction Fin-
     ance Corporation into the Small Business Administration.
     It is still the same old bureaucracy.

874. Caiden, Gerald E. "Reform and the Revitalization of the
     American Bureaucracy." QUARTERLY JOURNAL OF ADMINIS-
     TRATION, 13 (1979), 243-58.

     Predicts great things from the reforms of the Carter
     administration. Proposition 13 in California is another
     healthy sign of change. We are on the verge of entering
     a new era of administrative revitalization.

875. Campbell, Alan K. "Civil Service Reform as a Remedy for
     Bureaucratic Ills." MAKING BUREAUCRACIES WORK. Edited
     by Carol H. Weiss and Allen H. Barton. Beverly Hills,
     Cal.: Sage, 1980.

     The first director of the Office of Personnel Manage-
     ment describes the events leading up to the Civil Ser-
     vice Reform Act of 1978 and the major elements of that
     reform effort.

876. "CED's Plan to Nourish the Top Bureaucrats." BUSINESS
     WEEK, (July 25, 1964), 70, 72, 77.

     The Committee for Economic Development makes public
     its recommendations for civil service reform. Among
     the proposals is the creation of a senior civil ser-
     vice.

877. Herring, E. Pendleton. "Social Forces and the Reorgan-
     ization of the Federal Bureaucracy." SOUTHWESTERN
     SOCIAL SCIENCE QUARTERLY, 15 (1934), 185-200.

     Although it might be desirable to reorganize federal
     bureaus according to their major functions, this is not
     likely to happen because the existing arrangement is de-
     pendent upon interest group support.

878. Hoyt, Kendall K. "Branch Bureaucracy Affords Main Chance
     for Federal Economy and Efficiency." ANNALIST, 49
     (1937), 727.

     Recommends the decentralization of the federal govern-
     ment.

879. May, Geoffrey. "Daydreams of a Bureaucrat." PUBLIC AD-
     MINISTRATION REVIEW, 5 (1945), 153-61.

     A federal official suggests some reforms.

880. Medina, William A. CHANGING BUREAUCRACIES: UNDERSTANDING
     THE ORGANIZATION BEFORE SELECTING THE APPROACH. New
     York: Marcel Dekker, 1982. 160 pp.

     Examines the responses of organizations to the strat-
     egies used by management to effect change. Specifically,
     three major reform efforts were designed to change the
     operation of the entire federal government. They were
     PPB, management-by-objectives, and executive development.
     Departments and agencies responded differently to these
     mandated managerial changes. In the context of force
     field theory, 22 factors affecting acceptance or rejec-
     tion of reforms are identified. These factors can be
     either driving or restraining forces and are not inher-
     ently one or the other.

881. Nelson, Michael. "A Short, Ironic History of American
     National Bureaucracy." JOURNAL OF POLITICS, 44 (1982),
     747-78.

     Looks at the history of American bureaucracy since 1775.
     At every stage, efforts to make the administrative branch

more responsive to political control has tended to have
the opposite effect. Ironically, then, the more politicians have fought for control, the more power they have
lost.

882. Rourke, Francis E., ed. REFORMING THE BUREAUCRACY. Washington, D.C.: Government Research Corporation, 1977.
45 pp. Second edition, 1978. 45 pp.

A collection of articles from the *National Journal*
assessing the results of recent attempts at reform.

7. Bureaucracy in Action

883. Berthong, Donald J. "Legacies of the Dawes Act: Bureaucrats and Land Thieves at the Cheyenne-Arapaho Agencies of Oklahoma." ARIZONA AND THE WEST, 21 (1979),
335-54.

Describes how land speculators and indifferent bureaucrats destroyed the economic base for two Indian tribes
in the early 1900s.

884. Briggs, Jean. "The President Proposes, the Bureaucrats
Dispose." FORBES, 121 (June, 1978), 55-57.

On conflicts within the Carter administration over the
making of energy policy.

885. Carter, Luther J. "The Energy Bureaucracy: The Pieces
Fall into Place." SCIENCE, 185 (1974), 44.

Infighting over energy policy.

886. Carter, Luther J. "Energy: Cannibalism in the Bureaucracy." SCIENCE, 186 (1974), 511.

And the beat goes on. See Item 885.

887. Cloud, Preston. "The Improbable Bureaucracy: The United
States Geological Survey, 1879-1979." PROCEEDINGS

OF THE AMERICAN PHILOSOPHICAL SOCIETY, 124 (1980),
155-67.

A centennial history of the USGS. Over the years, the
agency has remained creative and resourceful.

888. Colfer, Carold. "Bureaucrats, Budgets, and the BIA:
      Segmented Opposition in a Residential School." HUMAN
      ORGANIZATION, 34 (1975), 149-56.

      Examines the operation of a school under the jurisdic-
      tion of the Bureau of Indian Affairs. The school was
      segmented along professional and service lines.

889. Danziger, Edmund. INDIANS AND BUREAUCRATS: ADMINISTER-
      ING THE RESERVATION POLICY DURING THE CIVIL WAR. Urb-
      ana: University of Illinois Press, 1974. 240 pp.

      Describes in great detail the implementation of the re-
      servation policy for Indians during the Lincoln adminis-
      tration.

890. DeMontigny, Lionel H. "The Bureaucratic Game and a Pro-
      posed Indian Ploy." INDIAN HISTORIAN, 8 (Fall, 1975),
      25-30.

      Argues that Indians are at a disadvantage in their re-
      lations with the Bureau of Indian Affairs. They should
      use contracting and employee assignment practices to
      cope with the officialdom.

891. Galliard, Frye. "The Indians and the Bureaucrats." PRO-
      RESSIVE, 37 (1973), 37-42.

      Looks at the tensions between Indians and the Bureau
      of Indian Affairs.

892. Gilmore, Kenneth O., and Eugene Methuin. "The REA--A
      Case Study of Bureaucracy Run Wild." READER'S DIGEST,
      83 (December, 1963), 81-87.

      What is the Rural Electrification Administration up to?

893. Graham, Hugh. "Short-Circuiting the Bureaucracy in the
      Great Society Policy Origins in Education." PRESIDEN-
      TIAL STUDIES QUARTERLY, 12 (1982), 407-20.

      Re-examines the use by President Johnson of secret
      task forces to design policy options. The formation of
      education policy was influenced by such groups. In
      the process, they served to strengthen the role of the
      bureaucratic actors in policy formulation.

894. Green, Harry A. "Bureaucracy and Functional Represen-
      tation: A Critique of the Urban Affairs Controversy."
      FLORIDA STATE UNIVERSITY RESEARCH REPORTS IN SOCIAL
      SCIENCE, 8 (February, 1965), 1-18.

      Examines the development of national housing policy.
      Housing interests have historically maintained a close
      relationship with the relevant federal agencies. This
      has led to fragmentation. The creation of a unified
      Department of Housing and Urban Development was contro-
      versial because no interest wanted to be deprived of its
      bureaucratic ally.

895. House, Karen Elliot. "Energy Agency Finds Bureaucracy
      Doesn't Work Energetically." WALL STREET JOURNAL, 191
      (January 17, 1978), 12.

      Troubles in the Department of Energy.

896. Jones, Augustus J. LAW, BUREAUCRACY, AND POLITICS: THE
      IMPLEMENTATION OF TITLE VI OF THE CIVIL RIGHTS ACT OF
      1964. Washington, D.C.: University Press of America,
      1982. 300 pp.

      Studies the dynamics and actors of the implementation
      of the Civil Rights Act. It was found that the three
      federal departments--Housing and Urban Development, HEW,
      and Labor--most involved have not been overly aggressive
      in enforcing the act. This is because of political pres-
      sure, lack of resources, and competing agency objectives.
      The fragmentation of civil rights legislation ensures
      that the problem is no one's responsibility.

897. Madison, Christopher. "He Makes the Bureaucracy Move by
      Breaking the Bureaucratic Rules." NATIONAL JOURNAL,
      12 (1980), 929-32.

      Describes how an Energy Department official makes
      things happen by the judicious granting of exemptions
      to departmental rules and regulations.

898. Metcalf, Linda, ed. "Bureaucracy: Formulating and Imple-
      menting National Indian Policy." MAKING PUBLIC POLICY:
      STUDIES IN AMERICAN POLITICS. Edited by J. Brigham.
      Lexington, Mass.: D.C. Heath, 1977.

      Includes cases and commentaries describing the rela-
      tionship between the federal government and the Indian
      community.

899. Moseley, John. "Democratic Gains from Wartime Bureau-
      cracy." SOUTHWESTERN SOCIAL SCIENCE QUARTERLY, 26
      (1945), 133-42.

      Concludes that we can learn from the Office of Price
      Administration, with its effective mixture of citizen
      volunteers and capable public officials.

900. Radin, Beryl A. IMPLEMENTATION, CHANGE, AND THE FEDERAL
      BUREAUCRACY: SCHOOL DESEGREGATION POLICY IN HEW, 1964-
      1968. New York: Teachers College Press, 1977. 239 pp.

      Investigates the making of federal policies against
      discrimination in federal grants, loans and contracts.
      Many problems arose because the issue emerged internal-
      ly without any prior discussion in the political arena.
      The making and implementation of the policy eventually
      became caught up in HEW's survival needs.

901. Rycroft, Robert W. "Bureaucratic Responsibility in the
      Federal Energy Administration." BUREAUCRAT, 6 (Fall,
      1977), 19-33.

      Examines the ways in which responsibility was estab-
      lished within the new Federal Energy Administration.
      External control devices were not important.

902. Rycroft, Robert W. "Bureaucratic Performance in Energy
      Policy-Making: An Evaluation of Output Efficiency in
      the Federal Energy Administration." PUBLIC POLICY,
      26 (1978), 599-627.

      Uses the criteria of equity and efficiency to measure
      the performance of the Federal Energy Administration.
      The FEA has not performed well.

                    C. Representative Bureaucracy

903. Akins, Carl. "Minority Perspectives on Bureaucracy."
      BUREAUCRAT, 2 (1973), 131-35.

      A general discussion of equal opporunity in employ-
      ment.

904. Barger, Harold M. "Images of Bureaucracy: A Tri-Ethnic
      Consideration." PUBLIC ADMINISTRATION REVIEW, 36
      (1976), 287-96.

      Finds that data from a survey of Anglo, black and Mex-
      ican-American junior high school students reveal differ-
      ences in attitudes about a career in the public service.
      White, middle-class youths are least impressed with a
      career in local government. There is, however, an in-
      consistency in the ideological view of bureaucracy and
      the image of government employment.

905. Clasen, Don, and James T. Jones. "Increasing Minority
      Representation in the Public Bureaucracies." BUREAU-
      CRAT, 2 (1973), 178-88.

      Discuss ways to upgrade and increase minority employ-
      ment in government. The development of minority intern-
      ships is urged.

906. Davis, Charles E., and Jonathan P. West. "Analyzing
      Perceptions of Affirmative Action Issues: A Study
      of Mexican-American Supervisors in a Metropolitan
      Bureaucracy." MIDWEST REVIEW OF PUBLIC ADMINISTRA-
      TION, 12 (1978), 246-56.

Examines the attitudes of Mexican-American administrators toward programs emphasizing minority opportunities. As might be expected, they were more favorable than the Anglos. However, within the minority group, attitudes were conditioned by demographic and work-related factors.

907. Dennard, Cleveland. "The Minority Bureaucrat." BUREAU-CRAT, 2 (1973), 127-30.

Says that minority males have special problems and special responsibilities in the bureaucracy.

908. Dock, Leslie. "An Uppity Woman's View of Bureaucracy." MANAGEMENT REVIEW, 67 (June, 1978), 45-49.

Suggests differences between men and women in their approaches to management.

909. Fischer, Paul B. "The 'War on Poverty' and the 'Blackening' of Urban Bureaucracies." POLICY STUDIES JOURNAL, 2 (1974), 179-86.

Argues that the War on Poverty largely benefited the black middle class by providing them access to positions within municipal government. This development tended to reduce the radical leadership within the local communities.

910. Fletcher, Arthur A. "Random Thoughts on the Bureaucracy." BUREAUCRAT, 2 (1973), 136-43.

Reflects on problems of minority representation, with emphasis on the Department of Labor. By the end of the century, minorities and females may be the dominant force in the bureaucracy.

911. Garcia, Philip L. "The Puerto Rican Experience with the Bureaucracy." BUREAUCRAT, 2 (1973), 158-65.

Reviews the status of Puerto Ricans in the federal government. Their situation is worse than other Spanish-speaking minorities.

912. Gomez, Rudolph. "Mexican Americans in American Bureau-
      cracy." MEXICAN AMERICANS: POLITICS, INFLUENCE, OR
      RESOURCE? Edited by Frank Baird. Lubbock: Texas
      Tech Press, 1977.

      Looks at the penetration of Mexican Americans into the
      higher levels of the federal civil service. They are
      grossly underrepresented.

913. Knox, Holly, and Mary Ann Millsap. "Sex Discrimination
      and Bureaucratic Politics: The U.S. Office of Educa-
      tion's Task Force on Women's Education." NATIONAL
      POLITICS AND SEX DISCRIMINATION IN EDUCATION. Edited
      by Andrew Fishel and Janice Pottker. Lexington, Mass.:
      Lexington Books, 1977.

      Describes the creation and the activity of a task force
      set up to examine the extent of sex discrimination in
      federal aid to education. Little progress was made in
      the implementation of its recommendations.

914. Kranz, Harry. THE PARTICIPATORY BUREAUCRACY: WOMEN AND
      MINORITIES IN A MORE REPRESENTATIVE PUBLIC SERVICE.
      Lexington, Mass.: Lexington Books, 1976. 244 pp.

      Contends that an unrepresentative elite has a dispro-
      portionate amount of power in government. This can be
      compensated for by making the bureaucracy more diverse.
      As the core of modern government, the administration
      needs to reflect the variety of society. Both the elite
      and the general public will find it to their advantage
      to promote a representative work force in the public
      service.

915. Krislov, Samuel. REPRESENTATIVE BUREAUCRACY. Englewood
      Cliffs, N.J.: Prentice-Hall, 1974.

      Argues that the American public service must be com-
      posed of diverse demographic categories in order to rep-
      resent different views within the policy process. How-
      ever, there are limits to representation in administra-
      tion. The experiences of other countries in handling
      questions of ethnic, religious, or linguistic variety
      in the public service are examined.

916. Krislov, Samuel, and David H. Rosenbloom. REPRESENTA-
   TIVE BUREAUCRACY AND THE AMERICAN POLITICAL SYSTEM.
   New York: Praeger, 1981. 208 pp.

   Conclude that the bureaucracy cannot be eliminated
   so the proper course is to maximize the political representativeness of public administration. In this context, personnel selection methods, interest group contacts, methods of accountability, and citizen interactions are discussed. No one method of achieving representation is sufficient by itself and must be reinforced
   by others.

917. Larson, Arthur D. "Representative Bureaucracy and Administrative Responsibility: A Reassessment." MIDWEST
   REVIEW OF PUBLIC ADMINISTRATION, 7 (1973), 79–89.

   Criticizes weaknesses in the theory of representative
   bureaucracy. It does not truly address the question of
   administrative responsibility.

918. Levine, Charles H. "Unrepresentative Bureaucracy: Or
   Knowing What You Look Like Tells You Who You Are (And
   Maybe What To Do About It)." BUREAUCRAT, 4 (1975),
   90–98.

   Develops a typology of unrepresentative bureaucracy,
   based on the elements of stratification and segmentation. The types are consociational, apartheid, strat-
   ified, and representative bureaucracies. In the representative model, both segmentation and stratification
   are low. Strategies for dealing with various types of
   unrepresentativeness are discussed.

919. Levy, Burton. "The Bureaucracy of Race: Enforcement of
   Civil Rights Laws and Its Impact on People, Process-
   es, and Organization." JOURNAL OF BLACK STUDIES, 2
   (September, 1971), 77–105.

   Examines American civil rights agencies to determine
   if these bureaucracies are different from the rest of
   administration. There seems to be a higher degree of
   strain and racial tension within the agencies.

920.   Levy, Burton.   "Effects of 'Racism' on the Racial Bur-
           eaucracy."   PUBLIC ADMINISTRATION REVIEW, 32 (1972),
           479-86.

       Looks at the stages of development of civil rights
       agencies and concentrates on the most recent challenges
       to such organizations.   The shift in emphasis from dis-
       crimination and prejudice to racism has affected the
       agency relationships with minorities and changed the
       internal dynamics.

921.   Levy, Burton.   "The Racial Bureaucracy, 1941-1971: From
           Prejudice to Racism to Discrimination."   JOURNAL OF
           INTERGROUP RELATIONS, 2 (1972), 3-32.

       Traces the development of civil rights agencies in
       the federal government through three stages.

922.   Long, Norton E.   "Bureaucracy and Constitutionalism."
           AMERICAN POLITICAL SCIENCE REVIEW, 46 (1952), 808-18.

       Argues that the bureaucracy is a positive part of the
       American constitutional system, especially since it is
       far more than an instrument for the execution of the
       will of elected officials.   It is more representative
       than Congress in terms of its composition.   It may also
       be more dedicated to the democratic ethos and the prin-
       ciples of constitutionalism than the other branches.

923.   Lynn, Naomi, and Richard Vaden.   "Toward a Non-Sexist
           Personnel Opportunity Structure: The Federal Exec-
           utive Bureaucracy."   PUBLIC PERSONNEL MANAGEMENT,
           8 (1979), 209-15.

       Survey career federal executives on civil service re-
       forms.   Little sex difference in attitudes was found.

924.   Marks, E.L.   REPRESENTATION IN THEORY, LEGISLATURES, AND
           BUREAUCRACIES.   Santa Monica: Rand, 1981.   41 pp.

       Reviews and integrates the literature on the concept
       of representatation, especially in bureaucracy.

925. Meier, August, and Elliot Rudwick. "The Rise of Segre-
        gation in the Federal Bureaucracy." PHYLON, 28 (1967),
        178-84.

        Trace the patterns of segregation of black employees
        in the federal government between 1900 and 1930.

926. Meier, Kenneth. "Representative Bureaucracy: An Empir-
        ical Assessment." AMERICAN POLITICAL SCIENCE REVIEW,
        69 (1975), 526-42.

        Criticizes the theories of representative bureaucracy
        on four different grounds. The empirical data do not
        support the theory of representative bureaucracy in Am-
        erican government; at the higher levels, the public ser-
        vice is unrepresentative. And even if it were more like
        the socioeconomic composition of the general public,
        there is no guarantee that it would reflect popular ideas
        when making policy.

927. Meier, Kenneth, and Lloyd G. Nigro. "Representative Bur-
        eaucracy and Policy Preferences: A Study in the Atti-
        tudes of Federal Executives." PUBLIC ADMINISTRATION
        REVIEW, 36 (1976), 458-69.

        Claim that the theory of representative bureaucracy
        is deficient both as a normative theory of political
        control and as an empirical description of reality. The
        composition of the civil service has little impact on
        public policy, and unrepresentative executives may hold
        representative values. The idea of representation is
        perhaps largely of symbolic value.

928. Nachmias, David, and David H. Rosenbloom. "Measuring
        Bureaucratic Representation and Integration." PUB-
        LIC ADMINISTRATION REVIEW, 33 (1973), 590-97.

        Suggest a "measure of variation" as a means for determ-
        ining the integration of groups into the bureaucracy.
        Numbers alone do not indicate more than the degree of
        "passive representation." A number of values must be
        used to supplement any measure of representation.

929. Nigro, Lloyd G., and Kenneth Meier. "Bureaucracy and
      the People: Is the Higher Federal Service Represent-
      ative?" BUREAUCRAT, 4 (1975), 300-08.

      Find that the federal supergrades are representative
      in terms of a set of values about key issues, even
      though they are unrepresentative in terms of background.
      Demographic representation does not necessarily trans-
      late into normative representation.

930. Rankin, Jerry, and Jose de la Isla. "Mexican Americans
      and the New Federalism: What Role for the Bureaucracy?"
      BUREAUCRAT, 2 (1973), 144-57.

      Urge Mexican Americans to concentrate their efforts
      at the state and local levels.

931. Reeves, Earl J. "Equal Employment and the Concept of the
      Bureaucracy as a Representative Institution." MIDWEST
      REVIEW OF PUBLIC ADMINISTRATION, 6 (1972), 3-13.

      Examines the bureaucracy as a representative institu-
      tion, with special emphasis on the hiring of blacks.
      If bureaucracy is to be representative, then minority
      members will face special pressures from inside and out-
      side the organization. Minorities, in any case, can
      bring a valuable sensitivity to issues.

932. Rodriguez, Armando. "A Chicano Looks at Bureaucracy."
      BUREAUCRAT, 2 (1973), 170-72.

      The personal experiences of a Mexican American.

933. Romzek, Barbara S., and J. Stephen Hendricks. "Organ-
      izational Involvement and Representative Bureaucracy:
      Can We Have It Both Ways?" AMERICAN POLITICAL SCIENCE
      REVIEW, 76 (1982), 75-82.

      Look at the involvement of minority employees in four
      federal agencies, including the Civil Rights Commission.
      CRC minority employees do not rank high in organization-
      al involvement, leading to speculation that there is a
      relationship between achieving goals and integration in-
      to the organization.

934. Rosenbloom, David H. "Forms of Bureaucratic Representa-
      tion in the Federal Service." MIDWEST REVIEW OF PUB-
      LIC ADMINISTRATION, 8 (1974), 159-77.

      Seeks to resolve some of the ambiguity in the concept
      of representative bureaucracy. Historically, the civil
      servants have been seen as representing the state, and
      doctrines have reinforced this idea. Active representa-
      tion, in the sense of a conscious pursuit of group goals,
      has become possible with changes in judicial thinking
      and personnel regulations. The linkage between active
      and passive representation, however, is still unclear.

935. Rosenbloom, David H., and Douglas Kinnard. "Bureaucrat-
      ic Representation and Bureaucrat's Behavior: An Explor-
      atory Analysis." MIDWEST REVIEW OF PUBLIC ADMINISTRA-
      TION, 11 (1977), 35-42.

      Analyze attitudes and behavior of minority bureaucrats
      in the Department of Defense. Minority representation
      in upper level positions can be an important means for
      achieving substantive representation for ethnic groups.

936. Rosenbloom, David H. "Representative Bureaucracy: Still
      Controversial after All These Years?" ADMINISTRATIVE
      CHANGE, 7 (July-December, 1979), 1-10.

      Says that the idea of representative bureaucracy is
      still questioned by many, even though it seems to be
      supported by the evidence. Political scientists, in par-
      ticular, discount the notion because of their faith in
      the importance of elections.

937. Saltzstein, Grace. "Representative Bureaucracy and Bur-
      eaucratic Responsibilities." ADMINISTRATION AND SOC-
      IETY, 10 (1979), 465-75.

      Discusses the theory of representative bureaucracy.
      It is a difficult idea to operationalize and so far
      little solid work has been done to link passive and
      active representation. Many ambiguities remain in the
      theory. Also discussed is the possibility that the the-
      ory is useful in legitimizing bureaucratic power.

938.   Sigelman, Lee, and Albert Karnig. "Black Representa-
       tion in the American States: A Comparison of Bureau-
       cracies and Legislatures." AMERICAN POLITICS QUART-
       ERLY, 4 (1976), 237-45.

       Investigate Long's thesis (Item 922) that the bureau-
       cracy is more representative than the legislature. In
       state governments, both institutions underrepresent the
       blacks.

939.   Sigelman, Lee, and Albert Karnig. "Black Education and
       Bureaucratic Employment." SOCIAL SCIENCE QUARTERLY,
       57 (1977), 858-63.

       Compare the educational status of blacks with majority
       public employees. Lower levels of education for blacks
       are not directly responsible for lower employment rates.
       Rather, both are indications of a general level of dis-
       crimination.

940.   Sigelman, Lee, and William G. Vanderbok. "The Saving
       Grace? Bureaucratic Power and American Democracy."
       POLITY, 10 (1978), 440-47.

       Refute the Long thesis (Item 922) about the represent-
       ative nature of bureaucracy. Bureaucrats and legislators
       are similar in background characteristics.

941.   Simpson, Richard L., and Ida H. Simpson. "Women and
       Bureaucracy in the Semi-Professions." THE SEMI-PRO-
       FESSIONS AND THEIR ORGANIZATION. Edited by Amitai
       Etzioni. New York: Free Press, 1969.

       Look for reasons to explain the pattern of bureaucrat-
       ic control within work groups with a preponderance of
       female members, for example, nursing, libraries, edu-
       cation, and social services. The public is less will-
       ing to grant professional autonomy to groups dominated
       by women.

942.   South, Scott J. "Sex and Power in the Federal Bureau-
       cracy: A Comparative Analysis of Male and Female Sup-
       ervisors." WORK AND OCCUPATIONS, 9 (1982), 233-54.

Tests the thesis that differences in supervisory behavior result from sex differentials in organization
power. The thesis is confirmed since differences between
male and female supervisors disappeared when variations
in organization power were controlled.

943.   Subramaniam, V. "Representative Bureaucracy: A Reas-
          sessment." AMERICAN POLITICAL SCIENCE REVIEW, 61
          (1967), 1010-19.

Concludes that it will be extremely difficult to ever
achieve a truly representative bureaucracy since the
middle class has greater access to administrative skills.
The familial background of higher civil servants in six
countries is analyzed. Only the United States appears
to have a representative civil service.

944.   Thompson, Frank J. "Bureaucratic Responsiveness in the
          Cities: The Problem of Minority Hiring." URBAN AFFAIRS
          QUARTERLY, 10 (1974), 40-68.

Expresses optimism about the ability of urban administrators to respond to the problems of minority representation.

945.   Thompson, Frank J. "Minority Groups in Public Bureau-
          cracies: Are Passive and Active Representation
          Linked? ADMINISTRATION AND SOCIETY, 8 (1976), 201-26.

Asks whether minority civil servants represent the view
of their ethnic group. It is concluded that, in some
circumstances, such representation does take place.

946.   Thompson, Frank J. "Types of Representative Bureaucracy
          and Their Linkage: The Case of Ethnicity." PUBLIC AD-
          MINISTRATION, 3rd. ed. Edited by Robert Golembiewski,
          Frank Gibson, and Geoffrey Cornog. Chicago: Rand Mc-
          Nally, 1976.

Sees representative bureaucracy as coming in three varieties: demographic, attitudinal, and substantive. The
attainment of one feature does not necessarily imply the
other two.

947.   Votaw, Don. "The New Equality: Bureaucracy's Trojan
       Horse." CALIFORNIA MANAGEMENT REVIEW, 20 (Summer,
       1978), 5-17.

       Claims that the requirements for equality in hiring
       practices within organizations will mean greater govern-
       mental control over the private sector.

948.   Washnis, George J. "Decentralization--Its Impact on
       the Bureaucracy and Minorities." BUREAUCRAT, 2
       (1973), 193-98.

       Review essay on Nordlinger, *Decentralizing the City*.

            D.   Bureaucracy and the Regulatory Process

949.   Adams, Charles M. "Bookkeeper for the Bureaucracy."
       NATION'S BUSINESS, 24 (October, 1936), 56-62.

       About the paperwork burden imposed on small business
       by the government.

950.   Blauvaelt, Howard. "Controlling the Federal Bureaucra-
       cy." CHEMICAL ENGINEERING PROGRESS, 74 (October,
       1978), 32-35.

       On environmental regulations that hurt industry.

951.   Buckley, James L. "Federal Bureauracy: Servant or Mas-
       ter?" VITAL SPEECHES OF THE DAY, 45 (1979), 715.

       Against excessive government regulation.

952.   "Bureaucracy under Fire." BROADCASTING, 74 (June 17,
       1968), 36-37.

       FCC Commissioner Lee Loevinger questions the use of
       commissions for the resolution of social problems. See
       Item 978.

953. "Bureaucratic Imperialism." FORBES, (November 15, 1977), 45.

     On a proposal to regulate foreign trade.

954. "The Bureaucrats Belt Us Again." FORTUNE, 88 (October, 1973), 128.

     About the National Highway Safety Administration's new rules on automobile standards.

955. Clark, Timothy. "It's Still no Bureaucratic Revolution, But Regulatory Reform Has a Foothold." NATIONAL JOURNAL, 11 (1979), 1596-1601.

     Examines the efforts of the Carter administration to lessen the impact of government regulations in the economy.

956. Clarkson, Kenneth W., and Timothy J. Muris, eds. THE FEDERAL TRADE COMMISSION SINCE 1970: ECONOMIC REGULATION AND BUREAUCRATIC BEHAVIOR. New York: Cambridge University Press, 1981. 379 pp.

     A collection of articles, largely case studies, looking at the performance of the Federal Trade Commission during the 1970s. The agency compiled a poor record of performance despite its broad powers and general lack of control by others. Proposals for reform, stressing improved economic analysis, are suggested.

957. "Costly New U.S. Super Bureaucracy in Offing, Farm Bureau Chief Warns." NATIONAL UNDERWRITER, 78 (December 2, 1974), 4, 17.

     The head of the Farm Bureau Federation attacks the Consumer Protection Agency.

958. Crosby, William H. "Bureaucratic Clout, and a Parable: The Iron-Enrichment-Now Brouhaha." JOURNAL OF THE AMERICAN MEDICAL ASSOCIATION, 228 (1974), 1651-52.

     Concerning the Food and Drug Administration.

959. Cross, Jennifer. "Smoking Out the Bureaucrats." NATION,
     221 (1975), 306-08.

     Describes how the California Department of Consumer Af-
     fairs has been forced to move energetically in the pro-
     tection of the public interest.

960. Dallas, Daniel. "The Bureaucratic Malaise." MANUFACT-
     URING ENGINEERING AND MANAGEMENT, 73 (November, 1974),
     8.

     Deplores the effect of the Environmental Protection
     Agency on industrial research and development.

961. Demkovich, Linda. "Government's Nursing Home Rules--
     Better Care or More Bureaucracy? NATIONAL JOURNAL,
     12 (1980), 1846-48.

     Discusses proposed regulations by Health and Human Ser-
     vices covering the nursing home industry.

962. Deutsch, Jan G. "Politics, Economics, and Corporate
     Power: The Challenge of Bureaucracy." TEXAS LAW RE-
     VIEW, 58 (1980), 777-87.

     Asks whether it is possible for the legal system alone
     to ensure the accountability of the modern corporation.
     The answer depends upon one's view of human self-develop-
     ment. The Marxist and Hegelian conception of innate
     human capacity are examined.

963. Downes, Peter. "Federal or State Regulation? Aren't
     Bureaucracies at Fault? BUSINESS INSURANCE, (August
     8, 1977), 2.

     How bureaucracy continues to thwart individual init-
     iative.

964. Dunne, Gerald. "Deregulation by Bureaucracy--The Fox
     and the Henhouse." BANKING LAW JOURNAL, 97 (1980),
     787.

     Questions the reform of banking by government.

965. Erickson, Don V. ARMSTRONG'S FIGHT FOR FM BROADCASTING: ONE MAN VS BIG BUSINESS AND BUREAUCRACY. University: University of Alabama Press, 1973. 226 pp.

Details how the inventor of FM radio had to fight with the broadcasting industry as well as the Federal Communication Commission in order to get his innovation accepted.

966. Etheridge, Obie L. "On Pumps, Explosions, and Government Bureaucracy." WATER AND WASTES ENGINEERING, 16 (November, 1979), 27.

On the complexity of OSHA codes.

967. Goldberg, Arthur J. "A Defense of the Bureaucracy in Corporate Regulation and Some Personel Suggestions for Corporate Reform." GEORGE WASHINGTON LAW REVIEW, 48 (1980), 514-20.

A former supreme court justice indicates that there is a need for government involvement in corporate affairs.

968. Hood, Arthur. "Shall Industry or Bureaucracy Plan Our Economic Development?" VITAL SPEECHES OF THE DAY, 9 (1943), 525-33.

The need to get government off our backs.

969. Howe, Warner, "The Growing Bureaucracy of State and National Building Regulation." CODE ADMINISTRATION REVIEW, 2 (Summer, 1974), 43-51.

On the administration of building codes, with emphasis on the situation in Tennessee.

970. Katzmann, Robert A. REGULATORY BUREAUCRACY: THE FEDERAL TRADE COMMISSION AND ANTITRUST POLICY. Cambridge, Mass.: MIT Press, 1980. 223 pp.

Uses organizational analysis to explain the selection of antitrust cases by the FTC. The commission decides to prosecute because of the distribution of organization power. The structure affects the making and implementation of antitrust policy.

971. Kaufman, Colin K. "Eliminating Bureaucracy from the Federal Bankruptcy Administration." AMERICAN BANKRUPTCY LAW JOURNAL, 49 (1975), 197-229.

Proposes modifications in pending changes of the federal bankruptcy laws in order to lessen the complexity of their administration.

972. Kinlaw, Dennis. "Of Equal Opportunity and Other Bureaucratic Intrustions." CHRISTIANITY TODAY, 21 (November 5, 1976), 16-18.

Discusses the dangers to academic freedom and religious liberty from regulations imposed on higher education by the federal government.

973. Klein, Jeffrey. "The Nuclear Regulatory Bureaucracy." SOCIETY, 18 (July-August, 1981), 50-56.

Describes the failures of the Nuclear Regulatory Commission and suggests ways of improvement.

974. Kuhn, Lawrence. "Unleashing the Bureaucrats." JOURNAL OF METALS, 24 (September, 1972), 3.

On Federal Power Commission interference in foreign trade.

975. "Lancaster Looks at Entrenched Bureaucracy." NATIONAL UNDERWRITER, 84 (November 21, 1980), 36-38.

Sees bureaucracy as opposed to private business.

976. Leigh, Robert D. "Politicians vs. Bureaucrats." HARPER'S, 190 (1945), 97-105.

A participant describes a skirmish between Congress and the Federal Communications Commission.

977. "Lifting the Bureaucratic Burden." FORBES, 125 (March
      31, 1980), 109.

      On a campaign to cut government paperwork.

978. Loevinger, Lee. "The Sociology of Bureaucracy." BUS-
      INESS LAWYER, 24 (1968), 7-18.

      Argues that lawyers participating in the regulatory
      process must be aware of the psychology of the bureau-
      crats. Several hypotheses about bureaucratic power are
      suggested.

979. Lutz, Philip. "The Growing Bureaucracy in State Gov-
      ernment." COMMERCIAL LAW JOURNAL, 43 (1938), 12-14.

      On the increase in the regulation of business by state
      governments.

980. McGuire, O.R. "Federal Administrative Decisions and
      Judicial Control Thereof, or, Bureaucracy under Con-
      trol." REPORT OF THE VIRGINIA STATE BAR ASSOCIATION,
      48 (1936), 301-07.

      Praises the vigilence of the courts in protecting bus-
      iness from needless regulation.

981. Mason, Lowell. "The Unauthorized Growth of Bureaucratic
      Power." THE NEW ARGUMENT IN ECONOMICS: THE PUBLIC VER-
      SUS THE PRIVATE SECTOR. Edited by Helmut Schoeck and
      James Wiggins. Princeton, N.J.: D. Van Nostrand,
      1963.

      Rails about the Federal Trade Commission and its as-
      sault on business prerogatives.

982. Moon, Becky F. "Bureaucracy vs. the Elders Council: The
      People in Doubt about the Regulatory Process." TEXAS
      REPORTS ON BIOLOGY AND MEDICINE, 37 (1978), 217-23.

      Questions the effectiveness of environmental protec-
      tion regulations. Greater public awareness, concern
      and participation are needed to make the system work.

983. Murphy, Thomas A. "Senate Bill Poses Threat: Freedom
      or Bureaucracy?" FINANCIAL EXECUTIVE, 44 (April,
      1976), 32-35.

      The Chairman of General Motors opposes a bill aimed at
      national economic planning.

984. Orton, Steve. "On the Nature of Bureaucracy." AMERICAN
      IMPORT-EXPORT BULLETIN, 92 (February, 1980), 37-39.

      Discusses recent reforms in customs procedures.

985. Phelan, Robin E. "The Proposed Bankruptcy Administra-
      tion (the 'FBA')--Bureaucratic Alphabet Soup Gets a
      Bigger Bowl." AMERICAN BANKRUPTCY LAW JOURNAL, 48
      (1974), 341-68.

      Argues against the creation of a federal agency to ad-
      minister bankruptcy laws.

986. Read Thomas. "Should Bureaucracy Rule Petroleum?"
      NATION'S BUSINESS, 29 (August, 1941), 17.

      Sees some sinister implications in emergency plans for
      control of the oil companies.

987. Schrag, Philip, and Michael Meltsner. "Class Action: A
      Way to Beat the Bureaucracies without Increasing Them."
      WASHINGTON MONTHLY, 4 (November, 1972), 55-61.

      Contend that the class-action suit is an effective way
      to control business. The consumers have access to a de-
      vice that does not depend upon the ponderous activity of
      a regulatory bureaucracy.

988. Strange, G.L. "HUD Registrations: The Good, the Bad,
      and the Merely Bureaucratic." INDUSTRIAL DEVELOPMENT
      AND MANUFACTURER'S RECORD, 144 (September-October,
      1975), 16-18.

      Grumbles about new federal rules pertaining to real
      estate sales.

989. Thompson, Frank J. "Deregulation by the Bureaucracy:
      OSHA and the Augean Quest for Error Correction."
      PUBLIC ADMINISTRATION REVIEW, 42 (1982), 202-12.

      Examines the difficulties faced by a federal agency
      in "standards deregulation" or the reduction in formal
      requirements for the deregulated area. Several propo-
      sitions about such regulations are formulated.

990. Thorpe, Merle. "The Bureaucrat Becomes Dictocrat."
      NATION'S BUSINESS, 27 (September, 1939), 13.

      Says that business dances to the whims of arbitrary
      administrators.

991. Thorpe, Merle. "Bureaucracy Lifts Its Mask." NATION'S
      BUSINESS, 28 (June, 1940), 13.

      Business needs protection from the regulators.

992. Weart, Spencer A. "Living with the Bureaucracy." BAR-
      RON'S, 23 (February 15, 1943), 7.

      Says that business should learn to live with increas-
      ing government regulation.

      E. Bureaucracy in State and Local Government

993. Alford, Robert R., with the collaboration of Harry M.
      Scoble. BUREAUCRACY AND PARTICIPATION: POLITICAL CUL-
      TURES IN FOUR WISCONSIN CITIES. Chicago: Rand McNal-
      ly, 1969. 244 pp.

      Develops a typology of urban political cultures, rang-
      ing from the bureaucratized, particpatory ("modern")
      to the nonbureaucratic, nonparticipatory ("traditional").
      Although participation and bureaucracy are incompatible,
      they are often the preferred package of the middle class.
      A community's political culture appears to be a function
      of governmental structure and socioeconomic conditions.
      A city that is both bureaucratized and participatory will
      have a more pluralistic power structure than one that is
      bureaucratic but nonparticipatory.

994. Alford, Robert R. "Bureaucracy and Participation in
      Four Wisconsin Cities." URBAN AFFAIRS QUARTERLY,
      5 (1969) 5-30.

      A shorter version of Item 993.

995. Alford, Robert R. "Ideological Filters and Bureaucrat-
      ic Responses in Interpreting Research: Community Plan-
      ning and Poverty." SOCIAL POLICY AND SOCIOLOGY. Ed-
      ited by N.J. Demerath, Otto Larsen, and Karl Schues-
      sler. New York: Academic Press, 1975.

      Argues that the dominant policy research paradigm, es-
      pecially in community studies, stresses consensus, inte-
      gration, and differentiation. The resulting analysis
      enables politicians and administrators to evade actual
      problem solving.

996. Alix, Ernest K. "A Case of Limited Debureaucratization
      of a Small Town Council." BUFFALO STUDIES, 3 (1967),
      71-102.

      Uses Eisenstadt's concept of debureaucratization (Item
      395) to describe a small city government manipulated by
      leading economic interests.

997. Antunes, George E., and John P. Plumlee. "The Distrib-
      ution of an Urban Public Service: Ethnicity, Socio-
      economic Status, and Bureaucracy as Determinants of
      the Quality of Neighborhood Streets." THE POLITICS
      AND ECONOMICS OF URBAN SERVICES. Edited by Robert
      L. Lineberry. Beverly Hills, Cal.: Sage, 1978.

      Find that the quality of streets in Houston is not re-
      lated to the ethnic or socioeconomic composition of the
      neighborhoods. Professional decision rules of the public
      roads officials are the most important determinant of the
      quality of the streets.

998. Archibald, R.W., and R.B. Hoffman. INTRODUCING TECHNO-
      LOGICAL CHANGE IN A BUREAUCRATIC STRUCTURE. Santa Mon-
      ica: Rand, 1969. 31 pp.

      Describe a procedure for introducing new technology.

999. Bingham, Richard D. "Innovation, Bureaucracy, and Public Policy: A Study of Innovation Adoption by Local Governments." WESTERN POLITICAL SCIENCE QUARTERLY, 31 (1978), 178-205.

Identifies the factors determining the innovation process. If given the proper incentives, local government can be innovative. Products, rather than processes, are most likely to be adopted.

1000. Blank, Blanche D. "The Battle of Bureaucracy." NATION, 203 (1966), 632-36.

On the difficulty of civil service reform in New York City.

1001. Blank, Blanche D., Rita J. Immerman, and C. Peter Rydell. "A Comparative Study of an Urban Bureaucracy." URBAN AFFAIRS QUARTERLY, 4 (1969), 343-54.

Apply the comparative method to branch libraries in New York City. Substantial inequalities in the distribution of resources were found. There were also differences in the satisfaction levels of both staff and clients.

1002. Brewer, Garry. POLITICIANS, BUREAUCRATS, AND THE CONSULTANT: A CRITIQUE OF URBAN PROBLEM SOLVING. New York: Basic Books, 1973. 291 pp.

Examines the failure of innovation in management in San Francisco and Pittsburgh. Consultants were unsuccessful in developing a problem-solving computer program for application to urban problems. The forces behind the innovations are described, and the attitudes of politicians and administrators are analyzed.

1003. Chackerian, Richard. "Community Influence and Bureaucratic Structure." CANADIAN PUBLIC ADMINISTRATION, 16 (1973), 652-61.

Studies the management of 59 American cities. When the political environment of the city is not highly differentiated, bureaucracy tends to emerge.

1004. Choi, Yearn. "Bureaucratic Phenomena in Southeast Vir-
       ginia Cities: Conflict or Consonance? INTRODUCTION
       TO PUBLIC ADMINISTRATION. By Yearn Choi. Virginia
       Beach, Va.: Donning, 1979.

       Tests empirically the degree of conflict between line
       and staff personnel. A high degree of conflict was not
       found within the cities studied. Psychological common-
       alities may explain the high degree of harmony among the
       officials.

1005. Cohen, David. "Bureaucracy in Crisis." BARRISTER, 4
       (Spring, 1977), 10-13.

       Praises sunset and sunshine laws as methods of reform
       in state government. These methods can free government
       from inaction through the interest group veto.

1006. Cook, Fred J. "Bureaucratic Follies." NATION, 227
       (1978), 565, 568-69.

       Fumes about his misadventures with the New Jersey
       Division of Taxation.

1007. Cooper, Alfred. "The Bureaucrat in Politics." PLAIN
       TALK, 4 (May, 1949), 39-43.

       A municipal employee confesses to engaging in polit-
       ical activity while on the job.

1008. Cooper, Terry L. "Bureaucracy and Community Organiza-
       tion: The Metamorphosis of a Relationship." ADMINIS-
       TRATION AND SOCIETY, 11 (1980), 411-43.

       Traces the transformation of a community organization
       from a militant advocacy group to a bureaucracy domin-
       ated by professionals.

1009. Downs, George. BUREAUCRACY, INNOVATION, AND PUBLIC POL-
       ICY. Lexington, Mass.: Lexington Books, 1976. 150
       pp.

       Examines the role of state bureaucracy in the flow

or diffusion of innovation in the U.S. The movement
toward deinstitutionalization of juvenile offenders is
used to determine the forces at work in the spread of
a new policy. The bureaucracy is critical, and an agency headed by a committed director in an autonomous position is most effective in innovation.

1010. Downs, George, and David Rocke. "Bureaucracy and Juvenile Corrections in the States." POLICY STUDIES
JOURNAL, 7 (1979), 721-28.

Tests the extent to which variations in the bureaucratic characteristics of state organizations have a
bearing on the adoption of new policies.

1011. Edwards, Robert. "Working with the Bureaucracy at the
Community or Village Level." JOURNAL OF THE COMMUN-
ITY DEVELOPMENT SOCIETY, 2 (Fall, 1971), 41-46.

Describes the relations between local community action
groups and state government.

1012. Edwards, William. "Bureaucracy and Administrative Organization in New Mexico." NEW MEXICO QUARTERLY, 13
(1943), 59-72

Finds that the state is badly in need of reorganization of its executive branch.

1013. Eisinger, Peter K. "The Economic Conditions of Black
Employment in Municipal Bureaucracies." AMERICAN
JOURNAL OF POLITICAL SCIENCE, 26 (1982), 754-71.

Maintains that the degree of black employment in city
government depends on several economic factors which
vary from city to city. It may be that blacks will
gain more access to policy making in economically ad-
vantaged cities than in those poor cities governed by
black mayors.

1014. Ermer, Virginia, and John H. Strange, eds. BLACKS AND
BUREAUCRACY: READINGS IN THE PROBLEMS AND POLITICS

OF CHANGE. New York: Thomas Y. Crowell, 1972. 342 pp.

A collection of previously published work on the interaction between urban bureaucracies and blacks, especially of the lower class.

1015. Ermer, Virginia. "Strategies for Increasing Bureaucratic Responsiveness: Internal Monitoring or an Executive-Clientele 'Alliance.'" MIDWEST REVIEW OF PUBLIC ADMINISTRATION, 9 (1975), 121-32.

Suggests that department heads and clients can join together to stimulate the urban bureaucracy. The experience of an agency in Baltimore is described.

1016. Fainstein, Norman I, and Susan S. Fainstein. "Innovation in Urban Bureaucracies: Clients and Change." AMERICAN BEHAVIORAL SCIENTIST, 15 (1972), 511-31.

Examine by way of a case study of the New York City schools the conditions under which clients are likely to be able to bring about change in bureaucracy.

1017. Faux, G. "Politics and Bureaucracy in Community-Controlled Economic Development." LAW AND CONTEMPORARY PROBLEMS, 36 (1971), 277-96.

Argues that bureaucratization prevents the local action programs from exercising much discretion in their activities. The poor will never have real independence until they acquire more political power.

1018. Fox, Douglas. THE POLITICS OF CITY AND STATE BUREAUCRACY. Pacific Palisades, Cal.: Goodyear, 1974. 124 pp.

Discusses the role of bureaucracy in the state and local policy process. The ways in which various political actors relate to the urban bureaucracy are examined.

1019.   Francis, Roy G., and Robert C. Stone.   SERVICE AND PRO-
        CEDURE IN BUREAUCRACY: A CASE STUDY.   Minneapolis:
        University of Minnesota Press, 1956.   201 pp.

        Present a case study of a state employment agency.
        Which was more important, service to clients or follow-
        ing procedures?   A random sample of documents indicated
        that a procedural orientation dominated.   Other evidence
        showed that service was as important as procedures.

1020.   Goldstein, Michael L.   "Black Power and the Rise of
        Bureaucratic Authority in New York City Politics: The
        Case of Harlem Hospital, 1917-1931."   PHYLON, 41
        (1980), 187-201.

        Investigates the displacement of political leadership
        by functionally fragmented bureaucracies.   The result
        was a loss of power by black political leaders.

1021.   Gonzales, Raymond.   "The Bureaucratic System Gets Pat
        on Its Red Tape."   THRUST, 9 (May, 1980), 28-29.

        On California state government.

1022.   Goudy, Willis J., and Robert O. Richards.   "Citizens,
        Bureaucrats, and Legitimate Authority: Some Unantic-
        ipated Consequences within the Administration of Soc-
        ial Action Programs."   MIDWEST REVIEW OF PUBLIC AD-
        MINISTRATION, 8 (1974), 191-202.

        Discuss the conflict between citizen boards and pro-
        fessionals in a Model Cities program, in terms of the
        disagreement over legitimate authority patterns.   The
        very idea of representation may be a new way for making
        legitimate the formal power of the bureaucracy.

1023.   Graves, Richard P.   "City Hall Revisited--Observations
        of a Bureaucrat Turned Businessman."   PUBLIC PERSON-
        NEL REVIEW, 27 (1966), 31-33.

        Believes that the merit system is vital to the preser-
        vation and extension of a free society.

1024. Greer, Scott. "Bureaucratization of the Emerging City."
       FISCAL RETRENCHMENT AND URBAN POLICY. Edited by John
       P. Blair and David Nachmias. Beverly Hills, Cal.:
       Sage, 1979.

       Says that the urban scene is dominated by large or-
       ganizations, public and private. These bureaucracies
       may not be very effective in achieving any single goal,
       but together they are an excellent means of control.
       A destabilizing politics of confrontation is avoided
       as these organizations provide to all groups a share
       of resources.

1025. Hackett, Bruce. "Emerging Patterns of Stratification
       and Integration in the California Bureaucracy." THE
       CHANGING PUBLIC SERVICE. Edited by Bruce Hackett.
       Davis: University of California, Institute of Govern-
       mental Affairs, 1968.

       A summary of personnel changes in the California civ-
       il service.

1026. Hudson, James R. "Municipal Bureaucracies and Municipal
       Power." INTELLECT, 105 (1977), 396-98.

       On the increasing strength of organized civil servants
       in local government.

1027. Illinois, Office of the Governor. BEYOND BUREAUCRACY:
       A PROGRAM FOR RESTRUCTURING THE EXECUTIVE BRANCH OF
       ILLINOIS STATE GOVERNMENT. Springfield: State of
       Illinois, 1972. 136 pp.

       A set of recommendations concerning the reorganization
       of state government.

1028. Jones, Bryan D., Saadia Greenberg, Clifford Kaufman,
       and Joseph Drew. "Service Delivery Rules and the
       Distribution of Local Government Services: Three De-
       troit Bureaucracies." JOURNAL OF POLITICS, 40 (1978),
       332-68.

       Study the impact of internal operating rules on the
       actual delivery of public services within the city.

1029. Jones, Bryan D., in association with Saadia Greenberg
       and Joseph Drew. SERVICE DELIVERY IN THE CITY: CIT-
       IZEN DEMAND AND BUREAUCRATIC RULES. New York: Long-
       man, 1980. 274 pp.

       Investigate the patterns of service delivery in De-
       troit. A theory of citizen demand and governmental
       response is presented.

1030. Jones, Bryan D. "Party and Bureaucracy: The Influence
       of Intermediary Groups and Urban Public Service De-
       livery." AMERICAN POLITICAL SCIENCE REVIEW, 75
       (1981), 688-700.

       Examines the effect of intermediary groups, espec-
       ially the political party, on the delivery of services
       in Detroit. The party structure seems to be efficac-
       ious in modifying bureaucratic behavior in at least
       three ways. Other groups were not so effective.

1031. Jowell, Jeffrey L. LAW AND BUREAUCRACY: ADMINISTRATIVE
       DISCRETION AND THE LIMITS OF LEGAL ACTION. Port Wash-
       ington, N.Y.: Dunellen, 1975. 214 pp.

       Analyzes the action of client advocates in three urb-
       an agencies. Advocacy can help to enforce uniformity
       and adherence to administrative rules, thus ensuring
       that deprived clients have equal access to services.

1032. Kaufman, Herbert. "Bureaucrats and Organized Civil Ser-
       vants." PROCEEDINGS OF THE ACADEMY OF POLITICAL SCI-
       ENCE, 29, No. 4 (1969), 41-54.

       Describes how the problems of the municipal bureau-
       cracy have been aggravated by the increased power of
       civil service unions in New York City.

1033. Kaufman, Herbert. "Robert Moses: Charismatic Bureau-
       crat." POLITICAL SCIENCE QUARTERLY, 90 (1975), 521-
       38.

       Review essay of Caro, *The Power Broker*.

1034. Kelley, Harry F., and Charles E. Patterson. THE TEN-
       NESSEE BUREAUCRAT: A SURVEY OF STATE ADMINISTRATORS.
       Knoxville: University of Tennessee, Bureau of Public
       Administration, 1970. 94 pp.

       Presents the results of a 1964 survey of state ex-
       ecutives just below the level of agency head. The
       areas examined are representativeness, career patterns,
       and role expectations and interests. Comparisons are
       made with California state officials.

1035. Kheel, Theodore. "Tyranny of a Bureaucracy." URBIA,
       1 (Winter, 1973-74), 3-6.

       Argues that the New York Port Authority is dominated
       by its permanent staff.

1036. Kristol, Irving. "Decentralization and Bureaucracy in
       Local Government." THINKING ABOUT CITIES. Edited
       by Anthony Pascal. Belmont, Cal.: Dickinson, 1970.

       Reviews the decentralization efforts of the 1960s and
       concludes that "antibureaucracy" can be as bad as bur-
       eaucracy, unless handled carefully. A workable system
       of decentralization should strengthen authority, not
       weaken it. Given the nature of some social problems,
       the idea of decentralization may have gained popular-
       ity at precisely the wrong time.

1037. Lambright, W. Henry, and Paul J. Flynn. "Bureaucratic
       Politics and Technological Change in Local Govern-
       ment." JOURNAL OF URBAN ANALYSIS, 4 (1977), 93-118.

       Contend that we must take into account the role of
       the bureaucrats in the adoption of technology in local
       government. The self-interest of the public official
       is most important. Innovation may not take place with-
       out some stimulation from outside.

1038. Levin, Melvin B., and Norman A. Abend. BUREAUCRATS IN
       COLLISION: CASE STUDIES IN AREA TRANSPORTATION PLAN-
       NING. Cambridge, Mass.: MIT Press, 1971. 295 pp.

       Use several case studies of transportation planning

to illuminate the sources of conflict between operating
agencies and area-wide planning units. The regional
planning units, supported by federal pressure, are, at
best, "one contender among many in a complicated game
involving an intricate mix of local, state, and federal
participants."

1039. McNee, Robert B. "Regional Planning, Bureaucracy and
Geography." ECONOMIC GEOGRAPHY, 46 (1970), 190-98.

Questions the reliance of much planning in geography
on an assumption about an individualistic, market-dom-
inated world rather than one driven by bureaucratic
planning agencies. Models which view locational decision-making as a function of bureaucratic behavior are
needed.

1040. Maney, Ardith. REPRESENTING THE CONSUMER INTEREST:
MAYORS, POLITICAL PARTIES, AND INTEREST GROUPS IN
BUREAUCRATIC POLITICS. Washington, D.C.: University
Press of America, 1978. 378 pp.

Discusses the politics surrounding the regulation of
business in New York City over the past several decades.

1041. Mann, Dean. THE CITIZEN AND THE BUREAUCRACY: COMPLAINT-
HANDLING PROCEDURES OF THREE CALIFORNIA LEGISLATORS.
Berkeley: University of California, Institute of Gov-
ernmental Studies, 1968. 52 pp.

Presents examples of the ways in which citizen complaints are handled.

1042. Miller, Ernest G. "Architects, Politics, and Bureau-
cracy: Reorganization of the California Division of
Architecture." GOVERNMENTAL REORGANIZATION: CASES
AND COMMENTARIES. Edited by Frederick C. Mosher.
Indianapolis: Bobbs-Merrill, 1967.

Describes in detail the 1958 reorganization of a state
agency with close ties to a professional group. The
case illustrates the uses and abuses of management consultants within a politically charged atmosphere.

1043. Miner, H. Craig. "'A Corps of Clerks:' The Bureaucracy
       of Industrialization in the Indian Territory, 1866-
       1907." CHRONICLES OF OKLAHOMA, 53 (1975), 322-51.

       Praises the role played by pioneer administrators in
       Oklahoma's territorial days.

1044. Mladenka, Kenneth R. "The Urban Bureaucracy and the
       Chicago Political Machine: Who Gets What and the
       Limits to Political Control." AMERICAN POLITICAL
       SCIENCE REVIEW, 74 (1980), 991-98.

       Tests the thesis that the Chicago political machine
       maintains itself by trading public services for votes.
       Little evidence was found of political influence in the
       distribution of resources. The bureaucracy tends to
       make its allocative decisions according to formula and
       professional standards.

1045. Mladenka, Kenneth R. "Citizen Demands and Urban Ser-
       vices: The Distribution of Bureaucratic Response in
       Chicago and Houston." AMERICAN JOURNAL OF POLITICAL
       SCIENCE, 25 (1981), 693-714.

       Asks whether municipal officials politicize citizen
       contacts with government; that is, do they reward or
       punish on the basis of election support? The evidence
       indicates that allocative outcomes do not depend on
       political action.

1046. Mohapatra, Manindra K. "Ombudsmanic Role of City Coun-
       cilmen and Urban Bureaucracy: An Empirical Study of
       the Perceptual Orientation of Officials and 'Attentive
       Citizens' in Tidewater." URBAN PROBLEMS IN A METRO-
       POLITAN SETTING. Edited by Thomas L. Wells. Norfolk,
       Va.: Old Dominion University, 1975.

       Measures how a number of political participants view
       the complaint-handling function of city council members.
       Most incumbent city council members did not see this as
       a major part of the job. Others, including city mana-
       gers, were more inclined to see the value of an "ombuds-
       manic" role for the elected officials. The interest
       groups held a similar position.

1047. Mott, Paul E. "Bureaucracies and Community Planning." SOCIOLOGICAL INQUIRY, 43 (1973), 311-23.

   Reviews the defects of bureaucracy in the planning process and urges greater decentralization of the whole planning function.

1048. Nash, Gerald D. "Bureaucracy and Economic Reform: The Experience of California, 1899-1911." WESTERN POLIT-ICAL QUARTERLY, 13 (1960), 678-91.

   Argues that many of the reforms instituted by Progres-sive politicians in California had been started earlier by civil servants.

1049. Nash, Gerald D. "Bureaucracy and Reform in the West: A Neglected Interest Group." WESTERN HISTORICAL QUART-ERLY, 2 (1971), 295-305.

   Claims that government officials were important in the taming of the West. They were also a major force in the passage of reform legislation by the states.

1050. Needleman, Martin L., and Carolyn E. Needleman. GUER-RILLAS IN THE BUREAUCRACY: THE COMMUNITY PLANNING EXPERIMENT IN THE UNITED STATES. New York: John Wiley, 1974. 368 pp.

   Describe the tension between, on the one hand, a city planning agency and community residents and, on the other hand, the traditional planning officials and other city departments. The members felt that it was neces-sary to hide their role as community advocates while they acted in the capacity of disinterested and impar-tial experts.

1051. Noel, James J. "On the Administrative Sector of Social Systems: An Analysis of the Size and Complexity of Government Bureaucracies in the American States." SOCIAL FORCES, 52 (1974), 549-58.

   Tests variables determining the size of the public service in the American states.

1052.   Parkin, Andrew. "Centralization, Bureaucracy, and Urban Services: A Comparative Perspective." THE POLITICS OF URBAN PUBLIC SERVICES. Edited by Richard C. Rich. Lexington, Mass.: Lexington Books, 1982.

Compares the urban governmental structures of the United States and Australia. The design of the Australian system has resulted in a high degree of interjurisdictional service equality without a loss of responsiveness to local demands.

1053.   Peirce, Neal. "Structural Reform of Bureaucracy Grows Rapidly." NATIONAL JOURNAL, 7 (1975), 502-08.

Examines the effort by governors, such as Carter of Georgia, to modernize and rationalize their organizational structures and budgeting systems.

1054.   Pindur, Wolfgang. "The Ungoverned Bureaucrat: A Time for a Change." DEMOCRACY AND THE PUBLIC SERVICE IN LOCAL GOVERNMENT. Edited by Richard Rutyna and Yearn Choi. Norfolk, Va.: Old Dominion University, 1976.

Argues in favor of greater community control as a way to achieve representative democracy.

1055.   Preston, M.B. "The New Urban Bureaucrats: A Case Study of Local CETA Administration in Illinois." JOURNAL OF HEALTH AND HUMAN RESOURCES ADMINISTRATION, 1 (1979), 557-69.

Says that CETA programs bring in a new type of relatively inexperienced bureaucracy. It was felt that this inexperience might account for less discretion being granted the staff. However, the evidence shows that discretion is not related to the experience of the personnel involved.

1056.   Quitmeyer, John M. "Sunset Legislation: Spotlighting Bureaucracy." UNIVERSITY OF MICHIGAN JOURNAL OF LAW REFORM, 11 (1978), 269-89.

Reviews recent experiments in the states with sunset legislation.

1057. Record, Wilson. "The Sociological Study of Municipal
       Bureaucracies." SOCIAL PROBLEMS, 11 (1964), 301-05.

       Examines some of the factors which inhibit the fruit-
       ful cooperation of sociologists and urban administra-
       tors. A major problem is that municipal bureaucrats
       are anti-intellectual and unsympathetic to the point
       of view of the academics.

1058. Rich, Wilbur C. THE POLITICS OF URBAN PERSONNEL POLICY:
       REFORMERS, POLITICIANS, AND BUREAUCRATS. Port Wash-
       ington, N.Y.: Kennikat, 1982. 190 pp.

       Looks at the development of public personnel policy
       in New York City. Originally the result of the inter-
       action of politicians and civil service reformers, the
       policy is now complicated by the growth of unions. As
       a major interest group, the union has had an impact on
       the level of productivity in urban government.

1059. Rosentraub, Mark S., and Lyke Thompson. "Bureaucratic
       Discretion and Surveys of Citizen Satisfaction." AN-
       ALYZING URBAN-SERVICE DISTRIBUTIONS. Edited by Rich-
       ard C. Rich. Lexington, Mass.: Lexington Books, 1982.

       Inquire into the usefulness of citizen curveys on cli-
       ent satisfaction as a way to assess the distribtuion
       of municipal services. No definite conclusions are ar-
       rived at.

1060. Schumaker, Paul D., and David M. Billeaux. "Group Repre-
       sentation in Local Bureaucracies." ADMINISTRATION AND
       SOCIETY, 10 (1978), 285-316.

       Look at the question why some groups are better rep-
       resented than others. Group and agency interactions
       in American cities are observed.

1061. Schutz, Charles E. "Bureaucratic Party Organization
       through Professional Political Staffing." MIDWEST
       JOURNAL OF POLITICAL SCIENCE, 8 (1964), 127-42.

       Looks at the role of the permanent staff in a state
       party organization.

1062.   Shapiro, H.R. THE BUREAUCRATIC STATE: PARTY BUREAUCRACY
         AND THE DECLINE OF DEMOCRACY IN AMERICA. New York:
         Samizdat Press, 1975.   366 pp.

         Concludes that party politicians have caused the ruin
         of local government in the United States. The loss of
         local control of schools is a case in point. A return
         to grass roots government is our salvation.

1063.   Skok, James E. "Participation in Decision Making: The
         Bureaucracy and the Community." WESTERN POLITICAL
         QUARTERLY, 27 (1974), 60-79.

         Examines the role of bureaucracies in "reformed" city
         government in two suburbs. The thesis that bureaucrats
         dominate the policy process in such cities is not con-
         firmed. The level of participation seems more related
         to the socioeconomic attributes of the community.

1064.   Spero, Sterling, and John M. Capozzola. THE URBAN COM-
         MUNITY AND ITS UNIONIZED BUREAUCRACIES: PRESSURE POL-
         ITICS AND LOCAL GOVERNMENT LABOR RELATIONS. New York:
         Dunellen, 1973.   361 pp.

         Describe the rise of public sector unionization in
         local government. The evolution of collective bargain-
         ing in several cities is sketched. The union movement
         is seen as another aspect of the trend toward greater
         bureaucratic autonomy. A review of the strike issue
         and other union interests indicates that all parts of
         the employee relationship have been affected. This may
         leave unresolved questions about the determination of
         public policy.

1065.   Starr, C.M. "California's New Office of Administrative
         Law and other Amendments to the California APA: A
         Bureau to Curb Bureaucracy and Judicial Review, Too."
         ADMINISTRATIVE LAW REVIEW, 32 (1980), 713-32.

         Is none too pleased with changes in the California
         Administrative Procedures Act.

1066.   Steinman, Michael. "The State Bureaucracy." NEBRASKA
         GOVERNMENT AND POLITICS. Edited by Robert Miewald.
         Lincoln: University of Nebraska Press, 1983.

Sketches developments in state administration since
WWII. Methods of controlling administration, such as
sunset legislation, are emphasized.

1067.   Sterne, Richard, James Phillips, and Alvin Rabashka.
        THE URBAN ELDERLY POOR: RACIAL AND BUREAUCRATIC CON-
        FLICT. Lexington, Mass.: Lexington Books, 1974.
        145 pp.

        Report on a study of the Model Cities program in Ro-
        chester, New York. It was found that there are major
        differences between black and white senior citizens, al-
        though these differences are not always recognized by
        program administrators.

1068.   Stone, Clarence N., Robert K. Whelen, and William J.
        Murin. URBAN POLICY AND POLITICS IN A BUREAUCRATIC
        AGE. Englewood Cliffs, N.J.: Prentice-Hall, 1979.
        399 pp.

        Consider urban policy in terms of the relationship
        between bureaucratic "micropolitics" and the "macro-
        politics" of the democratic process. The inner work-
        ings of the administrative agencies are seen as major
        determinants of local policies.

1069.   Stone, Marvin. "Yankee Who Tames Bureaucrats." U.S.
        NEWS AND WORLD REPORT, 85 (August 7, 1978), 79-80.

        On Governor James Longley of Maine.

1070.   Stowe, Eric L. "Defining a National Urban Policy: Bur-
        eaucratic Conflict and Shortfall." URBAN REVITALIZA-
        TION. Edited by Donald B. Rosenthal. Beverly Hills,
        Cal.: Sage, 1980.

        Enumerates the reasons for the failure of the Carter
        administration to frame a national urban policy. Bur-
        eaucratic rivalries were a major problem. The process
        of formulating a policy should have been focused out-
        side the bureaucracies. The policy makers relied too
        heavily on a "rational policy model."

1071. Thomas, William C. "Generalists versus Specialists:
       Careers in a Municipal Bureaucracy." PUBLIC ADMINIS-
       TRATION REVIEW, 21 (1961), 8-15.

       Reports on a study of bureau chiefs in New York City.
       Despite efforts to the contrary, most bureaus did not
       encourage the generalist administrator. The civil ser-
       vice remained a collection of separate career patterns.

1072. Viteritti, Joseph P. BUREAUCRACY AND SOCIAL JUSTICE:
       ALLOCATION OF JOBS AND SERVICES TO MINORITIES. Port
       Washington, N.Y.: Kennikat, 1979. 214 pp.

       Argues that local government must attempt to achieve
       both efficient operations and social justice. The pro-
       grams of New York City are examined. The ideologies of
       participation are analyzed in terms of the complaint
       that that city's politics have always been too decen-
       tralized.

1073. Viteritti, Josephy P. "Bureaucratic Environments, Ef-
       ficiency, and Equity in Urban-Service-Delivery Sys-
       tems." THE POLITICS OF URBAN PUBLIC SERVICES. Edited
       by Richard C. Rich. Lexington, Mass.: Lexington
       Books, 1982.

       Explores the assumptions underlying the studies of
       bureaucratic decision rules in the distribution of urb-
       an services. Efficiency and equity may be promoted by
       the civil service and the logic of the bureaucratic or-
       ganization may serve to harmonize those two elements
       of the quality of service.

1074. Wade, Alan D. "On Humanizing the Bureaucracies." POL-
       ITICS AND THE GHETTOS. Edited by Roland Warren. New
       York: Atherton, 1969.

       Advocates a humanized bureaucracy as a way of enlist-
       ing the community in solving problems. As it is, the
       welfare system is a means of oppression in the ghetto.

1075. West, Jonathan, and Charles E. Davis. "Images of Pub-
       lic Administration: A Study of Supervisors in a

Metropolitan Bureaucracy." PUBLIC PERSONNEL MANAGE-
MENT, 7 (1978), 316-22.

Ask city officials to compare the quality and efficiency of the public with the private organization. The
bureaucrats held favorable attitudes toward the caliber
of personnel in government. In general, job satisfaction was related to the perception of government as an
employer.

1076. "Where Bureaucracy Really Runs Riot." U.S. NEWS AND
WORLD REPORT, 87 (September 3, 1979), 31-32.

On the growth of state and local governments.

1077. White, Richard W. "The CAA Transition Task Force: How
Bureaucracy Responded to a Change in Presidential
Policy." POLICY ANALYSIS, 2 (1976), 623-34.

A case study on the reorganization of the Community
Action Agency.

1078. Willis, William. "Bureaucracy and the Bill of Rights."
STATE GOVERNMENT, 17 (1944), 278-79.

A governor criticizes the expansion of federal power
at the expense of the states.

1079. Wortman, Don. "Working with Bureaucracy at the Federal Level." JOURNAL OF THE COMMUNITY DEVELOPMENT SOC-
IETY, 2 (Fall, 1971), 47-52.

Describes problems in the relations between community
action programs and the federal agencies.

1080. Yarwood, Dean L., and Dan D. Nimmo. "Subjective Environments of Bureaucracy: Accuracies and Inaccuracies
in Role-Taking among Administrators." WESTERN POL-
ITICAL QUARTERLY, 29 (1976), 337-52.

Survey several groups to see how each is able to
evaluate the perceptions of the others. The groups

were administrators, legislators, and citizens. In
their perceptions of bureaucracy, a number of inaccuracies were discovered.

1081.   Yin, Robert K. "Production Efficiency versus Bureau-
        cratic Self-Interest: Two Innovative Processes."
        POLICY SCIENCES, 8 (1977), 381-99.

        Argues that policy innovation in state and local gov-
        ernment may take one of two forms: service improvements
        and the more permanent use of innovation.

1082.   Yin, Robert K., Suzanne Quick, Peter Bateman, and Ellen
        Marks. CHANGING URBAN BUREAUCRACIES: HOW NEW PRAC-
        TICES BEOMCE ROUTINIZED. Santa Monica: Rand, 1978.
        155 pp. Appendix, 193 pp.

        An early version of Item 1083.

1083.   Yin, Robert K., with the assistance of Suzanne Quick,
        Peter Bateman, and Ellen Marks. CHANGING URBAN BUR-
        EAUCRACIES: HOW NEW PRACTICES BECOME ROUTINIZED.
        Lexington, Mass.: Lexington Books, 1979. 395 pp.

        Investigates the ways in which local governments in-
        corporate innovations within the operational routines
        of their bureaucracies. The "life histories" of sev-
        eral innovations are examined to identify the factors
        accounting for routinization. A tentative explanation
        of routinization is offered.

V. BUREAUCRACY IN INTERNATIONAL AFFAIRS

A. American Foreign Policy

1084. Alger, Chadwick. "The External Bureaucracy in United
        States Foreign Affairs." ADMINISTRATIVE SCIENCE
        QUARTERLY, 7 (1962), 50-78.

        Analyzes the role of outside advisors, consultants,
        and researchers--the "external bureaucracy." The
        various functions of these outsiders are discussed.
        In general, these contacts between private groups and
        the foreign policy makers may serve an adaptive pur-
        pose by helping the integration of more elements into
        society.

1085. Allison, Graham T. "Conceptual Models and the Cuban
        Missile Crisis." AMERICAN POLITICAL SCIENCE REVIEW,
        63 (1969), 689-718.

        Takes the 1961 missile crisis as an illustration of
        the way in which foreign policy analysts apply concep-
        tual models. Three models--Rational Policy, Organiza-
        tional Process, and Bureaucratic Politics--are ident-
        ified and described. Using the third model, "national
        behavior in international affairs can be conceived of
        as outcomes of intricate and subtle, simultaneous, ov-
        erlapping games among players located in positions, the
        hierarchical arrangement of which constitutes the gov-
        ernment."

1086. Allison, Graham T. ESSENCE OF DECISION: EXPLAINING
        THE CUBAN MISSILE CRISIS. Boston: Little, Brown,
        1971. 338 pp.

        Expands upon the models of foreign affairs outlined

in Item 1085. The Organizational Process and Bureaucratic (Governmental) Politics models are advocated as
useful supplements to the classical Rational Actor conceptual model.

1087. Anderson, Irvine H. "The 1941 *De Facto* Embargo of Oil
       to Japan: A Bureaucratic Reflex." PACIFIC HISTORY
       REVIEW, 44 (1975), 201-31.

       Argues that, despite clear indications not to do so
       from President Roosevelt, officials cut off the export
       of oil to Japan. This move added to the momentum lead-
       ing to WWII.

1088. Arkes, Hadley. BUREAUCRACY, THE MARSHALL PLAN, AND THE
       NATIONAL INTEREST. Princeton, N.J.: Princeton Univer-
       sity Press, 1972. 395 pp.

       Contends that the idea of the national interest can
       be made concrete by looking at the values of the imple-
       menting agencies in foreign affairs. The values in-
       volved in the Marshall Plan program are described in
       terms of the "presumptions" that shaped the actions of
       the bureaucracy. The choices made by officials in im-
       plementing the plan defined the priorities of American
       policy.

1089. Art, Robert J. "Bureaucratic Politics and American For-
       eign Policy: A Critique." POLICY SCIENCES, 4 (1973),
       467-90.

       Maintains that the bureaucratic politics paradigm is
       of limited value in the study of the formulation of Am-
       erican foreign policy. Two "waves" of scholars using
       the paradigm are examined.

1090. Bacchus, William I. FOREIGN POLICY AND THE BUREAUCRAT-
       IC PROCESS: THE STATE DEPARTMENT'S COUNTRY DIRECTOR
       SYSTEM. Princeton, N.J.: Princeton University Press,
       1974. 350 pp.

       Investigates the role of the country officers in the
       making of policy within the State Department. The back-
       grounds, perceptions, and functions of the officers at

this level are investigated. The difficulty of significant reform in the system is discussed.

1091. Ball, Desmond. "The Blind Man and the Elephant: A
Critique of Bureaucratic Politics Theory." AUSTRAL-
IAN OUTLOOK, 28 (1974), 71-92.

Criticizes Allison (Item 1086) and Halperin (Item
1107) for their emphasis on the power of bureaucrats in
foreign policy. The president is still at the center of
American policy.

1092. Barron, Bryton. INSIDE THE STATE DEPARTMENT: A CANDID
APPRAISAL OF THE BUREAUCRACY. New York: Comet Press,
1956. 178 pp.

A veteran of the State Department is none too happy
with the way it is being run.

1093. Brady, Linda P., and Charles W. Kegley. "Bureaucratic
Determinants of Foreign Policy: Some Empirical Evidence." INTERNATIONAL INTERACTIONS, 3 (1977), 33-50.

Test the bureaucratic politics model of international
relations with cross-national comparisons.

1094. Bruun, Hans. "Miraculous Mandarins? Investigating the
Function of Bureaucracy in Foreign Policy." SCANDA-
NAVIAN POLITICAL STUDIES, 11 (1976), 113-29.

Outlines the research needed to identify the roles
of the bureaucracy in foreign affairs.

1095. Caldwell, Dan. "Bureaucratic Foreign Policy Making."
AMERICAN BEHAVIORAL SCIENTIST, 21 (1977), 87-110.

Discusses the development of the bureaucratic politics
model.

1096. Calkin, Homer. "Alvey A. Adee Comments on State Department Bureaucracy." SOCIETY FOR THE HISTORY OF AMER-
ICAN FOREIGN POLICY NEWSLETTER, 10 (Fall, 1979), 10-13.

Extracts some remarks on the management of the State
Department made by a official who served from 1870 to
1924.

1097.   Chai, Jai Hyung.   "Presidential Control of the Foreign
        Policy Bureaucracy: The Kennedy Case." PRESIDENTIAL
        STUDIES QUARTERLY, 8 (1978), 391-403.

        Discusses the changes in the foreign policy machinery
        made during the Kennedy administration.

1098.   Davis, David Howard.   HOW THE BUREAUCRACY MAKES FOREIGN
        POLICY: AN EXCHANGE ANALYSIS. Lexington, Mass.: Lex-
        ington Books, 1972. 164 pp.

        Develops a model of bureaucratic interaction for ap-
        plication in the sphere of foreign policy. The rela-
        tionship between the State Department and three domestic
        agencies is analyzed in terms of the exchange of "com-
        modities." In routine activity, agencies are willing
        to trade parts of their output for the products of other
        agencies. The resulting policy is an outcome of such
        bargaining.

1099.   Destler, I.M.   PRESIDENTS, BUREAUCRATS, AND FOREIGN POL-
        ICY: THE POLITICS OF ORGANIZATIONAL REFORM. Prince-
        ton, N.J.: Princeton University Press, 1972. 327 pp.

        Argues that foreign policy machinery has been shaped
        by considerations of bureaucratic politics, which is
        defined as "the process by which people inside govern-
        ment bargain with one another in complex policy ques-
        tions." It is naive to believe that a single organiza-
        tional reform, such as strengthening the role of the
        secretary of state, can bring order to this area. How-
        ever, through the judicious selection of available
        tools, a president may be able to cause the bureaucracy
        to respond to his policy initiatives. A loyal team of
        staff assistants promises the maximum of presidential
        influence in foreign affairs. Such a team can give
        the president the upper hand in the ongoing process
        of organizational negotiations.

1100. Feinberg, Richard E. "Bureaucratic Organization and
       United States Policy toward Mexico." PROCEEDINGS
       OF THE ACADEMY OF POLITICAL SCIENCE, 34, No. 1
       (1981), 32-42.

       Examines U.S.-Mexican relations in terms of three
       strategies, each with an attendant set of organization-
       al manifestations.

1101. Finger, Seymour M. YOUR MAN AT THE UN: PEOPLE, POLI-
       TICS, AND BUREAUCRACY IN MAKING FOREIGN POLICY. New:
       York: New York University Press, 1980. 320 pp.

       Reviews the performance of the U.S. representatives
       to the United Nations from 1946 to 1979, and discusses
       the role of the permanent mission staff. The personal
       qualities of the representative seems to be the most
       important determinant of the mission's success.

1102. Fisher, Francis D. "Foreign Meddling and Bureaucratic
       Nitpicking: Or Intergovernmental Relations in Over-
       seas and Domestic Aid Settings." JOURNAL OF COMPAR-
       ATIVE ADMINISTRATION, 2 (1970), 211-27.

       Argues that the experience gained in the administra-
       tion of foreign aid programs can be transferred to dom-
       estic assistance programs.

1103. Gelb, Leslie H., and Morton Halperin. "Diplomatic
       Notes: The Ten Commandments of the Foreign Affairs
       Bureaucracy." HARPER'S, 244 (June, 1972), 28-37.

       Describe the rules of the game by which the bureau-
       crats pursue their organizational and personal inter-
       ests. The outcome is the lack of presidential control
       of foreign affairs.

1104. Hafner, Donald L. "Bureaucratic Politics and 'Those
       Frigging Missiles': JFK, Cuba, and U.S. Missiles in
       Turkey." ORBIS, 21 (1977), 307-33.

       Reexamines President Kennedy's relations with the
       bureaucracy before and during the Cuban Missile Crisis.

1105.   Halperin, Morton. "Why Bureaucrats Play Games." FOR-
        EIGN POLICY, 2 (1971), 70-90.

        Contends that the president can control foreign policy
        only when aware of the organizational interests of all
        the participating agencies. Organizations strive to
        protect their autonomy, morale, "essence," mission, and
        budgetary position.

1106.   Halperin, Morton, and Arnold Kanter, eds. READINGS IN
        AMERICAN FOREIGN POLICY: A BUREAUCRATIC PERSPECTIVE.
        Boston: Little, Brown, 1973. 434 pp.

        A collection of previously published work stressing
        the bureaucrtic politics model.

1107.   Halperin, Morton, with Priscilla Clapp and Arnold Kant-
        er. BUREAUCRATIC POLITICS AND FOREIGN POLICY. Wash-
        ington, D.C.: Brookings Institution, 1974. 340 pp.

        Uses the antiballistic missile controversy as an ex-
        ample of the bureaucratic infighting between the Defense
        Department and the president's allies.

1108.   Heinrichs, Waldo H. "Bureaucracy and Professionalism
        in the Development of American Career Diplomacy."
        TWENTIETH CENTURY AMERICAN FOREIGN POLICY. Edited
        by John Braeman, Robert Bremner, and David Brody.
        Columbus: University of Ohio Press, 1971.

        Traces the growth of a career diplomatic service for
        the United States.

1109.   Hermann, Charles F. "What Decision Units Shape Foreign
        Policy: Individual, Group, Bureaucracy?" POLICY
        STUDIES JOURNAL, 3 (1974), 166-70.

        Reviews the recent literature on foreign policy and
        finds that three alternative explanations are popular.
        Policy can be seen as the result of bureaucratic organ-
        izations, the small group process, or the decisions of
        individuals. The applicability of any approach would
        seem to depend upon the nature of the situation and the
        stage of the development of the policy.

1110. Hornbostel, Peter. "Investment Guarantees: Bureaucracy Clogs the Flow." COLUMBIA JOURNAL OF WORLD BUSINESS, 4 (March-April, 1969), 37-47.

Maintains that a program to minimize the risk to private investors in the developing countries is not working.

1111. Johnson, E.A.J. AMERICAN IMPERIALISM IN THE IMAGE OF PEER GYNT: MEMOIRS OF A PROFESSOR-BUREAUCRAT. Minneapolis: University of Minnesota Press, 1971. 336 pp.

Relates the recent failures of American foreign policy to bureaucratic bungling, incompetence, and cowardice. The country blundered into its current imperialistic stance.

1112. Joseph, Paul. "The Politics of 'Good' and 'Bad' Information: The National Security Bureaucracy and the Vietnam War." POLITICS AND SOCIETY, 7 (1977), 105-26.

Discusses the quality of information used by policy makers during a critical phase of the Vietnam War.

1113. Kaplan, Stephen S. "The U.S. Arms Transfers to Latin America, 1945-74: Rational Strategy, Bureaucratic Politics, and Executive Parameters." INTERNATIONAL STUDIES QUARTERLY, 19 (1975), 399-43.

Combines a number of models to examine the American policy about arms transfers to Brazil and the Dominican Republic. Because of bureaucratic considerations, the State Department has been more likely to follow the lead of national security officers than the other agencies involved in arms transfers.

1114. Karas, Thomas H. "Secrecy as a Reducer of Learning Capacity in the U.S. Foreign Policy Bureaucracy." POLICY STUDIES JOURNAL, 3 (1974), 162-66.

Argues that secrecy reduces the ability of foreign policy officials to respond to new outside challenges. Secrecy distorts the processing of information.

1115. Kasurak, Peter C. "American 'Dollar Democrats' in Can-
       ada, 1927-1941: A Study in Bureaucratic Politics."
       AMERICAN REVIEW OF CANADIAN STUDIES, 9 (Autumn, 1979),
       57-71.

       Uses the bureaucratic politics approach to study the
       issue of the promotion of trade to Canada by the Amer-
       ican government.

1116. Kaufman, Burton I. "Wilson's 'War Bureaucracy' and
       Foreign Trade Expansion." PROLOGUE, 6 (1974), 19-31.

       Describes the long-range effects of various agencies
       set up during the latter years of the Wilson adminis-
       tration to promote foreign trade.

1117. "Henry Kissinger--Bureaucracy and Policy." WASHINGTON
       POST, September 17, 1973. Reprinted in AMERICAN GOV-
       ERNMENT: READINGS AND CASES, 6th. ed. Edited by Peter
       Woll. Boston: Little, Brown, 1978.

       An interview with Kissinger who reflects on the dif-
       ficulty in controlling the making of foreign policy.
       Policy is not planned, but rather results from the de-
       cisions of agencies in the pursuit of their individual
       self-interest.

1118. Krasner, Stephen D. "Are Bureaucrats Important? (Or Al-
       lison Wonderland)." FOREIGN POLICY, 7 (1972), 159-79.

       On the Allison thesis (Item 1086).

1119. Lowenthal, Abraham F. "United States Policy toward
       Latin America: 'Liberal,' 'Radical,' and 'Bureau-
       cratic' Perspectives." LATIN AMERICAN RESEARCH RE-
       VIEW, 8 (Fall, 1973), 3-25.

       Reviews the recent literature on U.S.-Latin American
       relations in order to identify the basis of the policy-
       making process. The Alliance for Progress is taken as
       an example. The question is whether the resulting pol-
       icy was the product of any particular intellectual
       orientation or a matter of organizational calculation.

1120. Madar, Daniel. "Planners, Influence, and Bureaucracy."
       INTERNATIONAL JOURNAL, 30 (1974-75), 57-59.

       Says that planners have little influence in the State
       Department's policy making.

1121. Miller, Linda. "Presidents and Bureaucrats." POLITY,
       9 (1970), 228-36.

       A review essay on several books about the politics
       and administration of foreign policy.

1122. Nathan, James A., and James K. Oliver. "Bureaucratic
       Politics: Academic Windfalls and Intellectual Pit-
       falls." JOURNAL OF POLITICAL AND MILITARY SOCIOLOGY,
       6 (1978), 81-91.

       Suggest that the bureaucratic politics model is in-
       adequate for the analysis of foreign policy. It does
       not take into account the role of the president or of
       other major actors, such as Congress and corporate in-
       terests. It requires, moreover, an enormous of data
       for its empirical validation.

1123. Nelson, Michael. "The White House, Bureaucracy and For-
       eign Policy: The Lesson from Cambodia." VIRGINIA
       QUARTERLY REVIEW, 56 (1980), 193-215.

       Uses the 1970 Cambodia invasion as an example of how
       the president may have lost control of the State Depart-
       ment machinery.

1124. Neu, Charles E. "The Emergence of a Foreign Policy Bur-
       eaucracy." REVIEWS IN AMERICAN HISTORY, 6 (1978),
       240-42.

       Review essay on R.H. Werking, *The Master Architects*.

1125. Perlmutter, Amos. "The Presidential Political Center
       and Foreign Policy: A Critique of the Revisionist and
       Bureaucratic-Politics Orientations." WORLD POLITICS,
       27 (1974), 87-106.

Claims that the president remains the major force in foreign policy. Theorists who argue that policy is a product of bureaucratic politics have not explained satisfactorily the role of the presidency. In reality, foreign policy is made by a "presidential court," the members of which are subject to the will of the president. The court is determined by the personal style of the president.

1126.   Rosati, Jerel. "Developing a Systematic Decision-Making Framework: Bureaucratic Politics in Perspective." WORLD POLITICS, 33 (1981), 234-52.

Finds a great deal of variability in the role of the bureaucracy in different decision-making situations.

1127.   Rourke, Francis. BUREAUCRACY AND FOREIGN POLICY. Baltimore: Johns Hopkins University Press, 1972. 80 pp.

On the involvement of the bureaucracy in the making and implementation of foreign policy.

1128.   Roy, W.G. "The Process of Bureaucratization in the U.S. State Department and the Vesting of Economic Interests, 1866-1905." ADMINISTRATIVE SCIENCE QUARTERLY, 26 (1981), 419-33.

Defines the vesting of interests as the extent to which a government agency takes into account the interests of nongovernmental actors. In the process of becoming more bureaucratic, the State Department vested a new set of interests. In conclusion, "the bureaucratization affected the pattern of vested interests through the institutionalization of particular tasks in routine administration."

1129.   Samuelson, Robert J. "The Move to Push U.S. Exports Becomes a Bureaucratic Nightmare." NATIONAL JOURNAL, 10 (1978), 1201-02.

Describes how one of Carter's policy initiatives has become bogged down in implementation.

1130.   Sherzer, Harvey, Michael Janik, and Allen B. Green.
        "Foreign Military Sales: A Guide to the United States
        Bureaucracy." JOURNAL OF INTERNATIONAL LAW AND ECON-
        OMICS, 13 (1979), 545-99.

        Review the substantive and procedural rules governing
        the sales of arms to foreign countries. The major
        roles are played by the president, Congress, and the
        Departments of State and Defense. There is a basic
        tension between questions of national security and the
        domestic economy.

1131.   Sigel, Leon V. "Bureaucratic Politics and Tactical Use
        of Committees: The Interim Committee and the Decision
        to Drop the Atomic Bomb." POLITY, 10 (1978), 326-34.

        Contributes to the development of the bureaucratic
        politics model by pointing out the importance of inter-
        agency committees in forging a policy decision. The
        decision to use the atomic bomb against Japan illus-
        trates this dimension of bureaucratic politics.

1132.   Suetonius (pseudonym). "King of the Bureaucrats." NEW
        REPUBLIC, 178 (June 17, 1978), 25-27.

        Describes the undersecretary of state for political
        affairs as the heart of the bureaucracy's power in for-
        eign policy making.

1133.   Szajkowski, Zosa. "The Consul and the Immigrant: A Case
        of Bureaucratic Bias." JEWISH SOCIAL STUDIES, 36
        (1974), 3-18.

        Claims that American diplomatic personnel exhibited
        anti-Jewish biases in the issuance of passports.

1134.   Thompson, James C. "On the Making of U.S.-China Pol-
        icy, 1961-69: A Study in Bureaucratic Politics."
        CHINA QUARTERLY, 50 (1972), 22-43.

        Argues that it was a core of officials in the Kennedy-
        Johnson administration that laid the groundwork for
        President Nixon's opening of relations with China.

1135. Warwick, Donald P. "Bureaucracy in the U.S. Department
       of State." SOCIOLOGICAL QUARTERLY, 44 (1974), 75-91.

       Emphasizes hierarchy and rules as the major components
       of the bureaucratization process in foreign affairs.
       See Item 1136.

1136. Warwick, Donald P., in collaboration with Marvin Meade
       and Theodore Reed. A THEORY OF PUBLIC BUREAUCRACY:
       POLITICS, PERSONALITY, AND ORGANIZATION IN THE STATE
       DEPARTMENT. Cambridge, Mass.: Harvard University
       Press, 1975. 252 pp.

       Studies major reorganization moves in the State De-
       partment between 1966 and 1974. Failure is inevitable
       unless reorganizations are perceived by the bureaucrats
       themselves as being in their own interest. Or, "you
       can lead a bureaucracy to slaughter, but you can't make
       it shrink." That is, only when officials perceive the
       hierarchy and rules as problems for themselves as actors
       will reform have much chance. The real way to reform
       is through the improvement of the work environment for
       the officials within the organization.

1137. Webb, James. "Cultural Attaché: Scholar, Propagandist,
       or Bureaucrat?" SOUTH ATLANTIC QUARTERLY, 71 (1972),
       352-64.

       Reflects on the ambiguous role of this foreign ser-
       vice officer.

1138. Werking, Richard H. "Bureaucrats, Businessmen, and
       Foreign Trade: The Origins of the United States Cham-
       ber of Commerce." BUSINESS HISTORY REVIEW, 52 (1978),
       321-41.

       Argues that the U.S. Chamber of Commerce was largely
       the creation of government officials, especially with-
       in the Department of Commerce and Labor.

1139. Yarmolinsky, Adam. "Bureaucratic Structures and Polit-
       ical Outcomes." JOURNAL OF INTERNATIONAL AFFAIRS,
       23 (1969), 225-35.

Contends that, in the struggle between the Departments of State and Defense, the military has a number of advantages with which to influence the direction of foreign affairs.

B. International Relations

1140. Allison, Graham T., and Morton H. Halperin. "Bureaucratic Politics: A Paradigm and Some Policy Implications." WORLD POLITICS, 24 (1972), 40-79.

Extend the bureaucratic politics model to the broader study of international relations. The motivation of the actors, as members of organizations, is stressed.

1141. Allison, Graham T. "Questions about the Arms Race: Who's Racing Whom? A Bureaucratic Perspective." CONTRASTING APPROACHES TO STRATEGIC ARMS CONTROL. Edited by Robert Pfalzgraff. Lexington, Mass.: Lexington Books, 1974.

Argues that the arms race is more than an action and reaction phenomenon. The behavior of the bureaucratic participants must be taken into account.

1142. Feld, Werner J., and Lewis B. Kilbourne. "The U.N. Bureaucracy: Growth and Diversity." INTERNATIONAL REVIEW OF ADMINISTRATIVE SCIENCES, 43 (1977), 321-33.

Examines the rapid growth, the recruitment patterns, and the compensation of the United Nations staff.

1143. Gonazales, Heliodoro. "UNCTAD III--Beggar's Opera: The Bureaucrats Overreach." INTER-AMERICAN ECONOMIC AFFAIRS, 26 (Autumn, 1972), 51-67.

Concludes that the United Nations Conference on Trade and Development was ineffective in generating support for a sustained approach to the problem of international economic development. The basic goals were undermined by the desire of the bureaucrats involved to protect the interests of their own orgnizations.

1144. Hopkins, Raymond F.   "The International Role of 'Domestic' Bureaucracy." INTERNATIONAL ORGANIZATION, 30 (1976), 405-32.

       Examines the international role of agencies with a mission related to domestic affairs, such as the Department of Agriculture. The study of international relations should not be confined to the traditional foreign affairs units.

1145. Hopkins, Raymond F.   "Global Management Networks: The Internationalization of Domestic Bureaucracies." INTERNATIONAL SOCIAL SCIENCE JOURNAL, 30 (1978), 31-46.

       Descibes the increasingly important ramifications of domestic government agencies, for example, those involved with food or energy.

1146. Jacobson, Harold K.   "ITU: A Potpourri of Bureaucrats and Industrialists." THE ANATOMY OF INFLUENCE: DECISION MAKING IN INTERNATIONAL ORGANIZATION. Edited by Robert W. Cox and Harold K. Jacobson.   New Haven, Conn.: Yale University Press, 1973.

       Describes the International Telecommunications Union, the oldest and one of the smallest international organizations. The organization is dominated by officials of national communications agencies and representatives of private firms.

1147. Lauren, Paul G.   DIPLOMATS AND BUREAUCRATS: THE FIRST INSTITUTIONAL RESPONSES TO TWENTIETH-CENTURY DIPLOMACY IN FRANCE AND GERMANY. Stanford, Cal.: Hoover Institution Press, 1976.   294 pp.

       Discusses the organization of modern diplomacy from a historical perspective. Critical administrative reforms in the two nations are detailed.

1148. Marshall, A.W.   "NATO Defense Planning: The Political and Bureaucratic Constraints." DEFENSE MANAGEMENT. Edited by Stephen Enke. Englewood Cliffs, N.J.: Prentice-Hall, 1967.

Inquires into the continuing military weakness of America's European allies. The reluctance to spend money for self-defense stems from the budgetary processes of the individual nations. The erection of a strong military alliance will be inhibited by the acts of the individual bureaucracies.

1149. Nashat, Mahyar. NATIONAL INTERESTS AND BUREAUCRACY VERSUS DEVELOPMENT AID: A STUDY OF THE UNITED NATIONS EXPANDED PROGRAMME OF TECHNICAL ASSISTANCE TO THE THIRD WORLD. Geneva: Tribune Editions, 1978. 213 pp.

Examines the spotty record of one of the first efforts to provide technical assistance of developing countries. The involvement of national and international bureaucracies reduced the effectiveness of the program.

1150. "Politics, Bureaucracy, and the Environment." NATURE, 237 (1972), 363-64.

Describes the positions of various international organizations taking part in the UN Conference on the Human Environment.

1151. Rattinger, Hans. "Armaments, Détente and Bureaucracy." JOURNAL OF CONFLICT RESOLUTION, 19 (1975), 571-95.

Investigates the level of defense spending for NATO and the Warsaw Pact in order to detect differences from a level that could be predicted by "bureaucratic momentum." Such momentum, and not the response of the actors to crises, is the most important determinant of spending in both camps.

1152. Sharp, Walter R. "International Bureaucracies and Political Development." BUREAUCRACY AND POLITICAL DEVELOPMENT. Edited by Joseph LaPalombara. Princeton, N.J.: Princeton University Press, 1963.

Examines the performance of the development programs sponsored by the United Nations. UN field agents tend to influence the host country, either by affecting the institutional structure or by impinging upon budgetary decisions.

1153.   Sommerfeld, Paul. "The UN Bureaucracy: The Need for
        Reform." VENTURE, 22 (November, 1970), 11-14.

        On proposed changes in the administrative staff of
        the United Nations.

1154.   Vittachi, Tarzie. "Newspeak among the Diplomats: A
        Concise Glossary to the Speech of International Bur-
        eaucracy." HORIZON, 18 (Autumn, 1976), 88-89.

        Looks at the strange way in which diplomats speak
        without saying anything.

1155.   Weiss, Thomas G. INTERNATIONAL BUREAUCRACY: AN ANALYSIS
        OF THE OPERATION OF FUNCTIONAL AND GLOBAL INTERNAT-
        IONAL SECRETARIATS. Lexington, Mass.: Lexington
        Books, 1975. 187 pp.

        Looks at the theory and practice of international ad-
        ministration, with emphasis on the nature of the civil
        service. Ideally, the international bureaucrat must be
        independent, impartial, and dedicated to the global in-
        terest. In fact, however, these administrators tend
        to be loyal to their functional organizations and to
        be nervous about questions of power. They are an elite
        group, often out of touch with the humanity they are
        supposed to serve. The management of ILO and UNICEF
        are used as case studies.

1156.   Weiss, Thomas G., and Robert S. Jordan. "Bureaucratic
        Politics and the World Food Conference: The Interna-
        tional Policy Process." WORLD POLITICS, 28 (1976),
        422-39.

        Investigate the role of the Food and Agriculture Or-
        ganization in promoting the World Food Conference. The
        conference is evidence that international organizations
        can transcend national interests to reach some greater
        goal. The officials involved with the problem of food
        were able to influence the governments of the member
        nations. Since the administrative sphere may become
        a major arena of international relations, it is impor-
        tant that scholars examine the dynamics of policy mak-
        ing at this level.

1157. Weiss, Thomas G. "International Bureaucracy: The Myth
       and the Reality of the International Civil Service."
       INTERNATIONAL AFFAIRS, 58 (1982), 287-306.

       Identifies the dominant theories about the interna-
       tional system of administration. There are several
       distinctive features of the international civil ser-
       vice which require a wholly new theoretical approach.
       A different paradigm for studying the international
       bureaucracy is needed.

VI.   HISTORICAL BUREAUCRACIES

1158.   Ali, Shaukat. "History of Egyptian Bureaucracy from
        the Earliest Times to French Occupation." PAKISTAN
        ADMINISTRATIVE STAFF COLLEGE QUARTERLY, 7 (December,
        1969), 1-37.

        Covers salient periods in the administration of the
        Pharohs, Romans, Arabs, and the Ottomans.

1159.   Antonio, Robert J. "The Introduction of Domination and
        Production in Bureaucracy: The Contribution of Organ-
        izational Efficiency to the Decline of the Roman Em-
        pire." AMERICAN SOCIOLOGICAL REVIEW, 44 (1979), 895-
        912.

        Uses the Weberian distinction between substantive and
        formal rationality to examine the Roman system of ad-
        ministration. The contradictions of these two types of
        rationality coexisted within a single system, leading
        to its eventual decline. In confusing ideology for the
        reality, the administrative structure was unable to re-
        spond to outside challenges.

1160.   Armstrong, John A. "Old Regime Governors: Bureaucratic
        and Patrimonial Attributes." COMPARATIVE STUDIES IN
        SOCIETY AND HISTORY, 14 (1972), 2-29.

        Operationalizes a definition of patrimonial adminis-
        tration and measures that factor within French and Rus-
        sian civil services in the 17th and 18th centuries.

1161.   Barnard, Frederick M. "Christian Thomasius: Enlight-
        enment and Bureaucracy." AMERICAN POLITICAL SCIENCE
        REVIEW, 59 (1965), 430-38.

        Describes the political thought of Thomasius, who

lived between 1655 and 1728. He was a leading German
Cameralist and his students were influential in the
formation of the Prussian bureaucracy.

1162. Bielenstein, Hans. THE BUREAUCRACY OF HAN TIMES. Cam-
       bridge: Cambridge University Press, 1980. 261 pp.

       On elements of Chinese administration from 206 B.C.
       to 221 A.D.

1163. Blake, Stephen P. "The Patrimonial-Bureaucratic Empire
       of the Mughals." JOURNAL OF ASIAN STUDIES, 39 (1974),
       77-94.

       Demonstrates that the Indian rulers illustrated the
       Weberian model of patrimonial-bureaucratic administra-
       tion.

1164. Bosher, J.F. FRENCH FINANCES, 1770-1795: FROM BUSINESS
       TO BUREAUCRACY. Cambridge: Cambridge University
       Press, 1970. 369 pp.

       Describes the growing bureaucratization of the French
       system of financial administration.

1165. Carney, T.F. "Two Contemporary Views of a Traditional
       Bureaucracy." JOURNAL OF COMPARATIVE ADMINISTRATION,
       2 (1970), 398-427.

       Reviews historical documents describing the working
       of the Byzantine administrative system at the time of
       Justinian (483-565).

1166. Carney, T.F. BUREAUCRACY IN TRADITIONAL SOCIETY: RO-
       MANO-BYZANTINE BUREAUCRACIES VIEWED FROM WITHIN.
       Lawrence, Kans.: Coronado Press, 1971. 538 pp.

       Discusses Roman and Byzantine administration. In-
       cluded are a survey of the subject, a more detailed
       view of the Byzantine situation, and a complete trans-
       lation of John the Lydian's "On the Magistracies of
       the Roman Constitution."

1167. Chamberlain, William H. "Bureaucracy Kills--A Lesson from Rome." FREEMAN, 13 (1963), 32-38.

Blames the decline and fall of the Roman Empire on the bureaucrats.

1168. Church, Clive. "The Social Basis of the French Central Bureaucracy under the Directory, 1795-1799." PAST AND PRESENT, 36 (April, 1967), 59-72.

Examines the social background of 4,300 ministerial clerks during the Directorate. There was a distinct administrative hierarchy which was comparable to the existing social pyramid. This period saw the beginning of a real bureaucracy in France.

1169. Creel, H.G. "The Beginnings of Bureaucracy in China: The Origins of the *Hsein*." JOURNAL OF ASIAN STUDIES, 23 (1964), 155-84.

Describes how, at about 600 B.C., the *hsein*, an administrative unit controlled by the central government, replaced more feudally based local entities. This move toward centralization strengthened bureaucratic tendencies.

1170. de Crespigny, Rafe. "The Recruitment System of the Imperial Bureaucracy of Later Han." CHUNG CHI JOURNAL, 6 (1966), 67-78.

Examines the importance of Confucian training in the dynasty in the years before 220 A.D.

1171. Dalby, Michael T., and Michael S. Werthman, eds. BUREAUCRACY IN HISTORICAL PERSPECTIVE. Glenview, Ill.: Scott, Foresman, 1971. 178 pp.

A collection of previously published work on the historical development of bureaucratic institutions. The emphasis is on bureaucracy as a governmental phenomenon. All historical periods are treated.

1172. Dorn, Walter. "The Prussian Bureaucracy in the Eight-
          eenth Century." POLITICAL SCIENCE QUARTERLY, 46
          (1931), 403-23; 47 (1932), 75-94, 259-73.

          Argues that the bureaucracy was the most creative
       force in Prussian history. Its relationship to the
       monarchy is emphasized.

1173. Eisenstadt, S.N. "Political Struggle in Bureaucratic
          Societies." WORLD POLITICS, 9 (1956), 15-36.

          Analyzes the social and political characteristics of
       bureaucratic polities such as China, the Byzantine Em-
       pire, and prerevolutionary France. Within such systems,
       there were two areas of legitimacy: that of the ruler
       and that of the bureaucrats. A major research question
       is the degree to which the officials acted as an auton-
       omous group, especially in relationship to the upper
       strata of society.

1174. Eisenstadt, S.N. "Internal Contradictions in Bureau-
          cratic Polities." COMPARATIVE STUDIES IN SOCIETY AND
          HISTORY, 1 (1958), 58-75.

          Identifies features leading to change in bureaucratic
       empires, ranging from the Egyptian system to the Span-
       ish colonies. A continuing problem in such societies
       was a condition of "free-floating resources" which had
       to be controlled to preserve the stability of the ex-
       isting order. An increase in resources often weakened
       the support of the ruling elite.

1175. Eisenstadt, S.N. "Political Orientations of Bureau-
          cracies in Centralized Empires." ESSAYS ON COMPAR-
          ATIVE INSTITUTIONS. New York: John Wiley, 1965.

          Examines the main types of social and political ori-
       entations of bureaucrats in historically centralized
       empires.

1176. Griffiths, R.A. "Public and Private Bureaucracies in
          England and Wales in the Fifteenth Century." TRANS-
          ACTIONS OF THE ROYAL HISTORICAL SOCIETY, 30 (1980),
          109-30.

Determines the backgrounds and careers of some early English clerks. As a highly trained profession in late medieval times, they formed a powerful force in society and politics. Patronage, however, was very crucial in the development of a career.

1177. Grossberg, Kenneth A. "Bakufu *bugyonin*: The Size of the Lower Bureaucracy in Muromachi Japan." JOURNAL OF ASIAN STUDIES, 35 (1976), 651-54.

On the problem of determining the number of lower level administrators in the years from 1336 to 1573.

1178. Hoberman, Louisa. "Bureaucracy and Disaster: Mexico City and the Flood of 1629." JOURNAL OF LATIN AM-ERICAN STUDIES, 6 (1974), 211-30.

Uses a natural disaster to illustrate some points concerning the role of the municipal government in the administration of the Spanish colonial empire.

1179. Hume, Leonard J. BENTHAM AND BUREAUCRACY. New York: Cambridge University Press, 1981. 320 pp.

Summarizes the thought of Jeremy Bentham (1748-1832) on the efficient and responsive organization of the executive branch of government. The complexity of 18th-century political thought is emphasized.

1180. Johnson, Hubert C. "The Concept of Bureaucracy in Cameralism." POLITICAL SCIENCE QUARTERLY, 79 (1964), 378-402.

Traces the major principles of early German administrative thought. The cameralists stressed the importance of an ethos stressing adherence of established routines in administration. Perhaps some elements of modern bureaucracy can be attributed to this school's insistence on the supremacy of internal regulations. Cameralism also provided a theoretical basis for the idea of the benevolent bureaucrat.

1181.   Kaplan, Frederick. "Tatiscev and Kantimir: Two Eight-
        eenth Century Exponents of a Russian Bureaucratic
        Style of Thought." JAHRBÜCHER FÜR GESCHICHTE OST-
        EUROPAS, 13 (1965), 497-510.

        On two officials under Peter the Great (1689-1725).

1182.   Liebel, Helen. "Enlightened Bureaucracy versus Enlight-
        ened Despotism in Baden, 1750-1792." TRANSACTIONS OF
        THE AMERICAN PHILOSOPHICAL SOCIETY, 55 (1965), 1-132.

        Investigates the rising middle class and the develop-
        ment of liberalism in a German state before the French
        Revolution. The emphasis is on the emergence and de-
        cline of a bourgeois bureaucracy within a monarchical
        context.

1183.   Liu, James T.C. "Eleventh-Century Chinese Bureaucrats:
        Some Historical Classifications and Behavioral Types."
        ADMINISTRATIVE SCIENCE QUARTERLY, 4 (1959), 207-26.

        Argues that the bases of classification used by the
        ancient Chinese administrators were moralistic rather
        than functional. In a matter relevant to modern con-
        ditions, it is suggested that perhaps moral behavior
        can be measured objectively.

1184.   Liu, James T.C. "Some Classifications of Bureaucrats
        in Chinese Historiography." CONFUCIANISM IN ACTION.
        Edited by David S. Nivison and Arthur F. Wright.
        Stanford, Cal.: Stanford University Press, 1959.

        Discusses how the Chinese in the 11th century clas-
        sified their officials on the basis of their moral
        and political behavior.

1185.   McKnight, Brian E. VILLAGE AND BUREAUCRACY IN SOUTHERN
        SUNG CHINA. Chicago: University of Chicago Press,
        1972. 219 pp.

        Examines the lower level bureaucrats during the South-
        ern Sung period (1127-1279). The village officials were
        a central element in the system of social control.

1186. Markoff, John. "Governmental Bureaucratization: Gener-
       al Processes and an Anomalous Case." COMPARATIVE
       STUDIES IN SOCIETY AND HISTORY, 17 (1975), 479-503.

       Admits that bureaucratization is usually promoted by
       social elites. However, there is some reason to sus-
       pect that the masses of citizens also have some influ-
       ence on the decisions to vest power in large organiza-
       tions. The period before the French Revolution offers
       evidence of widespread popular demands for the greater
       centralization of government.

1187. Miller, Richard J. JAPAN'S FIRST BUREAUCRACY: A STUDY
       OF EIGHTH-CENTURY GOVERNMENT. Ithaca, N.Y.: Cornell
       University, China-Japan Program, 1978. 310 pp.

       Studies the emergence of public administration in
       Japan, with emphasis on the differences with methods
       in contemporary China.

1188. Ooms, Herman. CHARISMATIC BUREAUCRAT: A POLITICAL BI-
       OGRAPHY OF MATSUDAIRA SADANOBU. Chicago: University
       of Chicago Press, 1974. 225 pp.

       Examines the life of the 18th-century reformer of the
       bakufu bureaucracy which ruled Japan until the Meiji Re-
       storation of 1868.

1189. Phelan, John L. "Authority and Flexibility in the Span-
       ish Imperial Bureaucracy." ADMINISTRATIVE SCIENCE
       QUARTERLY, 5 (1960), 47-65.

       Explains the remarkable stability of the Spanish col-
       onial system in terms of the ambiguous goals governing
       the conduct of administrators in the field. The over-
       riding concern was the preservation of the institution
       itself, a matter of priority because of the self-inter-
       est of the members. Comparisons are drawn with the
       management of the Soviet industrial system.

1190. Phelan, John L. THE KINGDOM OF QUITO IN THE SEVENTEENTH
       CENTURY: BUREAUCRATIC POLITICS IN THE SPANISH EMPIRE.
       Madison: University of Wisconsin Press, 1967. 432 pp.

       Takes the career of the official Antonio de Morga as

an example of the operation of the Spanish colonial bureacuracy from 1615 to 1636.

1191.   Poole, Stafford.   "Institutionalized Corruption in the
        Letrado Bureaucracy: The Case of Pedro Farfán, (1568-
        1588)."   AMERICAS, 38 (1981), 149-71.

        Discusses the *letrados*--the civil servants within the
        Spanish imperial bureaucracy--as an administrative elite
        and closed caste.   They tended to operate like "civilian
        plunderers."   A case study is made of the career of Ped-
        ro Farfán, illustrating the corrupt elements of the en-
        tire system.

1192.   Ransel, David L.   "Bureaucracy and Patronage: The View
        from an Eighteenth-Century Letter-Writer."   THE RICH,
        THE WELL-BORN, AND THE POWERFUL.   Edited by F.C.
        Jaher.   Urbana: University of Illinois Press, 1973.

        Describes the patronage groups which were established
        to lessen the rigors of administrative modernization
        during the 18th century.   These groups served to pro-
        tect the status of those connected with them.

1193.   Rosenberg, Hans.   BUREAUCRACY, ARISTOCRACY AND AUTOC-
        RACY: THE PRUSSIAN EXPERIENCE, 1660-1815.   Cambridge,
        Mass.: Harvard University Press, 1958.   237 pp.

        Traces the emergence of the bureaucracy as the cen-
        tral feature of the Prussian state.   Although origin-
        ally a tool of dynastic absolutism, the officialdom
        soon became an independent source of political power.
        The officials claimed to govern in the name of the gen-
        eral interest while they remained closely allied with
        the traditional landed aristocracy.   The result of the
        reforms by Stein was a benevolent absolutism which de-
        prived the people of any effective status in the polit-
        ical system.

1194.   Sa, Meng-wu.   "The Rise of Confucianists and the Form-
        ation of Bureaucracy in Han Times."   CHINESE BUREAU-
        CRACY AND GOVERNMENT ADMINISTRATION: SELECTED ESSAYS.
        Edited by Joseph Jiang.   Honolulu: East-West Center,
        1966.

Reviews the role of Confucian disciples in influencing administrative behavior in the first century, B.C.

1195. Sariti, Anthony. "Monarchy, Bureaucracy, and Absolutism in the Political Thought of Ssu-ma Kuang." JOURNAL OF ASIAN STUDIES, 32 (1972), 53-76.

Examines the political thought of an 11th-century Chinese scholar-official.

1196. Schiller, A. Arthur. "Bureaucracy and the Roman Law." SEMINAR, ANNUAL EXTRAORDINARY NUMBER OF THE JURIST, 7 (1949), 26-48.

Discusses the imperial bureaucracy of Rome, as well as the special role of personnel trained in the law.

1197. Shinder, Joel. "Career Line Formation in the Ottoman Bureaucracy." JOURNAL OF THE ECONOMIC AND SOCIAL HISTORY OF THE ORIENT, 16 (1973), 217-37.

Identifies the forces leading to the emergence of the prototypical Ottoman bureaucrat in the middle of the 16th century.

1198. Singham, A.W. "Historical Empires and Bureaucratic Development." PUBLIC ADMINISTRATION REVIEW, 24 (1964), 187-93.

A review essay on the features of non-Western administration.

1199. Smith, Clyde C. "Birth of Bureaucracy." BIBLICAL ARCHEOLOGIST, 40 (March, 1977), 24-28.

Summarizes the archeological evidence about the dawn of administration at about 4,000 B.C.

1200. Stein, Stanley J. "Bureaucracy and Business in the Spanish Empire, 1759-1804: Failure of a Bourbon Reform." HISPANIC AMERICAN HISTORICAL REVIEW, 61 (1981), 2-28.

Considers unsuccessful reforms in the colonial inten-
dency system in terms of the clash between imperial
bureaucrats and colonial merchants.

1201.   Stewart, Paul.   "The Soldier, the Bureaucrat, and Fisc-
          al Records in the Army of Ferdinand and Isabella."
          HISPANIC AMERICAN HISTORICAL REVIEW, 49 (1969), 281-
          92.

          Describes how King Ferdinand (1452-1516) reconciled
          his desire for frugality with the medieval disdain of
          his Spanish officers for strict accounting of public
          funds.   The outcome was an army that was a more relia-
          able instrument of national policy.

1202.   Twichett, Denis.   THE BIRTH OF THE CHINESE MERITOCRACY:
          BUREAUCRATS AND EXAMINATIONS IN T'ANG CHINA.   London:
          China Society, 1976.   33 pp.

          On the use of civil service exams from 618 to 907.

1203.   Wallace, Anthony F.C.   THE SOCIAL CONTEXT OF INNOVATION:
          BUREAUCRATS, FAMILIES, AND HEROES IN THE EARLY INDUS-
          TRIAL REVOLUTION AS FORESEEN IN BACON'S *NEW ATLANTIS*.
          Princeton, N.J.: Princeton University Press, 1982.
          175 pp.

          Presents three examples of technological innovation
          in the early stages of industrialization in England.
          At least one of them--the application of steam power--
          developed from early experiments conducted by members
          of the English army.

1204.   Wang, Ya-nan.   "The Social and Economic Bases of Chin-
          ese Bureaucracy."   CHINESE BUREAUCRACY AND GOVERNMENT
          ADMINISTRATION: SELECTED ESSAYS.   Edited by Joseph
          Jiang.   Honolulu: East-West Center, 1966.

          Examines various explanations for the rise of a power-
          ful central bureaucracy in China.   The major reason was
          the interaction of economics and politics as China began
          to emerge from feudalism.

1205. Wittfogel, Karl A. ORIENTAL DESPOTISM: A COMPARATIVE
      STUDY OF TOTAL POWER. New Haven, Conn.: Yale Univer-
      sity Press, 1957. 556 pp.

      Describes the total administrative systems of the so-
      called hydraulic societies. The roots of bureaucratic
      totalitarianism in many ancient empires are found in
      the need for the maintenance of a comprehensive irri-
      gation system. No competitors to the bureaucratic-man-
      agerial elite could be tolerated. The managerial bur-
      eaucracy, or the "men of the apparatus," formed a rul-
      ing class. The role of this Asiatic mode of production
      in Marxist-Leninist thought is critically analyzed.
      Modern communist regimes may be the inheritors of the
      system of managerial statism.

VII.   COMPARATIVE STUDY OF BUREAUCRACY

A.   General Approaches

1206.   Berkman, Ali.   "Comparative Public Administration and
the Study of Bureaucracy."   STUDIES IN DEVELOPMENT,
9 (Summer, 1975), 1-21.

Describes how comparative public administration has
made researchers aware of the special problems of bureaucracy in modernizing societies.   In those countries,
the officials tend to be a powerful social group with
values and goals separate from those of the rest of the
public.

1207.   Blank, Blanche.   A PROPOSAL FOR A STATISTICAL APPROACH
TO COMPARATIVE ADMINISTRATION: THE MEASUREMENT OF
NATIONAL BUREAUCRACIES.   Bloomington, Ind.: Compara-
tive Administration Group, 1965.   41 pp.

See Item 1210.

1208.   Buckley, William F.   "Reflections on Bureaucratic Mod-
alities."   NATIONAL REVIEW, 31 (1979), 579.

Muses about the differences in national attitudes
toward bureaucracy.

1209.   Diamant, Alfred.   "Innovation in Bureaucratic Institutions."   PUBLIC ADMINISTRATION REVIEW, 27 (1967), 77-
87.

A review essay on S.N. Eisenstadt's *Essays on Comparative Institutions*.   Eisenstadt's categories of bureaucracy are used as the basis for a model to be used in
studying both developed and developing systems.

1210.   Diamant, Alfred, and Blanche Blank. "Measuring National Bureaucracies: The Interaction of Theory and Research." JOURNAL OF COMPARATIVE ADMINISTRATION, 1 (1969), 114-27.

Present some preliminary considerations about the objective measurement, for comparative purposes, of the administrative systems of different countries. The project so far involves Western Europe and the U.S. Indicators for input and output variables are now being developed. Possible hypotheses concerning these variables are suggested.

1211.   Dubhashi, P.R. "Bureaucrats: An Empirical Typology." INDIAN JOURNAL OF PUBLIC ADMINISTRATION, 10 (1964), 230-34.

Suggests variations in bureaucratic types.

1212.   Heady, Ferrel. "Bureaucratic Theory and Comparative Administration." ADMINISTRATIVE SCIENCE QUARTERLY, 3 (1959), 509-25.

Argues that the reservations expressed by Morroe Berger (Item 1906) about the utility of classical bureaucratic theory in comparative administration may be based on confusion about the structural and behavioral features of organizations. Organizational structure may be the same in several countries, even if the behavior of the people within those structures shows some differences.

1213.   Jain, R.B. "Politicization of Bureaucracy: A Framework for Measurement." INDIAN JOURNAL OF PUBLIC ADMINISTRATION, 20 (1974), 790-810.

Contends that a neutral public service is highly unlikely. However, there are degrees of political involvement and the attempt is made to construct measures of those differences for comparative purposes. A model is suggested, based on four categories of administrative politicization: depoliticized, semi-politicized, committed, and fully politicized bureaucracies. Each of these types is discussed along four "dimensions of analysis."

1214. Jain, R.B. "Politicization of Bureaucracy: A Framework for Measurement." RES PUBLICA, 16 (1974), 279-302.

See Item 1213.

1215. LaPorte, Robert J., and James F. Petras. "Optimizing Research Opportunities: A Methodological Note on the Comparative Study of Bureaucracy." JOURNAL OF COMPARATIVE ADMINISTRATION, 2 (1969), 234-48.

Explain that the collection of data from a public organization depends upon the timing of requests. Based on cases studies, the optimal period for field research is suggested. In general, it is found that "time periods coinciding with unfavorable or adverse political conditions for agency survival tend to be the most advantageous ones for data collection on administrative behavior."

1216. Lowi, Theodore J. "Public Policy and Bureaucracy in the United States and France." COMPARING PUBLIC POLICIES: NEW CONCEPTS AND METHODS. Edited by Douglas E. Ashford. Beverly Hills, Cal.: Sage, 1978.

Suggests the need for greater differentiation in bureaucratic models since each national case has a different mission. The unitary Weberian model of bureaucracy must be adapted to take account of the factors specific to any organization. The two countries are compared in terms of a fourfold typology of policy analysis.

1217. Riggs, Fred W. "Bureaucratic Politics in Comparative Perspective." JOURNAL OF COMPARATIVE ADMINISTRATION, 1 (1969), 5-38.

Distinguishes among different meanings of bureaucracy on functional and structural grounds. In a comparative sense, one can then inquire whether administrative structures are performing the political functions of a society. This factor is especially important in developing countries because of a tendency toward imbalance among the organs of government. An unbalanced system, or a "bureaucratic polity," is one dominated by its administrative structures.

1218. Russett, Bruce M., and R. Joseph Monsen. "Bureaucracy
       and Polyarchy as Predictors of Performance: A Cross-
       National Comparison." COMPARATIVE POLITICAL STUDIES,
       8 (1975), 5-31.

       Test the relationship between societal control over
       big organizations and the realization of certain goals.
       The values are peace, equality, and economic improve-
       ment. A polyarchic system, in which there are compet-
       ing organizational entities, may be most closely related
       to a value like economic growth.

1219. Santos, Conrado. "The Use of Analytical Models in the
       Comparative Study of Bureaucratic Organizations."
       PHILIPPINE JOURNAL OF PUBLIC ADMINISTRATION, 9 (1965),
       195-208.

       Identifies bureaucracy as one form of human organiza-
       tion. It is marked by jurisdiction, hierarchy, official
       rules, and qualifications for appointment to a position.

1220. Sayre, Wallace C. "Bureaucracies: Some Contrasts in
       Systems." INDIAN JOURNAL OF PUBLIC ADMINISTRATION,
       10 (1964), 219-29.

       Finds that even within Western theories, there are
       divergent views of the bureaucrat. An analysis of ex-
       isting bureaucracies reveals that there is room for
       diversity in the operation of administrative units.
       Many options do exist in the building of bureaucracies
       and no one model is ready for direct imposition in for-
       eign countries.

1221. Sisson, Richard. "Bureaucratic Politics in Comparative
       Perspective: A Commentary and Critique." JOURNAL OF
       COMPARATIVE ADMINISTRATION, 1 (1969), 39-46.

       A comment on Riggs, Item 1217.

1222. Slesinger, Jonathan A. A MODEL FOR THE COMPARATIVE
       STUDY OF PUBLIC BUREAUCRACIES. Ann Arbor: University
       of Michigan, Institute of Public Administration, 1957.
       26 pp.

Proposes a model for the comparison of public services and their interaction with the social environment.

1223. Strayer, Joseph R. "The Development of Bureaucracies: A Review." COMPARATIVE STUDIES IN SOCIETY AND HISTORY, 17 (1975), 504-09.

A review essay on books about the history of European administrative systems. Since no bureaucracy is entirely self-sustaining, the characteristics of any system will depend largely upon the recruitment and educational patterns.

B. Developmental Bureaucracy

1224. Ashford, Douglas E. "Bureaucrats and Citizens." ANNALS OF THE AMERICAN ACADEMY OF POLITICAL AND SOCIAL SCIENCE, 358 (1965), 89-100.

Examines the problems of citizen participation in the developing countries.

1225. Barnett, Tony. "Why Are Bureaucrats Slow Adapters? The Case of Water Management in the Gezira Scheme." SOCIOLOGIA RURALIS, 19 (1979), 60-70.

Studies the frustrations involved in implementing development plans. In this case, Sudanese irrigators who wanted to innovate were thwarted by the behavior of the bureaucrats.

1226. Benjamin, Roger. "The Legal System, Public Bureaucracy, and Political Development." LAW AND SOCIETY REVIEW, 5 (1970), 293-97.

A review essay on A.W. Singham's *The Hero and the Crowd in a Colonial Polity*.

1227. Berkman, Ali. "Administrative Reform or Bureaucratic Reform: The Choice for Underdeveloped Countries." STUDIES IN DEVELOPMENT, 9 (Fall, 1975), 12-23.

Distinguishes between reform of administration, a technical matter, and the reform of the bureaucracy. This latter aspect involves the change of the power position of the bureaucratic elite.

1228.   Brown, David. "Toward a Model of Bureaucratic Development Planning." INDIAN JOURNAL OF PUBLIC ADMINISTRATION, 17 (1971), 232-37.

On the political role of the administration in the making and implementing of development plans.

1229.   Brown, David. "Modifying Bureaucratic Systems in the Developing World." ASIAN FORUM, 6 (January-March, 1974), 2-18.

Suggests difficulties inherent in the transformation of administrative structures in developing systems.

1230.   Chackerian, Richard. "From Bureaucratic to Open Systems: Models of Development Administration." POLITICAL DEVELOPMENT AND BUREAUCRACY IN LIBYA. By Omar I. el Fathaly, Monte Palmer, and Richard Chackerian. Lexington, Mass.: Lexington Books, 1977.

Suggests an open-systems perspective for the study of development administration.

1231.   Colletta, N.J. "Ponape Islands Central High School: A Case Study of Bureaucratic Organization and Cross-Cultural Conflict in a Micronesian High School." INTERNATIONAL REVIEW OF EDUCATION, 20 (1974), 178-99.

Looks at the impact in the change of transmission of knowledge from the extended family network to a formal organization. The family tended to enculturate, while the school acculturated. Cross-cultural conflict arose during this process. Students caught in this situation had several options in adjusting to the new circumstance. The could remain alienated, at one extreme, or they could adjust to a different educational system.

1232.   Cranse, R.C. "Bureaucratic Constraints in Technical
         Assistance Programs." FOCUS: TECHNICAL COOPERATION,
         No. 1978-3 (1978), 12-17.

         Argues that technical advice is usually mediated by
         a bureaucratic organization. What the advisor does will
         be structured by organization needs and may not really
         fulfill the needs of the host culture.

1233.   Diamant, Alfred. BUREAUCRACY IN DEVELOPMENTAL MOVEMENT
         REGIMES: A BUREAUCRATIC MODEL FOR DEVELOPING SOCITIES.
         Bloomington: University of Indiana, International De-
         velopment Research Center, 1964. 97 pp.

         See Item 1234.

1234.   Diamant, Alfred. "Bureaucracy in Developmental Movement
         Regimes." FRONTIERS OF DEVELOPMENT ADMINISTRATION.
         Edited by Fred W. Riggs. Durham, N.C.: Duke Univer-
         sity Press, 1970.

         Identifies and describes the "developmental movement
         regime" as a special type of polity. An ideal type
         of a bureaucracy for such a regime is constructed. The
         elements of the model include the factor of ideology,
         the mobilization process and the administrative staff.
         The structural, functional, and behavioral character-
         istics of the model are discussed.

1235.   Dube, S.C. "Bureaucracy and Nation Building in Tran-
         sitional Societies." INTERNATIONAL SOCIAL SCIENCE
         JOURNAL, 16 (1964), 229-36.

         Discusses some of the difficulties of adjustment to
         national independence. The colonial civil service was
         an elite body, existing in a cultural "twilight zone"
         because of its association with the foreign rulers.
         The bureaucratic ethos derived from that experience is
         not easily reconciled with the ideals of nationhood
         and mass politics.

1236.   Dube, S,C, "Bureaucracy and Economic Development."
         INDIAN JOURNAL OF PUBLIC ADMINISTRATION, 12 (1966),
         343-51.

Presents a model of the role of bureaucracies in economic development.

1237.   Dwivedi, O.P.   "Bureaucratic Corruption in Developing
        Countries."   ASIAN SURVEY, 7 (1967), 245-53.

        With special reference to the Indian case, argues
        that administrative corruption can be beneficial. The
        modernizing elite tends to be most upset with corrup-
        tion, but for the masses, it can be a form of public
        accountability. Within a centralized system, it helps
        to promote administrative action. It may also encourage
        the activity of interest groups and other types of vol-
        untary associations.

1238.   Eisenstadt, S.N.   "Bureaucracy and Political Develop-
        ment."   BUREAUCRACY AND POLITICAL DEVELOPMENT.   Ed-
        ited by Joseph LaPalombara.   Princeton, N.J.:   Prince-
        ton University Press, 1963.

        Defines political development as the increased capa-
        city of a government to absorb varieties of changing
        political demands and organizations. National bureau-
        cracies differ in their ability to contribute to such
        development. Especially important is whether the soc-
        iety is in the stage of early or of late modernization.

1239.   Eisenstadt, S.N.   "Problems of Emerging Bureaucracies
        in Developing Areas and New States."   INDUSTRIALIZA-
        TION AND SOCIETY.   Edited by Bert F. Hoselitz and Wil-
        bert E. Moore.   Paris: UNESCO, 1963.

        Discusses in a general way the problems facing bureau-
        cracies in the newer states. Developing countries tend
        to have several levels of traditions, and because of
        these intrinsic contradictions, it is not altogether
        clear that officials can remain outside of the politi-
        cal process. When they become political actors, the
        bureaucrats may inhibit development.

1240.   Feit, Edward.   THE ARMED BUREAUCRATS: MILITARY ADMINIS-
        TRATIVE REGIMES AND POLITICAL DEVELOPMENT.   Boston:
        Houghton Mifflin, 1973.   199 pp.

Studies comparatively examples of military regimes
from Spain, Argentina, Pakistan, Burma, Greece, and
Egypt. Military regimes tend to pass through several
stages. A critical point is when the soldiers, inexperienced in administration, form an alliance with the
civilian bureaucrats. The coalition is likely to break
down, leading to a collapse of the regime.

1241. Gable, Richard W. "Bureaucratic Transition: The Case
of the British Colonies." PUBLIC ADMINISTRATION RE-
VIEW, 27 (1967), 474-82.

A review essay on six books about the influence of
the British colonial tradition on new states. The colonial and post-independence stages are discussed.

1242. Haldipur, R.N. "Bureaucracy's Response to New Challenges." INDIAN JOURNAL OF PUBLIC ADMINISTRATION,
22 (1976), 1-14.

Urges the administrative elite to consider a wide
range of citizen values in the process of modernization.

1243. Haldipur, R.N. "On Debureaucratizing Bureaucracy."
INDIAN JOURNAL OF PUBLIC ADMINISTRATION, 23 (1977),
814-20.

Argues that development administrators must avoid
bureaucratic norms in their relations with citizens.

1244. Heady, Ferrel. "Bureaucracies in Developing Countries."
FRONTIERS OF DEVELOPMENT ADMINISTRATION. Edited by
Fred W. Riggs. Durham, N.C.: Duke University Press,
1970.

Assesses the comparative study of development bureaucracy. The preferred course of growth for such bureaucracies is often stated by the scholars. Foreign aid
should be designed to encourage an appropriate role for
administration. Outside aid should not be used in such
a way as to weaken political organs.

1245. Heeger, Gerald A. "Bureaucracy, Political Parties, and
       Political Development." WORLD POLITICS, 25 (1973),
       600-07.

       Disputes the reasons generally given to support the
       idea that bureaucracies are the dominant factors in de-
       veloping countries. Whether the party or the bureau-
       cracy becomes the leading institution depends to a large
       extent on the character of the incumbents. The offic-
       ials may have pre-empted the political role and mono-
       polized the key positions for the benefit of the bur-
       eaucratic elite.

1246. Heper, Metin. "Notes on Public Administration 'Train-
       ing' for the Potential Bureaucratic Elites of the
       Transitional Societies." INTERNATIONAL SOCIAL SCIENCE
       JOURNAL, 27 (1975), 163-73.

       Contends that the doctrine of Western public adminis-
       tration must be adapted to the peculiar circumstances
       of developing countries. The potential elite has to
       recognize the need to share its power with an emerging
       middle class.

1247. Hoselite, Bert F. "Levels of Economic Performance and
       Bureaucratic Structures." BUREAUCRACY AND POLITICAL
       DEVELOPMENT. Edited by Joseph LaPalombara. Prince-
       ton, N.J.: Princeton University Press, 1963.

       Argues that both the bureaucracy and the economic in-
       stitutions undergo structural differentiation during
       modernization. The integrative capacity of society is
       lessened as the goal-achievement motive is strength-
       ened. The development of the civil service in France
       is an example.

1248. Jabbra, Joseph G. "Bureaucratic Corruption in the Third
       World." INDIAN JOURNAL OF PUBLIC ADMINISTRATION, 22
       (1976), 673-91.

       Claims that administrative corruption stems from the
       values of the larger society. Reform will have to in-
       clude the complete resocialization of bureaucrats.

1249.   Jha, S.N., "Representative Bureaucracy: An Indicator
        of Political Development." INDIAN JOURNAL OF PUBLIC
        ADMINISTRATION, 25 (1979), 324-35.

        Argues that the degree to which the bureaucracy is
        composed of representative elements of society can be
        taken as a measure of political modernization. A way
        of operationalizing this factor is described. A repre-
        sentative bureaucracy will ultimately ensure democracy
        as well as the control of administration.

1250.   Korten, David C., and Felipe B. Alfonso, eds. BUREAU-
        CRACY AND THE POOR: CLOSING THE GAP. New York: Mc-
        Graw-Hill International Book Company, 1981. 258 pp.

        A collection of essays on the experiences, largely
        unsuccessful, with development programs in Asia, Africa,
        and Latin America. Bureaucratic structures and proced-
        ures have been major factors in the failures of economic
        development. Suggestions for improving the operation
        of the bureaucracy are provided.

1251.   Krishnamurthi, Sundaram. "The Bureaucrat and the Pol-
        itician in the Development Triangle: Three Sides to
        Every Story." INTERNATIONAL DEVELOPMENT, 21, No. 3
        (1979), 19-21.

        Uses the experiences of an Indian state to show that
        technocrats, politicians, and administrators must co-
        operate in effective development programs.

1252.   LaPalombara, Joseph, ed. BUREAUCRACY AND POLITICAL DE-
        VELOPMENT. Princeton, N.J.: Princeton University
        Press, 1963. 513 pp.

        A collection of original essays on development admin-
        istration. Contains Items 1238, 1247, 1253, 1254,
        1272, 1277, 1329, 1580 and 1618.

1253.   LaPalombara, Joseph. "An Overview of Bureaucracy and
        Political Development." BUREAUCRACY AND POLITICAL
        DEVELOPMENT. Princeton, N.J.: Princeton University
        Press, 1963.

Summarizes the key problems confronting bureaucracies
in the process of political development. Concepts such
as "bureaucracy," "development," and "modernity" are
evaluated.

1254. LaPalombara, Joseph. "Bureaucracy and Political Devel-
          opment: Notes, Queries, and Dilemmas." BUREAUCRACY
          AND POLITICAL DEVELOPMENT. Edited by Joseph LaPal-
          ombara. Princeton, N.J.: Princeton University Press,
          1963.

       Discusses the role of public administration in the
       process of modernization and political change. Change
       in a polity occurs along four dimensions: structural
       differentiation, magnitude, achievement orientation,
       and secularization. For modernizing elites, democracy
       is often perceived as an ineffective means of progress.

1255. Leff, Nathaniel. "Economic Development through Bureau-
          cratic Corruption." AMERICAN BEHAVIORAL SCIENTIST,
          8 (November, 1964), 8-15.

       Argues that corruption may help economic development
       and, even if there are negative consequences, any at-
       tempts to eliminate it will not succeed.

1256. Mathur, V.K. "Bureaucracy and Political Development."
          EASTERN ANTHROPOLOGIST, 19 (1966), 231-40.

       A review essay on LaPalombara, Item 1252.

1257. von der Mehden, Fred. COMMUNALISM, BUREAUCRACY AND AC-
          CESS TO PUBLIC SERVICES IN AFRO-ASIA: AN OVERVIEW.
          Houston: William Marsh Rice University, Program of
          Development Studies, 1978. 29 pp.

       Examines the supposed imbalance in the representa-
       tion of ethnic and religious groups in Third World
       bureaucracies.

1258. Melotti, Umberto. "Socialism and Bureaucratic Collect-
          ivism in the Third World." TELOS, 43 (1980), 174-81.

Says that bureaucratic collectivism is a new form of
production, coinciding with the state enslavement of
the labor force. Developing countries have mistaken
such collectivism for socialism and have installed an
endogenous form of the system.

1259. Milne, R.S. "Bureaucracy and Development Administration." PUBLIC ADMINISTRATION (SYDNEY), 51 (1973),
411-25.

Sees bureaucracy and its problems as inevitable in
the developing world. Improvements will not come easily and solutions will not be spectacular.

1260. Montgomery, John D. "Bureaucracy as a Modernizing
Elite: Can Government Routines Lead to Development?"
POLICIES FOR PROMOTING AGRICULTURAL DEVELOPMENT. Edited by David Hapgood. Cambridge, Mass.: MIT Center
for International Studies, 1965.

Maintains that, despite the success by some ad hoc
groups, the future of agricultural development rests
with the regular bureaucracies. Developmental bureaucracies, however, suffer from organizational patholo-
gies. Institutional and individual changes are needed.

1261. Montgomery, John D. "Sources of Bureaucratic Reform:
A Typology of Purpose and Politics." POLITICAL AND
ADMINISTRATIVE DEVELOPMENT. Edited by Ralph Brai-
banti. Durham, N.C.: Duke University Press, 1969.

Identifies the "annoyance principle" in personal orientations toward the need for reform. Within a particular political context, reform may be a negative
rather than a positive action.

1262. Montgomery, John D. "The Populist Front in Rural Development: Or Shall We Eliminate the Bureaucrats and Get
On with the Job?" PUBLIC ADMINISTRATION REVIEW, 39
(1979), 58-65.

Describes the "populist front" as the idea that rural
development should be locally based. An argument is
made for a balance between local and central control.

1263. Moore, Michael. "Public Bureaucracy in the Post-Colon-
          ial State: Some Questions on 'Autonomy' and 'Domi-
          nance' in South Asia." DEVELOPMENT AND CHANGE, 11
          (1980), 137-48.

          Disputes the argument that the colonial bureaucracy
          was the dominant political factor and that therefore
          post-colonial bureaucracies are autonomous.

1264. Murphy, Earl F. "Bureaucracy in the Contemporary
          World." TEMPLE LAW QUARTERLY, 38 (1964), 43-60.

          Argues that bureaucracy is related to the level of
          capital in a society. In "capitally underdeveloped"
          countries, the creation of bureaucracy is more of a soc-
          ial than an economic function.

1265. Nicolson, I.F. "Bureaucracy in Developing Countries."
          PUBLIC ADMINISTRATION (SYDNEY), 30 (1971), 184-92.

          Contends that the organizational hierarchy is not yet
          developed to the point where non-Western societies can
          help themselves.

1266. Oszlak, Oscar. "Indicators of Bureaucratic Performance
          in Third World Countries: Uses and Limitations."
          PHILIPPINE JOURNAL OF PUBLIC ADMINISTRATION, 17
          (1973), 334-53.

          Discusses the difficulties in establishing evaluation
          measures for the reliable comparison of non-Western ad-
          ministrative systems.

1267. Presthus, Robert V. "The Social Bases of Bureaucratic
          Organization." SOCIAL FORCES, 38 (1959), 103-09.

          Examines the social preconditions for the importation
          of Western administrative methods. Developing countries
          have a predisposition toward a more charismatic approach
          to administrative authority. In Turkey and Egypt, for
          example, there is a tendency to personal leadership and
          subjectivity.

1268. Presthus, Robert V. "Behavior and Bureaucracy in Many Cultures." PUBLIC ADMINISTRATION REVIEW, 19 (1959), 25-35.

Suggests some lines for the development of a comparative public administration. A reliance on Western models should be avoided.

1269. Presthus, Robert V. "Weberian vs. Welfare Bureaucracy in Traditional Society." ADMINISTRATIVE SCIENCE QUARTERLY, 6 (1961), 1-24.

Examines a Turkish public agency to test the applicability of Weberian theory to a non-Western setting. The formal structure may not explain all aspects of administrative behavior in the traditional society.

1270. Pye, Lucian W. "Bureaucratic Development and the Psychology of Institutionalization." POLITICAL AND ADMINISTRATIVE DEVELOPMENT. Edited by Ralph Braibanti. Durham, N.C.: Duke University Press, 1969.

Discusses the changes from the psychological motivation of clerks in colonial times to the more conflict-filled, adversary situations of development administration. The increased tensions have put a great deal of pressure on the administrators.

1271. Reidy, A. "Bureaucracies in Agricultural Extension: Autonomous Role?" PUBLIC ADMINISTRATION BULLETIN, 34 (December, 1980), 44-51.

Investigates the ineffectiveness of most extension programs in development projects. The bureaucratic elite concentrates on the more progressive farmers and thus isolates itself and its mission from the broader farming community.

1272. Riggs, Fred W. "Bureaucrats and Political Development: A Paradoxical View." BUREAUCRACY AND POLITICAL DEVELOPMENT. Edited by Joseph LaPalombara. Princeton, N.J.: Princeton University Press, 1963.

Looks at the conditions under which non-bureaucratic

centers flourish or decline in developing countries.
Executive bodies tend to dominate politics. The im-
portation of Western administration may have a negative
impact on political institutions. Strengthening of administration causes the political spheres to lag behind.
Separate political institutions may have a better chance
at developing if the bureaucracy is relatively weak.

1273.   al-Salman, Fakhri. "Some Observations on Developmental
        Change and Bureaucracy in Developing Countries." RES
        PUBLICA, 18 (1976), 237-50.

        Classifies types of social change and the differences
        in bureaucratic involvement in those changes.

1274.   Sigelman, Lee. "Do Modern Bureaucracies Dominate Un-
        developed Polities?" AMERICAN POLITICAL SCIENCE RE-
        VIEW, 66 (1972), 525-28.

        Tests the thesis that administrative modernity leads
        to greater political power for the bureaucracy. The
        thesis is not confirmed by data from Third World na-
        tions.

1275.   Sigelman, Lee. "Bureaucratic Development and Dominance:
        A New Test of the Imbalance Thesis." WESTERN POLIT-
        ICAL QUARTERLY, 28 (1974), 308-13.

        Finds that the less developed bureaucracies are often
        the politically dominant ones. Bureaucratic develop-
        ment may be consistent with greater political develop-
        ment.

1276.   Spengler, Joseph J. "Public Bureaucracy, Resources
        Structure, and Economic Development: A Note." KY-
        KLOS, 11 (1958), 459-89.

        Argues that one of the greatest needs for economic
        development are managers with the proper skills and
        entrepreneurial motivations. The expansion of the bur-
        eaucracy lures these people away from the private sec-
        tor. The result is a misuse of scarce managerial tal-
        ent.

1277.   Spengler, Joseph J.   "Bureaucracy and Economic Develop-
        ment."   BUREAUCRACY AND POLITICAL DEVELOPMENT.   Ed-
        ited by Joseph LaPalombara.   Princeton, N.J.: Prince-
        ton University Press, 1963.

        Studies the role of the public bureaucracy in econ-
        omic development. The most important function of the
        bureaucracy is to provide a long-range planning hori-
        zon. However, there is often a disparity between the
        desired role and actual capacity.

1278.   Tilman, Robert O.   "Emergence of Black-Market Bureau-
        cracy: Administration, Development, and Corruption
        in the New States."   PUBLIC ADMINISTRATION REVIEW,
        28 (1968), 437-44.

        Views formal bureaucratic systems as versions of a
        controlled economy. A "black market" for corrupt prac-
        tices arises when the demand becomes high enough. The
        effect of corruption on political economic development
        is still unclear.

1279.   Torry, William L.   "Bureaucracy, Community, and Natural
        Disasters."   HUMAN ORGANIZATION, 37 (1978), 302-08.

        Argues that disaster relief programs may have detri-
        mental effects by weakening the self-help mechanisms
        of the local community. A transitory bureaucracy is
        a poor substitute for an indigenous relief system, par-
        ticularly in developing countries.

1280.   Trimberger, Ellen Kay.   REVOLUTION FROM ABOVE: MILITARY
        BUREAUCRATS IN JAPAN, TURKEY, EGYPT, AND PERU.   New
        Brunswick, N.J.: Transaction Books, 1978.   196 pp.

        Examines two 19th-century and two 20th-century cases
        of social and economic revolutions led by administra-
        tive elites, and particularly by the military members.
        The question is: under what conditions can the state
        machinery pursue goals of progressive change for the
        society? The revolution led by the administrative elite
        is a specific type of revolutionary process; it in-
        cludes the destruction of the economic base of the old
        ruling class. This sort of revolution will become more
        common in developing countries.

1281. Valsan, E.H. "Development Bureaucracy: A Tentative
       Model." INDIAN JOURNAL OF PUBLIC ADMINISTRATION, 18
       (1972), 38-50.

       Details the roles and constraints of administrators
       in developing countries. A model based on the high-
       level, middle, and low-level bureaucrats is proposed.
       Each level has a different role and faces different
       sets of constraints. Each level, however, does have
       a distinctive political role.

1282. Valsan, E.H. "Tradition and Promise in Development
       Bureaucracy." ADMINISTRATIVE CHANGE, 2 (June, 1974),
       1-10.

       Argues that development administration cannot be re-
       garded as separate from the old function of the mainte-
       nance of law and order. The achievement of development
       jobs requires a level of stability.

1283. Weiss, Moshe. "The Role of Government Bureaucracies in
       Developing States." ADMINISTRATION IN ISRAEL AND
       ABROAD, 7 (1966), 112-20.

       Claims that there is little sub-system differentiation
       in developing states.

1284. Worsley, Peter. "Bureaucracy and Decolonization: Demo-
       cracy from the Top." THE NEW SOCIOLOGY. Edited by
       Irving Louis Horowtiz. New York: Oxford, 1964.

       Examines the impact of native social institutions and
       the colonial system on bureaucracy.

VIII. NATIONAL STUDIES

A. Africa

1. General

1285. Abernathy, David B. "Bureaucracy and Economic Development in Africa." AFRICAN REVIEW, 1 (1971), 93-107.

Inquires why African bureaucracies are relatively
powerful yet operating well below their capacity for
achievement. They have trouble in mobilizing popular
support for economic development. Strong political
parties might be a way to increase the administrative
capacity of these new nations.

1286. Adamolekun, 'Lapido. "Accountability and Control Measures in Public Bureaucracies: A Comparative Analysis
of Anglophone and Francophone Africa." INTERNATIONAL
REVIEW OF ADMINISTRATIVE SCIENCES, 40 (1974), 307-21.

Finds important differences in the French and British
contributions to the present administrative systems in
the new African states. The post-colonial experiences
of Nigeria, Senegal, Guinea, and Tanzania are traced,
showing the conservative and radical versions of each
legacy.

1287. Adamolekun, 'Lapido. "Toward Development-Oriented Bureaucracies in Africa." INTERNATIONAL REVIEW OF AD-
MINISTRATIVE SCIENCES, 42 (1976), 257-65.

Describes the conditions necessary for the effective
development of administration in Africa. The greatest
need is a strong and purposeful political leadership.

1288. Apthorpe, Raymond. "The Introduction of Bureaucracy
       into African Politics." JOURNAL OF AFRICAN ADMINIS-
       TRATION, 12 (1960), 126-34.

       Sees differences in the native polities, ranging from
       hierarchical systems to ones depending upon personal
       qualities. Western-style administration is more eas-
       ily integrated within those societies that were not
       hierarchically centralized.

1289. Burke, Fred G., and Peter L. French. "Bureaucracy and
       Africanization." FRONTIERS OF DEVELOPMENT ADMINIS-
       TRATION. Edited by Fred W. Riggs. Durham, N.C.:
       Duke University Press, 1970.

       Define Africanization as "the deliberate substitution
       in positions of authority, influence, and status of one
       category of persons for another. Persons termed and
       perceived as Africans are recruited and appointed to
       positions previously occupied by persons termed Euro-
       pean or Asian." Propositions are advanced concerning
       the impact of this process on the administration in
       new African states.

1290. Colson, Elizabeth. "The Role of Bureaucratic Norms in
       African Political Structure." SYSTEMS OF POLITICAL
       CONTROL AND BUREAUCRACY IN HUMAN SOCIETIES. Edited
       by Verne F. Ray. Seattle: American Ethnological
       Society, 1958.

       Reviews a number of pre-colonial bureaucratic struc-
       tures. There were some systems with a tendency to the
       appointment of officers by a central power. Since there
       was little specialization, these officers could be eas-
       ily replaced.

1291. Cottingham, Clement. CONTEMPORARY AFRICAN BUREAUCRACY:
       POLITICAL ELITES, BUREAUCRATIC RECRUITMENT, AND AD-
       MINISTRATIVE PERFORMANCE. Morristown, N.J.: General
       Learning Press, 1974. 28 pp.

       Examines Sub-Saharan states. The conclusion is that
       bureaucratic performance is related to the recruitment
       practices of the political elites, to the colonial

administrative practices, and to the relationship between bureaucratic and political elites. Based on this
model, questions are raised about earlier theories of
modernization.

1292. Davey, K.J. "Local Bureaucrats and Politicians in East
       Africa." JOURNAL OF ADMINISTRATION OVERSEAS, 10
       (1971), 268-79.

       Looks at developments in Kenya, Tanzania, and Uganda.
       These are new nations in which politicians have not yet
       assumed control over local bureaucrats.

1293. Ekpo, Monday U. ed. BUREAUCRATIC CORRUPTION IN SUB-
       SAHARAN AFRICA: TOWARD A SEARCH FOR CAUSES AND CON-
       SEQUENCES. Washington, D.C.: University Press of
       America, 1979. 449 pp.

       A collection of articles, most of them published pre-
       viously, covering theories of administrative corruption
       and manifestation of the problem in African politics.

1294. Enloe, Cynthia. "Ethnicity, Bureaucracy and State-
       Building in Africa and Latin America." ETHNIC AND
       RACIAL STUDIES, 1 (1978), 336-51.

       Argues that ethnicity is an important factor in the
       political activity of the bureaucracy in developing
       countries.

1295. Fleming, William G. "Authority, Efficiency, and Role
       Stress: Problems in the Development of East African
       Bureaucracies." ADMINISTRATIVE SCIENCE QUARTERLY,
       11 (1966), 386-404.

       Discusses the problems associated with finding the
       proper mix between external authority and internal ef-
       ficiency in colonial bureaucracy. The ambivalences
       inherent in the changes of traditional methods caused
       much stress for the native officials. In the cases
       of Tanganyika, Uganda, and Kenya, the maximization of
       authority tended to minimize the attainiment of the
       desired level of efficiency.

1296. Harris, Richard L. "The Effects of Political Change
       on the Role Set of Senior Bureaucrats in Ghana and
       Nigeria." ADMINISTRATIVE SCIENCE QUARTERLY, 13
       (1968), 386-401.

       Contends that political change in the two countries
       has affected the role of the senior bureaucrats. Ana-
       lysis is made on the basis of Homan's theory of ele-
       mentary social behavior. Senior bureaucrats have a
       great deal in common with members of the military
       elite who have taken power.

1297. Katako, J.Y. "Bureaucracy and Nation-Building in Af-
       rica." QUARTERLY JOURNAL OF ADMINISTRATION, 5
       (1971), 409-19.

       Sees the political involvement of the bureaucracy as
       a barrier to rational administration.

1298. Lochie, Michael F. "Representative Government, Bureau-
       cracy, and Political Development: The African Case."
       JOURNAL OF DEVELOPING AREAS, 2 (Ocobter, 1967),
       37-56.

       Suggests that the emergence of non-bureaucratic
       centers of power in developing countries will allow the
       administrators to perform their formal roles more ef-
       fectively.

1299. McLoughlin, Peter. "The Farmer, the Politician, and
       The Bureaucrat: Local Government and Cultural Devel-
       opment in Independent Africa." AFRICAN STUDIES RE-
       VIEW, 15 (1972), 413-36.

       Describes the several areas of conflict between tech-
       nical and professional civil servants with local polit-
       ical leadership.

1300. Markovitz, Irving L. "Bureaucratic Development and
       Economic Growth." JOURNAL OF MODERN AFRICAN STUDIES,
       14 (1976), 183-200.

       Argues that Africanized bureaucracies have done little

to promote broad-based economic development. The African administrators have not been sensitive to the needs of the lower class. By emphasizing industrial development, the rural poor have been neglected.

1301.   Tiger, Lionel. "Bureaucracy and Urban Symbol Systems."
THE CITY IN MODERN AFRICA. Edited by H. Miner. New
York: Praeger, 1967.

Suggests that, because of the central role of the state and administration, the city in modern Africa takes as its symbolic nucleus the bureaucracy.

1302.   White, C.M.N. "The Introduction of Western Bureaucracy
into African Politics." FROM TRIBAL RULE TO MODERN
GOVERNMENT. Edited by Raymond Apthorpe. Lusaka:
Rhodes-Livingston Institute, 1959.

On the confrontation of the colonial administrators with native polities.

1303.   Omitted.

2. Botswana

1304.   Picard, Louis. "Bureaucrats, Cattle and Public Policy:
Land Policy in Botswana." COMPARATIVE POLITICAL
STUDIES, 13 (1980), 313-56.

Sees the bureaucracy as the dominant socioeconomic elite. Those who execute and formulate policy may also be the major beneficiaries of those policies.

3. Ethiopia

1305.   Keller, Edmund. "The Revolutionary Transformation of
Ethiopia's Twentieth-Century Bureaucratic Empire."
JOURNAL OF MODERN AFRICAN STUDIES, 19 (1981), 307-
35.

Finds a connection between the contradictory nature of Haile Selassie's centralized government and the drastic changes brought about by the revolution of 1974.

4. Ghana

1306. Apter, David E., and Robert A. Lystad. "Bureaucracy,
       Party, and Constitutional Democracy: An Examination
       of Political Role Systems in Ghana." TRANSITION IN
       AFRICA: STUDIES IN POLITICAL ADAPTATION. Edited by
       Gwendolen M. Carter and William O. Brown. Boston:
       Boston University Press, 1958.

       Examine the development of role specificity among
       political and administrative actors as they worked their
       way through several interim constitutions. Party and
       bureaucracy exert opposing pressures on members of the
       parliament and cabinet. Post-independence governments
       will show greater instability until the roles are bet-
       ter defined.

1307. Dumett, Raymond. "Pressure Groups, Bureaucracy, and
       the Decision-Making Process: The Case of Slavery
       Abolition and Colonial Expansion in the Gold Coast,
       1874." JOURNAL OF IMPERIAL AND COMMONWEALTH HISTORY,
       9 (1981), 193-215.

       Describes the British reaction to the Asante War of
       1873-74.

1308. Kuklick, Henrika. THE IMPERIAL BUREAUCRAT: THE COLONIAL
       ADMINISTRATIVE SERVICE IN THE GOLD COAST, 1920-1939.
       Stanford, Cal.: Hoover Institution Press, 1979. 225
       pp.

       Investigates the culture of colonialism through a des-
       cription of the "occupational life cycle" of British
       administrators in the Gold Coast. The administrative
       impact of the colonial legacy on developments in Ghana
       is discussed.

1309. Price, Robert M. SOCIETY AND BUREAUCRACY IN CONTEMP-
       ORARY GHANA. Berkeley: University of California
       Press, 1975. 261 pp.

Traces the weaknesses of the bureaucracy of Ghana to the persistence of the ties of civil servants with their kinship groups. Bureaucrats are expected to honor familial obligations rather than look out for the welfare of the general public.

1310. Wilks, Ivor. "Aspects of Bureaucratization in Ashanti in the Nineteenth Century." JOURNAL OF AFRICAN HISTORY, 7 (1966), 215-32.

Studies the emergence of an administrative class in the Ashanti empire. The king gained power through the appointment and promotion of a group of officials on the basis of merit.

5. Kenya

1311. Berman, Bruce. "Bureaucracy and Incumbent Violence: Colonial Administration and the Origins of the 'Mau Mau' Emergency in Kenya." BRITISH JOURNAL OF POLITICAL SCIENCE, 6 (1976), 143-75.

Argues that the Mau Mau emergency was actually a pre-emptive action by colonial authorities against native Kenyan leadership.

1312. Blunt, Peter. "Bureaucracy and Ethnicity in Kenya: Some Conjectures for the Eighties." JOURNAL OF APPLIED BEHAVIORAL SCIENCE, 16 (1980), 336-53.

Suggests that ethnic homogeneity is likely to become an important part of organizations in Kenya.

1313. Nellis, John. "Is the Kenyan Bureaucracy Developmental? Political Considerations in Development Administration." AFRICAN STUDIES REVIEW, 14 (1971), 389-401.

Contends that although the Kenyan bureaucracy is politically powerful, it has not been active in promoting development. This is because of the conservative bias of the administrative elite.

1314. Parkin, David. "The Rhetoric of Responsibility: Bureau-
       cratic Communication in a Kenya Farming Area." POL-
       ITICAL LANGUAGE AND ORATORY IN TRADITIONAL SOCIETY.
       Edited by Maurice Bloch. New York: Academic Press,
       1975.

       Analyzes the official pronouncements of administra-
       tors in terms of their ideological or planning content.
       Bureaucrats could appeal to either dimension in their
       attempts to stimulate compliance with plans.

1315. Tiger, Lionel. "Bureaucracy and Charisma in Ghana."
       JOURNAL OF ASIAN AND AFRICAN STUDIES, 1 (1966),
       13-26.

       Describes the relations of Nkrumah and the senior
       civil service in the context of the routinization of
       charisma. The bureaucracy has not always adjusted to
       the leadership of the political head.

1316. Walguchu, Julius. "The Politics of Nation-Building in
       Kenya: A Study of Bureaucratic Elitism." THE ADMIN-
       ISTRATION OF CHANGE IN AFRICA: ESSAYS IN THE THEORY
       AND PRACTICE OF DEVELOPMENT ADMINISTRATION IN AFRICA.
       Edited by E. Philip Morgan. New York: Dunellen, 1974.

       Argues that the political neutrality of the adminis-
       tration is not now feasible in Kenya. This is espec-
       ially true since the decline of the role of political
       parties. But whatever the case, the bureaucracy as a
       power center has not been of great benefit to the pub-
       lic.

1317. Yambo, Mauri. "The Dialectic of Size and Structure:
       The Case of Kenya's State Bureaucracy." AFRICAN
       JOURNAL OF SOCIOLOGY, 1 (1981), 72-100.

       Disputes the contention that the Kenyan bureaucracy
       has not undergone significant change since independence.
       That bureaucracy is both more extensive and complex
       than in 1963. However, the dominant ideology of the
       nation has remained the same.

6. Liberia

1318. Nimley, Anthony J. THE LIBERIAN BUREAUCRACY: AN ANA-
LYSIS AND EVALUATION OF THE ENVIRONMENT, STRUCTURE,
AND FUNCTIONS. Washington, D.C.: University Press
of America, 1980. 314 pp.

A general description of the administrative system of
Liberia.

7. Mali

1319. Meillassoux, Claude. "A Class Analysis of the Bureaucratic Process in Mali." JOURNAL OF DEVELOPMENT STUD-
IES, 6 (1970), 97-110.

Concludes that the native aristocracy was able to assume important roles in the colonial bureaucracy. It
was thus able to continue its dominant role in society
after independence.

8. Nigeria

1320. Adamolekun, 'Lapido. "Inside Bureaucracy: Some Reflections on My Experiences within a Nigerian State Administration." QUARTERLY JOURNAL OF ADMINISTRATION,
9 (1975), 203-17.

Reports on his tour of duty in Nigerian public administration. An area of interest is success of administrative efforts at the local level. Political leadership seems to play a part in administrative success
in local government.

1321. Agbonifo, Peter O., and Ronald Cohen. "The Peasant
Connection: A Case Study in the Bureaucracy of Agri-
Industry." HUMAN ORGANIZATION, 35 (1976), 367-79.

Describe a plan for cooperation between local farmers

and a large food processing company. For economic reasons, the scheme did not work well, and the bureaucracy was unable to help in making adjustments. The mistakes might have been avoided through better planning.

1322. Aina, Sola. "Bureaucratic Corruption in Nigeria: Continuing Search for Causes and Cures." INTERNATIONAL REVIEW OF ADMINISTRATIVE SCIENCES, 48 (1982), 70-76.

Looks at the effect of corruption on Nigerian development programs. There is no single solution to the problem.

1323. Aluko, T.M. "Administrator in Our Public Services: A Professional Officer Speaks Up on Bureaucracy." NIGERIAN ADMINISTRATION AND ITS POLITCAL SETTING. Edited by A. Adedeji. London: Hutchinson Educational, 1968.

Presents the view of an expert technician about the bad effects of central control units in the Nigerian administration.

1324. Asobie, H.A. "Bureaucratic Politics and Foreign Policy: The Nigerian Experience, 1960-1975." CIVILISATIONS, 30 (1980), 253-75.

Uses the bureaucratic politics model to describe the foreign policy in the early years of independence.

1325. Cole, Taylor. "Bureaucracy in Transition: Independent Nigeria." PUBLIC ADMINISTRATION, 38 (1960), 321-37.

Describes the civil service at the beginning of nationhood, with special reference of the Nigerization process.

1326. Ekpo, Monday U. "Gift Giving and Bureaucratic Corruption in Nigeria." BUREAUCRATIC CORRUPTION IN SUB-SAHARAN AFRICA: TOWARD A SEARCH FOR CAUSES AND CONSEQUENCES. Edited by Monday U. Ekpo. Washington, D.C.: University Press of America, 1979.

Views bureaucratic corruption in Nigeria as a vestige of the traditional ritual of giving gifts to people in authority.

1327.   Green, Harry A.   "Administrative Capacity for Development: Proposals for Bureaucratic Reform in Nigeria."
        PHILIPPINE JOURNAL OF PUBLIC ADMINISTRATION, 20 (1976), 292-307.

        Describes the introduction of administrative reforms known as the "New Style Public Service."

1328.   Green, Harry A.   "Bureaucracy and Professionalism: Toward Management Improvement in Nigeria."   JOURNAL OF ADMINISTRATION OVERSEAS, 16 (April, 1977), 88-97.

        Discusses a reform movement in the Nigerian public service. Greater professionalism was the main concern. Staff training to meet this need was recommended.

1329.   Kingsley, J. Donald.   "Bureaucracy and Political Development, with Particular Reference to Nigeria."   BUREAUCRACY AND POLITICAL DEVELOPMENT.   Edited by Joseph LaPalombara.   Princeton, N.J.: Princeton University Press, 1963.

        Contends that bureaucracy, as the most advanced social institution in African states, is perceived as both an alien thing and as a necessary means for achieving progress.   This accounts for the political schizophrenia in these societies.

1330.   Kirk-Greene, Anthony.   "Bureaucartic Cadres in a Traditional Milieu."   EDUCATION AND POLITICAL DEVELOPMENT. Edited by James S. Coleman.   Princeton, N.J.: Princeton University Press, 1965.

        Examines the tension caused by the introduction of merit criteria, as found in the modern bureaucracy, into an established, heredity-centered tribal hierarchy during the process of political modernization.

1331. Kirk-Greene, Anthony. "The Merit Principle in an Afri-
       can Bureaucracy." NATIONS BY DESIGN: INSTITUTION-
       BUILDING IN AFRICA. Edited by Arnold Rivkin. New
       York: Anchor, 1968.

       Describes the conflict between administrators chosen
       according to the principle of "open merit" and those
       selected in accord with the traditional values of the
       Hausa tribe.

1332. O'Connell, James. "Bureaucratic 'Politics' in Niger-
       ia: The Problems of Inter-Class and Inter-Department-
       al Conflict in the Public Services." NIGERIAN ADMIN-
       ISTRATION AND ITS POLITICAL SETTING. Edited by A.
       Adedeji. London: Hutchinson Educational, 1968.

       Identifies sources of tension within the Nigerian
       civil service.

1333. Okali, Fidelis. "The Dilemma of Premature Bureaucrat-
       ization in the New States of Africa: The Case of Nig-
       eria." AFRICAN STUDIES REVIEW, 23 (September, 1980),
       1-16.

       Argues that Western formalism was superimposed on the
       traditional social norms. As a result, the bureaucracy
       is not a means for achieving the public interest. In-
       stead it is an instrument for the satisfaction of ethnic
       and other personal obligations.

1334. Olorunsola, Victor. "Pattern in Interactions between
       Bureaucratic and Political Leaders." JOURNAL OF
       DEVELOPING AREAS, 3 (1968), 51-65.

       Examines the relationship between politicians and
       civil servants in Nigeria. The power of the bureau-
       cracy varies with the power of other social groups.

                        9. Senegal

1335. Adamolekun, 'Lapido. "Bureaucrats and Senegalese Pol-
       itical Process." JOURNAL OF MODERN AFRICAN STUDIES,
       9 (1971), 543-59.

Discusses the growing involvement of the civil service in politics.

1336. Cruise O'Brien, Donal B. "Co-operators and Bureaucrats: Class Formation in a Senegalese Peasant Society." AFRICA, 41 (1971), 263-78.

Describes how peasant farmers are systematically exploited by a government development program.

1337. Schumacher, Edward J. POLITICS, BUREAUCRACY AND RURAL DEVELOPMENT IN SENEGAL. Berkeley: University of California Press, 1975. 279 pp.

Investigates the changes in Senegal's rural development plans. Originally the plans were socialist and predicated on massive changes in the psychology of the peasants. Adjustments to reality have toned down the ambitious nature of the rural sector ventures.

10. South Africa

1338. Cloete, J.J.N. "Saipa Conference on Bureaucracy: A Balanced Perspective." SAIPA, 12 (1977), 91-92.

On conditions in South Africa.

1339. Johnston, Thomas. "African Bureaucratization in Southern Africa: The Changana-Tsonga Migration as a Determinant." INTERNATIONAL REVIEW OF HISTORY AND POLITICAL SCIENCE, 18 (May, 1981), 20-30.

Looks at the migration of the Tsonga into the Northern Transvaal as a factor in the rise of bureaucracy among natives in the area.

11. Tanzania

1340. Finucane, James R. RURAL DEVELOPMENT AND BUREAUCRACY IN TANZANIA: THE CASE OF THE MWANZA REGION. Uppsala: Scandanavian Institute of African Studies, 1974. 192 pp.

Discusses the problems of rural development, and especially the difficulties caused by the imposition of bureaucratic norms. The lack of popular participation in development plans led to a program of administrative decentralization.

1341. McCarthy, D.M.P. "Organizing Underdevelopment from the Inside: The Bureaucratic Economy in Tanganyika, 1919-1940." INTERNATIONAL JOURNAL OF AFRICAN HISTORICAL STUDIES, 10 (1977), 573-99.

Examines development in Tanganyika as part of the capitalist world system.

1342. McCarthy, D.M.P. COLONIAL BUREAUCRACY AND CREATING UNDERDEVELOPMENT: TANGANYIKA, 1919-1940. Ames: Iowa State University Press, 1982. 151 pp.

Assesses the impact of the colonial administration on the Tanganyikan economy in the inter-war years. The various policies condemned the colony to a subordinate position in the international economic order. The bureaucracy was instrumental in perpetuating an underdeveloped economy.

1343. Samoff, Joel. "The Bureaucracy and the Bourgeoisie: Decentralization and Class Structure in Tanzania." COMPARATIVE STUDIES IN SOCIETY AND HISTORY, 21 (1979), 30-62.

Discusses the Tanzanian experiment in decentralization of the political system. The ideology of the bureaucratic elite prevented effective citizen participation.

1344. Stren, Richard. "Underdevelopment, Urban Squatting, and the State Bureaucracy: A Case Study of Tanzania." CANADIAN REVIEW OF AFRICAN STUDIES, 16 (1982), 67-91.

Uses a case study of squatter housing in Dar es Salaam to demonstrate the class features in an underdeveloped country. The proliferation of the bureaucratic culture has made an effective response to a housing shortage very difficult.

12. Uganda

1345. Apter, David. THE POLITICAL KINGDOM IN UGANDA: A STUDY
       IN BUREAUCRATIC NATIONALISM. Princeton, N.J.: Prince-
       ton University Press, 1961. 498 pp.

       An examination of the relationship between native pol-
       itical leadership and colonial administration.

1346. Fallers, Lloyd. BANTU BUREAUCRACY: A CENTURY OF POLIT-
       ICAL EVOLUTION AMONG THE BASOGA OF UGANDA. Chicago:
       University of Chicago Press, 1965. 283 pp.

       Investigates the patterns of political authority in
       tribal society during the introduction of Western col-
       onialism. The conflict and harmony of various insti-
       tutions are discussed. In 19th-century Basoga, legit-
       imate authority was based on either patrilineal kinship
       groups or on the tribal kingdom. Into this system, the
       British introduced the modern civil service at the local
       level. At the present time, both the traditional and
       modern systems of authority are accepted as legitimate
       by the members of the society. The power of the lineage
       groups will inhibit bureaucratic norms.

1347. Kiggundu, M.N. "Bureaucracy and Modernization: A Com-
       ment." INTERNATIONAL JOURNAL OF CONTEMPORARY SOCIO-
       LOGY, 11 (1974), 55-58.

       Criticism of Item 1349.

1348. Miller, Robert. "The Party-State and Bureaucratic/Pol-
       itics Relations in Africa." COMPARATIVE POLITICAL
       STUDIES, 8 (1975), 293-317.

       Compares Uganda with Tanzania in terms of the elite
       involvement in politics. The countries are examples
       of the growing scope of bureaucratic power in modern-
       izing regimes.

1349.   Rogers, Rolf, and Mally Odwori-Mboko. "Bureaucracy and
        Modernization in Uganda." INTERNATIONAL JOURNAL OF
        CONTEMPORARY SOCIOLOGY, 10 (1973), 89-108.

        Look at the impact of formal administration on differ-
        ent tribal organizations and the consequent impact on
        the process of modernization. See Item 1347.

1350.   Rogers, Rolf. "Bureaucracy and Modernization: A Reply
        to the Comment by Mr. M.N. Kiggundu." INTERNATIONAL
        JOURNAL OF CONTEMPORARY SOCIOLOGY, 11 (1974), 59-60.

        A response to Item 1347.

1351.   Southwold, Martin. BUREAUCRACY AND CHIEFSHIP IN BUGAN-
        DA: THE DEVELOPMENT OF APPOINTIVE OFFICE IN THE HIS-
        TORY OF BUGANDA. Kampala: East African Institute of
        Social Research, 1961. 20 pp.

        Tells how hereditary rulers gradually lost their power
        to an appointed group of officials.

                          13. Zaire

1352.   Golan, Tamar. EDUCATING THE BUREAUCRACY IN A NEW POL-
        ITY. New York; Teachers College Press, 1968. 78 pp.

        Examines the operation of the National School for Law
        and Administration in Zaire. It may be creating an
        elite that is divorced from the larger public. The
        value of Western educators in the development process
        is also questioned.

1353.   Gould, David J. BUREAUCRATIC CORRUPTION AND UNDERDE-
        VELOPMENT IN THE THIRD WORLD: THE CASE OF ZAIRE.
        New York: Pergammon, 1980. 181 pp.

        Develops a theoretical approach to the interrelation-
        ship of corruption and economic development. The
        model is applied to three stages in the history of
        Zaire.

1354. Schatzberg, Michael G. POLITICS AND CLASS IN ZAIRE:
       BUREAUCRACY, BUSINESS AND BEER IN LISALA. New York:
       Holmes and Meier, 1980. 228 pp.

       Uses the case study of the distribution of beer in
       a town in Zaire to illuminate the shifting patterns
       of class formation in a new state. Political and com-
       mercial power have become intertwined in the post-col-
       onial period, leading to a variety of coalitions.

1355. Schatzberg, Michael G. "Ethnicity and Class at the
       Local Level: Bars and Bureaucrats in Lisala, Zaire."
       COMPARATIVE POLITICS, 13 (1981), 461-78.

       Investigates the drinking habits of local officials
       and concludes that ethnic associations are useful to
       saloon owners in getting a share of the allocated beer.
       Ethnicity is still a major factor in administration,
       despite efforts to eliminate it.

                         14. Zambia

1356. Dresang, Dennis L. BUREAUCRACY AND DEVELOPMENT IN ZAM-
       BIA. New York: African Studies Association, 1970.
       41 pp.

       Examines the administrative dimensions of economic
       development in Zambia.

1357. Dresang, Dennis L. "Ethnic Politics, Representative
       Bureaucracy and Development Administration." AMER-
       ICAN POLITICAL SCIENCE REVIEW, 68 (1974), 1605-17.

       Tests the proposition that members of ethnic groups
       will represent their group's interest within the bureau-
       cracy. In Zambia, individual officials tended to make
       decisions on the basis of career advancement. However,
       the symbolic representation of ethnic groups is polit-
       ically important.

1358. Quick, Stephen A. "Bureaucracy and Rural Socialism
       in Zambia." JOURNAL OF MODERN AFRICAN STUDIES, 15
       (1977), 379-400.

Examines government policy toward the development
of rural cooperatives as a version of "microsocialism."
Enthusiasm was originally high, but the initiative failed
because of the lack of communication between the administrators and the citizens.

1359. Weinrich, A.K.H. CHIEFS AND COUNCIL IN RHODESIA: TRAN-
SITION FROM PATRIARCHIAL TO BUREAUCRATIC POWER. Columbia: University of South Carolina Press, 1971. 252
pp.

Looks at how the patriarchial position of the Karenga
chiefs became more bureaucratized and thus acquired elements incompatible with the nature of chiefship. The
forces of modernization affected the authority of the
chiefs and made their relationships with their people
more problematic.

B. Asia

1. General

1360. Braibanti, Ralph. "Elite Cadres in the Bureaucracy of
India, Pakistan, and Malaya since Independence." A
DECADE OF COMMONWEALTH. Edited by W.B. Hamilton,
Kenneth Robinson, and C.D.W. Goodwin. Durham, N.C.:
Duke University Press, 1966.

Sketches the emerging role of senior administrators
in three systems affected by the British.

1361. Braibanti, Ralph, ed. ASIAN BUREAUCRATIC SYSTEMS EMERG-
ENT FROM THE BRITISH IMPERIAL TRADITION. Durham,
N.C.: Duke University Press, 1966. 733 pp.

A collection of original essays on changes in the administrative systems of India, Pakistan, Burma, Ceylon,
Malaya, and Nepal since independence. The ways in which
the British legacy in administrative matters has been
retained or modified is the central theme.

1362. Braibanti, Ralph. "Conceptual Prerequisites for the Evolution of Asian Bureaucratic Systems." MANAGE-MENT TRAINING FOR DEVELOPMENT: THE ASIAN EXPERIENCE. Edited by Inayatullah. Kuala Lumpur: Asian Centre for Development Administration, 1975.

Urges development administrators to be aware of the transitory nature of knowledge. If this can be done, the new nations will not need to be dependent upon the ideas and cultures of outside forces.

1363. Farrar, Curtis. "American Aid and Asian Bureaucrats." INTERNATIONAL DEVELOPMENT REVIEW, 15, No 2. (1973), 15-20.

Suggests ways for upgrading the administration in developing countries.

1364. Kraus, Richard, William E. Maxwell, and Reeve Vanneman. "The Interests of Bureaucrats: Implications of the Asian Experience for Recent Theories of Development." AMERICAN JOURNAL OF SOCIOLOGY, 85 (1979), 135-55.

Look at officials in higher education in Thailand, India, and China to show how their self-interest shapes development.

1365. Quah, Jon S.T. "The Origins of Public Bureaucracies in the ASEAN Countries." INDIAN JOURNAL OF PUBLIC AD-MINISTRATION, 24 (1978), 400-29.

Initiates comparative research on the administrations of Indonesia, Malaysia, the Philippines, Singapore, and Thailand.

1366. Quah, Jon S.T. "Bureaucratic Corruption in the ASEAN Countries: A Comparative Analysis of the Anti-Corruption Strategies." JOURNAL OF SOUTHEAST ASIAN STUDIES, 13 (1982), 153-77.

Reviews recent anti-corruption efforts in Malaysia, the Philippines, Indonesia, Thailand, and Singapore.

1367. Quah, Jon S.T. "Tackling Bureaucratic Corruption: The
       ASEAN Experience." STRATEGIES FOR ADMINISTRATIVE RE-
       FORM. Edited by Gerald E. Caiden and Heinrich Sied-
       entopf. Lexington, Mass.: Lexington Books, 1982.

       Examines measures for solving corruption as applied
       in Indonesia, Malaysia, the Philippines, Singapore,
       and Thailand. A matrix of anti-corruption strategies
       is suggested. Strategies can be effective, ineffective,
       or hopeless.

1368. Springer, J. Fred, and Richard W. Gable. "The Impact
       of Informal Relations on Organizational Rewards: Com-
       paring Bureaucracies in Southeast Asia." COMPARATIVE
       POLITICS, 12 (1980), 191-210.

       Investigate informal relationships in the bureaucra-
       cies of the Philippines, Indonesia, and Thailand. The
       object of concern is the traditional personalist, dy-
       adic, hierarchical model. It is suggested that the im-
       portance of informal elements may have been exaggerated
       since close social ties with superiors are rather rare
       in the situations studied.

1369. Wood, Geoff. "Bureaucracy and the Post-Colonial State
       in South Asia. A Reply." DEVELOPMENT AND CHANGE, 11
       (1980), 149-56.

       A comment on Item 1263.

                    2. Afghanistan

1370. Dupree, Louis. "Afghanistan: 1968. Part I: Government
       and Bureaucracy." AMERICAN UNIVERSITIES FIELD STAFF
       REPORTS: SOUTH ASIA SERIES, 12 No. 4 (1968).

       Finds that reforms are often frustrated by the inef-
       ficiency of the administration. "Few bureaucracies
       in the world equal ... Afghanistan in its built-in
       slowdown mechanisms." Most civil servants remain ded-
       icated to preserving the old ways, and change of any
       sort is seen as a threat to their existence.

3. Bangladesh

1371. Ahamed, Emajuddin. "Dominant Bureaucratic Elites in
Bangladesh." INDIAN POLITICAL SCIENCE REVIEW, 13
(1979), 30-48.

Claims that the former members of the Pakistani system have regained their roles as the power wielders.
This is despite their disgrace suffered immediately
after the 1975 disorders.

1372. Blair, Harry. "Rural Development, Class Structure and
Bureaucracy in Bangladesh." WORLD DEVELOPMENT, 6
(1978), 65-82.

Argues that the program for rural development in the
former East Pakistan promoted class differences. The
administrators favored the local elites rather than
the masses of peasants.

1373. Coward, E. Walter, and Badaruddin Ahmed. "Village,
Technology and Bureaucracy: Patterns of Irrigation
Organization in Comilla District, Bangladesh." JOUR-
NAL OF DEVELOPING AREAS, 13 (1979), 431-40.

Use a case study to show the articulation of local
cooperatives societies with the national government.
The irrigation system has worked well because of local
discretion and bureaucratic flexibility.

1374. Kamaluddin, S. "The New Classless Bureaucracy." FAR
EASTERN ECONOMIC REVIEW, 109 (September 19, 1980),
32.

On administrative developments in Bangladesh.

1375. Khan, Mohammed, and Habib Mohammed Zafarullah. "Admin-
istrative Reforms and Bureaucratic Intransigence in
Bangladesh." STRATEGIES FOR ADMINISTRATIVE REFORM.
Edited by Gerald E. Caiden and Heinrich Siedentopf.
Lexington, Mass.: Lexington Books, 1982.

Report on the failure of structural changes to modify
the attitudes of elitist administrators. Self-interest
remains more important than the public interest. The
civil service resists any change in their system of
privileges.

1376. Maniruzzaman, Talukden. "Administrative Reform and Pol-
      itics within the Bureaucracy in Bangladesh." JOURNAL
      OF COMMONWEALTH AND COMPARATIVE POLITICS, 17 (1979),
      47-59.

      Examines the sources of tension within the civil ser-
      vice and between the society and its administrators.

                              4. Burma

1377. Guyot, James F. "Bureaucratic Transformation in Burma."
      ASIAN BUREAUCRATIC SYSTEMS EMERGENT FROM THE BRITISH
      IMPERIAL TRADITION. Durham, N.C.: Duke University
      Press, 1966.

      Traces the changes in the Burmese bureaucracy in the
      postwar period through the assumption by the military
      of political control.

                              5. China

1378. Balazs, Etienne. "China as a Permanently Bureaucratic
      Society." CHINESE CIVILIZATION AND BUREAUCRACY: VAR-
      IATIONS ON A THEME. New Haven, Conn.: Yale Univer-
      sity Press, 1964.

      Accounts for the durability of Chinese civilization
      by reference to the bureaucracy of mandarins. This
      small elite persisted because it possessed the know-
      ledge of how to govern, of how to keep the society in
      operation. The system they managed was totalitarian.
      The links between ancient and modern China are dis-
      cussed.

1379. Balazs, Etienne. "History as a Guide to Bureaucratic
          Practice." CHINESE CIVILIZATION AND BUREAUCRACY:
          VARIATIONS ON A THEME. New Haven, Conn.: Yale Uni-
          versity Press, 1964.

          Argues that the peculiar nature of Chinese historio-
          graphy was the result of a bureaucratic spirit. Among
          other things, history was always expressed as an offic-
          ial document. It was written by officials to be read
          by other officials.

1380. Balazs, Etienne. CHINESE CIVILIZATION AND BUREAUCRACY:
          VARIATIONS ON A THEME. New Haven, Conn.: Yale Univer-
          sity Press, 1964. 309 pp.

          A collection of essays on the scholar-official class
          of China.

1381. Barnett, A. Doak. "Social Stratifcation and Aspects of
          Personnel Management in the Chinese Communist Bureau-
          cracy." CHINA QUARTERLY, 28 (1966), 8-39.

          Discusses mechanisms for the control of the bureau-
          cracy by the Communist Party.

1382. Barnett, A. Doak. "Mechanisms for Party Control in the
          Government Bureaucracy in China." ASIAN SURVEY, 6
          (1966), 659-74.

          Views the Communist Party as the policy-making organ
          of government. Government organizations are controlled
          by, first, a party "shadow government," and second, the
          appointment of party members to government posts.

1383. Barnett, A. Doak. CADRES, BUREAUCRACY, AND POLITICAL
          POWER IN COMMUNIST CHINA. New York: Columbia Univer-
          sity Press, 1967. 563 pp.

          Uses case studies of a ministry, a local government
          organization, and a commune to illustrate the working
          of the Chinese bureaucracy. The party cadres are seen
          as integral parts of the administrative process. The
          leadership level has been able to impose its will on
          the entire society.

1384.   Burchill, C.S.   "Bureaucracy versus Democracy: The
        Chinese Cultural Revolution."   QUEEN'S QUARTERLY,
        79 (1972), 136-44.

        Speculates on the chances of success in the attempts
        to lessen the role of bureaucracy in Chinese society.

1385.   Chai, Trong.   "Communist Party Control over the Bureau-
        cracy; The Case of China."   COMPARATIVE POLITICS, 11
        (1979), 359-70.

        Discusses Mao's methods, during the 1960s, of main-
        taining party control over administration.   Party dom-
        ination may not have been as strong as is commonly be-
        lieved by Western observers.

1386.   Chan, Steve.   "Rationality, Bureaucratic Politics, and
        Belief System: Explaining the Chinese Policy Debate,
        1964-66."   JOURNAL OF PEACE RESEARCH, 16 (1979), 333-
        47.

        Applies the rational actor and bureaucratic politics
        models to the making of foreign policy in the People's
        Republic of China.   The cognitive bases of the various
        groups of Peking officials are analyzed.

1387.   Chan, Wellington K.K.   "Bureaucratic Capital and Chou
        Hsueh-hsi in Late Ch'ing China."   MODERN ASIAN STUD-
        IES, 11 (1977), 427-39.

        Discusses the mobilization of capital by the bureau-
        cracy for economic development prior to 1912.   The
        private sector was unable to match the government in
        this respect.

1388.   Chang, Chin-chien.   "Characteristics of Chinese Bureau-
        eaucracy."   CHINESE BUREAUCRACY AND GOVERNMENT ADMIN-
        ISTRATION: SELECTED ESSAYS.   Edited by Joseph Jiang.
        Honolulu: East-West Center, 1966.

        A general history of the imperial Chinese system of
        administration.

1389. Chen, Yung-fu. "Rural Elections in Wartime China: Democratization of Sub-Bureaucracy." MODERN CHINA, 6
(1980), 267-310.

Examines how the Communist Party used local politics
to infiltrate government during WWII.

1390. Chi, Madelaine. "Bureaucratic Capitalists in Operation:
Ts'ao Ju-lin and His New Communication Clique, 1916-
1919." JOURNAL OF ASIAN STUDIES, 34 (1975), 675-88.

Tells of the activity of a group of officials in the
early Chinese Republic, with emphasis on the relevance
of their policies for Japanese economic imperialism in
the next decades.

1391. Chiang, James K. "Chinese Bureaucratic Characteristics." CHINESE JOURNAL OF ADMINISTRATION, 21 (1973),
11-30.

Reports on the results of a survey of Taiwanese administrators.

1392. Dittmer, Lowell. "Revolution and Reconstruction in Contemporary Chinese Bureaucracy." JOURNAL OF COMPARA-
TIVE ADMINISTRATION, 5 (1974), 443-86.

Describes that attempt at bureaucratic reform known
as the Cultural Revolution. In the effort to recon-
stitute bureaucracy, the aim was to have an administration that was both responsive to leadership and to the
local community. Structural change and modifications
in the patterns of communication have had some effect.
Since 1980, there has been a trend toward the re-estab-
lishment of central authority.

1393. Handleman, John R. "Penetrating the Bureaucracy of the
Chinese People's Republic: The Role of Non-National
Actors." ASIAN SURVEY, 18 (1978), 956-66.

Assesses the potential penetrability of the Chinese
foreign relations bureaucracy by outside groups such as
multinational corporations.

1394.   Harding, Harry. ORGANIZING CHINA: THE PROBLEM OF BUR-
         EAUCRACY, 1949-1976. Stanford, Cal.: Stanford Univer-
         sity Press, 1981. 418 pp.

         Concentrates on the centrality of questions of organ-
         ization policy in contemporary Chinese politics up to
         the death of Mao. Chinese leaders have moved between
         the ideals of further rationalization of the bureaucra-
         cy and more participatory forms of administration. Even
         though effective administration has been maintained dur-
         ing this period, the basic dilemma of the bureaucracy
         has not been resolved.

1395.   Herson, Lawrence. "China's Imperial Bureaucracy: Its
         Direction and Control." PUBLIC ADMINISTRATION REVIEW,
         17 (1957), 44-53.

         Examines the performance of the traditional Chinese
         administrative system. It was good at creating and
         maintaining order but it could not adjust very well to
         change.

1396.   Hiniker, Paul J., and Jolanta Perlstein. "Alternation
         of Charismatic and Bureaucratic Styles of Leadership
         in Post-Revolutionary China." COMPARATIVE POLITICAL
         STUDIES, 10 (1974), 529-54.

         Applies the Weberian principles to the Chinese exper-
         ience since 1949. There was a tendency for leadership
         patterns to move between charisma and bureaucratic auth-
         ority.

1397.   Israel, John, and Donal W. Klein. REBELS AND BUREAU-
         CRATS: CHINA'S DECEMBER 9ERS. Berkeley: University
         of California Press, 1976. 305 pp.

         Describes the development of Chinese student activists
         in the 1930s into members of the administrative elite of
         the People's Republic after 1949. Biographical sketches
         serve to trace the careers of the individuals involved.

1398.   Jiang, Joseph. CHINESE BUREAUCRACY AND GOVERNMENT AD-
         MINISTRATION: AN ANNOTATED BIBLIOGRAPHY. Honolulu:
         East-West Center, 1964. 157 pp.

1399. Jiang, Joseph, ed. CHINESE BUREAUCRACY AND GOVERNMENT ADMINISTRATION: SELECTED ESSAYS. Honolulu: East-West Center, 1966. 90 pp.

A collection of translated articles by Chinese scholars on various periods in Chinese history.

1400. Kau, Ying-mao. "The Urban Bureaucratic Elite in Communist China: A Case Study of Wuhan, 1949-1965." CHINESE COMMUNIST POLITICS IN ACTION. Edited by A. Doak Barnett. Seattle: University of Washington Press, 1969.

Studies the bureaucratic elite in a Chinese local government. The system seems to be developing along lines predicted by Weber.

1401. King, Ambrose. "Maoist Anti-Bureaucratic Model: Historical and Comparative Perspectives." JOURNAL OF THE CHINESE JOURNAL OF HONG KONG, 2 (1974), 71-120.

Examines the tenets of the Cultural Revolution. A comparison of Maoist thought with other theories of organization and management reveals several similarities.

1402. Lampton, David M. "Administration of the Pharmaceutical, Research, Public Health, and Population Bureaucracies." CHINA QUARTERLY, 74 (1978), 385-400.

A look at a specialized part of Chinese public administration.

1403. Lee, Shu-ching. "Administration and Bureaucracy: The Power Structure in Chinese Society." TRANSACTIONS OF THE SECOND WORLD CONGRESS OF SOCIOLOGY, (1954), 3-15.

Claims that the Chinese imperial bureaucracy reflected an extension of the family roles into the formal organization.

1404. Lewis, John. "Leader, Commissar and Bureaucrat: The
       Chinese Political System in the Last Days of the
       Revolution." JOURNAL OF INTERNATIONAL AFFAIRS, 24
       (1970), 48-74.

       Describes the development of administrative doctrine
       in the years before the Chinese Communists assumed the
       control of government.

1405. Marsh, Robert M. "Bureaucratic Constraints on Nepot-
       ism in the Ch'ing Period." JOURNAL OF ASIAN STUDIES,
       19 (1960), 117-33.

       Examines the determinants of career advancement in
       the Ch'ing bureaucracy (1644-1912). Factors such as
       seniority were more important than extra-bureaucratic
       attributes such as family ties. The sons of commoners
       had the same chance of promotion as sons of the offic-
       ials or members of the local elite.

1406. Metzger, Thomas A. THE INTERNAL ORGANIZATION OF THE
       CH'ING BUREAUCRACY: LEGAL, NORMATIVE, AND COMMUNICA-
       TIONS ASPECTS. Cambridge, Mass.: Harvard University
       Press, 1973. 469 pp.

       On governmnental organization from 1644 to 1912.

1407. Michael, Franz. THE ORIGINS OF MANCHU RULE IN CHINA:
       FRONTIER AND BUREAUCRACY AS INTERACTION FORCES IN
       THE CHINESE EMPIRE. Baltimore: Johns Hopkins Press,
       1942. 127 pp.

       Discusses the evolution of the Manchu bureaucracy and
       its establishment in China.

1408. Morgan, Maria C. "Controlling the Bureaucracy in Post-
       Mao China." ASIAN SURVEY, 21 (1981), 1223-36.

       Investigates the anti-bureaucracy campaign in the
       years (1977-1980) following the death of Mao. Bureau-
       cratic control has become more difficult since the Cul-
       tural Revolution. Other aspects of the socialist ex-
       perience also cause problems. Legal-rational organiza-
       tions are not compatible with the economic system.

1409.   Nelson, Harvey W. "Military Bureaucracy in the Cultural
        Revolution." ASIAN SURVEY, 14 (1974), 372-95.

        Looks at the role of the military both during and
        after the Cultural Revolution.

1410.   Noumoff, S.J. "Bureaucracy and Revolutionary Continuity
        in China." POLITICAL SCIENCE REVIEW, 18 (April-June,
        1979), 1-34.

        Interprets recent Chinese politics as the struggle
        between politics and production. The emphasis on pro-
        duction has replaced revolutionary politics in the era
        following the Cultural Revolution.

1411.   Oksenberg, Michael. "Local Leaders in Rural China,
        1962-65: Individual Attributes, Bureaucratic Posi-
        tions, and Political Recruitment." CHINESE COMMUN-
        IST POLITICS IN ACTION. Edited by A. Doak Barnett.
        Seattle: University of Washington Press, 1969.

        Examines the recuitment of local leaders into offic-
        ial positions in rural China.

1412.   Oksenberg, Michael. "Methods of Communication within
        the Chinese Bureaucracy." CHINA QUARTERLY, 57 (1974),
        1-39.

        Looks at the unusual and elaborate system of covert
        communications within Chinese administration.

1413.   Pelzel, John C. "Notes on the Chinese Bureaucracy."
        SYSTEMS OF POLITICAL CONTROL AND BUREAUCRACY IN HUMAN
        SOCIETIES. Edited by Verne F. Ray. Seattle: Amer-
        ican Ethnological Society, 1958.

        Finds the roots of Chinese bureaucracy in Confucian
        thought. But while the doctrine was critical in over-
        coming feudal tendencies, it also led to decay since
        eventually Confucianism becomes more important than
        actually accomplishing anything.

1414. Shi, Zhongquan. "The 'Cultural Revolution' and the
        Struggle against Bureaucracy." BEIJING REVIEW, 24
        (December 7, 1981), 17-20.

        Contends that the Cultural Revolution did not really
        succeed in controlling the bureaucracy. The Communist
        Party, however, is still engaged in the fight against
        the emergence of bureaucracies.

1415. Sterba, Richard L. "Clandestine Management in the Im-
        perial Chinese Bureaucracy." ACADEMY OF MANAGEMENT
        REVIEW, 3 (1978), 69-78.

        Claims that the reputation of the mandarins was exag-
        gerated. They had a great deal of trouble in control-
        ling the clerical level of administration.

1416. Taraki, Bariman. "Institutionalization and Bureaucracy
        in China: The Relevance of the Maoist Experience."
        STUDIES IN INTERNATIONAL DEVELOPMENT, 13 (1978), 100-
        24.

        Examines the theory and practice of Maoist doctrines
        about institutionalization.

1417. Vogel, Ezra. "From Revolutionary to Semi-Bureaucrat:
        The 'Regularisation' of Cadres." CHINA QUARTERLY,
        29 (1967), 36-60.

        Says that while the Communist Party cadre has become
        more bureaucratized, the revolutionary vision is still
        an important element in administration.

1418. Vogel, Ezra. "Politicized Bureaucracy: Communist
        China." FRONTIERS OF DEVELOPMENT ADMINISTRATION.
        Edited by Fred W. Riggs. Durham, N.C.: Duke Univer-
        sity Press, 1970.

        Describes the way in which political and administra-
        tive concerns are fused; that is, there is no sharp di-
        viding line between politician and civil servant in the
        Communist Chinese system. This fusion leads to tension
        between power problems and the requirements of rational
        management.

1419. Wang, Gung-hsing. "Kuan-chung and His Philosopy of
Bureaucracy." THE CHINESE MIND. By Gung-hsing Wang.
New York: John Day, 1946.

Looks at the thought of the 7th-century philosopher
who was noted for his faith in the efficiency of administration. His ideas were revived in Chiang Kai-shek's
New Life Movement in the 1930s.

1420. Wang, Gung-wu. "Bureaucracy in Imperial China." PUB-
LIC ADMINISTRATION (SYDNEY), 32 (1973), 62-71.

Discusses dissimilarities between the traditional system and modern Western bureaucracy.

1421. Whyte, Martin King. "Bureaucracy and Modernization in
China: The Maoist Critique." AMERICAN SOCIOLOGICAL
REVIEW, 38 (1973), 149-63.

Compares Western and Maoist theories of organization
and concludes that non-Western models can be effective
tools in the process of modernization.

1422. Whyte, Martin King. "Bureaucracy and Antibureaucracy
in the People's Republic of China." HIERARCHY AND
SOCIETY: ANTHROPOLOGICAL PERSPECTIVES ON BUREAUCRACY.
Edited by Gerald M. Britan and Ronald Cohen. Philadelphia: Institute for the Study of Human Issues,
1980.

Argues that the bureaucratic and antibureaucratic im-
pulses in Chinese society are complementary rather than
contradictory. The Chinese are serious about finding
a method of organization that is productive yet is still
revolutionary. The Chinese version of the agricultural
commune is examined. This development seems to have resulted in relief from some bureaucratic tendencies.

1423. Wilson, I. "Bureaucratic Politics in the Chinese People's Republic." PUBLIC ADMINISTRATION (SYDNEY), 32
(1973), 72-82.

On the turbulence in the discussion of appropriate
organizational forms.

1424.   Yang, C.K.   "Some Characteristics of Chinese Bureau-
           cratic Behavior." CONFUCIANISM IN ACTION. Edited
           by David S. Nivison and Arthur F. Wright. Stanford,
           Cal.: Stanford University Press, 1959.

        Examines the classical Chinese administrative system
        from a Weberian perspective.

1425.   Zentner, Joseph L.   "Bureaucracy in the People's Repub-
           lic: Some Deviations from Weber." INDIAN JOURNAL OF
           SOCIAL RESEARCH, 13 (1972), 111-18.

        Compares the Weberian model with recent developments
        in China.

                          6.   Hong Kong

1426.   Burns, John P.   "'Representative Bureaucracy' and the
           Senior Civil Service in Hong Kong." HONG KONG JOUR-
           NAL OF PUBLIC ADMINISTRATION, 2 (June, 1980), 2-20.

        Argues that representative bureaucracy is desirable
        since it ensures responsiveness to social needs. How-
        ever, the Hong Kong senior civil service is not repre-
        sentative of ethnic groups or females. Women are es-
        pecially underrepresented.

1427.   Burns, John P.   "The Changing Pattern of Bureaucratic
           Representation: The Case of the Hong Kong Senior Civil
           Service." INDIAN JOURNAL OF PUBLIC ADMINISTRATION,
           27 (1981), 399-429.

        Asks if the Hong Kong bureaucracy is ethnically and
        sexually representative. The situation of local people
        and females has improved, but the highest levels are
        still unrepresentative. Better educated women held
        lower positions than men.

1428.   Harris, Peter.   HONG KONG: A STUDY IN BUREAUCRATIC POL-
           ITICS. Hong Kong: Heinemann Asia, 1978. 186 pp.

        Describes the politics of Hong Kong in terms of the
        idea of the bureaucratic state.

1429. Lee, Mary. "Bureaucratic Jigsaw." FAR EASTERN ECONOMIC REVIEW, 108 (March 18, 1980), 39-40.

On government reorganization in Hong Kong.

1430. Lethbridge, Henry J. "The Emergence of Bureaucratic Corruption as a Social Problem in Hong Kong." JOURNAL OF ORIENTAL STUDIES, 12 (1974), 17-29.

Discusses the institutionalization of administrative corruption in the 19th century and its implications for modern practice.

1431. Tasker, Rodney. "'Raw Deal' Angers Bureaucrats." FAR EASTERN ECONOMIC REVIEW, 92 (April 30, 1976), 38.

Hong Kong bureaucrats are unhappy about their pay.

7. India

1432. Arora, Satish K. "Political Policy and the Future of Bureaucracy." INDIAN JOURNAL OF PUBLIC ADMINISTRATION, 17 (1971), 355-66.

On problems of Indian administration, with emphasis on the public malaise about bureaucratic performance.

1433. Ashraf, A. "Bureaucracy, Leadership, and Rural Development in Uttar Pradesh." INDIAN JOURNAL OF POLITICS, 5 (July-December, 1971), 25-34.

Argues that the bureaucracy has stifled economic development. The administrative elite has monopolized power to the extent that an independent political leadership has been unable to emerge. The example is from an Indian state.

1434. Avasthi, Amreshwar, and Ramesh Arora, eds. BUREAUCRACY AND DEVELOPMENT: INDIAN PERSPECTIVES. New Delhi: Associated Publishing House, 1978. 267 pp.

A collection of essays on problems of administration

in an environment of change. Among the topics are the
idea of commitment, the need for specialization, and
the concept of rural development.

1435. Banerjee, R.N. "Should India Have a Committed Bureau-
       cracy? INDIAN POLITICAL SCIENCE REVIEW, 5 (1970-71),
       45-89.

       Summarizes the views of several Indian political sci-
       entists on the question of neutrality in the adminis-
       tration of development programs.

1436. Bhambri, Chandra. BUREAUCRACY AND POLITICS IN INDIA.
       Delhi: Vikas Publications, 1971. 349 pp.

       Argues that the weakness of Indian political leader-
       ship has left a void which is being filled by the bur-
       eaucracy. The myth of political neutrality cannot be
       sustained any longer since officials are obviously in-
       volved in politics. Several examples of confrontations
       between politicians and bureaucrats are reviewed.

1437. Bhambri, Chandra. "A Study of Relationship between
       Prime Minister and Bureaucracy in India." INDIAN
       JOURNAL OF PUBLIC ADMINISTRATION, 17 (1971), 367-82.

       Describes three phases in the relationship of Indira
       Gandhi with the civil service. Her relationship with
       the bureaucracy can be plotted on an independence-de-
       pendence curve, based on her political power.

1438. Bhatt, Anil. "Colonial Bureaucratic Culture and De-
       velopment Administration: Portrait of an Old-Fashioned
       Indian Bureaucrat." JOURNAL OF COMMONWEALTH AND COM-
       PARATIVE POLITICS, 17 (1979), 159-75.

       Traces the career of an Indian civil servant from the
       colonial era to the modern period of economic develop-
       ment and democratic politics.

1439. Bhattacharya, Mohit. "Bureaucrat's Reponse to Emergen-
       cy: An Empirical Study." INDIAN JOURNAL OF PUBLIC
       ADMINISTRATION, 20 (1974), 846-67.

Argues that, based on the responses to drought in India, a bureaucracy will evolve the structure appropriate for the solution of emergency situations.

1440. Bhattacharya, Mohit. "Bureaucratic Rules and Bureaucratic Behavior." ADMINISTRATIVE CHANGE, 3 (July-December, 1975), 73-80.

Reviews the administrative response to famine conditions in an Indian state. The level of cooperation between central and field offices was facilitated by a set of rules appropriate to the crisis conditions.

1441. Bhownik, Dhrubajyoti. "'Technocrats' Plea for Parity with Bureaucrats: A Case Study of West Bengal." INDIAN JOURNAL OF POLITICAL SCIENCE, 36 (1975), 161-76.

Considers the demands by specialists that they be granted parity with the administrative elite in the Indian Administrative Service.

1442. Bhownik, Dhrubajyoti. "Political Development in India and Bureaucracy: An Attitude Study," INDIAN JOURNAL OF PUBLIC ADMINISTRATION, 21 (1975), 109-18.

Calls for changes in the structure and ethos of the administration in order to reach the lower classes. The bureaucracy must penetrate the rural areas where change is needed the most.

1443. Braibanti, Ralph. "Reflections on Bureaucratic Reform in India." ADMINISTRATION AND ECONOMIC DEVELOPMENT. Edited by Ralph Braibanti and J.J. Spengler. Durham, N.C.: Duke University Press, 1963.

Concludes that "the program of administrative reform in India since 1947 has been unusually well conceived and has been marked by a firm sense of order, balance, and allocation of priorities." An administrative system is in a good position to bring to a successful conclusion the efforts for development.

1444. "Bureaucratic Acrobatics." COMMUNITY DEVELOPMENT JOUR-
       NAL, 4 (January, 1969), 5-6.

       Describes the tensions between district administrators
       and local officials in India.

1445. Chaturvedi, H.R. BUREAUCRACY AND LOCAL COMMUNITY: DY-
       NAMICS OF RURAL DEVELOPMENT. Columbia, Mo.: South
       Asian Books, 1977. 199 pp.

       Surveys Indian administrators at the district and the
       block levels to identify those factors which promote or
       impede developmental performance in Rajasthan. New
       roles and norms more appropriate to decentralization
       are needed.

1446. Chauhan, D.S. "India's Underprivileged Classes and the
       Higher Public Service: Towards Developing a Represent-
       ative Bureaucracy." INTERNATIONAL REVIEW OF ADMIN-
       ISTRATIVE SCIENCES, 42 (1976), 39-55.

       Evaluates attempts to broaden the base of recruit-
       ment for the Indian civil service.

1447. De, N.R. INDIAN BUREAUCRACY: OBSOLESCENCE AND INNOVA-
       TION. New Delhi: National Labour Institute, 1975.
       34 pp.

       Suggestions for reform of Indian administration.

1448. Dey, Bata K. "Bureaucracy and Development: Some Reflec-
       tions." INDIAN JOURNAL OF PUBLIC ADMINISTRATION, 15
       (1969), 228-48.

       Insists that development bureaucracy requires a new
       type of structure. But more important, it requires a
       new type of administrator. The development administra-
       tor must have a liberal frame of mind coupled with the
       necessary skills.

1449. Dey, Bata K. BUREAUCRACY, DEVELOPMENT, AND PUBLIC MAN-
       AGEMENT IN INDIA. New Delhi: Uppal Publishing House,
       1978. 334 pp.

Presents a critique of Indian administation. There
is a need for greater management ability. This may
necessitate more emphasis on the specialist and the
lessening of the role of the generalist.

1450. Dubhashi, P.R. "Committed Bureaucracy." INDIAN JOUR-
       NAL OF PUBLIC ADMINISTRATION, 17 (1971), 33-39.

       Argues in favor of greater dedication to democracy
       and development on the part of the Indian bureaucracy.
       This sense of commitment must arise out of professional
       pride and identification with the larger objectives of
       society.

1451. Eldersveld, Samuel J. "Bureaucratic Contact with the
       Public in India: Some Preliminary Findings in Delhi
       State." INDIAN JOURNAL OF PUBLIC ADMINISTRATION,
       11 (1965), 216-35.

       Reports on a survey of public attitudes about admin-
       istration. It seems that an increase in contacts be-
       tween citizens and administrators develops support for
       administration.

1452. Encarnation, Dennis J. "The Indian Central Bureaucra-
       cy: A Psychological Application." ASIAN SURVEY, 19
       (1979), 1126-45.

       Sees that the pressures of complexity are making ir-
       relevant the distinction between politics and adminis-
       tration. The Indian bureaucracy is heaviliy involved
       in making policy. The real question is what class in-
       fluences determine the nature of the bureaucracy.

1453. Fritz, Dan. "Bureaucratic Commitment in Rural India:
       A Psychological Application." ASIAN SURVEY, 16
       (1976), 338-54.

       Argues that the commitment of individual administra-
       tors to the goal of rural development will determine
       the impact of the program. Interviews were held with
       the relevant personnel. It was found that about one-
       quarter were committed while the remainder were more
       concerned with their own self-interest.

1454. Gaikwad, V.R. PANCHAYANTI RAJ AND BUREAUCRACY. Hyder-
       abad: National Institute of Community Development,
       1969. 76 pp.

       Discusses the Panchayati Raj as an element in India's
       program for local administration and democratic partic-
       ipation. The emphasis is on the stress that results
       from the interaction of local officials and the bureau-
       crats.

1455. Goyal, S.K. "Bureaucracy: A Sociological Study of Im-
       personal Orientations among Subordinates (Clerical
       Staff)." INTERDISCIPLINE, 4 (1967), 185-96.

       Operationalizes Weber's concept of impersonality and
       applies the instrument to Indian clerical workers.

1456. Goyal, S.K. "Bureaucracy: A Sociological Study of Level
       of Orientation of Clerks towards the Norms of Bureau-
       cracy." INDIAN SOCIOLOGICAL BULLETIN, 5 (1968), 248-
       57.

       Surveys lower-level bureaucrats. Most of them come
       from a relatively poor economic background and have a
       low level of orientation toward standard bureaucratic
       norms such as impersonality.

1457. Hager, Michael. "Bureaucratic Corruption in India:
       Legal Control of Maladministration." COMPARATIVE
       POLITICAL STUDIES, 6 (1973), 197-219.

       Concludes that corruption comes in several varieties,
       not all of which can be dealt with effectively by the
       law. Quasi-corruption, precorruption, and corruption
       are aspects of the problem. To solve the problem, the
       legal checks must be strengthened and supplemented by
       a free press, a sense of integrity among political
       leaders, and a mature political process.

1458. Haragopal, G., and K.M. Manohar. "Some Aspects of Mo-
       rale in the Rank and File of Indian Bureaucracy."
       INDIAN JOURNAL OF PUBLIC ADMINISTRATION, 22 (1976),
       705-29.

Survey clerks and find that morale is generally low,
although there are variations according to the level
of government. The rank and file feel that their work
is important although they are not highly involved in
their jobs.

1459. Heginbotham, Stanley J. CULTURES IN CONFLICT: THE
FOUR FACES OF INDIAN BUREAUCRACY. New York: Columbia University Press, 1975. 236 pp.

Investigates the Indian administration in terms of
four traditions: Dharmic, Colonial, Developmental, and
Gandhian. The thesis is supported by research on the
administrators in the state of Tamil Nadu.

1460. Iyer, Ramaswamy. "Understanding Our Bureaucracy."
INDIAN JOURNAL OF PUBLIC ADMINISTRATION, 12 (1966),
697-716.

Reviews deficiencies in Indian administration and
suggests changes. To prevent inefficiency, modern
management methods are needed. More important, there
must be a clear idea as to what the civil service is
all about.

1461. Jagannadham, Vedula, and N.S. Bakshi. CITIZENS AND THE
MUNICIPAL BUREAUCRACY: A SURVEY OF THE BUILDING DE-
PARTMENT OF THE DELHI MUNICIPAL CORPORATION. New
Delhi: Indian Institute of Public Administration,
1971. 124 pp.

Present an in-depth look at Indian administration at
the local level. The workings of the agency are studied and suggested changes are presented. In general,
it was found that officials were corrupt and used the
rules to harass the citizens.

1462. Jain, R.B. "Bureaucracy and Politics in India." INDIAN
JOURNAL OF POLITICAL SCIENCE, 32 (1971), 82-92.

A review essay on recent books about Indian administration. The authors make cogent arguments about the
deficiencies of the existing system.

1463.   Jain, R.B., and P.N. Chaudhuri. BUREAUCRACY AND DEVEL-
        OPMENT: A COMPARATIVE STUDY IN ORIENTATION AND BEHAV-
        IOR OF BUREAUCRACY ENGAGED IN DEVELOPMENTAL AND NON-
        DEVELOPMENTAL TASKS. New Delhi: Centre for Policy
        Research, 1981. 352 pp.

        Compare the values, orientations, and behavior of
        officials engaged in developmental and non-developmen-
        tal functions in two Indian states. The values of the
        bureaucrats, regardless of mission, show the same pat-
        terns. Bureaucracy, in any case, is not incompatible
        with development. Further reforms are still indicated,
        however.

1464.   Jeffrey, Robin. "Bureaucratic Politics in an Imperial
        System: The Rivalry between Two Indian Diwans."
        JOURNAL OF COMMONWEALTH AND COMPARATIVE POLITICS,
        15 (1977), 266-85.

        Uses the story of two prominant Indian politicians
        to make some points about the categories of bureau-
        cratic politics. The tactics can be outshining, dis-
        crediting, appealing, or ingratiating.

1465.   Joshi, R.C. "Bureaucrats and Politicians at the Rural
        Level." INDIAN JOURNAL OF PUBLIC ADMINISTRATION, 21
        (1975), 191-96.

        Says that the village politician may block or help
        development. This leaves the administrator with some-
        thing of a dilemma.

1466.   Joshi, R.C. "Bureaucrats and Politicians: Role Rela-
        tionships." INDIAN JOURNAL OF PUBLIC ADMINISTRATION,
        22 (1976), 15-22.

        Uses his experience as a civil servant to examine
        the relationship of politicians to administrators and
        its effect on the efficiency and responsiveness of the
        bureaucracy.

1467.   Khan, Iltija. "Bureaucracy in a Developing Country:
        India." PUBLIC ADMINISTRATION (SYDNEY), 32 (1973),
        352-65.

Describes the Indian bureaucracy as moving from the British hierarchical model to one more suited to the problems of development. Corruption is still a problem and the administrators are often too far removed from the public. There is little incentive for individuals to perform above the acceptable level.

1468. Khanna, B.S. "Bureaucracy and Development in India." DEVELOPMENT ADMINISTRATION IN ASIA. Edited by Edward Weidner. Durham, N.C.: Duke University Press, 1970.

Examines the capacity of the Indian bureaucracy for leading development, with emphasis on the changes in the structure and the recuitment patterns of the civil service. A number of modified personnel practices are analyzed.

1469. Khosla, R.P. "Bureaucrats--The Loss of Vision." INDIAN JOURNAL OF PUBLIC ADMINISTRATION, 11 (1965), 35-41.

Says that bureaucracy results when official functions become more important than actual results.

1470. Kumar, Khrishna. "The Bureaucratic Imagination." ECONOMIC AND POLITICAL WEEKLY, 16 (1981), 1413-15.

Argues that the educational bureaucracy has deprived parents of a role in shaping the policy pertaining to the operation of schools.

1471. Maheshwari, S.R. "The Indian Bureaucracy: Its Profile, Malady, and Cure." INDIAN JOURNAL OF POLITICAL SCIENCE, 31 (1970), 222-37.

Admits that the Indian bureaucracy is far from perfect but wonders whether a greater degree of "commitment" to development goals will cure what ails it. Its greatest weakness is the rampant careerism of its members, leading to the expansion of administration into areas where it is not needed. Improved morale might improve the situation.

1472.   Maheshwari, S.K.   "Bureaucracy and Political Develop-
        ment in India."   INDIAN JOURNAL OF POLITICAL SCIENCE,
        39 (1978), 331-48.

        Presents a model for improvements in development ad-
        ministration.

1473.   Marican, Y.M.   "Bureaucratic Power in India and Japan."
        PHILIPPINE JOURNAL OF PUBLIC ADMINISTRATION, 16
        (1972), 204-23.

        Argues that the power of the bureaucracy is greater
        in Japan than in India.

1474.   Mathur, Kuldeep.   BUREAUCRATIC RESPONSE TO DEVELOPMENT:
        A STUDY OF BLOCK DEVELOPMENT OFFICERS IN RAJASTHAN
        AND UTTAR PRADESH.   Delhi: National Publishing House,
        1972.   121 pp.

        Studies Indian administrative behavior at the grass-
        roots level.   The BDOs tend to have a rural background.
        They are suspicious of politicians and are not highly
        committed to the ideals of the public service.

1475.   Mathur, Kuldeep.   BUREAUCRACY AND THE NEW AGRICULTURAL
        STRATEGY.   New Delhi: Concept, 1982.   103 pp.

        Examines the administration of the "green revolution"
        policy in India.   The national machinery has discour-
        aged implementation of the program at the local level.
        The bureaucracy has been more interested in higher
        production than in total rural development.

1476.   Mazumdar, D.L.   "The Indian Bureaucracy--A Plea for
        a Sociological Study."   INDIAN JOURNAL OF PUBLIC AD-
        MINISTRATION, 12 (1966), 266-69.

        Calls for an objective and scientific study of admin-
        istration as the basis for reform.

1477.   Mehra, Om Prakash.   "Buraucrats and Self-Actualization."
        INDIAN JOURNAL OF PUBLIC ADMINISTRATION, 22 (1976),
        667-72.

Feels that Indian managers should pay more attention
to the theories of Abraham Maslow and other behavioral
scientists.

1478. Mehta, B. BUREAUCRACY AND CHANGE. Jaipur: Administrative Change, 1975. 84 pp.

A collection of essays by a former civil servant on
the reform of state government.

1479. Misra, Bankey. THE BUREAUCRACY IN INDIA: AN HISTORICAL
ANALYSIS OF DEVELOPMENTS TO 1947. Delhi: Oxford
University Press, 1977. 421 pp.

Details the development of Indian administration under
British rule. The story is one of modernity versus
traditionalism. A continuing problem has been the
promise of career mobility within a status-bound society. Despite their elitist training, the Indian administrators were often outsiders in the colonial bureaucracy.

1480. Montgomery, John D. "The Bureaucracy as a Modernizing
Elite: The Possibility of Reform." ADMINISTRATION,
POLITICS, AND DEVELOPMENT IN INDIA. Bombay: Lalvani
Publishing House, 1972.

An assessment of the developmental capacity of the
Indian bureaucracy with suggestions for change.

1481. Murao, Bahadur, R.M. Schroff, B.D. Sharma, and Ross
Pollock. "Comments: The Annual Assessment and Pro-
motion System in Indian Bureaucracy." INDIAN JOURNAL
OF PUBLIC ADMINISTRATION, 13 (1967), 128-37.

Reactions to Prakash, Item 1490.

1482. Muttalib, M.A. "Committed Bureaucracy or Positions of
Confidence." ADMINISTRATIVE CHANGE, 4 (July-December, 1976), 38-42.

Argues that the model of administrative neutrality
of the British needs to be modified in India.

1483. Nagar, Purushottam. "Lala Lajpat Rai on the Character
       of Bureaucracy in British India." ADMINISTRATIVE
       CHANGE, 2 (January-June, 1975), 179-82.

       Discusses the views on administration of a leader in
       the movement for Indian independence.

1484. Nayar, P.K.B. LEADERSHIP, BUREAUCRACY AND PLANNING IN
       INDIA: A SOCIOLOGICAL STUDY. New Delhi: Associated
       Publishing House, 1969. 176 pp.

       Based on the data from the state of Kerala and Andhra
       Pradesh, it is found that the Indian bureaucracy is
       not effective in its planning mission. An "institution-
       building" model is used to evaluate the data. In order
       to fulfill its planning responsibility, considerable
       structural and behavioral changes will be needed.

1485. Pai Panandiker, V.A., and S.S. Kshirsagar. "Bureaucra-
       cy in India: An Empirical Study: INDIAN JOURNAL OF
       PUBLIC ADMINISTRATION, 17 (1971), 187-208.

       Explore the characteristics of a sample of 723 Indian
       civil servants. There is some conformity with the Web-
       erian model, although there is a great deal of change
       taking place within the system.

1486. Pai Panandiker, V.A., and S.S. Kshirsagar. "A Profile
       of Development Bureaucracy in India." INDIAN JOUR-
       NAL OF PUBLIC ADMINISTRATION, 18 (1972), 505-32.

       Compare the development administrators with the other
       parts of the civil service and with other countries.
       Compared to other Indian bureaucrats, those involved
       in development tend to be younger, come from a rural
       background, and are more representative of the total
       population.

1487. Pai Panandiker, V.A., and S.S. Kshirsagar. BUREAUCRA-
       CY AND DEVELOPMENT ADMINISTRATION. New Delhi: Centre
       for Policy Research, 1978. 208 pp.

       Identify the characteristics of civil servants who

are involved in development. The evidence shows that
these bureaucrats are not predominantly from the upper
and upper-middle classes. Developmental personnel are
better educated than their counterparts in the traditional branches. In general, static models of bureaucracy are not sufficient for comprehending the dynamics
of development administration.

1488. Pant, Niranjar. "Status, Participation, and Evaluation
of Municipal Bureaucracy." JOURNAL OF CONSTITUTIONAL
AND PARLIAMENTARY STUDIES, 10 (1976), 314-25.

Measures the citizen evaluations of a municipal bureaucracy. Differences in perceptions were explained
by the socioeconomic status and level of participation
of the citizens.

1489. Potter, David C. "Bureaucratic Change in India." AS-
IAN BUREAUCRATIC SYSTEMS EMERGENT FROM THE BRITISH
IMPERIAL TRADITION. Durham, N.C.: Duke University
Press, 1966.

Examines Indian administration from the standpoint
of bureaucratic responsibility.

1490. Prakash, Kailash. "The Annual Assessment and Promotion
System in Indian Bureaucracy." INDIAN JOURNAL OF
PUBLIC ADMINISTRATION, 12 (1966), 770-809.

Studies the way in which members of the All India Service are evaluated and promoted. An alternative system is suggested.

1491. Prasad, G.K. BUREAUCRACY IN INDIA: A SOCIOLOGICAL
STUDY. New Delhi: Sterling Publishers, 1974. 152 pp.

Reports on a field survey in 1962-64 of the characteristics and attitudes of administrators in Bihar state.
The bureaucratism leads to lower morale. The service
is fragmented and limited in its outlook. Suggestions
include more decentralization, better leadership, and
more delegation of authority.

1492. Rai, Hardiwar, and Sakendra Singh. "Indian Bureaucra-
       cy: A Case for Representativeness." INDIAN JOURNAL
       OF PUBLIC ADMINISTRATION, 19 (1973), 1-15.

       Suggest that development administration needs wider
       participation, especially since the bureaucratic elite
       comes from restricted social groups. Educational oppor-
       tunities must be broadened and the promotion system
       needs to be changed.

1493. Rieger, Hans. "Bureaucracy and the Implementation of
       Economic Plans in India." INDIAN JOURNAL OF PUBLIC
       ADMINISTRATION, 13 (1967), 32-42.

       Identifies implementation as the most problematic
       part of planning for economic development.

1494. Roy, W.T. "Sahibs and Mandarins: A Comparative Study
       of Bureaucratic Elites in India and China in the
       Nineteenth Century." POLITICS, 2 (May, 1967), 36-47.

       Finds differences in the relationship between bureau-
       crats and politicians in the two societies.

1495. Rudolph, Suzanne, and Lloyd I. Ruudolph. "A Bureau-
       cratic Lineage in Princely India: Elite Formation
       and Conflict in a Patrimonial System." JOURNAL OF
       ASIAN STUDIES, 34 (1975), 717-54.

       Examines the growth of a bureaucratic elite in terms
       of the histories of three families.

1496. Sharma, G.B. "Representative Bureaucracy: The Need
       for Methodological Reformulation." INDIAN JOURNAL
       OF PUBLIC ADMINISTRATION, 27 (1981), 1019-33.

       Criticizes major theories of representative bureau-
       cracy. A number of factors go into determining repre-
       sentation. An especially important one is the gate-
       keeper function--the groups who determine the recruit-
       ment and selection procedures. Overall, representa-
       tion cannot be guaranteed by a single policy.

1497.   Singh, Nirmal. "Bureaucracy, Commitment, and Develop-
          ment in India." ADMINISTRATIVE CHANGE, 1 (December,
          1973), 62-75.

          Suggests that, despite the talk about the need for a
          committed bureaucracy, the facts indicate that most of-
          ficials do not believe in equality, democracy, or econ-
          omic planning. A majority of them are concerned mainly
          with material benefits.

1498.   Singhi, Narendra. "Job-Satisfaction amongst Bureau-
          crats in an Indian State." INDIAN POLITICAL SCIENCE
          REVIEW, 7 (1972-73), 32-38.

          Surveys Indian civil servants and finds that only half
          are satisfied with their work, although the level of
          dissatisfaction is related to one's position within the
          hierarchy.

1499.   Singhi, Narendra. "Job Satisfaction among Bureaucrats
          in an Indian State." PHILIPPINE JOURNAL OF PUBLIC
          ADMINISTRATION, 17 (1973), 227-41.

          Finds that public employees are less satisfied with
          their work than their counterparts in the private sec-
          tor.

1500.   Singhi, Narendra. "Bureaucracy and Corruption." AD-
          MINISTRATIVE CHANGE, 2 (December, 1974), 33-47.

          Surveys public and private managers in India to de-
          termine their perception of the extent of corrupt be-
          havior by public officials. The public managers were
          more likely than the private ones to believe that the
          public service was corrupt. A majority of both groups
          felt that private business was not corrupt. The organ-
          izations felt to be most corrupt were police, taxation,
          and public works. Moral weakness was cited most often
          as the cause of bureaucratic corruption.

1501.   Singhi, Narendra. BUREAUCRACY, POSITIONS AND PERSONS:
          ROLE STRUCTURES, INTERACTIONS, AND VALUE-ORIENTATIONS
          OF BUREAUCRATS IN RAJASTHAN. New Delhi: Abhinav
          Publications, 1974. 398 pp.

Measures the social backgrounds and value orientations of members in the bureaucratic hierarchy in an Indian state.

1502.   Spangenberg, Bradford.   BRITISH BUREAUCRACY IN INDIA: STATUS, POLICY AND THE I.C.S. IN THE LATE 19TH CENTURY.   New Delhi: Manohar, 1976.   380 pp.

Concentrates on the British members of the Indian Civil Service.   Despite the romantic notions about the ability of this organization, the truth is that it was staffed by insecure office politicians, nervous about their situation in a strange and foreign land.   The reputed efficiency of the service may have been a myth to justify the European monopoly of higher positions. The strengths and weaknesses of the present Indian Administrative Service stem from the ambiguous record of the ICS.

1503.   Taub, Richard P.   BUREAUCRATS UNDER STRESS: ADMINISTRATORS AND ADMINISTRATION IN AN INDIAN STATE.   Berkeley: University of California Press, 1969.   235 pp.

Studies members of the Indian Administrative Service on duty in the state of Orissa.   The service suffers from a clear dedication to goals larger than the maintenance of internal routines.   The transition from being a representative of the Crown, enforcing order, to a public servant in a democratically based development program has had profound effects on the members of the service.   Technical experts continue to threaten the traditional high status of the generalists.   Despite this and other problems in adjustment to nationhood, the IAS has performed well; it has helped to achieve national integration and to preserve the essence of the political process.

1504.   Umapathy, M. "Designing Bureaucracy for Development." INDIAN JOURNAL OF PUBLIC ADMINISTRATION, 27 (1982), 276-97.

Admits that the present bureaucracy is not doing a good job.   But development is not impossible with the proper design of an administrative system.

1505. Vajpey, Dhirendra. "Public Opinion on Bureaucratic
        Performance in Uttar Pradesh and Its Impact on Social
        Change and Modernization, 1966-76." INDIAN JOURNAL
        OF PUBLIC ADMINISTRATION, 23 (1977), 960-64.

        Finds that most Indians are favorably disposed toward
        their administrators.

1506. Vajpey, Dhirendra. "Public Opinion of Bureaucratic
        Performance in Uttar Pradesh (India) and Its Impact
        on Social Change and Modernization." PHILIPPINE
        JOURNAL OF PUBLIC ADMINISTRATION, 22 (1978), 169-95.

        Tests the hypothesis that greater citizen contact with
        administration creates more support for government pro-
        grams. The evidence seems to support the general prop-
        osition.

1507. Varma, V.P. "Bureaucracy in India: Image and Reality,"
        JOURNAL OF POLITICAL STUDIES, 8 (1975), 58-69.

        Urges several changes in Indian administration. There
        is a special need for greater specialization in the
        skills of the civil servants.

1508. Verma, S.L. "Lokpal, Bureaucracy, and the Common Man."
        INDIAN JOURNAL OF PUBLIC ADMINISTRATION, 24 (1978),
        1130-44.

        Discusses proposals for the handling of grievances
        about public administration in India. The lokpal is
        the equivalent of the ombudsman.

1509. Verma, S.L. "Bureaucratic Culture of the Higher Civil
        Services in India." JOURNAL OF CONSTITUTIONAL AND
        PARLIAMENTARY STUDIES, 12 (1978), 60-72.

        Sketches the norms and values of the Indian adminis-
        trative elite.

1510. Verma, S.L. "Bureaucratic Culture of Higher Civil Ser-
        vices in India." INDIAN JOURNAL OF PUBLIC ADMINISTRA-
        TION, 39 (1978), 188-201.

Argues that the higher civil service in India has developed its own culture. The beliefs of this group are
elitist and in favor of the status quo. The bureaucrats are also politically powerful.

1511.   Weiner, Myron. "Political Evolution--Party Bureaucracy
        and Institutions." INDIA: A RISING MIDDLE POWER.
        Edited by John Mellor. Boulder, Colo.: Westview,
        1979.

        Reviews recent political developments in India, with
        emphasis on the organization of the major political
        parties.

1512.   Wilcox, Wayne. "Politicians, Bureaucrats, and Develop-
        ment in India." ANNALS OF THE AMERICAN ACADEMY OF
        POLITICAL AND SOCIAL SCIENCE, 358 (1965), 114-22.

        Suggests that India's political system, in respect
        to development, is unique. The administrative struc-
        ture is capable, but removed from the masses. The pol-
        itical system has worked well in generating mass sup-
        port. There remains, however, a gap between the two
        elements, thus hindering development goals. The ad-
        ministration is not powerful enough to force massive
        development projects but it is still a major partner
        in the making of policy.

                        8.   Indonesia

1513.   Emmerson, Donald K. "The Bureaucracy in Political Con-
        text: Weakness in Strength." POLITICAL POWER AND
        COMMUNICATIONS IN INDONESIA. Edited by Karl Jackson
        and Lucian W. Pye. Berkeley: University of Calif-
        ornia Press, 1978.

        Argues that power is so concentrated in the bureau-
        cracy that the means of communication with the larger
        society have been lost. Through its monopoly of soc-
        ial authority, the elite has been weakened. Lacking
        effective feedback, the bureaucracy has worked itself
        into a vulnerable position.

1514. Emmerson, Donald K. "Bureaucratic Alienation in Indonesia: The 'Director General's Dilemma.'" POLITICAL PARTICIPATION IN MODERN INDONESIA. Edited by R.W. Liddle. New Haven, Conn.: Yale University Southeast Asia Studies, 1973.

   Uses reader responses to a magazine contest about the "Director General's Dilemma" as a measure of public attitudes about Indonesian administration. The public was found to be fairly knowledgeable about how government works and does not work.

1515. Hansen, Gary E. "Bureaucratic Linkages and Policy-Making in Indonesia: BIMAS Revisited." POLITICAL POWER AND COMMUNICATIONS IN INDONESIA. Edited by Karl Jackson and Lucian W. Pye. Berkeley: University of California Press, 1978.

   Describes the operation of the "green revolution" program--BIMAS--in terms of the patterns of communications between the peasants and the government officials. Without greater farmer participation, the success of the program is in doubt.

1516. Jackson, Karl. "Bureaucratic Polity: A Theoretical Framework for the Analysis of Power and Communication in Indonesia." POLITICAL POWER AND COMMUNICATIONS IN INDONESIA. Edited by Karl Jackson and Lucian W. Pye. Berkeley: University of California Press, 1978.

   Describes Indonesia as a polity in which power and political participation is limited almost entirely to the employees of the state, especially the military and bureaucratic elites. Mass political participation does not appear to be a likely development in the near future.

1517. Jackson, Karl. "The Prospects for Bureaucratic Polity in Indonesia." POLITICAL POWER AND COMMUNICATIONS IN INDONESIA. Edited by Karl Jackson and Lucian W. Pye. Berkeley: University of California Press, 1978.

   Concludes that "the present Indonesian bureaucratic polity is stable but weak, but difficult to modernize."

1518. Schulz, Lawrence. "Bureaucracy and Modernization: The
       Impact of Development Administration in Indonesia."
       ASIAN FORUM, 6 (January-March, 1974), 19-31.

       A description of development administration in Indo-
       nesia.

1519. Smith, Theodore A. "Stabilizing Performance in the
       Indonesian Bureaucracy: Gaps in the Administrator's
       Tool Kit." ECONOMIC DEVELOPMENT AND CULTURAL CHANGE,
       23 (1975), 719-38.

       Surveys Indonesian administrators to identify incen-
       tives for higher productivity.

1520. Soemardjan, Selo. "Bureaucratic Organization in a Time
       of Revolution." ADMINISTRATIVE SCIENCE QUARTERLY,
       2 (1957), 182-99.

       Describes the Indonesian civil service during a period
       of transition to independence from the Dutch. There
       was an emphasis on election of administrative positions
       rather than selection by merit. This process led to
       the formation of cliques within the organization and
       the politicization of the administration.

1521. Sutherland, Heather. THE MAKING OF A BUREAUCRATIC
       ELITE: THE COLONIAL TRANSFORMATION OF THE JAVANESE
       PRIYAYI. Exeter, N.H.: Heinemann, 1979. 182 pp.

       Describes how a native social group, the priyayi,
       was used by the colonial rulers as the basis for the
       formation of an administrative elite.

1522. Walker, Millidge, and Irene Tinker. "Development and
       Changing Bureaucratic Styles in Indonesia: The Case
       of the Pamong Praja." PACIFIC AFFAIRS, 48 (1975),
       60-73.

       Examines the pressures on the civil service for great-
       er involvement in rural development programs in Indo-
       nesia.

9. Japan

1523. Black, Cyril. "Japan and Russia: Bureaucratic Politics
        in a Comparative Context." SOCIAL SCIENCE HISTORY,
        2 (1978), 414-26.

        Compares the developmental aspects of the two nations
        as described by Silberman (Item 1548) and Rieber (Item
        2007).   A major theme is the capacity of the bureau-
        cratic system to take advantage of scientific and tech-
        nological advances from outside sources.

1524. Brown, Sidney. "Okubo Toshimichi and the First Home
        Rule Ministry Bureaucracy: 1873-78." MODERN JAPAN-
        ESE LEADERSHIP: TRANSITION AND CHANGE.   Edited by
        Bernard Silberman and H.D. Hartoonian.   Tucson:
        University of Arizona Press, 1966.

        Focuses on the top managerial group in a key minis-
        try during the early years of modernization in Japan.

1525. "Bureaucracy on the Move." JAPAN QUARTERLY, 6 (1959),
        1-5.

        There are signs of a revival of bureaucratism in
        postwar Japan.

1526. Dowdy, Edwin. "Aspects of Tokugawa Bureaucracy and
        Modernization." AUSTRALIAN JOURNAL OF POLITICS AND
        HISTORY, 16 (1970), 375-89.

        Inquires into the reasons for an effective transition
        to modernization in post-1868 Japan.   The elements of
        a modern bureaucracy were in place before the changes
        took place.

1527. Dowdy, Edwin. JAPANESE BUREAUCRACY: ITS DEVELOPMENT
        AND MODERNIZATION. Melbourne: Cheshire, 1973.   192
        pp.

        Examines the social system to identify those elements

of Japanese bureaucracy that facilitated economic modernization. Special emphasis is given to the beliefs,
values and symbols of the larger society.

1528.   Hackett, Roger. "Nishi Amane--A Tokugawa-Meiji Bureau-
        crat." JOURNAL OF ASIAN STUDIES, 18 (1959), 213-26.

        A portrait of a Japanese official.

1529.   Inoki, Masamichi. "The Civil Bureaucracy--Japan."
        POLITICAL MODERNIZATION IN JAPAN AND TURKEY. Edited
        by Robert Ward and Dankwart Rustow. Princeton, N.J.:
        Princeton University Press, 1964.

        Traces the history of the involvement of the Japanese
        bureaucracy in the modernization process.

1530.   Ito, Daiichi. "The Bureaucracy: Its Attitudes and Be-
        havior." DEVELOPING ECONOMIES, 6 (1968), 446-67.

        Describes the role of the bureaucracy in the planning
        and directing of the development of the Japanese econ-
        omy. In the process, some public agencies became close-
        ly identified with private industries.

1531.   Johnson, Chalmers. "The Re-employment of Retired Jap-
        anese Government Bureaucrats in Japanese Big Busi-
        ness." ASIAN SURVEY, 14 (1974), 953-65.

        Examines the extent of the practice of former offic-
        ials working for private industry. There is nothing
        sinister or conspiratorial about this practice.

1532.   Johnson, Chalmers. "Japan: Who Governs? An Essay on
        Official Bureaucracy." JOURNAL OF JAPANESE STUDIES,
        29 (1975), 1-28.

        Emphasizes the continuation of strongly authoritar-
        ian administrative values through several stages since
        1940. The bureaucratic mentality is firmly entrenched
        in political norms.

1533. Kakizawa, Koji. "The Diet and the Bureaucracy: The
       Budget as a Case Study." THE JAPANESE DIET AND THE
       U.S. CONGRESS. Edited by Francis R. Valeo and Charles
       E. Morrison. Boulder, Colo.: Westview, 1982.

       Discusses the oversight function of the Japanese Diet
       in terms of its role in budgetary politics. Comparisons
       are made with the American system.

1534. Koh, B.C., and Jae-on Kim. "Paths to Advancement in
       Japanese Bureaucracy." COMPARATIVE POLITICAL STUDIES,
       15 (1982), 289-313.

       Apply path analysis to biographical data on members
       of the higher civil service. An evaluation is made of
       three important elements of advancement--university
       background, field of study, and examinations. The
       importance of seniority is discussed; it is suggested
       that seniority does not reduce mobility nor produce
       stagnation in the ranks of the bureaucracy.

1535. Macrae, Norman. "The Most Intelligent Bureaucracy."
       ECONOMIST, 223 (May 27, 1967), xxiii-xxiv.

       On the role of the bureaucracy in economic planning.

1536. Maki, John. "The Role of Bureaucracy in Japan." PAC-
       IFIC AFFAIRS, 20 (1947), 391-406.

       Argues that the bureaucracy emerged from the military
       defeat as one of the most powerful segments of Japan-
       ese society.

   *   Marican, Y.M. "Bureaucratic Power in India and Japan."
       Cited above as Item 1473.

1537. Okada, Tadao. "The Unchanging Bureaucracy." JAPAN
       QUARTERLY, 12 (1965), 168-76.

       Sees the bureaucracy as a continuation of aristocrat-
       ic power from the Meiji Reform. The addition of demo-
       cratic institutions has not really modified the behav-
       ior of the administrative elite.

1538. "A Paradise Lost: Bureaucracy Shaken by Expense Scandals." JAPAN QUARTERLY, 27 (1980), 152-57.

On public reactions to allegations of corruption in administration. The impact on proposed reform efforts is assessed.

1539. Pempel. T.J. "The Bureaucratization of Policymaking in Postwar Japan." AMERICAN JOURNAL OF POLITICAL SCIENCE, 18 (1974), 647-64.

Devises four indicators which show a strong and growing role for the bureaucracy in the political process.

1540. Rice, Richard. "Economic Mobilization in Wartime Japan: Business, Bureaucracy and Military in Conflict." JOURNAL OF ASIAN STUDIES, 38 (1979), 689-706.

Describes the political struggle among the three major groups in adjusting the Japanese economy to wartime needs. All three were internally divided, which led to considerable conflict.

1541. Shirven, Maynard N., and Joseph L. Speicher. "Examination of Japan's Upper Bureaucracy." PERSONNEL ADMINISTRATION, 14 (July, 1951), 48-57.

Present the process leading to a new system of examinations for Japanese civil servants. The American influence stressed the measurement of more specialized skills. In general, the new examinations were designed to produce a bureaucracy more in tune with democratic ideals.

1542. Silberman, Bernard. "The Bureaucracy and Economic Development in Japan." ASIAN SURVEY, 5 (1965), 529-37.

Tests the validity of the proposition that a modern bureaucracy is necessary for economic development. The Japanese case suggests that a traditional system, at the beginning of the process, may be an asset. A fully developed bureaucracy along Weberian lines could be a disadvantage.

1543. Silberman, Bernard. "Criteria for Recruitment and Success in the Japanese Bureaucracy, 1868-1900. 'Traditional' and 'Modern' Criteria in Bureaucratic Development." ECONOMIC DEVELOPMENT AND CULTURAL CHANGE, 14 (1966), 158-73.

Examines the criteria for eligibility, recruitment, and advancement in the civil service between 1868 and 1900. A social background in the traditional political elite was critical for eligibility, but achievement-oriented factors were essential for recruitment and promotion. This combination of ascribed and achieved characteristics may have been valuable in the creation of an instrument for development.

1544. Silberman, Bernard. "Bureaucratic Development and the Structure of Decision-Making in the Meiji Period: The Case of the *Genrō*." JOURNAL OF ASIAN STUDIES, 27 (1967), 81-94.

Discusses the role of a group of elder statesmen in the bureaucratic elite.

1545. Silberman, Bernard. "The Role of the Prefectural Governors in Japanese Bureaucratic Development." DEVELOPMENT ADMINISTRATION IN ASIA. Edited by Edward Weidner. Durham, N.C.: Duke University Press, 1970.

Uses the administrative style in Meiji Japan to look at propositions about the role of bureaucracy in development. The administrative elite was successful because their innovations were not constrained by bureaucratic routines. Their commitment was to development instead of to bureaucratic values. They were loyal to their social class and the use of formal recruitment might have been dysfunctional in terms of development.

1546. Silberman, Bernard. "Bureaucratic Development and the Structure of Decision-Making in Japan, 1868-1925." JOURNAL OF ASIAN STUDIES, 29 (1970), 337-62.

Takes the case of Japan to make the point that a strong bureaucracy at the start of development might result in unstable, ambiguous decision-making patterns in government.

1547. Silberman, Bernard. "Bureaucratization in the Meiji
       State: The Problems of Succession in the Meiji Re-
       storation, 1868-1900." JOURNAL OF ASIAN STUDIES,
       35 (1976), 421-30.

       Applies organization theory to analyze the way in
       which the bureaucratic elite solved the problem of
       succession.

1548. Silberman, Bernard. "Bureaucratic Development and Bur-
       eaucratization: The Case of Japan." SOCIAL SCIENCE
       HISTORY, 2 (1978), 385-98.

       Argues that many pre-1945 features of Japanese gov-
       ernment were dependent upon the traditional bureaucrat-
       ic leadership style. All the apparent changes in Jap-
       anese government were only changes in style within a
       tradition of bureaucratic authoritarianism. Any var-
       iations resulted from modifications in the process of
       development.

1549. Spaulding, Robert. "The Bureaucracy as a Political
       Force, 1920-1945." DILEMMAS OF GROWTH IN PREWAR
       JAPAN. Edited by James W. Morley. Princeton, N.J.:
       Princeton University Press, 1971.

       An examination of the role of the bureaucratic elite
       in events leading up to WWII.

1550. Spinks, Charles. "Bureaucratic Japan." FAR EASTERN
       SURVEY, 10 (1941), 219-25.

       Describes Japan as a "dictatorship of the bureaucra-
       cy."

1551. Suttmeier, Richard. "Gikan Question in Japanese Gov-
       ernment: Bureaucratic Curiosity or Institutional
       Failure?" ASIAN SURVEY, 18 (1978), 1046-66.

       Discusses some of the differences between the gen-
       eralists and specialists in Japanese public adminis-
       tration.

1552. Suzuta, Atsuyuki. "The Way of the Bureaucrat." JAPAN
       ECHO, 5 (Autumn, 1978), 42-53.

       Speculates on the ability of bureaucrats to adjust to
       new political patterns.

1553. Tsuji, Kiyoaki. "The Cabinet, Administrative Organiza-
       tion and the Bureaucracy." ANNALS OF THE AMERICAN
       ACADEMY OF POLITICAL AND SOCIAL SCIENCE, 308 (1956),
       10-17.

       Finds that the bureaucracy is steadily regaining the
       power it had lost in the war.

                        10. Korea

1554. Bark, Dong-suh, and Chae-jin Lee. "Bureaucratic Elite
       and Development Orientation." POLITICAL LEADERSHIP
       IN KOREA. Edited by Dae-sook Suh and Chae-jin Lee.
       Seattle: University of Washington Press, 1976.

       Contend that the social background, administrative ex-
       perience, and developmental orientation of the senior
       bureaucrats are interrelated.

1555. Bark, Dong-suh. "The Korean Bureaucracy and Political
       Development in Korea." KOREA JOURNAL, 18 (January,
       1978), 10-15.

       Argues that the country has made remarkable economic
       progress but remains politically underdeveloped because
       of the power of the bureaucracy. Even within the bur-
       eaucracy, power tends to be distributed unequally among
       different bureaus.

1556. Cho, Chang-hyun. "Bureaucracy and Local Government
       in South Korea." GOVERNMENT AND POLITICS OF KOREA.
       Edited by Se-jin Kim and Chang-hyun Cho. Silver
       Springs, Md.: Research Institute on Korean Affairs,
       1972.

       Discusses the structure of South Korean administration
       and the recruitment and training of the higher cadre.

Under the Park administration, the power of the bureaucracy has grown at the expense of the legislature. Corruption remains a serious problem.

1557. Hahn, Bae-ho, and Ha-ryong Kim. "Party Bureaucrats and
       Party Development." POLITICAL LEADERSHIP IN KOREA.
       Edited by Dae-sook Suh and Cahe-jin Lee. Seattle:
       University of Washington Press, 1976.

       Study the South Korean case as an example of party
       building in a new nation.

1558. Hong, Soohn-ho. "Bureaucracy in Korea." KOREA JOURNAL,
       20 (August, 1980), 4-13, 20.

       A history of Korean administration since the 14th
       century.

1559. Jun, Jong-sup. "Some Considerations of the Role of Bur-
       eaucracy: Effecting Modernization of Korea." KOREANA
       QUARTERLY, 10 (1968), 26-33.

       About the work of the South Korean bureaucracy in the
       work of economic development.

1560. Kim, Il-sung. "On Eliminating Bureaucracy." ON THE
       BUILDING OF THE WORKER'S PARTY OF KOREA. Pyongyang:
       Foreign Language Publishing House, 1978.

       A 1955 speech by the leader of North Korea.

1561. Lee, Chae-jin, and Dong-suh Bark. "Political Percep-
       tion of Bureaucratic Elite in Korea." KOREA JOURNAL,
       13 (October, 1973), 29-41.

       Survey senior bureaucrats and conclude that the bur-
       eaucracy may have lessened the growth of competing cen-
       ters of political power in South Korea.

1562. Pae, Sung-moun. "Modernization and Bureaucracy: Kor-
       ean Administrators' Motivation and National Modern-
       ization." CHINESE JOURNAL OF ADMINISTRATION, 33
       (1982), 117-36.

        Surveys the most senior members of the South Korean
bureaucracy and finds that there is among this group
a high level of motivation for the further attainment
of modernization goals.

1563.   Yoon, Woo-kon. "Korean Bureaucrat's Behavior: An Ana-
        lysis of Personality and Its Effect." KOREA JOURNAL,
        14 (July, 1974), 22-39.

        Finds that South Korean bureaucrats score highly on
a measure of authoritarianism.

11. Laos

1564.   Coward, E. Walter. "Indigenous Organisation, Bureau-
        cracy and Development: The Case of Irrigation."
        JOURNAL OF DEVELOPMENT STUDIES, 13 (1976), 92-105.

        Examines the development of a new irrigation system
in Laos as an example of the problems of uniting local
users and the central administration. In this case,
indigenous irrigation experience was integrated within
the new system.

12. Malaysia

1565.   Allen, J. de Vere. "The Malayan Civil Service, 1874-
        1941: Colonial Bureaucracy/Malay Elite." COMPARATIVE
        STUDIES IN SOCIETY AND HISTORY, 12 (1970), 149-78.

        Traces the significant features of the growth of the
Malay civil service in the period before WWI. See Item
1573.

1566.   Chauhan, D.S., and Kenneth Hempel. "Bureaucracy and
        Development in Malaysia: The Ecology of Administra-
        tive Reform and Communal Constraints." PLURAL SOC-
        IETIES, 9 (Spring, 1978), 19-36.

        Discuss the strengths and weaknesses in administra-
tion caused by significant ethnic divisions within the
composition of the bureaucracy.

1567.   Hooker, M.B. "Law, Religion, and Bureaucracy in a Malay
        State: A Study in Conflicting Power Centers." JOUR-
        NAL OF COMPARATIVE LAW, 19 (1971), 264-86.

        Identifies four centers of power in a developing soc-
        iety: two traditional (land law or *adat* and religion)
        and two modern (politics and bureaucracy). The inter-
        action of these four elements causes tension.

1568.   Hussein, Ahmed, and Shabbir Cheema. "Leadership Co-
        hesion and Bureaucratic Dominance in Malaysia." IN-
        DIAN JOURNAL OF PUBLIC ADMINISTRATION, 23 (1977), 913-
        26.

        On relations between local leaders and administration.

1569.   Jomo, K.S. "Spontaneity and Planning in Class Forma-
        tion: The Ascendency of the Bureaucratic Bourgeoisie
        in Malaya." SPONTANEITY AND PLANNING IN SOCIAL DE-
        VELOPMENT. Edited by Ulf Himmelstrand. Beverly
        Hills, Cal.: Sage, 1981.

        Uses the case of Malaysia to show that the post-col-
        onial bureaucracy tends to serve the interests of in-
        ternational capitalism. The planning process serves
        to integrate the national economy into a larger sys-
        tem.

1570.   Milne, Robert S. "Bureaucracy and Bureaucratic Reform
        in Malaysia." PHILIPPINE JOURNAL OF PUBLIC ADMINIS-
        TRATION, 10 (1966), 375-88.

        Describes favorably the performance and political per-
        formance of the Malaysian administration.

1571.   Ness, Gayl. "Modernization and Indigenous Control of
        the Bureaucracy in Malaysia." ASIAN SURVEY, 5
        (1965), 467-73.

        Argues that native leadership in new countries is
        most effective in economic development. It helps to
        break down the isolation of local units and involve
        the public in the development process.

1572. Ness, Gayl. BUREAUCRACY AND RURAL DEVELOPMENT IN MAL-
AYSIA: A STUDY IN COMPLEX ORGANIZATIONS IN STIMULATING
ECONOMIC DEVELOPMENT IN NEW STATES. Berkeley: Uni-
versity of California Press, 1967. 257 pp.

Concentrates on the development activity of the Ministry of Rural Development. Malaysia seems to have
achieved a high level of success, at least in terms of
translating development plans into action. The secret
of this success lies in the ethnic composition of the
society which has fostered political control of development administration. Ethnic pluralism is reflected
in the conduct of the administration.

1573. Ness, Gayl. "The Malayan Bureaucracy and Its Occupa-
tional Communities: A Comment on James de Vere Allen's
'Malay Civil Service, 1874-1941.'" COMPARATIVE STUD-
IES IN SOCIETY AND HISTORY, 12 (1970), 179-87.

A comment on Item 1565.

1574. Tilman, Robert O. BUREAUCRATIC TRANSITION IN MALAYA.
Durham, N.C.: Duke University Press, 1964. 175 pp.

Discusses the development and composition of the Malayan civil service, with emphasis on the Malayaniza-
tion of the bureaucracy in the colonial period. The
racial composition of the current system is also analyzed.

1575. Tilman, Robert O. "Bureaucratic Development in Malaya."
ASIAN BUREAUCRATIC SYSTEMS EMERGENT FROM THE BRITISH
IMPERIAL TRADITION. Edited by Ralph Braibanti. Dur-
ham, N.C.: Duke University Press, 1966.

Examines remaining traces of British influence in the
Malayan civil service.

13. Mongolia

1576. Aberle, David F. CHAHAR AND DAGOR MONGOL BUREAUCRATIC
ADMINISTRATION, 1912-1945. New Haven, Conn.: HRAF
Press, 1962. 117 pp.

Studies the administrative styles of two tribal elements in Mongolia during the early years of the Republic of China.

14. Nepal

1577. Goodall, Merrill. "Bureaucracy and Bureaucrats: Some
        Theories Drawn from the Nepal Experience." ASIAN
        SURVEY, 15 (1975), 892-95.

        Finds that, despite attempts at modernization, there
        are two distinct groups in the bureaucracy of Nepal.
        One part is oriented toward performance, while the
        other is more traditional. The latter group is usually
        associated with the upper class and are conscious of
        threats to their status.

1578. Pradhan, Prachanda. "The Nepalese Bureaucracy: A His-
        torical Perspective." PHILIPPINE JOURNAL OF PUBLIC
        ADMINISTRATION, 17 (1973), 178-96.

        Tells us as much as we are ever likely to want to know
        about this particular subject.

15. Pakistan

1579. Ahamed, Emajuddin. "Exclusive Bureaucratic Elites in
        Pakistan: Their Socio-Economic and Regional Back-
        ground." INDIAN POLITICAL SCIENCE REVIEW, 15 (1981),
        52-66.

        Contends that the data show the Pakistan bureaucracy
        to be a closed group intimately related to the most
        powerful groups in society.

1580. Braibanti, Ralph. "Public Bureaucracy and Judiciary
        in Pakistan." BUREAUCRACY AND POLITICAL DEVELOPMENT.
        Edited by Joseph LaPalombara. Princeton, N.J.:
        Princeton University Press, 1963.

        Speculates on the fate of the British administrative

and judicial legacy in a new nation. Pakistan's administrative infrastructure was severely strained by
the partition with India. Environmental pressures on
the bureaucracy further decreased the responsiveness
of the traditional elite.

1581. Braibanti, Ralph. RESEARCH ON THE BUREAUCRACY OF PAK-
ISTAN: A CRITIQUE OF SOURCES, CONDITIONS, AND ISSUES,
WITH APPENDED DOCUMENTS. Durham, N.C.: Duke Univer-
sity Press, 1966. 569 pp.

Attempts to "identify, classify, and evaluate source
materials for the study of the bureaucracy of Pakistan
and to assess conditions for research there." A number
of government documents and public addresses are appended to the text.

1582. Braibanti, Ralph. "The Higher Bureaucracy of Pakistan."
ASIAN BUREAUCRATIC SYSTEMS EMERGENT FROM THE BRITISH
IMPERIAL TRADITION. Durham, N.C.: Duke University
Press, 1966.

Views Pakistan as an example of an administrative
state in which the bureaucracy remains at the center
of political power.

1583. Goodnow, Henry F. THE CIVIL SERVICE OF PAKISTAN: BUR-
EAUCRACY IN A NEW NATION. New Haven, Conn.: Yale
University Press, 1964. 328 pp.

Discusses the nature of the administrative elite in
Pakistan. Most of the material covers developments in
the 1950s. Items discussed include the attitudes, traditions, and procedures of the CSP. This group is important politically; it is conservative and jealous of
its prestige and power. The administrative system needs
to be brought under greater control by other elements
of the polity.

1584. Jan, Saeed Ullah. "Bureaucracy." CONCEPT OF PAKISTAN,
4 (Summer, 1968), 17-21.

On facts and fictions about the bureaucracy.

1585. Khan, Mohammed Mohabbat. BUREAUCRATIC SELF-PRESERVA-
       TION: FAILURE OF MAJOR ADMINISTRATIVE REFORM EFFORTS
       IN THE CIVIL SERVICE OF PAKISTAN. Dacca: University
       of Dacca, 1980. 167 pp.

       Examines the pre-1973 reform efforts in Pakistan.
       Most of the reforms failed because they were not con-
       sidered within the context of political leadership by
       the bureaucratic elite. Real reform came about only
       after the defeat in the war over Bangladesh.

1586. Syed, Anwar. "Bureaucratic Ethics and Ethos in Pak-
       istan." POLITY, 4 (1971), 159-94.

       Argues that the Pakistani bureaucracy has a bad re-
       putation and that there are few ways, short of a mass
       movement, for the people to demand change.

1587. Syed, Anwar. ISSUES OF BUREAUCRATIC ETHICS: TWO ES-
       SAYS. Lahore: Progressive Publishers, 1975. 49 pp.

       See Item 1586.

1588. Ziring, Lawrence, and Robert LaPorte. "The Pakistan
       Bureaucracy: Two Views." ASIAN SURVEY, 14 (1974),
       1086-1103.

       Discuss the factors leading up to and the implemen-
       tation of reform efforts in the civil service under the
       Bhutto regime.

16. Philippines

1589. Abueva, Jose. "Bureaucratic Politics in the Philip-
       pines." CASES IN COMPARATIVE POLITICS. Edited by
       Lucian W. Pye. Boston: Little, Brown, 1970.

       On the political role of the civil service.

1590. Clemente, F.A. "Philippine Bureaucratic Behavior."
       PHILIPPINE JOURNAL OF PUBLIC ADMINISTRATION, 15
       (1971), 119-47.

Discusses the operation of Philippine administration
at the local level.

1591. Conception, Mercedes B. "Mitigated Bureaucracy." PHIL-
IPPINE SOCIOLOGICAL REVIEW, 8 (July-October, 1960),
22-25.

Argues that the effect of bureaucratic formalism is
lessened because of the influence of paternalism. There
is a strong strain of familism which encourages citizens to appeal government decisions.

1592. Corpuz, Onofre. THE BUREAUCRACY OF THE PHILIPPINES.
Manila: Institute of Public Administration, 1957.
268 pp.

Describes the evolution of the Philippine administrative system since the days of Spanish colonialism. The
system is now fairly stable, but increased requirements
for better training and greater specialization are becoming evident.

1593. Krauss, Wilma R. "Toward a Theory of Political Participation of Public Bureaucrats." ADMINISTRATIVE SCI-
ENCE QUARTERLY, 16 (1971), 180-91.

Compares the electoral and legislative behavior of
Philippine and Hawaiian bureaucrats. The behavior was
found to vary with the hierarchical structure and the
length of service in a merit system.

1594. Krauss, Wilma R. "Some Aspects of the Influence Process of Public Bureaucrats: An Ideal-Typical Model
and Cross-Cultural Guttman Scale." WESTERN POLITICAL
QUARTERLY, 25 (1972), 323-39.

Investigates the process by which bureaucrats influence electoral and legislative decision. The breadth,
range, and frequency of political activity is corre-
lated with the background characteristics of bureaucrats in the Philippines and Hawaii.

17. Singapore

1595. Meow, Seah. "Public Relations in the Singapore Bureau-
           cracy: A Neglected Aspect in Administration." INDIAN
           JOURNAL OF PUBLIC ADMINISTRATION, 19 (1973), 612-26.

       Argues that improved public relations programs would
       make bureaucracy more effective, resilient, and respon-
       sive to the citizens.

18. Sri Lanka

1596. Kearney, Robert N. "Ceylon: The Contemporary Bureau-
           cracy." ASIAN BUREAUCRATIC SYSTEMS EMERGENT FROM
           THE BRITISH IMPERIAL TRADITION. Edited by Ralph
           Braibanti. Durham, N.C.: Duke University Press,
           1966.

       Examines the characteristics and problems of the
       bureaucracy during a period of rapid political change.

1597. Kearney, Robert N., and Richard L. Harris. "Bureau-
           cracy and Environment in Ceylon." JOURNAL OF COMMON-
           WEALTH STUDIES, 2 (1964), 253-66.

       Find that the bureaucracy is not well integrated into
       society. The elitist and exclusive tendencies resulted
       from both traditional and colonial influences. Adjust-
       ments to independence and other expressions of nation-
       alism by the higher civil service have been rather dif-
       ficult.

19. Thailand

1598. Bowornwathana, Bidhya. "Multiple Superiors in the
           Thai Public Health Bureaucracy." CHINESE JOURNAL OF
           ADMINISTRATION, 33 (1982), 6-55.

       Explores aspects of administrative control when one
       reports to more than one superior.

1599. Evers, Hans-Dieter. "The Formation of a Social Class Structure: Urbanization, Bureaucratization, and Social Mobility in Thailand." AMERICAN SOCIOLOGICAL REVIEW, 31 (1966), 480-88. *Also:* JOURNAL OF SOUTHEAST ASIAN HISTORY, 7 (September, 1966), 110-15.

Does not find evidence to support the contention that social mobility in a developing society is increased by such aspects of modernization as urbanization or bureaucratization.

1600. Haas, David. INTERACTION IN THE THAI BUREAUCRACY: STRUCTURE, CULTURE, AND SOCIAL EXCHANGE. Boulder, Colo.: Westview, 1979. 180 pp.

Describes and compares the patterns of social exchange of two groups of Thai officials: local bureaucrats and physicians in a provincial hospital. The way in which administrative behavior is constrained and channeled is presented as a matter of individual maximization of benefits.

1601. King, John K. "Thailand's Bureaucracy and the Threat of Communist Subversion." FAR EASTERN SURVEY, 23 (1954), 169-73.

Feels that because the bureaucracy is a major center of power in Thai society it is a likely target for Communist infiltration and subversion.

1602. Krannich, Ronald L., and Caryl Krannich. "Anonymous Communications and Bureaucratic Politics in Thailand." ADMINISTRATION AND SOCIETY, 11 (1979), 227-48.

Examine the significance of anonymous letters within a Thai municipal organization. These letters are important elements of bureaucratic politics and serve to keep the organization from becoming too rational.

1603. Krannich, Ronald L. "The Politics of Street-Level Bureaucracy in Thailand." PHILIPPINE JOURNAL OF PUBLIC ADMINISTRATION, 22 (1978), 113-30.

Applies street-level theory to local administrators.

1604. Krannich, Ronald L. "The Politics of Personnel Manage-
        ment: Competence and Compromise in the Thai Bureau-
        cracy." HONG KONG JOURNAL OF PUBLIC ADMINISTRATION,
        3 (June, 1981), 32-55.

        Finds that the insistence on formal improvements of
        the personnel system have not overcome the political
        content. The realities of politics have forced gov-
        ernment officials to modify the application of merit
        considerations in municipal organizations.

1605. Mosel, James. "Fatalism in Thai Bureaucratic Decision-
        Making." ANTHROPOLOGICAL QUARTERLY, 39 (1966), 191-
        99.

        Concludes that Thai administrators have a low sense
        of self-efficacy because of the nonrational elements
        of the culture.

1606. Neher, Clark D. "A Critical Analysis of Research on
        Thai Politics and Bureaucracy." ASIAN THOUGHT AND
        SOCIETY, 2 (April, 1977), 13-27.

        Argues that most analyses of other writers "tend to
        oversimplify the complexity of Thai politics and to un-
        derestimate the pluralistic forces in Thai sociopolit-
        ical activity." Conflict theory is advocated as a way
        to approach the study of Thai political affairs.

1607. Riggs, Fred W. THAILAND: THE MODERNIZATION OF A BUREAU-
        CRATIC POLITY. Honolulu: East-West Center Press,
        1966. 470 pp.

        Examines the historical bases of the rise of the pol-
        itical power of the Thai bureaucracy. As a bureaucrat-
        ic polity, "the energy of officials is directed toward
        activities designed to enhance their own power and pres-
        tige." If the Thai system is to be directed toward
        larger ends, it must be checked by other political or-
        gans which are, at the present time, non-existent in
        the society. In the meantime, complete modernization
        will be difficult because of the complete power of the
        bureaucracy.

1608.   Rubin, Herbert J.   "Modes of Bureaucratic Communica-
          tions." SOCIOLOGICAL QUARTERLY, 15 (1974), 212-30.

          Identifies four modes of communications in Thai public
          administration. The social status of the officials is
          particularly important in official communications.

1609.   Rubin, Herbert J.   "Rules, Regulations, and the Rural
          Thai Bureaucracy." JOURNAL OF SOUTHEAST ASIAN STUD-
          IES, 11 (1980), 50-73.

          Compares the "bargaining" over the enforcement of
          bureaucratic rules in France and the U.S. with govern-
          ment in rural Thailand.

1610.   Shor, Edgar.   "The Thai Bureaucracy." ADMINISTRATIVE
          SCIENCE QUARTERLY, 5 (1960), 66-86.

          Finds that the Thai bureaucracy is well insulated
          from society. Its concerns are narrow and somewhat
          introverted.

1611.   Siffin, William J.   "Personnel Processes of the Thai
          Bureaucracy." PAPERS IN COMPARATIVE PUBLIC ADMINIS-
          TRATION. Edited by Ferrel Heady and Sybil Stokes.
          Ann Arbor: University of Michigan, Institute of Pub-
          lic Administration, 1962.

          Examines the combination of traditional and modern
          practices in Thai administration.

1612.   Siffin, William J.   THE THAI BUREAUCRACY: INSTITUTIONAL
          CHANGE AND DEVELOPMENT. Honolulu: East-West Center
          Press, 1966. 291 pp.

          Argues that the Thai bureaucracy has been shaped in
          large part by cultural factors, including Buddhist
          thought and a tradition of royal absolutism. The ac-
          complishment of specific goals in the most efficient
          manner is not a major value. The emphasis is on the
          maintenance of routines and innovation is not rewarded
          or encouraged. It is predicted that the pressures of
          modernization will force the modification of official
          attitudes and behaviors.

1613.   Somvichian, Kamol. "'The Oyster and the Shell:' Thai
        Bureaucrats in Politics." ASIAN SURVEY, 18 (1978),
        829-37.

        A former Thai politician reflects on the relationship
        of civilian officials and the military since the coup
        of 1977.

1614.   Springer, J. Fred, and Richard W. Gable. "Moderniza-
        tion and Sex Roles: The Status of Women in Thai Bur-
        eaucracy." SEX ROLES, 7 (1981), 723-37.

        Assess the position of women in Thai public adminis-
        tration. In general, females hold lower positions and
        are paid less than males with comparable qualifications.
        Women may be influential in an informal way, but this
        source of influence may be less effective in the mod-
        ern organization.

1615.   Thomas, Ladd. "Bureaucratic Attitudes and Behavior as
        Obstacles to Political Integration of Thai Muslims."
        SOUTHEAST ASIA, 3 (1974), 545-66.

        Concludes that the officials who most often come in
        contact with Muslims have the lowest opinion of them,
        thus hampering political integration.

1616.   Zimmerman, Robert. "Student 'Revolution' in Thailand:
        The End of the Bureaucratic Polity?" ASIAN SURVEY,
        14 (1974), 509-29.

        A survey of recent political developments.

                        20. Vietnam

1617.   Brown, Douglas R. "Bureaucracy and Dependency in the
        Third World: The Soc Son Refugee Project in South
        Viet Nam." NEW SCHOLAR, 3 (1971), 103-23.

        Examines a failed resettlement program. The Vietnam-
        ese bureaucracy was unhelpful because of the desire of
        the officials to preserve the social status of their
        urban patrons.

1618. Dorsey, John T. "The Bureaucracy and Political Devel-
          opment in Viet Nam." BUREAUCRACY AND POLITICAL DEVEL-
          OPMENT. Edited by Joseph LaPalombara. Princeton,
          N.J.: Princeton University Press, 1963.

       Constructs a model of political development based on
       a theory of energy conversion, with energy defined as
       the acquisition of information organized as knowledge.
       The distribution and circulation of knowledge in a soc-
       iety determine the amounts of energy within the system
       that can be converted from one form to another. Look-
       ing at the case of South Vietnam, it is found that the
       power of the bureaucracy tended to monopolize the energy
       exchange process, thus preventing the emergence of other
       sources of political action. The bureaucracy failed to
       establish effective articulation with other important
       sectors.

1619. Joiner, Charles, and Roy Jumper. "Organizing Bureau-
          crats: South Viet Nam's Revolutionary Civil Servant's
          League." ASIAN SURVEY, 3 (1963), 203-15.

       Describes the role of organized civil servants in
       consolidating the interests within the bureaucracy and
       thus increasing the control of the Diem regime.

1620. Jumper, Roy. "Mandarin Bureaucracy and Politics in
          South Viet Nam." PACIFIC AFFAIRS, 30 (1957), 47-58.

       Says that the bureaucracy is a power center because
       it was one of the few groups to come out of the French
       period with some degree of internal organization. It
       has, in turn, inhibited the growth of any competing
       groups.

1621. Weil, Herman M. "Can Bureaucracies Be Rational Actors?
          Foreign Policy Decision-Making in North Vietnam."
          INTERNATIONAL STUDIES QUARTERLY, 19 (1975), 432-68.

       Addresses some of the problems raised by Allison's
       model (Item 1086) of foreign policy making. How can
       one evaluate the action of members of closed societies
       such as North Vietnam? Data for the years 1971-73 are
       derived from secondary sources. From this information,
       the key actors are identified.

C. Australia and New Zealand

1622. Benda, H.J. "Bureaucrats and Politicians." NEW ZEA-
        LAND JOURNAL OF PUBLIC ADMINISTRATION, 11 (Summer,
        1950), 72-79.

        Wonders if the administrators are gaining power at
        the expense of political leadership in New Zealand.

1623. Borehan, Paul, Michael Cass, and Michael McCallum.
        "The Australian Bureaucratic Elite: The Importance
        of Social Backgrounds and Occupational Experience."
        AUSTRALIAN AND NEW ZEALAND JOURNAL OF SOCIOLOGY, 15
        (July, 1979), 45-55.

        Survey Australian civil servants. This body is not
        representative of the general population. The group
        is fairly homogeneous.

1624. Brown, Allen. "The Improper and Arbitary Use of Power:
        A Case Study of an Australian Bureaucracy." AUSTRAL-
        IAN PLANNING INSTITUTE JOURNAL, 5 (October, 1967),
        93-98.

        On the bureaucracy of planning in Australia.

1625. Caiden, Gerald. "The Political Role of the Commonwealth
        Bureaucracy." PUBLIC ADMINISTRATION (SYDNEY), 24
        (1965), 310-28.

        Considers the four major periods in the growth of
        the Australian national bureaucracy, with emphasis on
        its participation in the political process.

1626. Caiden, Gerald. THE COMMONWEALTH BUREAUCRACY. Mel-
        bourne: Melbourne University Press, 1967. 445 pp.

        Describes the personnel system of the national govern-
        ment. Following an account of the environment of the
        bureaucracy, the specific personnel practices such as

recruitment and fringe benefits are covered. Proposals
for improving the service are included, and emerging
problems in the public service are touched upon.

1627. Caiden, Gerald. "Tackling Bureaucratic Inertia: Some
Personal Reflections on the Royal Commission on Aus-
tralian Government Administration." AUSTRALIAN QUART-
ERLY, 49 (1977), 5-16.

Reviews the recommendations of a commission studying
the improvement of public administration.

1628. Collins, Hugh. "The 'Coombs Report:' Bureaucracy, Diplomacy, and Australian Foreign Policy." AUSTRALIAN
OUTLOOK, 30 (1976), 387-413.

Is not happy with the recommendations made by a panel
looking at the machinery of foreign affairs.

1629. Cravens, Fadjo. "Bureaucracy in Australia." CONGRES-
SIONAL RECORD, 90 (1944), A4715-16.

A reprint from the *New York Times Magazine*.

1630. Gibbons, P.J. "Milk Quality Control: An Example of
Bureaucratic Growth." PUBLIC ADMINISTRATION, 40
(1978), 62-71.

On the wild and wacky world of dairy regulations in
New Zealand.

1631. Hawker, Geoffrey. "The Bureaucracy under the Whitlam
Government--And Vice Versa." POLITICS, 10 (May 10,
1975), 15-23.

Suggests that it is hard to tell who is winning the
battle of the Labour government to control the bureaucracy.

1632. Hill, Larry B. "Affect and Interaction in an Ambiguous Authority Relationship: New Zealand's Bureaucrats and the Ombudsman." JOURNAL OF COMPARATIVE

ADMINISTRATION, 4 (1972), 35-48.

Measures attitudes of officials toward the ombudsman.
The bureaucrats were found to be favorably inclined toward the institution.

1633.   Hill, Larry B.   "Institutionalization, the Ombudsman,
        and Bureaucracy." AMERICAN POLITICAL SCIENCE RE-
        VIEW, 68 (1974), 1075-85.

        Examines the office of ombudsman in New Zealand in
        terms of a theory of institutionalization, which is
        measured as an authority-based phenomenon. The offen-
        sive capability of an organization against its envir-
        onment is an important factor. On the basis of the
        data, it is shown that the ombudsman has been estab-
        lised as an authority figure within the bureaucracy and
        can be considered institutionalized.

1634.   Juddery, Bruce. AT THE CENTRE: THE AUSTRALIAN BUREAU-
        CRACY IN THE 1970S. Melbourne: Cheshire, 1974.   272
        pp.

        A survey of Australian national government.

1635.   Lyall, E.A.   "Dr. Caiden's View of the Commonwealth Bur-
        eaucracy." PUBLIC ADMINISTRATION (SYDNEY), 26 (1967),
        377-83.

        A review essay on Item 1626.

1636.   Macdonald, John S., and Leatrice Macdonald.   "Italian
        Migration to Australia: Manifest Functions of Bureau-
        cracy versus Latent Functions of Informal Networks."
        JOURNAL OF SOCIAL HISTORY, 3 (1970), 249-76.

        Argue that the anti-migration policies of the bureau-
        cracy were subverted by the development of informal net-
        works among the migrants. The groups provided inform-
        ation and assistance to other migrants. The ostensible
        function of the bureaucracy resulted in a dysfunctional
        outcome.

1637. McMartin, Arthur. "'Born Bureaucrat:' Thomas Cudbert Harington." AUSTRALIAN JOURNAL OF PUBLIC ADMINIS-TRATION, 38 (1979), 263-78.

A sketch of the life of a 19th-century official.

1638. Mediansky, Fedor A., and James A. Nockels. "The Prime Minister's Bureaucracy." PUBLIC ADMINISTRATION (SYD-NEY), 34 (1975), 202-15.

Argue that party changes in Australian government encouraged the new leadership to set up a number of ad-visory bodies and other extra-bureaucratic units. The new government was suspicious of the permanent bureau-cracy and uncertain of its own ability to manage. It may be that the prime minister's bureaucracy has now outlived its purpose. The regular agencies can now be relied upon for implementation of the program of the government.

1639. Mediansky, Fedor A., and James A. Nockels. "Malcolm Fraser's Bureaucracy." AUSTRALIAN QUARTERLY, 53 (1981), 394-418.

Assess the administrative changes that have taken place under Prime Minister Fraser. His style of admin-istration is based on a hierarchical concentration of power in the cabinet. The personal staff of the prime minister has given him an advantage over the other min-isters.

1640. Milne, R.S., ed. BUREAUCRACY IN NEW ZEALAND. Welling-ton: New Zealand Institute of Public Administration, 1957. 137 pp.

A collection of original essays on the civil service, with emphasis on problems of popular control of the ad-ministration.

1641. Newell, William. "Australian and Japan: A Study in Com-parative Bureaucracies." JOURNAL OF INDUSTRIAL RE-LATIONS, 17 (1975), 265-71.

> Compares the bureaucratic system of the two nations. The many differences result from the distinctive recruitment patterns.

1642. Pringle, Rosemary. "Feminists and Bureaucrats." REFRACTORY GIRL, 18-19 (1979-80), 58-60.

On employment practices and women's rights.

1643. Simms, Marian. "Bureaucrats and Businessmen: The Changing Composition of Boards and Commissions from Curtin to Menzies." AUSTRALIAN JOURNAL OF PUBLIC ADMINISTRATION, 40 (1981), 254-56.

Investigates the social backgrounds of appointees to governing boards of public corporations.

1644. Skertchley, Allan R. NEW BUREAUCRACY: RECONSTRUCTION OF STATE GOVERNMENT BUREAUCRACIES TO MEET THE NEEDS AND EXPECTATIONS OF THE POST-INDUSTRIAL SOCIETY. Perth: W.C. Brown, Government Printer, 1977. 123 pp.

On state government administration.

1645. Smith, Thomas B. "Salient New Zealand Bureaucratic Norms." POLITICAL SCIENCE, 25 (1973), 26-36.

On features of New Zealand administration.

1646. Smith, Thomas B. THE NEW ZEALAND BUREAUCRAT. Wellington: Cheshire, 1974. 162 pp.

Discusses the characteristics of administrators in the New Zealand bureaucracy.

1647. Spann, R.N. "Studies in Bureaucracy." PUBLIC ADMINISTRATION (SYDNEY), 25 (1966), 163-69.

A review essay on two books about the Australian civil service.

1648. Spann, R.N. "The Commonwealth Bureaucracy." AUSTRAL-
        IAN POLITICS. Edited by Henry Mayer. Melbourne: F.
        W. Cheshire, 1966.

        An overview of the national administrative system.

1649. Wettenhall, R.L. "Savings Banks, Bureaucracy and the
        Public Corporation." AUSTRALIAN JOURNAL OF POLITICS
        HISTORY, 10 (1964), 54-69.

        Attempts to discover the origin of the public corp-
        oration in Australia.

1650. Wettenhall, R.L., and J.M. Power. "Bureaucracy and Dis-
        aster." PUBLIC ADMINISTRATION (SYDNEY), 28 (1969),
        263-77.

        Discuss the administrative response to a bushfire dis-
        aster in Tasmania.

1651. Wilenski, Peter. "The Left and State Bureaucracy."
        AUSTRALIAN QUARTERLY, 52 (1980), 398-414.

        Looks at the efforts of the Australian Labour Party
        to promote a reform oriented bureaucracy.

                        D. Canada

1652. Angus, W.H. "The Individual and the Bureaucracy: Jud-
        icial Review--Do We Need It?" MCGILL LAW REVIEW, 20
        (1974), 177-212.

        Concedes that judicial review of administrative action
        is necessary in Canada, but its scope should be nar-
        rowed. Other means of maintaining oversight of the
        bureaucracy, such as the ombudsman, will gradually de-
        velop.

1653. Atkinson, Michael M., and Kim Nossal. "Bureaucratic
        Politics and the New Fighter Aircraft Decisions."
        CANADIAN PUBLIC ADMINISTRATION, 24 (1981), 531-58.

Apply the bureaucratic politics model of foreign policy making to the decisions concerning the acquiring of
fighter aircraft. Three departments engaged in the policy are examined. There is no clear evidence support-
ing the contention that policy is the result of conflict among bureaus. It may be that a parliamentary
system imposes greater restraints on bureaucratic infighting.

1654. Bakvis, Herman. "French Canada and the 'Bureaucratic
       Phenonmenon.'" CANADIAN PUBLIC ADMINISTRATION, 21
       (1978), 103-24.

       Identifies some unique French-Canadian characterist-
       ics and inquires whether they have any effect on bureau-
       cratic behavior, using Crozier's theory (Item 309).

1655. "Basford's Bureaucracy for Consumers." CANADIAN BUSI-
       NESS, 42 (August, 1969), 16-18, 23-24.

       A profile of the Canadian Minister for Consumer and
       Corporate Affairs.

1656. Baum, Daniel J., ed. THE INDIVIDUAL AND THE BUREAU-
       CRACY. Toronto: Osgoode Hall Law School, York Uni-
       versity, 1975. 135 pp.

       A collection of essays on the rights of the individ-
       ual in the administrative state.

1657. Beattie, Christopher, and B.G. Spencer. "Career At-
       tainment in Canadian Bureaucracies: Unscrambling the
       Effects of Age, Seniority, Education, and Ethnolin-
       guistic Factors on Salary." AMERICAN JOURNAL OF SOC-
       IOLOGY, 77 (1971), 472-90.

       Find that ethnic and linguistic factors account for
       many aspect of the career of a Canadian administrator.

1658. Beattie, Christopher, Jaques Désy, and Stephen Long-
       staff. BUREAUCRATIC CAREERS: ANGLOPHONES AND FRANCO-
       PHONES IN THE CANADIAN PUBLIC SERVICE. Ottawa: In-
       formation Canada, 1972. 652 pp.

Describe the careers, education patterns, and social backgrounds of French and English speaking members of the federal civil service.

1659.   Brown, M. Paul. "A Lesson in Bureaucratic Persistence: The Provision of Rehabilitation and Resource Management Services in the Maritimes, 1943–81." CANADIAN PUBLIC ADMINISTRATION, 25 (1982), 130–46.

Examines the phenomenon of "bureaucratic persistence" or the ability of organizations to survive. The object of study is a Nova Scotian agency involved in resources management. It endured over several decades, despite changes in its name and charter. Among the factors accounting for such durability is the nature of the cabinet in legislation and the dynamics of federalism. Finally, to survive any agency must have some valid function.

1660.   Campbell, Colin, and George J. Szablowski. THE SUPER-BUREAUCRATS: STRUCTURE AND BEHAVIOR IN CENTRAL AGENCIES. New York: New York University Press, 1979. 286 pp.

Look at the Canadian version of a new group of public officials--the super-bureaucrats. These are members of government-wide coordinating agencies such as finance offices. These officials differ in many respects from traditional line bureaucrats. Problems of accountability may arise since these groups tend to avoid public scrutiny. Methods of increasing the political accountability of these officials are suggested.

1661.   Cole, Taylor. THE CANADIAN BUREAUCRACY--A STUDY OF CANADIAN CIVIL SERVANTS AND OTHER PUBLIC EMPLOYEES, 1939–1947. Durham, N.C.: Duke University Press, 1949. 292 pp.

Describes the administration of the federal government of Canada, with emphasis on major issues of personnel administration. The period under consideration was a formative one in the national bureaucracy.

1662.   Cole, Taylor. CANADIAN BUREAUCRACY AND FEDERALISM,
        1947-1965. Denver: University of Denver, 1966.
        35 pp.

        Reflections on the importance of the bureaucracy in
        the maintenance of Canadian federalism.

1663.   Corbett, D.C. "The Politics of Bureaucracy in Canada."
        PUBLIC ADMINISTRATION (SYDNEY), 32 (1973), 42-55.

        Sketches the shifts in the power center of Canadian
        bureaucracy in the past few decades.

1664.   Friedmann, Karl A. "Controlling Bureaucracy: Attitudes
        in the Alberta Public Services toward the Ombudsman."
        CANADIAN PUBLIC ADMINISTRATION, 19 (1976), 51-87.

        Measures the opinions of provincial administrators
        toward the office of the ombudsman. In general, there
        was a favorable attitude toward the office.

1665.   Gopalakrishna, K.C. "The Role of Bureaucracy in Can-
        ada." INDIAN JOURNAL OF PUBLIC ADMINISTRATION, 16
        (1970), 557-74.

        A survey of the operation of administration in Can-
        adian goverment.

1666.   Grey, Rodney. "Bureaucracy and Citizens." QUEEN'S
        QUARTERLY, 57 (1950), 88-98.

        Surveys the Canadian federal bureaucracy and its con-
        tinuing problems.

1667.   Guindon, Hubert. "Social Unrest, Social Class, and
        Quebec's Bureaucratic Revolution." QUEEN'S QUARTER-
        LY, 71 (1964), 150-62.

        Argues that the continued integration of the new mid-
        dle class in French Canada will depend upon the response
        of the government for more public services.

1668. Hodgetts, J.E. "Adolescent Bureaucracy: Some Features of the Canadian Civil Service before Confederation." CANADIAN JOURNAL OF ECONOMICS AND POLITICAL SCIENCE, 18 (1952), 419-30.

Examines the roots of the Canadian civil service and traces the path of its relationship with the political leadership of the central government.

1669. Hodgetts, J.E. "The Liberals and the Bureaucrats: A Rose by Any Other Name." QUEEN'S QUARTERLY, 62 (1965), 176-83.

Wonders what the long tenure in office of the Liberal Party will do to the neutrality of the bureaucracy. Will the officials be able to respond to the leadership of a different party?

1670. Johnson, A.F. "A Minister as an Agent of Policy Change: The Case of Unemployment Insurance in the Seventies." CANADIAN PUBLIC ADMINISTRATION, 24 (1981), 612-33.

Describes the interaction of cabinet ministers and senior civil servants in the policy-making process. An analysis of unemployment policy indicates that the minister can be at a disadvantage in the formative stages of a policy. However, by performing the functions of surveillance and legitimation, the minister can remain a major actor in policy change.

1671. Johnson, Walter S. "The Reign of Law under an Expanding Bureaucracy." CANADIAN BAR REVIEW, 22 (1944), 380-90.

Argues that Canadians can live with bureaucracy if lawyers are allowed to keep check on administration.

1672. Jones, J.C.H. "The Bureaucracy and Public Policy: Canadian Merger Policy and the Combines Branch, 1960-71." CANADIAN PUBLIC ADMINISTRATION, 18 (1975), 269-96.

Hypothesizes that bureaus attempt to maximize private

rather than social utility in the conduct of administration. The elements of the private utility function
are described and applied to the performance of an agency. Security maximization best explains the conduct of
the bureau. Whether a bureau is doing any good depends
upon the congruence of the private utility function with
the larger public interest.

1673. Kernaghan, W.D.K, ed. BUREAUCRACY IN CANADIAN GOVERN-
MENT. Toronto: Methuen, 1969. 190 pp. Second edition, 1973. 181 pp.

A collection of readings on the activity of the Canadian civil service.

1674. Mallory, J.R. "Parliament, the Cabinet, and the Bureaucrats in Canada." POLITICS, 15 (1980), 249-63.

Details the decline of cabinet authority and the rise
of a powerful civil service in the national government.

1675. Morley, J. Terence. "The Justice Development Commission: Overcoming Bureaucratic Resistance to Innovative Policy-Making." CANADIAN PUBLIC ADMINISTRATION,
19 (1976), 121-39.

Examines a special unit of the British Columbia Attorney General's office to see the limits of innovation in organizations.

1676. Nossal, Kim R. "Allison through the (Ottawa) Looking
Glass: Bureaucratic Politics and Foreign Policy in
a Parliamentary System." CANADIAN PUBLIC ADMINISTRA-
TION, 22 (1979), 610-26.

Test the applicability of Allison's model (Item 1086)
of bureaucratic politics to the Canadian foreign policy-
making process. There is some support for the notion
that the model can be applied in a parliamentary system.
However, one must keep in mind the differences between
the presidential and parliamentary systems. These differences will have an impact on the tone of bureaucratic
politics and its effects on policy.

1677.   Pickersgill, J.W.   "Bureaucrats and Politicians."   CAN-
        ADIAN PUBLIC ADMINISTRATION, 15 (1972), 418-27.

        Reflects on personal experiences concerning the inter-
        play of administrators and politicians.

1678.   Porter, John.   "Higher Public Servants and the Bureau-
        cratic Elite in Canada."   CANADIAN JOURNAL OF ECONO-
        MICS AND POLITICAL SCIENCE, 24 (1958), 483-501.

        Investigates the characteristics of the Canadian bur-
        eaucratic elite as of 1953.   The group appears to have
        a monopoly of skills and knowledge and is more closed
        than open.   The higher civil servants form a homogen-
        eous group and are not representative of the majority
        of Canadians.

1679.   Porter, John.   "The Bureaucratic Elite: A Reply to Pro-
        fessor Rowat."   CANADIAN JOURNAL OF ECONOMICS AND
        POLITICAL SCIENCE, 25 (1959), 204-09.

        A response to Item 1683.

1680.   Presthus, Robert, and William V. Monopoli.   "Bureaucra-
        cy in the United States and Canada: Social, Attitud-
        inal, and Behavioral Variables."   INTERNATIONAL JOUR-
        NAL OF COMPARATIVE SOCIOLOGY, 18 (1977), 176-90.

        Surveys the senior civil service in the U.S. and Can-
        ada.   Among other things, the Canadian administrators
        tend to have a more general educational background.

1681.   Probyn, Stephen.   "The Boom Town Bureaucracy Built."
        CANADIAN BUSINESS, 51 (October, 1978), 36-45.

        Describes how Ottawa has become a wealthy city because
        of the growth of government.

1682.   Rich, Harvey.   "The Canadian Case for a Representative
        Bureaucracy."   POLITICAL SCIENCE, 27 (1975), 97-100.

        Suggests that there is a possible conflict between

representativeness and merit in a society without equal
educational opportunities. The growth of the merit system in Canada has led to the appointment of French-
speaking citizens in smaller numbers. Equality of opportunity for education is a prerequisite for a truly
representative public service.

1683.   Rowat, Donald C. "On John Porter's 'Bureaucratic Elite
        in Canada.'" CANADIAN JOURNAL OF ECONOMIC AND POLIT-
        ICAL SCIENCE, 25 (1959), 204-209.

        Argues that Porter (Item 1678) overemphasizes the ele-
        ment of efficiency in administration. There should be
        more effort to recruit people from underrepresented
        groups. Such a move need not reduce the efficiency of
        the Canadian public service.

1684.   Savoie, D.J. "The General Development Agreement Ap-
        proach and the Bureaucratization of Provincial Gov-
        ernments in the Atlantic Provinces." CANADIAN PUB-
        LIC ADMINISTRATION, 24 (1981), 116-31.

        Explores the implications of the use of general devel-
        opment agreements between the national and provincial
        governments. These agreements significantly alter the
        role of local organizations. The relationships between
        provincial officials and the provincial ministers have
        also been changed.

1685.   Schultz, Richard. FEDERALISM, BUREAUCRACY, AND PUBLIC
        POLICY: THE POLITICS OF HIGHWAY TRANSPORT REGULATION.
        Montreal: McGill-Queen's University Press, 1980. 228
        pp.

        Looks at the implementation of the National Transport-
        ation Act of 1967 from a bureaucratic politics model.

1686.   Sigelman, Lee, and William Vanderbok. "Legislators,
        Bureaucrats, and Canadian Democracy: The Long and
        Short of It." CANADIAN JOURNAL OF POLITICAL SCIENCE,
        10 (1977), 615-23.

        Tests the thesis of Norton Long (Item 922) that the
        bureaucracy is more representative than legislatures.

The data show that the thesis does not hold true for
Canada.

1687.   Smith, Larry.   "Getting Your Way with a Bureaucrat."
        CANADIAN BUSINESS, 53 (September, 1980), 104-07, 110-
        15.

        Lists seven ways to deal with government officials.

1688.   Smith, Larry.   "Counterattack: How to Wage War against
        the Bureaucrats, and Win." CANADIAN BUSINESS, 55
        (February, 1982), 108, 110.

        Advice to owners of small businesses.

1689.   Snell, James G.   "The Deputy Head in the Canadian Bur-
        eacuracy: A Case Study of the Registrar of the Supreme
        Court of Canada." CANADIAN PUBLIC ADMINISTRATION, 24
        (1981), 301-09.

        A historical note on the development of a powerful
        office in Canadian government.

1690.   "Streamlining Canada's Bureaucracy." BUSINESS WEEK,
        (March 28, 1964), 100-03.

        On the Glassco Commission recommendations on adminis-
        trative reorganization.

1691.   Sudama, Trevor.   "PPBS and Theories of Decision-Making,
        Bureaucracy and Politics." INDIAN JOURNAL OF PUBLIC
        ADMINISTRATION, 23 (1977), 319-39.

        Looks at the application of program budgeting in Can-
        ada. The approach--PPBS--has had greater success in
        Canada than in the U.S., largely because Canadian ex-
        ecutives have a greater control over the bureaucratic
        political process than their American counterparts.

1692.   Wilson, Seymour, and Willard Mullins.   "Representative
        Bureaucracy: Linguistic/Ethnic Aspects in Canadian

Public Policy." CANADIAN PUBLIC ADMINISTRATION, 21 (1978), 513-38.

Explore the development of the policy designed to en-sure the representation of French-speaking citizens in the public service. Crucial events leading up to the present policy are described. In the final analysis, sociological diversity is a positive value, but the use of quotas to achieve this desirable end cannot be re-commended.

1693. Winham, Gilbert R. "Bureaucratic Politics and Canadian Trade Negotiations." INTERNATIONAL JOURNAL, 34 (1978-79), 64-89.

Identifies the participants in the renegotiation of Canada's protectionist trade policy.

1694. Winslow, J.J. Fraser. "Bureaucracy." CANADIAN BAR RE-VIEW, 8 (1930), 278-82.

Finds that Hewart's *The New Despotism* (Item 70) ap-plies to Canada as well as Great Britain.

E. European Democracies

1. General

1695. Anderson, Eugene, and Pauline Anderson. POLITICAL IN-STITUTIONS AND SOCIAL CHANGE IN CONTINENTAL EUROPE IN THE NINETEENTH CENTURY. Berkeley: University of Cal-fornia Press, 1967. 451 pp.

Describe the major developments in governmental in-stitutions. The rise of bureaucracy was a major fea-ture of the century, with changes taking place in the composition and social role of administration. The administrative elite in many countries created an of-ficial mentality which, in many cases, was at odds with the ordinary lives of citizens. The anti-bureaucratic literature of the time is reviewed. The relationship of administration to other organs of government in a time of democratization is explored.

1696. Armstrong, John A. THE EUROPEAN ADMINISTRATIVE ELITE. Princeton: Princeton University Press, 1973. 406 pp.

Examines the growth of the administrative elites in Great Britain, France, Germany, and Russia from the 17th century up to the present time. The basic thesis is that, despite considerable changes in social and political conditions, the elites have remained exclusive corporations whose activity is devoted to promotion of their own group interests.

1697. Diamant, Alfred. "Bureaucracy in Western Europe: A Review." PUBLIC ADMINISTRATION REVIEW, 19 (1959), 198-203.

A review essay on Chapman's *The Profession of Government.*

1698. Diamant, Alfred. "European Models of Bureaucracy and Development." INTERNATIONAL REVIEW OF ADMINISTRATIVE SCIENCES, 32 (1966), 309-20.

Discusses the European experience in terms of its relevance to economic development in other parts of the world.

1699. Diamant, Alfred. "Bureaucracy and Administration in Western Europe: A Case of Not-So-Benign Neglect." POLICY STUDIES JOURNAL, 1 (1973), 133-38.

Claims that American political scientists have not given enough attention to the question of administration, thus getting a distorted view of the European political scene.

1700. Diamant, Alfred. "Bureaucracy and Public Policy in Neocorporatist Settings: Some European Findings." COMPARATIVE POLITICS, 14 (October, 1981), 101-24.

A review essay on the theme of the management of the developed welfare states by an administrative elite. Implications for the U.S. are explored.

1701.   Frankel, Charles. "Bureaucracy and Democracy in the
        New Europe." DAEDALUS, 93 (1964), 471-92.

        Compares a rather dispirited democracy with a vital
        bureaucracy in the countries of Western Europe in the
        postwar era. A major problem remains the bringing in-
        to the open the bureaucratic decision process. The
        system of recruitment into the public service must be
        broadened so more segments of society can have access
        to this important part of the political system.

1702.   Krygier, Martin. "State and Bureaucracy in Europe:
        The Growth of a Concept." BUREAUCRACY: THE CAREER
        OF A CONCEPT. Edited by Eugene Kamenka and Martin
        Krygier. London: Edward Arnold, 1979.

        Examines the growth of European bureaucratic systems,
        the theories of administration derived from this de-
        velopment, and the emergence of the concept of bureau-
        cracy.

1703.   Putnam, Robert D. "Bureaucrats and Politicians: Con-
        tending Elites in the Policy Process." PERSPECTIVES
        IN POLICY-MAKING. Edited by William B. Gwyn and
        George Edwards. New Orleans: Tulane University Press,
        1975.

        Finds that the politicians and the bureaucrats in
        European democracies are uncertain partners in the
        business of governing. Survey data from several West-
        ern European states indicate that the two groups are
        different in their backgrounds and perceptions.

1704.   Strauss, Eric. THE RULING SERVANTS: BUREAUCRACY IN
        RUSSIA, FRANCE--AND BRITAIN? London: George Allen
        and Unwin, 1961. 307 pp.

        Describes the "many imperfections in the structure
        and functioning of big organizations" in the three
        countries. Because of a number of historical reasons,
        France and Russia developed bureaucracies which have
        remained beyond popular control. There is still some
        hope for avoiding a similar situation in Great Britain,
        although there are some ominous developments.

2. The European Economic Community

1705. Coombes, David. POLITICS AND BUREAUCRACY IN THE EURO-
PEAN COMMUNITY: A PORTRAIT OF THE COMMISSION OF THE
E.E.C. Beverly Hills, Cal.: Sage, 1970. 343 pp.

Studies the operation of the Commission of the EEC.
The career patterns of the officials are investigated.
It is argued that the more the Commission develops and
practices its administrative routines, the less able
it will be to show initiative and creativity in the
further integration of Europe.

1706. Feld, Werner. "The National Bureaucracies of the EEC
Member States and Political Integration: A Prelimin-
ary Inquiry." INTERNATIONAL ADMINISTRATION: ITS EVO-
LUTION AND CONTEMPORARY APPLICATIONS. Edited by
Robert Jordan. New York: Oxford University Press,
1971.

Describes the attitudes of bureaucrats toward further
integration within the Common Market. There is not much
enthusiasm among these officials for closer political
ties with other member nations. More centralization
might threaten their positions within the national
bureaucracies. These findings probably extend to other
sorts of multi-national organizations.

1707. Michelmann, Hans J. ORGANISATIONAL EFFECTIVENESS IN
A MULTINATIONAL BUREAUCRACY. New York: Praeger, 1978.
259 pp.

Examines the functioning of five directorates within
the Commission of the European Community. The variables
affecting the performance of the sub-units of a multi-
national organization are emphasized. It is found that
two directorates have been effective and are likely to
remain effective. The other three probably will not
achieve the degree of autonomy or national support to
imrprove the level of their performance. Autonomy seems
to be the critical variable.

1708. Peterson, R.L. "European Bureaucrats in European Reg-
       ional Organizations." INTERNATIONAL REVIEW OF ADMIN-
       ISTRATIVE SCIENCES, 36 (1970), 333-46.

       Describes the relationship of members of national ad-
       ministrative units to multinational organizations.

1709. Scheinman, Lawrence. "Some Preliminary Notes on Bureau-
       cratic Relationships in the European Economic Commun-
       ity." INTERNATIONAL ORGANIZATION, 20 (1966), 750-73.

       Suggests the conditions under which bureaucratic in-
       terpenetration or the intermingling of efforts by nat-
       ional agencies is likely to occur. The impact of such
       intermingling on further integration is considered. It
       is found that such interpenetration does have an effect
       in the making of policy but that it is seldom the de-
       cisive factor.

                            3. Denmark

1710. Damgaard, Erik. "The Political Role of Nonpolitical
       Bureaucrats in Denmark." THE MANDARINS OF WESTERN
       EUROPE: THE POLITICAL ROLE OF TOP CIVIL SERVANTS.
       Edited by Mattei Dogan. New York: Halsted, 1975.

       Argues that permanent officials exert considerable
       power in Danish policy making. Politicians, moreover,
       have not been eager to challenge this power. The sys-
       tem moves along in an incremental way, with little ov-
       erall planning.

                  4. Federal Republic of Germany

1711. Adam, Uwe D. "Persecution of the Jews: Bureaucracy and
       Authority in the Totalitarian State." LEO BAECK IN-
       STITUTE YEAR BOOK, 23 (1978), 139-48.

       Examines the inherent irrationality of one of the last
       anti-Jewish measures of the Nazi administrative system.

1712. Aronson, Shlomo. "The Nazi Bureaucracy." PUBLIC ADMIN-
       ISTRATION IN ISRAEL AND ABROAD, 8 (1968), 84-99.

Examines bureaucratic elements in the Nazi method of organization.

1713. Bartholdy, Albrecht. "Bureaucracy in a Nation's Lean Years: The German Experience." THE NEW SOCIAL SCIENCE. Edited by Leonard D. White. Chicago: University of Chicago Press, 1930.

Praises the German bureaucracy as a repository of national values and the defender of the republic. It has been the backbone of the nation during a period of extreme stress. The survival of German culture depends on administration.

1714. Bendersky, Joseph. "Ernst Wilhelm Bohle and the Nazi Foreign Organization: Bureaucratic Self-Preservation in a Totalitarian State." INTERNATIONAL REVIEW OF HISTORY AND POLITICAL SCIENCE, 15 (August, 1978), 31-40.

Discusses the bureaucratic infighting within the Nazi party. This sort of diversion led to a great deal of bureaucratic bungling.

1715. Bosetzky, Hans. "Forms of Bureaucratic Organization in Public and Industrial Administrations." INTERNATIONAL STUDIES OF MANAGEMENT AND ORGANIZATION, 10 (Winter, 1980-81), 58-73.

Finds that there is a tendency toward debureaucratization in West German society. Ironically, this trend seems more powerful in public organizations than it does in industry. This may be because of a shift in the factor of social autonomy, with private firms becoming less concerned with market performance.

1716. Caplan, Jane. "Bureaucracy, Politics and the National Socialist State." THE SHAPING OF THE NAZI STATE. Edited by Peter Stachura. London: Croom Helm, 1978.

Argues that we should re-examine the relationship between the civil service and the Nazi party. The tension between the two may not have been as great as commonly supposed.

1717.   "Democracy versus Bureaucracy--An Example from Germany."
        COUNTY OFFICER, 15 (November, 1950), 14-15, 31-32.

        On local government in Germany.

1718.   Dyson, Kenneth. PARTY, STATE, AND BUREAUCRACY IN WEST-
        ERN GERMANY. Sage Professional Papers in Comparative
        Politics No. 01-063. Beverly Hills, Cal.: Sage, 1977.
        65 pp.

        Identifies significant political changes since WWII.
        Parties have assumed some of the legitimacy of the state
        because of the tradition that combines state power with
        executive action. As a result, party and bureaucracy
        have become fused.

1719.   Frank, Elke. "The Role of Bureaucracy in Transition."
        JOURNAL OF POLITICS, 28 (1966), 724-53.

        Examines the role of the bureaucracy in German pol-
        itics during several critical stages in the years be-
        tween 1910 and 1932.

1720.   Gillis, John R. "Aristrocracy and Bureaucracy in Nine-
        teenth Century Prussia." PAST AND PRESENT, 41 (1968),
        105-29.

        Describes how the high ideals of the Prussian official
        class were corrupted through their association with the
        landed aristocracy. Eventually, they could no longer
        claim to represent an impartial view of the national in-
        terest.

1721.   Gillis, John R. THE PRUSSIAN BUREAUCRACY IN CRISIS,
        1840-1860: ORIGINS OF AN ADMINISTRATIVE ETHOS. Stan-
        ford, Cal.: Stanford University Press, 1971. 269 pp.

        Discusses the role of the bureaucracy during a time
        of revolution. During this period, the Prussian offic-
        ials developed an internal code of conduct that made
        them problematic political elements for many years to
        come. It became increasingly difficult for them to
        maintain their neutrality in politics.

1722. Harris, Richard L. "The Government Bureaucracies of
West Germany and Italy." PHILIPPINE JOURNAL OF PUB-
LIC ADMINISTRATION, 9 (1965), 209-20.

Compares the decentralization of German administration
with the centralized Italian system.

1723. Kent, B. "Bureaucracy in Nazi Germany." PUBLIC ADMIN-
ISTRATION (SYDNEY), 32 (1973), 56-61.

Examines the peculiar manifestations of bureaucracy
during the Nazi regime.

1724. Mayntz, Renate, and Fritz W. Scharpf. POLICYMAKING IN
THE GERMAN FEDERAL BUREAUCRACY. New York: Elsevier,
1975. 184 pp.

Argue that the highly industrialized nations face the
problem of "overload" as they strive to deal with a variety of complex policy issues. The policy system, including administration, must play a more active role in
ensuring the long-range survival of the society. In
this context, the nature of bureaucracy in Bonn is examined. Reforms needed to improve the German system,
including budgeting and information processing, are
discussed.

1725. Morstein Marx, Fritz. "German Bureaucracy in Transition." AMERICAN POLITICAL SCIENCE REVIEW, 28 (1934),
467-80.

On the early years of the Nazi regime.

1726. Neunreither, Karl-Heinz. "Politics and Bureaucracy in
the West German *Bundesrat*." AMERICAN POLITICAL SCI-
ENCE REVIEW, 53 (1959), 713-31.

Discusses the role of administrators in the operation
of the upper house of the West German parliament. The
functioning of federalism is dependent upon the cooperation of the bureaucrats. The differentiation among
levels of government is a continuing source of tension
within the system.

1727. Neunreither, Karl-Heinz. "Federalism and West German
       Bureaucracy." POLITICAL STUDIES, 7 (1959), 233-45.

       See Item 1726.

1728. Peterson, E.N., "The Bureaucracy and the Nazi Party."
       REVIEW OF POLITICS, 28 (1966), 172-92.

       Argues that the Nazis failed to absorb the bureaucra-
       cy. The public officials were a highly flexible group
       and retained at most times the capacity to thwart the
       plans of the party.

1729. Pinney, Edward L. "Latent and Manifest Bureaucracy in
       the West German Parliament: The Case of the Bundes-
       rat." MIDWEST JOURNAL OF POLITICAL SCIENCE, 6 (1962),
       149-64.

       Describes the rather considerable influence of admin-
       istrators in the German upper house of parliament.

1730. Pinney, Edward L. FEDERALISM, BUREAUCRACY, AND PARTY
       POLITICS IN WESTERN GERMANY: THE ROLE OF THE BUNDES-
       RAT. Chapel Hill, N.C.: University of North Carolina
       Press, 1963. 268 pp.

       Discusses the role of the Bundesrat in the West Ger-
       man federal system, including the effect on the bureau-
       cratic structure. This legislative body plays a crit-
       ical part in the maintenance of the nation's federal-
       ism.

1731. Scharpf, Fritz W. "Does Organization Matter? Task
       Structure and Interaction in the Ministerial Bureau-
       cracy." ORGANIZATION AND ADMINISTRATIVE SCIENCES,
       8 (1977), 149-67.

       Reports on a study of the reorganization of the West
       German Ministry of Transport. It was found that, in
       implementing a national transportation policy, there
       were serious deficiencies in interministerial coordina-
       tion. The reformulation of jurisdictional boundaries
       was recommended.

1732. Tower, Charles. "Bureaucracy and 'Social Service.'"
ENGLISH REVIEW, 50 (1930), 587-91.

Reflects on the state of German bureaucracy as described in a book by General von Seeckt.

5. France

1733. Church, Clive. REVOLUTION AND RED TAPE: THE FRENCH
MINISTERIAL BUREAUCRACY, 1770-1850. New York: Clarendon, 1981. 425 pp.

Traces the growth of French administration in terms
of the development of the ministries. The roots of the
bureaucracy are found in the patrimonial practices of
the *ancien regime*. The Revolution had a profound impact on administration and its implications were still
being worked out well into the 19th century. The outlines of modern centralized administration were already
firmly established by 1850. Throughout, a central concern has been the establishment of reliable means for
the control of administration.

1734. Diamant, Alfred. "The French Council of State: Compar-
ative Observations on the Problem of Controlling the
Bureaucracy of the Modern State." JOURNAL OF POLI-
TICS, 13 (1951), 562-88.

Compares the common law approach in the United States
with the administrative code of France.

1735. Ehrmann, Henry. "French Bureaucracy and Organized Interests." ADMINISTRATIVE SCIENCE QUARTERLY, 5 (1961),
534-55.

Reports on interviews with high-ranking French civil
servants. The question is whether interest groups have
any access to the making of administrative rules. Several bureaus rely heavily on organized interests for
political support; in return, the groups may have a dis-
proportionate amount of influence. There is some feel-
ing that the groups may distort an appreciation of the
larger public interest.

1736. Ehrmann, Henry. "Bureaucracy and Interest Groups in
       the Decision-Making Process of the Fifth Republic."
       FAKTOREN DER POLITISCHEN ENTSCHEIDUNG. Edited by
       G.A. Ritter and G. Ziebura. Berlin: Walter de Gruy-
       ter, 1963.

       Describes the emergence of "administrative pluralism"
       as a move toward an "economic parliament" in which a
       system of group representation is more open and regu-
       larized.

1737. Lloyd, Andrew. "Freedom to Fight the Research Bureau-
       cracy." NEW SCIENTIST, 83 (1979), 645.

       On the use of the French freedom of information laws
       by scientists.

1738. Milder, N. David. "Some Aspects of Crozier's Theory
       of Bureaucratic Organizations: Charles de Gaulle as
       an Authoritarian Reformer Figure." JOURNAL OF COM-
       PARATIVE ADMINISTRATION, 3 (1971), 61-82.

       Uses concepts from Crozier's *The Bureaucratic Pheno-
       menon* (Item 309) to analyze French politics during the
       early period of the Fifth Republic.

1739. Morse, David. "The French and British Views of Bureau-
       crats." PERSONNEL ADMINISTRATION, 9 (January, 1947),
       17-19.

       Looks at differences in the status and prestige of
       the public service.

1740. Osborne, Thomas. "Social Science at the *Sciences Po*:
       Training the Bureaucratic Elite in the Early Third
       Republic." HISTORICAL REFLECTIONS, 8 (1981), 51-76.

       Describes the role of the Ecole Libre de Sciences
       Politique in the education of the administrative elite.
       in France. This institution had an impact on the lib-
       eral thought of the administrators. The height of its
       influence came before the turn of the century.

1741. Rogers, Richard, Mike Davies, and Alan Stanton. "The Differences between French and English Bureaucratic Systems." ROYAL INSTITUTE OF BRITISH ARCHITECTS JOURNAL, 84 (1977), 13-16.

Discuss the problems faced by British architects in working in other states of the EEC, especially France.

1742. Sharp, Walter. THE FRENCH CIVIL SERVICE: BUREAUCRACY IN TRANSITION. New York: Macmillan, 1931. 588 pp.

Describes the structure of the French civil service. The country is moving away from the administrative stagnation encouraged by the Napoleonic legacy. There is a greater need for a public service capable of dealing with the demands of modern technology.

1743. Spitzer, Alan B. "The Bureaucrats as Procounsul: The Restoration Prefect and the *Police Géneralé*." COMPARATIVE STUDIES IN SOCIETY AND HISTORY, 7 (1965), 371-92.

Examines how the French officials used the Napoleonic system of administrative centralization even though opposed to the underlying political principles of the system.

1744. Suleiman, Ezra. "The French Bureaucracy and Its Students: Toward the Desanctification of the State." WORLD POLITICS, 23 (1970), 121-70.

Reviews the recent work of French scholars in public administration. Only recently has there been a movement away from a strictly legal approach.

1745. Suleiman, Ezra. POLITICS, POWER, AND BUREAUCRACY IN FRANCE. Princeton, N.J.: Princeton University Press, 1974. 440 pp.

Studies the composition and role of the modern French higher civil service. The recruitment and training of the administrative elite is described. The role of the elite corps in French politics is analyzed. Data were derived from interviews with 135 ranking officials.

1746. Thoenig, Jean-Claude. "State Bureaucracies and Local
       Government in France." INTERORGANIZATIONAL POLICY
       MAKING: LIMITS TO COORDINATION AND CENTRAL CONTROL.
       Edited by Kenneth Hanf and Fritz Scharpf. Beverly
       Hills, Cal.: Sage, 1978.

       Offers a model of French bureaucracy as a system of
       open and non-autonomous organizations operating with-
       in local society. The situation is referred to as a
       "honeycomb system."

1747. Thoenig, Jean-Claude. "Local Subsidies in the Third
       Republic: The Political Marketplace and Bureaucratic
       Allocation." FINANCING URBAN GOVERNMENT IN THE WEL-
       FARE STATE. Edited by Douglas Ashford. London:
       Croom Helm, 1980.

       Examines the elements in the French model of trans-
       fer of funds from the central government to localities.
       An assessment of the real degree of decentralization is
       made.

1748. Wall, Irwin M. "Socialists and Bureaucrats: The Blum
       Government and the French Administration, 1936-37."
       INTERNATIONAL REVIEW OF SOCIAL HISTORY, 19 (1974),
       325-46.

       Argues that the failure of Blum's Popular Front may
       have been due to the reluctance of the politicians to
       deal with the problem of bureaucracy. By not democrat-
       izing the public service, the government disillusioned
       its followers and guaranteed a continuation of conser-
       vative public policy.

                        6. Great Britain

1749. Abbotson, Martin. BUREAUCRACY RUNS MAD. London: Watts
       and Company, 1940. 88 pp.

       A compilation of complaints about the official stup-
       idity of the British government. There seems to be
       little that bureaucrats can do well.

1750. Aiken, Charles. "The British Bureaucracy and the Origins of Parliamentary Policy." AMERICAN POLITICAL SCIENCE REVIEW, 33 (1939), 26-46, 219-33.

Identifies the factors influencing the decisions of the legislature. The bureaucracy is found to play a large role. However, the civil service is a responsible one, because the permanent staff is always loyal to a political leader.

1751. Allen, Carleton. "Bureaucracy on Trial." QUARTERLY REVIEW, 254 (1930), 321-41.

A review essay on Hewart, *The New Despotism* (Item 70) and Port, *Administrative Law*.

1752. Allen, Carleton. BUREAUCRACY TRIUMPHANT. London: Oxford University Press, 1931. 148 pp.

A collection of essays on bureaucracy, including Items 33, 34 and 1751.

1753. Anderson, John. "Bureaucracy." PUBLIC ADMINISTRATION, 7 (1929), 3-19.

Offers a defense of the British civil service. The British have always stressed public service as a personal thing and not the product of a mechanized system.

1754. Aylmer, G.E. "From Office-Holding to Civil Service: The Genesis of Modern Bureaucracy." TRANSACTIONS OF THE ROYAL HISTORICAL SOCIETY, 30 (1980), 91-108.

Develops the outlines of pre-bureaucratic administration. True bureaucracy developed in England during the 18th century. A major change came about when public office was perceived not as a private interest but as a public entity.

1755. Brogan, Colm. "Bureaucracy in Practice." FREEMAN, 5 (1955), 269-70.

The bureaucrats overstep their bounds.

1756. "The Bureaucrat." ECONOMIST, 140 (1941), 264.

Examines defects of the British civil service.

1757. "Bureaucratic Control." NEW STATESMAN, 23 (1942), 269-70.

On deficiencies in wartime administration.

1758. "The Bureaucrats." LISTENER, 67 (1962), 280.

About the morale of civil servants.

1759. "Bureaucrats at School." ECONOMIST, 209 (1963), 48.

Describes a program of post-entry training for British civil servants.

1760. "Bureaucrat's Bugbear." NEWSWEEK, 66 (October 25, 1965), 54.

On the British ombudsman.

1761. Carr, Cecil. "Bureaucracy." COLUMBIA UNIVERSITY QUARTERLY, 33 (1941), 105-20.

Compares the civil service of Great Britain with that of the U.S.

1762. Christopher, Allan. "On Becoming a Bureaucrat." NEW STATESMAN, 49 (1955), 880.

Reflects on life in the civil service.

1763. Cripps, Leonard. BRASS SCREWS: JUSTICE AND FREEDOM OR BUREAUCRACY AND SLAVERY. London: C. Birchall and Sons, 1941. 30 pp.

Denounces the interference of government in more and more spheres.

1764. Dandeker, Christopher. "Patronage and Bureaucratic Con-
trol--The Case of the Naval Officer in English Society,
1780-1850." BRITISH JOURNAL OF SOCIOLOGY, 29 (1978),
300-20.

Examines the movement from patronage appointments to
a system based more on qualifications in the British
Navy. This movement, beginning about 1815, led to a
more bureaucratic service.

1765. Davidson, Roger, and Rodney Lowe. "Bureaucracy and Innovation in British Welfare Policy." THE EMERGENCE
OF THE WELFARE STATE IN BRITAIN AND GERMANY, 1850-
1950. Edited by Wolfgang Mommsen. London: Croom
Helm, 1981.

Survey British social policy from 1870 to 1945. Although the government grew in size during this period,
careful analysis reveals considerable variation over
time and among bureaus.

1766. Davies, B., and O. Coles. "Electoral Support, Bureaucratic Criteria, Cost Variations, and Intra-Authority
Allocations: A Home Help Case." POLITICAL STUDIES,
29 (1981), 415-24.

Test whether the desire for electoral support or the
use of rationalistic criteria is the most important
factor in the allocation of public service. The major
variable is the degree of monopoly enjoyed by the public agency. A case of assistance for the elderly is
analyzed.

1767. Davies, Jon G. THE EVANGELISTIC BUREAUCRAT: A STUDY OF
A PLANNING EXERCISE IN NEWCASTLE UPON TYNE. London:
Tavistock, 1972. 239 pp.

Investigates an unsuccessful planning effort in an
English community. Local leaders left the technical
questions to the planners who, in turn, applied values
inappropriate to local conditions. Consequently, there
was a breakdown in communications.

1768.   "The Discreet Agony of the Bureaucracy." ECONOMIST,
        273 (December 8, 1979), 17-18.

        On fears about a threatened reduction in the size of
        the civil service.

1769.   Elliot, Frank. "More Bureaucracy." CORNHILL, 73 (1932)
        334-43.

        Deplores the growth of government.

1770.   Emeritus. "Forty Years of Bureaucracy." CORNHILL, 72
        (1932), 187-207.

        A veteran reflects on a career in the civil service.

1771.   Finer, Samuel. "Patronage and the Public Services: Jef-
        fersonian Bureaucracy and the British Tradition."
        PUBLIC ADMINISTRATION, 30 (1952), 329-60.

        Discusses differences between the personnel systems
        of the U.S. and Great Britain in light of Leonard D.
        White's history of the American system.

1772.   Foot, Dingle. "The Advance of Bureaucracy." SPECTATOR,
        155 (1935), 216.

        More concern about the size of government.

1773.   George, Stephen. "Too Much Bureaucracy." BUILT ENVIR-
        ONMENT, 1 (June, 1975), 38-41.

        Complains about the combination of administrative in-
        terference and political influence that sometimes pre-
        vent the architect from providing the best available
        in public housing. The result is too often mediocre
        and poorly planned projects.

1774.   Gladden, E.N. CIVIL SERVICE OR BUREAUCRACY? London:
        Staples Press, 1956. 224 pp.

        Describes the operation of the British civil service.

The system has many admirable features, but there is a
crisis looming as the officials become more involved in
political questions.

1775. Gregory, Roy. "Bureaucracy Observed." NEW SOCIETY,
23 (1973), 58-60.

Reviews what can be learned about the British civil
service from the reports of the parliamentary commissioner for administration, the British ombudsman.

1776. Gwyn, William B. "Labour Party and the Threat of Bureaucracy." POLITICAL STUDIES, 19 (1971), 383-402.

Describes how the governing Labour Party approached
the question of creating an ombudsman. The party was
interested in showing that, despite its emphasis on
planning and an active government, it was sensitive to
threats to individual liberties by abuses by the administration.

1777. Halsey, A.H. "Authority, Bureaucracy, and the Education Debate." OXFORD REVIEW OF ADMINISTRATION, 3
(1977), 217-33.

Discusses the rise of bureaucratic authority and its
impact on the British school system.

1778. Harries-Jenkins, Gwyn. "Bureaucracy in Great Britain
in the 1980s." JOURNAL OF APPLIED BEHAVIORAL SCIENCE,
16 (1980), 317-35.

Says that despite the general public resentment of
bureaucracy the existing condition is actively being
promoted by the dominant elite. By pursuing a managerial ideology that stresses formal rationality, this
elite makes use of its own type of subjectivity in its
continued control of society. This elite includes elements from several organizations that accept the nec-
essity of greater rationality. This may result eventually in better management or complete collapse. More
likely, the system will continue in the same way without any resolution of the current sources of tension
and anxiety.

1779. Hudson, H.R. "A Responsible Bureaucracy in Great Brit-
       ain." PUBLIC ADMINISTRATION (SYDNEY), 12 (1953), 42-
       55.

       Examines the use of discretion by administrators.
       Formal means of establishing responsibility are becom-
       ing less effective.

1780. Jay, Anthony. THE HOUSEHOLDER'S GUIDE TO COMMUNITY
       DEFENCE AGAINST BUREAUCRATIC AGGRESSION: A REPORT ON
       BRITAIN'S GOVERNMENT MACHINE. London: Cape, 1972.
       64 pp.

       A review of the British system and means for citizen
       control.

1781. Jones, Cedric. "Bureaucracy." CONTEMPORARY REVIEW,
       192 (1957), 342-44.

       Comments on a recently released official report on
       the civil service.

1782. Jowell, Jeffrey. "Law, Discretion and Bureaucracy."
       LISTENER, 99 (1978), 261-62.

       Explores the extent to which British law can control
       the exercise of official discretion.

1783. Kinglsey, J. Donald. REPRESENTATIVE BUREAUCRACY: AN
       INTERPRETATION OF THE BRITISH CIVIL SERVICE. Yellow
       Springs, Ohio: Antioch Press, 1944. 324 pp.

       Dismisses the idea of bureaucratic despotism in Great
       Britain. The civil service, because of its composition,
       is an integral part of that same middle-class mentality
       dominating British life. The essence of administrative
       responsibility is a psychological rather than a mechan-
       ical factor; it is a state of mind which "leads the
       agent to act as though he were the principal." The
       postwar civil service will continue to mirror the as-
       piration of a majority of British citizens; adjustments
       to the need for a more active, planning state will be
       made.

1784. Lee, J.M. "The British Civil Service and the War Economy: Bureaucratic Conceptions of the 'Lessons of History' in 1918 and 1945." TRANSACTIONS OF THE ROYAL HISTORICAL SOCIETY, 30 (1980), 183-98.

Attempts to identify the self-perception of the senior civil servants in the two postwar periods. The question is important since it goes to define the boundaries of the British constitution's conception of the rights and duties of administrators. It was during this period that the British became aware that they did in fact have a bureaucracy.

1785. Levy, Thomas. "How Bureaucracy is Created." LAW JOURNAL, 94 (1944), 43-44.

A member of parliament laments the loss of legislative power to the bureaucracy.

1786. Mackal, Paul. "Trends in British Governmental Bureaucratization and Sub-Bureaucratization." BRITISH JOURNAL OF SOCIOLOGY, 23 (1971), 66-76.

Defines sub-bureaucratization as the counterproductive competition among units of bureaus. Political and social trends are described as contributing to the major structural deficiencies of the British civil service.

1787. Macpherson, Hugh. "Spreading the Bureaucratic Jam." SPECTATOR, 228 (1972), 150.

Muses about the congregation of the great majority of British civil servants in London.

1788. Martin-Leake, H. "Agriculture and Bureaucracy." FORTNIGHTLY REVIEW, 182 (1954), 238-40.

Deplores the interference of government in British agriculture.

1789. Middleton, Charles R. "The Emergence of Constitutional Bureaucracy in the British Foreign Office." PUBLIC

ADMINISTRATION, 53 (1975), 365-81.

Traces changes in the British Foreign Office between
1782 and 1841. In this period, greater mobility among
the clerks contributed to a sense of career.

1790. Montague, Joel B. "Bureaucracy and British Socialism."
SOCIOLOGY AND SOCIAL RESEARCH, 37 (1953), 164-68.

Argues that while bureaucratization was a product of
capitalism and aristocracy, it will expand more rapidly
under a Labour government. This is because they are
in favor of more public functions. As a result there
will be less mass participation in government. A modification of the base for recruitment and a broadening
of access to education by the working class may introduce new elements into the civil service.

1791. Morris-Jones, Myndraeth. SOCIALISM AND BUREAUCRACY.
London: Fabian Publications, 1949. 29 pp.

An explanation of the socialist position on the civil
service.

1792. Mount, Ferdinand. "The Bureaucracy That Kills." SPEC-
TATOR, 239 (September 24, 1977), 4.

Denounces the rigidity of bureaucracy and the damage
it does to the morale of the public.

1793. Parris, Henry. CONSTITUTIONAL BUREAUCRACY: THE DEVEL-
OPMENT OF BRITISH CENTRAL ADMINISTRATION SINCE THE
EIGHTEENTH CENTURY. London: George Unwin, 1969. 324
pp.

Presents a history of the British central administration. A great change came over the civil service in
the middle of the 19th century, as new functions were
added and the personnel became better qualified for the
offices. The pattern for development between 1830 and
1870 was by no means inevitable and it could have turned
out differently. The result, however, was not as dangerous to individual liberties as predicted by people
such as Dicey.

1794. Perry, Percival. BEWARE BUREAUCRACY! London: Individualist Bookshop, 1941. 30 pp.

An attack on the actions of government.

1795. Pitt, Douglas. BUREAUCRATIC ADAPTATION. Farnsborough: Saxon House, 1979. 206 pp.

A case study of change and adaptation in the British postal service.

1796. Rex, John. "Is There Good in Bureaucracy?" LISTENER, 67 (1972), 275-77.

An analysis of the meaning of bureaucracy.

1797. Rowan, R. "Beleaguered by Bains and Bureaucrats." TIMES EDUCATIONAL SUPPLEMENT, 3324 (March 18. 1977), 20-21.

On a government proposal for the reform of local government with emphasis on education.

1798. Russell-Smith, Enid. MODERN BUREAUCRACY: THE HOME CIVIL SERVICE. London: Longman, 1974. 122 pp.

Sketches the structure and composition of the civil service. Overall, the system is just a little bit of all right.

1799. Ryan, Alan. "Utilitarianism and Bureaucracy: The Views of J.S. Mill." STUDIES IN THE GROWTH OF NINETEENTH-CENTURY GOVERNMENT. Edited by Gillian Sutherland. Totowa, N.J.: Rowman and Littlefield, 1972.

Examines John Stuart Mill's thoughts about the civil service and its reform. His approach to the topic was not clearly derived from utilitarian philosophical principles.

1800. Sayre, Wallace C. "Bureaucracies: Some Contrasts in Systems." INDIAN JOURNAL OF PUBLIC ADMINISTRATION, 10 (1964), 219-29.

Contrasts the administrative systems of the U.S. and Great Britain.

1801.   Sheriff, Peta. "Unrepresentative Bureaucracy." SOCIO-
         LOGY, 8 (1974), 447-62.

Contends that the attitudes of higher civil servants are more important than the social or educational background of recruits. Changes in the past few decades have not resulted in a significant modification in the nature of the civil service, since they were more technical in nature and not related to a basic change in values. Concentration must be placed on the discovery of the factors which ultimately shape the values of public administrators.

1802.   Sites, James N. "Why Bureaucrats Can't Run a Business."
         NATION'S BUSINESS, 54 (October, 1966), 35, 76-78.

How the British made an awful mess of their nationalized railroads.

1803.   Skevington, Leonard. "The Crisis of the Bureaucracy."
         PILOT PAPERS, 2 (1947), 71-84.

A civil servant reflects on emerging problems in the British bureaucracy. So far, the officials have not been intimately involved in politics, but that is likely to change.

1804.   Smith, J.H. "The Rise of a Bureaucracy." TRANSACTIONS
         OF THE THIRD WORLD CONGRESS OF SOCIOLOGY, (1956),
         56-70.

Describes changes in the industrial management after the nationalization of the transportation industry. The trucking industry had been quite chaotic, with a number of small operators engaged in intense competition. After nationalization, a regular bureaucratic hierarchy was imposed, causing a great deal of antagonism and tension. The truckers were reluctant to adjust to the changed conditions.

1805. Stokes, E.T. "Bureaucracy and Ideology: Britain and India in the Nineteenth Century." TRANSACTIONS OF THE ROYAL HISTORICAL SOCIETY, 30 (1980), 131-56.

Reconsiders the impact of ideas on the development of British administration. Were the bureaucrats pure pragmatists or were they motivated by a belief in some vision of their role in society? The teachings of J. Bentham are of importance here. The example of the course of Indian administration is indicative of the power of ideals.

1806. Torrance, John R. "Sir George Harrison and the Growth of Bureaucracy in the Early Nineteenth Century." ENGLISH HISTORICAL REVIEW, 83 (1968), 52-88.

Reviews the life and times of the first permanent secretary of the Treasury.

1807. Torrance, John R. "Social Class and Bureaucratic Innovation: The Commissioners for Examining the Public Accounts, 1780-1787." PAST AND PRESENT, 78 (1978), 56-81.

Examines how middle-class officials established administrative practices for the auditing of public accounts. This was the beginning of a major change in British administrative style. The officials stressed uniformity, service to the public, and economy in public expenditure. They were also ethical and insisted on strict obedience to the law.

1808. "Triumphant Bureaucracy." NEW STATESMAN, 25 (1943), 315.

On problems within the civil service.

1809. Veale, Douglas. "Civil Service or Bureaucracy? NINETEENTH CENTURY, 110 (1931), 453-63.

Another critical account of the problems involved in the expansion of government.

1809a. "What Kind of Bureaucracy?" SPECTATOR, 222 (1968), 878.

On the Fulton Commission report on suggested changes in the nature of the civil service.

1810. Wigglesworth, Alfred. "Bureaucratic Control." NATIONAL REVIEW, 119 (1942), 330-32.

Says that the education of the civil servants does not prepare them for the regulation of industry, as wartime experience shows. The cooperation of business is needed in shaping postwar policy.

1811. Wilson, David J. "Party Bureaucracy in Britain: Regional and Area Organisation." BRITISH JOURNAL OF POLITICAL SCIENCE, 2 (1972), 373-81.

Describes the relationship of the intermediate level of party organization with the central headquarters in London.

1812. Wilson, David J. POWER AND PARTY BUREAUCRACY IN BRITAIN: REGIONAL ORGANISATION IN THE CONSERVATIVE AND LABOUR PARTIES. London: Saxon House, 1975. 171 pp.

Focuses on the role of the regional level of party organization between the central offices and the constituency parties at the local level.

1813. Winder, George. "British Bureaucrats Kill Some Cows." FREEMAN, 2 (1952), 273-75.

A minor scandal in British administration.

7. Ireland

1814. Pyne, Peter. THE IRISH BUREAUCRACY: ITS POLITICAL ROLE AND THE ENVIRONMENTAL FACTORS INFLUENCING THIS ROLE: SOME PRELIMINARY REMARKS. Londonderry: New University of Ulster, 1973. 43 pp.

Outlines the nature of Irish administration. A major

problem is the fragmentation of the service. The administrative structure is divided vertically and horizontally. The Department of Finance is the elite ministry. While the civil service is dedicated to the idea of political subordination, the nature of legislation is such that many opportunities exist for bureaucratic influence in the policy process.

1815. Pyne, Peter. "The Bureaucracy in the Irish Republic: Its Political Role and the Factors Influencing It." POLITICAL STUDIES, 22 (1974), 15-30.

See Item 1814.

8. Italy

1816. Clark, Burton. ACADEMIC POWER IN ITALY: BUREAUCRACY AND OLIGARCHY IN A NATIONAL UNIVERSITY SYSTEM. Chicago: University of Chicago Press, 1977. 205 pp.

Examines the development of Italian higher education. The major theme concerns the tension caused by the efforts of the central government to regulate the behavior of the locally oriented, guild-like faculties in the universities.

1817. Clark, Martin. "Italy: Regionalism and Bureaucratic Reform." THE FAILURE OF THE STATE. Edited by James Cornfold. London: Croom Helm, 1975.

Describes attempts in Italy to solve some of the basic problems in administration. To relieve the pressure of centralization, many functions were transferred from Rome to the regions, and a new set of managerial techniques were introduced in the central offices. The reforms have been resisted by the bureaucrats.

1818. Cole, Taylor. "Italy's Fascist Bureaucracy." AMERICAN POLITICAL SCIENCE REVIEW, 32 (1938), 1143-57.

Argues that although the bureaucracy is central to the attainment of many of Mussolini's goals, its career patterns have not changed since pre-fascist days.

1819. Cole, Taylor. "Reform of the Italian Bureaucracy."
       PUBLIC ADMINISTRATION REVIEW, 13 (1953), 247-56.

       Reviews developments since the collapse of the fas-
       cist regime. Things are not moving too swiftly.

1820. Freddi, Giorgio. "Regional Devolution, Administrative
       Decentralisation, and Bureaucratic Performances in
       Italy." POLICY AND POLITICS, 8 (1980), 383-98.

       Looks at the record of regional autonomy. Overall,
       the regional structures have not done well and, most
       of all, they have done little to improve the nature of
       Italian public administration.

    * Harris, Richard L. "The Government Bureaucracies of
       West Germany and Italy." Cited above as Item 1722.

1821. Hellman, Stephen. "Generational Differences in the
       Bureaucratic Elite of Italian Communist Party Provin-
       cial Federations." CANADIAN JOURNAL OF POLITICAL SCI-
       ENCE, 8 (1975), 82-106.

       Describes the selection and promotion practices of
       the party structure.

1822. LaPalombara, Joseph, and John T. Dorsey. "On the Ital-
       ian and French Bureaucracies." PROD, 1 (September,
       1957), 35-40.

       A comparison of the administrative systems of the two
       countries.

1823. Passigli, Stefano. "The Ordinary and Special Bureau-
       cracies in Italy." THE MANDARINS OF WESTERN EUROPE:
       THE POLITICAL ROLE OF TOP CIVIL SERVANTS. Edited by
       Mattei Dogan. New York: Halsted, 1975.

       Compares the old-line "ordinary" bureaus and the new-
       er, economically oriented "special" agencies. The new
       bureaus have made some progress in economic development.
       Neither type, however, is particularly effective in a
       political sense.

1824. Sabetti, Philip. "The Politics and Bureaucracy of Planning Modern Rome." IL POLITICO, 43 (1978), 144-49.

Discusses problems of city planning in an ancient municipality.

9. The Netherlands

1825. Rosenthal, Uriel. "Communalism and Clientele Bureaucracy: Research into the Relations between the Administration and the Administered in the Netherlands." SOCIOLOGIA NEERLANDICA, 12 (1976), 79-88.

Examines the effects of a low level of client involvement in public administration.

10. Norway

1826. Hoff, Ole-Jacob. "Of Blueberries and Bureaucrats." POLICY REVIEW, 14 (Fall, 1980), 157-59.

Reflections on the Norwegian berry tax.

11. Spain

1827. Burnham, James. "Bureaucracy in Spain." FREEMAN, 4 (1954), 629-30.

Finds the Spanish civil service to be huge, corrupt and cumbersome.

1828. Medhurst, Keith. "The Political Role of the Spanish Bureaucracy." GOVERNMENT AND OPPOSITION, 4 (1969), 235-49.

Speculates on the role of the bureaucracy in post-Franco Spain.

1829. Press, Irwin. "The City of Context: Cultural, Historical, and Bureaucratic Determinants of Behavior in

Seville." URBAN ANTHROPOLOGY, 4 (1975), 27-34.

Looks at the Spanish city as preindustrial and provincial. The various pressures on behavior, including
bureaucratic mechanisms, may cause as much constraint
on people as the elements of rural life.

12. Sweden

1830. Albrecht, Sandra L. "Politics, Bureaucracy, and Worker
        Participation: The Swedish Case." JOURNAL OF APPLIED
        BEHAVIORAL SCIENCE, 16 (1980), 299-315.

        Looks at recent moves in Sweden to increase worker
        participation in industry as a matter of public policy.
        Sweden developed an extensive system in the 1960s as
        demands for democratic participation led to legislation
        favoring that approach. In the 1980s, there will be
        more pressure to increase the role of workers in the
        control of the firm.

1831. Anton, Thomas J., Claes Linde, and Anders Mellbourn.
        "Bureaucrats in Politics: A Profile of the Swedish
        Administrative Elite." CANADIAN PUBLIC ADMINISTRATION,
        16 (1973), 627-65.

        Describes the attitudes of Swedish civil servants,
        with special emphasis on generational differences.

1832. Meijer, Hans. "Bureaucracy and Policy Formulation in
        Sweden." SCANDINAVIAN POLITICAL STUDIES, 4 (1969),
        103-16.

        Examines the role of Royal Commissions as a prelimin-
        ary stage in the making of policy proposals.

1833. Schiff, Martin. "The Welfare State Bureaucracy and
        Democratic Control in Sweden." ADMINISTRATION, 22
        (1974), 298-314.

        See Item 1834.

1834. Schiff, Martin. "Welfare State Bureaucracy and Demo-
      cratic Control in Sweden: Its Implications for the
      United States." POLITICAL SCIENCE, 27 (1975), 82-96.

      Considers the dilemma of the welfare state: as the
      attempts to improve the lives of citizens increase,
      there is greater public resentment about the officials
      of the state. Reform attempts in Sweden and the U.S.
      still stress rationality rather than humanity.

1835. Stearns, L.R. "Fact and Fiction of a Model Enforce-
      ment Bureaucracy: The Labour Inspectorate of Sweden."
      BRITISH JOURNAL OF LAW AND SOCIETY, 6 (1979), 1-23.

      Examines the administration of occupational safety
      laws.

13. Switzerland

1836. Friedrich, Carl J., and Taylor Cole. RESPONSIBLE BUR-
      EAUCRACY: A STUDY OF THE SWISS CIVIL SERVICE. Cam-
      bridge, Mass.: Harvard University Press, 1932. 93 pp.

      Argue in favor of a balanced, scientific approach to
      the study of bureaucracy. In examining the operation
      of the Swiss system, they find that good administration
      is compatible with popular government.

F. Latin America and the Caribbean

1. General

1837. Collier, David. "Overview of the Bureaucratic-Author-
      itarian Model." THE NEW AUTHORITARIANSM IN LATIN AM-
      ERICA. Edited by David Collier. Princeton, N.J.:
      Princeton University Press, 1979.

      Reviews the elements of the model designed by O'Donnell
      (Item 1851) to explain the emergence of authoritarian
      regimes in economically advanced Latin American coun-
      tries.

1838.   Collier, David. "The Bureaucratic-Authoritarian Model:
        Synthesis and Priorities for Future Research." THE
        NEW AUTHORITARIANISM IN LATIN AMERICA. Princeton,
        N.J.: Princeton University Press, 1979

        A summary of the discussion about the O'Donnell model
        (Item 1851).

1839.   Dishman, Robert. "Cultural Pluralism and Bureaucratic
        Neutrality in the British Caribbean." ETHNICITY,
        5 (1978), 274-99.

        Argues that the British concept of administrative neu-
        trality was unable to survive in the newly independent
        nations of the Caribbean.

    *   Enloe, Cynthia. "Ethnicity, Bureaucracy and State-
        Building in Africa and Latin America." Cited above
        as Item 1294.

1840.   Garcia-Zamor, Jean-Claude. "A Typology of Creole Bur-
        eaucracies." INTERNATIONAL REVIEW OF ADMINSTRATIVE
        SCIENCES, 38 (1972), 49-60.

        Studies the political role of bureaucracy in Cuba,
        the Dominican Republic, Haiti, Puerto Rico, and the
        Commonwealth states.

1841.   Garcia-Zamor, Jean-Claude. "Micro-Bureaucracies and
        Development Administration." INTERNATIONAL REVIEW
        OF ADMINISTRATIVE SCIENCES, 39 (1973), 417-23.

        Defines mico-bureaucracies as "small and informal or-
        ganisations of bureaucrats who have the broad common aim
        of wishing changes that would benefit the entire social
        and political system." The role of such groups in the
        states of the Caribbean is examined.

1842.   Geller, Daniel S. "Economic Modernization and Political
        Instability in Latin America: A Causal Analysis of
        Bureaucratic Authoritarianism." WESTERN POLITICAL
        QUARTERLY, 35 (1982), 33-49.

Explores the relationship between economic development and political decay and the rise of authoritarianism. The "timing" of development seems to be more important in this process than the level of development as a determinant of political climate.

1843. Graham, Lawrence. "Democracy and the Bureaucratic State in Latin America." THE CONTINUING STRUGGLE FOR DEMOCRACY IN LATIN AMERICA. Edited by Howard Wiarda. Boulder, Colo.: Westview, 1980.

Discusses the rise of authoritarianism in Latin America since 1964. The 1980s may see a breakdown of such regimes and a return to more democratic systems.

1844. Handman, Max. "The Bureaucratic Cultural Pattern and Political Revolution." AMERICAN JOURNAL OF SOCIOLOGY, 39 (1933), 301-33.

Offers an explanation for political revolutions in bureaucratically oriented societies such as Latin America. The outbursts are necessary in order to satisfy those persons otherwise excluded from official positions.

1845. Hanson, Mark. "Organizational Bureaucracy in Latin America and the Legacy of Spanish Colonialism." JOURNAL OF INTER-AMERICAN STUDIES AND WORLD AFFAIRS, 16 (1974), 199-219.

Traces the defects of modern development administration to the traditions of Spanish colonialism.

1846. Hopkins, Jack W. "Contemporary Research on Public Administration and Bureaucracies in Latin America." LATIN AMERICAN RESEARCH REVIEW, 9 (1974), 109-40.

Reviews the recent literature and finds deficiencies in the study of Latin American public administration--or, public administration in Latin America. Further systematic study is needed since the subject has lagged behind other branches of political science.

1847.   Kaufman, Robert R.   "Industrial Change and Authoritar-
           ian Rule in Latin America: A Concrete Review of the
           Bureaucratic-Authoritarian Model."   THE NEW AUTHOR-
           ITARIANISM IN LATIN AMERICA.   Edited by David Collier.
           Princeton, N.J.: Princeton University Press, 1979.

           Examines the economic bases of repressive political
        regimes in Latin America.

1848.   Laba, Roman.   "Fish, Peasants, and State Bureaucracies:
           The Development of Lake Titicaca."   COMPARATIVE POL-
           ITICAL STUDIES, 12 (1979), 335-61.

           Studies the joint effort of Peru, Bolivia, and the
        U.S. to create a commercial fishing industry in the
        Andes.   The project was a failure for both technical
        and normative reasons, but none of the agencies involved
        in the project has been able to admit that the whole
        thing was a bad idea.

1849.   de Marquez, Viviane.   "Politics, Bureaucracy, and In-
           dustrial Democracy: A Comparative Framework for the
           Analysis of Worker Control in Latin America."   SOCIO-
           LOGY OF WORK AND OCCUPATIONS, 8 (1981), 165-79.

           Discusses the probability of achieving worker control
        through industrial democracy in a stage of late or mar-
        ginal capitalism.   Peru, Chile and Mexico are examples.

1850.   Mills, G.E.   "The Environment of Commonwealth Caribbean
           Bureaucracies."   INTERNATIONAL REVIEW OF ADMINISTRA-
           TIVE SCIENCES, 39 (1973), 14-24.

           Explores the role of the civil service in the nations
        of the Caribbean influenced by the British.

1851.   O'Donnell, Guillermo A.   MODERNIZATION AND BUREAUCRATIC-
           AUTHORITARIANISM: STUDIES IN SOUTH AMERICAN POLITICS.
           Berkeley: University of California, Institute of In-
           ternational Studies, 1973.   219 pp.

           Develops a model to investigate the impact of modern-
        ization on Latin American political systems.   The social

differentiation that results from economic growth has
led to the emergence of "a new type of political authoritarianism," namely, bureaucratic-authoritarianism.
This is in contrast to the predictions that economic
growth would promote greater democracy. Argentina and
Brazil are examples.

1852. O'Donnell, Guillermo A. "Reflections on the Patterns
of Change in the Bureaucratic-Authoritarian State."
LATIN AMERICAN RESEARCH REVIEW, 13 (1978), 3-38.

Describes the bureaucratic-authoritarian state, with
emphasis on its manifestations in Brazil and Argentina.

1853. O'Donnell, Guillermo A. "Tensions in the Bureaucratic-
Authoritarian State and the Question of Democracy."
THE NEW AUTHORITARIANISM IN LATIN AMERICA. Edited by
David Collier. Princeton, N.J.: Princeton University
Press, 1979.

Speculates on the possibilities of democratizing the
authoritiarian regimes of Latin America.

1854. Oszlak, Oscar. "Critical Approaches to the Study of
State Bureaucracy: A Latin American Perspective."
INTERNATIONAL SOCIAL SCIENCE JOURNAL, 31 (1979), 661-
81.

Sketches an approach to the study of the public organization, with special reference to the changing bureaucracies of Latin America.

1855. Rajbansee, Joseph. "Size and Bureaucracy in the Caribbean." JOURNAL OF COMPARATIVE ADMINISTRATION, 4
(1972), 205-24.

Examines how small size affects administration in the
state of the Caribbean. Size presents several challenges to effective development action. The smallness of
the service has negative sociopsychological implications
for the members. Small organizations will never be as
effective as large ones in the process of national development.

1856.   Remmer, Karen, and Gilbert Merkx. "Bureaucratic-Auth-
        oritarianism Revisited." LATIN AMERICAN RESEARCH RE-
        VIEW, 17 (1982), 3-50.

        Assess the theory (Item 1851), with emphasis on the
        more recent formulations. A response from Guillermo
        O'Donnell is included.

1857.   St. Hill, C.A.P. "Reform of the Public Services: Prob-
        lems of Transitional Bureaucracy in Commonwealth Car-
        ibbean States." SOCIAL AND ECONOMIC STUDIES, 19
        (1970), 135-44.

        Argues that the existing administrative systems may
        not be able to promote economic development.

1858.   Scott, Robert E. "The Government Bureaucrat and Polit-
        ical Change in Latin America." JOURNAL OF INTERNAT-
        IONAL AFFAIRS, 20 (1966), 289-305.

        Contends that Latin American bureaucracies are called
        upon to fill conflicting roles. They are responsible
        for maintaining order while promoting social change.
        At the same time, they are expected to be agents of de-
        mocratization. Different responses of the administra-
        tors to this challenge are discussed.

1859.   Sloan, John W. "Bureaucracy and Public Policy in Latin
        America." INTER-AMERICAN ECONOMIC AFFAIRS, 34
        (Spring, 1981), 14-47.

        Maintains that, despite the high level of mutual mis-
        trust between officials and the public, the government
        continues to dominate the development process, thus
        inhibiting the growth of widespread citizen support.

1860.   Weaver, Jerry L. "Role Expectations of Latin American
        Bureaucrats." JOURNAL OF COMPARATIVE ADMINISTRATION,
        4 (1972), 133-66.

        Approaches the study of Latin American administration
        in terms of role expectation theory. Data from Chile,
        Ecuador, Peru, Venezuela, and Guatemala are reviewed.

1861.   Wright, Freeman. BUREAUCRACY AND POLITICAL DEVELOPMENT:
        AN APPLICATION OF ALMOND AND POWELL TO LATIN AMERICA.
        Tucson: University of Arizona, Institute of Government
        Research, 1970. 22 pp.

        Tests the thesis that political development takes
        place with "increased differentiation and specializa-
        tion of political structures and increased seculariza-
        tion of political culture." Latin America does not ap-
        pear to support the Almond and Powell argument. Despite
        the power of the bureaucracy, popular political insti-
        tutions have not emerged.

2. Argentina

1862.   Jordan, David C. "Argentina's Bureaucratic Oligarchs."
        CURRENT HISTORY, 62 (1972), 70-75.

        Describes the negative consequences of concentrating
        power in the hands of closed, well organized groups.

3. Barbados

1863.   Parris, Ronald G. "Inequality and Control in a Colon-
        ial Bureaucracy: Barbados, 1955-1962." JOURNAL OF
        BLACK STUDIES, 3 (1972), 57-74.

        Examines the role of multinational corporations in the
        social structure of colonial society.

4. Bolivia

1864.   Lofstrom, William. "From Colony to Republic: A Case
        Study of Bureaucratic Change." JOURNAL OF LATIN AM-
        ERICAN STUDIES, 5 (1973), 177-97.

        Explores the years from 1825 to 1828 as turning points
        in the political development of Bolivia. Changes in
        the administrative style made possible the rejection of
        direct control by Spain.

5. Brazil

1865. Daland, Robert T.   "Attitudes toward Change among Braz-
         ilian Bureaucrats." JOURNAL OF COMPARATIVE ADMINIS-
         TRATION, 4 (1972), 167-203.

         Bases a report on the attitudinal data derived from
         interviews with 325 top-level bureaucrats. The poten-
         tial of this group to achieve political and social de-
         velopment is examined. The predominant groups within
         the bureaucracy have the most negative attitude toward
         change. The recruitment and socialization patterns do
         not seem to encourage innovative persons. The impact
         of the military on the bureaucracy is considered.

1866. Daland, Robert T.   EXPLORING BRAZILIAN BUREAUCRACY: PER-
         FORMANCE AND PATHOLOGY. Washington, D.C.: University
         Press of America, 1981.   455 pp.

         Describes the contemporary Brazilian administrative
         system. As part of an authoritarian regime, the bureau-
         cracy is perceived as an instrument for the achievement
         of the goals of the leaders.

1867. Haddad, Paulo.   "Brazil: Economists in a Bureaucratic-
         Authoritarian System." HISTORY OF POLITICAL ECONOMY,
         13 (1981), 656-80.

         Examines the rise in prestige and power of economists
         in Brazilian government. Their backgrounds and atti-
         tudes about policy issues are explored.

1868. Manchester, Alan K.   "The Growth of Bureaucracy in Bra-
         zil." JOURNAL OF LATIN AMERICAN STUDIES, 4 (1972),
         77-83.

         Finds the roots of Brazilian bureaucracy in the Portu-
         guese government-in-exile in the 19th century. The
         transfer of power from Lisbon to the new country set
         the foundation of the further expansion of administra-
         tion.

1869.   Miller, Darrel. "Entrepreneurs and Bureaucrats: The
        Rise of an Urban Middle Class." THE DILEMMA OF AMA-
        ZONIAN DEVELOPMENT. Edited by Emilio F. Moran.
        Boulder, Colo.: Westview, 1982,

        Discusses the human dimensions of Amazonian develop-
        ment in terms of the growth of new elements within the
        urbanized portions of the area.

1870.   Uricoechea, Fernando. THE PATRIMONIAL FOUNDATIONS OF
        THE BRAZILIAN STATE. Berkeley: University of Calif-
        ornia Press, 1980. 233 pp.

        Examines the rise of the Brazilian political system
        during the 19th century. Throughout much of the century,
        there was a bitter struggle between the central gov-
        ernment and the patrimonial systems at the local level.
        The national bureaucracy was eventually able to over-
        whelm the local militias.

                        6.   Chile

1871.   Cleaves, Peter S. BUREAUCRATIC POLITICS AND ADMINIS-
        TRATION IN CHILE. Berkeley: University of Calif-
        ornia Press, 1974. 352 pp.

        Concludes, after interviewing 150 Chilean officials,
        that bureaucrats are engaged in a wide range of polit-
        ical activity in order to meet the goals of their organ-
        ization. Budgetary politics and planning are central
        reasons for their activity. The reform of government
        housing agencies is explored.

1872.   Menges, Constantine. POLITICS AND AGRARIAN BUREAUCRA-
        CIES IN CHILE: 1962-1964. Santa Monica: Rand, 1968.
        34 pp.

        Describes the performance of three government agen-
        cies implementing agrarian reform laws. Once a reform
        is passed, the politics of bureaucracy make it diffi-
        cult to assign responsibility for poor results. The
        potential beneficiaries of reform need their own organ-
        ization to check on the government bureaucracies.

1873. Parrish, Charles J. "Bureaucracy, Democracy, and De-
          velopment: Some Considerations Based on the Chilean
          Case." DEVELOPMENT ADMINISTRATION IN LATIN AMERICA.
          Edited by Clarence Thurber and Lawrence Graham. Dur-
          ham, N.C.: Duke University Press, 1973.

       Recommends the use of organization theory as an ap-
       proach to the study of bureaucracy in less developed
       countries. Incrementalism versus central planning is
       reconsidered in light of the Chilean experience. Be-
       cause development bureaucracy must respond to so many
       pressures from established interests, progress is halt-
       ing and uncertain. A comprehensive planning model may
       accomplish more, but it would also require a source of
       independent power for the administrators.

                          7. Colombia

1874. Bailey, John. "Bureaucratic Politics and Social Secur-
          ity Policy in Colombia." INTER-AMERICAN ECONOMIC AF-
          FAIRS, 29 (Spring, 1976), 3-20.

       Shows how administrative policy making is conditioned
       by the political environment. When political capabil-
       ity is dispersed among competing groups, the outcomes
       will reflect a number of variables.

1875. Ruhl, J. Mark. "An Alternative to the Bureaucratic-
          Authoritarian Regime: The Case of Colombia." INTER-
          AMERICAN ECONOMIC AFFAIRS, 35 (Autumn, 1981), 43-69.

       Describes how Colombia has managed to avoid the im-
       position of an authoritarian military regime. The
       reasons may lie in the unique history of the country's
       politics and thus does not provide a guide for a model
       to be used by other nations.

1876. Schmidt, Steffen W. "Bureaucrats as Modernizing Brok-
          ers? Clientelism in Colombia." COMPARATIVE POLITICS,
          6 (1974), 425-50.

       Applies a model of patron-broker-client relationships
       to Colombia administration. The brokerage function may

be a major factor in modernizing society, by allowing
a more technically oriented administration to introduce
modern solutions into the process of development.

8. Costa Rica

1877. Poitras, Guy E., and Charles Denton. "Bureaucratic
Performance: Case Studies from Mexico and Costa Rica."
JOURNAL OF COMPARATIVE ADMINISTRATION, 3 (1971), 169-
87.

Measure and compare the bureaucrat's perception of
development goals, bureaucratic performance, and the
environmental constraints on that performance.

1878. Denton, Charles. "Bureaucracy in an Immobilist Society:
The Case of Costa Rica." ADMINISTRATIVE SCIENCE QUAR-
TERLY, 14 (1969), 418-25.

Finds no support for the idea that the bureaucrats can
take the lead in economic and political development when
the society is dominated by an immobilist political
elite. The existence of strong political parties is no
guarantee of greater institutional modernization.

9. Cuba

1879. Aguirre, Neigno. "Women in the Cuban Bureaucracies:
1968-1974." JOURNAL OF COMPARATIVE FAMILY STUDIES,
7 (1976), 23-40.

Finds that sexual equality has not been established
in the Cuban civil service and that women are still un-
derrepresented.

1880. LeoGrande, William. "A Bureaucratic Approach to Civil-
Military Relations in Communist Political Systems:
The Case of Cuba." CIVIL-MILITARY RELATIONS IN COM-
MUNIST SYSTEMS. Edited by Dale Herspring and Ivan
Volgyes. Boulder, Col.: Westview, 1978.

Applies a model of bureaucratic politics to the Cuban

civil-military relations. The various organizational
participants are identified.

1881.   Valdés, Nelson. "The Cuban Revolution: Economic Organ-
        ization and Bureaucracy." LATIN AMERICAN PERSPEC-
        TIVES, 6 (Winter, 1979), 13-37.

        Traces changes in Cuban doctrine about economic or-
        ganization in a revolutionary society. Bureaucratiza-
        tion is increasing under current policy.

                        10.   Guatemala

1882.   Lujan, Herman D. "The Bureaucratic Function and Sys-
        tem Support: A Comparison of Guatemala and Nicaragua."
        COMPARATIVE POLITICS, 7 (1975), 559-76.

        Investigates the perception of citizens of the bureau-
        cracy as an element of the larger political system. In
        both the Central American cases, there was evidence
        that contact with administration lessens support for
        the regime.

1883.   Weaver, Jerry L. "Value Patterns of a Latin American
        Bureaucracy." HUMAN RELATIONS, 23 (1970), 225-33.

        Measures empirically the values of members of the
        Guatemalan civil service.

1884.   Weaver, Jerry L. "Bureaucracy during a Period of Soc-
        ial Change: The Case of Guatemala." DEVELOPMENT AD-
        MINISTRATION IN LATIN AMERICA. Edited Clarence Thur-
        ber and Lawrence Graham. Durham, N.C.: Duke Univer-
        sity Press, 1973.

        Examines the role of the bureaucracy in the planned
        social change in a developing country. The results of
        interviews with Guatemalan officials are analyzed. Is
        social rationalization a product of the actions of the
        bureaucracy? The civil service seems to have lagged be-
        hind other sectors in society and has been a defective
        vehicle for national development.

11. Guyana

1885. Luchtman, Harold A. "Race and Bureaucracy in Guyana."
JOURNAL OF COMPARATIVE ADMINISTRATION, 4 (1972),
225-52.

Examines the effect of racial imbalance in the composition of the civil service. The situation has led
to bureaucratic tension. The condition will not improve until the establishment of a true socialist society.

12. Mexico

1886. Alisky, Martin. "Mexico's Steel Industry: Getting Bureaucrats to Work Together." INTELLECT, 104 (1976),
462-64.

On a public corporation to produce steel.

1887. Alisky, Martin. "Mexico's 'Watergate' Investigations
Ousts Hundreds of High-Level Bureaucrats." USA TODAY,
107 (January, 1979), 10-12.

The Mexicans crack down on corruption.

1888. Bailey, John J. "Presidency, Bureaucracy and Administrative Reform in Mexico: The Secretariat of Programming and Budget." INTER-AMERICAN ECONOMIC AFFAIRS,
34 (Summer, 1980), 27-59.

Analyzes the creation and not altogether successful
early years of a planning and budgeting agency set up
by the Portillo administration.

1889. Benveniste, Guy. BUREAUCRACY AND NATIONAL PLANNING:
A SOCIOLOGICAL CASE STUDY IN MEXICO. New York: Praeger, 1970. 141 pp.

Studies the national planning of education in Mexico.

The purpose is to describe the reality of the political process, especially as the experts attempt to impose their rational plans on a rather untidy world. In order to gain access to political power, the planners must form coalitions with other actors within government.

1890. Greenberg, Martin H. BUREAUCRACY AND DEVELOPMENT: A MEXICAN CASE STUDY. Lexington, Mass.: Lexington Books, 1970. 158 pp.

Tests the thesis that bureaucracy in developing societies is ineffective through a study of the Mexican Ministry of Hydraulic Resources. There is a great deal of tension between the technical experts and the more partisan administrators. Even though the agency was marked by informality, nepotism, and corruption, it was not necessarily inefficient.

1891. Grimes, C.E., and Charles Simmons. "Bureaucracy and Political Control in Mexico: Towards and Assessment." PUBLIC ADMINISTRATION REVIEW, 29 (1969), 72-79.

See the emergence of a body of technically oriented professionals as a threat to the political control of the Mexican bureaucracy. The potential of the "tecnicos" makes it hard to predict the future role of the bureaucracy.

1892. Grindle, Merilee. "Patrons and Clients in the Bureaucracy: Career Networks in Mexico." LATIN AMERICAN RESEARCH REVIEW, 12 (1977), 37-66.

See Item 1893.

1893. Grindle, Merilee. BUREAUCRATS, POLITICIANS, AND PEASANTS IN MEXICO: A CASE STUDY IN PUBLIC POLICY. Berkeley: University of California Press, 1977. 220 pp.

Concludes, after the study of a single agency, that Mexican bureaucrats have made a distinctive adjustment to the conditions of political leadership in that nation. The system is stable in spite of its authoritarian and exploitive character.

* Poitras, Guy E., and Charles Denton. "Bureaucratic Performance: Case Studies from Mexico and Costa Rica." Cited above as Item 1877.

1894. Poitras, Guy E., "Welfare Bureaucracy and Clientele Politics in Mexico." ADMINISTRATIVE SCIENCE QUARTERLY, 18 (1973), 18-26.

Contends that the Mexican welfare bureaucracy has not achieved the goals of social development because of the representation, within its structure, of the elites of important clientele groups. Elite consensus comes at the expense of the goal of promoting social change for those most in need of welfare services.

13. Nicaragua

* Lujan, Herman D. "The Bureaucratic Function and System Support: A Comparison of Guatemala and Nicaragua." Cited above as Item 1882.

14. Peru

1895. Cleaves, Peter, and Martin Scurrah. AGRICULTURE, BUREAUCRACY, AND MILITARY GOVERNMENT IN PERU. Ithaca, N.Y.: Cornell University Press, 1980. 329 pp.

Analyze the agrarian reforms initiated in 1968. The reforms failed as an experiment although there were some important beneficiaries.

1896. Dietz, Henry. "Bureaucratic Decision-Making and Clientelistic Participation in Peru." AUTHORITARIANISM AND CORPORATISM IN LATIN AMERICA. Edited by James Malloy. Pittsburgh: University of Pittsburgh Press, 1977.

Examines how the urban poor (squatters) in Peru make demands and otherwise participate in the administrative system in local government.

1897. Handelman, H. PEASANTS, LANDLORDS AND BUREAUCRATS: THE
       POLITICS OF AGRARIAN REFORM IN PERU. Hanover, N.H.:
       American Universities Field Staff, 1981. 23 pp.

       Argues that, after land reform, the Peruvian peasants
       may still be in a subservient position, but greater op-
       portunites exist under state management. The reforms
       seem to have lessened peasant discontent and enabled
       the system to survive during a period of economic de-
       pression.

1898. Hopkins, Jack W. "Comparative Observations on Peruvian
       Bureaucracy." JOURNAL OF COMPARATIVE ADMINISTRATION,
       1 (1969), 301-20.

       Compares Peru with the U.S.

15. Trinidad and Tobago

1899. Nancoo, Stephen. "Administrative Theory and Bureaucra-
       tic Control: A Study of the Ombudsman Idea in Trini-
       dad and Tobago." INDIAN JOURNAL OF PUBLIC ADMINIS-
       TRATION, 23 (1977), 242-54.

       Examines the feasibility of an ombudsman for Trini-
       dad and Tobago. Developing countries seem to be in
       particular need for such an institution.

16. Venezuela

1900. Silva Michelena, Jose. "The Venezuelan Bureaucrat."
       A STRATEGY FOR RESEARCH ON SOCIAL POLICY. Edited by
       Frank Bonilla and Jose Silva Michelena. Cambridge,
       Mass.: MIT Press, 1967.

       Analyzes the administrators with emphasis on the
       high turnover rates among the more competent. Role
       stress seems to be the most critical problem for the
       members of the Venezuelan bureaucracy and accounts for
       the departure of many qualified people from the public
       service.

1901. Stewart, Bill. CHANGE AND BUREAUCRACY: PUBLIC ADMINIS-
TRATION IN VENEZUELA. Chapel Hill, N.C.: University
of North Carolina Press, 1978. 140 pp.

Looks at the interrelationships of Venezuela's increased revenue from oil, national development, and the
administrative system. Socioeconomic and career variables are used to study the performance of the bureaucracy and the possibility of administrative reform.

G. The Middle East

1. General

1902. Roos, Leslie L., and Noralou Roos. "Bureaucracy in the
Middle East: Some Cross-Cultural Relationships."
JOURNAL OF COMPARATIVE ADMINISTRATION, 1 (1969), 281-
99.

Compare the job satisfaction of bureaucrats in Egypt,
Turkey, and Pakistan. Developing countries exhibit a
"bureaucratic syndrome," featuring low morale and a
concern with job security.

1903. Weinbaum, Marvin G. "Agricultural Constraints and Bur-
eaucratic Politics in the Middle East." FOOD POLI-
TICS: THE REGIONAL CONFLICT. Edited by David N.
Balaam and Michael J. Carey. Totowa, N.J.: Allanheld,
Osman and Company, 1981.

Reviews the impediments posed by bureaucratic politics to increasing the production of food in the states
of the Middle East. These bureaucracies tend to reflect
the major national divisions and controversies and are
defective tools for the implementation of agrarian reform plans.

2. Egypt

1904. Akhavi, Shahrough. "Egypt: Diffused Elite in a Bureaucratic Society." POLITICAL ELITES IN ARAB NORTH AF-
RICA. New York: Longman, 1982.

Says that Egypt is a bureaucratic polity, but one without policy direction from a monolithic elite. The social and political power is diffused among several major groups.

1905. Ayubi, N.M.M. BUREAUCRACY AND POLITICS IN CONTEMPORARY EGYPT. London: Ithaca Press, 1980. 547 pp.

Argues that the Nasser regime was a bureaucratic polity. Political parties and popular participation were replaced by organizational concerns. Technology took the place of ideology. This emphasis on development in a technical sense led to a failure to solve the real problems of inequality and poverty.

1906. Berger, Morroe. "Bureaucracy East and West." ADMINIS-TRATIVE SCIENCE QUARTERLY, 1 (1957), 18-29.

Examines the Egyptian bureaucracy as illustrative of the differences between Western and non-Western admin-istration. A survey of officials indicates that profes-sional and bureaucratic predispositions are not as re-lated as they are in the West.

1907. Berger, Morroe. BUREAUCRACY AND SOCIETY IN MODERN EG-YPT: A STUDY OF THE HIGHER CIVIL SERVICE. Princeton, N.J.: Princeton University Press, 1957. 231 pp.

Describes the Egyptian civil service in terms of bur-eaucratic theory. It is found that Western concepts are of questionable utility in the study of non-Western or-ganizational behavior.

1908. Sharp, Walter R. "Bureaucracy and Politics--Egyptian Model." TOWARD THE COMPARATIVE STUDY OF PUBLIC ADMIN-ISTRATION. Edited by William J. Siffin. Bloomington: Indiana University Press, 1959.

Discusses the administrative system of Egypt, with emphasis on the years between 1952 and 1956. The land has inherited a highly personalized pattern of administra-tration. A truly efficient bureaucracy may be at least a generation in the future.

3. Iran

1909. Bakhash, Shaul. "The Evolution of Qajar Bureaucracy: 1779-1879." MIDDLE EASTERN STUDIES, 7 (1971), 139-68.

Portrays the history of the Qajar dynasty in Persia in terms of the power struggle between the shah and his ministers.

1910. Gable, Richard W., and William B. Storm. "Public Administration in Iran: Sketches of a Non-Western Transitional Bureaucracy." PHILIPPINE JOURNAL OF PUBLIC ADMINISTRATION, 5 (1961), 226-34.

Look at the modernization efforts of the Iranian administration.

4. Israel

1911. Avni-Segre, Dan V. "The Breakdown of Israel's Bureaucratic System in October, 1973." PUBLIC ADMINISTRATION IN ISRAEL AND ABROAD, 14 (1974), 123-30.

Contends that the inability of the system to respond to a crisis in an effective manner was the result of the prevailing mood of "immobilism."

1912. Avruch, Kevin. "Becoming Traditional: Socialization to Bureaucracy among American Immigrants in Israel." STUDIES IN COMPARATIVE INTERNATIONAL DEVELOPMENT, 16 (Fall-Winter, 1981), 64-83.

Describes how American immigrants developed a sense of personal influence in their encounters with the Israeli bureaucracy.

1913. Globerson, Arye. "A Profile of the Bureaucratic Elite in Israel." PUBLIC PERSONNEL MANAGEMENT, 2 (January-February, 1973), 9-15.

Identifies the salient characteristics of the Israeli
bureaucracy. This group has traits in common with both
advanced and developing countries.

1914. Katz, David, and Aaron Antonovsky. "Bureaucracy and Im-
      migrant Adjustment." INTERNATIONAL MIGRATION REVIEW,
      7 (1973), 247-56.

      Discuss how newcomers to Israeli learn to deal with
      the administrative system.

1915. Nachmias, David, and David H. Rosenbloom. "Antecedents
      of Public Bureaucracy: The Case of Israel." ADMINIS-
      TRATION AND SOCIETY, 9 (1977), 45-80.

      Inquire into the reasons why public officials leave
      public service. A survey of 630 Israeli bureaucrats
      indicates that self-image, a sense of efficacy, and
      a perception of political involvement in administration
      are the major causes. Ways of dealing with these de-
      terminants of turnover are suggested.

1916. Nachmias, David, and David H. Rosenbloom. "Bureaucracy
      and Ethnicity." AMERICAN JOURNAL OF SOCIOLOGY, 83
      (1978), 967-74.

      Ask whether attitudes toward public administration are
      determined by ethnic background. It appears that be-
      coming a public employee does not change attitudes de-
      rived from ethnicity.

1917. Nachmias, David, and David H. Rosenbloom. BUREAUCRATIC
      CULTURE: CITIZENS AND ADMINISTRATORS IN ISRAEL. New
      York: St. Martin's, 1978. 212 pp.

      Use data from interviews with over 2,000 Israeli cit-
      izens and administrators in order to identify the per-
      ceptions of and attitudes toward bureaucracy. Citizen
      orientations are classified as "bureautic," "bureau-
      phile," and "bureau-tolerant." Officials are classified
      according to their perceptions of personnel practices
      as based on ascriptive or achieved aspects.

1918. Raphaeli, Nimrod. "The Absorption of Orientals into
       the Israeli Bureaucracy." MIDDLE EASTERN STUDIES,
       8 (1972), 84-91.

       Finds that Oriental migrants are represented in pro-
       portion to their numbers in the general population.

1919. Rosenbloom, David H., and David Nachmias. "Bureaucratic
       Representation in Israel." PUBLIC PERSONNEL MANAGE-
       MENT, 3 (1974), 302-13.

       Examine the Israeli bureaucracy in terms of represen-
       tativeness. The results indicate that passive under-
       representation of some groups may not always be ex-
       plained in terms of discrimination. The findings have
       implications for the theory of representative bureau-
       cracy.

1920. Rosenbloom, David H., and David Nachmias. "Why Exit
       The Public Bureaucracy? An Exploratory Study." AD-
       MINISTRATIVE CHANGE, 3 (January-June, 1976), 1-19.

       Examine the reasons why Israeli bureaucrats decide to
       go into the private sphere. Among other factors, the
       negative attitude toward the bureaucracy by citizens
       and a sense of alienation were important. Ethnicity
       also seems to play a role.

1921. Sharkansky, Ira. "How to Cope with Bureaucracy." JERU-
       SALEM QUARTERLY, 6 (Winter, 1978), 80-93.

       Describes varieties of citizen discontent with the
       Israeli bureaucracy.

1922. Shokeid, Moshe. "Reconciling with Bureaucracy: Middle
       Eastern Immigrants' *Moshav* in Transition." ECONOMIC
       DEVELOPMENT AND CULTURAL CHANGE, 29 (1980), 187-205.

       Explores the patterns of accommodation to bureaucracy
       through a study of the smallholders cooperative. The
       moshav was a bridge between traditional society and a
       bureaucratic organization. Traditional roles such as
       rabbi were transformed into positions resembling a
       civil service pattern.

5.　Lebanon

1923.　Nakib, Khalil, and Monte Palmer.　"Traditionalism and
Change among Lebanese Bureaucrats."　INTERNATIONAL RE-
VIEW OF ADMINISTRATIVE SCIENCES, 42 (1976), 15-22.

Measure elements of modernity within a Middle Eastern
bureaucracy.　The forces of modernization do not seem
to have changed the orientation of the administrators.

6.　Libya

1924.　el Fathaly, Omar I., Monte Palmer, and Richard Chackerian.　POLITICAL DEVELOPMENT AND BUREAUCRACY IN LIBYA.
Lexington, Mass.: Lexington Books, 1977.　122 pp.

A collection of original studies on facets of political development in an oil-rich country.　The major
theme is the revolutonary leader's attempt to build an
institutional framework capable of diversifying the
economic base.　The erection of an administrative cadre
at the local level is a special problem.　However, the
traditional behavior reinforced by tribal leaders is
being overcome.

7.　Morocco

1925.　Shuster, James R.　"Bureaucratic Transition in Morocco."
HUMAN ORGANIZATION, 24 (1957), 53-58.

Considers the bureaucracy as both the object and the
instrument of modernization.

8.　Saudi Arabia

1926.　al Nimir, Saud, and Monte Palmer.　"Bureaucracy and Development in Saudi Arabia."　PUBLIC ADMINISTRATION AND
DEVELOPMENT, 2 (1982), 93-104.

Evaluate the development potential of the Saudi bureaucracy by measuring the innovative and developmental
attitudes of its members. The results indicate that
there is a low level of innovative behavior.

1927. Othman, Osman A. "Saudi Arabia: An Unprecedented Growth
of Wealth with an Unparalled Growth of Bureaucracy."
INTERNATIONAL REVIEW OF ADMINISTRATIVE SCIENCES, 43
(1979), 234-40.

Notes the special features of the Saudi administrative
system: lack of tradition, no colonial background, and
great wealth.

1928. al Sadhan, Abdulrahman. "Modernisation of the Saudi
Bureaucracy." KING FAISAL AND THE MODERNISATION OF
SAUDI ARABIA. Edited by Willard Beling. London:
Croom Helm, 1980.

Describes the work of King Faisal in changing the
bureaucracy.

1929. Sheean, Vincent. "Birth of a Bureaucracy." ARAMCO
WORLD, 21 (January-February, 1970), 2-5.

On the Saudi civil service.

9. Turkey

1930. Abadan-Unat, Nermin. "Women in Government as Policy-
Makers and Bureaucrats: The Turkish Case." WOMEN,
POWER AND POLITICAL SYSTEMS. Edited by Margherita
Rendel. London: Croom Helm, 1981.

Assesses the impact of legal and educational reform
on the status of women in public administration. Open-
ing up education for females has not significantly
changed their representation in the bureaucracy.

1931. Alvarez, David J. BUREAUCRACY AND COLD WAR DIPLOMACY:
THE UNITED STATES AND TURKEY, 1943-1946. Thessalon-
iki: Institute for Balkan Studies, 1980. 147 pp.

Investigates the determinants of Turkish-American relations in the years after WWII. It is found that "American policy toward Turkey was not the product of a
monolithic decision-making process but, rather, reflects
the interaction of a number of semiautonomous actors,
both human and organizational. Middle-level bureaucrats
in the State Department were ultimately the most important in shaping the policy."

1932. Bent, Frederick. "The Turkish Bureaucracy as an Agent
    of Change." JOURNAL OF COMPARATIVE ADMINISTRATION,
    1 (1969), 47-64.

    Inquires into the reasons inhibiting the role of the
    bureaucracy in social innovation.

1933. Chambers, Richard. "The Civil Bureaucracy--Turkey."
    POLITICAL MODERNIZATION IN JAPAN AND TURKEY. Edited
    by Robert Ward and Dankwart Rustow. Princeton, N.J.:
    Princeton University Press, 1964.

    Traces the history of administration from the Ottoman
    era to the present. Now the bureaucracy is both an
    agent of change and an object for political moderniza-
    tion.

1934. Findley, Carter. "The Foundation of the Ottoman Foreign
    Ministry: The Beginnings of Bureaucratic Reform under
    Selim III and Mahmud II." INTERNATIONAL JOURNAL OF
    MIDDLE EAST STUDIES, 3 (1972), 388-416.

    An episode in Ottoman administration.

1935. Findley, Carter. BUREAUCRATIC REFORM IN THE OTTOMAN
    EMPIRE: THE SUBLIME PORTE, 1789-1922. Princeton,
    N.J.: Princeton University Press, 1980. 455 pp.

    Sorts out the several efforts at reforming the Otto-
    man Empire from the late 18th to the early 20th century.
    The subject is of special importance because the imper-
    ial style was significant in establishing the adminis-
    trative tradition throughout the Muslim world.

1936. Heper, Metin. "Traditional Tendencies in the Upper
Reaches of the Bureaucracy in Changing Turkey."
TURKISH PUBLIC ADMINISTRATION, 2 (1975), 121-53.

Identifies sources of resistance to change in the
Turkish civil service.

1937. Heper, Metin. "Political Modernization as Reflected in
Bureaucratic Change: The Turkish Bureaucracy and a
'Historical Bureaucratic Empire' Tradition." INTER-
NATIONAL JOURNAL OF MIDDLE EAST STUDIES, 7 (1976),
507-21.

Discusses the major influences of the Ottoman tradition on the present Turkish civil service. The modernization movement was originally induced rather than
organic, but the bureaucratic elite is giving up some
of its attachment to the non-democratic values of the
earlier era.

1938. Heper, Metin. "The Recalcitrance of the Turkish Public
Bureaucracy to 'Bourgeois Politics:' A Multifactor
Political Stratification Analysis." MIDDLE EAST JOUR-
NAL, 30 (1976), 485-500.

Argues that the change from a royal to a public bureaucracy was "induced" rather than "organic." This led
to tension between the middle class and the administrators.

1939. Heper, Metin. "Patrimonialism in the Ottoman Turkish
Public Bureaucracy." ASIAN AND AFRICAN STUDIES, 13
(1979), 13-21.

Looks at the durability of traditional features of
the Turkish administration.

1940. Heper, Metin, Ching-lim Kim, and Seong-tong Pai. "The
Role of Bureaucracy and Regime Types: A Comparative
Study of Turkish and South Korean Higher Civil Servants." ADMINISTRATION AND SOCIETY, 12 (1980), 137-
57.

Inquire into the differences in bureaucracies caused by variety in regime types.

1941. Weiker, Walter F. "The Ottoman Bureaucracy: Modernization and Reform." ADMINISTRATIVE SCIENCE QUARTERLY,
13 (1968), 451-70.

Discusses the attempts by Ottoman rulers to modernize
the society from 1826 to 1877. The efforts failed because the main goal was the preservation of "Ottoman-
ism," which resulted in the lack of change within an
authoritarian state system, including the bureaucracy.
Without sufficient political commitment to change, bureaucratic behavior inconsistent with modernization per-
sisted.

H. The Soviet Union and Eastern Europe

1. General

1942. Beck, Carl. "Bureaucracy and Political Development in
Eastern Europe." BUREAUCRACY AND POLITICAL DEVELOP-
MENT. Edited by Joseph LaPalombara. Princeton, N.J.:
Princeton University Press, 1963.

Considers the impact of bureaucratization on the political systems of Eastern Eruope, with emphasis on the
political doctrine, the administrative system, and the
political elite. Bureaucratic theory is not found to
be an effective tool for the analysis of these societies. The ideology of a revolutionary movement prevents
the creation of a wholly independent bureaucracy.

1943. Beck, Carl. "Bureaucratic Conservatism and Innovation
in Eastern Europe." COMPARATIVE POLITICAL STUDIES,
1 (1968), 275-94.

Examines the relationship of government officials to
innovation. There is a trend toward wider participation by a variety of political actors and social forces.
Because of the internal dynamics of communist regimes,
it is likely bureaucracy will assume an advocacy role.

1944. Carlo, Antonio. "The Crisis of Bureaucratic Collectivism." TELOS, 43 (1980), 3-31.

Describes the recurring crises brought on the by failure of central planning in the USSR and Eastern Europe.

1945. Cocks, Paul. "Bureaucracy and Party Control." COMPAR-
ATIVE SOCIALIST SYSTEMS: ESSAYS ON POLITICS AND ECON-
OMICS. Edited by Carmelo Mesa-Lago and Carl Beck.
Pittsburgh: University of Pittsburgh Center for In-
ternational Studies, 1975.

Looks at the problems that communist systems have always had in regularizing control mechanisms over the
bureaucracy.

1946. Djilas, Milovan. THE NEW CLASS: AN ANALYSIS OF THE
COMMUNIST SYSTEM. New York: Frederick A. Praeger,
1957. 214 pp.

Argues that the party bureaucracy in communist society has become a new ruling class. Its power comes
from its collective ownership of the nation's property,
administered in the name of the state and society. The
new class cannot permit participation in the sharing of
power for their monopoloy is the means to their survival
as a group. It cannot afford to implement that ideological promise of transition to a better society.

1947. Harman, Chris. BUREAUCRACY AND REVOLUTION IN EASTERN
EUROPE. London: Pluto, 1974. 296 pp.

Sees the Soviet Union and its satellites as systems
of bureaucratic state capitalism for which the Marxist
theory of revolution is still relevant. A revolution
against the bureaucracy by the working class is inevitable as the many postwar crises in Eastern Europe tend
to suggest.

1948. Hirszowicz, Maria. THE BUREAUCRATIC LEVIATHAN: A STUDY
IN THE SOCIOLOGY OF COMMUNISM. Oxford: Martin Robinson, 1980. 208 pp.

Discusses the relationship between state power and

society in the Soviet Union and Eastern Europe, with emphasis on the gulf between Marxist theory and reality. Several dimensions of the problem of bureaucratic power are analyzed, including the Stalinist roots of bureaucracy and the weakness of bureaucratic rationality in a planned economy.

1949.   Horowitz, Gus. "Dynamics of Antibureaucratic Stuggle in the USSR and East Europe." INTERNATIONAL SOCIALIST REVIEW, 33 (November, 1972), 18-29.

Discusses the popular opposition to the bureaucracy in socialist states.

1950.   Lendvai, Paul. THE BUREAUCRACY OF TRUTH: HOW COMMUNIST GOVERNMENTS MANAGE THE NEWS. Boulder, Colo.: Westview, 1981. 285 pp.

Analyzes the operation of the mass media in the countries of Eastern Europe, including Yugoslavia. International broadcasts into the area by Western countries and the consequences of the Helsinki Accords are also discussed.

1951.   Mallet, Serge. BUREAUCRACY AND TECHNOCRACY IN THE SOCIALIST COUNTRIES. Nottingham: Bertrand Russell Peace Foundation, 1974. 63 pp.

On administration and the capacity for innovation.

1952.   Sajo, Andras. "Why Do Public Bureaucracies Follow Legal Rules?" INTERNATIONAL JOURNAL OF THE SOCIOLOGY OF LAW, 9 (1981), 69-84.

Examines the relationship between the rule of law and public administration in socialist countries, particularly in Hungary. Bureaucracies abide by the law because of the economic environment, the internal organization, and the socialization of the officials.

1953.   Steigerwald, Robert. "Bureaucracy and Real Socialism." EAST-WEST DIALOGUES: FOUNDATIONS AND PROBLEMS OF REVOLUTIONARY PRAXIS. Edited by Paul Crosser, David

DeGrood, and Dale Riepe. Amsterdam: B.R. Grüner, 1973.

Defends the centralization of administrative power in the socialist states. The critics show their basically petty bourgeois nature.

1954. "The Superfluous Men: The Latest 'Fight against Bureaucracy.'" EAST EUROPE, 7 (July, 1958), and (August, 1958), 3-16 and 15-26.

Part I describes the attempts at bureaucratic reform in Poland and Bulgaria. Part II covers Hungary, Romania and Czechoslovakia.

2. Albania

1955. Raicevic, Jovan. "Ideological Grounds for Albanian Irredentism and Bureaucratic Nationalism in Kosovo." SOCIALIST THOUGHT AND PRACTICE, 21 (September, 1981). 22-37.

On recent political conditions in Albania.

3. Czechoslovakia

1956. Beck, Carl. "Party Control and Bureaucratization in Czechoslovakia." JOURNAL OF POLITICS, 23 (1961), 279-94.

Argues that the role of party and ideology have made some modifications in traditional bureaucratic practice. The bureau is controlled by units outside of the formal structure. Party loyalty is at least as important as technical or professional qualifications. A major problem is the management of the conflict between the public administrator and the party leaders.

1957. Korbonski, Andrzej. "Bureaucracy and Interest Groups in Communist Societies: The Case of Czechoslovakia." STUDIES IN COMPARATIVE COMMUNISM, 4 (January, 1971), 57-79.

Contends that the communist societies can be seen in terms of interest group models. The Czech case resembles the structure of Western states in the degree of group involvement in administration.

1958.   Sik, Ota. CZECHOSLOVAKIA: THE BUREAUCRATIC ECONOMY. White Plains, N.Y.: International Arts and Sciences Press, 1972. 138 pp.

Uses the Czech example to show why the communist system of economic planning cannot work in advanced industrial nations. Communist regimes are not really socialist but instead are "state-capitalist systems in which the working people are governed, repressed, and exploited by a power elite relying on a party and a state bureaucracy of unprecedented proportions."

1959.   Svitak, Ivan. "The Czech Bureaucratic Collectivist Class." NEW POLITICS, 11, No. 2 (1974), 81-92.

New class theory applied to Czechoslovakia.

4. German Democratic Republic

1960.   Ludz, Peter C. "Marxism and Systems Theory in a Bureaucratic Society." SOCIAL RESEARCH, 42 (1975), 661-74.

Discusses the theoretical ambiguities in the ideology of the dominant elite in the GDR.

1961.   Sinclair, Peter. "Bureaucratized Agriculture: Planned Social Change in the GDR." SOCIOLOGIA RURALIS, 19 (1979), 211-26.

Argues that centralized planning has alienated the East German farmers, leading to lower productivity as compared to farmers in Western Germany.

5. Hungary

1962.   Marrese, Michael. "The Bureaucratic Response to Economic Fluctuation: An Econometric Investigation of of Hungarian Investment Policies." JOURNAL OF POLICY MODELING, 3 (1981), 221-43.

Attempts to measure the causes of deviations from long-term trends in investment policies in a socialist state.

6. Poland

1963. Hirszowicz, Maria. "Intelligentsia versus Bureaucracy? The Revival of a Myth in Poland." SOVIET STUDIES, 30 (1978), 336-61.

Rejects the idea that the intellectuals will force a change in Polish bureaucracy. The educated strata are already a major component of the bureaucracy and are dependent upon it.

1964. Maneli, Mieczyslaw. "From Gomulka to Gierek: The Moral Decay of the Polish Bureaucracy." DISSENT, 18 (1971), 230-34.

On recent political developments in Poland.

1965. Piotrowski, Jerzy. "Old People, Bureaucracy, and the Family in Poland." FAMILY, BUREAUCRACY, AND THE ELDERLY. Edited by Ethel Shanas and Marvin Sussman. Durham, N.C.: Duke University Press, 1977.

On the administration of social services for the elderly.

1966. "Technocrats, Bureaucrats, and Democrats." EAST EUROPE, 18 (May, 1969), 32-33.

Extracts from a Polish symposium. It is agreed that the rise in the influence of technical experts has led to a decrease in the viability of worker self-government. Greater participation by the workers in a system of political democracy is required to bring the bureaucracy back into line.

7. Soviet Union

1967.   Armstrong, John A. THE SOVIET BUREAUCRATIC ELITE: A
        CASE STUDY OF THE UKRAINIAN APPARATUS. New York:
        Praeger, 1959. 174 pp.

        Studies the background, careers and turnover rate
        of the members of the higher levels of the Ukrainian
        administration. A major question is the importance of
        communist ideology in the conduct of administrative
        activity.

1968.   Berliner, Joseph S. "Russia's Bureaucrats: Why They're
        Reactionary." TRANS-ACTION, 5 (December, 1967) 53–58.

        Argues that Soviet managers resist innovation because
        of the relatively low payoffs for success compared to
        the high cost of failure to meet regular quotas.

1969.   Berliner, Joseph S. "Bureaucratic Conservatism and
        Creativity in the Soviet Economy." FRONTIERS OF DE-
        VELOPMENT ADMINISTRATION. Edited by Fred W. Riggs.
        Durham, N.C.: Duke University Press, 1970.

        Discusses weaknesses in the administrative level be-
        tween the central bureaucracy and the industrial plants.
        This is the "planning bureaucracy."

1970.   Cocks, Paul. "The Policy Process and Bureaucratic Pol-
        itics." THE DYNAMICS OF SOVIET POLITICS. Edited by
        Paul Cocks, Robert Daniels, and Nancy Heer. Cam-
        bridge, Mass.: Harvard University Press, 1976.

        Describes the elements of the Soviet decision making
        process, with emphasis on the use of advanced manager-
        ial techniques.

1971.   Constas, Helen. "The USSR--From Charismatic Sect to
        Bureaucratic Society." ADMINISTRATIVE SCIENCE QUART-
        ERLY, 6 (1961), 282–98.

Suggests that the USSR is a new social type: bureaucratic totalitarianism based on charismatic authority.
Charismatic bureaucracies are inherently authoritarian and unlike the pluralism in the bureaucracies in the
West. The Soviet system is comparable to the ancient
empires of Egypt, China or the Incas.

1972. Dawisha, Karen. "The Limits of the Bureaucratic Politics Model: Observations on the Soviet Case." STUD-
IES IN COMPARATIVE COMMUNISM, 13 (1980), 300-26.

Claims that the bureaucratic politics model is not
sufficient to explain outcomes in Soviet foreign policy
making. The party and communist ideology undermine the
usefulness of the model.

1973. Dolenko, A., and Y. Feofanov. "Bureaucrat in the
Dock." CURRENT DIGEST OF THE SOVIET PRESS, 13 (May,
1961), 33-34.

Tell of a Soviet housing manager who was brought to
trial on the charge of "bureaucracy."

1974. Fainsod, Merle. "Bureaucracy and Modernization: The
Russian and Soviet Case." BUREAUCRACY AND POLITICAL
DEVELOPMENT. Edited by Joseph LaPalombara. Prince-
ton, N.J.: Princeton University Press, 1963.

Analyzes the potential of the bureaucracy as a modernizing force by examining the Russian and Soviet experiences. Based on their relationship to political authority, bureaucracies may be classified as military-
dominated, ruler-dominated, and ruling. The communist
elite made the transition from a ruling to a party-
state bureaucracy.

1975. Field, Daniel. THE END OF SERFDOM: NOBILITY AND BUREAU-
CRACY IN RUSSIA, 1855-1861. Cambridge, Mass.: Harvard
University Press, 1976. 472 pp.

Traces the antecedents of the great reforms which
ended serfdom in Russia. The eventual impact of the
reformers within the bureaucracy is assessed.

1976. Field, Daniel. "Three New Books on the Imperial Bur-
      eaucracy." KRITIKA, 15 (1979), 119-47.

      A review essay on works by Soviet historians.

1977. Galli, Giorgio. "Whither Russia?--A Bureaucracy under
      Fire." PROBLEMS OF COMMUNISM, 15 (September-October,
      1966), 31-35.

      Says that the Soviet bureaucracy is powerful but very
      static. Intellectuals and technocrats may force it to
      share some of its power.

1978. Ganguly, Shivaji. "A Comparative Paradigm of Western
      and Soviet Bureaucracies." INDIAN JOURNAL OF PUBLIC
      ADMINISTRATION, 23 (1977), 100-13.

      Develops a model for use in the comparison of the Sov-
      iet system with Western countries.

1979. Hollander, Paul. "Observations on Bureaucracy: Total-
      itarianism and the Comparative Study of Communism."
      SLAVIC REVIEW, 26 (1967), 302-07.

      Discusses various models for the study of Soviet soc-
      iety. The totalitarian model is still valid.

1980. Hollander, Paul. "Politicized Bureaucracy: The Soviet
      Case." NEWSLETTER ON COMPARATIVE STUDIES OF COMMUN-
      ISM, 4 (May, 1971), 13-22.

      Argues that the Soviet case "is a type of bureaucracy
      largely undreamed of in the philosophy of Western soc-
      iologists and students of bureaucracy, a type which de-
      fies many of our major preconceptions about bureaucra-
      cy." The peculiar interaction of ideology, politics,
      and economics has created a new type of organizational
      form. It is most of all an instrument of control and
      only secondarily a means for social modernization. As
      a means for the maintenance of the bureaucratic elite,
      it is incapable of sanctioning values which threaten
      its existence.

1981. Hough, Jerry F. "The Bureaucratic Model and the Nature of the Soviet System." JOURNAL OF COMPARATIVE ADMIN- ISTRATION, 5 (1973), 134-67.

Discusses the difficulties of applying a single model of bureaucratic behavior to the study of Soviet admin- istration and politics.

1982. Jahn, Egbert. "Armaments and Bureaucracy in Soviet Society." BULLETIN OF PEACE PROPOSALS, 10 (1979), 108-15.

Asks whether there are socially and politically rele- vant system differences between Eastern and Western policies on armaments and international relations.

1983. Keep, John. "Programming the Past: Imperial Russian Bureaucracy and Society under the Scrutiny of Mr. George Yaney." CANADIAN-AMERICAN SLAVIC STUDIES, 8 (1974), 569-80.

Review essay on Yaney's *The Systematization of Russian Government*.

1984. Kipp, Jacob W. "M. Kh. Reutern on the Russian State and Economy: A Liberal Bureaucrat during the Crimean Era, 1854-1960." JOURNAL OF MODERN HISTORY, 47 (1975), 437-59.

Summarizes the liberal economic thought of Mikhail Reutern, a Russian official.

1985. Kipp, Jacob W., and W. Bruce Lincoln. "Autocracy and Reform: Bureaucratic Absolutism and Political Modern- ization in Nineteenth-Century Russia." RUSSIAN HIS- TORY, 6 (1979), 1-21.

Discuss contradictory tendencies in the adminsitra- tion of the Czarist system.

1986. Levin, Alfred. "Russian Bureaucratic Opinion in the Wake of the 1905 Revolution." JAHRBÜCHER FÜR GE- SCHICHTE OSTEUROPAS, 11 (1963), 1-12.

Describes the reactions of Russian offials to the
trend of political liberalization.

1987. Lieven, Dominic. "The Russian Civil Service under Nicholas II: Some Variations on the Bureaucratic Theme."
JAHRBÜCHER FÜR GESCHICHTE OSTEUROPAS, 29 (1981), 366-
403.

Examines the ethnic, social and educational background
of civil servants during the reign of Nicholas II. The
typical career pattern is identified. Considerable variation is found in the characteristics of the members of
the civil service.

1988. Lieven, Dominic. "Bureaucratic Liberalism in Late Imperial Russia: The Personality, Career and Opinions
of A.N. Kulomzin." SLAVONIC AND EAST EUROPEAN RE-
VIEW, 60 (1982), 413-32.

Uses a biographical sketch of a career official to
illuminate the activity of enlightened bureaucrats during the reign of Nicholas II.

1989. Lincoln, W. Bruce. "Russia's 'Enlightened' Bureaucrats
and the Problem of State Reform, 1848-1856." CAHIERS
DU MONDE RUSSE ET SOVIETIQUE, 12 (1971), 410-21.

Discusses the bureaucratic involvement in the prepar-
atory stages of modernization.

1990. Lincoln, W. Bruce. "The Genesis of an 'Enlightened'
Bureaucracy in Russia, 1825-1856." JAHRBÜCHER FÜR
GESCHICHTE OSTEUROPAS, 20 (1972), 321-30.

Looks at the beginning of liberalization in Russian
society.

1991. Lincoln, W. Bruce. NIKOLAI MILIUTIN: AN ENLIGHTENED
RUSSIAN BUREAUCRAT. Newtonville, Mass.: Oriental
Research Partners, 1977. 130 pp.

On the career of a 19th-century administrator.

1992. Lincoln, W. Bruce. "A Profile of the Russian Bureaucracy on the Eve of the Great Reforms." JAHRBÜCHER
FÜR GESCHICHTE OSTEUROPAS, 27 (1979), 181-96.

Examines the composition of the civil service in the
middle of the 19th century.

1993. Loeber, Dietrich A. "Bureaucracy in a Worker's State:
E.B. Pashukanis and the Struggle against Bureaucratism in the Soviet Union." SOVIET UNION, 6 (1979),
154-65.

Considers bureaucracy as a special problem for a socialist society since, theoretically, there are no social
roots for such a form of organization. The thought of
a legal theorist, writing in the 1930s, is summarized.
His suggestions for fighting bureaucratism are included
in the discussion.

1994. Luke, Timothy W., and Carl Boggs. "Soviet Subimperial-
ism and the Crisis of Bureaucratic Centralism." STUD-
IES IN COMPARATIVE COMMUNISM, 15 (1982), 95-124.

Sees the present crisis in Soviet-type societies to
be the result of a convergence of domestic and international pressures. A centralized bureaucratic system
is rather fragile as it tries to maintain its position
in the international economic order. The political
system has lost its energy as a leading example of a
developmental form.

1995. McClelland, James. "The Bureaucrats and *The Intelligent*." SOVIET STUDIES, 24 (1973), 588-93.

A review essay on books about Soviet education policy.

1996. MacDonald, Dwight. "Bureaucratic Culture: Nicholas I
and Josef I." POLITICS, 5 (Spring, 1948), 109-13.

Compares the censorship of the arts under the czar
and Stalin. The communist regime has been much more
effective in stifling creative thought and putting a
chill on artistic work.

1997. Meehan-Waters, Brenda. "The Evolution of the Russian
       Bureaucracy in the Nineteenth Century." SOVIET STUD-
       IES IN HISTORY, 18 (1979), 3-10.

       Review essay on a history by a Soviet writer.

1998. Melman, Seymour. "Management and Bureaucracy in the
       Russian Factory." DISSENT, 6 (1959), 275-79.

       Compares American and Soviet industrial management,
       based on Berliner's *Factory and Managers in the USSR*.

1999. Mosse, Werner E. "Aspects of Tsarist Bureaucracy: Re-
       cruitment to the Imperial State Council, 1855-1914."
       SLAVONIC AND EAST EUROPEAN REVIEW, 57 (1979), 240-54.

       Investigates how members were brought into the highest
       and most important body in the Russian bureaucracy.

2000. Mosse, Werner E. "Russian Bureaucracy at the End of the
       Ancien Régime: The Imperial State Council, 1897-1915."
       SLAVIC REVIEW, 39 (1980), 616-32.

       Examines the role of traditional and developmental
       elements within the czarist bureaucracy during its last
       years. An analysis of the background of the members of
       the Imperial State Council reveals that the influence
       of the landed aristocracy had decreased. However, there
       was enough infighting that the stability of the entire
       regime was threatened.

2001. Odom, William E. THE SOVIET VOLUNTEERS: MODERNIZATION
       AND BUREAUCRACY IN A PUBLIC MASS ORGANIZATION.
       Princeton, N.J.: Princeton University Press, 1973.
       360 pp.

       Describes a large-scale paramilitary organization in
       the 1920s and 1930s. Despite the implications of or-
       ganization theory, it was found that the voluntary as-
       pects of the operation were compatible with direction
       of activity from a bureaucratic center. The system was
       an effective one in reaching certain goals.

2002. Orlovsky, Daniel T.   "Recent Studies on the Russian
        Bureaucracy." RUSSIAN REVIEW, 35 (1976), 448-67.

        A review essay on several books about bureaucracy in
        the years before the Russian Revolution.

2003. Perrins, Michael.   "The Council for State Defence, 1905-
        1909: A Study in Russian Bureaucratic Politics."
        SLAVONIC AND EAST EUROPEAN REVIEW, 58 (1980), 370-98.

        On an organization within the Russian bureaucracy.

2004. Pintner, Walter M.   "The Social Characteristics of the
        Early Nineteenth-Century Bureaucracy." SLAVIC RE-
        VIEW, 29 (1970), 429-43.

        An analysis of the background of administrators.

2005. Pintner, Walter M., and Don K. Rowney, eds.   RUSSIAN
        OFFICIALDOM: THE BUREAUCRATIZATION OF RUSSIAN SOCIETY
        FROM THE SEVENTEENTH TO THE TWENTIETH CENTURY. Chapel
        Hill, N.C.: University of North Carolina Press, 1980.
        396 pp.

        A collection of original articles on various dimen-
        sions of the growth of the size, scope and power of
        the Russian bureaucracy.

2006. Raeff, Marc.   "The Bureaucratic Phenomenon of Imperial
        Russia, 1700-1905." AMERICAN HISTORICAL REVIEW, 84
        (1979), 399-411.

        A review essay on several books on Russian bureaucra-
        tic systems. Recent scholarship has identified two
        major period, with the dividing line somewhere between
        the years 1815 and 1848. One still wonders, however,
        how the imperial system survived for so long.

2007. Rieber, Alfred J.   "Bureaucratic Politics in Imperial
        Russia." SOCIAL SCIENCE HISTORY, 2 (1978), 399-413.

        Argues that the tsarist bureaucracy was fragmented
        and not suited to a stable political system.

2008. Rigby, T.H.   "The Birth of the Central Soviet Bureau-
       cracy." POLITICS, 7 (1972), 121-35.

       Examines the continuity between pre- and post-revo-
       lutionary administrative conditions.

2009. Rigby, T.H.   "Bureaucracy and Democracy in the USSR.
       AUSTRALIAN QUARTERLY, 42 (March, 1970), 5-14.

       Sees the possibility for the introduction of a form
       of democracy into the authoritarian-bureaucratic pol-
       itical system of the Soviet Union.

2010. Rowney, Don.   "Structure, Class and Career: The Problem
       of Bureaucracy and Society in Russia, 1801-1917."
       SOCIAL SCIENCE HISTORY, 6 (1982), 87-110.

       Looks at the policies covering the recruitment and
       assignment of high level personnel as an example of
       the interaction between administration and society.

2011. Seeger, Murray.   "Secrecy about Air Crashes: The Typi-
       cal Response of the Bureaucrats." COMPUTERS AND
       AUTOMATION, 22 (February, 1973), 38.

       On the coverup of air disasters in the USSR.

2012. Shachtman, Max.   THE BUREAUCRATIC REVOLUTION: THE RISE
       OF THE STALINIST STATE. New York: Donald Press, 1962.
       360 pp.

       A collection of essays on the theme that the Stalinist
       regime represented a form of social organization called
       "bureaucratic collectivism." The Soviet bureaucracy is
       a unique form of class exploitation and oppression.
       This new class does not own the means of production but
       rather, in a sense, owns the state itself. For its own
       self-preservation, it cannot afford to permit any form
       of popular political participation.

2013. Silverman, Roger, and Ted Grant.   BUREAUCRATISM OR WORK-
       ER'S POWER? London: Militant, 1975. 52 pp.

2014. Sinel, Allen A. "The Socialization of the Russian Bur-
eaucratic Elite, 1811-1917: Life at the Tsarskoe Selo
Lyceum and the School of Jurisprudence." RUSSIAN HIS-
TORY, 3, Pt. 1 (1976), 1-31.

Describes the role of two schools set up to train
future bureaucrats.

2015. Smith, Gordon B. "Bureaucratic Politics and Public Pol-
icy in the Soviet Union." PUBLIC POLICY AND ADMINIS-
TRAION IN THE SOVIET UNION. Edited by Gordon B.
Smith. New York: Praeger, 1980.

Presents an overview of bureaucratic politics in the
Soviet Union.

2016. Spiro, George. MARXISM AND THE BOLSHEVIK STATE: WORKERS
DEMOCRATIC WORLD GOVERNMENT VERSUS NATIONAL-BUREAUCRA-
TIC 'SOVIET' AND CAPITALIST REGIMES. New York: Red
Star Press, 1951. 1077 pp.

Goes on and on about the betrayal of the revolution
by bureaucrats of any sort.

2017. Sternheimer, Stephen. "Administering Development and
Developing Administration: Organizational Conflict in
the Tsarist Bureaucracy, 1906-1914." CANADIAN-AMER-
ICAN SLAVIC STUDIES, 9 (1975), 277-301.

Uses the Russian case to test some propositions about
what makes the bureaucracy of a nation help or hinder
modernization.

2018. Sternheimer, Stephen. "Soviet Cities: Bureaucratic De-
generation, Bureaucratic Politics, or Urban Management?" PUBLIC POLICY AND ADMINISTRATION IN THE SOV-
IET UNION. Edited by Gordon B. Smith. New York:
Praeger, 1980.

Considers local administration in the Soviet Union
in terms of three models. Local government is a combination of technical and political questions.

2019.   Sternheimer, Stephen. "Administration for Development:
        The Emerging Bureaucratic Elite, 1920-1930." RUSSIAN
        OFFICIALDOM: THE BUREAUCRATIZATION OF RUSSIAN SOCIETY
        FROM THE SEVENTEENTH TO THE TWENTIETH CENTURY. Edited
        by Walter M. Pintner and Don K. Rowney. Chapel Hill,
        N.C.: University of North Carolina Press, 1980.

        Examines the transition from an imperial to the sov-
        iet bureaucracy. While personnel changed rather rapid-
        ly, the character of the old bureaucracy remained large-
        ly untouched.

2020.   Strong, Anna Louise. "The Soviets Fight Bureaucracy."
        AMERICAN MERCURY, 33 (1934), 86-89.

        Describes how the Soviet Union keeps a check on inef-
        fective administration.

2021.   Taubman, William. GOVERNING SOVIET CITIES: BUREAUCRATIC
        POLITICS AND URBAN DEVELOPMENT IN THE USSR. New York:
        Praeger, 1973. 116 pp.

        Considers local government in the USSR as a function
        of bureaucratic politics involving local officials, the
        managers of industrial plants, and the party leadership.
        The plant managers--the "economic notables" of the com-
        munity--have often been able to pursue their goals of
        greater production without much control by the officials
        of the municipality.

2022.   Theen, Rolf H.W. "Party and Bureaucracy." PUBLIC POL-
        ICY AND ADMINISTRATION IN THE SOVIET UNION. Edited
        by Gordon B. Smith. New York: Praeger, 1980.

        Looks at the role of the Communist Party in terms
        of its three basic functions: recruitment, policy mak-
        ing, and the control of administration.

2023.   Torke, Hans J. "Continuity and Change in the Relations
        between Bureaucracy and Society in Russia, 1613-1861."
        CANADIAN-AMERICAN SLAVIC STUDIES, 5 (1971), 457-76.

        Finds the roots of Russian bureaucracy in the decision
        to exclude the nobility from service to the state.

2024. Urban, Michael E. "Bureaucracy, Contradiction, and Id-
          eology in Two Societies." ADMINISTRATION AND SOCIETY.
          10 (1978), 49-85.

          Contends that the doctrine of modern administration
          is an ideology designed to cover up basic contradic-
          tions involved in the conduct of large-scale efforts.
          A review of administrative literature from the U.S. and
          the Soviet Union reveal that, regardless of the myths
          of the social system, the managers approach problems
          in a similar manner.

2025. Urban, Michael E. "Bureaucratic Ideology in the United
          States and the Soviet Union: Some Empirical Dimensi-
          ons." ADMINISTRATION AND SOCIETY, 14 (1982), 139-62.

          Interviews two groups of people in both the U.S. and
          the Soviet Union--the practitioners and the academics
          in public administration--in order to measure the di-
          mensions of the ideology of administration. The data
          indicate that there are differences in outlook in both
          countries between the academics and the practitioners
          of public administration.

2026. Valenla, Jiri. "The Bureaucratic Politics Paradigm and
          the Soviet Invasion of Czechoslovakia." POLITICAL
          SCIENCE QUARTERLY, 94 (1979), 55-76.

          Contends that the rational actor model is not an ade-
          quate explanation of Soviet foreign policy. The Czech
          case indicates that bureaucratic interests and the per-
          spectives of senior leaders were critical factors in
          the decision to invade.

2027. Weissman, Neil B. REFORM IN TSARIST RUSSIA: THE STATE
          BUREAUCRACY AND LOCAL GOVERNMENT, 1900-1914. New
          Brunswick, N.J.: Rutgers University Press, 1981.
          292 pp.

          A case study of local government in pre-revolutionary
          Russia dealing with the attempts at administrative re-
          form. The efforts at reform proposed by the Ministry
          of Interior were aimed at the preservation of the role
          of a strong central bureaucracy. The isolation of the
          bureaucracy from society is emphasized.

2028. Whelan, Heide W. ALEXANDER III AND THE STATE COUNCIL
       BUREAUCRACY AND COUNTER-REFORM IN LATE IMPERIAL RUS-
       SIA. New Brunswick, N.J.: Rutgers University Press,
       1982. 258 pp.

       Examines the efforts to lessen the impact of earlier
       reforms during the reign of Alexander III (1881-1894).
       There were basic inconsistencies in the sources of auto-
       cratic authority and these were represented within the
       bureaucracy, which had become the governing class in
       Russia.

2029. Yaney, George. "Bureaucracy and Freedom: N.M. Korku-
       nov's Theory of the State." AMERICAN HISTORICAL RE-
       VIEW, 71 (1966), 468-86.

       Describes a Russian thinker (1853-1904) who tried to
       reconcile the authoritarian state with individual lib-
       erty. His argument was that administration, and not
       law, was the best guarantee of freedom.

2030. Yaney, George. "Bureaucracy as Culture: A Comment."
       SLAVIC REVIEW, 41 (1982), 104-11.

       Finds fault with those scholars who view Russian or
       Soviet administration as largely goal oriented. Rather,
       administrative action is often determined by a broader
       bureaucratic culture. It is that culture, rather than
       administrative rationality, that is the reality for
       the citizens and officials alike.

IX. BUREAUCRATIC MANAGEMENT

2031. Aiken, Michael, and Samuel B. Bacharach. "The Urban
       System, Politics, and Bureaucratic Structure: A
       Comparative Analysis of 44 Local Governments in Bel-
       gium." ORGANIZATION AND ENVIRONMENT: THEORY, ISSUES,
       AND REALITY. Edited by Lucien Karpik. London: Sage,
       1978.

       Test several hypotheses concerning the relationship
       between environmental factors and the size and admin- ·
       istrative complexity of local government organizations
       in Belgium. It was found, among other things, that
       the size of the city is an important determinant of the
       size of the bureaucracy.

2032. Aiken, Michael, Samuel B. Bacharach, and J. Lawrence
       French. "Organizational Structure, Work Processes,
       and Proposal Making in Administrative Bureaucracies."
       ACADEMY OF MANAGEMENT JOURNAL, 23 (1980), 631–52.

       Study lower level officials in several Belgium mun-
       icipalities to see the effect of structure and process
       on the degree of innovation. The determinants of the
       actor's proposal making depended upon the level of the
       operation.

2033. Ali, Shaukat. "Bureaucratic Leadership: A Theoretical
       Perspective." PAKISTAN ADMINISTRATIVE STAFF COLLEGE
       QUARTERLY, 7 (March–June, 1969), 44–46.

       Notes the lack of a concrete theoretical framework
       for the study of administrative leadership.

2034. Allen, David. BUREAUCRATIC POLITICS: DECISION MAKING
       IN ORGANISATIONS. Manchester: University of Man-
       chester, 1979. 15 pp.

2035. Bacharach, Samuel B., and Michael Aiken. "Communica-
       tions in Administrative Bureaucracy." ACADEMY OF
       MANAGEMENT JOURNAL, 20 (1977), 365-77.

       Measure verbal communication within local government
       units. Organizational variables explain most of the
       differences in the amount of communication.

2036. Bar-Yosef, Rivka, and E.O. Schild. "Pressures and De-
       fenses in Bureaucratic Roles." AMERICAN JOURNAL OF
       SOCIOLOGY, 71 (1966), 665-73.

       Argue that line bureaucrats are under pressure from
       superiors and clients. Two structural mechanisms for
       dealing with this pressure are joint defense and buf-
       fer defense. Without some defense, the bureaucrat may
       react only to the heaviest pressure.

2037. Blair, John P. "Bureaucratic Behavior at Feeding Time."
       BUREAUCRAT, 5 (1977), 459-62.

       On setting salaries in the public organization.

2038. Blau, Peter. THE DYNAMICS OF BUREAUCRACY. Chicago:
       University of Chicago Press, 1955. 269 pp.

       Conducts a study on small groups in formal organiza-
       tions. The members of a state employment agency and a
       federal labor law unit were observed. A dependence on
       hierarchical authority is found to enhance overconform-
       ity and resistence to change. Such tendencies, however,
       were relieved, in some cases, by employment security,
       allegiance to the work group, professional attitudes,
       and organizational goals. The informal adjustments to
       dysfunctional formal rules often permitted the organ-
       ization to function effectively.

2039. Blau, Peter, Wolf V. Heydebrand, and Robert E. Stauffer.
       "The Structure of Small Bureaucracies." AMERICAN
       SOCIOLOGICAL REVIEW, 31 (1966), 179-91.

       Summarize data from 156 public personnel agencies.
       It is found that the existence of a professional staff
       tends to increase the need for management services.

2040. Blau, Peter. "Decentralization in Bureaucracies."
POWER IN ORGANIZATIONS. Edited by M. Zald. Nash-
ville, Tenn.: Vanderbilt University Press, 1970.

The effect of decentralization on the distribution
of power within formal organizations.

2041. Bozeman, Barry. "Organization Design in the Public
Bureaucracy." AMERICAN REVIEW OF PUBLIC ADMINISTRA-
TION, 15 (1981), 107-118.

Discusses the assimilation of organization design concepts from the public sphere into public administration.
Business concepts are not immediately transferable to
all public organizations.

2042. Brix, V.H. "Control, Bureaucracy, and Power." HUMAN
SYSTEMS MANAGEMENT, 2 (1981), 316-21.

Advocates the use of models based on systems and control theory to bridge the gap between the theory and
practice of management. Such an approach would enable
one to reconsider the nature of power within bureaucratic organizations.

2043. Brouillette, John, and E.L. Quarantelli. "Types of
Patterned Variation in Bureaucratic Adaptation to
Organizational Stress." SOCIOLOGICAL INQUIRY, 41
(1971), 39-46.

Dispute the view that organizational adaptation to
change results from informal patterns of interaction
among members. A study of disaster-impacted organizations reveals that there is a definite structure of organizational adaptation.

2044. Burke, W. Warner. "Organizational Development and Bureaucracy in the 1980s." JOURNAL OF APPLIED BEHAVIOR-
AL SCIENCE, 16 (1980), 423-37.

Explores the future of Organization Development (OD).
The method of promoting change has not been favorably
received by public and private organizations.

2045. Carew, Donald K., Sylvia Carter, Janice M. Gamache,
       Rita Hardiman, Bailey W. Jackson, and Eunice M. Par-
       isi. "New York Division for Youth: A Collaborative
       Approach to the Implementation of Structural Change
       in a Public Bureaucracy." JOURNAL OF APPLIED BEHAV-
       IORAL SCIENCE, 13 (1977), 327-40.

       Report on an Organizational Development (OD) applica-
       tion in a public agency. Agency output and staff mor-
       ale were improved by the intervention. The experience
       indicates that a bureaucracy changes when top manage-
       ment is committed and has the proper attitude.

2046. Casburn, Edwin H. "Bureaucracy vs. Shared Decision
       Making." NASSP BULLETIN, 60 (April, 1976), 62-68.

       Says that shared decision making is an art to be prac-
       ticed by administrators.

2047. Coates, Charles H., and Roland J. Pellegrin. "Execu-
       tives and Supervisors: Informal Factors in Differ-
       ential Bureaucratic Promotion." ADMINISTRATIVE SCI-
       ENCE QUARTERLY, 2 (1957), 200-15.

       Investigate the importance of informal factors, such
       as religion, political activity, social standing, and
       hobbies, in promotion within an organization. Differ-
       ences were found in the importance of several of the
       informal factors.

2048. Deutsch, Karl W., and William A. Madow. "A Note on the
       Appearance of Wisdom in Large Bureaucratic Organiza-
       tions." BEHAVIORAL SCIENCE, 6 (1961), 72-78.

       Apply a mathematical formula to determine the prob-
       ability of members with wisdom, that is, the ability
       to make an organizationally correct decision in the ap-
       propriate situation.

2049. Dimock, Marshall. "Bureaucracy Self-Examined." PUB-
       LIC ADMINISTRATION REVIEW, 4 (1944), 197-207.

       Discusses problems of public management.

2050. Dimock, Marshall. ADMINISTRATIVE VITALITY: THE CONFLICT WITH BUREAUCRACY. New York: Harper and Brothers, 1959. 298 pp.

Examines questions of institutional growth and decay. Leadership is needed if the organization is to retain its vitality, while making use of the positive aspects of the bureaucratic structure.

2051. Dubin, Robert. "Technical Characteristics of Bureaucracy." HUMAN RELATIONS IN ADMINISTRATION. Edited by Robert Dubin. New York: Prentice-Hall, 1951.

Describes the basic features of bureaucracy.

2052. Dunsire, Andrew. IMPLEMENTATION IN A BUREAUCRACY. Oxford: Martin Robinson, 1978. 260 pp.

Volume I of a two-part study of the "execution process" in public organizations. It is argued that the process of carrying out decisions can be separated from the actual making of decisions. Structural design, regardless of the incumbents, is the crucial factor. The emphasis can be placed on formal authority and jurisdiction, the nature of the required knowledge, and information processing. A case study of the closing of a British rail line is used to illustrate models of implementation.

2053. Dunsire, Andrew. CONTROL IN A BUREAUCRACY. Oxford: Martin Robinson, 1978. 263 pp.

Volume II of the project on the "execution process."

2054. Dyer, Frederick C., and John M. Dyer. BUREAUCRACY VS. CREATIVITY: THE DILEMMA OF MODERN LEADERSHIP. Coral Gables, Fla.: University of Miami Press, 1965. 153 pp.

Discuss how large organizations can maintain orderly routines while encouraging creativity among its members. Some of the methods for stimulating creative behavior in organizations are mentioned.

2055.   Eccles, Robert. "Bureaucratic versus Craft Administra-
        tion: The Relationship of Market Structure to the Con-
        struction Firm." ADMINISTRATIVE SCIENCE QUARTERLY,
        26 (1981), 449-69.

        Raises questions about the validity of Stinchcombe's
        thesis (Item 2115) that construction firms are based
        on the model of crafts administration.

2056.   Evan, William M., and Morris Zelditch. "A Laboratory
        Experiment on Bureaucratic Authority." AMERICAN SOC-
        IOLOGICAL REVIEW, 26 (1961), 883-93.

        Set up a laboratory experiment to test the relation-
        ship between ability and authority. Authority of know-
        ledge and the authority of office were compared.

2057.   Flemming, Roy B. "Search for Process Theories of Bur-
        eaucratic Innovation." URBAN AFFAIRS QUARTERLY, 16
        (1980), 245-54.

        Review essay on books about bureaucratic innovation.

2058.   Fromm, Erich. "Thoughts on Bureaucracy." MANAGEMENT
        SCIENCE, 16 (1970), B699-B705.

        Argues that the essence of bureaucracy in management
        is the treatment of others as things. A more humanist-
        ic management style is necessary and possible.

2059.   Gannon, Martin, and Frank Paine. "Unity of Command
        and Job Attitudes of Managers in a Bureaucratic Or-
        ganization." JOURNAL OF APPLIED PSYCHOLOGY, 59
        (1974), 392-94.

        Test the attitudes of government employees toward the
        principle of the unity of command. The violation of
        the principle was related to dysfunctional consequences
        for organizations.

2060.   Gerhardt, Uta. "The Emergence of 'Situated Roles' in
        a Bureaucratic Setting: Role Reduction and the Limits

of Social Reform." SOCIOLOGY OF WORK AND OCCUPATIONS, 2 (1975), 257-83.

Compares the formal role requirements with actual job performance in a West German public agency. Much of the formal job specification was not relevant to the performance of the necessary work.

2061. Glueck, William, and David Dennis. "Bureaucratic, Democratic, and Environmental Approaches to Organization
Design." JOURNAL OF MANAGEMENT STUDIES, 9 (1972),
196-205.

Maintain that neither bureaucratic nor democratic structures are appropriate in all managerial situations. Most significantly, the environment (complexity/volatility, size, technology, and personnel) must be taken into account.

2062. Gouldner, Alvin W. PATTERNS OF INDUSTRIAL BUREAUCRACY.
Glencoe, Ill.: Free Press, 1954. 282 pp.

Investigates the operation of an industrial plant in an attempt to resolve some of the ambiguities in the Weberian model of bureaucracy. Bureaucratization occurs at variable intervals within an organization, depending upon a number of internal factors. Three patterns of bureaucracy--mock, representative, and punishment-centered--are identified and described. The enforcement of bureaucratic rules depends upon the attitudes of the subordinates toward power. The rules can be used to increase or decrease organizational tensions. Leadership succession is an important variable in the setting of the mood of an organization.

2063. Gray, Thomas, and Cynthia Roberts-Gray. "Structuring
Bureaucratic Rules to Enhance Compliance." PSYCHO-
LOGICAL REPORTS, 45 (1979), 579-89.

Conduct an experiment with changes in the formal rule structure. The results indicate that bureaucratic rules add to the desire for compliance on the part of members of an organization. Group goals are reinforced through the association with rules.

2064. Grinyer, Peter, and Masoud Yasai-Ardekani. "Strategy,
       Structure, Size and Bureaucracy." ACADEMY OF MANAGE-
       MENT JOURNAL, 24 (1981), 471-86.

       Study British firms to measure the correlations among
       diversification strategy, structure, size and bureau-
       cratization. Strategy and structure seem most likely
       to result in greater bureaucratization.

2065. Grusky, Oscar. "Corporate Size, Bureaucratization, and
       Managerial Succession." AMERICAN JOURNAL OF SOCIO-
       LOGY, 67 (1961), 261-69.

       Compares large and small businesses in terms of the
       frequency of succession in higher offices. Frequency
       of succession was positively related to size. As an
       organization became bigger, the more likely it was that
       the process of succession will be routinized.

2066. Gusfield, Joseph R. "Equalitarianism and Bureaucratic
       Recruitment." ADMINISTRATIVE SCIENCE QUARTERLY, 2
       (1958), 521-41.

       Argues that while the notion of bureaucracy may be
       based on equality of opportunity, the reality of the
       recruitment process is to the contrary. The middle
       class has an advantage in that it is more likely to
       have the attitude and training for a career within the
       bureaucracy.

2067. Halaby, Charles N. "Bureaucratic Promotion Criteria."
       ADMINISTRATIVE SCIENCE QUARTERLY, 23 (1978), 466-
       84.

       Examines data on the role of evaluations, examina-
       tions, and seniority in promotions within public organ-
       izations. Length of service was the most powerful in-
       ternal factor. Promotion criteria are ultimately de-
       termined by extraorganizational factors such as the
       socioeconomic conditions within a region.

2068. Hall, Richard H. "Interorganizational Structural Var-
       iation: Application of the Bureaucratic Model." AD-
       MINISTRATIVE SCIENCE QUARTERLY, 7 (1962), 295-308.

Measures variations in organization structure using a six-factored model of bureaucratization. Bureaucracy is conceived of as a number of dimensions such as the division of labor, the system of rules covering the position, and the existence of a hierarchy. The model is applied to organizations to obtain for each its position on a continuum of more or less bureaucratized.

2069.   Hall, Richard H. "Bureaucracy and Small Organizations." SOCIOLOGY AND SOCIAL RESEARCH, 48 (1963), 38-46.

Asks whether the concept of bureaucracy is useful in the study of small organizations. Such organizations are found to be only slightly less bureaucratic than larger ones.

2070.   Hamilton, Gary G., and N.W. Biggart. "Making the Dilettante an Expert: Personal Staff in Public Bureaucracies." JOURNAL OF APPLIED BEHAVIORAL SCIENCE, 16 (1980), 192-210.

Examine the growth of the personal staffs of political leaders. These groups of professionals are seen as an effective means for amateurs--the politicians--to enhance their power in relation to the bureaucracy.

2071.   Hetzler, Stanley. "Variations in Role-Playing Patterns among Different Echelons of Bureaucratic Leaders." AMERICAN SOCIOLOGICAL REVIEW, 20 (1955), 700-06.

Measures difference in relations with other leaders of officers within the U.S. Air Force.

2072.   Homer, Frederic D., and Garth Massey. "On Being Canned: Personnel Decisions in Democratic Bureaucracies." BUREAUCRAT, 8 (Spring, 1979), 33-39.

Argue that attempts to democratize the personnel decisions of a large organization may lead to anxiety and frustration for the individual. The entire process is seen as more irrational and unpredictable, thus leading to lower morale.

2073. Jennings, Eugene. "How Managers Become Bureaucrats."
       NATION'S BUSINESS, 47 (February, 1959), 38-39, 86-87.

       Advises business leaders to avoid the "civil service
       mentality" among their management cadre.

2074. Jennings, Eugene. THE EXECUTIVE: AUTOCRAT, BUREAUCRAT,
       DEMOCRAT. New York: Harper and Row, 1962. 272 pp.

       Identifies a number of ambiguities in the self-image
       of the modern business leader. The executive has three
       choices of style to use: autocrat, bureaucrat, or demo-
       crat. The bureaucrat is one who handles all responsib-
       ilities according to organizational procedures.

2075. Juran, J.M. BUREAUCRACY: A CHALLENGE OF BETTER MANAGE-
       MENT. New York: Harper and Brothers, 1944. 138 pp.

       Describes bureaucratic inefficiencies in the federal
       government. Better management practices, based on the
       principles of Scientific Management, are suggested.
       Each agency should have an "administrative management
       group" to evaluate the organization's performance and
       to make improvements.

2076. Kumalo, C. "African Elites in Industrial Bureaucracy."
       THE NEW ELITES OF TROPICAL AFRICA. Edited by P.C.
       Lloyd. London: Oxford University Press, 1966.

       Studies 27 Ugandan industrial executives. Their or-
       ientation toward bureaucratic norms such as hierarchy
       and formal rules was somewhat weak.

2077. Landsberger, Henry. "The Horizontal Dimension in Bur-
       eaucracy." ADMINISTRATIVE SCIENCE QUARTERLY, 6 (1961)
       299-332.

       Identifies commonalities in attitudes among people
       on the same managerial level in different organiza-
       tions. Members of middle management in three sep-
       arate companies shared many of the same problems and
       faced the same sort of organizational opponents. Con-
       flict, then, is not necessarily the result of any spec-
       ific company policy.

2078.   Leese, Joseph.   "The Bureaucratic Model's Weakness."
        NASSP BULLETIN, 60 (February, 1976), 90-94.

        Claims that subordinates should not be permitted to
        evaluate their superiors.

2079.   Litwak, Eugene.   "Models of Bureaucracy Which Permit
        Conflict."   AMERICAN JOURNAL OF SOCIOLOGY, 67 (1961),
        177-84.

        Classifies models of bureaucracy as Weberian, human
        relations, or professional.   The latter has become the
        most prevalent today.   There is a need for a model of
        the complex organization which will help to integrate
        conflicting forces within a single structure.

2080.   Litwak, Eugene.   "Technological Innovation and Theoret-
        ical Function of Primary Groups and Bureaucratic
        Structures."   AMERICAN JOURNAL OF SOCIOLOGY, 73 (1968),
        468-81.

        Contends that advanced technology will not eliminate
        either primary groups or bureaucratic tendencies with-
        in organizations.

2081.   Lyden, Fremont.   "Innovation in Bureaucracy?"   PUBLIC
        ADMINISTRATION REVIEW, 29 (1969), 84-85.

        Says that control procedures in organizations seem
        to inhibit innovation.

2082.   Lyden, Fremont.   "Can Bureaucrats Be Creative?"   PUBLIC
        ADMINISTRATION REVIEW, 32 (1972), 255-56.

        Yes, if they work at it.

2083.   Lyden, Fremont.   "How Bureaucracy Responds to Crisis."
        PUBLIC ADMINISTRATION REVIEW, 34 (1974), 597-99.

        A digest of Brouillette and Quarantelli (Item 2043).

2084. McNulty, James E. "Organized Decision-Making: A Pro-
       posal for Studying the Influence of Entrepreneurial
       Aversiveness to Risk-Taking on Bureaucratic Struc-
       ture." NEW PERSPECTIVES IN ORGANIZATION RESEARCH.
       Edited by William Cooper, Harold Leavitt, and M.W.
       Shelly. New York: John WIley, 1964.

       Suggests, but does not conduct, an experiment to test
       the manager's aversion to risk as a factor in the struc-
       ture of the organization.

2085. Maniha, John K. "Organizational Demotion and the Pro-
       cess of Bureaucratization." SOCIAL PROBLEMS, 20
       (1972), 161-73.

       Examines the function of demotion as an organizational
       sanction in the process of bureaucratization.

2086. Maniha, John K. "The Standardization of Elite Careers
       in Bureaucratizing Organizations." SOCIAL FORCES,
       53 (1974), 282-88.

       Defines standardization as the process whereby the
       organization deliberately decreases the level of in-
       ternal social diversity. The concept is used to ana-
       lyze career patterns in a police department.

2087. Maniha, John K. "Universalism and Particularism in
       Bureaucratizing Organizations." ADMINISTRATIVE SCI-
       ENCE QUARTERLY, 20 (1975), 177-90.

       Looks at the effect of seniority and merit as pro-
       motion criteria within a bureaucratic setting. Bur-
       eaucracy has an effect on an organization's mobility
       patterns. Seniority tends to become more important at
       the higher levels as bureaucratization occurs.

2088. Marvick, Dwaine. "Expectations Concerning Power in a
       Bureaucratic Arena." ADMINISTRATIVE SCIENCE QUART-
       ERLY, 2 (1958), 542-49.

       Examines the problem of consensus within work groups
       and program units about power relations.

2089. Meyer, Marshall W. "Two Authority Structures of Bureaucratic Organization." ADMINISTRATIVE SCIENCE
QUARTERLY, 13 (1968), 211-28.

Uses data from 254 public finance offices. Authority
is more highly centralized as the number of organizational sub-units increase.

2090. Meyer, Marshall W. "Automation and Bureaucratic Structure." AMERICAN JOURNAL OF SOCIOLOGY, 74 (1968),
256-64.

Finds that the data processing sections of public
agencies are structurally different than other parts
of the organization. The deviations from classical
organization theory suggest a major point: "as interdependence in an organization increases, non-hierarchical
forms of cooperation and the coordinator's role tend to
emerge." The advance of automation in all organizations
may have a dramatic impact on structural features.

2091. Meyer, Marshall W. BUREAUCRATIC STUCTURE AND AUTHORITY:
COORDINATION AND CONTROL IN 254 GOVERNMENT AGENCIES.
New York: Harper and Row, 1972. 134 pp.

A survey of city, county and state finance offices.
The effect of organizational size and such structural
features as the levels of hierarchy on the system of
internal control is investigated. The impact of comput-
erization is also considered. The data processing unit
of an organization has several unique features. Self-
containment of units in government does not have the
same effect as in business.

2092. Meyer, Marshall W., and Craig Brown. "The Process of
Bureaucratization." AMERICAN JOURNAL OF SOCIOLOGY,
83 (1977), 264-85.

Find that the degree of formalization of personnel
procedures in government agencies is a function of the
era of origin and the further impact of environmental
features. Bureaucratization starts with the organization's response to enviromental pressures.

2093. Meyer, Marshall W. CHANGE IN PUBLIC BUREAUCRACIES.
       London: Cambridge University Press, 1979. 251 pp.

       Reports on data from a study of American finance of-
       fices, in an attempt to measure influences from within
       and from the environment on public organizations. The
       emphasis is on the capacity for survival of public bur-
       eaus. Stable leadership is an important protective de-
       vice for the bureau. Non-market organizations may be
       more vulnerable to environmental forces since they lack
       the justification provided by market criteria.

2094. Michelson, Stephen. "The Working Bureaucrat and the
       Non-Working Bureaucracy." MAKING BUREAUCRACIES WORK.
       Edited by Carol Weiss and Allen H. Barton. Beverly
       Hills, Cal.: Sage, 1980.

       Admits that government employees appear to work hard
       and accomplish little. The reason for this unproduc-
       tive activity may be the faulty conception and design
       of public programs.

2095. Miles, Robert H., and M.M. Petty. "Leader Effective-
       ness in Small Bureaucracies." ACADEMY OF MANAGEMENT
       JOURNAL, 20 (1977), 238-50.

       Test elements of leadership in organizations of small
       size.

2096. Miller, George. "Dimensions of Bureaucracy: A Smallest
       Space Analysis." WESTERN SOCIOLOGICAL REVIEW, 6
       (1975), 20-32.

       Uses spatial analysis to define the dimensions of bur-
       eaucracy within formal organizations.

2097. Murray, V.V., and Allan F. Corenbaum. "Loyalty to Im-
       mediate Superior at Alternate Hierarchical Levels in
       a Bureaucracy." AMERICAN JOURNAL OF SOCIOLOGY, 72
       (1966), 77-85.

       Test for the relationship of loyalty to superiors to
       position in the hierarchy. No difference was found in
       the loyalty to alternate levels of the hierarchy.

2098. Muttalib, M.A. DEMOCRACY, BUREAUCRACY AND TECHNOCRACY: ASSUMPTIONS OF PUBLIC MANAGEMENT THOUGHT. New Delhi: Concept Publishers, 1980. 132 pp.

> Argues that administration has three essential components and consequent administative roles: the political administrator, the generalist administrator, and the technical specialist.

2099. Perrow, Charles. "The Bureaucratic Paradox: The Efficient Organization Centralizes in Order to Decentralize." ORGANIZATION DYNAMICS, 5 (Spring, 1977), 3-14.

> Maintains that managers should concentrate on controlling the premises for decision making. If that can be done, then decentralization is feasible.

2100. Pokorny, Gary, and Steven C. Carter. "Organization Development: One Way to Get Control of Your City Bureaucracy." PUBLIC MANAGEMENT, 60 (September, 1978), 11-13.

> Describe the use of Organization Development (OD) in Sioux City, Iowa. The intervention resulted in personal growth, especially among top managers.

2101. Rehfuss, John, and Debra Furtado. "Bureaucratized Executive Management Reform: The California CEA case." INTERNATIONAL JOURNAL OF PUBLIC ADMINISTRATION, 4 (1982), 381-94.

> Describe the California Career Executive Assignment system. The reform was a forerunner of the federal Senior Executive Service. The CEA has been accepted by officials in the years since its initiation in 1963.

2102. Reimann, Bernard. "On the Dimensions of Bureaucratic Structure: An Empirical Reappraisal." ADMINISTRATIVE SCIENCE QUARTERLY, 18 (1973), 462-76.

> Uses an empirical study of 19 U.S. manufacturing operations to measure aspects of organizational structure.

Decentralization, specialization, and formalization are the major variables. The results suggest that a multidimensional model of bureaucracy is preferable to the traditional Weberian model.

2103.   Rigby, T.H.   "Bureaucratic Politics: An Introduction." PUBLIC ADMINISTRATION (SYDNEY), 32 (1973), 1-21.

Reviews the contributions to organization theory of Gouldner, Dalton, Crozier and Burns and Stalker.

2104.   Rossel, Robert D.   "Autonomy in Bureaucracies." ADMINISTRATIVE SCIENCE QUARTERLY, 16 (1971), 308-14.

Reports on data from nine organizations. Autonomy, defined as a negative attitude toward bureaucracy, was more typical of middle management than other positions. The orientation toward autonomy is seen as a sign of frustration over lower career mobility among those who perceive little chance for further advancement in their organizations.

2105.   Schein, Virginia, and Larry Greiner.   "Can Organization Development Be Fined Tuned to Bureaucracies?"   ORGANIZATION DYNAMICS, 5 (Winter, 1977), 48-61.

Argue that bureaucracy is unlikely to fade away so OD practitioners must adjust to the reality of formal organizations.

2106.   Shaheen, Thomas A., "Choice: Bureaucracy or Curricular Renaissance?" EDUCATIONAL LEADERSHIP, 31 (1974), 492-95.

Suggests that managers must become leaders.

2107.   Sharma, Jitendra, and Jack Rombouts.   "Bureaucracy and Innovation."   JOURNAL OF HUMAN RELATIONS, 20 (1972), 450-58.

Describe the detrimental effects of bureaucracy on efficiency and morale. Changes for the improvement of innovation are suggested.

2108. Sheane, Derek. BEYOND BUREAUCRACY. Bolton: Organisation Research, 1976. 44 pp.

On industrial management.

2109. Shomper, Richard, and Victor Phillips. MANAGEMENT IN BUREAUCRACY. New York: Amacom, 1973. 35 pp.

An American Association of Manufacturer's briefing paper for management training.

2110. Sigelman, Lee. "Bureaucratization and Organization Effectiveness: A Double-Dip Hypothesis." ADMINISTRATION AND SOCIETY, 13 (1981), 251-64.

Advances an explanation to reconcile two contradictory ideas about the impact of bureaucracy on organization performance.

2111. Singer, D.A. "Flexible Bureaucracy." ADULT LEADERSHIP, 24 (1976), 201-02.

A plea for less rigidity in management style.

2112. Smith, Edmund A. "Bureaucratic Organization: Selective or Saturative." ADMINISTRATIVE SCIENCE QUARTERLY, 2 (1957), 361-75.

Compares a public agency, the Catholic Church, and the military. Recruitment into different organizations can be from a single social group (selective) or from the general population (saturative). Each of the organizations seems attractive to a particular personality type.

2113. Smith, Howard R. THE CAPITALIST IMPERATIVE: THE NEW BIOLOGY AND THE OLD BUREAUCRACY. Hicksville, N.Y.: Exposition Press, 1975. 301 pp.

Explores current issues in industrial psychology, with reference to sociobiology.

2114.   Stahl, O. Glenn.   "What a Bureaucrat Thinks about Ex-
        ecutives." JOURNAL OF SOCIAL ISSUES, 1 (December,
        1945), 52-61.

        Stresses the importance of leadership in the perform-
        ance of organizations.

2115.   Stinchcombe, Arthur L.   "Bureaucratic and Craft Admin-
        istration of Production: A Comparative Study." AD-
        MINISTRATIVE SCIENCE QUARTERLY, 4 (1959), 168-87.

        Compares mass production and construction industries
        in order to identify forms of organization other than
        the bureaucratic. The construction industry is charac-
        terized by activity by autonomous sub-contractors, who
        are professional craft workers. In alternative modes,
        status in the labor market rather than status in the
        organization is the source of legitimacy in decisions.
        See Item 2055.

2116.   Taylor, Jack E., and Elizabeth Bertinot.   "An OD Inter-
        vention to Install Participative Management in a Bur-
        eaucratic Organization." TRAINING AND DEVELOPMENT
        JOURNAL, 27 (January, 1973), 18-21.

        Describe the use of management-by-objectives (MBO)
        in Harris County, Texas. The experiment appears to have
        been successful.

2117.   Thompson, Victor A. MODERN ORGANIZATION. New York:
        Alfred A. Knopf, 1961. 197 pp.

        Sees society as dominated by highly rationalized or-
        ganizations. This leads to problems of coordination
        in the face of greater specialization. Bureaucracy
        attempts to integrate this specialization within the
        traditional hierarchy, leading to the "most symptomatic
        characteristics of modern bureaucracy": the growing im-
        balance between ability and authority. "Bureaupatho-
        logical" behavior arises because of the demands from
        the formal authority which conflict with the abilities
        and needs of the individual members. One pathological
        condition is "bureausis," or low tolerance for ration-
        ality and other features of bureaucracy.

2118. Thompson, Victor A. "Bureaucracy and Innovation." AD-
MINISTRATIVE SCIENCE QUARTERLY, 10 (1965), 1-20.

Finds that bureaucratic structures are not conducive
to innovation. Bureaucracy, however, is evolving into
a condition which can promote creativity.

2119. Thompson, Victor A. BUREAUCRACY AND INNOVATION. University of Alabama Press, 1969. 167 pp.

Questions whether greater rationality within organizations can lead to more creative responses to problems. Innovation may be a largely nonrational process.
Despite the dangers, public management is reverting to
rigorous management science. An agenda for research
on organizational innovation is suggested.

2120. Thompson, Victor A. THE DEVELOPMENT OF MODERN BUREAU-
CRACY: TOOLS OUT OF PEOPLE. Morristown, N.J.: General
Learning Press, 1974. 29 pp.

Sees the organization as a tool designed to achieve
certain ends. The job of the manager is to ensure that
members exhibit behavior that leads to unified action.
In this striving for uniformity, power arrangements
give the advantage to management. The informal system
of the organization continues to resist the artificial
system of formal control.

2121. Thorsrud, Einar. "Democratization of Work as a Process
of Change towards Non-Bureaucratic Types of Organization." EUROPEAN CONTRIBUTIONS TO ORGANIZATION THE-
ORY. Edited by Geert Hofsted and Sami Kassen. Amsterdam: Van Gorcum, 1976.

Describes programs desinged to make Norwegian industrial organizations more democratic.

2122. Thorsrud, Einar. "Democracy at Work: Norwegian Experiences with Non-Bureaucratic Forms of Organization."
JOURNAL OF APPLIED BEHAVIORAL SCIENCE, 13 (1977),
410-21.

Looks at worker participation in Norway. The process of introducing industrial democracy is detailed.

2123. Toedtman, James. "Bureaucracy Blues." PERSONNEL JOURNAL, 58 (1979), 742.

Advocates more federal support for research into personnel management.

2124. Udy, Stanley. "'Bureaucratic' Elements in Organization: Some Research Findings." AMERICAN SOCIOLOGICAL REVIEW, 23 (1958), 418-20.

Inquires whether all production organization exhibit similar bureaucratic traits.

2125. Williams, Virgil. "Bureaucratic Proliferation: A Theoretical Approach." AMERICAN JOURNAL OF ECONOMICS AND SOCIOLOGY, 22 (1963), 337-45.

Argues that the creation of new bureaus is a solution to the problem of bureaucratic rigidity. A theory of deviant behavior is applied to organizations.

X. BUREAUCRACY AND THE CONTROL OF KNOWLEDGE

2126. Altheide, David L., and John Johnson. BUREAUCRATIC
        PROPAGANDA. Boston: Allyn and Bacon, 1980. 256 pp.

        Examine bureaucratic communications from the stand-
        point of "impression management." Official reports
        prepared by an organization are not so much a reflec-
        tion of the truth as exercises in dramaturgy. The
        resulting "bureaucratic propaganda" is a major determ-
        inant of the modern view of reality. Examples from
        welfare and the military are used.

2127. Ballew, Van, and Paul Frishkoff. "Bureaucracy and State
        Audit." STATE AUDIT: DEVELOPMENTS IN PUBLIC ACCOUNT-
        ABILITY. Edited by B. Geist. London: Macmillan,
        1981.

        Discuss the evolving nature of the auditing function
        in modern administration.

2128. Barnes, Henry A. "The Language of Bureaucracy." LAN-
        GUAGE IN AMERICA. Edited by Neil Postman, Charles
        Weingartner, and Terence Moran. New York: Pegasus,
        1969.

        On the way bureaucrats abuse the English language.

2129. Beckman, Norman. "The Planner as Bureaucrat." JOUR-
        NAL OF THE AMERICAN INSTITUTE OF PLANNERS, 30 (1964),
        323-27.

        Advises public planners to accept a position that is
        subordinate to political leadership. They must be pre-
        pared to follow the wishes of the public.

2130.   Bennett, James T., and Manuel Johnson. "Paperwork and
         Bureaucracy." ECONOMIC INQUIRY, 17 (1979), 435-51.

         Develop a model to explain the proliferation of paper-
         work. Federal officials find it profitable to pass on
         the cost of administration to the private sector. One
         way to solve this problem would be to compensate the
         private sector for its compliance.

2131.   Broadnax, Walter D. "Zero-Base Budgeting: New Direc-
         tions for the Bureaucracy?" BUREAUCRAT, 6 (1977),
         56-66.

         Describes the new budgeting technique. It may have
         some impact but government remains resistant to exces-
         sive rationalization.

2132.   Brown, Richard H. "Bureaucratic Bathos: Or How to Be
         a Government Consultant without Really Trying." AD-
         MINISTRATION AND SOCIETY, 10 (1979), 477-92.

         Finds that consulting has become a big business, even
         if there are few guidelines about how to do it. Some
         suggestions for government consultants are provided.

2133.   "The Bureaucrat at the Luncheon Table." BUREAUCRAT,
         6 (1977), 121-30.

         An anonymous tale about zero-base budgeting.

2134.   Carley, Michael. "Political and Bureaucratic Dilemmas
         in Social Indicators for Policy Making." SOCIAL IN-
         DICATORS RESEARCH, 9 (1981), 15-33.

         Identifies several important constraints, both pol-
         itical and bureaucratic, on the application of social
         indicators. Means for overcoming these limits are de-
         scribed. Improved policy modeling would cause the most
         improvement.

2135.   Cohen, David K., and Charles Lindblom. "Solving Prob-
         lems of Bureaucracy: Limits on Social Science." AM-
         ERICAN BEHAVIORAL SCIENTIST, 22 (1979), 547-60.

Question the contention that improved information will
solve many of the problems of bureaucracy. It is argued
that the sort of basic knowledge produced and consumed
by large organizations is expensive and necessarily in-
complete.

2136. Daneke, Gregory. "Policy Analysis in Bureaucratic Re-
        form." SOUTHERN REVIEW OF PUBLIC ADMINISTRATION, 1
        (1977), 108-28.

        Considers the potential of policy development and as-
        sessment techniques. The most promising are those which
        attempt to go beyond pure economic considerations. Soc-
        ial indicators is one encouraging device.

2137. Deitschman, Seymour J. "Implementation of New Ideas
        in Bureaucracies." OPERATIONS RESEARCH, 19 (1971),
        989-90.

        Speculates that, in large bureaucracies, the probab-
        ility of a new idea being implemented depends on the
        number of persons in the chain leading up to implemen-
        tation.

2138. Dery, David. "The Bureaucratic Side of Computers: Mem-
        ory, Evocation, and Management Information." OMEGA,
        9 (1981), 25-32.

        Argues that management information systems do not sup-
        port managers because they are not flexible enough to
        cope with unstructured problems. A survey of welfare
        agencies found managers keeping their own records to
        supplement their memories.

2139. Diener, Richard. "Ethics and the Information Special-
        ist in a Bureaucratic Milieu." PROCEEDINGS OF THE
        AMERICAN SOCIETY FOR INFORMATION SCIENCE, 13 (1976),
        131.

        Urges information specialists to pay attention to the
        content of the material they process. There is a moral
        obligation involved here and the specialist is not tot-
        ally neutral.

2140.   Dürr, W.T.   "Information as a Source of Bureaucratic
        Power in the Political Decision-Making Process."   PRO-
        CEEDINGS OF THE AMERICAN SOCIETY FOR INFORMATION SCI-
        ENCE, 15 (1978), 199-22.

        Stresses a still evolving role of bureaucracies as
        gatekeepers for social knowledge.   They have the power
        to create what people will know.

2141.   Dutton, William H., and Kenneth L. Kraemer.   "The Bur-
        eaucratic Politics of Computing."   COMPUTERS AND POL-
        ITICS: HIGH TECHNOLOGY IN AMERICAN LOCAL GOVERNMENTS.
        James N. Danziger, William H. Dutton, Rob Kling, and
        Kenneth L. Kraemer.   New York: Columbia University
        Press, 1982.

        Identify four stages in the development of computer
        technology in local government.   A dynamic and changing
        politics of computing has led to shifts in the power
        within organizations.

2142.   Eisenstadt, S.N.   "Information, Decision Making and Bur-
        eaucratization."   ETHICS IN AN AGE OF PERVASIVE TECH-
        NOLOGY.   Edited by Melvin Kranzberg.   Boulder, Colo.:
        Westview, 1980.

        Points out the perils in the concentration of power
        in the hands of experts.

2143.   Elgin, Duane S., and Robert A. Bushnell.   "The Limits
        to Complexity: Are Bureaucracies Becoming Unmanage-
        able?"   FUTURIST, 11 (1977), 337-49.

        Suggest that organizations can become too big to ac-
        complish their basic missions.   Among the problems of
        size: lack of measurements, the technological impera-
        tive, and responding to the needs of clients.   Large
        organization are also more prone to disruption at key
        points.   The problems are most intense in public or-
        ganizations, but they can also be found in the private
        sector.   Bureaucratic growth takes place in stages,
        with the final stage a period of systems crisis and the
        era of despair.   A number of stragegies for coping with
        this phenomenon are discussed.

2144.   Grossbard, S.   "Closing the Loop: A Critical Assessment
        of the Role of Evaluation in the Federal Bureaucracy."
        JOURNAL OF HEALTH AND HUMAN RESOURCES ADMINISTRATION,
        1 (1979), 538-56.

        Identifies some of the constraints on the use of eval-
        uation in federal organizations, with emphasis on the
        Department of HEW.   Suggestions for improving current
        use of evaluation and assessments are made.

2145.   Hargrove, Erwin.   "The Bureaucratic Politics of Eval-
        uation: A Case Study of the Department of Labor."
        PUBLIC ADMINISTRATION REVIEW, 40 (1980), 150-59.

        Details the attempts of elements within the Depart-
        ment of Labor to evaluate the CETA program.   Attitudes
        toward knowledge will influence bureaucratic behavior.
        Within the organization, the division of labor will
        tend to make any knowledge incomplete.

2146.   Haveman, Joel.   "Taking Up the Tools to Tame the Bureau-
        cracy." NATIONAL JOURNAL, 9 (1977), 514-20.

        On zero-base budgeting and sunset legislation.

2147.   Henry, Nicholas.   "Bureaucracy, Technology and Know-
        ledge Management." PUBLIC ADMINISTRATION REVIEW, 35
        (1975), 572-78.

        Considers the bureaucracy's control of knowledge in
        a technological society.   It is argued that the "bur-
        eaucracy, as a public policymaking institution in a
        technological society, is antithetical to the pluralist
        paradigm of the democratic process originally conceived
        by James Madison and perpetuated by most of his intel-
        lectual progeny in political science departments."

2148.   Holzman, David L.   A CONCEPTUAL FRAMEWORK OF INFORMA-
        TION PROCESSES: A MEANS OF IMPROVING BUREAUCRATIC
        PERFORMANCE. Santa Monica: Rand, 1978.   32 pp.

        Concludes that decision makers often lack the right
        information because of structural distortions within
        organizations.

2149. Laudon, Kenneth C. COMPUTERS AND BUREAUCRATIC REFORM:
       THE POLITICAL FUNCTIONS OF URBAN INFORMATION SYSTEMS.
       New York: John Wiley, 1974.   325 pp.

       Examines the impact of computer applications in four
       state and local governments. The principal use of com-
       puters has been to collect, store and process data in
       the routine operations of government. The conclusion
       is that advanced technology in information processing
       tends to perpetuate the role of the existing bureau-
       cratic arrangements rather than leading to greater or-
       ganizational creativity. There has been little impetus
       to a reconsideration of major public policy questions.
       In fact, computers may make the public more inclined to
       accept the status quo.

2150. Leese, Joseph. "The Bureaucratic Colander." PERSON-
       NEL JOURNAL, 53 (1974), 757-60.

       Studies the extent to which, and in what ways, the
       information is communicated from supervisors to members
       of the work group.

2151. Little, Dennis L. "Thinking the Unthinkable: Or Fore-
       casting the Future in the Federal Bureaucracy." PUB-
       LIC ADMINISTRATION REVIEW, 34 (1974), 78-82.

       A review essay on books about the application of fut-
       urism in the federal government. Forecasting techniques
       are described.

2152. Lively, D. "Government Housekeeping Authority: Bureau-
       cratic Privileges without a Bureaucratic Privilege."
       HARVARD CIVIL RIGHTS LAW REVIEW, 16 (1981), 495-517.

       Examines the "housekeeping authority" of federal
       agencies which enables them to set up internal rules
       for the "custody, use and preservation" of records.
       This authority can be used by officials to deny to cit-
       izens access to documents. The proper scope of the
       government's rights to refuse to present documents or
       allow employees to testify is discussed. The question
       is important in the conduct of trials in which the gov-
       ernment is not a party.

2153. Lutzker, Michael. "Max Weber and the Analysis of Modern
       Bureaucratic Organization: Notes toward a Theory of
       Appraisal." AMERICAN ARCHIVIST, 45 (1982), 119-30.

       Discusses the Weberian model as the basis of a theory
       for archivists. The bureaucracy which produces the
       records handled by archivists is a complex proposition
       and many of the documents are the product of internal
       dynamics rather than a straightforward presentation of
       the official record.

2154. Martin, Margaret E. "Statistical Practice in Bureau-
       cracies." JOURNAL OF THE AMERICAN STATISTICAL ASSOC-
       IATIONS, 76 (1981), 1-8.

       Argues that data collection by government agencies,
       for distribution to others as a product, differs sig-
       nificantly from applying statistics as a science or a
       methodology. Special problems are encountered in bur-
       eaucratic fact gathering and dissemination.

2155. Meltsner, Arnold J. "Bureaucratic Policy Analysis."
       POLICY ANALYSIS, 1 (1975), 115-31.

       Examines the behavior of policy analysts working for
       the federal government. Politics is a part of the use
       of analysis. The present policy analyst is more bureau-
       crat than analyst.

2156. Meltsner, Arnold J. POLICY ANALYSIS IN THE BUREAUCRACY.
       Berkeley: University of California Press, 1976.   310
       pp.

       Describes the reality confronting the policy analyst
       in government. In general, the doing of analysis is
       never as easy as the textbooks make out. Government
       analysts are employed by a specific agency that wants
       analysis to serve specific ends. Analysts can be clas-
       sified as technicians, politicians or entrepreneurs.

2157. Rhodabarger, Dale. "Are They Calling You a Bureaucrat?"
       COMPUTER DECISION, 13 (March, 1981), 66-71.

       Users should not see the EDP unit as bureaucratic.

2158. Rich, Robert. "Use of Social Science Information by
       Federal Bureaucrats: Knowledge for Action versus Know-
       ledge for Understanding." USING SOCIAL RESEARCH FOR
       PUBLIC POLICY MAKING. Edited by Carol Weiss. Lex-
       ington, Mass.: Lexington Books, 1977.

       Discusses the use of public opinion polls by policy
       makers. Although not directly action oriented, such
       data may influence the outcome through impacting the
       way administrators view their goals and the larger soc-
       iety.

2159. Rich, Robert. "Systems of Analysis, Technology Assess-
       ment, and Bureaucratic Power." AMERICAN BEHAVIORAL
       SCIENTIST, 22 (1979), 393-416.

       Argues that the method known as technology assessment
       has been used by the bureaucracy for political reasons.

2160. Rich, Robert. SOCIAL SCIENCE INFORMATION AND PUBLIC
       POLICY MAKING: THE INTERACTION BETWEEN BUREAUCRATIC
       POLITICS AND THE USE OF SURVEY DATA. San Francisco:
       Jossey-Bass, 1981. 205 pp.

       Describes an experiment in applying social science sur-
       vey data to public issues. The use of such data depend-
       ed to a large extent on bureaucratic politics since the
       information was accepted or rejected according to its
       importance in promoting the interests of an agency or
       an individual career.

2161. Rieger, Hans. "Innovations in Bureaucratic Systems."
       INDIAN JOURNAL OF PUBLIC ADMINISTRATION, 16 (1970),
       506-20.

       Sees the information processing aspects of organiza-
       tions as capable of improvement through further automa-
       tion.

2162. Schick, Allen. "A Death in the Bureaucracy: The Demise
       of Federal PPB." PUBLIC ADMINISTRATION REVIEW, 33
       (1973), 146-56.

       Analyzes the failure of planning-programming-budgeting

in the federal government. PPB never penetrated the
routines of government and remained a thing apart from
the form and content of the budget.

2163.   Shuman, Jack N. "Mathematical Model Building and Public
        Policy: The Games Some Bureaucrats Play." TECHNOLOG-
        ICAL FORECASTING AND SOCIAL CHANGE, 9 (1976), 309-34.

        Suggests that formal model building for the making of
        decisions is "an exercise in unreality." Other ap-
        proaches to solving complex social and economic issues
        must be developed. The actions of policymakers during
        the Vietnam War are used to illustrate the point.

2164.   Singer, James W. "It Seems to Be a Bureaucratic Rule--
        When in Doubt, Hire a Consultant." NATIONAL JOURNAL,
        11 (1979), 1932-34.

        On the boom in the consulting business in Washington.

2165.   Stephens, Thomas W. "Bureaucracy, Intelligence, and
        Technology: A Reappraisal." WORLD AFFAIRS, 139
        (1976-77), 231-43.

        Suggests ways of improving the capability of national
        intelligence gathering functions.

2166.   Stockfisch, Jacob A. "The Genesis of Systems Analysis
        within the Bureaucracy." THE CHALLENGE OF SYSTEMS
        ANALYSIS: PUBLIC POLICY AND SOCIAL CHANGE. Edited
        by Grace Kelleher. New York: John Wiley, 1970.

        Examines the "special sociology" of the bureaucracy,
        with emphasis on the Defense Department. Special con-
        trol mechanisms were needed, thus leading to systems
        analysis. The lessons learned in military management
        can be applied to any public organization.

2167.   Stockfisch, Jacob A. "The Bureaucratic Pathology."
        FEDERAL STATISTICS: REPORT OF THE PRESIDENT'S COM-
        MISSION. Washington, D.C: Government Printing Of-
        fice, 1971.

Argues that bureaucratic motivations affect the statistical information processed by government. Bureaus
depend on budgets for their existence and so their information is designed to enhance their position in the
budgetary negotiations.

2168. Sudama, Trevor. "PPBS and Theories of Decision-Making,
       Bureaucracy and Politics." POLITICAL SCIENCE, 29
       (July, 1977), 39-56.

       Reviews the theory of planning-programming-budgeting
       systems. The operation of the systems in both the U.S.
       and Canada is compared.

2169. Viteritti, Joseph P. "Policy Analysis in the Bureau-
       cracy: An Ad Hoc Approach." PUBLIC ADMINISTRATION
       REVIEW, 42 (1982), 466-74.

       Describes the development and operation of a policy
       analysis unit within the New York City school system.
       The unit was ad hoc in that it was temporary and re-
       moved from the daily operations of the bureaucracy.
       Such a unit is able to raise important issues and to
       improve the quality of decision making.

2170. Wade, L.L. "Communications in a Public Bureaucracy:
       Involvement and Performance." JOURNAL OF COMMUNICA-
       TION, 18 (March, 1968), 18-25.

       Finds that, in the U.S. Bureau of the Budget, effec-
       tive performance is related to personal involvement in
       the communications networks.

2171. Wanat, John. "Bureaucratic Politics in the Budget Form-
       ulation Arena." ADMINISTRATION AND SOCIETY, 7 (1975),
       191-212.

       Reports on the "interbureaucratic political process
       of budget formulation in the Labor Department from
       FY 1959 to FY 1968." The agency reacted to external
       obstacles to its programs in the determination of its
       budgetary requests.

XI.   BUREAUCRACY IN BUSINESS

2172.   Bendix, Reinhard.   "Bureaucratization in Industry."
        INDUSTRIAL CONFLICT.   Edited by Arthur Kornhauser,
        Robert Dubin, and Arthur Ross.   New York: McGraw-Hill,
        1954.

        Argues that the traditional entrepreneur has been re-
        placed by the bureaucratic manager, with a drastic mod-
        ification of the ideology of business.

2173.   Bendix, Reinhard.   WORK AND AUTHORITY IN INDUSTRY: ID-
        EOLOGIES OF MANAGEMENT IN THE COURSE OF INDUSTRIALIZA-
        TION.   New York: John Wiley, 1956.   464 pp.

        Seeks to identify the ideologies of management--those
        ideas that justify the subordination of employees to
        the heads of organization within a formal organization.
        Examples of managerial thought are taken from England,
        Russia, and the United States.   The progressive ration-
        alization of the management function is emphasized.

2174.   Black, Paul V.   "Experiment in Bureaucratic Centraliza-
        tion: Employee Blacklisting on the Burlington Rail-
        road, 1877-1892."   BUSINESS HISTORY REVIEW, 51 (1977),
        444-59.

        On the beginnings of centralized supervision of the
        workforce in the railroad industry.

2175.   Bosetzky, Horst.   "Forms of Bureaucratic Organization
        in Public and Industrial Administration."   INTERNA-
        TIONAL STUDIES OF MANAGEMENT AND ORGANIZATIONS, 10
        (Winter, 1980-81), 58-73.

        Questions whether industry is less bureaucratic than

those in the public sphere. The argument is made that
in any society, both government and private organizations develop to the same level of bureaucratization.

2176. Brady, Robert A. "Bureaucracy in Business." JOURNAL
       OF SOCIAL ISSUES, 1 (December, 1945), 32-43.

       Discusses bureaucratic tendencies in business organ-
       izations.

2177. "Bureaucrats Meet Company Brass." BUSINESS WEEK, (May
       22, 1965), 176-78.

       On Brookings Institutions conferences of federal of-
       ficials with corporation leaders.

2178. "Businessman Bureaucrats." BUSINESS WEEK, (May 18,
       1963), 120.

       Business leaders reportedly do not feel that their
       background prepares them for public office.

2179. Dimock, Marshall E., and Howard K. Hyde. BUREAUCRACY
       AND TRUSTEESHIP IN LARGE CORPORATIONS. Washington,
       D.C.: Government Printing Office, 1940. 144 pp.

       Inquire whether large business corporations still
       are capable of efficiency and resiliency. The owner-
       ship of business has become diffused and separated from
       management, with power centralized in the hands of the
       trustees. A number of structural causes of bureaucracy
       in business are discovered. Business leaders are en-
       couraged to recognize the signs of bureaucracy and take
       action to improve management. Such steps will increase
       production as well as maintain a high level or morale
       among employees.

2180. Donavid, J.D. "The Bureaucracy Lives." DUNS REVIEW,
       99 (April, 1972), 93-96.

       A horror tale about red tape in industry.

2181. Dugger, William M. "Corporate Bureaucracy: The Incidence of the Bureaucratic Process." JOURNAL OF ECONOMIC ISSUES, 14 (1980), 399-409.

Inquires whether the Weberian model describes the bureaucratization of the modern corporation.

2182. Gersuny, Carl. "The Honeymoon Industry: Rhetoric and Bureaucratization of Status Passage." FAMILY COORDINATOR, 19 (1970), 260-66.

Maintains that the service sector now administers many formerly intimate aspects of human life. The honeymoon industry is a well organized example. The sales messages of the industry are analyzed.

2183. Goldman, Paul, and Donald Van Houton. "Bureaucracy and Domination: Managerial Strategy in Turn-of-the-Century American Industry." THE INTERNATIONAL YEARBOOK OF ORGANIZATION STUDIES 1979. Edited by David Dunkerley and Graeme Salaman. London: Routledge and Kegan Paul, 1980.

Argue that bureaucratization was pursued by industrialists not simply for its addition to efficient production. It also served to deprive the skilled workers of their power as they were reduced to replaceable cogs in in the system. Bureaucratic arrangements also enhanced the domination by managers.

2184. Gordon, Myron J. "Corporate Bureaucracy, Productivity Gain, and Distribution of Revenue in U.S. Manufacturing, 1947-77." JOURNAL OF POST-KEYNESIAN ECONOMICS, 4 (1982), 483-96.

Speculates on the impact of the absorption of corporate revenue by the bureaucratic staff. The extra money spent on administrative staff does not seem to have been compensated for by any increased productivity of the organization.

2185. Gross, Edwin J. "Bureaucracy, the 'Gatekeeper' Concept and Consumer Innovation." JOURNAL OF RETAILING, 43 (Spring, 1967), 9-16, 64-65.

Examines buyer motivation and behavior in terms of the organizational structure within which they work.

2186.   Halverson, W. Stanton. "How to Manage the Management Bureaucracy." MANAGEMENT REVIEW, 67 (July, 1978), 39-40.

Urges stronger control of executives by a company's board of directors.

2187.   Hathaway, James W. "Insurers Must Fight Bureaucracy." NATIONAL UNDERWRITER, 82 (August 4, 1978), 31, 34-35.

Warns of the dangers of increasing bureaucratization within the insurance industry.

2188.   Hlavacek, James D., and Victor A. Thompson. "Bureaucracy and New Product Innovation." ACADEMY OF MANAGEMENT JOURNAL, 16 (1973), 361-72.

Ask how large organizations can overcome their bureaucratic tendencies and improve their records in product innovation. The concept of the "venture team" is advanced. See Item 2189.

2189.   Hlavacek, James D., and Victor A. Thompson. "Bureaucracy and Venture Failure." ACADEMY OF MANAGEMENT REVIEW, 3 (1978), 242-50.

Examine the reasons for the failure of "venture teams" in the process of product innovation. See Item 2188.

2190.   Kocka, Jürgen. "Family and Bureaucracy in German Industrial Management, 1850-1914: Siemens in Comparative Perspective." BUSINESS HISTORY REVIEW, 45 (1971), 133-56.

Analyzes the development of pre-industrial bureaucratic traditions as an important factor in the early successes of German industry.

2191. Kocka, Jürgen. "Capitalism and Bureaucracy in German Industrialization before 1914." ECONOMIC HISTORY REVIEW, 34 (1981), 453-68.

Explains the reasons for the adoption of bureaucratic managerial systems by the early industrialists. This style adapted from the public sphere seems to have facilitated economic rationality and effectiveness.

2192. Lindo, David. "Coping with Business' Own Bureaucracies." ADMINISTRATIVE MANAGEMENT, 39 (January, 1978), 38-40.

On reorganizations in business.

2193. Livesay, Harold C. "Entrepreneurial Persistence through the Bureaucratic Age." BUSINESS HISTORY REVIEW, 51 (1977), 415-43.

Argues that the individual is still decisive in the operation of business organizations.

2194. Lutchen, Mark. "Protecting the Company from Bureaucratic Slowdown." MANAGEMENT REVIEW, 69 (April, 1980) 41-45.

On bureaucracy in the business world.

2195. McFarland, Dalton. "Whatever Happened to the Efficiency Movement? In Which Some Questions Are Raised about Bureaucracy and the Human Condition." CONFERENCE BOARD RECORD, 13 (June, 1976), 50-55.

Discusses the Scientific Management movement. Today, the human costs of efficiency cannot be ignored and so management must be redefined in more humanistic terms.

2196. Main, Jeremy. "How to Battle Your Own Bureaucracy." FORTUNE, 103 (May 12, 1981), 54-58.

Reports on one company that was able to raise the productivity of its office workers.

2197. Mayer, Caroline E. "For Businessmen in the Bureaucracy,
       Life is No Bed of Roses." U.S. NEWS AND WORLD REPORT,
       85 (June 12, 1978), 56-58.

       On differences between business and government.

2198. Miller, William. "The Business Elites in Business Bur-
       eaucracies: Careers of Top Executives in the Early
       Twentieth Century." MEN IN BUSINESS. Cambridge,
       Mass.: Harvard University Press, 1952.

       Describes how lawyers and other professional types
       became the chief executives of major businesses in
       the U.S.

2199. "Profile of a Bureaucratic Company." HYDROCARBON PRO-
       CESSING, 50 (January, 1971), 143-48.

       Examines how the poorly planned organization struc-
       ture and managerial system caused reduced production.
       The personnel of the company had become a loosely con-
       nected mass of individuals rather than a unit.

2200. Rayner, Derek. "A Battle Won in the War on Paper Bur-
       eaucracy." HARVARD BUSINESS REVIEW, 53 (January-
       February, 1975), 8-14.

       Tells how one firm cut down on the amount of internal
       paperwork.

2201. Sanders, Elizabeth. "Business, Bureaucracy, and the
       Bourgeoisie: The New Deal Legacy." THE POLITICAL
       ECONOMY OF PUBLIC POLICY. Edited by Alan Stone and
       J. Edward Harpham. Beverly Hills, Cal.: Sage, 1982.

       Inquires into the reasons for the rapid increase in
       a "bureaucracy-intensive" approach to the regulation
       of economic affairs during the New Deal. This move
       was endorsed by business, labor, and the middle class.
       In particular, "the federal government nurtured the
       middle-class intelligentsia by providing its members
       with economic security and status and excitement of a
       new mission."

2202.   Seligson, Harry.   "Bureaucracy in Big Business."   GOOD
        GOVERNMENT, 74 (September-October, 1957), 41-44.

        Even business has problems with bureaucratic features.

2203.   Shamier, Boas.   "Between Bureaucracy and Hospitality--
        Some Organizational Characteristics of Hotels."
        JOURNAL OF MANAGEMENT STUDIES, 15 (1978), 285-307.

        Discusses the ambiguities in the world of hotel man-
        agement.

2204.   Wallace, William M.   HOW TO SAVE FREE ENTERPRISE FROM
        BUREAUCRATS, AUTOCRATS, AND TECHNOCRATS.   Homewood,
        Ill.: Dow Jones-Irwin, 1974.   282 pp.

        Argues that the bureaucratic structure is based on
        coercion and fear, thus leading to a number of problems
        in and out of the organization: unemployment, govern-
        ment expansion, loss of efficiency, and alienation.   A
        fraternal model of cooperative effort, drawn from soc-
        iobiology, is discussed as the "unbureaucracy."

2205.   Westerfield, William.   "Bureaucratic Bloat."   CHAIN
        STORE AGE EXECUTIVE, 57 (August, 1981), 14.

        Says retail trade organizations can suffer from bur-
        eaucracy.

XII. CRIMINAL JUSTICE

2206. Bordua, David J., and Albert J. Reiss. "Command, Con-
       trol and Charisma" Reflections on Police Bureaucra-
       cy." AMERICAN JOURNAL OF SOCIOLOGY, 72 (1966), 68-
       76.

       Examine changes in the occupational status of police
       under the pressure of bureaucratization. The command
       structure of the chief has also shifted toward more
       formality.

2207. Brickey, Stephen L., and Dan Miller. "Bureaucratic
       Due Process: An Ethnography of a Traffic Court."
       SOCIAL PROBLEMS, 22 (1975), 689-97.

       Investigate the operation of a traffic court and find
       various routines that stress speed and efficiency in
       the handling of cases. Justice may be impaired by the
       consideration of organizational needs.

2208. Cloyd, Jerald. "The Processing of Misdemeanor Drinking
       Drivers: The Bureaucratization of Arrest, Prosecution
       and Plea Bargaining Situations." SOCIAL FORCES, 56
       (1977), 385-407.

       Argues that the courts have forced the police to be-
       have more formally with the people they arrest.

2209. Dickson, Donald T. "Bureaucracy and Morality: An Or-
       ganizational Perspectives on a Moral Crusade." SOC-
       IAL PROBLEMS, 16 (1968), 143-56.

       Contends that the passage of laws to regulate mari-
       juana was promoted by the Narcotics Bureau in order to
       bolster its position within the federal bureaucracy.

The classification of marijuana users as criminals created a new job for the bureau and justified larger budget requests. In turn, societal attitudes toward the drug were changed as the bureau enforced the law.

2210. Dickson, Donald T. "Narcotics and Marijuana Laws: Two
        Case Studies in Bureaucratic Growth and Survival."
        DRUG ABUSE CONTROL: ADMINISTRATION AND POLITICS. Edited by Richard Rachin and Eugene Czajkoski. Lexington, Mass.: Lexington Books, 1975.

        Argues that the Marijuana Tax Act of 1937 was a survival strategy of the U.S. Narcotics Bureau and its director. The law made more work for the agency and gave it a greater claim to budget increases.

2211. Edwards, Harry T. "A Judge's View on 'Justice, Bureaucracy, and Legal Method.'" MICHIGAN LAW REVIEW, 80
        80 (1981), 259-69.

        A reply to Vining (Item 2236).

2212. Erickson, Richard V. "Police Bureaucracy and Decision-Making: The Function of Discretion in Maintaining the Police System." POLICE, 16 (June, 1972), 59-65.

        Suggests that the dynamics of police discretion can be best understood within the context of a rigid command bureaucracy.

2213. Ferdinand, Theodore. "Criminal Justice: From Colonial Intimacy to Bureaucratic Formality." HANDBOOK OF CONTEMPORARY URBAN LIFE. Edited by David Street and Associates. San Francisco: Jossey-Bass, 1978.

        Discusses the development of American criminal justice as a function of the urbanization process.

2214. Gazell, James A. "State Trial Courts: An Odyssey into a Faltering Bureaucracy." SAN DIEGO LAW REVIEW, 8 (1971), 275-332.

        Court management needs greater scholarly attention.

2215. Gazell, James A. "Indication of Managerial Consciousness in an Urban Judicial Bureaucracy." DENVER LAW REVIEW, 49 (1973), 489-528.

Develops a model of "managerial consciousness" and applies it to state trial judges in San Diego.

2216. Gazell, James A. STATE TRIAL COURTS AS BUREAUCRACIES: A STUDY IN JUDICIAL MANAGEMENT. Port Washington, N.Y.: Dunellen, 1975. 168 pp.

Urges greater attention to the managerial aspects of the American judiciary.

2217. Gross, Soloman. "Bureaucracy and Decision Making Viewed from a Patrol Precinct." POLICE CHIEF, 42 (January, 1975), 59-64.

Examines the dysfunctional results of a rigid organizational structure in police work. Several means of improving police administration are suggested.

2218. Hagan, John. "Criminal Justice in Rural and Urban Communities: A Study in the Bureaucratization of Justice." SOCIAL FORCES, 55 (1977), 597-612.

Measures the effects of urbanization and bureaucratization on judicial sentencing. Data come from the patterns of sentencing of Indians and whites in Canada. Rural jurisdictions tended to sentence Indians more severely.

2219. Heydebrand, Wolf V. "The Context of Public Bureaucracy: An Organizational Analysis of Federal District Courts." LAW AND SOCIETY REVIEW, 11 (1977), 759-821.

Considers the U.S. district court system as a formal organization. As organizations, they must be understood within the context of their environments. The environment generates their workload and otherwise affects the task structure of the courts.

2220.   Higginbotham, Patrick E.   "Bureaucracy--The Carcinoma
        of the Federal Judiciary."   ALABAMA LAW REVIEW, 31
        (1980), 261-72.

        Claims that the judicial branch has become too en-
        cumbered with auxiliary personnel and units.

2221.   Hoffman, Richard B.   "The Bureaucratic Spectre: Newest
        Challenge to the Courts."   JUDICATURE, 66 (August,
        1982), 60-72.

        Argues that the increase in caseload and judicial
        staff has made the courts so complex that the judges
        have been forced to emphasize administration at the ex-
        pense of judicial decision making.   More of the admin-
        istrative function should be delegated to the staff by
        the judges.

2222.   Howton, F.W.   "Bureaucracy, Summary Punishment, and the
        Uniform--Roles of Correction Officers and His [sic]
        Work."   CRIMINOLOGICA, 7 (November, 1969), 59-67.

        Stresses the importance of wearing a uniform for the
        corrections officer.   It creates a sense of membership
        in the group, thus inhibiting the bureaucratization of
        this occupational group.

2223.   Jackson, Bruce.   THE BUREAUCRATIC CRISIS: PUBLIC INSTI-
        TUTIONS--WHOM DO THEY SERVE?   Huntsville, Tex.: Sam
        Houston State University, Institute of Contemporary
        Corrections and the Behavioral Sciences, 1978.   11
        pp.

        Looks at prison administration as an example of the
        displacement of public goals by bureaucratic needs and
        incentives.

2224.   Jerimer, John M., and Leslie J. Berkes.   "Leader Be-
        havior in a Police Command Bureaucracy: A Closer
        Look at the Quasi-Military Model."   ADMINISTRATIVE
        SCIENCE QUARTERLY, 24 (1979), 1-23.

        Evaluate the role of supervision in building morale

in police departments. The bureaucratic leadership role
had few supporters. The leader's attitude toward participation and the variability of the job were better
predictors of job satisfaction. The findings cast some
doubt on the stereotypes of the quasi-military basis
of police organization.

2225. Kinder, Douglas. "Bureaucratic Cold Warrior: Harry J.
Anslinger and Illicit Narcotic Traffic." PACIFIC
HISTORICAL REVIEW, 50 (1981), 169-91.

Argues that the Federal Narcotics Commissioner exploited the anti-communist scare of the 1950s to promote
the interests of his agency. His claim was that the
international communist conspiracy was behind the use
of drugs.

2226. Kingsnorth, Rodney. "Decision-Making in a Parole Bureaucracy." JOURNAL OF RESEARCH IN CRIME AND DELIN-
QUENCY, 6 (1969), 210-18.

Describes the factors that parole agents use in making their decisions. The process is far removed from
an exercise in formal rationality.

2227. Landau, Simcha. "Essential Problems in the Functioning
of the Prison as a Formal-Bureaucratic Organization."
DELINQUENCY AND SOCIETY, 4 (1969), 6-26.

Identifies the limits to the application of the bureaucratic model to prison administration.

2228. Levi, Margaret. BUREAUCRATIC INSURGENCY: THE CASE OF
POLICE UNIONS. Lexington, Mass.: Lexington Books,
1977. 165 pp.

Describes police unionization in New York City, Detroit and Atlanta. The police officers are the insurg-
ents. The spectre of a crisis in urban government is
caused by the agitation of the various unions for no-
thing more than a monetary advantage. There are no
other political implications of the unions in American
urban affairs.

2229. Lindesmith, Alfred R. "The Federal Narcotic Bureau-
       cracy and Drug Policy." JOURNAL OF DRUG ISSUES,
       8 (1978), 157-72.

       Advocates returning the regulation of narcotics to
       the states. The record of the federal agencies in this
       area is not impressive. They have such a reputation
       for lobbying for their own interests that they are in-
       capable of leading significant reforms aimed at solving
       the drug problem.

2230. Litrell, W. Boyd. BUREAUCRATIC JUSTICE: POLICE, PRO-
       SECUTORS, AND PLEA BARGAINING. Beverly Hills, Cal.:
       Sage, 1979. 284 pp.

       Examines the way in which justice has been bureau-
       cratized as the system continues to impose formal cat-
       egorizations upon the people caught up in it. The
       processing of criminal offenders has undergone great
       change. The use of plea bargaining is used as an ex-
       ample of the bureaucratic response to the strains now
       experienced by the system.

2231. McCree, Wade. "Bureaucratic Justice: An Early Warning."
       UNIVERSITY OF PENNSYLVANIA LAW REVIEW, 129 (1981),
       777-97.

       Warns about the increasing bureaucratization of the
       work of the judges.

2232. Murphy, Walter F. "Chief Justice Taft and the Lower
       Court Bureaucracy: A Study in Judicial Administra-
       tion." JOURNAL OF POLITICS, 24 (1962), 453-76.

       Explores the methods by which a chief justice was
       able to influence the administration of lower federal
       courts.

2233. Petrick, Richard. "Bureaucratic Decentralization and
       the Redistricting of Urban Services: The Case of
       Team Policing." POLICY STUDIES JOURNAL, 1 (1981),
       581-95.

       Uses an example of team policing in St. Paul to argue

that there are moderate positions in the debate about the decentralization of urban government. Many of the advantages of decentralization are obtainable without complete community control of services.

2234. Polk, Kenneth. "Social Class and the Bureaucratic Response to Youthful Deviance." HUMBOLDT JOURNAL OF SOCIAL RELATIONS, 1 (1973), 2-7.

Looks at the class bias in the "labeling" mechanisms of bureaucracy.

2235. Skolnick, Jerome, and Richard Woolworth. "Bureaucracy, Information and Social Control: A Study of a Morals Detail." THE POLICE: SIX SOCIOLOGICAL ESSAYS. Edited by David Bordua. New York: John Wiley, 1967.

Examine police enforcement of statutory rape laws, an area in which complaints are reluctantly made by the victims. Police information-gathering techniques are featured. The police ultimately tend to serve a mediating role between the lives of the citizens and the rigors of the law.

2236. Vining, Joseph. "Justice, Bureaucracy, and Legal Method." MICHIGAN LAW REVIEW, 80 (1981), 248-58.

Deplores the bureaucratization of the U.S. Supreme Court, and especially the inferior quality of the written decisions because of the influence of the law clerks. See Item 2211.

XIII. EDUCATION

A. General

2237. Allen, Jack. "Bureaucracy in Education: A Symposium."
      PEABODY JOURNAL OF EDUCATION, 55 (1977), 39-40.

      An introduction to a discussion of the problem.

2238. Anderson, Barry. "Socioeconomic Status of Students and
      School Bureaucratization." EDUCATIONAL ADMINISTRATION
      QUARTERLY, 7 (Spring, 1971), 12-24.

      Finds that schools attended by students of the lower
      class are operated differently in comparison to those
      with a majority of middle-class students. Since the
      bureaucratic system is designed to control behavior,
      the emphasis on rules may have a negative effect on the
      achievement of lower-class students.

2239. Anderson, Barry. "School Bureaucratization and Alien-
      ation from High School." SOCIOLOGY OF EDUCATION, 46
      (1973), 315-34.

      Concludes that a substantial proportion of students
      who perceive their schools as being bureaucratic also
      have a greater sense of alienation.

2240. Anderson, Barry, and Ronald Tissier. "Social Class,
      School Bureaucratization and Educational Aspirations."
      EDUCATIONAL ADMINISTRATION QUARTERLY, 9 (Spring, 1973),
      34-49.

      Suggest a causal relationship between social class,
      school structure and the desire of students to continue
      their education.

2241. Anderson, Barry. "An Application of the Bureaucratic
       Model to the Study of School Administration." JOUR-
       NAL OF EDUCATIONAL ADMINISTRATION, 12 (1974), 63-75.

       Determines that the student perception of bureaucrat-
       ization is related to a sense of alienation from school,
       especially among lower-class students. Student percep-
       tion of bureaucracy is not correlated with that of the
       teaching staff.

2242. Anderson, James G. "Bureaucratic Rules: Bearers of
       Organizational Authority." EDUCATIONAL ADMINISTRA-
       TION QUARTERLY, 2 (1966), 7-34.

       Argues that the structural arrangements as defined
       by the formal rules ensure that organizational behav-
       ior will be consistent with stated goals. However,
       the rules can also be dysfunctional in terms of the
       objectives of the organization. The rules can have
       latent and manifest functions. See Item 2277.

2243. Anderson, James G. "Bureaucratic Rules: A Final Word."
       EDUCATIONAL ADMINISTRATION QUARTERLY, 3 (1967), 7-10.

       A response to the criticisms in Item 2277.

2244. Anderson, James G. "The Teacher: Bureaucrat or Profes-
       sional?" EDUCATIONAL ADMINISTRATION QUARTERLY, 3
       (1967), 291-300.

       On the conflict between the organizational and pro-
       fessional roles of teachers.

2245. Anderson, James G. BUREAUCRACY IN EDUCATION. Balti-
       more: Johns Hopkins Press, 1968. 217 pp.

       Surveys the teaching staffs in public junior high
       schools. Rules are major measures of bureaucratization.
       It is found that the types of rules within a school will
       vary directly with the size of the school. Bureaucra-
       tization is also dependent upon environmental, organiza-
       tional, departmental, and individual variables. The
       socioeconomic status of the community has a bearing on
       the level of bureaucratization of its schools.

2246. Arnstine, Donald. "Freedom and Bureaucracy in the
Schools." FREEDOM, BUREAUCRACY AND SCHOOLING. Edited by Vernon F. Haubrich. Washington, D.C.: Association for Supervision and Curriculum Development,
1971.

Considers the relationship between education and liberty in a free society. Freedom in education is more
than the curriculum and the techniques of teaching; it
is a matter of social and political structure of the
school. Moreover, freedom will not be granted volun-
tarily by the bureaucratic establishment within education. Other groups will have to earn their right to
it through the exercise of power.

2247. Bates, Richard. "Bureaucracy, Professionalism and Knowledge: Structure, Authority, and Control." EDUCATION
RESEARCH AND PERSPECTIVES, 7 (December, 1980), 66-76.

Analyzes the varieties in authority structures within
schools. Professional knowledge is seen as a source of
bureaucratic legitimacy.

2248. Bixler, Paul. "The Librarian--Bureaucrat or Democrat?"
LIBRARY JOURNAL, 79 (1954), 2274-79.

On the appropriate role for the librarian.

2249. Bjork, Robert. "How Useful is the American Educational
Bureaucracy?" PEABODY JOURNAL OF EDUCATION, 55 (1977),
51-55.

Not very, really. The administrative overhead, despite its great size, has not been productive.

2250. Brennan, Barrie. "Principals as Bureaucrats." JOURNAL
OF EDUCATIONAL ADMINISTRATION, 11 (1973), 171-78.

Tests Australian secondary school principals and finds
that their attitudes are largely non-bureaucratic. The
principals tended to take as their administrative model
the role of the leader.

2251.   Bridges, Edwin M.   "Bureaucratic Role and Specializa-
        tion: The Influence of Experience on the Elementary
        Principal."   EDUCATIONAL ADMINISTRATION QUARTERLY,
        1 (Spring, 1965), 19-28.

        Concludes that the bureaucratic role of the principal
        may vary with the scope of the position and the person-
        ity of the incumbent.   Experience is the most important
        determinant of organizational behavior and outlook.

2252.   Brubaker, Dale, and Roland H. Nelson.   CREATIVE SURVIVAL
        IN EDUCATIONAL BUREAUCRACIES.   Berkeley, Cal.: McCut-
        chan Publishers, 1974.   205 pp.

        Argue that teachers must understand the reality of
        the formal organization within which they operate.   Ef-
        fective guidelines for understanding the decision-making
        process are discussed.

2253.   Button, Warren.   "Bureaucracy This, Bureaucracy That."
        URBAN EDUCATION, 7 (1972), 107-08.

        Protests that not all the problems of education are
        caused by this thing people are so eager to call bureau-
        cracy.

2254.   Clark, Ann D.   "Special Education: A Microcosm of Bur-
        eaucracy."   FREEDOM, BUREAUCRACY, AND SCHOOLING.   Ed-
        ited by Vernon F. Haubrich.   Washington, D.C.: Assoc-
        iation for Supervision and Curriculum Development,
        1971.

        Looks at the organization of special educational pro-
        grams for students who deviate intellectually, socially,
        physically, or emotionally.   This new aspect of public
        administration has been dominated by an extensive bur-
        eaucracy from its inception.

2255.   Clark, Geraldine.   "Bureaucracy or Commitment?"   LIB-
        RARY JOURNAL, 95 (1970), 209-10.

        Contends that the school librarian must reach out
        to new clients, especially among minority students and
        the lower class.

2256. Cohen, Louis. "School Size and Head Teacher's Bureaucratic Role Conceptions." EDUCATIONAL REVIEW, 23 (1970), 50-58.

Confirms that the size of the school is related to the bureaucratic role conceptions of the head teachers in the British school system.

2257. Davis, Arthur K. "Defining Bureaucracy." SOCIAL EDUCATION, 8 (1944), 309-11.

Says that teachers have a special responsibility for making students understand the realities of modern society, including bureaucracy.

2258. Dean, Jonathan. "Empty Classrooms: The Bureaucratic Response in New York City." EDUCATION AND URBAN SOCIETY, 13 (1981), 459-85.

Examines how the New York City school system reacted to a decline in enrollments.

2259. Dershimer, Richard A. "Will the Bureaucrats and Engineers Ruin NIE?" PHI DELTA KAPPAN, 53 (1971), 250-51.

Expresses dismay about the type of people who appear to be taking control of the new National Institute of Education.

2260. Dokecki, Paul. "Bureaucratic Schools and Families: Toward a Renegotiation with Policy Implications." PEABODY JOURNAL OF EDUCATION, 55 (1977), 56-62.

Claims that the family is still the "key human development enhancing system in our society." However, families and neighborhoods have been disenfranchised by an educational bureaucracy. Steps must be taken to bring the family back into the process.

2261. Ecklund, Bruce K. "Public Participation, Innovation, and School Bureaucracies." PUBLIC ADMINISTRATION REVIEW, 29 (1969), 218-25.

A review essay on books concerning citizen participation in education.

2262. English, Fenwick. "Matrix Management in Education:
       Breaking Down School Bureaucracy." EDUCATIONAL TECH-
       NOLOGY, 17 (January, 1977), 19-26.

       Offers advice on alternative management styles to
       avoid bureaucratization.

2263. Fantini, Mario D. "On Effecting Change in Educational
       Bureaucracies." EDUCATION AND URBAN SOCIETY, 13
       (1981), 399-416.

       Gives several examples of how change can be brought
       about in large school systems.

2264. Feld, Marcia M. "The Bureaucracy, the Superintendent,
       and Change." EDUCATION AND URBAN SOCIETY, 13 (1981),
       417-44.

       Identifies some of the elements which must be present
       if the educational bureaucracy is to accept recommenda-
       tions for innovation. The role of the superintendent is
       critical.

2265. Fuller, Henry J. "The Bureaucracy of Education." AMER-
       ICAN BIOLOGY TEACHER, 18 (1956), 119-23.

       Claims that potential teachers are not attracted to
       the profession because of their aversion to working in
       a bureaucratic setting.

2266. Furtwengler, Willis. "Energy for the Causes of the
       Creation and Maintenance of Bureaucracies." PEABODY
       JOURNAL OF EDUCATION, 55 (1977), 41-44.

       Argues that bureaucracy, for all its faults, is still
       the best vehicle for the provision of mass education.
       No matter what we do, bureaucracy will remain the es-
       sence of a highly technological society.

2267. Gidney, R.D., and D.A. Lawr. "Bureaucracy vs. Community? The Origins of Bureaucratic Procedures in the Upper Canadian School System." JOURNAL OF SOCIAL HISTORY, 13 (1980), 438-57.

On early Canadian education policy.

2268. Gracey, Harry L. CURRICULUM OR CRAFTSMANSHIP: ELEMENTARY SCHOOL TEACHERS IN A BUREAUCRATIC SETTING. Chicago: University of Chicago Press, 1972. 208 pp.

Examines the organizational structure of an East Coast elementary school and its relationship to the teaching methods of the staff and pupil responses. Most of the teachers were curriculum oriented and were thus part of a pupil-processing bureaucracy. A minority of teachers, however, retained a sense of craftsmanship--they cared for the pupil as a person and as a unique individual, deserving of special attention. The craft approach is becoming harder to maintain in the increasingly bureaucratic educational system.

2269. Hamm, Russell, and Glen Brown. "Educational Bureaucracy: What To Do About It?" CLEARING HOUSE, 53 (September, 1979), 40-43.

Explode a myth or two about bureaucracy.

2270. Hanson, E. Mark. "The Modern Educational Bureaucracy and the Process of Change." EDUCATIONAL ADMINISTRATION QUARTERLY, 11 (Autumn, 1975), 21-36.

Concludes that authority in the modern school is a factor shared by superiors and subordinates. Each is trying to control the other. The result is a balancing act, with each side striving to maintain its own sphere of influence.

2271. Hanson, E. Mark. "The Professional/Bureaucratic Interface: A Case Study." URBAN EDUCATION, 11 (1976), 313-32.

Argues that the mechanisms of bureaucratic control within the modern school are mitigated by professional

norms. An "interacting spheres model" (ISM) best describes the system of educational governance. The
model sees two spheres of authority within the organization. Both teachers and administrators adopt defen-
sive strategies for the protection of their spheres of
influence.

2272.   Hanson, E. Mark. "Beyond the Bureaucratic Model: A
        Study of Power and Autonomy in Educational Decision-
        Making." INTERCHANGE, 7 (February, 1977), 27-38.

        Expands on the Interacting Spheres Model (Item 2371).
        The model stresses the two decision-making systems in
        schools. The model is more accurate than the tradition-
        al bureaucratic model.

2273.   Harper, Dean. "The Growth of Bureaucracy in School Sys-
        tems." JOURNAL OF ECONOMICS AND SOCIOLOGY, 24 (1965)
        261-72.

        Finds that several factors have contibuted to the
        growth of bureaucracy in American schools. These in-
        clude an increase in size and the number of specialized
        programs. Another factor is the decrease in the motiva-
        tion of the staff, requiring the establishment of more
        elaborate patterns of rules.

2274.   Hartley, H.J. "Educational Bureaucracy, Teacher Orien-
        tation, and Selected Criterion Variables." JOURNAL
        OF EDUCATIONAL RESEARCH, 60 (1966), 54-57.

        On a relationship of teacher attitudes toward the
        bureaucratic factors of the organization.

2275.   Haubrich, Vernon F., ed. FREEDOM, BUREAUCRACY, AND
        SCHOOLING. Washington, D.C.: Association for Super-
        vision and Curriculum Development, 1971. 293 pp.

        A collection of essays looking at the problems in-
        herent in the administration of mass education. Edu-
        cation has become one of the largest "industries" in
        the country and the control of all its complex elements
        requires more administration.

2276. Hechinger, Fred M. "Challenge: De-bureaucratizing without De-schooling." PERSPECTIVES ON EDUCATION, 5 (Fall,
1971), 1-4.

   On improvements in education administration.

2277. Hills, Jean. "Some Comment on James G. Anderson's 'Bur-
eacucratic Rule--Bearers of Organizational Authority.'"
EDUCATIONAL ADMINISTRATION QUARTERLY, 2 (1966), 243-
61.

   A critique of Item 2342. See Item 2343.

2278. Hollister, C. David. "School Bureaucratization as a
Reponse to Parent's Demand." URBAN EDUCATION, 14
(1979), 221-35.

   Argues that schools tend to become more bureaucratic
in order to deflect the demands of parents while ap-
pearing to comply with them.

2279. Horn, Roger. "Think Big: The Bad Side of Bureaucracy."
COLLEGE AND RESEARCH LIBRARIAN, 33 (1972), 13-17.

   Claims that librarians tend to expand their operations
to the point where they "lose sight of any objective
for existence except existence itself."

2280. Hoy, Wayne K., Wayne Newland, and Richard Blazovksy.
"Subordinate Loyalty to Superiors, Esprit and Aspects
of Bureaucratic Structure." EDUCATIONAL ADMINISTRA-
TION QUARTERLY, 13 (1977), 71-78.

   Study the relationship of centralization and formalization to loyalty and esprit among the professional
staff of secondary schools. There was a relationship
but it was more complex than originally anticipated.
In fact, the more highly codified the job description,
the higher the sense of esprit among teachers.

2281. Isherwood, Geoffrey, and Wayne K. Hoy. "Bureaucratic
Structure Reconsidered." JOURNAL OF EXPERIMENTAL ED-
UCATION, 41 (Fall, 1972), 47-50.

A survey of teachers reveals that many of them have a dualistic view of organizational control.

2282. Isherwood, Geoffrey, and Wayne K. Hoy. "Bureaucracy, Powerlessness and Teacher Work Values." JOURNAL OF EDUCATIONAL ADMINISTRATION, 11 (1973), 124-38.

Find that professionally oriented teachers experience a greater sense of powerlessness in an authoritarian setting as compared to a collegial one. Conversely, organizationally or socially oriented teachers are most powerless in a collegial setting. Overall, however, the authoritarián setting leads to the highest level of feelings of alienation.

2283. Jain, Tek. "Bureaucracy and Work Motivation: An Empirical Assessment of the Conceptualization of Max Weber and Warren Bennis." ADMINISTRATIVE CHANGE, 4 (1977), 191-212.

Surveys school superintendents to find the motivation for work. The Weberian notion that bureaucracy is itself a motivator was not substantiated.

2284. Johnson, Eldon. "Education: Antidote for Bureaucracy." SCHOOL AND SOCIETY, 60 (December 16, 1944), 385-87.

Argues for post-entry training for administrators.

2285. Katz, Michael B. "The Emergence of Bureaucracy in Urban Education: The Boston Case, 1850-1884." HISTORY OF EDUCATION QUARTERLY, 8 (1968), 155-88, 319-57.

Uses the Boston example to illustrate the separation of education from laymen and its capture by the education profession allied with government.

2286. Katz, Michael B. "From Volunteerism to Bureaucracy in American Education." SOCIOLOGY OF EDUCATION, 44 (1971), 297-332.

On the elimination of the non-professionals from the control of American education.

2287. Katz, Michael B. CLASS, BUREAUCRACY, AND SCHOOLS: THE
       ILLUSION OF EDUCATIONAL CHANGE IN AMERICA. New York:
       Praeger, 1971. 158 pp.

       Contends that the American educational system has long
       been a bureaucracy whose main function is "the creation
       of attitudes that reflect dominant social and industrial
       values." For many years now, the public school system
       has been designed and operated to make the children or-
       derly, industrious, and respectful of authority. The
       school bureaucracy is a tool for controlling social mob-
       ility and keeping the lower class in its place. This
       function of American education can be traced back to
       developments in the 19th century.

2288. Kimbrough, Ralph, and Eugene Todd. "Bureaucratic Organ-
       ization and Educational Change." EDUCATIONAL LEADER-
       SHIP, 25 (1967), 220-29.

       Argues that a more open structure will encourage an
       attitude of inquiry, even though some control remains
       necessary.

2289. Kirp, David L. "Proceduralism and Bureaucracy: Due Pro-
       cess in the School Setting." STANFORD LAW REVIEW, 28
       (1976), 841-76.

       Focuses on the consequences of applying traditional
       due process standards, especially formal adversary
       hearings, to the public schools.

2290. Kliebard, Herbert M. "Bureaucracy and Curriculum The-
       ory." FREEDOM, BUREAUCRACY, AND SCHOOLING. Edited
       by Vernon F. Haubrich. Washington, D.C.: Association
       for Supervision and Curriculum Development, 1971.

       Claims that manufacturing concepts and Scientific
       Management influenced the American educational process.
       The curriculum was designed to produce a standard out-
       put. Schools were viewed as factories to transform
       a raw material into socially useful products. This
       bureaucratic model threatens to destroy intellectual
       curiosity in the name of efficiency, while the pro-
       duction metaphor means dehumanization of education.

2291. Kuhlman, Edward L., and Wayne K. Hoy. "The Socializa-
       tion of Professionals into Bureaucracies: The Begin-
       ning Teacher in the School." JOURNAL OF EDUCATIONAL
       ADMINISTRATION, 12 (October, 1974), 18-27.

       Find that the experiences of new teachers lead to
       greater bureaucratic and less professional orientations.
       There was little indication of a dual orientation which
       would allow the interpenetration of the two cultures.

2292. Levesque, George. "White Bureaucracy, Black Community:
       The Contest over Local Control of Education in Ante-
       bellum Boston." JOURNAL OF EDUCATION THOUGHT, 11
       (August, 1977), 140-55.

       Describes the history of early school desegregation
       in Boston in the 1840s.

2293. Levine, Daniel. "Concepts of Bureaucracy in Urban
       School Reform." PHI DELTA KAPPAN, 52 (1971), 329-
       33.

       Urges school reform stressing the cooperation of the
       clients rather than traditional bureaucratic authority.
       Decision making authority should be shared with members
       of the community.

2294. Lind, Loren. "The Rise of Bureaucracy in Ontario
       Schools." THIS MAGAZINE IS ABOUT SCHOOLS, 6 (Summer,
       1972), 104-19.

       An example from Canada.

2295. Louis, Karen. "Dissemination of Information from Cen-
       tralized Bureaucracies to Local Schools: The Role
       of the Linking Agent." HUMAN RELATIONS, 30 (1977),
       25-42.

       Examines the conditions under which the dissemination
       and application of research by local school personnel
       can be improved. A model of the "linking agent" is
       proposed. This mechanism would operate out of a cen-
       tral office and help local teachers with new material.

2296. Louis, Karen, and Sam Sieber. BUREAUCRACY AND THE DIS-
PERSED ORGANIZATION: THE EDUCATIONAL EXTENSION EXPER-
IMENT. Norwood, N.J.: Ablex Publications, 1979. 249
pp.

Describe an organizational innovation intended to improve the use of new information by local teachers. The
creation of an educational extension agent is analyzed.
The result was a hybrid organization, with the agent operating without many constraints within a highly bureaucratic central organization. That dispersed organization is a method of getting around some of the problems
of excessive bureaucratization.

2297. Luebbering, Ken. "The Emergence of Bureaucracy: The
Missouri School Law of 1853." MISSOURI HISTORICAL
REVIEW, 74 (1980), 300-22.

Uses the thesis of Michael Katz (Item 2287) to show
how the 1853 law deprived local schools of authority
and led to a centralized bureaucracy dominated by a
professional group.

2298. Lynch, Beverly. "Libraries as Bureaucracies." LIBRARY
TRENDS, 27 (1979), 259-67.

States that libraries have to be bureaucratic in order
to control their environment and not because of the in-
nate pettiness of the librarians.

2299. McCorry, Jeese J. MARCUS FOSTER AND THE OAKLAND PUBLIC
SCHOOLS: LEADERSHIP IN AN URBAN BUREAUCRACY. Berkeley:
University of California Press, 1978. 163 pp.

Details the successes and failures of a black superintendent of schools in a large urban system. Among
his accomplishments was parent participation, although
the long-range impact of this change on staff routines
is questionable.

2300. Mackay, D.A. "Research on Bureaucracy in Schools: The
Unfolding Strategy." JOURNAL OF EDUCATIONAL ADMINIS-
TRATION, 7 (1969), 37-44.

Discusses several approaches to organization theory, including classical and modern approaches. Education research needs to adopt more fluid theories.

2301. Marjoribanks, Kevin. "Bureaucratic Structure in Schools and Its Relationship to Dogmatic Leadership." JOURNAL OF EDUCATIONAL RESEARCH, 63 (1970), 355-57.

Applies the Rokeach Attitude Scale to 50 elementary school principals and relates the scores on the level of dogmatism to the level of bureaucracy in the schools. Overall, there seems to be little correlation between the two factors.

2302. Marjoribanks, Keven. "Bureaucratic Orientations, Autonomy, and the Professional Attitudes of Teachers." JOURNAL OF EDUCATIONAL ADMINISTRATION, 15 (1977), 104-13.

Finds that the relationship of bureaucracy to professionalism is complex but the organization and professional attitudes are not necessarily incompatible. In conclusion, "bureaucratic orientations and professional attitudes need not be in conflict if schools increase the autonomy allowed teachers."

2303. Meyer, John W., David Tyack, Joane Nagel, and Audri Gordon. "Public Education as Nation-Building in America: Enrollments and Bureaucratization in the American States, 1870-1930." AMERICAN JOURNAL OF SOCIOLOGY, 85 (1979), 591-613.

Argue that industrialization and bureaucratization were not prime factors in public education since, at the outset of the movement, most of the country was rural. Instead, the best explanation for the push for education is a combination of religious and political considerations.

2304. Michaelson, Jacob B. "Revision, Bureaucracy, and School Reform: A Critique of Katz." SCHOOL REVIEW, 85 (1977) 229-46

A critical review of Katz, Item 2287.

2305. Miskel, Cecil, and Ed Gerhardt. "Perceived Bureaucracy, Teacher Conflict, Central Life Interests, Volunteerism, and Job Satisfaction." JOURNAL OF EDUCATIONAL ADMINISTRATION, 12 (1974), 84-97.

Study the extent to which conflicts within schools are the result of a professional-bureaucratic tension. Teachers tend to define the proper administrative role as a matter of coordination and not direction. Administrators thus need to reduce the sharpness of authority in professional settings.

2306. Moeller, Gerald. "Bureaucracy and Teacher's Sense of Power." ADMINISTRATOR'S NOTEBOOK, 11 (November, 1962), 1-4.

Finds that bureaucracy provides a stable environment for teachers within which they can seek personally acceptable levels of power.

2307. Moeller, Gerald, and W.W. Charters. "Relations of Bureaucratization to Sense of Power among Teachers." ADMINISTRATIVE SCIENCE QUARTERLY, 10 (1966), 444-65.

Measure the sense of power and relation to the degree of bureaucratization within the school. Contrary to expectations, the sense of power was greater in the highly bureaucratized organizations.

2308. Murphy, Jerome T. "Title V of ESEA: The Impact of Discretionary Funds on State Education Bureaucracies." SOCIAL PROGRAM IMPLEMENTATION. Edited by Walter Williams and Richard Elmore. New York: Academic Press, 1976.

Investigate the behavior of administrators in the relationship with other organizations within a federally funded program.

2309. Neve, Brian. "Bureaucracy and Politics in Local Government: The Role of Local Authority Education Officers." PUBLIC ADMINISTRATION, 55 (1977), 291-303.

Looks at the impact of local participation in education, especially in terms of the power of the chief
education officer in the community. Such local administrators will have great influence in shaping the direction of local politics.

2310. Newberg, Norman A., and Richard H. De Lone. "The Bur-
       eaucratic Milieu." EDUCATION AND URBAN SOCIETY, 13
       (1981), 445-58.

       Examine how the constraints imposed by school bureau-
       cracy can be overcome.

2311. Pellicano, Roy R. "Teacher Unionism and Bureaucracy:
       A Case Study." EDUCATIONAL FORUM, 44 (1980), 304-19.

       Concentrates on the conflict between unionized teach-
       ers and school administrators.

2312. Praetz, Helen. "The Birth of a Bureaucracy: The Victor-
       ian Catholic Education Office." AUSTRALIAN AND NEW
       ZEALAND JOURNAL OF SOCIOLOGY, 16 (July, 1980), 20-24.

       Describes how, within a short period, parochial edu-
       cation came to resemble the Weberian model of bureau-
       cracy.

2313. Punch, Keith F. "Interschool Variation in Bureaucrat-
       ization." JOURNAL OF EDUCATIONAL ADMINISTRATION, 8
       (1970), 124-34.

       Studies some variations in bureaucratic structure in
       public schools. Leader behavior is found to be the
       single biggest determinant of the level of bureaucrat-
       ization. The size of the school was inversely related
       to bureaucracy. It is would seem to be true that "as
       goes the principal, so goes the school." Bureaucratic
       leaders will create bureacratic organizations.

2314. Pusey, Michael. DYNAMICS OF BUREAUCRACY: A CASE ANA-
       LYSIS IN EDUCATION. New York: John Wiley, 1976.
       160 pp.

Discusses in great detail the recommendations made by the Tasmanian Education Department. Many of the recommendations have since been adopted.

2315. Rees, Richard. "Caution: Bureaucracy Ahead." CONTEMPORARY EDUCATION, 46 (1975), 140-42.

Warns of increased formalization as teachers become more unionized.

2316. Rogers, David. 110 LIVINGSTON STREET: POLITICS AND BUREAUCRACY IN THE NEW YORK CITY SCHOOL SYSTEM. New York: Random House, 1968. 584 pp.

Describes the attempts to achieve desegregation within the New York City school system. The interest groups involved with the issue had varying degrees of access to the system. Generally, the bureaucratic structure was more responsive to anti-desegregation forces and the professionals delayed the implementation of policy mandates from political leadership. This indicates the power of bureaucrats to veto policy directives.

2317. Rogers, David. "New York City Schools: A Sick Bureaucracy." SATURDAY REVIEW OF LITERATURE, (July 20, 1968), 47-49.

A version of Item 2316.

2318. Russell, James W. "Adult Education and Bureaucratic Proneness." ADULT LEADERSHIP, 10 (1962), 290.

Adult education can lessen bureaucracy.

2319. Schlechty, Philip C., and Ann Turnbull. "Bureaucracy or Professionalism: Implications of P.L. 94-142 for Teacher Education." JOURNAL OF TEACHER EDUCATION, 29 (November-December, 1978), 34-38.

State that the new law will enhance bureaucracy at the same time that it decreases the traditional autonomy of the classroom teacher.

2320. Sergiovanni, Thomas J. "Rational, Bureaucratic, Col-
       legial, and Political Views of the Principal's Role."
       THEORY INTO PRACTICE, 18 (1979), 12-20.

       Summarizes in table form the four major leadership
       models.

2321. Shapiro, Lillian. "Bureaucracy and the School Library."
       SCHOOL LIBRARY JOURNAL, 20 (1973), 1346-51.

       Librarians must guard against being bureaucratic.

2322. Shaw, Archibald. "Banish the Bureaucrat." EDUCATIONAL
       EXECUTIVE'S OVERVIEW, 3 (July, 1962), 9.

       Uplifting words for the principal.

2323. Sidnell, Michael. "Towards Bureaupolitocracy." JOUR-
       NAL OF CANADIAN STUDIES, 7 (May, 1972), 3-18.

       Criticizes the recommendations of an Ontario govern-
       ment study commission on education.

2324. Smith, Joan K. "Educational Innovations and Institu-
       tional Bureaucracy." JOURNAL OF THOUGHT, 9 (1974),
       219-27.

       Argues that federal education officials have under-
       mined innovative approaches to education such as per-
       formance contracting and experimental schools.

2325. Sousa, David, and Wayne K. Hoy. "Bureaucratic Struc-
       tures in Schools: A Refinement and Synthesis in Mea-
       surement." EDUCATIONAL ADMINISTRATION QUARTERLY, 17
       (Fall, 1981), 21-39.

       Apply several suggested measures of bureaucracy to
       55 secondary schools. A synthesis of the results led
       to the identification of the four underlying dimensions
       of school organization: organizational control, ration-
       al specialization, formalization of routines, and sys-
       tem centralization.

2326. Sproull, Lee, Stephen Weiner, and David Wolf. ORGAN-
IZING AN ANARCHY: BELIEF, BUREAUCRACY, AND POLITICS
IN THE NATIONAL INSTITUTE OF EDUCATION. Chicago:
University of Chicago Press, 1978. 282 pp.

Study the early rocky years of NIE. As an agency dominated by enthusiasts, it was hard for members to adjust
to policy failures. Solutions to problems were sought
in a series of reorganizations, with little success. A
more realistic perception of the mission of the agency
eventually filtered through the belief system of the organization. Learning about needed corrective action was
then possible.

2327. Staaf, Robert J. "The Growth of the Educational Bureaucracy: Do Teachers Make a Difference?" BUDGETS AND
BUREAUCRATS: THE SOURCES OF GOVERNMENT GROWTH. Edited by Thomas E. Borcherding. Durham, N.C.: Duke
University Press, 1977. 291 pp.

Takes the absence of competition in the schools as
a major factor in the growing salaries of educational
personnel, especially those in administration. The
general public has little information about schools
and their output; neither does it have strong incentives to enforce restraint on the members of the educational system.

2328. Stamp, Robert M. "The Response to Urban Growth: The
Bureaucratization of Public Education in Calgary,
1884-1914." JOURNAL OF EDUCATION THOUGHT, 19 (1976),
49-61.

About conditions in pioneer days in Canada.

2329. Tesconi, Charles, and Van Cleve Morris. THE ANTI-MAN
CULTURE: BUREAUTECHNOCRACY AND THE SCHOOLS. Urbana:
University of Illinois Press, 1972. 232 pp.

Define bureautechnocracy as the new sociocultural
milieu. The defects of the school system are traced
to its central role in maintaining the new view of the
world. A more humane philosophy is proposed.

2330. Thomas, A. Ross. "Innovation within a Bureaucratic
       Education System." JOURNAL OF EDUCATIONAL ADMINIS-
       TRATION, 6 (1968), 116-31; 7 (1969), 20-36.

       Measures the extent and direction of innovation with-
       in the Australian education system. Upward movement
       is noted in the rate of innovation. New leadership also
       tends to stimulate change. Innovation is least likely
       to take place because of the decisions of centralized
       offices.

2331. Thomas, Norman C. "Bureaucratic-Congressional Inter-
       action and the Politics of Education." JOURNAL OF
       COMPARATIVE ADMINISTRATION, 2 (1970), 52-80.

       Examines the centrality of administrative agencies
       in policy making, using the analysis of communication
       in the educational subsystem as a case.

2332. Toma, Eugenia F. "Bureaucratic Structures and Educa-
       tional Spending." SOUTHERN ECONOMIC JOURNAL, 47
       (1981), 640-54.

       Examines the impact of state departments of education
       on the level of financing for education.

2333. Tyack, David. "Bureaucracy and the Common School: The
       Example of Portland, Oregon, 1851-1913." AMERICAN
       QUARTERLY, 19 (1967), 475-98.

       Describes the challenge to formalism by an Oregon
       school reformer.

2334. Willers, Jack. "A Philosophical Perspective of Bureau-
       cracy." PEABODY JOURNAL OF EDUCATION, 55 (1977).
       45-50.

       Asks how an environment based on rigidity can foster
       growth and creativity. Perhaps it is true that edu-
       cation is supposed to produce compliance with bureau-
       cratic authority. Bureaucracy in any case is not an
       ethically neutral concept; rather it brings to any sit-
       uation a powerful set of values.

2335. Winter, Richard. "Keeping Files: Aspects of Bureaucra-
cy and Education." EXPLORATIONS IN THE POLITICS OF
SCHOOL KNOWLEDGE. Edited by Geoff Whitty and Michael
Young. Nafferton: Nafferton Books, 1976.

Looks at how school files on students facilitate the
process of bureaucratization.

2336. Wise, Arthur E. LEGISLATED LEARNING: THE BUREAUCRATIZA-
TION OF THE AMERICAN CLASSROOM. Berkeley: University
of California Press, 1979. 219 pp.

Argues that increased demands by state and federal
governments for accountability and greater productivity
in the public schools has led to counterproductive moves
to rationalize education. The proliferation of regulations and of quantification thus results in an emphasis
on formal outcomes. The mandated changes reduce the
role of teachers and community leadership. It probably
also reduces the actual quality of education.

2337. Yudof, Mark. "Procedural Fairness and Substantive Justice: Due Process, Bureaucracy, and the Public
Schools." FUTURE TRENDS IN EDUCATION POLICY. Edited
by Jane Newitt. Lexington, Mass.: Lexington Books,
1979.

Speculates about the future of the legalization of
the rights of students and parents. There must be some
balance between legal prescriptions and less formal
means of social control. Such a balance is not now in
sight.

B. Higher Education

2338. Anderson, G. Lester. "Bureaucracy, Idiosyncrasy, Tol-
erability, and Academic Personnel Administration."
JOURNAL OF THE COLLEGE AND UNIVERSITY PERSONNEL AS-
SOCIATION, 24 (Summer, 1973), 32-44.

On major administrative aspects of the conduct of the
personnel function in higher education.

2339. Artandi, Susan. "Big University--Humane or Bureaucra-
       tic?" SCIENCE, 191 (1976), 1129.

       Sees higher education at a crossroads. It could be-
       come a machine for cranking out graduates.

2340. Blank, Blance. "Bureaucracy or Democracy: Which Is
       the Enemy in Campus Confrontations? AAUP BULLETIN,
       55 (1969), 257-58.

       On student disorders of the 1960s.

2341. Conant, Miriam. "The Academic Dean as Subversive Bur-
       eaucrat." EDUCATIONAL RECORD, 48 (1967), 276-84.

       Describes the dean as an administrator who must main-
       tain order while stimulating creative thought.

2342. Daalder, Hans, and Edward Shils, eds. UNIVERSITIES,
       POLITICIANS AND BUREAUCRATS: EUROPE AND THE UNITED
       STATES. New York: Cambridge University Press, 1982.
       520 pp.

       A collection of essays concentrating on the increas-
       ing involvement of government in higher education. The
       period covered begins with the student agitation of the
       1960s.

2343. Dufty, N.F. "Bureaucracy in a College of Advanced Edu-
       cation." JOURNAL OF EDUCATIONAL ADMINISTRATION, 12
       (October, 1974), 123-34.

       Reports on the attitudes of Australian college teach-
       ers toward the bureaucratic aspects of their schools.

2344. Finn, Chester E. SCHOLARS, DOLLARS, AND BUREAUCRATS.
       Washington, D.C.: Brookings Institutions, 1978. 238
       pp.

       Examines the rather piecemeal fashion in which the
       federal government has become involved in higher edu-
       cation. Despite the large dollar amounts involved,
       there is no central direction.

2345. Friedman, Milton. "Bureaucracy Scorned." NEWSWEEK, 86
       (December 29, 1975), 47.

       On federal aid to education.

2346. Henry, Nicholas, ed. "Innovating the Academic Bureau-
       cracy." JOURNAL OF RESEARCH AND DEVELOPMENT IN EDU-
       CATION, 6 (1972), 1-116.

       A special issue on the question of bureaucracy in
       higher education.

2347. Hoebel, E. Adamson. "The University as Bureaucracy."
       SYSTEMS OF POLITICAL CONTROL AND BUREAUCRACY IN HUMAN
       SOCIETIES. Edited by Verne F. Ray. Seattle: American
       Ethnological Society, 1958.

       Looks at university governance from an anthropological
       perspective. College administration is threatened by
       non-academic managers.

2348. Jacobson, Lewis A. "The Insolence of Office, or My War
       with the Bureaucrats." COLLEGE AND UNIVERSITY, 41
       (1965-1966), 353-55.

       An episode in the life of a college administrator.

2349. McGrath, Earl J. "Bureaucracy in Higher Education."
       JOURNAL OF SOCIAL ISSUES, 1 (December, 1945), 44-51.

       On the postwar problems of higher education.

2350. MacIntyre, Alasdair. "Bureaucratising a University."
       OXFORD REVIEW, 3 (1966), 67-71.

       A critical look at some proposals for the reform of
       administration at Oxford.

2351. Page, Charles. "Bureaucracy and Higher Education."
       JOURNAL OF GENERAL EDUCATION, 5 (1951), 91-100.

       On the growth of administration in the colleges.

2352. Rehder, Robert R. "The Bureaucratic Drift in the Gov-
       ernance of Higher Education: Insights from Organiza-
       tion Theory." EDUCATIONAL TECHNOLOGY, 19 (July, 1979)
       7-15.

       Argues that organization theory indicates that bureau-
       cratization will be dysfunctional in reaching university
       and college goals. The mission of the academy cannot
       be managed in a traditional manner.

2353. Roche, George. "Bureaucracy versus the Private Sector:
       What Sort of Society?" VITAL SPEECHES OF THE DAY,
       42 (1976), 265-68.

       Denounces the IRS treatment of tax exempt status for
       colleges as well as a number of other indignities im-
       posed on higher education by the federal government.

2354. Seabury, Paul, ed. BUREAUCRATS AND BRAINPOWER: GOVERN-
       MENT REGULATION OF UNIVERSITIES. San Francisco: In-
       stitute for Contemporary Studies, 1979. 171 pp.

       A collection of original essays on the threat of gov-
       ernment interference to the autonomy and integrity of
       higher education.

2355. Simpson, George. "Bureaucracy, Standardization, and
       Liberal Arts: Evidence of Mass Production in Higher
       Education." JOURNAL OF HIGHER EDUCATION, 20 (March,
       1949), 129-36.

       Warns that "higher education has become part and par-
       cel of that social process which is its very business
       to transvaluate, criticize, and establish on sound lib-
       eral principles." The liberal arts must avoid assembly
       line techniques and continue to teach students about
       what is happening to their society.

2356. Stroup, Herbert. BUREAUCRACY IN HIGHER EDUCATION.
       New York: Free Press, 1966. 242 pp.

       Considers American higher education in terms of the
       theory of bureaucratization.

2357. Sullivan, Timothy. "The Education Bureaucracy's Credibility Gap." SOUTHWESTERN JOURNAL OF PHILOSOPHY, 3 (Winter, 1972), 85-91.

Argues that universities face a crisis because of their dual nature. They are supposed to turn out highly trained technocrats for employment in a business society. At the same time, they are engaged in a search for truth.

2358. Wilson, H.T. "Academic Bureaucracy." QUEEN'S QUARTERLY, 78 (1971), 343-52.

Looks at the modern university as a bureaucracy. Improvement might come through the recreation of closer primary group relationships within the institution.

XIV. THE ENVIRONMENT

2359. Andrews, Richard. "Environment and Bureaucracy: Pro-
gress and Prognosis." JOURNAL OF ENVIRONMENTAL EDU-
CATION, 6 (1974), 1-6.

Assesses the impact of the National Environmental Policy Act (NEPA) of 1969. This act was designed to increase the awareness of federal administrators about
environmental problems. Any change in agency behavior
since 1969 is best explained in terms of outside pressures.

2360. Baden, John, and Rodney D. Fort. "Natural Resources
and Bureaucratic Predators." POLICY REVIEW, 11
(1980), 68-81.

Look at the administration of natural resources in
terms of the "logic of bureaucratic irrationality."
A system of incentives--bureaucratic predators--is suggested as a way of improving agency decision making.

2361. Baden, John, and Richard L. Stroup, eds. BUREAUCRACY
VS. ENVIRONMENT: THE ENVIRONMENTAL COSTS OF BUREAU-
CRATIC GOVERNANCE. Ann Arbor: University of Michigan
Press, 1981. 238 pp.

A collection of original essays exploring the reasons
for the persistence of problems in resources management. Despite the larger share of public funds dedicated to environmental questions, effective policies
are not common. The theme is that the self-interests
of the bureaucrats are not likely to provide the incentives for finding long-range solutions. There must
be a change in the sort of calculations made by resource
administrators.

2362. Bhattacharya, Mohit. BUREAUCRACY AND DEVELOPMENT AD-
       MINISTRATION. New Delhi: Uppal Publishing, 1979.
       152 pp.

       Discusses major organizational issues in rural devel-
       opment in India. There are particularly unstable com-
       binations of competing units at the local level.

2363. "Bureaucracy." JOURNAL OF FORESTRY, 33 (1935), 831-33.

       On government activity in forestry.

2364. Byrd, Harry F. "Bureaucracy and the Farmers." SCIEN-
       TIFIC AMERICAN, 151 (1934), 85.

       Against New Deal agricultural programs.

2365. Coyer, B.W., and D.S. Schwerin. "Bureaucratic Regula-
       tion and Farmer Protest in the Michigan PBB Contam-
       ination Case." RURAL SOCIOLOGY, 46 (1981), 703-23.

       Examine how farmers attempted to ease the burden of
       regulation of contaminants in the environment through
       contacts with state regulatory agencies. The case had
       both administrative and electoral ramifications.

2366. Cramton, Roger, and Richard K. Berg. "On Leading a
       Horse to Water: NEPA and the Federal Bureaucracy."
       MICHIGAN LAW REVIEW, 71 (1973), 511-36.

       Argue that the National Environmental Policy Act of
       1969 (NEPA) is an example of the possibilities of or-
       derly social change.

2367. Day, Robert D. "Archeologists in Agriculture: A New
       Bureaucracy." JOURNAL OF FORESTRY, 76 (1978), 765.

       Wonders if the Department of Agriculture needs as
       many archeologists as it has, especially since nobody
       seem to be in charge of them or what they are doing--
       if anything.

2368. LeLuna, P.R. "Bureaucratic Opposition as a Factor in Truman's Failure to Achieve a Columbia River Authority." CANADIAN HISTORICAL ASSOCIATION HISTORICAL PAPERS, (1975), 231-56.

Finds that the Corps of Engineers and the Bureau of Reclamation lobbied Congress to kill a TVA-like system for the Columbia River.

2369. "The Department of Antiagriculture: Letters to and from a Bureaucracy." POLITICS, 3 (1946), 158-60.

A case of bureaucratic bumbling in agriculture.

2370. Hanke, Steve H. "Bureaucratic Supply Legislative Demand: Implications for Water Resources Planning." JOURNAL OF SOIL AND WATER CONSERVATION, 30 (1975), 158-59.

Expresses disenchantment with planning for water projects. The bureaus and Congress seldom use benefit-cost analysis in their determinations about water projects. A stricter budget would make some hard choices necessary.

2371. Hardin, Charles. "Agricultural Price Policy: The Political Role of Bureaucracy." POLICY STUDIES JOURNAL, 6 (1978), 467-72.

Describes the agricultural subsystem at the federal level.

2372. Inglis, David R. "The Potential Must Be Stressed to Get the Bureaucracy Moving." BULLETIN OF THE ATOMIC SCIENTISTS, 32 (March, 1976), 60.

On governmental opposition to wind power research.

2373. Johnson, M. Bruce. "The Environmental Costs of Bureaucratic Governance: Theory and Cases." BUREAUCRACY VS ENVIRONMENT: THE ENVIRONMENTAL COSTS OF BUREAUCRATIC GOVERNANCE. Edited by John Baden and Richard L. Stroup. Ann Arbor: University of Michigan Press, 1981.

Argues that the public interest may not be served
simply by turning areas of the environment over to regulation by administrators. The decisions they make may
be in their interest but not in the welfare of the public.

2374. Jones, Clifford A. "Environmental Backlash and the Illinois EPA: Perceptions of the Bureaucratic Elite."
PUBLIC AFFAIRS BULLETIN, 6 (May-October, 1973), 1-6.

Examines how the resistance to environmental protection laws were perceived by officials in Illinois. The
administrators did not seem to be affected by the so-
called public "backlash" against the laws.

2375. Lamb, Berton, and Harvey Doerksen. "Bureaucratic Power
and Instream Flows." JOURNAL OF POLITICAL SCIENCE, 6
(1978), 35-50.

Look at several public agencies which regulate the
flow of water in streams in terms of their impact on
the natural environment.

2376. Libecap, Gary. "Bureaucratic Opposition to the Assignment of Property Rights: Overgrazing on the Western
Range." JOURNAL OF ECONOMIC HISTORY, 41 (1981), 151-
58.

Analyzes the role of the Departments of Agriculture
and Interior in restricting the use of rangeland in
the Western states. Jurisdictional disputes between
the two agencies delayed the imposition of effective
control on range use until 1934.

2377. Lowitt, Richard, ed. JOURNAL OF A TAMED BUREAUCRAT:
NILS A. OLSEN AND THE BAE, 1925-1935. Ames: Iowa
State University Press, 1980. 245 pp.

Nils Olsen was in charge of the Bureau of Agricultural Economics during a critical times in American
agriculture. His diary gives details on many of the
battles revolving around the framing of an acceptable
farm policy.

2378. McPherson, William. "Wilderness and Organized Recreation: The Development of Bureaucratic Constraints and Conflicts." HUMBOLDT JOURNAL OF SOCIAL RELATIONS, 2 (1974), 27-30.

Explores the tensions between the organized and the spontaneous enjoyment of natural wilderness areas.

2379. Mason, Alpheus T. BUREAUCRACY CONVICTS ITSELF: THE BALLINGER-PINCHOT CONTROVERSY OF 1910. New York: Viking, 1941. 224 pp.

Describes the relationship between the professionals and the politicians in the famous scandal within the Department of Interior. A major theme is the course of Louis Brandeis's "struggle for an honest and efficient public service under qualified and accepted leaders."

2380. Meier, Kenneth J. "Building Bureaucratic Coalitions: Client Representation in USDA Bureaus." THE NEW POLITICS OF FOOD. Edited by Don Hadwiger and William Browne. Lexington, Mass.: Lexington Books, 1978.

Develops measures of clientele support for bureaus within USDA in order to determine the impact of recent environmental changes on bureau politics.

2381. Murphy, Earl F. "Environmental Bureaucracies Appraised." EKISTICS, 44 (1977), 156-64.

Doubts whether bureaucracy can be an effective means for protecting the environment. At best, it is only one tool and one whose weakness is a mechanical approach to what is a constantly changing problem. The natural system has a great effect on human culture and major changes are needed in how we react to the environment.

2382. Nader, Ralph, and Ronald Brownstein. "Beyond the Love Canal: Bureaucracy Has Compounded the Chemical Mess." PROGRESSIVE, 44 (May, 1980), 28-31.

Describe how jurisdictional disputes hindered getting help to the victims of the Love Canal disaster.

2383.   Nienaber, Jeanne.   "Two Faces of Scarcity: Creativity
        in and Constraints on Bureaucratic Behavior." NATURAL
        RESOURCES SCARCITY: THE CHALLENGE TO PUBLIC POLICYMAK-
        ING. Edited by Susan Welch and Robert Miewald. Bev-
        erly Hills, Cal.: Sage, 1983.

        Argues that scarcity depends upon perceptions, many
        of which are determined by existing bureaucracies. The
        major focus is on the linkages among the resources
        base in the U.S., political orientations of the public,
        and the resulting bureaucratic behavior.

2384.   Nugent, Tom.   "The Pollution of Bureaucracy." NATION,
        221 (1975), 434-36.

        How the EPA lost the war against auto pollution.

2385.   Oyugi, Walter.   "Bureaucracy and Rural Development in
        Africa." INDIAN JOURNAL OF PUBLIC ADMINISTRATION,
        26 (1980), 418-42.

        Reviews the sorry record of rural development efforts
        in African states. Most programs suffer from uncertain-
        ty, instability, and lack of resources.

2386.   Poirot, Paul.   "Bureaucratic Decisions." FREEMAN, 13
        (October, 1962), 46-48.

        Says that surpluses in American agriculture are caused
        by government interference in supply and demand.

2387.   Reich, Charles A. BUREAUCRACY AND THE FORESTS. Santa
        Barbara, Cal.: Center for the Study of Democratic In-
        stitutions, 1962. 12 pp.

        Argues that resources-related agencies operate with
        much discretion. Congress delegates its power to the
        professionals and related interest groups. As a re-
        sult, the general public is excluded from participation.
        Methods of increasing citizen involvement in resource
        decisions are discussed.

2388. Schlebecker, John T. "Farmers and Bureaucrats: Reflec-
         tions on Technological Innovation in Agriculture."
         AGRICULTURAL HISTORY, 51 (1977), 641-55.

         Sees technology and advanced administration as respon-
         sible for much of the innovation that has taken place
         in agriculture throughout history.

2389. Siffin, William J. "Bureaucracy, Entrepreneurship, and
         Natural Resources: Witless Policy and the Barrier
         Islands." CATO JOURNAL, 1 (1981), 293-311.

         On the management of the coastal islands of the At-
         lantic and Gulf Coasts.

2390. Smith, Frederick C. "The Bureaucrat's Gift to the
         Farmers--Russian Whiskers and Leather Boots." CON-
         GRESSIONAL RECORD, 87 (1941), A3102-03.

         American's rural yeomen are well on the way to be-
         coming serfs because of the New Deal.

2391. Trelease, Frank J. "The Model Water Code, the Wise Ad-
         ministrator, and the Goddamn Bureaucrat." NATURAL
         RESOURCES JOURNAL, 14 (1974), 207-29.

         Warns about the dangers inherent in a system of water
         rights administered by a central body. The traditional
         system of "prior appropriation" is preferred because
         it ensures a minimum of centralized control in the dis-
         tribution of water.

2392. Wade, Nicholas. "Bird Lovers and Bureaucrats at Log-
         gerheads over Peregrine Falcon." SCIENCE, 199 (1978),
         1053-55.

         The Audubon Society takes on the U.S. Fish and Wild-
         life Service.

2393. Wandesforde-Smith, Geoffrey. "The Bureaucratic Response
         to Environmental Politics." NATURAL RESOURCES JOUR-
         NAL, 11 (1971), 479-88.

Claims that American environmentalists are forcing
resources administrators to reconsider whether they
can continue to do "business as usual." The established
bureaucracies are finding it hard to respond to the demands of the conservationist movement.

2394.   Whittington, William. "Bureaucracy Rides the Rivers."
        NATION'S BUSINESS, 33 (September, 1945), 31-34, 76-78.

Warns against expanding the concept of the Tennessee
Valley Authority to other parts of the country.

XV.   THE HEALTH CARE SYSTEM

2395.   Adams, Thomas M.   "Medicine and Bureaucracy: Jean Col-
        ombier's Regulations for *Depôts de Méndicté*."   BUL-
        LETIN OF THE HISTORY OF MEDICINE, 52 (1978), 529-41.

        On reforms in French hospitals in the 1780s.

2396.   Ben-David, Joseph.   "The Professional Role of the Phys-
        ician in Bureaucratized Medicine: A Study of Role Con-
        flict."   HUMAN RELATIONS, 11 (1958), 255-74.

        Examines the motivational factors for physicians in
        public clinics in Israel.   Many of the doctors were
        dissatisfied, but those who were most adjusted had ac-
        cepted a service or a scientific role.

2397.   Bergland, Richard M.   "American Neurosurgery and the
        Federal Government: Bureaucracy versus Ad Hocracy."
        CURRENT CONTROVERSIES IN NEUROSURGERY.   Edited by
        T.P. Morley.   Philadelphia: W.B. Saunders, 1976.

        Warns about the growing federal involvement in medical
        education.   Toffler's "ad hocracy" (Item 558) is recom-
        mended as an alternative form of cooperation between
        doctors and government.

2398.   Crandall, Sandra.   "How an FNP Won Over the Bureaucra-
        cy."   AMERICAN JOURNAL OF NURSING, 76 (1976), 1963-
        64.

        Describes how a family nursing practitioner (FNP) set
        up a health care facility in a public housing project.
        The administrators were eventually won over.

2399. Deegan, Mary Jo, and Larry Nutt. "The Hospital Volun-
       teers: Lay Persons in a Bureaucratic Setting." SOC-
       IOLOGY OF WORK AND OCCUPATIONS, 2 (1975), 338-53.

       See the hospital as using universalistic and imper-
       sonal criteria of performance, while most volunteers
       are motivated by a vague desire to "help the patient."
       Problems of adjustment are thus created.

2400. Draper, Peter, and Tony Smart. "Social Science and
       Health Policy in the United Kingdom: Some Contribu-
       tions to the Bureaucratization of the National Health
       Service." INTERNATIONAL JOURNAL OF HEALTH SERVICES,
       4 (1974), 453-70.

       Look at recent reforms in the NHS, many of which have
       led to greater centralization and bureaucratization.
       Social science has contributed significantly to these
       changes. A new "sociology of health" is needed.

2401. Engel, Gloria. "The Effect of Bureaucracy on the Pro-
       fessional Autonomy of the Physician." JOURNAL OF
       HEALTH AND SOCIAL BEHAVIOR, 19 (1969), 30-40.

       Surveys doctors in several organization settings.
       Perceived professional autonomy was lowest in the most
       bureaucratic organizations.

2402. Evans, Therman. "Taxation with Representation: On the
       Health Bureaucracy and Black People." NEW ENGLAND
       JOURNAL OF MEDICINE, 295 (1976), 1013-14.

       Finds that blacks are underrepresented in the health
       policy-making process.

2403. Falkson, Joseph L. AN EVALUATION OF ALTERNATIVE MODELS
       OF CITIZEN PARTICIPATION IN URBAN BUREAUCRACY. Ann
       Arbor: University of Michigan, School of Public
       Health, 1971. 212 pp.

       Reviews the problems created by the participation of
       citizen advisory boards in community health services.

2404. Friedson, Eliot. "Dominant Profession, Bureaucracy and Client Services." ORGANIZATION AND CLIENTS. Edited by William Rosengren and Mark Lefton. Columbus, Ohio: Charles E. Merill, 1970.

Argues that, in the case of health care administration, many of the negative facets of relations with the clients result "from its professional organization instead of its bureaucratic characteristics."

2405. Green, Stephen. "Professional/Bureaucratic Conflict: The Case of the Medical Profession in the National Health Service." SOCIOLOGICAL REVIEW, 23 (1975), 121-41.

Contends that there are four potential areas of conflict within hospitals: goals, controls, incentives, and influence. A study of hospitals in Scotland did not find, in the areas of goals and control, that there were serious professional and bureaucratic tensions.

2406. Harris, John W. "The Effects of Bureaucratic versus Familistic Environment on the Role Definition of Chronic Mental Patients." SOCIOLOGICAL FOCUS, 1 (1970), 24-37.

Examines the negative effects of bureaucratic features in mental health institutions. Patients seem to suffer from the lack of close personal contact with the staff.

2407. Hedley, R. Alan. "Professional Bureaucracy: Community Mental Health Care Teams." ORGANIZATION AND ADMINISTRATIVE SCIENCES, 8 (1977-78), 61-76.

Discusses the mental health services in Vancouver in terms of the negotiations between the professionals and bureaucrats.

2408. Heydebrand, Wolf V. HOSPITAL BUREAUCRACY: A COMPARATIVE STUDY OF ORGANIZATIONS. Port Washington, N.Y.: Dunellen, 1973. 362 pp.

Investigates the modern hospital in terms of theories

of organizations. Because of their task complexity and
extensive use of technology, as well as the mix of various organizational forms, hospitals have become distinctive organizational models. The problem of coordination is particularly acute. An examination of several types of hospitals helps to identify the prototypical form of a postbureaucratic organization. Data are
derived from a survey of employees in American hospitals.

2409.   Jaffe, Dennis T. "Therapy Types: Bureaucrats, Healers,
        and Communities." JOURNAL OF HUMANISTIC PSYCHOLOGY,
        16 (Summer, 1976), 15-28.

        Argues that bureaucratic therapy prevails in mental
        hospitals and works mainly as a mechanism of social con-
        trol.

2410.   Johnson, Elmer. "Bureaucracy in the Rehabilitation
        Institution: Lower Level Staff as a Treatment Re-
        source." SOCIAL FORCES, 30 (1960), 355-59.

        Suggests that the informal interaction between staff
        and inmates at lower levels should be regarded as a re-
        source in the humanization of mental hospitals and the
        prisons.

2411.   Kahne, Morton. "Bureaucratic Structure and Impersonal
        Experience in Mental Hospitals." PSYCHIATRY, 22
        (1959), 363-75.

        Contends that the bureaucratic elements of the mental
        hospital have an effect on the relation of doctors with
        patients. The inmates are regarded in a formal stereo-
        typical way, with little possiblity for close, personal
        contact. Mental hospitals should attempt to create a
        social environment in which patients are in personal
        relationships with other people.

2412.   Karasu, Toksoz B. "Proving the Efficacy of Psychother-
        apy to Government: A Bureaucratic Solution?" AMERI-
        CAN JOURNAL OF PSYCHIARTRY, 139 (1982), 789-90.

        On government attempts to evaluate psychotherapy.

2413. Kernaghan, Salvinija. "The 'Organic Approach' to Cutting through Bureaucracy." HOSPITAL, 51 (September, 1977), 71-74.

Describes the application of democratic management to a hospital. The staff was more satisfied and patients received better treatment.

2414. Kilpatrick, James. "Hospitals and the Bureaucrats." NATION'S BUSINESS, 63 (May, 1975), 11-12.

Views with alarm the interference of the federal government with health care.

2415. Lister, John. "A Call for Change--Bureaucracy and the Profession--Dependent Patients." NEW ENGLAND JOURNAL OF MEDICINE, 279 (1968), 1441-43.

Paints a dark picture of the private practitioner in the British National Health Service.

2416. Malone, Mary F. "The Dilemma of a Professional in a Bureaucracy." NURSING FORUM, 3, No. 4 (1964), 36-60.

Looks at the nurse in general hospitals as being constrained by other professionals and the organization.

2417. Martin, Morgan. "The Bureaucrat: The Taming of the DHEW." JOURNAL OF THE AMERICAN MEDICAL ASSOCIATION, 233 (1975), 976-78.

Edifies doctors about their new partners in health care. Rules of dealing with bureaucrats are given.

2418. Mechanic, David, with the collaboration of Linda Aikens, James Greenley, Doris Slesinger, Bonnie Svarstad, and Richard Tessler. THE GROWTH OF BUREAUCRATIC MEDICINE: AN INQUIRY INTO THE DYNAMICS OF PATIENT BEHAVIOR AND THE ORGANIZATIONS OF MEDICAL CARE. New York: John Wiley, 1976. 345 pp.

Examines the role of the clients and medical staff

in the emerging health care system in the United States. Improvements needed in the system as a "helping institution" are stressed.

2419. Mechanic, David. "The Growth of Medical Technology and Bureaucracy: Implications for Medical Care." MILBANK MEMORIAL FUND QUARTERLY, 55 (1977), 61-78.

Looks at the way in which advanced medical technology has modified traditional doctor-patient relations.

2420. Mellett, D.J. "Bureaucracy and Mental Illness: The Commissioners in Lunacy, 1845-90." MEDICAL HISTORY, 25 (1981), 221-50.

Describes the organizational arrangements for treating mental illness in Britain. The system led to the "medicalization" of insanity and enhanced the role of doctors in treating mental disorders.

2421. Mirelowitz, Seymour. "Alienation and Bureaucratization of Mental Health Organizations." AMERICAN JOURNAL OF ORTHOPSYCHIATRY, 41 (1971), 217-18.

Warns of the dehumanizing effect on clients of bureaucratic systems of mental health care.

2422. Mirelowtiz, Seymour. "Alienation and Bureaucratization of Mental Health Organization." MENTAL HYGIENE, 56 (1972), 6-12.

Finds alienation and anomie to be the dysfunctional consequences of bureaucracy in mental health care. The mental health facilities need to explore organizational forms that are more humanistic.

2423. Novack, Steven J. "Professionalism and Bureaucracy: English Doctors and the Victorian Health Administration." JOURNAL OF SOCIAL HISTORY, 6 (1973), 440-62.

Explains the motives of the doctors in aligning with government in the provision of health services.

2424. Press, Irwin. "Bureaucracy versus Folk Medicine." URBAN ANTHROPOLOGY, 2 (1973), 232-47.

Suggests that the broader the services provided the modern health care system, the better it can compete with traditional folk medicine. The examples are taken from Spain.

2425. Schwartzman, Helen B. "The Bureaucratic Context of a Community Mental Health Center: The View from 'Up.'" HIERARCHY AND SOCIETY: ANTHROPOLOGICAL PERSPECTIVES ON BUREAUCRACY. Philadelphia: Institute for the Study of Human Issues, 1980.

Analyzes the "paper context" of a change in the treatment of the mentally ill.

2426. Shuval, Judith. "Ethnic Stereotyping in Israeli Medical Bureaucracies." SOCIOLOGY AND SOCIAL RESEARCH, 46 (1962), 455-65.

Examines the conflict between professional norms and societal prejudices which is built into the organizational structure of an Israeli medical organization. The results of a survey indicate that it is easier to maintain universalistic standards in smaller units.

2427. Strong, P.M. THE CEREMONIAL ORDER OF THE CLINIC: PARENTS, DOCTORS AND MEDICAL BUREAUCRACIES. Hanley-on-Thames: Routledge and Kegan Paul, 1979. 267 pp.

Discusses the interactions of doctors with patients in a British children's clinic.

2428. Tatalovich, Raymond. "After Medicare: The Politics of Bureaucratic Adaptation in the American Medical Association." INTERNATIONAL REVIEW OF HISTORY AND POLITICAL SCIENCE, 22 (February, 1974), 1-18.

Analyzes the leadership of the American Medical Association. The elite was found to be rather conservative and reactive.

2429. Thompson, Frank J.   HEALTH POLICY AND THE BUREAUCRACY:
       POLITICS AND IMPLEMENTATION.   Cambridge, Mass.: MIT
       Press, 1981.   334 pp.

       Examines the post-legislative phase of policy making
       in several areas of health policy.   Included are Medic-
       aid, Medicare, health maintenance organizations, health
       systems planning, the National Health Service Corps, the
       Veterans Administration, Hill-Burton, and occupational
       health and safety regulation.   Policies are described
       as regulatory or distributive.   Elements influencing
       policy outcomes, including the degree of commitment
       and professionalism, are discussed.

2430. Thompson, Frank J.   "Bureaucratic Discretion and the
       National Health Service Corps."   POLITICAL SCIENCE
       QUARTERLY, 97 (1982), 427-45.

       Uses the agency as a case of goal evolution within
       a context of vague laws and relaxed oversight.   In this
       case, the lack of strict hierarchical control led to
       benign policy changes.

2431. Watts, Geoff.   "The Healthy Bureaucracy."   NEW SCIEN-
       TIST, 83 (1979), 462-63.

       On the British National Health Service.

2432. Weitzel, William D.   "A Psychitrist in a Bureaucracy:
       The Unsettling Compromise."   PSYCHIATRY, 27 (1976),
       644-47.

       Studies Army psychiatrists.   Three general modes of
       adaptation to the needs of the organization are elabo-
       rated.

XVI. LABOR

2433. Clawson, Dan. BUREAUCRACY AND THE LABOR PROCESS: THE
       TRANSFORMATION OF U.S. INDUSTRY, 1860–1920. New York:
       Monthly Review Press, 1980. 284 pp.

       Argues that the doctrine of capitalist management did
       not develop along bureaucratic lines simply because of
       technical reasons. Rather, bureaucracy was seen as an
       effective means for the control of the working force.
       The rise of the factory deprived workers of control
       over their jobs. Taylorism, or Scientific Management,
       was a particularly important instrument for depriving
       the workers of their autonomy.

2434. DiTomaso, Nancy. "Class Politics and Public Bureaucra-
       cy: The U.S. Department of Labor." CLASSES, CONFLICT
       AND THE STATE: EMPIRICAL STUDIES IN CLASS ANALYSIS.
       Edited by Maurice Zeitlin. Cambridge, Mass.: Win-
       throp, 1980.

       Describes how the political demands of the lower class
       were deflected by institutionalization. While purport-
       ing to represent workers, the DOL actually limits their
       access to government.

2435. Dobbs, Farrell. TEAMSTER BUREAUCRACY. New York: Monad
       Press, 1977. 304 pp.

       Concludes a three-part history of the Teamsters Union
       up to the end of WWII. A major theme is the defeat of
       the radical elements within the labor movement by the
       more conservative leadership which built itself into
       a self-perpetuating bureaucracy. Rank-and-file members
       have not been able to challenge the power of the insti-
       tutional elite.

2436. Friedman, Samuel. TEAMSTER RANK AND FILE: POWER, BUR-
       EAUCRACY, AND REBELLION AT WORK IN A UNION. New York:
       Columbia University Press, 1982. 320 pp.

       Examines how an insurgent group within a local of the
       Teamsters Union led their struggle against their leader-
       ship. Local union organizations can resist the indif-
       ference of bureaucratized national headquarters toward
       their interests.

2437. Dubofsky, Melvyn. "George Meany: The Perfect Bureau-
       crat." NEW POLITICS, 10, No. 2 (1973), 30-36.

       Review essay on Joseph Goulner's *Meany*.

2438. Herberg, Will. "Bureaucracy and Democracy in Labor
       Unions." ANTIOCH REVIEW, 3 (1943), 405-17.

       Notes the paradox in the centralization of labor
       unions despite their commitment to the freedom of their
       members. Institutional reforms will not be as effective
       as the "moral dynamics" of their leaders in changing
       this trend towards bureaucracy.

2439. Masters, Nicholas. "The Organized Labor Bureaucracy as
       a Base of Support for the Democratic Party." LAW AND
       CONTEMPORARY PROBLEMS, 27 (1965), 252-65.

       Assesses the power of the AFL-CIO in terms of produc-
       ing votes for presidential candidates.

2440. Moses, John. "Bureaucrats and Patriots: The German Soc-
       ialist Trade Union Leadership from Sarajevo to Ver-
       sailles, 1914-1919." LABOR HISTORY, 30 (1976), 1-21.

       Examines the policies of the German labor movement
       during WWI and the reaction of the unions to the Nov-
       ember Revolution and the Treaty of Versailles.

2441. Popiel, Gerald. "Bureaucracy in the Mass Industrial
       Union." AMERICAN JOURNAL OF ECONOMICS AND SOCIOLOGY,
       15 (1955), 49-58.

Identifies the factors unique to the bureaucratization of labor unions. Several aspects of union activity, including the need for constant negotiation, mitigate against the creation of the bureaucratic personality. Union leaders are marginal types since they are constantly under pressure from both the rank and file and from management. This also prevents the emergence of bureaucratic leadership.

2442. Schrade, Paul. "Growing Bureaucratization of the UAW." NEW POLITICS, 10, No. 2 (1973), 13-21.

On the Woodcock leadership of the auto workers.

2443. Van Tine, Warren R. THE MAKING OF THE LABOR BUREAUCRAT: UNION LEADERSHIP IN THE UNITED STATES, 1870-1920. Amherst: University of Massachusetts Press, 1973. 230 pp.

Explores the development of union leadership before 1920. The question is examined in terms of social background, the ideology of unionism, union-management relations, and the general bureaucratization of American society.

2444. Won, George, and Douglas Yamamura. DEMOCRACY WITHIN A BUREAUCRACY: A LABOR UNION DILEMMA. Honolulu: University of Hawaii, Industrial Relations Center, 1967. 13 pp.

On the difficulty of establishing democracy within a bureaucratically structured organization.

XVII. MILITARY AFFAIRS

2445. Alter, Jonathan. "Tinker, Tailor, Soldier, Bureaucrat:
       The Apprenticeship of Alexander Haig." WASHINGTON
       MONTHLY, 13 (March, 1981), 14-22.

       Traces the career of the master careerist. Haig is
       typical of the bureaucratic survivor, with loyalty and
       getting ahead more important than accomplishment.

2446. Axelrod, Robert. BUREAUCRATIC DECISIONMAKING IN THE
       MILITARY ASSISTANCE PROGRAM: SOME EMPIRICAL FINDINGS.
       Santa Monica: Rand, 1968. 36 pp.

       Uses the responses of officers in a MAP to answer
       questions about the generation of alternatives, the role
       of bureaucratic bargaining, and the issue of organiza-
       tional learning. The data suggest a new set of research
       questions.

2447. Baldwin, Hanson. "The Growing Risks of Bureaucratic In-
       telligence." REPORTER, 29 (August 15, 1963), 48-52.

       Discusses the bureaucratic infighting among the in-
       telligence agencies which leads to, among other things,
       impediments to the open evaluation of military infor-
       mation.

2448. Beard, Edmund. DEVELOPING THE ICBM: A STUDY IN BUREAU-
       CRATIC POLITICS. New York: Columbia University Press,
       1976. 273 pp.

       Looks at the failure of the American military, between
       1946 and 1954, to develop an effective ballistic mis-
       sile. The major reason for the delay was the internal
       bureaucratic politics of the Air Force.

2449.   Bergerson, Frederick A.   THE ARMY GETS AN AIR FORCE:
        TACTICS OF INSURGENT BUREAUCRATIC POLITICS.   Balti-
        more: Johns Hopkins Press, 1980.   216 pp.

        Describes how Army officers--the insurgents--were able
        to obtain an air capability for their service despite
        the presence of the Air Force.   Insurgency is a fairly
        mild form of bureaucratic machinations.   Although loyal
        to the organization, the insurgent takes advantage of
        all opportunities to maximize a particular point of
        view.   Insurgency may activate a bureaucracy to move
        in a certain direction, but it does raise grave ques-
        tions about political control.

2450.   Butterworth, Robert.   "Bureaucratic Politics and Con-
        gress' Role in Weapons Development: The Arms Control
        Impact Statement."   POLICY STUDIES JOURNAL, 8 (1979),
        76-84.

        Considers the general failure of the impact statement
        required in weapons systems funding.   The dynamic of
        the bureaucratic process has been misunderstood by the
        policy makers.

2451.   Chirillo, Louis D.   "Shipbuilding: Building Ships or
        Bureaucracies?   UNITED STATES NAVAL INSTITUTE PRO-
        CEEDINGS, 101 (August, 1975), 38-45.

        Argues that naval shipyards and private shipbuilders
        have become more bureaucratic in response to perceived
        pressures from Washington.

2452.   Davis, Arthur K.   "Bureaucratic Patterns in the Navy
        Officer Corps."   SOCIAL FORCES, 27 (1948), 143-53.

        Contends that the rigors of military bureaucracy pro-
        duce a strict sense of discipline and formalization.
        These factors, in turn, result in dysfunctional aspects
        such as avoiding responsibility, legalism, insulation,
        and ceremonialism.   The military variant of bureaucracy
        is affected by unique types of strains.

2453.   Deitchman, Seymour J.   THE BEST-LAID SCHEMES: A TALE OF
        SOCIAL RESEARCH AND BUREAUCRACY.   Cambridge, Mass.:
        MIT Press, 1976.   483 pp.

A participant describes his role in the military's attempt to apply social science research to problems of revolutionary movements in the Third World. The lesson to be learned is that the desires of administrators and the researchers diverge from the very beginning of such a project.

2454. Funk, Sherman, and Mark McBriarty. "Decline and Fall of the Bureaucratic Image." DEFENSE MANAGEMENT JOURNAL, 6 (Summer, 1970), 5-9.

On improvements in military management.

2455. Gabriel, Richard. "Acquiring New Values in Military Bureaucracy: A Preliminary Model." JOURNAL OF POLITICAL AND MILITARY SOCIOLOGY, 7 (1979), 89-102.

Argues that the cohesion of military units is largely a matter of primary group loyalty. This cohesion is important for military effectiveness. The U.S. Army has moved from a corporate institution into an entrepreneurial bureaucracy. If the Army is to remain effective in combat, there is a need to redevelop a sense of corporate cohesion. The ways to establish these values are considered.

2456. Heurling, Bertel. "Notes on Bureaucratic Politics in National Security Policy." COOPERATION AND CONFLICT, 10 (1975), 237-59.

Tests the bureaucratic politics model with the decision on the ABM system. The model does not explain the policy outcome.

2457. Katz, David. "The Network Overlay: Helping Large Bureaucracies Do Things Better." BUREAUCRAT, 9 (Fall, 1980), 24-29.

Describes the use of a "network model" in defense intelligence work. The system is such that it can be applied to other organizations.

2458. Kinghorn, Alan. "Bureaucracy in Military Headquarters."
       MILITARY REVIEW, 49 (June, 1969), 54-61.

       Examines the staff officers as bureaucrats. The com-
       mander must take care to see that there is a healthy at-
       titude if the operation of his unit is not to deterio-
       rate.

2459. Komer, R.W. BUREAUCRACY DOES ITS THING: CONSTRAINTS
       ON US-GVN PERFORMANCE IN VIETNAM. Santa Monica:
       Rand, 1972. 179 pp.

       Analyzes the failures in the Vietnam War in terms of
       the sluggish response to events by officials in the
       government of Vietnam and their American counterparts.

2460. Lind, William. "Bureaucratic Tactics." AIR UNIVERSITY
       REVIEW, 31 (January-February, 1980), 87-89.

       Suggests that the tactician must keep in mind that the
       enemy is part of a bureaucracy.

2461. Mauer, George. "Bureaucrats in Reserve." PUBLIC PER-
       SONNEL REVIEW, 30 (1969), 130-35.

       On the National Defense Executive Researve.

2462. Miewald, Robert D. "Weberian Bureaucracy and the Mil-
       itary Model." PUBLIC ADMINISTRATION REVIEW, 30
       (1970), 129-33.

       Argues that Weber put too much emphasis on the ration-
       al components of military organizational doctrine. Mil-
       itary thought is examined to show that the irrational
       plays a large role in the conduct of military affairs.

2463. Miewald, Robert D. "The Army Post Schools: A Report
       from the Bureaucratic Wars." MILITARY AFFAIRS, 39
       (February, 1975), 8-11.

       Discusses a 19th-century dispute over the operation
       of post schools as an example of the bureaucratic strug-
       gles over jurisdiction among the staff officers.

2464. Moley, Raymond. "Indestructible Bureaucracy." NEWS-
       WEEK, 46 (December 12, 1955), 128.

       On the Department of Defense.

2465. Moley, Raymond. "Bureaucracy's Nine Lives." NEWSWEEK,
       46 (December 19, 1955), 100.

       And more on the Department of Defense.

2466. Nash, Henry T. "The Bureaucratization of Homicide."
       BULLETIN OF THE ATOMIC SCIENTISTS, 36 (April, 1980),
       22-27.

       Reflects on how defense analysts can "plan to incin-
       erate vast numbers of unknown human beings without any
       sense of moral revulsion."

2467. Odiorne, George. "The Military as a Bureaucracy: The
       Super Activity Trap." SOUTHERN REVIEW OF PUBLIC AD-
       MINISTRATION, 1 (1977), 74-87.

       Deplores the emphasis on activity rather than out-
       put in the military.

2468. Page, Charles H. "Bureaucracy's Other Face." SOCIAL
       FORCES, 25 (1946), 88-94.

       On bureaucratic elements in the U.S. Navy.

2469. Pollitt, Ronald. "Bureaucracy and the Armada: The Ad-
       ministrator's Battle." MARINER'S MIRROR, 60 (1974),
       119-32.

       Claims that the efficient administration of the Eng-
       lish was critical in the defeat of the Spanish Armada.

2470. Rycroft, Robert. "The Military Reform Movement, 1969-
       1972: The Development of a Bureaucratic Control Sys-
       tem." JOURNAL OF POLITICAL AND MILITARY SOCIOLOGY,
       3 (1975), 179-89.

       Discusses recent developments in the U.S. military.

2471.   Sabrosky, Alan, James C. Thompson, and Karen McPherson.
        "Organized Anarchies: Military Bureaucracy in the
        1980s." JOURNAL OF APPLIED BEHAVIORAL SCIENCE, 18
        (1982), 137-53.

        Argue that the American military is overburdened by
        its organizational complexity and internal politics.
        Several of the bureaucratic features detract from its
        responsiveness to such an extent that it is questionable
        if it could succeed in war.

2472.   Sanders, Ralph. "Bureaucratic Ploys and Strategems:
        The Case of the U.S. Department of Defense." JERU-
        SALEM JOURNAL OF INTERNATIONAL AFFAIRS, 4 (1979), 1-
        15.

        Describe the behavior of the Defense Department in
        the making of foreign policy.

2473.   Sapolsky, Harvey M.   THE POLARIS SYSTEM DEVELOPMENT:
        BUREAUCRATIC AND PROGRAMMATIC SUCCESS IN GOVERNMENT.
        Cambridge, Mass.: Harvard University Press, 1972.
        261 pp.

        Presents a case study of the development of the Pol-
        aris missile by a unit of the U.S. Navy. The invention
        of an elaborate decision-making tool--PERT--was more of
        a self-serving ritual than a serious means for the co-
        ordination of complexity and greater rationality. This
        bureaucracy survived because of the political astute-
        ness of its leaders.

2474.   Sherman, Edward F.   "Army Blues: A Bureaucracy Adrift."
        NATION, 212 (1971), 265-75.

        Finds the American military in a state of crisis. In
        his view, "a powerful institution finds itself unable
        to cope with the times."

2475.   Stirling, Yates. "Bureaucracy Rules the Navy." CURRENT
        HISTORY, 51 (March, 1940), 30-32.

        The U.S. Navy needs a general staff.

2476. Trott, Harlan. "Does Bureaucracy Rules the Waves?"
    CHRISTIAN SCIENCE MONITOR MAGAZINE, (June 15, 1940),
    3, 13.

    On needed reorganization in the Navy command struc-
    ture.

2477. Turner, Ralph. "The Navy Disbursing Officer as a Bur-
    eaucrat." AMERICAN SOCIOLOGICAL REVIEW, 12 (1947).
    342-48.

    Discusses the informal pressures on a formal bureau-
    cratic role. The disbursing officer is in a position
    of conflict regarding the official rules and commands
    of superiors. Informal pressures from colleagues may
    also divert the officer from purely formal action.
    The result may be "personal functioning within systems
    of power and status in which rules become of secondary
    importance."

XVIII. PROFESSIONALS AND BUREAUCRACY

2478. Badura, Bernhard. "Self-Help Groups as an Alternative
        to Bureaucratic Regulation and Professional Dominance
        of the Human Services." WELFARE OR BUREAUCRACY? PROB-
        LEMS OF MATCHING SOCIAL SERVICES TO CLIENT'S NEEDS.
        Edited by Dieter Grunow and Friedhard Hegner. Cam-
        bridge, Mass.: Oelschlager, Gunn and Hain, 1980.

        Advocates the organization of social service clients
        into self-help groups as a defense against the excessive
        control of their lives by bureaucratic professionals.

2479. Benson, J. Kenneth. "The Analysis of Bureaucratic-
        Professional Conflict: Functional versus Dialectical
        Approaches." SOCIOLOGICAL QUARTERLY, 14 (1973), 376-
        94.

        Proposes a dialectical approach which links the bur-
        eaucratic-professional conflict to basic contradictions
        within the organization.

2480. Billingsley, Andrew. "Bureaucratic and Professional Or-
        ientation Patterns in Social Casework." SOCIAL SER-
        VICE REVIEW, 38 (1964), 400-07.

        Compares social workers with the standard model of
        professionalization.

2481. Bloom, Joan R., and Jeffrey A. Alexander. "Team Nurs-
        ing: Professional Coordination or Bureaucratic Con-
        trol?" JOURNAL OF HEALTH AND SOCIAL BEHAVIOR, 23
        (1982), 84-95.

        Examine the possible uses of team nursing. Under cer-
        tain conditions, it can be bureaucratic or professional.

2482. Christie, Paul A. "Engineers in a Bureaucracy." ASHRAE
       JOURNAL, 15 (July, 1973), 41-42.

       Suggests how the conscientious professional can avoid
       the pitfalls of work in the big organization.

2483. Daniels, Arlene. "The Captive Professionals: Bureau-
       cratic Limitations to the Practice of Military Psych-
       iatry." JOURNAL OF HEALTH AND SOCIAL BEHAVIOR, 10
       (1969), 255-65.

       Argues that military psychiatrists perform largely
       for the organization and not for the benefit of the
       patient. However, any tension can be relieved if the
       organization is regarded as the object of the care.

2484. Danziger, James N. "The 'Skill Bureaucracy' and Intra-
       organizational Control: The Case of the Data Proces-
       sing Unit." SOCIOLOGY OF WORK AND OCCUPATIONS, 6
       (1979), 204-26.

       Surveys data processing units in local government to
       see the degree of tension the members feel in their re-
       lations with the rest of the organization. The EDP unit
       was fairly independent; it has "a distinctive perspective
       regarding its own role responsibilities, anchored in
       the standards of its professional group. This skill
       bureaucracy is remarkably expansionist, and is autono-
       mous in its operation."

2485. Donaldson, Lex, and Malcolm Warner. "Bureaucratic and
       Electoral Control in Occupational Interest Associa-
       tions." SOCIOLOGY, 8 (1974), 47-58.

       Find that a high degree of electoral control over
       full-time officers of trade unions and professional
       associations is related to a lower level of standard-
       ized procedures.

2486. Elliot, Clifford, and David Kuhn. "Professionals in
       Bureaucracies: Some Emerging Areas of Conflict."
       UNIVERSITY OF MICHIGAN BUSINESS REVIEW, 30 (January,
       1978), 12-16.

Maintain that professions and bureaucracy are based
on fundamentally different principles of organization.

2487.   Engel, Gloria V.   "Professional Autonomy and Bureau-
        cratic Organization."   ADMINISTRATIVE SCIENCE QUART-
        ERLY, 15 (1970), 12-21.

        Presents an empirical study of the proposition that
        bureaucracy limits professional autonomy.   Physicians
        in a variety of organizational settings were analyzed.
        The results suggest that "the professional type of bur-
        eaucratic organization is not necessarily detrimental
        to professional autonomy."   The members of moderate
        bureaucracies tended to have the greatest sense of
        professional autonomy.

2488.   English, Horace B.   "Professional Guilds and Bureaucra-
        cy."   JOURNAL OF SOCIAL ISSUES, 1 (December, 1945),
        62-65.

        Warns against the "guild spirit" in administration.

2489.   Fielding, A.G., and D. Portwood.   "Professions and the
        State--Towards a Typology of Bureaucratic Professi-
        ons."   SOCIOLOGICAL REVIEW, 28 (1980), 23-53.

        Develops a typology with which to analyze the rela-
        tions of bureaucratized professions with the state.

2490.   Foreman, James.   "The Professionalization-Bureaucrati-
        zation Dilemma: The Case of the Funeral Director."
        INTERNATIONAL JOURNAL OF CONTEMPORARY SOCIOLOGY,
        11 (1974), 229-44.

        Measures bureaucratization in the undertaking profes-
        sion by reviewing the content of the *Embalmer's Monthly*.

2491.   Frost, David.   "Professionalism and Bureaucracy."   BUILT
        ENVIRONMENT, 3 (1974), 578-80.

        Discusses the position of town planner in terms of
        the theory of professionalization.

2492. Hall, Richard. "Professionalization and Bureaucratiza-
       tion." AMERICAN SOCIOLOGICAL REVIEW, 33 (1968), 92-
       104.

       Studies several professions in organizational set-
       tings. There is a reciprocal relationship between the
       professions and the organizational structure.

2493. Hardcastle, David. "The Indigent Nonprofessional in the
       Social Service Bureaucracy: A Critical Examination."
       SOCIAL WORK, 16 (1971), 56-64.

       Questions whether the use of nonprofessionals will
       add much to the debureaucratization of social welfare
       agencies.

2494. Hobson, Wayne K. "Professionals, Progressives and Bur-
       eaucratization: A Reassessment." HISTORIAN, 39 (1977),
       639-58.

       Finds fault with the contention that the Progressives
       were representative of a "new middle class" of techno-
       crats. In looking at the degree to which occupational
       groups supported bureaucratization, variations among
       the professions were found.

2495. Lawler, Edward J., and Jerald Hage. "Professional-
       Bureaucratic Conflict and Intraorganizational Power-
       lessness among Social Workers." JOURNAL OF SOCIOLOGY
       AND SOCIAL WELFARE, 1 (1973), 92-102.

       Conclude that the sense of powerlessness among pro-
       fessionals will vary with the degree of organizational
       constraint.

2496. Littleton, A.C. "'An Inevitably Mediocre Bureaucracy.'"
       JOURNAL OF ACCOUNTANCY, 60 (1935), 264-69.

       Looks at the question whether accountants should be
       regarded as autonomous professionals. As a guardian
       of the integrity of the organization, accountants have
       a larger responsibility.

2497.   Malone, David, and Janet Wedel.   "Professional Orienta-
        tion and Bureaucratic Forms: Variations among Three
        Social Work Agencies."   PROCEEDINGS OF THE SOUTHWEST-
        ERN SOCIOLOGICAL ASSOCIATION, 19 (1969), 237-41.

        Find that a professional orientation was more pro-
        nounced in the less structured organizations.

2498.   Merton, Robert.   "Role of the Intellectual in Public
        Bureaucracy."   SOCIAL FORCES, 23 (1945), 405-15.

        Formulates hypotheses about the educated professional
        in the public service.

2499.   Michael, Jack.   "Can the Professional Maintain His Role
        in a Bureaucratic Organization?"   PROFESSIONAL ENGIN-
        EERS, 27 (December, 1973), 8-9.

        An excellent question.

2500.   Michael, J.A.   "Professional Practice in a Bureaucratic
        Organization."   PUBLIC ADMINISTRATION (SYDNEY), 33
        (1974), 147-66.

        On the problems of integrating the professional into
        the large organization.   Even though working in a bur-
        eaucracy is not the same as private practice, there
        is no reason why a professional has to be restrained
        in pursuing appropriate conduct.

2501.   Miller, George.   "Professionals in Bureaucracy: Aliena-
        tion among Industrial Scientists and Engineers."   AM-
        ERICAN SOCIOLOGICAL REVIEW, 32 (1967), 755-68.

        Examines the professional in the aerospace industry.
        Alienation in this group is associated with the type
        of organization structure.

2502.   Moneypenny, Philip.   "Professional Organizations and
        Bureaucratic Government."   SOUTHWESTERN SOCIAL SCI-
        ENCE QUARTERLY, 32 (1952), 257-63.

        Expresses confidence that the professionals will be

able to counteract the rigidity of the bureaucracy because of their sensitivity to the needs of the public.

2503.   Montagna, Paul. "Professionalization and Bureaucrat-
        ization in Large Professional Organizations." AMER-
        ICAN JOURNAL OF SOCIOLOGY, 74 (1968), 138-45.

        Examines the conflicts between professionalization and
        bureaucratization in a large public accounting firm.
        The double processes are complementary and develop in
        a sequential manner. Professionalization is related
        to centralization and the size of the administrative
        component of the organization.

2504.   Morrissey, Elizabeth, and David Gillespie. "Technology
        and the Conflict of Professionals in Bureaucratic Or-
        ganizations." SOCIOLOGICAL QUARTERLY, 16 (1975), 319-
        32.

        Suggest that bureaucracy and professionalism are not
        incompatible.

2505.   Ritzer, George. "Professionalization, Bureaucratiza-
        tion: The Views of Max Weber." SOCIAL FORCES, 53
        (1975), 627-34.

        Argues that Weber saw professionalism as part of the
        rationalization of society and thus was not an imped-
        iment to bureaucratization.

2506.   Rourke, Francis E. "Bureaucracy in Conflict: Adminis-
        trators and Professionals." ETHICS, 70 (1960), 22-
        27.

        Finds in American universities many examples of the
        inherent conflict between bureaucrats and profession-
        alism. The administrators resent the lack of discip-
        line among the professionals. The professionals feel
        they are doing the work for which the organization was
        established; in their view, the bureaucrat is useful
        only in taking care of the housekeeping functions of
        the organization. The administrators seem to be win-
        ning the struggle.

2507.   de Schweinitz, Karl. "Antidote for Bureaucracy." SUR-
        VEY, 80 (1944), 319-20.

        Says that bureaucracy results when people in organ-
        izations displace ends with means. Professionalism is
        a way to restore to organizations a sense of purpose.

2508.   Scott, Richard. "Professionals in Bureaucracies--Areas
        of Conflict." PROFESSIONALIZATION. Edited by Howard
        Vollmar and Donald Mills. Englewood Cliffs, N.J.:
        Prentice-Hall, 1966.

        A review of the outlines of the problem.

2509.   Shipman, George. "The New Bureaucracy." PUBLIC ADMIN-
        ISTRATION REVIEW, 25 (1965), 250.

        About professionals in organizations.

2510.   Smigel, Erwin O. "Professional Bureaucracy and the
        Large Wall Street Firms." ESTUDIOS DE SOCIOLOGIA,
        2 (1962), 155-65.

        Suggests that the "professional bureaucracy" is an
        important variation in the basic bureaucratic model.
        Large law firms function effectively because of the
        control provided by formal and informal professional
        norms. The occupational rules replace many of the
        control aspects of bureaucracy.

2511.   Sorensen, James E., and Thomas L. Sorensen. "The Con-
        flict of Professionals in Bureaucratic Organizations."
        ADMINISTRATIVE SCIENCE QUARTERLY, 19 (1974), 98-106.

        Describe a study of 264 certified public accountants
        in four national firms. It was found that professionals
        in the bureaucratic organization suffer from conflict
        and deprivation, leading to job dissatisfaction and job
        migration.

2512.   Stone, Robert C. "The Sociology of Bureaucracy and Pro-
        fessions." CONTEMPORARY SOCIOLOGY. Edited by J.S.
        Roucek. New York: Philosophical Library, 1958.

Reviews the literature on professionalization and bureaucracy. Problems in the relationship of the two are
discussed.

2513. Wardwell, Walter I. "Social Integration, Bureaucratiza-
       tion, and the Professions." SOCIAL FORCES, 33 (1955),
       356-59.

       Discusses the trend of bureaucratization in various
       occupational groups, including the free professions,
       crafts, and business. There remains a number of serious
       problems with the social integration of various work
       groups within the large organization.

2514. Williams, James O. "Professionalism and Bureaucracy:
       Natural Conflict." NASSP BULLETIN, 55 (December,
       1971), 61-68.

       The problem in the education profession.

2515. Willis, Evan. "Professionalism and Bureaucracy: The
       Changing Context of Primary Medical Care." COMMUN-
       ITY HEALTH STUDIES, 2 (October, 1978), 1-12.

       On the situation in New Zealand.

XIX.   RELIGION AND PHILANTHROPY

2516.   Brouwer, Arie R.   "Tower of Babel: Communications Myth-
         ology-in-the-Making for the Church Bureaucracy."
         CHRISTIAN CENTURY, 94 (1977), 276-79.

         Wonders about the value of the increase in technical
         jargon in organized religion.

2517.   Carey, Margaret D.   "A 'Democratic Authority' for Bur-
         eaucracy."   JOURNAL OF EDUCATIONAL ADMINISTRATION,
         9 (1971), 48-65.

         Argues that bureaucracy can be democratized.   The
         Catholic Church since Vatican II is an example of what
         can be done.

2518.   Chapin, Stuart.   "The Growth of Bureaucracy: A Hypo-
         thesis."   AMERICAN SOCIOLOGICAL REVIEW, 16 (1951),
         835-36.

         Sees the formalization process creeping into voluntary
         associations.

2519.   Donahue, Francis M., and Norman D. Humphrey.   "Changing
         Bureaucracy and Social Power in a Chicago Ukrainian
         Parish."   HUMAN ORGANIZATION, 11 (Summer, 1952), 23-
         36.

         Describe the transformation of a traditional sacred
         role into a more formal type of ethnic group leader.

2520.   Glover, Robert.   "Life among the Bureaucrats."   CHRIST-
         IAN CENTURY, 90 (1973), 19-20.

Describes some of the joys and frustration of being
a church bureaucrat.

2521. Karl, Barry D. "Philanthropy, Policy Planning, and
        the Bureaucratization of the Democratic Ideal."
        DAEDALUS, 105 (1976) 129-49.

        Identifies important traits of the private and pub-
        lic managerial elites in the U.S. The early philan-
        thropists believed in central planning but were in-
        terested in stimulating activity at the local level.
        Government bureaus later took on some of the aspects
        of an intermediary between the foundations and the
        professionalized bureaucracies requesting funds. All
        of this served to stimulate a creative tension between
        popular democracy and the managerial elites.

2522. Lorig, Arthur N. "The Growth of a Bureaucracy." WEST-
        ERN POLITICAL QUARTERLY, 12 (1959), 932-38.

        Traces the development of bureaucratic tendencies in
        the United Community Fund. Operating almost as a gov-
        ernmental entity, the Fund has acquired a great deal of
        power in the raising and spending of contributions.
        The best way to induce greater restraint in the organ-
        ization would be for contributors to withhold their
        donations.

2523. Luidens, Donald A. "Bureaucratic Control in a Protes-
        tant Denomination." JOURNAL FOR THE SCIENTIFIC STUDY
        OF RELIGION, 21 (1982), 163-75.

        Analyzes the power of the central staff of the Re-
        formed Church of America. Despite the traditional re-
        jection of the ecclesiastical exercise of power, it
        was found that bureaucratic demands have created a
        general perception of a highly centralized system of
        control.

2524. Mills, Robert. "Religion and Bureaucracy: A Spiritual
        Dialogue." JOURNAL OF RELIGION AND HEALTH, 15 (1976),
        291-96.

        Argues that the increasing bureaucratization of the

church may hinder spiritual purposes. Family living centers may be one way to overcome the tensions between spirituality and administrative efficiency.

2525. Page, Charles H. "Bureaucracy and the Liberal Church." REVIEW OF RELIGION, 17 (1952), 137-50.

On developments in church administration.

2526. Palacek, Marvin A. BATTLE OF THE BUREAUCRACIES: THE UNITED DEFENSE FUND. New York: Vantage, 1972. 291 pp.

Describes the tensions within the organization of a philanthropic agency.

2527. Shokeid, Moshe. "From Personal Endowment to Bureaucratic Appointment: The Transition in Israel of the Communal Religious Leaders of Moroccan Jews." JOURNAL FOR THE SCIENTIFIC STUDY OF RELIGION, 19 (1980), 105-13.

Traces the decline of traditional religious leadership and the adjustment of the community to more bureaucratically selected rabbis.

2528. Stoddard, Ellwyn. "Some Latent Consequences of Bureaucratic Efficiency in Disaster Relief." HUMAN ORGANIZATION, 28 (1968), 177-89.

Compares two relief organizations (Red Cross and the Salvation Army) in terms of internal operating procedures and perceived effectiveness by clients.

2529. Thompson, Kenneth A. BUREAUCRACY AND CHURCH REFORM: THE ORGANIZATIONAL RESPONSE OF THE CHURCH OF ENGLAND TO SOCIAL CHANGE, 1800-1965. Oxford: Clarendon Press, 1970. 264 pp.

Examines how the church adapted its organization in order to respond to changes in the larger society. Three periods of organizational change are noted. In all the periods, efficiency and sacred values clashed.

XX. SCIENCE AND TECHNOLOGY

2530. Abelson, Philip H. "Proliferation and Bureaucracy."
        SCIENCE, 163 (1969), 883.

        On the growth of grants-in-aid for research.

2531. Badaway, M.K. "Bureaucracy in Research: A Study of
        Role Conflict of Scientists." HUMAN ORGANIZATION,
        32 (1973), 123-33.

        Examines the role perceptions of scientists in an
        industrial plant. Are they creative people or mere fac-
        tors in the production process?

2532. Bensman, Joseph. "Who Writes What in the Bureaucratic
        University?" DISSENT, 15 (1968), 347-50.

        Protests the difficulty of determining authorship
        in modern research.

2533. Boffey, Philip. "Scientists and Bureaucrats: A Clash
        of Cultures on FDA Advisory Panel." SCIENCE, 191
        (1976), 1244-46.

        On the Red Dye No.2 controversy.

2534. Boulden, Larry L. "Can Technology Survive Bureaucracy:
        Models for Change." MACHINE DESIGN, 45 (June 12,
        1973), 104-08.

        Describes the "technology-enhancement" capabilities
        of various federal agencies.

2535.   Brown, Paula. "Bureaucracy in a Government Laboratory."
        SOCIAL FORCES, 32 (1954), 259-68.

        Studies the reaction of scientists to the conflicts
        concerning professional norms, bureaucratic rules and
        personal standards. In the observation of the work
        of a scientific unit, it is found that scientists
        find their rationality in the profession and not in
        the bureaucracy. However, impersonal factors tend to
        moderate both professionalism and bureaucracy.

2536.   "Bureaucracy Strikes U.S. Research Community, NSB Says."
        PHYSICS TODAY, 30 (January, 1977), 93-94.

        The National Science Board finds that basic research
        is threatened by federal rules.

2537.   "Of Bureaucrats and Bombs." NATION, 225 (1977), 131.

        On the development of the neutron bomb.

2538.   Carter, Luther J. "Reshuffling the Bureaucracy: Nixon
        Proposes Pollution, Ocean Agencies." SCIENCE, 168
        (1970), 1433-35.

        On reorganization plans for EPA and NOAA.

2539.   Carter, Luther J. "'Excessive Bureaucracy' Found in
        R&D at EPA." SCIENCE, 186 (1974), 32.

        A National Academy of Science report on research in
        the Environmental Protection Agency.

2540.   Cressey, D.R., "Crime, Science, and Bureaucratic Rule."
        CENTER MAGAZINE, 11 (July, 1978), 40-48.

        Sees similarities between the bureaucratization of
        law enforcement and scientific research. In either
        case, bureaucratic regulations threaten that creative
        use of discretion which has been so successful in the
        past.

2541. Driscoll, Everly. "Bureaucratic Odyssey of a Space-Mapping Camera." SCIENCE NEWS, 110 (L971), 363-63.

Describes how military secrecy and interagency politics have delayed civilian uses of space mapping.

2542. Hatch, Orrin G. "The Bureaucratization of Science." INNOVATION AND U.S. RESEARCH: PROBLEMS AND RECOMMENDATIONS. Edited by Charles F. Larson. Washington, D.C: American Chemical Society, 1980.

A U.S. senator supports decreasing the involvement of government in non-defense R&D.

2543. Haynes, William. "Unbridled Bureaucracy Would Kill Research." SATURDAY EVENING POST, 216 (October 16, 1943), 116.

Against federal support of research.

2544. Herzberg, Gerhard. "Bureaucracy and the Republic of Science." IMPACT OF SCIENCE ON SOCIETY, 22 (1972), 105-10.

Examines a Canadian legislative report on science policy. It is said that politicians do not understand science or scientists.

2545. Jennings, Feenan, and Lauristan King. "Bureaucracy and Science: The IDOE and the National Science Foundation." OCEANUS, 23 (Spring, 1980), 12-19.

Finds that the NSF, despite adding more paperwork, has been helpful in promoting the International Decade of Ocean Exploration.

2546. Katz, Amron. "A Retrospective on Earth-Resource Surveys: Arguments about Technology, Analysis, Politics, and Bureaucracy." PHOTOGRAMMETRIC ENGINEERING AND REMOTE SENSING, 42 (1976), 189-99.

Traces how aerial photography was caught up in a bureaucratic battle and the politics of national security.

2547.   Khol, Ronald. "Can Technology Survive Bureaucracy?
        Uncle Sam at the Helm." MACHINE DESIGN, 45 (April 5,
        1973), 98–104.

        On the interaction of engineers and government.

2548.   Lavoie, Francis. "Can Technology Survive Bureaucracy?
        Professionals on a Yo-yo." MACHINE DESIGN, 45 (March
        17, 1973), 118–23.

        Claims that engineers must lessen their dependence
        upon the policies of the federal government.

2549.   Leopold, A.C. "Heroic or Bureaucratic Science?" BIO-
        SCIENCE, 31 (October, 1981), 707.

        Says that the current structure of research funding
        involves so many scientists reviewing and compiling
        scores on the work of others that there will be a de-
        crease in revolutionary scientific breakthroughs.

2550.   Mellanby, Keith. "Neglected Research and the Power of
        Bureaucracy." NATURE, 255 (1975), 374.

        Feels that unorthodox research proposals stand little
        chance of support from the British government.

2551.   "Nom de Plume" and Donald Nilson. "Politics of Research
        Ethics in a Federal Bureaucracy." DEVIANCE AND DECEN-
        CY: THE ETHICS OF RESEARCH ON HUMAN SUBJECTS. Edited
        by Carl Klockars and Finbarr O'Connor. Beverly Hills,
        Sage, 1979.

        Present the case of a social scientists in the fed-
        eral government who was torn between the norms of sci-
        ence and the realities of agency politics.

2552.   Price, Don K. "Endless Frontiers or Bureaucratic Mo-
        rass?" DAEDALUS, 107 (1978), 75–92.

        Discusses the bureaucratization of scientific research.
        Planning should be done by generalist administrators.

2553. Record, Wilson. "Some Reflections on Bureaucratic
Trends in Sociological Research." AMERICAN SOCIO-
LOGICAL REVIEW, 25 (1960), 411-14.

Urges sociologists to study the implications of the
trend toward more organized research efforts.

2554. Redfearn, Judy. "UK Union Attacks GMAG Bureaucracy."
NATURE, 278 (1979), 3.

British professors protest limits on genetic research.

2555. Rich, Vera. "No Agreement Yet over Minimising Bureaucratic Barriers to Exchange." NATURE, 283 (1980), 805.

On scientific exchanges with the Soviet Union.

2556. Salsburg, David, and Andrew Heath. "When Science Pro-
gresses and Bureaucracy Lags--The Case of Cancer
Research." PUBLIC INTEREST, 65 (1981), 30-39.

Argue that the scientific enterprise is based on a
self-correcting mechanism that requires scientists to
acknowledge their mistakes; that there will be mistakes
is part of the scientific credo. However, problems
may arise when those mistakes are given concrete form
in a bureaucracy. Then the corrections may take much
longer and in the meantime, the public may be harmed.
Developments in cancer research are used to illustrate
the lag between scientific research and bureaucratic
policy.

2557. Szalai, A. "Research on Research and Some Problems of
Research Bureaucracy." SCIENTOMETRICS, 1 (1979), 247-
60.

Contends that the study of science must include more
than a sociology of knowledge. The organization of
scientific efforts must also be taken into account since
science does not take place in some sort of vacuum.
The impact of the research establishment on what gets
studied is all the more important today.

2558. Wheeler, Harvey. "The Challenge of 'Bureaucratized'
       Science." BULLETIN OF THE ATOMIC SCIENTISTS, 20
       (January, 1964), 14-17.

       Claims that the close relationship of science to gov-
       ernment is giving rise to a policy-making system that
       bypasses traditional legislative arenas. We need a
       "new science of politics" that will enable more citi-
       zens to participate in the making of science policy.

2559. Wise, Clare. "Can Technology Survive Bureaucracy?
       Who Pulls the Strings?" MACHINE DESIGN, 45 (Febru-
       ary 8, 1973), 119-27.

       On the problems of government involvement in tech-
       nological development.

XXI. SOCIAL SERVICES

2560. Auletta, Ken. "Babes in Bureaucracyland." HARD FEEL-
        INGS. New York: Random House, 1980.

        Tells how a creative child-care center was able to
        survive in spite of government interference.

2561. Berger, Brigitte. "Family, Bureaucracy, and the 'Spe-
        cial Child.'" PUBLIC INTEREST, 40 (1975), 96-108.

        Examines the increase in programs for children whose
        unusual learning problems are hard to explain. A num-
        ber of agencies have started to concentrate on these
        children. The major competitors are the mental health,
        the special education, and the legal areas. The con-
        fusion has created a number of conflicting definitions
        and procedures.

2562. Billis, David. "Reforming Welfare Bureaucracy: The See-
        bohm Report Outcome." POLICY STUDIES JOURNAL, 9
        (1980-81), 1250-61.

        Reviews the reform effort in Britain during the 1960s.
        Frustration resulted when the members of the welfare
        bureaucracy became unsure of their agency and profes-
        sional boundaries.

2563. Black, K. Dean, and Vern L. Bengston. "Implications
        of Telecommunications Technology for Old People, Fam-
        ilies, and Bureaucracies." FAMILY, BUREAUCRACY, AND
        THE ELDERLY. Edited by Ethel Shanas and Marvin B.
        Sussman. Durham, N.C.: Duke University Press, 1977.

        Examines the potential of new telecommuncations as a
        way for helping the family care for the elderly.

2564. Blumenthal, Richard. "The Bureaucracy: Antipoverty and
the Community Action Program." AMERICAN POLITICAL IN-
STITUTIONS: FIVE CONTEMPORARY STUDIES. Edited by
Allan P. Sindler. Boston: Little, Brown, 1969.

Recounts the personalities and policies going into
the launching of the War on Poverty in the 1960s. The
outcome was the result of infighting between bureaucratic guerillas and the welfare establishment.

2565. "Bureaucracy in the Saddle." CATHOLIC WORLD, 156
(1943), 104-05.

Bureaucracy is a threat to the family.

2566. Cloward, Richard A., and Frances Fox Piven. "The Professional Bureaucracies: Benefit Systems as Influence
Systems." THE ROLE OF GOVERNMENT IN PROMOTING SOCIAL
CHANGE. Edited by Murray Silberman. New York: Columbia University School of Social Work, 1965.

Maintain that the welfare bureaucracies strive to protect the conditions of their stability and expansion.
Public agencies want to avoid becoming vulnerable to
external groups, including the clients. Most of all,
client acquiesence in agency policy must be ensured.
Despite the emphasis on participation, low-income clients have little access to the bureaucracy.

2567. Cole, Robert F. "Social Reform Frustrated by Bureaucratic Routines: Title XX in Massachusetts." PUBLIC POL-
ICY, 27 (1979), 273-99.

Studies the failure of the Title XX provisions for
greater client participation in distribution of funds
for social programs. The federal administrators failed
to provide the flexibility and capacity for executing
the mandates of the program.

2568. Coughlin, Bernard. "Private Welfare in the Public Welfare Bureaucracy." SOCIAL SERVICE REVIEW, 35 (1961),
184-93.

Examines the role of private welfare agencies at

a time of growth in public efforts. Mutually advantageous relationships between the two sectors are necessary.

* Davies, Bleddyn, and Oliver Coles. "Electoral Support,
   Bureaucratic Criteria, Cost Variation, and Intra-Authority Allocations." Cited above as Item 1766.

2569. Denvir, John. "Controlling Welfare Bureaucracy: A Dy-
      namic Approach." NOTRE DAME LAWYER, 50 (1975), 457-
      82.

      Says that lawyers must understand the dynamics of bur-
      eaucratic motivation.

2570. Downs, George, and David Rocke. "Bureaucracy and Juve-
      nile Corrections in the States." POLICY STUDIES JOUR-
      NAL, 7 (1979), 721-28.

      Investigate the impact of bureaucracy in the policy-
      making process. Administrative units are important in
      the transfer of innovation from one jurisdiction to
      another.

2571. Finch, Wilbur. "Social Workers versus Bureaucracy."
      SOCIAL WORK, 21 (1976), 370-75.

      Gives advice about how to cope with organizational
      constraints on serving the social service clientele.

2572. Glasgow, Douglas. "Patterns in Welfare: Bureaucracy
      in Neighborhood Service." JOURNAL OF BLACK STUDIES,
      2 (1971), 171-87.

      Argues that the welfare bureaucracy perpetuates de-
      pendency in the black ghettoes. Moreover, the bureau-
      cratic structure has prevented the emergence of any
      community-based agencies for the provision of social
      services. A report on welfare in Southern California
      is presented. Methods for breaking out of the poverty
      syndrome are suggested.

2573. Glastonbury, Bryan, ed. SOCIAL WORK IN CONFLICT: THE
       PRACTITIONER AND THE BUREAUCRAT. London: Croom Helm,
       1980. 178 pp.

       Examines the tension in Great Britain between social
       workers who strive for professional autonomy and the
       organizations for which they work.

2574. Goodsell, Charles T. "Conflicting Perceptions of Wel-
       fare Bureaucracy." SOCIAL CASEWORK, 61 (1980), 354-
       60.

       Disputes the picture of the welfare bureaucracy as an
       impersonal oppresser of the poor. A survey indicates
       that clients and workers have a positive attitude to-
       ward welfare work.

2575. Goodsell, Charles T. "Looking Once Again at Human Ser-
       vice Bureaucracy." JOURNAL OF POLITICS, 43 (1981),
       763-78.

       Explores the thesis that lower-level bureaucrats in
       the human services are inhumane, incompetent, and abu-
       sive. A study of welfare workers in Appalachia reveals
       that clients are often given special attention, which
       is called "positive discrimination." This occurs even
       though the agency operates within a very narrow range
       of discretion.

2576. Green, A.D., "The Professional Social Worker in the
       Bureaucracy." SOCIAL SERVICE REVIEW, 40 (1966), 71-
       83.

       Delineates the sources of tension within welfare bur-
       eaucracies.

2577. Grunow, Dieter, and Friedhard Hegner. WELFARE OR BUR-
       EAUCRACY? PROBLEMS OF MATCHING SOCIAL SERVICES TO
       CLIENT"S NEEDS. Cambridge, Mass.: Oelschlager, Gunn
       and Hain, 1980. 238 pp.

       A collection of articles on the delivery of social
       services in industrial societies, with emphasis on the
       deficiencies of bureaucracy and professionalism.

2578. Gryski, Gerard S., and Charles L. Usher. "The Influence of Bureaucratic Factors on Welfare Policy Implementation." JOURNAL OF SOCIOLOGY AND SOCIAL WELFARE, 7 (1980), 817-30.

Insist that welfare policy research must take into account bureaucratic implementation, especially at the sub-state level. The degree of centralization and the professionalism of the staff were found to be important variables in the service delivery process.

2579. Handlen, Joel, and Ellen Hollingsworth. "Reforming Welfare: The Constraints of the Bureaucracy and the Clients." UNIVERSITY OF PENNSYLVANIA LAW REVIEW, 118 (1970), 1167-87.

Present a picture of the major characteristics of the welfare bureaucracy and welfare recipients as aspects of the problem of system reform.

2580. Hanlan, Archie. "Counteracting the Problem of Bureaucracy in Public Welfare." SOCIAL WORK, 12 (July, 1967), 88-94.

Suggest that informal rules may act to overcome many dysfunctional aspects of formal rules.

2581. Hanlan, Archie. "Casework beyond Bureaucracy." SOCIAL CASEWORK, 52 (1971), 195-99.

Urges caseworkers to exercise their professional judgment and seek autonomy in the performance of services for clients.

2582. Hartnett, Bruce. "Advocacy Planning and Bureaucratic Guerillas." EKISTICS, 42 (1976), 241-44.

Describes working with a squatter's rights group in London.

2583. Jacobs, Jerry. "'Symbolic Bureaucracy:' A Case Study of a Social Welfare Agency." SOCIAL FORCES, 47 (1969), 413-22.

Argues that there is a great discrepency between how
work is actually carried out and the formal rules of
the organization. The question then becomes how one
can explain the way in which an organization carries
out its function.

2584. Kakabadse, Andrew. "Bureaucracy and Social Services:
       A Comparative Study of English Social Service De-
       partments." INDIAN JOURNAL OF PUBLIC ADMINISTRATION,
       25 (1979), 190-201.

       Tries to determine the organizational structure that
       is most appropriate for social sowrk. British case-
       workers were dissatisfied with traditional bureaucratic
       forms.

2585. Kreps, Juanita. "Intergovernmental Transfers and the
       Bureaucracy." FAMILY. BUREAUCRACY, AND THE ELDERLY.
       Edited by Ethel Shanas and Marvin B. Sussman. Dur-
       ham, N.C.: Duke University Press, 1977.

       Looks at the bureaucratization of income supports for
       the elderly.

2586. Kroeger, Naomi. "Bureaucracy, Social Exchange, and
       Benefits Received in a Public Assistance Agency."
       SOCIAL PROBLEMS, 23 (1975), 182-97.

       Tests whether social exchange criteria were signif-
       icant in determining the benefits granted to clients.
       The demographic and personality characteristics of the
       clients had little bearing on the question. The bureau-
       cratic model was the best predictor of outcomes in
       the caseworker-client relationship.

2587. LeGates, Richard T. "Can the Federal Welfare Bureau-
       cracies Control Their Programs? The Case of HUD and
       Urban Renewal." URBAN LAWYER, 5 (1973), 228-63.

       Argues that newer welfare programs have been captured
       by special interest groups placed between the agency and
       the recipients of aid. This often leads to a displace-
       ment of program goals.

2588. Leonard, Peter. "Social Workers and Bureaucracy."
NEW SOCIETY, 7 (June 2, 1966), 12-13.

Professional and organization tensions observed.

2589. Leonard, Peter. "Professionalization, Community Action,
and the Growth of Social Service Bureaucracies."
SOCIOLOGICAL REVIEW MONOGRAPH, 20 (1973), 103-17.

Describes the challenge to professionalism in the
administration of British social welfare services.
As social welfare advances as a profession, there may
be a tendency to confuse bureaucratic norms with professionally right behavior. Social workers must be
trained in organization theory so they can avoid some
of the harmful pressures of the bureaucracy.

2590. Lightman, Ernie S. "Professionalization, Bureaucratization, and Unionization in Social Work." SOCIAL
SERVICE REVIEW, 56 (1982), 130-43.

Asks whether social workers see professionalism and
unionism as incompatible. An attitudinal survey indicates that the union is regarded as a means of protecting professional standards from the bureaucracy.

2591. Martin, Patricia, and Brian Segel. "Bureaucracy, Size,
and Staff Expectations for Client Independence in
Halfway Houses." JOURNAL OF HEALTH AND SOCIAL BE-
HAVIOR, 18 (1977), 376-90.

Studies the relationship of organization structure of
a social agency and the member's orientation toward client independence.

2592. Munnichs, M.A. "Linkages of Old People with Their Families and Bureaucracy in a Welfare State: The Netherlands." FAMILY, BUREAUCRACY, AND THE ELDERLY. Edited
by Ethel Shanas and Marvin B. Sussman. Durham, N.C.:
Duke University Press, 1977.

On the administration of service to the elderly in
the Netherlands.

2593.   Muris, Timothy. "Scaling the Welfare Bureaucracy: Ex-
        panding the Concepts of Government Employee Liabil-
        ity." UCLA LAW REVIEW, 21 (1973), 624-64.

        Suggests tort suits by welfare recipients as one way
        to enforce administrative responsibility and a sense of
        restraint.

2594.   Naturale, Cynthia. "Aging in America--Battling Stereo-
        types and Bureaucracy." TRIAL, 13 (May, 1977), 13.

        On the legal problems of the elderly.

2595.   O'Connor, Robert E., and Larry D. Spence. "Communica-
        tion Disturbances in a Welfare Bureaucracy: A Case
        for Self-Management." JOURNAL OF SOCIOLOGY AND SOC-
        IAL WELFARE, 4 (1976), 178-204.

        Find that white-collar workers are alienated from the
        communication process. Much of the information they re-
        ceive was not very relevant to the view of how to pro-
        vide service to the poor.

2596.   Paillat, Paul. "Bureaucratization of Old Age: Determin-
        ants of the Process, Possible Safeguards, and Reor-
        ientation." FAMILY, BUREAUCRACY, AND THE ELDERLY.
        Durham, N.C.: Duke University Press, 1977.

        Discusses the growing dependence of the elderly on
        public assistance.

2597.   Prottas, Jeffrey M. TECHNIQUES OF THE WEAK IN BUREAU-
        CRATIC CONFLICT. THE CASE IN PUBLIC HOUSING. Cam-
        bridge, Mass.: Harvard University, Department of City
        and Regional Planning, 1978. 34 pp.

        Examines how tenents and public housing managers inter-
        acted in two projects.

2598.   Prugar, Robert. "The Good Bureaucrat." SOCIAL WORK,
        18 (July, 1973), 26-32.

        Says that social workers must recognize the context

of their profession is an organizational one and learn
to use the proper bureaucratic skills in order to cope
with that reality.

2599. Rosenblum, Victor G. "Controlling the Bureaucracy of
the Anti-Poverty Program." LAW AND CONTEMPORARY
PROBLEMS, 31 (1966), 187-210.

Examines several instruments, including the ombudsman, for the control of the welfare bureaucracy. Judicial review is another important option.

2600. Scott, W. Richard. "Professional Employees in a Bureaucratic Structure: Social Work." THE SEMI-PROFES-
SIONS AND THEIR ORGANIZATION. Edited by Amitai Etzioni. New York: Free Press, 1969.

Uses a case study of a county welfare agency to examine the tension between professional and bureaucratic
work norms.

2601. Senay, Edward C., M. Blaine Walker, Sandra Rowton, and
Herman Lancaster. "Bureaucracy and the Human Needs
Approach." JOURNAL OF DRUG ISSUES, 3 (1973), 171-77.

Describe an alternative to bureaucracy in the drug
treatment process.

2602. Shanas, Ethel, and Marvin B. Sussman, eds. FAMILY,
BUREAUCRACY, AND THE ELDERLY. Durham, N.C.: Duke
University Press, 1977. 233.

A collection of articles examining the growing involvement of public agencies in providing care for the
elderly. The process in the U.S. as well as several
European countries is covered.

2603. Stein, Herman. "Administrative Implications of Bureaucratic Theory." SOCIAL WORK, 6 (July, 1961), 14-21.

Says that bureaucratic theory indicates some areas
of possible stress which the manager in welfare situations should recognize.

2604.   Taggart, Jane. "Is There a Solution to'Bureaucratic
        Violence'?" POLICE CHIEF, 45 (February, 1978), 48-
        49.

        Deplores how needs of the disabled are often ignored
        by officials in their desire to administer programs in
        an impartial manner.

2605.   Waldhorn, Steven. "Pathological Bureaucracies." GOVERN-
        MENT LAWLESSNESS IN AMERICA. Edited by Theodore Beck-
        er and Vernon Murray. New York: Oxford University
        Press, 1971.

        Defines "pathological bureaucracies" as those agencies
        "which have displaced a major part of their goals orig-
        inally assigned to them by the broader society." The
        convenience of the officials is more important than al-
        leviating social problems, and this indifference fur-
        ther exacerbates the problem. Public welfare is a case
        in point.

2606.   Wasserman, Harry. "The Professional Social Worker in a
        Bureaucracy." SOCIAL WORK, 16 (1971), 89-96.

        Looks at the problems facing the professional enter-
        ing a public welfare agency.

2607.   Weed, Frank J. "Bureaucratization as Reform: The Case
        of the Public Welfare Movement, 1900-1929." SOCIAL
        SCIENCE JOURNAL, 16 (1979), 79-89.

        Views the growth of bureaucratic social services as
        a solution to the problem of providing relief to the
        poor.

2608.   Whatcott, Weston. "Bureaucratic Focus and Service De-
        livery." SOCIAL WORK, 19 (1974), 432-38.

        Suggests that service delivery systems which are or-
        iented toward the rehabilitation of clients may have
        to be more rather than less bureaucratic.

XXII. ARTS AND HUMANITIES

2609. Adler, Renata. "Sartre, Saint Genet, and the Bureau-
        crat." TOWARD A RADICAL MIDDLE: FOURTEEN PIECES OF
        REPORTING AND CRITICISM. New York: Random House,
        1969.

        Reviews motifs in the works of Jean Genet.

2610. Arian, Edward. BACH, BEETHOVEN, AND BUREAUCRACY: THE
        CASE OF THE PHILADELPHIA ORCHESTRA. University:
        University of Alabama Press, 1971. 158 pp.

        Traces the development of a symphony orchestra into
        a bureaucratic organization. The way in which the arts
        are financed determine the structure and, eventually,
        the sort of music performed. The consequences of this
        are a distortion of artistic values and the alienation
        of performers. Federal funding may serve to liberate
        the artists.

2611. Bakema, J.B. "Bureaucracy Puts Architecture into Cold
        Storage." ROYAL INSTITUTE OF BRITISH ARCHITECTS JOUR-
        NAL, 83 (1976), 424-26.

        Says that architecture as a creative art is too much
        caught up in an establishment system designed for the
        control of "anonymous man."

2612. de Balzac, Honoré. BUREAUCRACY: OR, A CIVIL SERVICE
        REFORMER. Boston: Roberts Brothers, 1889. 333 pp.

        A translation of *Les Employés*, a novel describing the
        working of the bureaucracy in 19th century France.

2613. Carter, Malcolm. "The FDR Memorial: A Monument to Pol-
       itics, Bureaucracy, and the Art of Accommodation."
       ART NEWS, 77 (October, 1978), 51-57.

       On the problems involved in erecting a memorial to
       President Roosevelt.

2614. Courteline, Georges. THE BUREAUCRACY: SCENES FROM
       FRENCH OFFICIAL LIFE. London: Constable, 1928. 220
       pp.

       A translation of a farce about bureaucracy in the
       Third Republic.

2615. Davis, Douglas. "Artists versus Bureaucracy." NATIONAL
       SCULPTURE REVIEW, 26 (Summer, 1977), 7, 49.

       On federal support of the arts.

2616. Diamant, Alfred. "Anti-Bureaucratic Utopias in Highly
       Industrialized Societies: A Preliminary Assessment."
       JOURNAL OF COMPARATIVE ADMINISTRATION, 4 (1972), 3-34.

       Argues that 20th-century utopian literature reveals
       a reaction against large-scale organizations.

2617. Erlich, R.D. "Trapped in the Bureaucratic Pinball Ma-
       chine: Views of Dystopia in the Twentieth Century."
       SELECTED PROCEEDINGS OF THE 1978 SCIENCE FICTION RE-
       SEARCH ASSOCIATION NATIONAL CONFERENCE. Edited by
       T.J. Remington. Cedar Falls: University of Northern
       Iowa, 1979.

       Says that bureaucracy plays a big part in the view of
       the future held by science fiction writers.

2618. Fess, G.M. "*Les Employés* and *Scenes de la vie bureau-
       cratique.*" MODERN LANGUAGE NOTES, 43 (1928), 236-42.

       Points out the influences of the novels of Henri Mon-
       nier on the novels of Balzac.

2619. Flannery, James, "Taking Theatre to the Bureaucrats: An Experimental Production of *The Memorandum* by Vaclaw Havel." EDUCATIONAL THEATRE JOURNAL, 29 (1977), 526-34.

Describes a staging of a play about the absurdity of bureaucracy in a Canadian government office.

2620. Friedsam, H.J. "Bureaucrats as Heroes." SOCIAL FORCES, 32 (1954), 269-74.

Argues that the bureaucratization of American life has led to a body of fiction with heroes who are in conflict with the big organization. The needs of the organization are portrayed by novelists as conflicting with personal integrity.

2621. Holzer, Marc, Kenneth Morris, and William Ludwin, eds. LITERATURE IN BUREAUCRACY: READINGS IN ADMINISTRATIVE FICTION. Wayne, N.J.: Avery Publishing, 1979. 239 pp.

A collection of examples from fiction and other sources illustrating the problems of bureaucracy. The literature tends to be rather pessimistic about the organization, but students of administration should be aware of this darker side of the world of organized life.

2622. Joyner, Russell. "Artists versus the Bureaucracy." HUMANIST, 38 (September-October, 1978), 50.

On resistence to urban renewal plans in San Francisco.

2623. Kroll, Morton. "Galbraith and Bureaucratic Pathology." PUBLIC ADMINISTRATION REVIEW, 29 (1969), 85-86.

A review of *The Triumph*, a novel by John Kenneth Galbraith about life in the foreign service.

2624. Lippard, Lucy. "Beauty and the Bureaucracy." HUDSON REVIEW, 20 (1967-68), 650-56.

Discusses the problems of placing public sculptures in an urban environment.

2625.   McDaniel, Thomas R.   "Weber and Kafka on Bureaucracy:
        A Question of Perspective."   SOUTH ATLANTIC QUARTER-
        LY, 78 (1979), 361-75.

        Argues that Max Weber, the scientist, and Franz Kafka,
        the artist, had contrasting yet complementary views of
        modern bureaucracy.

2626.   Matanle, Stephen.   "The Bureaucracy of Ballroom Dancing."
        GEORGIA REVIEW, 31 (1977), 207-10.

        A short story.

2627.   Miewald, Robert D.   "The Humanities: Antidote for Bur-
        eaucracy."   NEBRASKA HUMANIST, 2 (Spring, 1979), 16-
        20.

        States that the humanities can undermine the knowledge
        base of modern bureaucracy and thus mitigate some of its
        harsher features.

2628.   Myer, Chuck.   "Christo and the Art of Bureaucracy."
        PLANNING, (July, 1981), 10-13.

        Describes how the sculptor famous for his large-
        scale projects has dealt with zoning and environmental
        regulations.

2629.   Neuse, Steven.   "Bureaucratic Malaise in the Modern Spy
        Novel: Deighton, Greene, and LeCarre."   PUBLIC ADMIN-
        ISTRATION, 60 (1982), 293-306.

        Contends that the modern spy novel, as represented
        by three major writers, portrays a rather dismal view
        of bureaucracy. Specifically, they present a world
        in which heroism is flawed, principles are suspect and
        evil is more than the actions of an external enemy.
        The bureaucratic state is the cause of all these rather
        unhappy consequences. The novels indicate that we are
        slipping into an uncertain but organizationally domin-
        ated future. The novels also offer a wealth of detail
        about the operation of large organizations and the in-
        tricacies of bureaucratic politics.

2630. New, W.H., "Bureaucratic Management." CANADIAN LITER-
ATURE, 79 (1978), 2-4.

Warns about bureaucracy creeping into literature and
other arts.

2631. Price, Julia. "Bureaucrats and Bedlam in Pavel Kohout's
White Book." CRITIQUE, 22, No. 2 (1980), 61-68.

Studies the Czech author's satire on bureaucracy.

2632. Provine, Robert. "Who's in Charge Here? The Musical
Bureaucracy in the Early Yi Dynasty Court." ASIAN
MUSIC, 9 (1978), 45-58.

Examines the organization of the musicians at the
court of the Korean emperor during the early years of
the dynasty.

2633. Saunders, George. REBELS AND BUREAUCRATS: SOVIET CON-
FLICT AS SEEN IN SOLZHENITSYN'S *CANCER WARD*. New
York: Merit Publishers, 1969. 59 pp.

Treats the novel as a parable of Soviet society under
Stalin.

2634. Schwarts, Francis. "The Bureaucracy of Music in Puerto
Rico." CARIBBEAN REVIEW, 9 (November-December), 14-21.

Examines sources of tension in government aid to the
arts in Puerto Rico.

2635. Sederberg, Peter C. "Bureaucratic Pathology: A Diagnos-
tic Vision of Catch-22." BUREAUCRAT, 2 (1973), 316-
24.

Considers Joseph Heller's novel, *Catch-22*, as an introduction to the study of bureaucracy. It shows an
organization gone mad, with a number of extreme patho-
logies.

2636.   Soeborg, Finn. FOUR CHEERS FOR BUREAUCRACY. London:
        Sidgewick and Jackson, 1952. 196 pp.

        A novel translated from the Danish.

2637.   Soutian, Peter. "Bureaucratic Brute." NEW YORK TIMES
        BOOK REVIEW, (July 28, 1968), 5, 16.

        A review of Bulgakov's *The Heart of a Dog*.

2638.   Waldo, Dwight. THE NOVELIST ON ORGANIZATIONAL ADMINIS-
        TRATION: AN INQUIRY INTO THE RELATIONSHIP BETWEEN TWO
        WORLDS. Berkeley: University of California, Insti-
        tute of Governmental Studies, 1968. 158 pp.

        An annotated bibliography of fictionalized accounts
        of administration, public and private.

2639.   Wechsberg, Joseph. "The Bureaucrat." NEW YORKER, 23
        (July 19, 1947), 25-28.

        An ironic look at the capacity for bureaucrats to sur-
        vive in any sort of environment.

2640.   West, Rebecca. "A Nineteenth-Century Bureaucrat." THE
        COURT AND THE CASTLE: SOME TREATMENTS OF A RECURRENT
        THEME. New Haven, Conn.: Yale University Press, 1957.

        On the works of Anthony Trollope.

2641.   West, Rebecca. "The Twentieth-Century Bureaucracy."
        THE COURT AND THE CASTLE: SOME TREATMENTS OF A RE-
        CURRENT THEME. New Haven: Yale University Press,
        1957.

        On the works of Franz Kafka. *The Trial* and *The Castle*
        are more than satires on bureaucracy. They can also be
        read as religious allegories.

2642.   Wormsor, Baron. "Bureaucrats Investigated." POETRY,
        138 (May, 1981), 65-66.

XXIII. BUREAUCRATIC RESPONSIBILITY

2643. Braibanti, Ralph. "Reflections on Bureaucratic Cor-
        ruption." PUBLIC ADMINISTRATION, 40 (1962), 357-72.

        Reviews many of the arguments made about administra-
        tive corruption. A number of positive measures for
        limiting corruption in government are put forward.

2644. Broadnax, Walter D. "The Tuskegee Health Experiment:
        A Question of Bureaucratic Morality?" BUREAUCRAT,
        4 (1975), 45-55.

        Describes the role of the U.S. Public Health Service
        in the Tuskegee Syphilis Study in which several black
        subjects were denied medical treatment in the name of
        scientific research.

2645. Bunn, Ronald F. "Notes on the Control and Responsib-
        ility of the Bureaucrat." SOUTHWESTERN SOCIAL SCIENCE
        QUARTERLY, 41 (1961), 407-14.

        Suggests that the idea of responsibility includes the
        idea of accountability, responsiveness, and explicabil-
        ity. The latter notion, perhaps the most important,
        refers to the adherence to scientific principles in
        carrying out one's duties.

2646. Caiden, Gerald E. "Public Maladministration and Bureau-
        cratic Corruption." HONG KONG JOURNAL OF PUBLIC AD-
        MINISTRATION, 3 (1981), 56-71.

        Argues that defects of administration attributable
        to corruption exist everywhere. Attempts at reform are
        generally unsuccessful. Deviant bureaucratic conduct
        is promoted by a number of factors.

2647.   Chambliss, William J.   "Vice, Corruption, Bureaucracy,
        and Power."   WISCONSIN LAW REVIEW, 2 (1971), 1150-73.

        Examines the corruption of local law enforcement sys-
        tems.   The discretionary power of such bureaucracies
        makes corruption almost inevitable.   In carrying out
        their routine activity, selective application of rules
        is necessary, a point well understood by organized
        crime.

2648.   Divine, Dona R.   "A Political Theory of Bureaucracy."
        PUBLIC ADMINISTRATION, 57 (1979), 143-58.

        Investigates the connection between bureaucracy and
        the notion of justice.

2649.   Douglas, Jack D.   "Living Morality versus Bureaucratic
        Fiat."   DEVIANCE AND DECENCY: THE ETHICS OF RESEARCH
        WITH HUMAN SUBJECTS.   Edited by Carl Klockars and
        Finbarr O'Connor.   Beverly Hills, Cal.: Sage, 1979.

        Argues that imposed codes of professional conduct,
        such as those proposed for the conduct of social re-
        search, are deadening in their effect on free inquiry.
        Much more desirable are types of "living morality"
        which spring from and are enforced by the informal norms
        of the group.

2650.   Finer, Herman.   "Administrative Responsibility in Demo-
        cratic Government."   PUBLIC ADMINISTRATION REVIEW, 1
        (1941), 335-50.

        A rejoinder to Friedrich (Item 2652).   The reliance
        on the conscience of the administrators is rejected.
        History shows that there will be abuses of power if
        external checks are removed.   The role of the officials
        must be subordinate to the elected leaders in a demo-
        cratic society.   Moral responsibility is proportional
        to the severity of political responsibility

2651.   Foster, Gregory D.   "Legalism, Moralism, and the Bur-
        eaucratic Mentality."   PUBLIC PERSONNEL MANAGEMENT,
        10 (1981), 93-97.

Maintains that a moralistic rather than legalistic
outlook will best enable public administrators to
respond to a changing environment.

2652. Friedrich, Carl J. "Public Policy and the Nature of
       Administrative Responsibility." PUBLIC POLICY. Ed-
       ited by Carl Friedrich and Edward Mason. Cambridge,
       Mass.: Harvard University Press, 1940.

       Argues that the inevitability of administrative dis-
       cretion makes questionable the effectiveness of any
       formal arrangement for ensuring responsibility. The
       expertise and professionalism of the officials must be
       trusted. Moreover, administrators are as capable of
       discerning the public will as politicians. Administra-
       tive responsibility is not so much enforced as it is
       elicited from officials.

2653. Hill, Larry B. "Bureaucracy, the Bureaucratic Auditor,
       and the Ombudsman: An Ideal-Type Analysis." STATE
       AUDIT: DEVELOPMENTS IN PUBLIC ACCOUNTABILITY. Edited
       by B. Geist. London: Macmillan, 1981.

       Examines the ombudsman as a type of check, or audit,
       on bureaucracy. The Israeli experience is emphasized.

2654. Hill, Larry B. "Bureaucratic Monitoring Mechanisms."
       THE PUBLIC ENCOUNTER: WHERE STATE AND CITIZENS MEET.
       Edited by Charles Goodsell. Bloomington: Indiana
       University Press, 1981.

       Develops a conceptual framework for identifying and
       measuring those mechanisms which play a role "in check-
       ing, controlling, watching, regulating, reviewing, sup-
       ervising, evaluating, auditing, or otherwise attending
       to those actions of public bureaucracies that have an
       impact on citizens."

2655. Hodgetts, J.E. "Bureaucratic Initiative, Citizen In-
       volvement, and the Quest for Administrative Account-
       ability." TRANSACTIONS OF THE ROYAL SOCIETY OF CAN-
       ADA, 12 (1974), 227-36.

       Sees a sense of professional ethics as the best way
       to keep the bureaucracy accountable.

2656. Kernaghan, Kenneth. "Responsible Public Bureaucracy:
       A Rationale and Framework for Analysis." CANADIAN
       PUBLIC ADMINISTRATION, 16 (1973), 572-603.

       Distinguishes between the objectively and subjectively
       responsible bureaucracy.

2657. Kickinski, Walter T. "The Future of Bureaucracy as
       Existential Experience." BUREAUCRAT, 3 (1974), 353-
       60.

       Argues that bureaucrats must exercise personal respon-
       sibility in their acts. An awareness of the bureaucrat-
       ic life as an existential experience is the best strat-
       egy for individual survival.

2658. Kohlberg, Lawrence, and Peter Scharf. "Bureaucratic
       Violence and Conventional Moral Thinking." AMERICAN
       JOURNAL OF ORTHOPSYCHIATRY, 42 (1972), 294-95.

       Examine the "life and death" decision as an interac-
       tion between moral beliefs of the individual and the
       context within which the decision is made.

2659. Loucks, Edward A. "Bureaucratic Ethics from Washington
       to Carter: An Historical Perspective." PUBLIC PERSON-
       NEL MANAGEMENT, 10 (1981), 77-82.

       Traces the stages in the growth of American ideas
       about public accountability.

2660. MacIntyre, Alasdair. "Utilitarianism and Cost-Benefit
       Analysis: An Essay on the Relevance of Moral Philo-
       sophy to Bureaucratic Theory." VALUES IN THE ELEC-
       TRIC POWER INDUSTRY. Edited by Kenneth Sayres.
       Notre Dame, Ind.: University of Notre Dame Press,
       1977.

       Examines the value premises of the philosophy em-
       bodied in cost-benefit analysis. The concept is a
       version of the theory of utilitarianism as applied
       within the complex organization.

2661. Mainzer, Lewis C. "Injustice and Bureaucracy." YALE
      REVIEW, 51 (1962), 559-73.

      Speculates on the reasons for a general absence of
      justice in the bureaucracy. Considerations of the needs
      of others is not promoted by hierarchical arrangements
      and other aspects of bureaucracy.

2662. Mainzer, Lewis C. "Honor in the Bureaucratic Life."
      REVIEW OF POLITICS, 26 (1964), 70-90.

      Asks whether bureaucracy serves to destroy the idea of
      personal responsibility.

2663. Miller, James. "What Happens When Bureaucrats Blow the
      Whistle?" READER'S DIGEST, 113 (July, 1978), 197-
      204.

      Some cases of public employees going public about the
      misdeeds of their superiors.

2664. Nadel, Mark V., and Francis E. Rourke. "Bureaucracies."
      HANDBOOK OF POLITICAL SCIENCE, VOL. V.: GOVERNMENTAL
      INSTITUTIONS AND PROCESSES. Edited by Fred Greenstein
      and Nelson Polsby. Reading, Mass.; Addison-Wesley,
      1975.

      Summarize the research on the sources of bureaucratic
      power. Issues of bureaucratic responsibility, as de-
      fined in the literature, are emphasized.

2665. Odegard, Peter H. "Toward a Responsible Bureaucracy."
      ANNALS OF THE AMERICAN ACADEMY OF POLITICAL AND SOC-
      IAL SCIENCE, 292 (1954), 18-29.

      Identifies several aspects of responsible bureaucracy
      in a democratic society.

2666. Rohr, John. "Ethics for Bureaucrats." AMERICA, 128
      (1973), 488-91.

      Says that schools and churches should do more to in-
      still in administrators a sense of moral values.

2667.   Rohr, John. ETHICS FOR BUREAUCRATS: AN ESSAY ON LAW
AND VALUES. New York: Marcel Dekker, 1978. 292 pp.

Suggests a program for educating public administrators in a sense of political values. The opinions of
the U.S. Supreme Court are recommended for study as a
source of "regime values." These are the values that
the American political system is designed to serve;
the democratic official should promote them in the exercise of administrative discretion. The issues of
equality, freedom, and property, as defined by the
courts, are looked at as specific examples of some important regime values.

2668.   Rourke, Francis E. "Bureaucratic Autonomy and the Pub-
lic Interest." MAKING BUREAUCRACIES WORK. Edited by
Carol H. Weiss and Allen H. Barton. Beverly Hills,
Cal.: Sage, 1980.

Notes that there has been a change in the thrust of
administrative reform; where once it was wanted to give
bureaucracy more independence, now there is a desire to
bring administration back under public control. This
is especially true of "constituency agencies" and the
"self-directing agencies." It is also suggested that
the public interest may be best served by a large degree of administrative independence.

2669.   Smigel, Erwin O., and H. Laurence Ross, eds. CRIMES
AGAINST BUREAUCRACY. New York: Van Nostrand, 1970.
142 pp.

A reader on the topic of crimes by members of large
organizations against their place of work. Both public
attitudes toward bureaucracy and the opportunities of-
fered by an organization routine contribute to this
sort of crime.

2670.   Rutledge, Philip J. "Bureaucratic Risk-Taking: What
Role for ASPA?" BUREAUCRAT, 2 (1973) 294-95.

Wonders if the professional association of public administrators should issue a statement about their responsibility for speaking out on issues.

2671. Smoot, Peter C. "Never Trust a Bureaucrat: Estoppel against the Government." SOUTHERN CALIFORNIA LAW REVIEW, 42 (1969), 391-406.

Wonders why judges have been so reluctant to apply the doctrine of estoppel against government actions.

2672. Spence, Larry. "Moral Judgment and Bureaucracy." MORAL DEVELOPMENT AND POLITICS. Edited by R. Wilson and G. Shochet. New York: Praeger, 1980.

Present a theory, centered on the rise of bureaucracy, to explain the moral deficiencies of modern public life.

2673. Stavins, Ralph L. "Transforming the Bureaucracy." BUREAUCRAT, 6 (Winter, 1977), 9-22.

Suggest steps to promote whistle-blowing in government.

2674. Weinstein, Deena. "Bureaucratic Opposition: The Challenge to Authoritarian Abuses in the Workplace." CANADIAN JOURNAL OF POLITICAL AND SOCIAL THEORY, 1 (1977), 31-46.

See Item 2675.

2675. Weinstein, Deena. BUREAUCRATIC OPPOSITION: CHALLENGING ABUSES AT THE WORKPLACE. New York: Pergamon, 1979. 145 pp.

Argues that bureaucracies are political entities within which members may want to defy authority in order to oppose administrative abuses. Opposition to the formal authority structure can arise over feelings that there has been a deviation from bureaucratic norms. Abuses may include injustice, incompetency, or immoral and unfair policies. Suggested strategies for resistence, including informing the public and direct action, are featured.

2676. Wyner, Alan. "Executive Ombudsman, and Criticisms of Contemporary Public Bureaucracy." EXECUTIVE OMBUDSMEN

IN THE UNITED STATES. Edited by Alan Wyner. Berkeley: University of California, Institute of Governmental Studies, 1973.

Examines the effect of the executive ombudsman--those directly to an elected executive--in the U.S.

2677. Wyner Alan. "Complaint Resolution in Nebraska: Citizens, Bureaucrats and the Ombudsman." NEBRASKA LAW REVIEW, 54 (1975), 1-26.

Reviews the creation and early operation of the ombudsman in Nebraska. The experience with the office indicates that the ombudsman idea can operate within the American political environment.

2678. Yates, Douglas T. "Hard Choices: Justifying Bureaucratic Decisions." PUBLIC DUTIES: THE MORAL OBLIGATIONS OF GOVERNMENT OFFICIALS. Edited by Joel Fleischman, Lance Liebman, and Mark Moore. Cambridge, Mass.: Harvard University Press.

Argues that American bureaucrats play a major role in making value choices and establishing the processes by which values are considered by the public. The ways in which bureaucrats perform this role must be made more open to public scrutiny.

XXIV. A LITTLE HUMOR

2679. Bennett, James T., and Manuel H. Johnson. "The Defin-
       ition of Bureaucrats by Bureaucratic Definitions."
       BUREAUCRAT, 7 (Spring, 1978), 77-78.

       On the pomposity of bureaucratic communications.

2680. Bennett, James T. "Trends in Bureaucratic Exposition:
       A Case Study." BUREAUCRAT, 7 (Summer, 1978), 47-48.

       An example of clear government prose.

2681. Bennett, James T., and Eddie R. Mayberry. "Bureaucrats
       and Social Science: Policy from Imponderables." BUR-
       EAUCRAT, 7 (Fall, 1978), 59-60.

       Funny stuff in the census data revealed.

2682. Bennett, James T., and Manuel H. Johnson. "Laws of
       Committee Organization and Management in Bureaucra-
       cies." BUREAUCRAT, 8 (Fall, 1979), 50-55.

       Provide some hints for successful "committee person-
       ship."

2683. Bennett, James T., and Manuel H. Johnson. "Thoughts
       on Bureaucracy." BUREAUCRAT, 8 (Winter, 1979-80) 57.

       Some doggerel.

2684. Boren, James H. WHEN IN DOUBT MUMBLE: A BUREAUCRAT'S
       HANDBOOK. New York: Van Nostrand Reinhold, 1972.
       172 pp.

This and the following five items are from the collected wit and wisdom of the founder and president of
the National Association of Professional Bureaucrats
(NATAPROBU).

2685.   Boren, James H. "The Art of Being a Bureaucrat." IN-
        TERNATIONAL MANAGEMENT, 27 (August, 1972), 50-53.

2686.   Boren, Hames H. "Call Me Indispensable, Or: How to Sur-
        vive in the Washington Bureaucracy." NATION'S BUSI-
        NESS, 60 (December, 1972), 50-52.

2687.   Boren, James H. "Making the World Safe for Bureaucra-
        cy." NASSP BULLETIN, 57 (May, 1973), 19-23.

2688.   Boren, James H. HAVE YOUR WAY WITH BUREAUCRATS: THE
        LAYMAN'S GUIDE TO PYRAMIDING FEATHERHEADS AND OTHER
        STRANGE BIRDS. Radnor, Pa.: Chilton Books, 1975.
        183 pp.

2689.   Boren, James H. THE BUREAUCRATIC ZOO: THE SEARCH FOR
        THE ULTIMATE MUMBLE. McLean, Va.: EPM Publications,
        1976. 118 pp.

2690.   Callan, J. Brady. "Sanctuary for Bureaucrats, or An
        Unsung Function of Government Libraries." WILSON
        LIBRARY BULLETIN, 50 (1975-76), 472.

        Concludes that the office library is a good place for
        bureaucrats to hide out when they do not want to be
        found.

2691.   Hambrick, Ralph S. "Organizational Politics: An Exer-
        cise in Pidgeonholing Bureaucrats." BUREAUCRAT, 4
        (1975), 104-06.

        Categorizes administrators according to the way they
        play bureaucratic games.

2692. Honadle, George H. "The Bureaucratic Imagination: Ex-
      cerpts from a Bureaucratologist's Notebook." BUREAU-
      CRAT, 7 (Winter, 1978), 38-39.

      Provides some hints on how to identify *Homo bureau-
      cratis*.

2693. I. "The Sensuous Bureaucrat." BUREAUCRAT 1 (1972)
      282-87.

      On lust in the office.

2694. Kidner, John. A GUIDE TO CREATIVE BUREAUCRACY: THE KID-
      NER REPORT. Washington, D.C.: Acropolis Books, 1972.
      168 pp.

      A satiric look at the foolishness that goes on in
      Washington.

2695. Kirschbaum, Joel. "The Bible for Born-Again Bureau-
      crats." BUREAUCRAT, 6 (Fall, 1977), 120-23.

      About the style of the Carter administration.

2696. Knowlton, Don. "Ballade for Bureaucrats." FREEMAN,
      3 (1952), 232.

      A poem.

2697. Lee, Ronald B. "The Law of Bureaucratic Assimilation."
      PUBLIC ADMINISTRATION REVIEW, 29 (1969), 203-04.

      A humorous look at the time it takes to get a new
      idea accepted in the bureaucracy.

2698. Love, Edmund G. ARSENIC AND RED TAPE. London: Victor
      Gollancz, 1961. 175 pp.

      A collection of vignettes about the inhabitants of
      the bureaucracy.

2699. Lusky, Sam. "Bureaucrats Nix Revolution." ADVERTISING
       AGE, 50 (May 28, 1979), 45.

       What would have happened if today's bureaucrats had
       been in charge of the American Revolution in 1776?

2700. McCurdy, Howard E. "The Rubber Hose Theory of Bureau-
       cracy." BUREAUCRAT, 2 (1973), 122-25.

       Bureaucrats should be forced to use their own ser-
       vices. That should straighten them out.

2701. Moldava, Gyorgy. "The Day the Bureaucrats Froze Stiff."
       ATLAS, 19 (January, 1970), 31-32.

       A satiric look at bureaucracy in Hungary.

2702. Parkinson, C. Northcote. PARKINSON'S LAW AND OTHER
       STUDIES IN ADMINISTRATION. Boston: Houghton Mifflin,
       1957. 113 pp.

       A collection of semiserious laws about life in big
       organizations, public and private. The most famous
       of these, of course, states: "Work expands so as to
       fill the time available for its completion."

2703. Peake, H.J. "Proven Patterns of Effective Behavior in
       Meetings and Attendeeship for Bureaucratic Fun and
       Profit." BUREAUCRAT, 9 (Fall, 1980), 54-56.

       How to score points at committee meetings.

2704. Peter, Laurence F., and Raymond Hull. THE PETER PRIN-
       CIPLE. New York: William Morrow, 1969. 185 pp.

       On the elements of the science of hierarchology, in-
       cluding the law that, "In a hierarchy, every employee
       tends to rise to his level of incompetence."

2705. Peter, Laurence F. "Dodge and Delay--Rules of Thumb
       for Bureaucratic Survival." HUMAN BEHAVIOR, 8 (May,
       1979), 68-69.

2706. Shafer, Ronald. "No Bureaucrat Wants Award of 'The Bird.' Not even Its Winners." PUBLIC ADMINISTRATION REVIEW, 32 (1972), 251-53.

On James Boren's (Item 2684) awards for breakthroughs in creative bureaucracy.

2707. "A Successful Bureaucrat's Advice to His Son, on the Occasion of the Latter's Embarkation upon a Lifelong Journey in His Father's Footsteps." BUREAUCRAT, 2 (1973), 207-12.

Provides a number of ploys with which to take out one's rivals in the organization.

2708. "Tales from the Bureaucratic Woods." DUN'S REVIEW, 111 (March, 1978), 94-96.

On the work of James Boren (Item 2684).

* * *

Der Bureaukrat
Tut seine Pflicht
Von neun bis eins.
Mehr tut er nicht!

INDEX OF AUTHORS